WHY THE NOVEL MATTERS

WHY THE NOVEL MATTERS

A POSTMODERN PERPLEX

Mark Spilka
and
Caroline McCracken-Flesher
Editors

INDIANA UNIVERSITY PRESS ● *Bloomington and Indianapolis*

The paper used in this publication meets the minimum requirements of American
National Standard for Information Sciences—Permanence of Paper for Printed
Library Materials, ANSI Z39.48-1984.
∞ ™

Manufactured in the United States of America

Library of Congress Cataloging-in-Publication Data
Why the novel matters : a postmodern perplex / Mark Spilka and
Caroline McCracken-Flesher, editors.
      p.   cm.
   ISBN 0-253-35554-0 (alk. paper)
   1. Fiction—History and criticism.   2. Postmodernism.   I. Spilka,
Mark.   II. McCracken-Flesher, Caroline.
PN3331.W54   1990
809.3—dc20   89-45857
                                                                 CIP

CONTENTS

II. Four Precursors

III. The Conference

KEYNOTE ADDRESS

THE NOVEL AS SUBJECTIVE MODE

Contents

ACKNOWLEDGMENTS

We owe thanks especially for the immediate existence of this volume to our colleagues at *Novel:* managing editor Roger Henkle, book review editor Richard Pearce, and editorial assistant Pam Hardman. We owe long-range thanks to editor emeritus Edward Bloom and British editor Park Honan for furthering the journal's existence over the past two decades; and to associate editor Ellen Rooney for extending its future promise. For our recent twentieth-anniversary conference, which contributes so heavily to the materials of this volume, we owe special thanks to former assistant editor Carol Singley and former editorial assistant Rosemary Colt, who helped to organize and run the conference, and to their predecessors Michelle Massé and Christina Crosby, who participated in it. We are grateful also to the National Endowment for the Humanities for sponsoring that conference and to the University Lectureship Fund and the Wetmore Lecture Fund at Brown for supplementary aid; to participating departments and programs such as Spanish, French, Comparative Literature, Women's Studies, American Studies, and Modern Culture and Media Studies; and to helpful deans such as Harriet Sheridan and Maurice Glicksman. There are also many people behind the scenes—*Novel's* manuscript checkers, indexers, and computer typists; the secretarial and administrative staff of the Brown English Department— too many, alas, to mention, but from among them we would like to single out computer ace Beth Sweeney and former administrative aide Ruth Oppenheim for special thanks. To our original backer Richard Saloman, our original designer Malcolm Grear, and our present helpful associates at Indiana University Press, we extend also our long-range and future thanks for this testament to common faith and effort.

To the readers, contributors, editors, advisers, friends, and abettors of Novel *since 1967*

WHY THE NOVEL MATTERS

Preliminaries

MARK SPILKA in creative conflict with
CAROLINE McCRACKEN-FLESHER

Revise, re-view
To see things anew

Susan Rubin Suleiman

Those who identify themselves by means of privileged positions based on hidden hierarchies and teleologies may be irritated, but their irritation is not about the end of morality or humanism; it is about the end of hegemony.

Elizabeth Deeds Ermarth

I keep thinking about the postmodern answering machine messages that, I am told, now abound in New York City. "You know what to do," the machines say. "You know when to do it."

Patricia Meyer Spacks

Back in the 1960s, when the journal *Novel: A Forum on Fiction* was founded, the aesthetic and humane value of fiction studies seemed so evident that a variety of new journals devoted to the genre soon sprang up. Thus, with *Nineteenth-Century Fiction* (1945) and *Modern Fiction Studies* (1955) already in the field, *Novel*'s more broadly generic precedent (1967) was either matched, anticipated, or reflected by *Studies in the Novel* (1969), *Studies in Short Fiction* (1963), *Studies in American Fiction* (1973), and (more broadly still) *The Journal of Narrative Technique* (1971). In the twenty-plus years since *Novel*'s inception, however, the face of criticism itself has been constantly changing. Repeatedly the journal's contributors have found themselves struggling to define not only their text but also their task—and indeed, in the context of recent reader response and much poststructuralist criticism, even themselves. And over and over, as the field of literature and the concept of the critic have come increasingly under question, *Novel*'s editors and contributors, along with those of other journals, have been forced to recognize that their generic concerns, however humanly or humanely pursued, have now become politically and culturally suspect. They have been forced, in effect, to wrestle with the question of how—or even whether—the novel continues to "matter" to individual and social lives in postmodern times. Our book collects from *Novel*'s pages a sampling of this critical generation's struggles to redefine their task and perhaps, in the end, to reappropriate the humanist heritage by rewriting humanism.

Of course, it is not new for critics to struggle with their role, or with a confused relation to the human/humane/humanities. We need cast our minds back only across this yet uncompleted century, across the historical critics, the New Critics, the structuralists and poststructuralists, to appreciate our field's constant and somewhat circular process of self-doubt, of critique and critical renewal.

Consider the 1940s. In those relatively simpler days, when the New Critics began to storm the academies with demands for a reconceived literary study, they defined their opponents, the entrenched historical scholars, by their apparent loss of confidence in literature. To the New Critics, these academic incumbents seemed in retreat before the truth-claims of modern science. On the one hand, because by scientific standards literature seemed unquantifiable and unqualifiable, the historical scholars had abandoned any attempt to define its nature and its value. Instead they distinguished it by its persistence, that is, by its contemporary popularity and its survival over time. On the other hand, while they failed to qualify literature scientifically, they paradoxically tried to acquire some of science's prestige by focusing their attention on a more "scientifically" accessible area of literary study, literary backgrounds. That is, although they laudably aimed to gain for literary study some of science's authority and discipline, in adopting scientific standards they effectively degraded and abandoned any specifically literary study of the text, any programmatic humanism.

This is the argument propounded by Allen Tate, the New Critics' advance guard, in his provocative essay "Miss Emily and the Bibliographer."[1] According to Tate, the historical "betrayal" began in the nineteenth century, when American and British scholars in the humanities followed the example of their German colleagues and began to model themselves upon scientists. Tate presents this momentous shift in a satiric light, but nonetheless with considerable cultural insight. He writes:

> The rise of the sciences, their immense practical successes, even their moral failures, intimidated the scholars and I seem to hear them say, at first secretly and late at night when black questions cannot be gainsaid: "Milton's science is false, and the scientists say that his moral and religious ideas have no empirical validity. But if I give up Milton I give up my profession, so I had better bestir myself to study scientifically Milton's unscientific science. We must get in on the wonderful scientific triumphs of the age. Nobody believes today that the arts give us a sort of cognition at least equally valid with that of scientific method; so we will just take the arts as fields of data for more scientific investigation." (Tate, 111–12)

Tate was probably wrong, certainly ungenerous, in attributing historical scholarship only to his predecessors' desire to preserve professional status and income. A more likely explanation is that earlier criticism took on the coloration of the dominant sciences as a protective strategy to preserve literature. Indeed, the New Critics in their turn would emulate science in order to preserve literature in all its "universality," not to save old jobs or beget new ones. But Tate was surely right in suggesting that at some point in the historical movement confidence in literature and in its human reference was lost, and that it was lost through lack of any going theory of cognition in literature, any workable defense

---

[1] Allen Tate, "Miss Emily and the Bibliographer," in *Reason in Madness: Critical Essays* (New York: Putnam, 1941), pp. 100–116. Page references in the text are to this edition.

against prevailing scientific assaults on normative absolutes, or against the moral and religious confusions advanced by those assaults. The study of literature did become background study; literary objects did consequently stand at risk of dissolution into the determinism of surrounding forces, as Tate maintained (109).

Literature, of course, would survive such risks, and most scholars would continue to profess their love for it. But Tate was again right to claim that historical criticism lacked any appropriate means for evaluating texts in themselves, and so undermined their literary specificity. In the matrix of historical criticism, with all its gaps, its hesitations, its omissions, literary works had been reduced, in effect, to mere stimuli for romantic effusions. Abandoned to the claims of the popular impressionistic criticism of the day, they now functioned as emotional grab bags, as it were, encouraging a diffuse variety of responses in the reader, some of them contradictory, none of them invalid, and none helping to illuminate the work or define its form. As Tate wrote, historical critics had effectively abdicated their critical responsibility, allowing readers—of whatever sophistication—"to feel as [they] please[d]" about literary works (107). The human had displaced the humanist. And yet, paradoxically enough, such "human" criticism would anticipate the democratic emphasis on the subjective nature of literary experience of recent reader response analysis—though decidedly, in its diffuse impressionism, it lacked the responsible approach of such analysis to how readers were in fact pleased to feel.

In his partisan zeal Tate had labeled his predecessors' reluctance to judge the text, their tendency to allow the human to assess the humanity, the Great Refusal. We might now more generously term it the Great Abstinence. How so? First, lacking more rigorous and more truly critical standards, unable to establish specifically literary value, historical scholars had bowed to the selective function of history and had simply accepted that body of literature which, by (somewhat wayward) popular acclaim, had survived into their own time. Second, on that basis they had refrained from judging or even teaching contemporary works, for those needed time to pass the survival test. But whether by refusal or by abstinence, these scholars paradoxically stood without any means of appraising literature *qua* literature.

It is not surprising, then, that historical criticism should precipitate from its abstinences and inabilities a criticism determined to appraise literature *qua* literature, a criticism deeply hostile to the easy subjectivities of impressionism and the flaws and fallacies of background study, a New Criticism, with Allen Tate as its angry advance guard.

For the next few decades the New Critics returned attention to the text and tried to judge the text by universal standards. Though they eschewed the backgrounds and impressionism behind which their predecessors had retreated, they similarly bowed to science (Tate to the contrary notwithstanding) through their exhaustive and supposedly objective explications of literary texts. Thus, where the historical scholars had supposedly deferred to scientism, the New Critics embraced it and revalued literature by adopting scientific standards as the basis for its evaluation. They nonetheless pursued the old humanist goals of truth and beauty by elevating literary texts into "verbal icons," revered aesthetic objects whose meanings might provide a kind of contemplative knowledge not available through science and whose forms might be universally judged by their coherence. It was that aesthetic formula, in its ready applicability, which enabled New Critics to storm the expanding academies after World War II. Returning veterans and their booming families had then created a sustained demand for advanced literacy in those humane/humanist studies, arts and letters, that the old historical scholars were unprepared to meet. Consequently the New Critics presided over a quasi-democratic and apparently humanist critical revolution—a revolution unmatched in previous literary history.

Now the wheel has come full circle. Between 1945 and 1960 the New Critics themselves became entrenched in the academies. In the 1960s, their doctrines were modified by a series of critical reforms into an eclectic pluralism still centered on formalism. Then, in the 1970s and after, the movement was displaced, if not altogether disempowered, by new theoretical ferment on an unprecedented scale. Its hegemony, in any case, had ended; humanism itself now seemed suspect; and the triumphant new theorists had themselves begun to wrestle with the human across the humanities.

Thus, where texts like René Wellek and Austin Warren's *Theory of Literature* once described the extrinsic and intrinsic blend of theoretical approaches to literature by which the old formalism flourished, now texts like Terry Eagleton's *Literary Theory* speak to the new hegemony of theory itself, in all its bewildering variety. In the main, moreover, these new theorists seem even more radically skeptical about humanism and aesthetics than the old historical scholars. Many semioticians and poststructuralists, for instance, now seem to deny the novel its traditional normative functions, its moral mediations between self and society, and its hard-won status as a literary art form. Like the old scholars, moreover, they derive their authority for denial from the scientific study of those background codes that literature supposedly records and/or transmits. Often they see those social codes as paradoxically antisocial—as with the literary depiction of women and minorities; often they question the privileged nature of literary texts on more broadly political grounds, as with their historical survival or their canonical elevation at the expense of less socially privileged texts or readers; or they focus on the intertextuality of all literary forms, or on their ideological gaps, and so deny their universal status and coherence as "verbal icons"; or they insist upon the wholly subjective nature of literary experience, or upon their own culturally constituted subjectivity as readers, their own role as intertexts, and so deny the normative authority, the cognitive objectivity, of such forms. Such denials and questionings, however legitimate as critical enterprises, suggest a new and radical distrust either of literature or of the ways we have previously conceived and dealt with it; to some humanist observers, they suggest also a curious failure to imagine any positive functions for literature. They accordingly raise the equally legitimate question as to why novels matter in postmodern times.

On the other hand, the extraordinary sophistication and undeniable vitality of the new theoretical movement set it off from the equally undeniable flaccidities of the old literary humanism. The whole field of literary theory is obviously booming, particularly in its feminist and Marxist branches, where its democratic impulses give evidence of a criticism that is newly and excitingly humane. Nor is there anything smug or flaccid about the negations of such theorists. Indeed, they pride themselves on their subjective honesty; they vigorously embrace their doubts and limitations; they acknowledge and proceed from their own biases. Eschewing the false comforts of an aging literary formalism, they now adopt more bracing attitudes like Keats's "negative capability"—the ability, that is, to confront and cope with manifold uncertainties, whether in life or in literature. After half a century of grimly cultivated wasteland alienations, such defiant braveries are refreshing, tonic, even heartening. It is not surprising, then, that today's critics speak of *jouissance* and carnivalistic joy as endemic to their pursuits.

Nor is it surprising that all the literary forms, but especially the novel, with its more immediate stake in social interchange and political subjectivity, are thriving from consideration as cultural rather than literary artifacts. Novels especially are still very much with us; they have not disappeared. Yet the negations of literary worth and meaning that accompany their newly politicized presence are also very much with us. The critical perplex also has not disappeared; indeed, the critical perplex prospers. Why and how do novels "matter" in postmodern times? What kind of confidence, if any, do they inspire as literary artifacts or even as newly democratized cultural artifacts? Is the novel alive and well amid competing texts and contemporary uncertainties? Is is still empowered with some of its old socio-literary clout?

This book selects from *Novel*'s pages those essays and proceedings which explore the seeming standoff between old humanist and new "posthumanist" responses to such questions, and which demonstrate some possible modes of resolution. For instance, in papers reprinted from a 1985 Modern Language Association panel on the future of novel criticism, Don Bialostosky, Bernard Duyfhuizen, and Mark Spilka examine, respectively, the polyphonic possibilities for carnivalistic joy in literary uncertainties (as championed by Bakhtin), the importance of literary process as an inclusive and comprehensive manifestation of perpetually changing judgment, and the growing evidence of practical new fusions between humanist and (as we are loosely terming them) "posthumanist" assumptions about literary experience.

As Spilka notes in his panel remarks, that evidence can be demonstrated by a series of *Novel* essays that precede the MLA conference. Attempts to cope with new theories lead here to lively cultural extensions of humanist positions. Thus Roy Pascal finds Frank Kermode's assumption of the utility rather than the truth of fictions too arbitrary and subjective in *The Sense of an Ending*. In opposition, he defines narrative as essential to our understanding of human relationships and to our appreciation of the relation between things coherent and contingent, manageable and unmanageable. He goes on to show, moreover, that the experience of reading such narratives involves a process of continually modified assumptions like that defined by Bernard Duyfhuizen. The crucial difference for Pascal, however, is the value of that process for life itself—its relevance, that is, as a type of experiential knowledge not available through science.

Similarly Terrence Doody, Steven Cohan, and Nancy Armstrong each to an extent repeat Pascal's concern for human relevance. Doody defines the idea of realism at work in *Ulysses* and *Don Quixote* as multivocal in its ambivalent mediations between fact and essence, self and world—or better still, as balanced in its mediations of the self's multiplicities in a detailed world—and therefore like those polyphonic and dialogic novels championed by Bakhtin. Steven Cohan finds readable characters where texts and readers work together to create virtual existences in the reader's imaginative space—characters become phenomenological objects, that is, as well as representational subjects in the reader's mind. Finally, Nancy Armstrong speaks boldly to the rise of female authority that accompanied the novel's rise in the eighteenth century, and attempts to account for the gendered contradictions distributed across that new literary form and its reception: the majority of the novel's authors were women; the majority of its readers were men; its characteristic subject—domestic conflict—was feminine; its rise occurred "at precisely the time when British society . . . seemed to want women confined to the home, their labor devalued, and their political rights perpetually denied to them."

When panelists at *Novel*'s twentieth-anniversary conference (spring 1987) apply old and new approaches to the novel's several functions, and focus on issues rather than on warring theories, they similarly honor the new sense of problematics in literary discussion while strenuously wresting provisional values out of literary conundrums. But perhaps the most interesting point is that these hard-won values, however provisional, are in new ways humanistic. Consider Elizabeth Deeds Ermarth's remarks as she concludes the final paper on the final panel, "The Novel as Narrative Process." Ermarth argues that humanism may not be in crisis, as some suppose. Rather, she suggests it may have been identified incorrectly with causality, Judeo-Christian morality, and premodern notions of historical time. Accordingly, it may be necessary now to redefine it:

> If humanism can be defined in philological terms . . . if it involves care for textuality and language, attention to difference between textual moments, an expanded sense of language as a model not just for well-made urns but for each human system in all its complex multivalence, then perhaps humanism is only just finding its own demystified way. In any case, the current emphasis on semiosis does move us well beyond some complacencies and does dispute the privilege of representational language; however, this does not seem tantamount to a cultural bonfire. Those who identify themselves by means of privileged positions based on hidden hierarchies and teleologies may be irritated, but their irritation is not about the end of morality or humanism; it is about the end of hegemony.

If humanism has been demystified and decentered, as Ermarth here suggests, then perhaps we should look for it in unexpected places and new guises. Leo

Bersani shines his critical light into one such unexpected place and reveals humanism in an extraordinary guise in his essay on Flaubert's encyclopedic subjectivism in *Bouvard and Pécuchet*. Bersani views the novel's inapplicable and alienating discourse as a political strategy, a form of resistance, "a defense against the manipulative seductions of political language" whereby "style caresses an encyclopedic culture out of its projects of mastery and into a liberalizing impotence." Similarly, exploring the novel as psychosocial design, Robert Caserio finds a healthy masochism, a kind of painfully energizing and erotogenic stimulus for writing and written subjects in the otherwise wholly ambiguous and bewilderingly disruptive contemporary novels of Christine Brooke-Rose and J. G. Ballard. Or skeptical decoder Robert Scholes himself takes on a surprising new guise, while waxing nostalgic on the novel as ethical paradigm, and finds a valid sense of consciousness as conscience in the nineteenth-century novels of George Eliot—one no longer tenable, apparently, in our own more politically encoded times.

Other critics move boldly beyond such marginally humane conclusions; they compromise and reinvent the notion of humanism by confronting the humanities with the specifically human. Most notably Charles Altieri and Susan Suleiman write their textualized selves across and against the literary text.

Altieri sets himself up as an intertext to Joyce's amazing "collideorscapes" (colliding, fragmenting, and escaping moments of historical awareness) in *Finnegans Wake*. He consequently arrives at an imagined Joycean social order "based on the pursuit of collective identifications that are knowable only in and as our differences as we [readers] make and unmake particular histories." More boldly still, Susan Suleiman establishes herself as a (female) intertext for (male) texts by co-opting even the form of critical discourse. She applies an exemplary "metapolylogue," an imagined conversational exchange between Daughter, Daddy, and various literary stand-ins for the missing Mother, to passages from sexist stories, films, and critical or psychological pronouncements about playfulness by such as Georges Bataille, Robbe-Grillet, Derrida, Winnicott, and Barthes. Though Suleiman's implied critique of these textualized speakers is negative, the exchange itself foregrounds and invigorates the missing Mother and implicates the reader in both her subjection and her resurgence. Refiguring the missing Mother, molded daughter, and reluctant reader each as writer, reader, and text, it transforms gendered absence into a decidedly vexed and vexing, and very present, question. It creatively distributes gendered anxieties across the field of literary play.

As these examples of freewheeling intertextuality indicate, it is the critic or reader who becomes privileged, or if not privileged then empowered, through postmodern considerations of text, reader, and circumambient world. Accordingly, we are forced to rethink the relations between the world, the text, and the critic, as Edward Said so wisely recommends.[2] And this may well be what *Novel*'s 1987 conference helps to accomplish. In the relatively new category

---

[2] Edward Said, *The World, the Text and the Critic* (Cambridge: Harvard University Press, 1983).

of the novel as discourse, for instance, panelists George Levine and Khachig Tölölyan along with panelist Altieri find places for the world's discourses within Conrad's novels, Tolstoy's *War and Peace*, Pynchon's *Gravity's Rainbow*, and, as noted, Joyce's *Finnegans Wake*. Further, they argue effectively that novels impinge on the world, even as the world and these critics impinge upon novels. Novels comprise dynamic meditations on the discourses of science, technology, war, and history as they affect all human lives—even those of critics!

Of course, these global impingements import risk into the writer's/reader's personal life. They bring discomfort foreign to traditional criticism in its limited focus on morals and manners. Morals and manners never caused us such critical anxiety. Yet even ethical concerns stand reconceived and reinvigorated in our time. They are not as flaccid and irrelevant to this twentieth century as Robert Scholes's nostalgic essay seems to indicate. Rather, as novelist David Lodge and others insisted during the windup session of the conference, the novel continues to flourish in ethical form, and to problematize ethics throughout the world, but especially in Africa and Latin America, and wherever the problems of women and minorities are taken seriously as fictional subjects. Moreover, it continues to deal coherently with such issues in terms of personal as well as social life.

There is no crisis, then, in the world of fiction, and though there are many differences about how to approach that world, there may be less academic controversy than supposed. What is important is the applicability of old and new approaches to progressive causes and to their literary expression. In this regard, it is particularly important that, as Daniel Schwarz observes, deconstructionists have no monopoly on socially progressive positions toward (for example) women, minorities, apartheid, or nuclear weapons. Humanists in literature departments had preceded them in advancing such concerns and their literary expression. By the same token, it is equally important that, as Susan Suleiman has shown, humanists have no monopoly on sexism or racism. Such problems exist among deconstructionists too. Thus, there is still room for humane criticism of a familiar order, especially as refreshed and revised by new democratizations, new extensions of the old western struggle for personal dignity and personal places in the social sun.

This is particularly evident in the American wing of feminist studies and in Afro-American studies, both of which have thrived in humanistic departments even as they have called those departments' tenets into question. However radical, feminist and black studies offer trenchant reworkings of humanistic concerns. Indeed, when critics like Patricia Meyer Spacks and Joseph Gold defend directly the novel's necessary stake in such traditional concerns, its continuing ethical and therapeutic functions, they imply its durable value for the moral and emotional lives of marginal as well as socially "centered" readers. It is on grounds like these, moreover, that Daniel Schwarz makes the case for an ongoing and revised humanist poetics in his lengthy contribution to *Novel*'s series on why the novel matters. His approach cannot be too easily dismissed by those who continue to read avidly, and with an irrepressible concern for the value of individual life, the feminist, minority, holocaust, anti-apartheid, gay, and lesbian fictions of our marginalizing and disjointed age.

Many of today's critics are not only mindful of opposing views but also willing to stretch their own positions in light of them. Thus the humanistically oriented Joseph Gold and Murray Schwartz invoke semiotics while discussing the novel's therapeutic functions; thus postmodern critics of various persuasions reach for humanist solutions, however newly conceived, to the politicized problematics of current literary studies. And all address literary texts from a widened—if not fractured—canon while so doing. Clearly, we may see today's critics as engaged in cognitive meditations on a far more ambitious cultural and literary scale than Allen Tate imagined when he spoke out in the late 1930s and early 1940s for both the moral and the aesthetic value of literary studies. And we may even see them as meditating on and through a modified and broadened humanism.

Evidently, postmodern critics have not lost confidence in the novel. Rather, they have relocated the novel within a broader and more dynamic cultural context and subjected it to new and searching (rather than destructive) interrogation. Indeed, in refiguring themselves as human/humane intertexts, these inquiring and newly empowered critics emulate, invigorate, and perhaps honor the novel's creative powers and its social functions, and more often than not they strenuously attempt to keep them alive, honest, and at least marginally applicable.

In such varied heroic ways, at any rate, and from such oddly uncomfortable angles, it seems evident that bridges are being built between old and new approaches, that the gap between them is not as impassable as previously supposed, and that further accommodations are now not only possible but very likely.

I

✣ ✣ ✣

The New Series

Poetics Panel

"The Present and Future States of Novel Criticism":
A Hopeful Overview

MARIANNA TORGOVNICK, *Moderator*

In 1967, the journal *Novel* began publication with the goal (articulated in a later collection of essays) of moving "Towards a Poetics of Fiction." Both the publication and its goal were accurate signs that the novel was becoming a widely and intensely studied, as well as a widely and pleasurably read, kind of literature. In 1985, it is easy to forget how recently the novel has risen to academic respectability. But not so very long ago novels were to be avidly read by graduate students, but not taught in graduate courses or written about in dissertations, and the field of academic publishing featured far more work on poetry than on fiction.

Some statistics presented by George H. Ford at the 1983 Modern Language Association meeting tell the story compellingly: of the 144 Ph.D. theses on English and American literature in this country in 1947, none were on the Victorian novel; in 1982, fully 47 of 817 theses were on Victorian novels. Similarly, in 1948, letters and biographies of major Victorian novelists were, by and large, unavailable. Only Thackeray's letters, for example, had received full publication; now volumes of letters by the Brontës, Eliot, Dickens, and Hardy are taken very much for granted. The same dearth or plenty situation existed for novels of other periods and for critical literature on fiction. In fact, 1948 saw the publication of F. R. Leavis' *The Great Tradition;* five more years would pass before publication of Dorothy Van Ghent's *The English Novel*, and eight years beyond that for Wayne Booth's *The Rhetoric of Fiction*.[1]

In the years when literary history alone organized staffs and course offerings in English departments, when the novel was considered "popular" rather than canonical art, and when New Criticism dominated critical discourse, a commonplace in books about novels was a statement to the effect that while the issue of language (or point of view, or style, or image) has been satisfactorily discussed in the criticism of poetry, it has received little attention in criticism of the novel. Such statements will not do in 1985, for many issues long neglected have now been treated and re-treated. For the critic of the novel, defining originality of critical approach has become a matter of rigor, sometimes even of anxiety. While poetry predominated in the New Critical endeavor, the novel has been at the center of more recently popular schools—the revived Russian Formalism, for ex-

---

[1] Ford's talk, "Looking Backward: The Victorian Novel," is now in print. See *Victorian Studies Newsletter* (Spring 1984), 3–6.

ample, and Structuralism. No longer neglected, the novel is amply discussed. We would seem to have moved a long way towards a poetics of fiction.

Indeed, since 1967, there have been many new directions in novel criticism, many efforts at a poetics of fiction or parts of one, directions and efforts in which *Novel* has played a vital role. At the same time, and especially in the late seventies and eighties, there have been significant challenges to the very idea of describing or defining genres (central, after all, to a journal like *Novel* and to the validity of novel study as a field), as well as challenges to the idea of a stable poetics. Sometimes viewed both by those within and without post-structuralist camps as radically subversive, as logos- and world-threatening, post-structuralism has, in practice and in important ways, reinfused energy and freedom into literary criticism.

At the tail-end of the New Criticism, criticism of the novel, like American and English criticism in general, was for a time in the doldrums. Others will remember, as I do, the dreariness of articles on subjects like (to cite only one sad example) dog imagery in *The Mill on the Floss*. But critical discourse in this country is back—back in vitality, back in importance, back in the liveliness and diversity of participating voices, back, often due to the influence of voices once perceived as threatening. Hence the time seemed right for a session at the Modern Language Association glancing back briefly, looking around, and looking ahead at novel criticism. Called "The Present and Future States of Novel Criticism: Still Towards a Poetics of Fiction?" the session included the papers that follow, as well as a lively question and discussion period. The session aimed not so much at specific interpretations of texts or at presentation of work in progress by the panelists, as at an overview of developments along various theoretical lines. It tried, moreover, to acknowledge the diverse points of view of specialists in the novel.

In my last sentence I used a term standard in the criticism and theory of the novel, but a term whose history in recent years itself suggested the need for a session on the current and future states of novel criticism—the term "point of view." Until fairly recently, "point of view" was synonymous with the names of two great critics of the novel: Henry James, whose writings first sensitized readers to its importance, and Wayne Booth, whose *The Rhetoric of Fiction* articulated distinctions that became in America absolutely basic, both widely accepted and widely used. Like the ghosts in some of his eerier fiction, James is always with us; and as recently as spring 1984, Booth's study was the subject of a conference—it is a long way from discarded and forgotten. But Booth's work is now only one of many approaches to the concept of point of view.

Consider the alternatives (all either new in the last decade or available in English only within the last decade): Gérard Genette's system of focalization, voice, and mode in *Narrative Discourse* (part of *Figures III*); Bakhtin's vocabulary of monologic and dialogic form; somewhat less influential but also notable voices, like Dorrit Cohn's in *Transparent Minds*, Seymour Chatman's in *Story and Discourse* and Susan Snyder Lanser's in *The Narrative Act*. Most of these alternative

systems and contributions to the poetics of point of view are still being absorbed
and evaluated, their relationships to the older, once dominant systems still being
mapped. Hence, the value of one of the papers to follow, Don Bialostosky's
analysis of Booth's reactions to Bakhtin.

The other papers at the session, printed after this introduction, also take up
approaches and issues raised by the work of the last decade. Bernard Duyfhuizen's essay assumes as its background both the debates about mimesis, the
nature of the author, and the question of narrative belief stimulated, in large
part, by the post-structuralist contribution and the large body of concerns raised
by reader-response approaches of the seventies. His exploration of narrative
transmission depends, moreover, on the work of continental critics like Roman
Jakobson. Mark Spilka, a voice associated from its beginnings with *Novel*, also
addresses the post-structuralist challenge to eclectic humanism, revising the too
facile notion that the former will continue to represent an adventurous avant-
garde and the latter a conservative rear-guard. His remarks reinforce my sense
that both post-structuralism and eclectic humanism have been and continue to
be essentially enabling approaches to literature, producing at their worst sterile
and repetitious applications of critical formulae (can a deconstruction of dog images in *The Mill on the Floss* be far behind?), but at their best approaches that
enable sensitive critics to discuss literary theory and novelistic texts freshly and
with illuminating results.

Inevitably, in selecting papers for this panel, I have omitted significant issues
and significant new directions in novel criticism, sometimes for lack of space on
the panel, sometimes because the proper proposal did not come. In his response, Richard Pearce points out some of these omissions and much else of
value. Without stealing his thunder, let me note some specific and regretted
omissions: first, feminist criticism—amply represented at 1984's MLA, but certainly important in this area; second, the role played by the veritable explosion
in the last fifteen years of biographical documents, like letters, biographies, di-
aries; third, the question of where the current impetus in novel criticism rests, in
this country or largely abroad; fourth, the role of the new literary history and of
political approaches, including Marxist approaches. Most readers can supply
other issues that might have been addressed in a session on the current and future states of novel criticism.

Finally, the goal or purpose of the session itself ought perhaps to be addressed. As a stopping-place, the session runs the risk of implying that we have
reached either a poetics of fiction or a point at which that desire is forever behind
us. The summing-up impulse of all stopping points risks becoming prescriptive.
Prescription was not the goal of the session but points towards a further, subtler,
danger. Those at the 1984 MLA may have been struck, as I was, by the recurrence of the word *synthesis* as a theme word at many sessions. The *Columbia History of American Literature* was to reflect and synthesize the "post-modernist"
multiplicity of views and voices in American studies. Women's studies were to
enter the mainstream. Once peripheral texts were to become canonical. The

name of Bakhtin was being uttered with admiration at many sessions, some of them having nothing to do with narrative theory.

The popularity of Bakhtin in a sense indicates what I am trying to get at. No one reading Bakhtin can fail, I think, to find his overall theories a bold and stimulating addition to the study of literature; I know that I have been sensitized to many effects in the novel, especially in novelists like Stendhal or Lawrence always stigmatized under reigning theories of authorial voice and point of view. But in reading Bakhtin I am also struck by how much he takes for granted that post-structuralism has challenged—the idea of literary history, the idea of genre and genre progression, for example, perhaps most of all the idea of authorial intention—senselessly discarded (as Paul de Man among others observed) by the New Critics and vigorously challenged by various critical schools even while academic courses and studies blithely continued to use the author as a structuring device and the industry of biographical documents proliferated.

We have been, clearly, a divided profession, sometimes a schizophrenic one pursuing theoretical debates that did not affect, really, our day to day lives as critics and teachers. Time then for a synthesis? The desire for one is clear and the usefulness of one evident in books like J. Hillis Miller's *Fiction and Repetition*. But synthesis at what price? Not, one hopes, at the price of effacing the truly original, truly idiosyncratic, truly liberating developments of the past decade. To do that would be to return criticism—of the novel as well as more generally—to the doldrums most of us remember. And the future of novel criticism holds, one hopes, the ability to absorb without neutralizing the exciting work behind and ahead.

"Still Towards a Poetics of Fiction?"
No—And Then Again Yes

MARK SPILKA, *Panelist*

In the spring of 1977 the journal *Novel: A Forum on Fiction* conducted a two-day conference at Brown University on the current state of fiction studies. The title of the conference—"Towards a Poetics of Fiction"—was taken from the title given to a series of essays the journal had published during its first ten years of existence. An anthology of essays from the journal, also called *Towards a Poetics of Fiction*, would be published by Indiana University Press in the same year. Both conference and anthology were designed to celebrate what had seemed like a successful effort, over the journal's first decade, to create for the study of fiction the kind of theoretical support that poetry had received in preceding decades of theoretical ferment. Though these celebratory measures were indeed justified, they were also anti-climatic. In retrospect they seem to me to mark the end of one theoretical movement, which I am going to call for want of better terms eclectic humanism, and the beginning of another, which we now loosely label structuralism or post-structuralism. Of course these movements overlap in time, and the rivalry between them has scarcely ended; but the climactic nature of the humanistic trend which *Novel* celebrated, and the triumphant spread of post-structuralism in the years since 1977, seem to me the obvious conditions which any discussion of the present state of novel criticism must accommodate.

I am saying then that the center of theoretical ferment has shifted from one movement to the other, and that eclectic humanism, though it co-exists with the new dispensation and may well absorb it in future decades, no longer exists as a generative source of exciting new theories. But if this is true, then the question posed by the subtitle for this panel—"Still Towards a Poetics of Fiction?"—calls for a double answer—something like "NO, we are not moving further towards the poetics of fiction originally envisioned by eclectic humanists; but then again, YES, we are witnessing a proliferation of structuralist and semiotic theories which have taken over the question of poetics and have given it new meanings and new directions."

For many of us those new meanings and directions are not altogether pleasing. Indeed, the 1977 conference arranged by *Novel* was designed, in effect, to stem the overwhelming tide. Some of the discussion panel topics—In Defense of Authors, In Defense of Readers, In Defense of Realism, Character as a Lost Cause—will suggest the embattled nature of our enterprise. Of course there were other panels—Structuralism and Marxism, Hermeneutics and the Novel, Feminists on Fiction—designed to represent the new dispensations, but in one way or another each of these approaches could then be legitimately claimed by either camp. The terms of conflict were anything but clear in 1977, though they have since crystallized in ways which make our impromptu lines of defense seem rather naive. A panel "In Defense of Organic Fictions," or "On Works vs. Texts," would have been more to the point, since it is on these grounds that the great shift in theoretical interest has been chiefly made. The old New Critical tendency to sacralize "works" into "verbal icons" has been replaced by the post-structural stress on deconstruction, on dissolving individual works into their intertextual constituents or codes, and therein lies a considerable change in outlook. The ontological status which John Crowe Ransom granted to works of poetry in the 1940s, by which they provided a kind of knowledge not available to science, has been by-passed with regard to fiction and poetry alike by the new dispensation, which no longer sees any connection between meaning and truth, which indeed accepts the prison house of language as its habitat, and which has now moved into those oddly comfortable quarters, replacing the old fictional analogues for truth with cultural codes for decoding, replacing the old cherished artifacts with intertextual documents of no special merit. A panel "In Defense of Fictional Truths" might also have been devised to meet *that* enormous challenge, but in fact the humanist camp had long since abandoned its serious defenses of such matters and had set the stage for the takeover we have all witnessed, whether with alarm or satisfaction.

Among our panelists in 1977, Wayne Booth and Julian Moynahan spoke with some eloquence to the value of authors, to their superiority over critics, and thus to the implicit value of the works they created, and to the ontological or aesthetic status by which such works provide what the old New Critics called experiential knowledge or what the Chicago critics saw as higher forms of pleasure. On the other side of the verbal icon Wolfgang Iser also spoke to the interrelations between novels and readers and the kinds of control and limitation that works place on readers as they actively help to reconstruct meanings worthy of contemplation. And I myself introduced the panels on Character and Realism with none too subtle plugs for the blend of realism and individualism by which the novel rose—at least according to panelist Ian Watt—and by which its ongoing stake in the nature and value of personal life might best be defended. But none of us spoke at any length to the change of works into texts which the new order assumes, nor to the related epistemological assumption that such texts bear on reality not as analogues or symbols or experiential models but as cultural codes for decoding, nor to the supporting political assumption that bourgeois individualism as explored through such texts is and always has been a dead liberal duck. Indeed, we did not at that point understand that the superiority of the reader as sociological decoder over texts, authors, characters, and the worlds they nominally share was just around the political—if not metaphysical—corner.[1]

A similar fate was in store for the anthology, *Towards a Poetics of Fiction*, which appeared that year, and which even went into a second printing, but which never made it to that supreme signifier, the paperback stage. Foremost among its several features were six approaches "Towards a Poetics of Fiction"—through structure, language, history, narrative, genre, and time—and a seventh essay warning against the dangers of a poetics for a genre which inherently resists systematic study. In that seventh essay, called "The Problem with a Poetics for the Novel," Walter Reed argues that the novel is an "outsider" form, "a deliberate stranger to literary decorum," and that it "opposes the forms of everyday life to the conventional forms of literature inherited from the past."[2] This type of literature, he says, is always "suspicious of its own literariness"; consequently it opposes literary paradigms and canons with paradigms from other areas of culture, such as forms of speech, subliterature, commerce, science, architecture, landscape gardening, and the like. By its very nature, then, the novel continues to resist the tendency toward systematization, structuration, and canonization that a poetics properly involves.

At stake here is the traditional conception of a poetics that Reed assumes: its

---

[1] For a partial record of the 1977 *Novel* conference, see Edward Bloom, ed., "In Defense of Authors and Readers," *Novel* 11 (Fall 1977), 5–25; Mark Spilka, ed., "Character as a Lost Cause," *Novel* 11 (Spring 1978), 197–217; and Edward Bloom, ed., "Hermeneutic Hesitation: A Dialogue between Geoffrey Hartman and Julian Moynahan," *Novel* 12 (Winter 1979), 101–112.

[2] Reed's essay originally appeared in *Novel* 9 (Winter 1976), 101–113. See also Mark Spilka, ed., *Towards a Poetics of Fiction* (Bloomington: Indiana University Press, 1977), pp. 62–74.

fundamental concern with "judging literature according to some standard of aesthetic good and bad." He goes on to say that "recent Structuralist *poetiques* of literary discourse, with their claim to a more value-free systematics, may challenge this traditional conception"; but in his concluding remarks he questions the applicability of the term "poetics" to this new approach because of its "apparent lack of concern with a canon or with aesthetic value" and its "lack of focus on the literary specificity of the texts that are being analyzed." Then, in an unusual paragraph which I want to quote in full, he makes a case for it as a counter-poetics:

> *Nevertheless* [he argues], *one may use the term 'poetics' to describe the systematics of Structuralists like Todorov and Barthes if one realizes that there has been a transvaluation of critical values. The literary humanism of traditional poeticians like Aristotle, Sidney, Staiger, or Frye, is replaced by a scientific holism which explicitly rejects the humanist assumptions. Rather than a defense, the Structuralists offer an attack on poesy, a counter-poetics which takes as its field not "poetry" or "literature" but a much broader range of narrative discourse—popular, classical, informal, formal, oral and written. This is a valuable contribution in its own right and a serious challenge to traditional methods of literary study, but as it deliberately ignores the inherited notions of literary form against which the novel has struggled, it would not seem able to grasp the novel's dialectical nature. In fact, in its opposition to the idea of a literary canon and to the idea of literary value judgment, the Structuralist* poetique *can be seen as a novelization of traditional poetics—a poetics by the novel, or at least by the* nouveau roman.[3]

Reed goes on to find a more adequate dialectical sense at work, if not a full-blown poetics, in Jakobson and some of the Russian Formalists; and in line with such findings he suggests also that an adequate theory of the novel must combine a poetics with a semiotics. In the book that follows, for which his essay from *Novel* forms the introduction, he tries to write *An Exemplary History of the Novel* based on that prescription.[4] His approach there is intertextual, and though he quietly replaces the term "semiotics" with "prosaics" so as to avoid systematic rigidity, he proves to be a semiotician in disguise rather than a humanist with structuralistic leanings. He too traffics in literary fictions and codes versus non-literary fictions and codes, and so maintains that explicit rejection of humanist assumptions which characterizes the structuralist enterprise.

In my review of Reed's book for *Studies in the Novel* (Spring 1982) I registered the complaint that it is the opposition of forms of life, rather than of literary with non-literary fictions, which constitutes the novel's determining thrust, and that it is the experience of felt life rather than of opposing fictions which matters for most readers, even if we grant the contributions which such fictions make to that meaningful experience. I also pointed out that the novel becomes an "in-

---

[3] *Novel* 9 (Winter 1976), 112; *Towards a Poetics of Fiction*, p. 73.

[4] Walter L. Reed, *An Exemplary History of the Novel: The Quixotic versus the Picaresque* (Chicago: University of Chicago Press, 1981).

sider" form in the nineteenth century, when its large popular audience displaces coterie readers and their favored genres; and that it then becomes an "outsider" form again with the art novels of Conrad, Ford, and James, as the century turns, and with the experimental novel and its new "uncommon" readers in our time. But this new outsider form is distinctly artful; it is *the* literary form prized by its new audience of academically trained readers, and so reverses and perhaps even undercuts the terms of Reed's dialectic.[5] In my introduction to *Novel's* tenth-year anthology, moreover, I had argued that Reed's supposedly unsystematic dialectic is only another version of the play between contingency and pattern, dream and truthtelling, on which other contributors had remarked, and that these opposing traits seemed to me to be generic and therefore rich matter for a poetics.[6] In his book, of course, Reed holds that even the word "genre" is too canonical for the novel, and that the word "protocol" speaks more aptly to its individualistic ways. But again such quarrels over terminology disguise larger differences than those of loose description versus tight prescription. At stake here is the question, as D. H. Lawrence puts it, of why the novel matters.

Reed himself is more sensitive to that question than many current practitioners of the semiotic arts. He believes, for instance, that modern novels may reflect and perhaps even redeem our desperate times through pluralistic and mythopoeic forms. There is a hidden value agenda to his descriptive history, and this seems to me to be the case also for the new *poetiques* and their value-free assumptions. The fact that feminists, Marxists, and Lacanian neo-Freudians have adopted these systems tends to belie their rejection of value-claims for literary works. If deconstruction proceeds in the name of the embattled humanism of the feminist movement, for instance, there must be something in those intertextual documents and codes worth fighting for; as there is, of course, in the Marxist concern with the social dynamics at work in literary texts, or the Lacanian concern with how we cure ourselves of this or that phallocentric obsession. During my own limited reading of the new approaches I was at first appalled by how quickly they have moved to the old medieval condition of determining how many angels in the house can dance on the head of an absent penis, and by how quickly the new terminologies have themselves hardened into unexamined formulas and rigid terms of discourse between initiated specialists. But lately, as an editor for *Novel* and in other capacities, I have noticed how some of those initiates are struggling toward painful acknowledgement that something of value may indeed be present in new and old texts, surviving their deconstructive shredding; and perhaps even more significantly, how some of those initiates are even beginning to write quite readable prose, using that common language by which all previous critical discourse used to proceed—at least outside of Chicago.

On the other side of the spectrum, I have also noticed how our embattled humanists are beginning to take concrete issue with their opponents by absorbing their methods and reasserting old claims within new contexts. In the years since

[5] See *Studies in the Novel* 14 (Spring 1982), 128–132.

[6] *Towards a Poetics of Fiction*, p. ix.

1977, for instance, over twenty theoretical essays have appeared in *Novel*, about seven of which might figure as extensions of our original "Poetics" series; and of those seven, at least four take arms against the writings of post-structuralists whose theories they have to some degree absorbed. This turning of attention of the old school to the new, in order to make its humanistic points, may help to explain my earlier contention that the generating force of the old school has subsided. Instead of focussing directly on the problems of a humanist poetics, such writers are forced to meet the challenge of the new dispensations. This weakens the thrust of the original movement, and indeed, none of the seven essays I have mentioned has the force and freshness of our original seven essays; they are marginal or peripheral or supplementary in their various concerns with realism, generic identity, readers, characters, feminine authority, and the structure of black fictions. Of course the original humanist contributions also had their arguments with older theories and with each other; but the discourse, as I have said, at least proceeded in a common language and with a number of shared assumptions about works, authors, and readers, and about real and novelistic worlds. The new discourse proceeds by such radically different views on all these matters as to make dialogue difficult; and indeed the humanists engaged with it write in less accessible prose than their predecessors. But at least they rise to the challenge.

Thus, in "Narrative Fiction and Reality" (Fall 1977), Roy Pascal takes on Frank Kermode's changing views in *The Sense of an Ending*, in which Kermode adopts Vaihinger's "as if" philosophy of useful fictions which are in themselves arbitrary and unreal, though they help to "make sense of the world."[7] Pascal is concerned with the implicit subjectivism and arbitrariness assigned to narrative fictions, and finds Kermode himself inconsistent in his handling of these borrowed ideas, accepting them at some points at face value and at others suggesting that "adequate respect for real time" or for "the End as a fact of life" must be observed in the novel's concern with time and endings. Pascal quarrels with similar inconsistencies in the philosophies of Vaihinger and Nietzsche on which Kermode relies, and uses the ideas of such philosophical or literary scholars as W. B. Gallie and H. R. Jauss to demonstrate that literary fictions are both objective and subjective in makeup, that attachment to reality is necessary to their usefulness. He postulates that literary fictions show things in relationship to other things, and that stories are and always have been processes through which universal understanding of human relationships is made possible; they engage us, that is, in models of human relationships which involve "anticipations and surprises, wishes and setbacks, judgments that require correction, a series that is somewhat altered with every new reading and involves, like life, alternations of expectations and revisions until the ending." The stuff of such stories is, moreover, the contingent; their purpose is "the discovery of some coherence within the great mass of the contingent." Literary fictions give us then an interplay be-

---

[7] See *Novel* 11 (Fall 1977), 40–50.

tween accident and coherence, and so further our "understanding of the manageable and the unmanageable."

Far from being arbitrary, then, the imposition of patterns, whether in art or life, is a condition of existence required of all forms of social life; there is nothing bourgeois about it; it is the way we go about coping with the contingencies which have always confronted human beings. Perhaps the unmanageability of such contingencies has increased in modern times; hence the influx of our current cynicisms as to the relations between language and reality. Yet the interplay of coherence and contingency still obtains in the modern fictions of a Kafka, or in more recent times, a Pynchon. Even happy endings, for Pascal, have an attachment to reality in that we have all experienced closures in experience, whether partial or provisional, which involve fulfillment. Thus, the effectiveness or usefulness of fictions is not arbitrary or opposed to truth, Pascal concludes, but depends rather "on the fact that they embody an aspect of reality."

I review this essay at length because it seems to me to offer a way out of the prison house of language and the code approach to literary fictions in which our current semioticians and poststructuralists are engaged, and toward which Kermode's book might be called a way station. I do not have space to reconstruct the similar attempts to rescue humanist assumptions from the new cynicisms in Terrence Doody's "Don Quixote, Ulysses, and the Idea of Realism" (Spring 1979), Steven Cohan's "Figures Beyond the Text: A Theory of Readable Character in the Novel" (Fall 1983), and Nancy Armstrong's "The Rise of Feminine Authority in the Novel" (Winter 1982). I can only commend them to your attention as I move on to my own final comments on that problem with a poetics posed by Walter Reed, its judgmental nature. In my own naivete I have always considered that a poetics may be both descriptive and, if not exactly prescriptive, at least concerned with problems of both aesthetic and moral valuation. I am an incorrigible believer in the novel's orienting functions from its origins to the present time, its concern with showing us how to live, or even how not to live, in terms of the value-conflicts which have always beset us, but which have been expressed through the individual lives of ordinary as well as extraordinary people since the rise of the middle classes in the eighteenth century. I am not personally or politically offended myself by the idea of bourgeois individualism because it seems to me a continually self-correcting fiction with some basis in the realities by which current feminists and Marxists and other value-free theorists not only earn their livings but are free to deny their own obvious heritage. Indeed, these new cultural commissars seem suspiciously like the rest of us, as they go about their imperial business, so perhaps I may be pardoned for thinking of them as bourgeois individualists in disguise.

The sweeping corrections they supply are accordingly quite welcome, if only because they force us to examine their disguises and revive and revise our own dormant views. But I do think there will have to be some accommodation on their part also of the aesthetic and moral value of literary fictions, in this case novels, some restoration of their status as works worthy of contemplation as well

as texts for deconstruction. We eclectic humanists have after all been engaged
for some time with the weaknesses and dangers of the works we cherish as well
as with their moral and aesthetic merits; and we have been engaged also in
broader and deeper approaches to fiction than mere formalism allows. The verbal icon is no longer a sacred object for us, but rather a richly meaningful object
which repays repeated study through a variety of extrinsic and intrinsic approaches. Its autonomy is relative rather than absolute, and I think that the new
schools will have to accept that relative value and its person-centered uses, even
as we learn to accept their descriptive systems and cultural codes as tools of
great sociological utility—as indeed they are when applied to those "privileged
texts" we all know and love, which as I understand it our American poststructuralists now treat as "works" even while professing otherwise.[8] If this seems
like another liberal ploy for compromise and absorption, I can only say—why
not? I think authors, works, readers, and cultures alike will benefit by it in the
long run; and if that is unduly optimistic, I can only say that this is an optimistic
as well as a skeptical and pragmatic culture in which we bourgeois individualists
also live, breathe, earn our salaries, and prepare our papers for each other's edi-
fication on socially regressive panels like this one. At least my own sense of a
happy ending tells me so.

[8] See, for example, Mario Valdes, ed., *The Identity of the Literary Text* (Toronto: University of Toronto Press, 1985); and for the
counter-tendency, see Charles Altieri, *Act & Quality: A Theory of Literary Meaning and Humanistic Understanding* (Amherst: University of Massachusetts Press, 1981). For other humanist defenses, see Robert Alter's brilliant assessment of the present conflict, "Mimesis and the Motive for Fiction," in *Motives for Fiction* (Cambridge: Harvard University Press, 1984), pp. 3–21; H. M.
Daleski's *Unities: Studies in the English Novel* (Athens: University of Georgia Press, 1985); and Daniel Schwarz's work in progress,
The Humanistic Heritage: Critical Theories of the English Novel from James to Hillis Miller.

Booth's Rhetoric, Bakhtin's Dialogics
and the Future of Novel Criticism*

DON H. BIALOSTOSKY, *Panelist*

When we ask, "Where do we go from here?" it helps to know where we are. In
novel criticism today, one place from which we can take our bearings on the future is Wayne Booth's *Rhetoric of Fiction*. It is not the only source of rhetorical
approaches to fiction on which current criticism draws, but since it remains the
most self-consciously rhetorical and the most widely known place in which to
learn about rhetorical criticism of fiction, I will take it as the place from which I
try to chart some future directions for novel criticism.

* This essay was provoked by and is indebted to a paper by Hendrik van Gorp on "Theories of Novelistic Polyphony: Bakhtin vs.
Stanzel, Genette, and Booth" presented at an International Colloquium on Mikhail Bakhtin: His Circle, His Influence, at
Queen's University, Kingston, Ontario, October 7–9, 1983. I have also benefited from conversation and correspondence with
Wayne Booth. Homer Goldberg and Marianna Torgovnick helped with close critical readings.

In the afterword to the 1983 second edition of *The Rhetoric of Fiction,* Booth has had occasion to ask himself where novel criticism has gone since 1961 and to point directions it might now take. Of the more than 400 new entries in his bibliography, he singles out four critics for their special pertinence to his project; of those four, one above all not only enriches Booth's inquiry but challenges some of its fundamental premises. Booth finds Mikhail Bakhtin's dialogic poetics of the novel especially impressive on the topics of language and style, historical and implied authors and readers, objectivity and technique, and ideology and form.[1]

Booth's acknowledgment of Bakhtin in his afterword is remarkable for its willingness to see him as a challenge on the same issues that *The Rhetoric of Fiction* raises rather than to quarantine him as a theorist of some other critical mode with its own distinctive but unrhetorical questions. In this he shows the effects of the responsive and open-ended pluralism he invents in *Critical Understanding.*[2] But in his foreword to Caryl Emerson's new translation of Bakhtin's *Problems of Dostoevsky's Poetics*—an essay he sees as spilling over from the afterword to his own book—Booth combines this stance with the more defensive pluralism of his 1968 essay on *"The Rhetoric of Fiction* and the Poetics of Fictions": he generously acknowledges Bakhtin's challenge to the rhetoric of fiction, but he also isolates that challenge in a critical mode distinct from his own.[3]

Booth begins his foreword to the Dostoevsky book by establishing a common ground between his Chicago Aristotelianism and Bakhtin's dialogism on the question of ideology and form. Both positions, he claims, reject the opposition between abstract form and ideological content for an idea of form charged with value or ideology. Booth distinguishes his Chicago Aristotelianism, however, for its focus on the distinction between the effects authors intend in their ideologically charged formal unities and the technical means they use to achieve them. According to the Chicago premises Booth worked under in *The Rhetoric of Fiction,* "Authors were . . . in charge of created unities that consisted of choices exemplified and judged."[4]

In this Aristotelian framework, Booth conceived the rhetoric of fiction as focused on technique, on "the rhetorical resources available to the writer . . . as he tries, consciously or unconsciously, to impose his fictional world upon the reader."[5] Booth assumed the end of imposing a unified fictional world of a given kind—like the tragic, comic, or horrific—and concerned himself with advocating the unrestricted use of all rhetorical means to impose that world upon the reader. He argued, accordingly, that it is an arbitrary and unnecessary restric-

[1] Wayne C. Booth, *The Rhetoric of Fiction,* 2nd ed. (Chicago: University of Chicago Press, 1983), pp. 409, 410n., 415–17, 419. The other three critics Booth pays special attention to are Peter Rabinowitz, Sheldon Sacks, and Gérard Genette.

[2] Wayne C. Booth, *Critical Understanding: The Powers and Limits of Pluralism* (Chicago: University of Chicago Press, 1979).

[3] Wayne C. Booth, "Introduction," in Mikhail Bakhtin, *Problems of Dostoevsky's Poetics,* ed. and trans. Caryl Emerson (Minneapolis: University of Minnesota Press, 1984), pp. xiii-xxvii; Wayne C. Booth, *"The Rhetoric of Fiction* and the Poetics of Fictions," *Novel* 1 (Winter, 1968), pp. 105–117; rpt. in *Towards a Poetics of Fiction,* ed. Mark Spilka (Bloomington: Indiana University Press, 1977), pp. 77–89.

[4] Booth, "Introduction," p. xviii.

[5] Booth, *Rhetoric of Fiction,* p. xiii.

tion on artists and readers to confine them to using or appreciating only "objective" techniques.

Booth's afterword presents Bakhtin's position as if it transcended the whole question of fictional techniques and their relation to artistic ends. Bakhtin's challenge, he writes, "has nothing at all to do with the author's effort to produce a single unified effect. Its subject is not the ordering of technical means toward certain effects so much as the quality of the author's imaginative gift—the ability or willingness to allow voices into the work that are not fundamentally under the 'monological' control of the novelist's own ideology."[6] As Booth recognizes, he has assimilated Bakhtin's position to the Longinian alternative to Aristotle that the Chicago school has long acknowledged—an alternative concerned to demonstrate the presence of genius or greatness or sublimity in the author rather than to articulate the functioning of parts in the whole in a given work.[7] Booth repeatedly emphasizes Bakhtin's transcendence of mere technical concerns for more profound and important issues, making his challenge to the rhetoric of fiction seem more like a moral and spiritual challenge to its questions than a technical and artistic challenge to Booth's answers to them.[8]

Booth thus diminishes his direct encounter with Bakhtin by conceding him the high ground and holding onto the low, but we shall see that the dialogics and the rhetoric of fiction challenge one another more directly on the common grounds of the author's role, the author's chosen artistic task, and the technical means of realizing it than Booth's account of Bakhtin allows. In outlining what I take to be their points of confrontation, I think I am also mapping terrain on which novel criticism may discover much that needs to be said about both its theoretical resources and the body of texts with which it is concerned.

Though Booth argues in *The Rhetoric of Fiction* for the author's use of all available technical means in imposing a fictional world on the reader, his polemical emphasis is on the uses of the author's voice. He shows the usefulness of direct authorial commentary and the price of renouncing it. And he argues that when such commentary is lacking and the author resorts to the "hundreds of devices [that] remain for revealing judgment and molding responses," "the author's voice is still dominant in a dialogue that is at the heart of all experience with fiction."[9] Booth's idea of the novel as dialogue among the author, narrators, characters, and readers links him with Bakhtin's dialogic model of novelistic discourse,[10] but his repeated insistence on the dominance of the author over narrators, characters and readers differentiates the rhetorical novel Booth examines from the dialogic Dostoevskian novel Bakhtin describes.[11]

[6] Booth, "Introduction," p. xx.

[7] *Ibid.*, pp. xx, xxvii.

[8] *Ibid.*, pp. xx, xxiv–xxv, xxvii.

[9] Booth, *Rhetoric of Fiction*, p. 272.

[10] *Ibid.*, p. 155.

[11] This insistent subordination of hero to author or story to discourse is widely assumed in contemporary novel and narrative theory. I have contrasted Seymour Chatman's reliance upon it with Bakhtin's challenge to it in "Bakhtin versus Chatman on Narrative: The Habilitation of the Hero," *University of Ottawa Quarterly* 53 (January, 1983), 109–116.

While Booth repeatedly posits a dialogue in which "the author sees more deeply and judges more profoundly than his presented characters,"[12] Bakhtin explicitly examines the novel in which not the author's superior consciousness but the hero's self-consciousness is the dominant of representation.[13] Booth would see such a move as a shift in technical devices that "turns the character whose mind is shown into a narrator,"[14] but Bakhtin's self-conscious hero is not a "center of consciousness" through whose perspective a story is told but the object of representation itself. The hero's discourse in its response to discourses of the other characters *and* the discourse of the author is, for Bakhtin, the novel's principal object of representation.[15]

Bakhtin's dialogics of fiction thus reopens the question of what is means and what is end in the novel and suggests that in some cases at least the choices Booth advocates as technically effective would not serve the end Bakhtin imagines. If the hero's self-consciousness is to be the dominant of representation, the author's position must be shifted from the finalizing and judging role Booth defends to an actively dialogic interchange with the hero. "Only in the light of this artistic project," Bakhtin writes, "can one understand the authentic function of such compositional elements as the narrator and his tone . . . and the . . . narration direct from the author."[16] This is not the critical language of someone unconcerned with "unified effect" and the "technical means toward certain effects"[17] but of someone who posits a different kind of effect that calls for a radical reconsideration of fictional means and ends.

Bakhtin's account of the genre of the Dostoevskian novel gives us an idea how the ends toward which it is organized differ from more familiar tragic or comic or rhetorical ends with which he contrasts it. Bakhtin traces Dostoevsky's generic sources along several lines of what he calls the "serio-comic" or carnivalized genres. In all these genres, he writes, "there is a strong rhetorical element, but in the atmosphere of *joyful relativity* characteristic of a carnival sense of the world this element is fundamentally changed: there is a weakening of its one-sided rhetorical seriousness, its rationality, its singular meaning, its dogmatism."[18] The "stylistic unity . . . of the epic, the tragedy, high rhetoric, [and] the lyric" is replaced by mixed styles in the serio-comic genres,[19] as "the epic and tragic wholeness of a person and his fate" is replaced by self-division in which the hero "ceases to mean only one thing."[20] Carnival familiarization suspends the usual hierarchies of social values and destroys "epic and tragic

[12] Booth, *Rhetoric of Fiction*, p. 74.

[13] Bakhtin, *Problems of Dostoevsky's Poetics*, pp. 49–50.

[14] Booth, *Rhetoric of Fiction*, p. 164.

[15] Bakhtin, *Problems of Dostoevsky's Poetics*, pp. 63–65, 266.

[16] *Ibid.*, p. 64.

[17] Booth, "Introduction," p. xx.

[18] Bakhtin, *Problems of Dostoevsky's Poetics*, p. 107.

[19] *Ibid.*, p. 108.

[20] *Ibid.*, pp. 116–17.

distance."[21] Deeply ambivalent responses to fundamental contradictions replace the clarified responses of separate tragic and comic genres; promiscuous participation replaces the conventional "division into performers and spectators."[22]

Even this highly compressed summary of the serio-comic genre can show us how Bakhtin gives positive character to a literary effect that Booth reads as a lack of the "clarity about distance" provided by the "traditional forms."[23] To the critic who argues for the reader's right to know whether to "approve or disapprove, laugh or cry,"[24] Bakhtin's "*joyful relativity* of all structure and order"[25] and his "ambivalent laughter"[26] are a challenge to fundamental distinctions of literary effect. The clarification of response one seeks in Aristotelian tragedy or comedy depends upon the audience's recognition of the hero's standing and the audience's distance from the hero's situation, but the participatory response Bakhtin envisions puts the hero and the audience in a carnivalized proximity to one another that replaces definitive judgment with mutual openness and responsiveness.

In such a fictional world, the author does not design characters to provoke laughter, tears, or admiration but to provoke articulate responsiveness of one person to another on common human ground. Instead of issuing in a non-verbal recognition or feeling or attitude, the unfinalized interplay of value-charged discourse in the dialogic work continues in the diverse verbal responses it provokes in its readers. Booth's rhetorical emphasis on determinate and generally nonverbal effects leads him to call "the critical disagreement" provoked by stories "a scandal."[27] For Bakhtin that unsettled controversy is a mark of success in a work designed to dialogic rather than rhetorical specifications.

In Bakhtin's serio-comic genre, then, it is not, as Booth says, that the characters defy "any temptation the author may have to fit them into his superior plans"[28] but rather that, as Bakhtin says, "the freedom of a character is an aspect of the author's design" and "is just as much a created thing as is the unfreedom of the objectivized hero."[29] Bakhtin has not forfeited an interest in artistic design and the technique that serves it but has radically enlarged the field of such designs and so has not only shifted the possible functions of techniques but has shifted the very boundaries between technique and design.

One of the most important shifts in these boundaries concerns the role of language or discourse or diction in the novel. In his afterword Booth remains insistently Aristotelian in treating language not as the object of imitation but as the

[21] *Ibid.*, p. 124.

[22] *Ibid.*, p. 122.

[23] Booth, *Rhetoric of Fiction*, p. 331.

[24] *Ibid.*

[25] Bakhtin, *Problems of Dostoevsky's Poetics*, p. 124.

[26] *Ibid.*, p. 166.

[27] Booth, *Rhetoric of Fiction*, p. 315.

[28] Booth, "Introduction," p. xxiii.

[29] Bakhtin, *Problems of Dostoevsky's Poetics*, pp. 64–65.

means for realizing the object of "characters-in-action,"[30] and he regrets that he did not place more emphasis on the primacy of plot in *The Rhetoric of Fiction*.[31] Bakhtin just as firmly declares that the "main object of [Dostoevsky's] representation is the word itself" understood as the discourse of the ideologist-hero in its responsiveness to the words addressed to it by other characters and by the author as well.[32] Bakhtin's analysis of the various ways in which one person's word can be related to the word of another provides perhaps his richest contribution to our critical vocabulary. His chapter on "Discourse in Dostoevsky" as well as his section on reported speech in *Marxism and the Philosophy of Language* enrich our understanding not only of novelistic techniques like free indirect discourse but of interesting novelistic objects in the very verbal interplay among the languages of characters, authors, and narrators.[33] His typology of verbal interactions is most immediately useful for analyzing local verbal events in the novel and leaves as yet unanswered the question Bakhtin himself thought remained most open at the end of his inquiries, the question "of *the whole* in a polyphonic novel."[34] That question remains open and important for future novel criticism.[35]

Introducing Bakhtin's dialogics of fiction into our discussion of the novel does not rule out the effects Booth considers or the techniques he defends, but it does tempt me to identify them and his rhetorical criticism of them as appropriate principally to the monologic novel. I shall resist the temptation, however, to set up a dialectical opposition between Booth's monologism and Bakhtin's dialogism, because the dialogic perspective finally does not allow for such an opposition in critical theory any more than in novelistic practice. Though Bakhtin himself, despite his dialogic principles, habitually makes use of this heightened opposition and tempts me to emulate him, he writes in the essay "Discourse in the Novel" that "even in those places where the author's voice seems at first glance to be unitary and consistent, direct and unmediatedly intentional, beneath that smooth single-languaged surface we can nevertheless uncover prose's three-dimensionality, its profound speech diversity, which enters the project of style and is its determining factor."[36] For Bakhtin, then, neither "monologic" novelists nor critical theorists would "mean only one thing" any more than does the hero of the Dostoevskian novel. While dialectical arguments reduce their participants to representing such single meanings, dialogic criticism must be

---

[30] Booth, *Rhetoric of Fiction*, p. 409.

[31] *Ibid.*, pp. 436–440.

[32] Bakhtin, *Problems of Dostoevsky's Poetics*, p. 266.

[33] Mikhail Bakhtin, *Marxism and the Philosophy of Language*, trans. Ladislav Matejka and I. R. Titunik (New York: Seminar Press, 1973), pp. 109–159. This volume was originally published under the name of V. N. Voloshinov.

[34] Bakhtin, *Problems of Dostoevsky's Poetics*, p. 4.

[35] For an effort in the Chicago Aristotelian and rhetorical tradition to come to terms with "the problem of completeness in the open-ended novel," see David Richter, *Fable's End: Completeness and Closure in Rhetorical Fiction* (Chicago: University of Chicago Press, 1974). James Phelan, writing in the same tradition, provides its most thorough analysis of the place of language in fiction but does not take up Bakhtin's contribution to the question. See his *Worlds from Words: A Theory of Language in Fiction* (Chicago: University of Chicago Press, 1981).

[36] Mikhail Bakhtin, "Discourse in the Novel," in *The Dialogic Imagination*, ed. Michael Holquist, trans. Caryl Emerson and Michael Holquist (Austin: University of Texas Press, 1981), p. 315.

alert to what remains to be said from the unfolding positions of its concrete participants.

Viewed in this dialogic perspective, Booth's linking of Bakhtin to the Longinian tradition may be seen as part of another agenda. Booth's current inquiries into the ethics of fiction make him less interested in Bakhtin's bearings on the technical issues of the rhetoric of fiction than on the evaluative issues that now concern him. In his feminist critique of Bakhtin and Rabelais in "Freedom of Interpretation: Bakhtin and the Challenge of Feminist Criticism," he subordinates technical issues to moral judgment of the "quality of . . . laughter" Rabelais evokes and political criticism of the exclusion of female voices from his text.[37] Booth recognizes the carnival effects Bakhtin dwells upon, but he challenges Bakhtin's celebration of them as ideologically limited rather than as formally unclear. But even in *The Rhetoric of Fiction* itself Booth opened the question of "the moral, not merely the technical, angle of vision from which the story is to be told," and his identification of Bakhtin's argument with that "more profound" question may serve to acknowledge Bakhtin's challenge where it matters most to him now, rather than to deflect it from the issues of the rhetoric of fiction in which he is no longer engaged.[38]

Bakhtin, too, has more to say than my reductive opposition between his theory and Booth's allows. Especially in his essay "Discourse in the Novel," he shows himself aware of a heterogeneity of novelistic genres not reducible to the Dostoevskian model dominated by the hero's self-consciousness and organized to carnivalized effects. His definition of the novel in that essay as "a diversity of social speech types . . . and a diversity of individual voices, artistically organized" preserves the emphasis on the imitation of language and on artistic organization that I have brought out, but it allows for other arrangements of diverse voices and other artistic effects than the Dostoevskian.[39]

His acknowledgment of this diversity also permits him to present the history of novelistic genres without making it seem to culminate in Dostoevsky's achievement—which reminds *me* to acknowledge that Booth in his foreword to Bakhtin finds his "own greatest challenge" in Bakhtin's historically and socially situated alternative to Booth's "ahistorical treatment of forms."[40] Though Bakhtin too, as I have argued, has his contribution to make to such an ahistorical theory of novelistic possibilities, I would not want the emerging conversation between his position and Booth's to confine itself to that formalistic purview. If we cannot rest in a dialectical opposition between a Boothian monologics and a Bakhtinian dialogics of fiction, perhaps we can have a historically specified Boothian "Rhetoric of Pre-Modern Fiction" to go along with a Bakhtinian "Prob-

---

[37] Wayne C. Booth, "Freedom of Interpretation: Bakhtin and the Challenge of Feminist Criticism," *Critical Inquiry* 9 (September, 1982), 60.

[38] Booth, *Rhetoric of Fiction*, p. 265.

[39] Bakhtin, "Discourse in the Novel," p. 262.

[40] Booth, "Introduction," p. xxvi.

lems of Dostoevsky's Poetics" and an Aristotelian "Problems of Athenian Tragic Poetics."

But such a historical formulation would be as fatal to the dialogue I wish to promote as its dialectical counterpart. For it should be clear that all these arguments bear on one another as accounts of the poetics of fiction, and that each of the theories is at least as conditioned by its responses to its theoretical predecessors as by its choice of specific historical subjects. We can no more isolate them from one another by specifying them historically than by defining their distinctive theoretical modes; we must engage them as they have engaged others on the perpetually open ground of what needs to be said next.

Booth, following Bakhtin in his foreword, writes that "to *state* the future would belie its openness,"[41] but I will venture a few speculations about the directions our conversations will take after Bakhtin. Formally, we will have to talk more about how an imitation of discourse rather than action finds that degree of wholeness it embodies. Historically, we will want to discuss novelistic discourses as both responses to and provocations of other social discourses. Theoretically, we may find ourselves reexamining novel criticism itself as a response to and a continuation of novelistic discourse. Other voices will surely contribute to these inquiries and remind us that we were engaged in them before Bakhtin was translated for us, but however the conversation proceeds some of it will go on from what Bakhtin, and what Booth's engagement with him, leaves to be said about the poetics of fiction.[42]

[41] *Ibid.*

[42] The conversation has, of course, already begun. The bibliography of essays and books on the novel influenced by Bakhtin begins in the West with Julia Kristeva's "Bakhtine, le mot, le dialogue et le roman" in *Critique* (April 1967), 438–65, and most recently includes Caryl Emerson's "The Tolstoy Connection in Bakhtin" in *PMLA* 100 (January, 1985), 68–80, and Victor Brombert's *Victor Hugo and the Visionary Novel* (Cambridge: Harvard University Press, 1984). Readers of *Novel* have already entered the conversation through David Hayman's essay and review in 16 (Winter, 1983), 101–120, 173–77. The most complete and convenient bibliography of Bakhtin's reception and influence is available in *The Bakhtin Newsletter* from Clive Thomson, Department of French, Queen's University, Kingston, Ontario, Canada K7L 3N6.

Mimesis, Authority, and Belief in Narrative Poetics: Toward a Transmission Theory for a Poetics of Fiction

BERNARD DUYFHUIZEN, *Panelist*

To examine the current state of narrative poetics and to speculate on its future, we need first to recall Aristotle's *Poetics* and its substantial place in the theory of the novel. The *Poetics* presents a systematic theory of rules for composition, for critical evaluation, and for production of the proper effect of tragedy on the audience. Central to Aristotle's theory is the concept of *mimesis*. For tragedy to produce the proper effect of fear and pity, it must represent plausible characters, situations, and actions, and these must convince the audience of their potential reality. Although Greek tragedy's highly stylized literary form could scarcely serve as a model for a naive realism, Aristotle's concept of *mimesis* contributed greatly to a sixteenth- and seventeenth-century concern with realism in drama and prose discourse.

Recently J. Paul Hunter and Lennard Davis have demonstrated that a constituent element in the novel's emergence was the blending of factual and fictional narratives in the popular press of the late seventeenth and early eighteenth centuries.[1] As these narratives became more involved and expansive the "novel" emerged as a suitable form for these extended tales of characters and society. Though no "poetics of fiction" existed *per se*, the principle of *mimesis* can be distinguished as the novel's central organizing force. *Don Quixote, Tom Jones, Clarissa, Tristram Shandy,* and other novels associated with the "rise of the novel" all have *mimesis*—or at least the question of it—as one of their main focuses. A cursory history of the novel confirms that a significant organizing principle of the genre has been the linguistic representation of life, thus marking a significant distinction between the novel and drama. Although Greek tragedy and the drama that followed was highly stylized, it held within it the potential for imitation as well as representation, whereas the novel is bound by the linguistic signs printed on a page and may only approach imitation in highly self-conscious novels within novels.

Such self-consciousness, of course, lays bare the devices of the novel and thereby estranges the reader's experience of a represented life. When Victor Shklovsky recognized the concept of estrangement (*ostraneniye*, sometimes translated as "defamiliarization") in literary texts, he and his fellow Russian Formalists momentarily redirected perception away from representation and toward the "literariness" of literary devices. The concept of estrangement, however, ultimately reinscribes itself in a "higher *mimesis*"; Shklovsky writes, "art exists that one may recover the sensation of life; it exists to make one feel things, to make the stone *stony*. The purpose of art is to impart the sensation of things as they are perceived and not as they are known. The technique of art is to make objects '[strange]'. . . ."[2] The literary device still functions to "represent life," only the reproduction no longer simply depends on the pretext of familiar presence. Representation has become an effect of discourse, of literariness—an effect of rhetoricity rather than a naive notion of referentiality.

The structural linguistics of Ferdinand de Saussure endorses the Russian Formalist conception of literary devices. When Saussure postulated the arbitrari-

[1] J. Paul Hunter, "News, Novelty, and the Novel," Div. on English III: General Topics, SCMLA Convention, Biloxi, 26 October 1984; Lennard J. Davis, *Factual Fictions: The Origins of the English Novel* (New York: Columbia University Press, 1983). Though focusing on letters rather than early newspapers, Ruth Perry's *Women, Letters, and the Novel* (New York: AMS, 1980) also presents a nonfictional model for the novel's origin.

[2] "Art as Technique," *Russian Formalist Criticism: Four Essays*, ed. and trans. Lee T. Lemon and Marion J. Reis (Lincoln: University of Nebraska Press, 1965), p. 12. On the translation of *ostraneniye* I am indebted to Tzvetan Todorov, with whom I studied at the School of Criticism and Theory in 1981.

ness of the linguistic sign, the bond between language (signifiers) and the world (signifieds) became a matter of convention and agreement rather than immanent relation. The power of convention, however, has been extremely strong, and as Levi-Strauss's early readings of myth made clear, the ties between literature and life (culture) still serve as a basic premise for critical activity. Structural linguistics may have provided a new model for critical inquiry, but the basic assumptions of mimetic reading were only redefined by structuralism's privileging of language.

When *Novel* began publication in the Fall of 1967, its first issues contained essays that questioned whether a poetics of fiction is possible, and whether a particular approach (through structure, language, history, narrative, genre, or time) could be fixed as the primary ground for such a poetics.[3] Not surprisingly, some of the contributors had reservations about such a project—by 1967 the novel and criticism of the novel had evolved to a stage of remarkable diversity, making the hope of a common ground for poetics appear distant. Still, a common ground, possibly a uniquely Anglo-American common ground, can be found in these early *Novel* essays: each depends to some degree on the novel's assumed relation to life and its seemingly inherent foundation in "realism."

For example, Eleanor Hutchens, in presenting an approach through temporal structure in the novel, writes, "Time is not mere successiveness; it is the very matrix of life" (53), hence its central place in any poetics of the novel. Or, as Robert Scholes puts it in setting forth an approach through genre, the "primary modes of fiction [satire, history, romance] are themselves based on the three possible relations between any fictional world and the world of experience. A fictional world can be better than the world of experience, worse than it, or equal to it" (44). Even David Lodge, whose approach through language shakes the novel's mimetic underpinnings, concludes his contribution with a cautionary note: "[I]n recommending an approach to the novel through language I am not seeking to deny or sever its connection with 'life,' but merely asking that the crucial role of language in presenting life to us in literary fiction be adequately recognized" (22). The foundation of novel theory in these essays was the depiction of a fictional universe that, even at its most absurd, resembles our everyday existence, conjoins life and language, and speaks to the human condition.

Meanwhile in France in the late 60s two critical movements that have significantly influenced the project of a poetics of fiction were being established. The first, narratology, developed out of early structuralist and semiotic theories to provide a seemingly scientific analysis of textual units, and in its extremest manifestation, a "mathematics" for textual analysis. Narratology has done much to improve formal and linguistic analyses of texts; yet in its move away from *mimesis*, such analysis tends to reduce texts to abstract formulae of "deep structure," which seemingly have little relation to how a text is consciously written or read—the structures discovered have significance but little meaning. In a sense, there is a mimetic trap in criticism: to be considered "meaning-full," a reading

---

[3] These essays were later collected in *Towards a Poetics of Fiction*, ed. Mark Spilka (Bloomington: Indiana University Press, 1977); references cited in the text below are to this collection.

must recount the story of a real reader's engagement with the text, and conventionally we tend to value that story as it clarifies our own mimetic assumptions. The epistemologies Western philosophy has devised to help us understand our world support the valorization of mimetic reading.

The second French critical movement, deconstruction, developed as a radical critique of conventional epistemologies, such as mimetic assumptions in reading, and as a response to structuralism's reductive logocentrism. Differing from more traditional ways of thinking, deconstruction seeks to question the accepted givens of all epistemologies, including its own. Thus, whereas structuralist narratology moves away from *mimesis* by shifting the focus of its inquiry, deconstruction questions the very concept of *mimesis*. Following this line of inquiry, we see that *mimesis* is conventionally understood by the phrase "art imitates life." This phrase marks the opposition reality/representation, in which reality (life) is both prior and privileged with relation to representation (art), which is both derivative and parasitic. This opposition appears logically natural, but it can be deconstructed to reveal representation as always already coexistent with reality; moreover, the representations (texts) that contain our culture also overdetermine our existence. Therefore, art imitates life and life imitates art. Neither is privileged or prior, both are parasitic and derivative. By overturning the accepted understanding of *mimesis*, deconstruction can question the referential foundation of the novel and most novel criticism, thus making problematic any poetics of fiction using *mimesis* as a basic, unquestioned premise.

The traditional establishment of *mimesis* as center for a poetics of fiction relied on two necessary commonplaces: (1) the author's authority and intentions, and (2) the reader's willingness (longing) to believe that the text's illusion of reality could be translated into a meaning with referential force in the reader's world of experience—hence the power of religious allegories to lead the flock in the proper path toward salvation. If we recall, for the moment, Roman Jakobson's famous communications model,[4] then my comments so far have been directed at the vertical axis of the model, the code-message-context (referent). Deconstruction also questions the horizontal axis of addresser-contact-addressee. Conventionally in narrative poetics, the producer of the text and his or her surrogates fill the role of the addresser. This addresser (author or narrator) is also seen as the originator of the textual speech act and therefore the sole authority over meaning. The problem for any poetics based on this premise is twofold: (1) *The belatedness of the author to his or her text*. Because language has paradigmatic/syntagmatic aspects and synchronic/diachronic aspects, the words of the text have neither their origin nor their referent exclusively with the writer's intention. Though the arrangement of signs in a particular text might appear unique, every text is always already written, a reiteration of what has already been said. (2) *The problem of distance and doubling*. By working in words the author always creates other selves that represent the authorial voice (narration) or the thematic focus (characters). The question of a minimal construal for the text becomes more problem-

---

[4] "Closing Statement: Linguistics and Poetics," *Style in Language*, ed. Thomas A. Sebeok (Cambridge: M.I.T. Press, 1960).

atic the more complex the narration—signifiers float free, open to an endless play of signification. If the addresser cannot support the center of a poetics, then what about the addressee?

The question of a reader-based poetics is equally vexed, since the central term—reader—also relies on either a unifying *mimesis* or a theoretical abstraction, and therefore cannot be adequately defined. Though we have theories of ideal, implied, characterized, and superreaders, all are theoretical constructs that only approximate actual reading. These theoretical readers and readings still assume, however, a correspondence between the text and the real world. Fictions can only mean if they reflect, or are found to reflect, conventional experience, and if they solicit the reader's participation in concretizing the fictional world and his or her belief in the "reality" depicted. As Clayton Koelb recently observed, "an article of hermeneutic faith" is "that fiction, no matter how outlandish, conceals some hidden kernel of truth."[5] Koelb deconstructs this article of faith in his book *The Incredulous Reader* by showing how some texts ask readers to maintain disbelief rather than suspending it. This mode of "lethetic" reading, to use Koelb's term, reveals a "logomimesis" in texts that claim no correspondence with the real world.[6] The reader's pleasure comes precisely from his or her disbelief, and it occurs in reading as process rather than reading as product, thus leading us back into the narrative act and the transmission/reception process.

This brings us to Jakobson's communication concept of "contact." Within the narrow confines of Jakobson's definition—"a physical channel and psychological connection between the addresser and the addressee, enabling both of them to enter and stay in communication"[7]—contact would appear to be as mimetically grounded and as problematic as any of the other concepts. However, I would like to close by suggesting that a theory of narrative transmission and textuality derived from a broader understanding of the concept of contact may produce another direction for the quest toward a poetics of fiction—though I would quickly add that I am not proclaiming, "Eureka, I've found the answer"; instead, I intend my suggestion as an additional approach to narrative texts.

The first step in a theory of transmission and textuality is to understand "contact" as process rather than a thing. If we consider "contact" as merely the channel for a particular message, its function in any theory will be narrow and easily dismissed. But as process, "contact" engages the activities of sending, receiving, coding, referring, and meaning that occur in any communication. Therefore, by the term "transmission" I am not bringing the author back in through the backdoor to a place of privilege; transmission must include reception for any full definition of process and contact in literary texts. Narrative, and the novel in particular, presents a clear situation in which we can observe transmission occurring.

---

[5] *The Incredulous Reader: Literature and the Function of Disbelief* (Ithaca: Cornell University Press, 1984), p. 125.

[6] "Lethetic" reading "renounces any claim to discover the 'true' reference of the text it disbelieves" (Koelb, pp. 38–39); therefore, it is opposed to "alethetic" reading, which seeks meaning through reference everywhere in the text. "Logomimesis" refers to texts that "reproduce or elaborate structures found not in the nonlinguistic world but in the resources of language itself" (Koelb, p. 41).

[7] Jakobson, p. 353.

All narratives include a "narrating," a "narrated," and a "reception,"[8] which are usually given the names discourse, story, and reading. But again process and not the product concerns us here, for telling is never a simple or innocent task, the thing told is a product of language and thus always in a condition of becoming rather than stasis, and reading or hearing narrative actively constructs a text that is often markedly different from the one intended by the author, denoted or connoted by the language, or read by any number of other readers. This constructed text can never be a totalization of the narrative; although, as we have all seen, such totalizations are often the goal of critical readings. To produce "a reading" is to eliminate the transmission process of reading by constraining the text within a limited and exclusionary range of interpretive structures.

Transmission in its fullest sense should be seen as a process that brings a text into momentary being, though never into a finally determinant form. A reason for this essential indeterminacy is that transmission incorporates a theory of textuality that recognizes the plurality of transmission processes. The text undergoing transmission is never an autonomous artifact; instead, by its intertextuality, the text includes all previous and later texts within its universe of possible significance and potential meaning. The transmission process rejects those intertexts that appear irrelevant but never banishes them totally. This last point is significant because in opening texts to the play of transmission there is a risk that by considering everything as meaningful we reach a point of entropy and meaninglessness. Real readers, however, will always select those aspects of their reading experiences that contribute to meaning. The aim of a transmission theory in the poetics of fiction is to understand how the process is motivated by and maintained in the reading of narrative texts.

To make what I am proposing a bit more concrete, consider *Don Quixote*, a novel overwhelmingly concerned with questions of literature's relationship to reality and the process of transmission and textuality. Throughout his adventures, Quixote tests literary *mimesis* as he attempts to live the life of chivalry he has read in books. In so doing, he actively engages and immerses himself in the transmission process of knightly romances to test the limits of their truth (fictionality). Similarly, the profusion of narrators, historians, and translators makes any assumptions of textual authority yet another fiction built on the one already in the novel's narrative of transmission. I would also contend that *Don Quixote* asks us not to suspend our disbelief but to maintain it and to enjoy fully the narrative process as it unfolds. That we can feel for Quixote yet also recognize the narratorial games of the text and our own shifting perception between the narrating and the narrated is, indeed, a unique experience that does not ask to be reduced to a fixed meaning in order to be understood.

Instead, I have in mind here something larger than just a single act of reading

---

[8] I will avoid the temptation to coin a process variant for "narratee" to suit the parallelism of my series; however, as should be clear to anyone working on a poetics of fiction, the terminological problems in narrative theory are occasionally insurmountable. Often the problem with theory and poetics is in turn the exactness and inexactness of our nomenclature. It is not my place here to attempt to resolve this issue, and I ask my reader's indulgence as I try to make do with some of the terms we already have.

or even a single reader's lifetime experience with a single text. Whatever sense a reader might have of *Don Quixote* at a particular moment is conditioned by literary and linguistic experience, particularly experience with novels and critical commentary. To deny this is to create a fiction of reading that would be impossible to reproduce. We are always learning to read texts differently (sometimes for better, sometimes for worse), and any poetics of fiction must contribute to and remain dynamic and flexible within this learning process. Thus the poetics of fiction can neither be singular in its focus nor depend on a fixed center always already present in readers. Each of us develops a poetics of fiction, but it develops over time and is altered with each reading experience.

If we are still moving toward "a poetics of fiction," that poetics would have to be capable of accommodating ever expanding textual universes and numerous personal poetics. Although we may "deconstruct" previous theories, these theories too belong to the universe of textuality and can never be banished. Thus the aim of this paper, to echo the closing of David Lodge's 1968 *Novel* article, has not been to eliminate the concepts of *mimesis*, authority, or reader from our discussions of a poetics of fiction. I would contend, instead, that these concepts are constituent elements for a theory of transmission and textuality. By broadening the theoretical horizon for a poetics of fiction, we can also attend to major questions, such as gender and ideology, that are now facing the theory of interpretation. The questions facing a theory of transmission focus on where in the process large scale differences or categories of response can be located. To date our efforts at a poetics have produced finer and finer tools of analysis, yet our goal is still as elusive as Dulcinea is to Quixote. The significance of such analysis is in its process of engaging textuality and transmission in a dynamic play of reading.

"The Present and Future States of Novel Criticism": Our Two-Headed Profession

RICHARD PEARCE, *Respondent*

In the old days we would have a sudden insight that opened up a novel, quickened it to life, generated a new understanding about a character, a social situation, or the use of language. Then we would search for a rationale—or a theory—to support our new reading. The meaning and value, we assumed, were discovered by opening ourselves more fully to the literary work. Now we have come to realize that no one reads without at least an implicit set of assumptions about the nature of language and literature and at least an implicit set of political values. And that these assumptions and values determine what we look for and what we find—however unexpected. For many critics this awareness is accompanied by a sense that theory takes precedence over reading. We can spend hours, even days, at meetings of a professional literary society and never hear the name of a single literary work.

To understand our dilemma, we may have to go back to the sixties. Not because this was the period that undermined historical sensibility by insisting on "relevance." But because we had reason to question much of what history had passed down to us. Imperialism, we had been taught, was a term denigrating European colonialist powers and Asian countries seeking more land. It was hard to accept the fact that America was acting imperialistically in Vietnam—that we had a long history of imperialism going back to the settling of the frontier, that indeed we now had to read Walt Whitman with new eyes.

Nor was it a difficult step from there to a full realization of what we should have always known: that words like "humanism" and "objectivity" are loaded. "Humanism" carries connotations of "universality" (applying to all humans) and "humane" (caring for all humans), but it was a system of education designed to teach young *men* how to rule and maintain power. Its values were not as broad as it claimed but limited by the position if not the experience of the ruling class. And it consolidated its power in the study of English literature as England was establishing its empire. Humanism was open to neither the great majority of people nor to their experiences.

And "objectivity" was practiced best by those who had the power to decide what should be examined and how to examine it objectively. Think of the mainline scientific studies documenting the inferiority of black people and women. We should have begun to wonder about objectivity much earlier, when Heisenberg demonstrated that the very act of looking at an electron caused a disturbance, or distortion, in what we saw. We would soon discover that ideology also causes a disturbance in "neutral" paradigms. What brought the problem to our attention was the way newspapers were reporting "objectively" about what they still called the "conflict" in Vietnam, calling our troops "advisors" and our bombing missions "protective reaction." Or what they were choosing not to report. Which ushered in the "new journalism" based on a notion that making one's position explicit and using the novelist's "unobjective" rhetoric was being more objective than masking an implicit position—or assuming you didn't have one.

The questioning of terms like "humanism" and "objectivity" reflected a growing distrust of authority, especially when its power was disguised—as democracy, liberal education, good English, close reading, or the omniscient narrator.

What all this led to, once the economy began to fail and the new conservatism set in, was a two-headed skepticism. One head remembered its lesson from the sixties: that values, or ideology, cannot be separated from one's approach. This led to the recognition that the sudden insight—which opened up a novel, quickened it to life, and generated new understanding—did not arise only from opening oneself more completely to the literary work. It arose also from a set of shared values disguised by what we called sensibility and derived from a very limited view of what could be called literature.

The other head remembered the lesson of Heisenberg and was nourished on the development of linguistics and anthropology, as well as the skepticism of Watergate. If the act of looking and the medium through which one looked affected what we saw, a new area should be examined. We should learn the way language actually works, what it can actually refer to. Moreover, we should focus not only on the language of the author and the characters but on all the codes that mediate between the text and the reader—as well as on the interrelationships or the process. Philosophers were discovered or rediscovered. Epistemological questions were sharpened. Critical languages were formed with unpronounceable words. And the new enthusiasm was fed on one side of the ocean by the joys of theoretical argument and on the other by the excitement of technology and of opening up new fields— did I say markets?—where one could stake a claim.

Let me hasten to admit that the paradigm, or parable, I have been developing—of our two-headed profession—is oversimplified. It does not account for what we learned about race and poverty in our land of opportunity. It is also extreme. Politically sensitive scholars climb the professional ladder as eagerly as the epistemological cynics. And cynical scholars have been motivated by a kind of interdisciplinary learning that makes traditional literary study appear very narrow. But this paradigm or parable gives me a way to express my own ambivalence—and will serve as a springboard into the papers we have just heard.

Let me first observe that my parable is not fully reflected by the panel of papers. No one speaks out of the head that feeds on political ideology. Most notably absent are the feminist voices, which have so invigorated novel criticism in the last ten years. And let me also observe that the panelist most responsive to questions of ideology is also the most concerned about their intrusion into literary study. Further, all three of these clear, thoughtful, and extremely useful papers aim toward some middle position. Therefore, I will leap in as an ideologue to draw them apart—not just for the joy of battle but to focus positions and opposition that should not be blurred.

The two attacks on traditional poetics are two ways of rejecting the authority of the author and his work. Through a lucid and incisive account of much difficult and wide-ranging material, Don Bialostosky focuses on the dialogue between Wayne Booth and Mikhail Bakhtin. Booth has developed a rhetoric for the author to gain maximum authority over his novel, to establish a unity of all its elements that will convey his views and ideology most forcefully. Bakhtin champions the kind of novel where the voice of the author is only one among many voices that speak, argue, harangue, cajole, mock, imply, ignore, and take joy in their contradictoriness. Bialostosky astutely distinguishes *dialectic*, which reduces the field to one of simple opposition, from *dialogic*, where the contradictions are multiple and irresolvable. And he warns against reducing criticism into camps of the monologic and dialogic novels. Indeed, he seeks a unified field of critical discourse, which can illuminate competing voices in what seems like a monologic narrative and, I take it, reveal the disguised authority of a novel that seems dialogic. One question I would ask is whether these two systems can share the same field. Granted, Bakhtin has developed a very sophisticated poetics of narratology. But wouldn't the energy of carnival be tamed in a unified corral? Or wouldn't Bakhtin's radical ideology be co-opted? I am surprised that the ideological differences between Booth and Bakhtin were expressed in only the most abstract terms. Can the middle ground be reached only by suppressing the clash between them?

Bernard Duyfhuizen clearly traces the postmodern fate of *mimesis* and makes compelling use of Jakobson's communications model. If we consider his vertical axis running from code to message to referent, we see that these three terms are not so easily separable as is assumed by readers who look for reflections of life in the text of a novel, since life itself is composed of texts. If we look along the horizontal axis from addresser to contact to addressee we see that the addressers (whether authors or narrators) have lost authority over the text because the language they speak is controlled by so many other sources. Nor can we turn to the reader (or addressee) as a source of authority because there are so many kinds of readers. The contact, then, is where we can pin our hopes. But we cannot *pin* them, for the contact is fluid: it is a process of transmission. All novels are like the *Quixote* copied from the original word for word by Borges' Pierre Menard, and which is radically new because the words have accumulated so many layers of meaning in the last 400 years.

Thomas Docherty has developed a model like Duyfhuizen's in a recent book called *Reading (Absent) Character.*[1] Characters, he insists, are not fixed—by either a pattern in the author's mind or the language on the printed page. They evolve as they are depicted point by point through time and space, in a field created by the interplay between reading and writing. After finishing Docherty's book, I was left with two questions that maybe Duyfhuizen can answer. First, though the novels gained a great deal by attending to what we may call the dynamics of the contact, there was no way of telling that one work was richer, more disturbing, more enlightening—I almost said better—than another. Second, at a time when students are coming to us less literate—that is, with few skills in reading and almost no literary stock upon which to draw—how are we going to make use of criticism that is getting more sophisticated, and more abstract, and that insists on examining the assumptions of reading before one reads?

Which leads us to Mark Spilka. Spilka speaks out of neither mouth of our two-headed profession. He cogently traces the recent evolution of novel criticism and poignantly expresses the anguish of a liberal humanist over its cost: the way writers and readers thought novels could expand the possibilities of feeling and thinking about life. It is refreshing to see someone unashamed of being middle class, of valuing individualism, and capable of showing how those who repudiate our system most strenuously are making their living and their individual reputations within it. From this position Spilka is also able to reflect on how the novel itself has always struggled against inherited notions of literary form and of

---

[1] Thomas Docherty, *Reading (Absent) Character: Towards a Theory of Characterization in Fiction* (Oxford: Oxford University Press, 1983).

political ideology. Still, he feels that what constitutes a novel is the experience and oppositions of *felt forms of life* rather than kinds of fiction. The question I would ask is what constitutes *felt forms of life*? Or isn't this, like "humanism," a term that pretends to be universal but is nonetheless defined by those who taught us how to read and passed down a particular literary tradition? If we feel the urge to impose order on chaos, don't we also feel the exclusion that certain forms of order impose? Robert Scholes points out that a generation of women had to stifle their reactions to Hemingway or be told they had not learned the lessons of "close reading." [2] And Nancy Miller defines the *Bildungsroman* as an "ambitious text"—which traces the development of a young man, not just from youth to maturity, but from powerlessness to a position of power. [3] So where does that leave the young woman, except to marry or die at the end of her story? Or consciously or unconsciously to oppose the "ambitious text" with an "erotic" one—the opposition being so silent that it has taken three hundred years for readers to discover it?

OK, he may answer. You see liberal humanism is self-correcting. But the correction has resulted from a foregrounding of ideology. We have no problem in accepting the need for our students to understand how they are being manipulated by advertising and mass media entertainment. That is, becoming sensitive to systems of meaning and value that precede the felt life of, say, *General Hospital's* Luke and Laura. Why shouldn't we demand the same attention to assumptions and ideology prior to their engagement with great novels?

[2] Robert Scholes, *Semiotics and Interpretation* (New Haven: Yale University Press, 1982), pp. 110–126.

[3] Nancy K. Miller, "Emphasis Added: Plots and Plausibilities in Women's Fiction," *PMLA* 96 (1981) 36–48.

The Case for a Humanistic Poetics

DANIEL R. SCHWARZ

In answering *Novel's* call for responses to the panel discussion "Still Towards a Humanistic Poetics?" I should make clear that I believe that we are on the threshold of a return to the concerns of traditional humanism—what a work means, who created it and why, and how it reflects the world beyond it. Moreover, it is the purpose of this essay, as it was of my recent study, *The Humanistic Heritage: Critical Theories of the English Novel from James to Hillis Miller,* to contribute to that return. Since I was unable to accept Marianna Torgovnick's invitation to be a member of the original panel, I feel particularly grateful to be getting a second chance to join that discussion.

At many major universities, deconstruction basks in the consensual glow of a dominant trend. With the influence of deconstruction spreading like fire in dry grass on a windy day, we are in a feisty time when we have the opportunity to debate the values, purposes, and future of literary studies in America. We should be grateful to deconstruction for opening up the canon and for questioning the notion of one authoritative reading; we should also be grateful to it for raising fundamental questions about the direction of literary studies in America and England. Yet we must thoughtfully consider in what directions deconstruction is taking literary studies. We must do more than querulously assert, as many traditionally oriented critics do even in our major universities, that deconstruction has reached high tide and, if I may change metaphors, that a benign critical teleology will express itself by—in a critical version of the Big Bang theory—expunging the evil influence of deconstruction.

By promising nothing less than a new ideology of reading, deconstruction has brought excitement to literary studies in America. In its efforts to apply philosophic texts and linguistics to the study of literature, it offers the seductive appeal of the complex and learned. Its major practitioners—the late Paul de Man, J. Hillis Miller, Geoffrey Hartman, Harold Bloom—are often brilliant in their insights, if elusive in their arguments. Deconstruction has transformed the way we talk about our literary experiences and has given us new and fresh stories of reading. But I believe that we need to take stock of the current critical mindscape and retrieve some important principles that have become submerged.

In this essay, my goals are to define what I believe to be valuable in deconstruction and to help clarify and define the principles of what I call humanistic formalism. In discussing deconstruction, I shall focus on Jonathan Culler's *On Deconstruction* because it has become the explanatory midrash for deconstruction, especially for the puzzling works of Jacques Derrida and Paul de Man. I would like to play the role of the English Brother William of Baskerville in Umberto Eco's *The Name of the Rose* and make a rather pragmatic and Aristotelian inquiry into the mysteries and thickets of continental theories; like the tolerant Brother William, I am less concerned with heresies than with fallacies. After reviewing the claims of deconstruction, I shall articulate my own neo-humanistic credo.

It behooves traditional Anglo-American humanistic criticism to resist the onslaught of deconstruction and to defend the ground of its own formalism. It is essential to define the theory and method of a criticism that owes its roots to Plato and Aristotle and that has in its various guises stimulated the serious study of literature in the twentieth century. We should begin by acknowledging what we have learned from deconstruction. Deconstruction has introduced the valuable idea that interpretations are stories of our reading experience—that is, interpretations are shaped by our particular personality and historical situation. Furthermore, it has warned us that these stories of reading, although they may pose as objective commentaries, are really, like all writing, to some degree at least, a disguise for idiosyncratic troping. But its practitioners have not sufficiently stressed the infinite gradations of metaphoricity within a complex work, nor how our reading involves a continual process of determining the precise gradations of literal and figurative language. As readers we organize even the most literal and realistic passages into narrative units of reading experience; these units always have something of a metaphorical component because they represent our understanding of the absent world and of the absent author who breathed life into that world and who represents himself/herself in it. As we read and organize the literal and determine the degree of metaphoricity, our reading process resembles the author's original organization of his/her experience.

One of deconstruction's virtues is that it reminds us to question the concepts of monolithic explanations for complex literary texts and issues; in a passage Culler twice quotes approvingly, de Man tells us: "The possibility of reading . . . can never be taken for granted" (1982, 224). Deconstruction has been helpful in its stress on the process of reading, on the dialogue between text and reader, on the need to stand outside a work. It has helped us understand that moral hierarchies within imagined worlds are in flux, particularly within the spacious worlds of novels, where subsequent episodes modify prior ones and vice versa.

Deconstruction reminds us that we cannot use language to summon reality absolutely. Using the English positivist William as his mouthpiece, Eco puts it nicely in *The Name of the Rose:* "I had thought each book spoke of the things, human and divine, that lie outside books. Now I realize that not infrequently books speak of books; it is as if they spoke among themselves" (342). To be sure, we read better when we know what is in other books, particularly the books that the author has read. Textuality, the idea that books take their meaning from other books, challenges the assumption that language summons reality and contends that such an assumption is an example of the logocentric fallacy.

Deconstruction has become a cult with its own prophets—Roland Barthes, Michel Foucault, Jacques Derrida—who speak a strange language. It has its own history and its own critical rites. One seminal rite is to quote obscure passages of Derrida, often translated into ungrammatical English, and to pretend that these statements are readable—as in the following passage: "for we have read *in the text* that the absolute present, Nature, what is named by words like 'real mother' etc., have always already escaped, have never existed; that what inaugurates meaning and language is writing as the disappearance of natural presence" (quoted in Culler, 1982, 106). Like other elite cults, deconstruction has fathered and mothered its own exotic vocabulary; it has also generated an extremely fulsome syntax which yields its meaning only to its acolytes and devotees. Perhaps most dangerously, it has created modes of inquiry which consign the literary work to the back burner.

Let us turn briefly to the Derridean idea that Western culture has privileged the "metaphysics of presence" by allowing itself to believe that language can summon or evoke a prior reality. If I, for example, write "Derrida," he does not appear in the room as a presence; nor does his name mean exactly the same thing to every reader. But it does not follow that his name is merely a series of sounds, a moment of pure textuality, whose significance can derive from its play on "derision" or "dadaism" or an inversion of "arid" or "Ariadne" (as in, to use a favorite deconstructive trope, "Ariadne's thread"). Even though words cannot absolutely summon reality, they can approach reality.

In its search for absolutely clean distinctions and definitions, deconstruction totalizes and becomes conservative if not totalitarian. While acknowledging that meaning cannot be stable and determinate, we do not need go the much further distance and concede that meaning is impossible. Just because a text fails to yield one unambiguous reading does not mean that most skilled readers do not agree on the major formal and thematic principles of most works. Merely because one can argue that language does not invoke presence, it does not follow that—to recite a shibboleth of recent theory—"There is nothing outside the text."[1] Or as Michael Riffaterre puts it, "Representation of reality is a [merely] verbal construct in which meaning is achieved by reference from words to words, not things" (230).

I am calling for a new humanism that—without abandoning its stress on such formal matters as rhetoric and close scrutiny of narrative codes—turns its attention to the content, meaning, and significance of imaginative literature. Rather than using literature as an occasion for speculation about the *text's* implications for semiotics, Marxism, or deconstruction, this new humanism would seek to understand the essential experience of the *work's* imaginative world. I am a formalist, nonetheless, in the sense that I believe content and meaning are inextricable functions of form. My credo is based on the belief that an interest in the contents of literary works is part of the reason we read them, that sophisticated readers respond to an inextricable relationship between form and content. When reading or when listening, we respond to the thoughts, feelings, and values of an ego or a consciousness or a presence. We hear a human voice that has tone, timbre, attitudes, gender, and values.

Literary theory, I believe, is important only insofar as it addresses methods of reading literary works, and only insofar as it enables us to think conceptually about how literary works cohere. Insofar as theory produces readings of literary works and helps us to understand how the works we read behave and how we behave when we read, it has a valuable function. In my judgment, a criticism that fails to produce powerful interpretations of complex works and fails to give us a fresh reading of major authors is not very important. Among other things, one feels in reading Culler that deconstruction is not sufficiently interested in works of literature. Or, as Eco's nominalist Brother William puts it, "[T]rue learning must not be content with ideas which are, in fact, signs, but must discover things in their individual truth" (382).

It may be time to propose the term Theoretical Fallacy for the phenomenon of speculating about works from such a remote distance and at such an abstract level of discussion that the theories do not help the reader understand what is within such works. Culler writes, "Critical categories are not just tools to be employed in producing sound interpretations but problems to be explored through the interaction of text and concept" (1982, 180). But all too often the concepts and categories are privileged over the critical activity of recreating what it feels like to read a work. But, then, Culler has told us in "Against Interpretation" (the

---

[1] Thus this work is "an intertextual event," and the reader becomes a "space," a "place," or a "function." See Culler, pp. 32–33.

opening essay of *The Pursuit of Signs*): "One thing we do not need is more interpretation of literary works" (1981, 6). Surely the title, "Against Interpretation," throws down the gauntlet to Anglo-American formalism to define its purposes and goals. For I believe that interpretation is central to the study of literature. In *On Deconstruction*, Culler writes, "The notion that the goal of analysis is to produce enriching elucidations of individual works is a deep presupposition of American criticism" (1982, 22). I proudly share that benighted notion.

I. Deconstruction and Its Implications

Deconstruction depends upon rejection of the possibility of moving toward an authoritative reading; it rejects the idea that reading can recover the author's intent, values, themes, or understanding of the world which his or her work imitates. By contrast, what I call humanistic formalism believes that we can approach the author's values and vision by attending to the rhetorical effects within the imagined world created by the author. In its disbelief in the hermeneutical circle—the circle by which the reader recreates the text that the author wrote through the mediation of the literary work—deconstruction is cynical. Even while disagreeing among its practitioners about the importance of intentionality, humanistic formalism recognizes the folly of the effort to deconstruct the author: "If, as Barthes claims, 'the birth of the reader must be at the cost of the death of the author,' many have been willing to pay that price" (Culler, 1982, 31). I wonder if anyone who has tried to teach *Ulysses* without having read Joyce's prior work or Ellmann's biography could write that. Put baldly, a work more readily yields a determinate meaning to those who know about the author's other works, life, and historical context.

A revitalized humanistic formalism would eschew such New Critical orthodoxies as the biographical fallacy and the shibboleth "exit author" and discover how to speak of the author as a formal presence in the text in ways that go beyond equating the omniscient narrator or implied author with the biographical author. For we need an aesthetic that takes account of how, particularly in such modern works as *The Rainbow* and *Ulysses*, the author's struggle with his subject becomes a major determinant of fictional form. In the process of reading we respond to an *imitation*, a *representation* of the real creator of the work. The author is in the imagined world as a distortion—at times, an idealization, a clarification, a simplification, an obfuscation—of the creating psyche. As Patricia Meyer Spacks has noted, "[I]f poets create themselves as figures in their poems, readers choose, consciously or unconsciously, to accept such figures as more or less appropriate to reality" (xii).

Thus the new humanistic formalism must part company with a parochial formalism—either New Critical or deconstructive—that excludes authors from the critical dialogue. The process of locating a human being within a work recognizes that reading is not merely a verbal game but a shared experience between reader and writer. Do we not seek and respond to a human voice within a work because it expresses the energy and values of the author? Voice validates lan-

guage, gives it shape, connects it with our experiential world. Even when reading letters and newspapers, we ask, "Who is speaking to whom?" and "On what
occasion?" and "For what purpose?" For that reason jesuitical discussions that
ignore authorial voice or reduce speech to a kind of writing should be met with
great skepticism. Because a complete explanation of the relationship between
authors and both their alter egos and their characters is not possible, because we
cannot provide a mathematical equation for each work, does it follow that we
should abandon our inquiry into such matters?

In its quest to undermine, to question, and to displace, deconstruction is a
kind of radical skepticism. Both deconstruction and skepticism depend on the
quite accurate perception that nothing is perfect and that certainty is impossible.
Put another way, deconstruction is a modern urban phenomenon in an age of
anxiety and disbelief. Just as the urban Wise Guy (the modern picaro) lives on
the margin and knows how to exploit every event for a profit, the deconstructive
picaro is an academic wise guy who sees the fly in the ointment, the problem
with any idea, and the faults in every person or situation; he verbally transforms
the specter of a remote possibility into what might actually happen and makes
us aware that the inconceivable might happen just this once. He inverts the
meaning of meaning, the significance of significance, by (to use one of the new
terms) "valorizing" the marginal, the inessential, the digressive, the false. For
example, Culler writes in praise of misunderstanding and misreading: "Reading
and understanding preserve or reproduce a content or meaning, maintain its
identity, while misunderstanding and misreading distort it. . . . We can thus
say, in a formulation more valid than its converse, that understanding is a special
case of misunderstanding, a particular deviation or determination of misunderstanding" (1982, 176). What Culler is doing is inverting the meaning of the words
understanding and misunderstanding. If we are going to reassign meanings to
words and reinvent the language, then of course there will be a free play of signifiers and of course we will be hard put to make connections with the world
outside the text.

In *Saving the Text*, Hartman coined the word derridadism with some relevance; if not reducible to dada, surely deconstruction is like a *fin de siecle* movement which responds to boredom and ennui (33) by adding excitement to reading. It does so not only by making the inconceivable possible, but also by
discovering patterns of sexuality and violence which import into reading repressed emotions that may be lacking in real life; and beyond that, in its conceit
of the critic's control over texts, it offers readers fantasies of power. As Culler
remarks, "the effect of deconstructive analyses, as numerous readers can attest,
is knowledge and *feelings of mastery*" (1982, 225). Similarly, he also sees the major
task of criticism as "that of making the text interesting, of combating the boredom which lurks behind every work, waiting to move in if reading goes astray or
founders. . . . A semiological criticism should succeed in reducing the possibilities of boredom by teaching one to find challenges and peculiarities in works
which the perspective of pleasure alone would make boring" (1978, 262). But for
humanistic formalism, the critic's task is to discover meaning and significance

within the imagined world, often by focusing on how the author has created a structure of effects for the reader. The critic's task is to recover meaning and report it intelligibly to other readers who have shared the experience of reading a work. The critic seeks to explain literature in terms of experiences that authors, fictional characters, and readers might possibly share. Such a criticism believes that words signify and that they can create an imagined world which temporarily displaces the reader's consciousness of the real one. For this criticism, reading—entering into the imagined world of another—is itself pleasurable.

Humanistic formalism believes that critics may convey but can never create the pleasures of a work, which come from the work itself. Ultimately, while not indifferent to the calls of textuality, humanistic formalism also stresses the signified over the signifier; the text's silences, gaps, and opacities are important for the most part because they, too, signify something about the imagined world outside the text. For this criticism, moreover, the representative is important, but so also is "the strange, the formal, the fictional" (Culler, 1978, 134). Indeed, humanistic formalism stresses the necessity for including the strange (experiences, particularly psychological ones that defy ordinary experience or reflect the dimly acknowledged needs of characters and authors); the formal (the aesthetic organization of experience); the fictive (imaginary experience which, in the form of dream, fantasy, and plans for the future, is part of human life).

Deconstruction stresses that each reading contains the seeds of its own undoing. It privileges the reader rather than the author without quite acknowledging that it does so. Put another way, the text is consubstantial with the reader rather than the author and/or the anterior world on which the text is based. Deconstruction emphasizes that every reader discovers heterogeneous readings in the same text, a situation that leads to an irreconcilable paradox or *aporia*. Deconstruction believes that all reading is misreading because no reading can take account of all the possibilities of a text. Humanistic formalism believes that reading is a quest toward the goal of an accurate reading, even though, like Zeno's paradox, it is a goal which we can only approach but never reach. But we can make very substantial progress toward that goal. Deconstruction views accurate reading as a mirage which continually recedes in proportion to that which is seemingly approached.

In *On Deconstruction*, Culler writes: "[T]o deconstruct a discourse is to show how it undermines the philosophy it asserts, or the hierarchical oppositions on which it relies, by identifying in the text the rhetorical operations that produce the supposed ground of argument, the key concept or premise" (1982, 86). But why does *identifying* its rhetorical operations undermine a discourse? If one identifies the rhetorical operations in *Emma* or *The Rape of the Lock*, isn't one finding what reinforces or supports the philosophy it asserts? For most works, identifying the rhetorical operations will show how a coherent, organic work is produced. But even if one identifies tensions within the rhetorical operations— tropes that pull in diverse directions—are we moving in a direction necessarily different from the old formalism? Finally, the act of identification is only prelude to the imposition of some pattern of reading or interpretation, even if it is a pattern of reading that challenges prior readings. As the excesses of the New Criticism taught us, cataloguing tropes for its own sake has little real value; the same may be said for cataloguing gaps.

We may even want to reconsider whether, like lemmings, we want to use the term "text" for novels. Isn't text a term which blurs the difference between signifier and signified and between foreground and background and deflects us from thinking of a novel as an "imagined world"? It may also be time to ask whether in novels order and unity are not preferable to disorder and incoherence. We should also be concerned with the standard that privileges works that tear themselves apart and regards as hierarchically superior those works that say something other than what they mean to say.

One problem with the concept of textuality is that it releases the critic from the responsibility of describing what a work says; when language is merely the interplay of signifiers, canniness and wit become the goals rather than truth or mimesis. Those who lost families in the Holocaust or their friends in the Viet Nam War will find it puzzling to have experience reduced by deconstruction to a rhetorical figure: "'experience' is divided and deferred—already behind us as something to be recovered, yet still before us as something to be produced" (Culler, 1982, 82). What I find most striking about *On Deconstruction* is its failure to deal with both political and social causes and effects and with human behavior—its causes, personal motives, and its consequences.

Many of the advances claimed by deconstruction are not so different from the progressive strains of humanistic criticism. Empsonian ambiguity as well as the New Critical emphases on tension and paradox are more like than unlike *aporia*. Nor is it news that the history of the criticism of a literary work will repeat the tensions within the work; it would be surprising if many, if not most, important critical readings did not in some way enact if not "repeat the structures it is analyzing," since much good criticism seeks to enact the process of reading (Culler, 1982, 139). Nor did we have to wait for deconstruction to tell us that the best literary criticism often "enacts what it asserts" (Culler, 1982, 138–39).

What is new is the change in the critic's stature from humble middleman who is midwife to meaning created by the author in his work, to a kind of imaginative *übermensch* who uses the work as a stimulus for whatever re-creation—I use the pun on recreation deliberately—occurs to her or him. Just as Romantic poets perceived the world according to the lamp of their imagination, these critics perceive literary works in light of their imaginative needs. They use the work or text as a pretext for their own text; the test is not whether a reading is true but whether it is "interesting." There is much evidence as well that they give the critic's commentary equal status with—if not privileged status over—the original work. Perhaps we should also note in this regard an important difference between the older and newer movement: unlike deconstruction, which values *aporia* and heterogeneous readings, the New Criticism valued the resolution of the contending readings into a unified one.

Do we feel while reading that "experience . . . has always already occurred and yet is still to be produced—an indispensable point of reference, yet never simply there" (Culler, 1982, 63)? If, as I believe, the human mind seeks coherent, logical explanations for its experiences, including its reading experiences, then it is a rather damaging admission for Culler to tell us that "deconstructive readings show scant respect for the wholeness or integrity of individual works" (1982, 220). Again, in the following assertion, where is the joy in reading about the representation of human experience, or, indeed, where is the joy in either language or aesthetic form? "The deconstructive questioning of categories and assumptions leads back repeatedly to a small group of problems and gives conclusions that function as knowledge" (Culler, 1982, 223). But knowledge *of what* and *for what?* Can we really hold out the possibility of a morphology of the marginal, the illogical, and the fissures within either a text or an intellectual tradition? As soon as such phenomena are "regularized" in a deconstructive grammar, is not deconstruction in danger of adopting the codification and unilateral explanations that it objected to in structuralism? Does not deconstruction create its own Platonic models by the very nature of its abstract speculations about how texts behave?

II. The Effects of Deconstruction on Literary Studies

The appeal of the New Criticism was that it made works accessible and exciting to high school students and young undergraduates; in a way, it was an enticement to two generations of students who were taught that if they used their analytic powers, sensibility, and judgment they would be able to understand a work of literature as a coherent self-contained ontology that related to their own experiential world. I have always told my students that my courses were subtitled "In Defense of Reading" and have urged that learning how to read well was as important as learning the details of an interpretation. What, we should ask, does deconstruction *say* to freshmen who are studying literature at a college or university for the first time? Among other things, it says that a negative process—"deconstruction"—is more important than a positive one—"reading" or "construing." It encourages students to describe their reading in abstract terms that belie their experiential base; it implies, if only by practice, that such diction should take precedence over detailed discussion; and, in its efforts to privilege the reader and to deflect attention from literary works to personal responses, it implies that any story of reading is as good as any other.

I have heard reports of less than successful sections of freshmen humanities where young teachers deconstructed such moving love poems as "To His Coy Mistress" without first construing them, using arcane language to present exotic rhetorical phenomena, codes, moves, and intertextual resonances. Yet the appeal of such poems to undergraduates derives—does it not—from their resemblance to questions of love and sexuality that students recognize as having something to do with their own lives. Deconstruction fathers/mothers abstractions in the classroom which make young undergraduates feel that the instructor has reached his or her thirties without ever having been eighteen, nineteen, twenty, or twenty-one; this apparent experiential gap creates the feeling in freshmen that their teacher has no empathy for their responses to the literature being read. While I would hasten to add that deconstruction has no monopoly on puzzling freshmen, it is a rather striking irony that deconstructionist colleagues often acknowledge that they have had their greatest success in teaching undergraduates when they use traditional methods of reading, including the very "thematizing" that they disdain in graduate seminars.

In what are now regarded as "advanced" literary studies, graduate students are encouraged to indulge in the kind of textuality which fuses one's own reading onto a prior reading without any regard to the original text; the effect of this process is to give the critical article or book more prestige than the work it analyzes and to claim in the name of semiotics that the critical activity of analyzing the secondary material is equal to if not greater than the powerful activity of reading complex works. Thus in supposedly "state-of-the-art" graduate courses, whole seminar sessions are spent applying Foucault's or Barthes's theories to a work or discussing the critical "strategies" and rhetorical "moves" of a single critical essay. In a kind of parody of traditional criticism, the language of the critical article or book is analyzed in depth to discover meanings of which the critic was unaware. For the first time in my teaching career, two of the graduate papers in a seminar devoted to Joyce's *Ulysses*—papers which were described to me beforehand in vastly different terms—focused almost exclusively on analyzing the "texts" of prior critics rather than the actual text of *Ulysses*.

A healthy interest in recent theory should be accompanied by a healthy skepticism that literary criticism has made in recent years a Great Leap Forward. We should be wary of a criticism that speaks in arcane diction and neologisms—indeed, at times, in tongues. Of course, in freeing readers to do what they wish with works and to redefine the canon as they please, deconstruction offers a handy tool for graduate students to say something *different* and seemingly original. For we should not underestimate how awed graduate students are by the sheer volume of critical materials that have accumulated in the past two decades. Deconstruction also offers an enticement to American and English professors of foreign literatures and European and Third World students of English and American literature for whom questions of tone and irony are very difficult. It is possible that we are developing a generation of graduate students who are tone-deaf, who—rather than respond to the voice and irony of *Emma*—will be interested primarily in indicting the novel for what is omitted in the way of sociological analysis of the class structure. The canon of the traditional English and American novel, with its emphasis on the incongruity between the values of a narrator who has a coherent self and the major characters, an incongruity dependent on subtle irony and nuances of voice, is particularly resistant to deconstructive readings.

The question of why we should spend endless hours and course time reading Derrida is a real one. Once we have learned the basic lessons of deconstruction, are we not better off reading literary texts? After spending several hours reading "Cogito and the History of Madness" (in *Writing and Difference*) for an informal colloquium, I asked myself whether this does not deflect us from attention that should be spent elsewhere. Once one knows the basic distinctions of deconstruction, is it worth the time to read volumes of Derrida with the same attention as Yeshiva students read Torah? I think I speak for many university literature professors when I say that, had I been confronted in my undergraduate or graduate years with Derrida, Nietzsche, and Marx as primary texts—instead of *Paradise Lost, Hamlet, Crime and Punishment, Lord Jim,* and *Ulysses*—I would not be teaching literature today.

In literature as in life we find what we look for. This is another way of saying theory is disguised autobiography. Just as Aristotelian critics such as R. S. Crane and Wayne Booth found in eighteenth-century texts the order and meaning that they sought in their criticism and discovered that authors built into texts both the rhetorical effects and moral values that they admired, deconstructive critics find *aporia*—moments of irreconcilable impasse—in modern texts. On the one hand, reading is defined by critics such as Barthes in terms akin to sexual orgasm; on the other, reading enacts the angst, marginality, frustration, and self-division that at times we are all prone to feel not only in our own critical and teaching activities, but in our lives. Perhaps, for deconstruction, interpretation has become in some instances no more than, to paraphrase T. S. Eliot, fragments that we each create to shore against our fears that our reading, like our lives, may end in ruins.

Questioning and redefining the canon to include works by women and minorities and works that have been undeservedly neglected is one of the exciting developments of the last decade; without canon reevaluation, the study of "modern literature" might have remained confined to the period from the sixteenth century through the Victorian with the heavy stress on the 1500–1880 years. But, believing as I do that some works have more artistic value and interest than others, I worry about using minor works as the centerpieces of syllabi for students who take very few literature courses. I also worry about the current practice of using eccentric and idiosyncratic works to make vast statements about cultural history.

III. The Novel as Mimesis: The Question of Realism

To return to *The Name of the Rose,* Eco knows that there is a reality beyond words, even if one cannot quite define or reach it. Brother William's quest for the murderer of real dead bodies is a quest to go beyond signs to discover the anterior reality—what Marianne Moore would call "imaginary gardens with real toads in them." Within the abbey in Eco's novel there are texts, but there are dead bodies—murdered bodies—which make a mockery of immersion in the world of books. As Brother William puts it, "If the [foot]print exists, there must have existed something whose print it is" (381). Or perhaps more to my point, "The good of a book lies in its being read. A book is made up of signs that speak of other signs, which in their turn speak of things" (478).

As we read, we enter into an imagined world whose significance depends on some relation to the world we recognize. The very conventions of grammar and syntax are mimetic of writing and speech patterns with which we are familiar; these conventions help embed us comfortably in the text. The things of the world—chairs, apples, sunny and rainy days—conform to what we know prior to the text. To reduce reading to linguistic games falsifies and trivializes what happens when we read and when we write. In concluding his section on the novel in *Structuralist Poetics*, Culler writes of structuralism's contribution: "By focusing on the ways in which it complies with and resists our expectations, its moments of order and disorder, its interplay of recognition and dislocation, it opens the way for a theory of the novel which would be an account of the plea-sures and difficulties of reading. In place of the novel as mimesis we have the novel as a structure which plays with different modes of ordering and enables the reader to understand how he makes sense of the world" (1982, 238). I know of no novelists who, in the above passage, would find anything recognizable in their stories of writing novels, and few readers who would find much that is recognizable in their own stories of reading novels. What happens to the passion of Ursula Brangwen, the pride of Leopold Bloom, the perspicacity and sen-sitivity of Mrs. Ramsay, the disillusionment of Mrs. Dalloway, and the subtle cowardice of Conrad's Jim? What does criticism that refuses to discuss the hu-man characters and moral issues in literature say about itself?

E. D. Hirsch, one of the more eloquent defenders of the mimetic function of literature and one of the most thoughtful about how literature means, writes in *Validity in Interpretation* that "Validity implies the correspondence to a meaning which is represented by the text," and "[T]he only compelling normative prin-ciple that has ever been brought forward is the old-fashioned ideal of rightly understanding what the author meant" (10, 26). Where he oversimplifies is in his failure to distinguish between the historical and ahistorical aspects of read-ing. For good readers stand outside the work and think about what the author means to contemporary readers as well as what the work meant to the original audience. We try to recuperate the original work—the world it represents as well as the world which shaped its creation (which may as in Eco's tale about the four-teenth century be quite different)—as much as we can, but as time passes the attempt to do so becomes more difficult. But we also read in terms of our own historical and personal position and, from that perspective, are aware of changes and similarities between the author's *Zeitgeist* and our own. To the extent that books liberate us from a sense of tick-tock time in our world and put us inside an imagined world where we are immersed in the narrative time of that world and of the people who inhabit it, reading is ahistorical.

In his later study *The Aims of Interpretation*, Hirsch writes, "Meaning . . . refers to the whole verbal meaning of a text, and 'significance' to textual meaning in relation to a larger context, i.e., another mind, another era, a wider subject matter" (2–3). But can meaning be separated from significance? As soon as one describes what is inherent in the text it becomes significance; the "isness" or meaning of a work cannot be separated from its "doesness" or significance. To use Hirsch's distinctions, literary criticism should not be content with meaning, but needs to concern itself with significance. Literary theory purports to codify the search for meaning as a kind of knowledge. But is this kind of knowledge possible except insofar as a trained reader will respond with greater sensitivity and perspicacity? If knowledge means knowing which are the right critical questions, then theory can teach it. But if it means constructing elaborate hypotheses by which literary works are tested and subsequently organized, then I am skeptical.

In his important recent study, *A New Mimesis: Shakespeare and the Representation of Reality,* A. D. Nuttall has defined the principles for his version of a new mimesis. He believes that major topoi—such as recurring moments in the literary tradition when the poet speaks of the generations of dead—need be read not simply as recurrences of the same formal conventions but as genuinely felt emotions. He calls for both a "renewed sense of the variety of reality" and "a renewed sense of evidence," as well as what he calls "the license to ask 'Is this true?' or 'Is this likely?' when reading fiction" (182). For Nuttall realism includes "precise visual description and psychological insight," but it also responds "to the more fugitive aspects of the real; in particular to shifting *appearances* as distinct from more stable entities" (186). He is arguing not for the superiority of realistic fiction but for the premise that "no form of literature be regarded as wholly insulated from this varying world" (193). What we need is a criticism that understands that "text" includes *the texture* of the moral and emotional experience it describes.

Some authors wish to approximate reality more than others; traditionally, we have called them realists. By the very nature of its selection and arrangement of its data from all the possible data, realism presents a perspective which is inevitably something of an illuminating distortion. But all authors depend on some recognition on the part of the reader that an act of mimesis is occurring. To invoke the model of Zeno's paradox, even the most realistic texts can approach but never quite reach reality. (The contrasting metaphor for deconstruction is a mirage where reality continually recedes by approximately the distance that language seems to approach it.)

While I believe all literature has *some* realistic component, I want to stress that realism is not an evaluative term and that we should not assume that the more realism the better. On the contrary, I understand realism as a descriptive term. Moreover, realism is more a process than an end. It involves the attempt to approach an historical or individual world. While ultimately language will not create a world prior to the text, the world evoked by language will have its own verisimilitude. As we read, the reality of the imagined world continually modifies and transforms itself. But always the imagined world will have a continually changing relation both to the anterior world which provided its tentative ground and to the anterior world in which the reader lives—the world that provides the ground for his or her responses.

Obviously within any work some aspects are more grounded in reality than others. For example, the depiction of a character depends upon the selection of one individual from among many possible residents of a city or geographical area, among many possible professions, among many members of the social class. By convention we understand that a major character—say, in Hardy's *Jude the Obscure*, a young aspiring uneducated male from the lower social classes who would rather be a scholar or clergyman than a stone carver—represents or typifies various groups and categories to which he belongs. In other words, under certain circumstances created by the author, readers perceive characters as signs with referents. By contrast, the simple descriptions of objects within a room generally have much less of a signifying function. Representation of humans almost differs in kind if not degree; it is both more metaphorical than other kinds of representation because of how we understand characters in their typifying function, and less metaphorical because the creation of people often short-circuits their putative metaphorical function and creates odd kinds of empathy with readers. Moreover, within novels characters are often so individualized and so idiosyncratic that they in fact represent only themselves and undermine the author's patterns of signification; put another way, the infinite variety of complex characters may deflect them from their signifying function. (As I argue in my recent *Reading Joyce's "Ulysses,"* Leopold Bloom is an example.)

Realism has lately been called into question on the grounds that there is no possible agreement about what constitutes reality since we as modernists believe that each person perceives in terms of his own experience and psychic needs. This is another version of Conrad's insistence that "Another man's truth is a dismal lie to me."[2] We not only all read a different text, but we are aware that even authors who thought they were creating omniscient narrators are really only creating anonymous first-person perspectives since what the omniscient narrator tells us is really only one possible explanation. (As my use of the word "tells" indicates, I believe that the mimetic model of storyteller, of a person speaking to another through the written word, more adequately explains what happens than elaborates theories that insist on writing as a sharply *different*, recondite activity.)

Readers and authors do their work in isolation from their fellows and are always lone perceivers; yet rhetorical convention depends upon an author creating a social reality based upon the possibilty of implied mutual understanding of author and reader. Rhetorical convention implies that the author is a representative of a larger community—the omniscient narrator, in particular, calls attention to the author as a representative figure. The reader is a representative of a larger community of readers who are being addressed. Realism depends upon the possibility of creating a hermeneutical circle in which author and reader participate. It depends on the possibility of a shared ontology, an agreed-upon system of language—usually with a varying but relatively low metaphorical quotient. It depends on the belief in an *a priori* world, even if the relation between the anterior world and the imagined ontology continually varies.

In addition to the empirical world, realism also needs to address dreams, hopes, and plans whose linear narratives may have more in common with the

---

[2] November 2, 1985, letter to Edward Noble in Georges Jean-Aubrey's *Joseph Conrad: Life and Letters*, 2 vols. (Garden City: Doubleday, 1927).

simplified plots of fictions than with the disruptions, abundance, and plotlessness of everyday life. Among other things, what makes *Ulysses* so compelling is its presentation in lieu of a traditional monolithic plot of Bloom's, Molly's, and Stephen's fantasies, hopes, and dreams—often in the form of half-told, dimly acknowledged, and contradictory plot fragments. One reason that twentieth-century writers such as Lawrence and Joyce return to myths for their plots is that our lives seem more and more to lack the kind of coherent forward movement that plots require. As Eliot understood, the mythic dimension orders the futility and anarchy of contemporary history. But myth also introduces a level of metaphoricity that breathes new life into and endows with greater complexity what may at first seem lifeless or sterile reality.

In the face of the threat of nuclear war, the breakdown of moral and religious certainties, the proliferation of divorces, the proclivity for multiple and simultaneous relationships, and even for overnight encounters, our lives no longer follow traditional linear plots. While our parents followed—indeed, were shaped by—the plots of marriages that were expected to last to the death of one partner, with the mother in the role of caretaker and the father in the role of provider, the uncertainties of our culture have made it much more difficult to embrace a monolithic plot. If the English novel is a genre of manners written by and for a culture whose paradigmatic plot is the quest for the appropriate marriage partner, then the so-called sexual revolution has changed not only the novel's authors but its readers. The fictions produced by our unstable culture reflect the intrusion of uncertainty, qualification, and disruption, but I think humanistic formalism has demonstrated that it has the critical tools to cope with such changes.

Marxist critics want to expand reality to include the historical and social patterns implied by the imagined world and to stress how that imagined world's circumstances relate to the anterior one. They want to find a pattern behind the "real" world, a kind of historical grammar that would give an explanation for what is presented as "reality" or, put another way, would provide a kind of knowledge for explaining the individual instances of realism within a novel. Fredric Jameson has been calling this reality beyond or behind the empirical reality the "political unconscious."[3] This conceptual pattern is a hypothetical schematic version not merely of what happens within the novel's imagined world, but of both what has happened prior to the events of the novel and what might happen after the events of the novel are over. It has the same relation to the actual presence of history—say, the Napoleonic Wars in *War and Peace* or the first World War in *To the Lighthouse*—as form does to content. But like form, history cannot be described except in the most metaphorical terms; thus historicity always has about it something of the ineffable.

On the whole the current critical emphasis on historicity in novels is an attempt to bridge gaps that have not been articulated and to fill in spaces that the novelist with his compulsive concern for human life has ignored. At times is not

---

[3] Fredric Jameson, *The Political Unconscious* (Ithaca: Cornell University Press, 1981).

the hypothesis of an historical pattern beyond the experiential level of the literary work a kind of New Platonism? Novels may be able to make some progress in creating an historical or economic cause and effect; surely, some novels do this much better than others. But we must differentiate between, on the one hand, discussions of the historical dimensions in such novels as *War and Peace* or *Ragtime*, in which historical events are dramatized or described with the same degree of verisimilitude as characters and episodes and, on the other, discussions of the historical implications drawn from a scintilla of material within the novel and then elaborated, developed, and indeed, *created* by what the reader knows about the period in which the novel is written. In these later discussions, it seems as if critics were drawing lines to invisible dots.

IV. Feminism and Humanism

Deconstruction has sought to appropriate the position of beleaguered minorities and to claim that it speaks on behalf of Third World nations and economically exploited masses. The implication that aligning oneself with socially progressive opinions somehow validates one's way of reading or one's way of discussing theory might be called the Fallacy of the Good and Beautiful.

While welcoming its support of enlightened positions, traditional humanistic critics should resist the polemical contention that in opposition to a "conservative" benighted humanism, deconstruction not only aligns itself with, but also is the intellectual counterpart and offensive arsenal for, the women's movement, minorities, and the socially oppressed. Recently deconstruction has sought to adopt anti-apartheid and divestment as its own, although these positions were strongly advocated well before the arrival of deconstruction by humanists in literature departments who were often in the vanguard of the civil rights movement and the anti–Viet Nam War movement. Widely circulated among True Deconstruction Believers is Derrida's statement on apartheid, as if his Word legitimized a political position and as if he spoke *ex cathedra* from the Holy See of Deconstruction. Indeed, his opinions have the very authority and presence that are anathema to deconstruction in other moments. Isn't Derrida cited by his followers as an apostolic text in day-to-day teaching and critical discourse?

In *On Deconstruction* Culler claims that feminist studies are a branch of deconstruction. But surely in England and America most work in feminist studies is concerned not with textuality and rhetorical moves but with the representation of experience: with the social implications of how women characters and authors have been and are being treated; with criticism that reduces women to passive objects and consigns women characters to the cupboards of male imagination; and with the need to adjust the canon to take account of women writing and women reading.

Indeed, feminist criticism often assumes the presence of an author and an historical cause and effect both between texts and the anterior world, and within imagined worlds. Certainly, Anglo-American feminist criticism is rooted in what

Joanne Frye has called "its experiential basis" and "a concern for women's lives";
it examines representation of women in literature and takes account of cultural
change (21, 24). In their influential *The Mad Woman in the Attic*, Gilbert and Gubar
proceed on the assumption that a self-conscious "I" can be defined: "For all literary artists, of course, self-definition necessarily precedes self-assertion: the creative 'I am' cannot be uttered if the 'I' knows not what it is" (17). Their concerns
are the difficulty and necessity of recovering the female "I" from an antagonistic
or indifferent literary culture and society.

Moreover, it is worth noting that the humanistic study of the English novel
has recognized the strong contribution of women writers and critics. It was almost a shibboleth of the late fifties and early sixties that the three greatest—or,
in a less provocative version, three of the greatest—English novels of the nineteenth century were written by women: *Emma, Wuthering Heights,* and *Middlemarch.* In her essay "Emphasis Added: Plots and Plausibilities in Women's Fiction," Nancy Miller writes that "sensibility, sensitivity, 'extravagance'—so many
code words for feminine in our culture that the attack is in fact tautological—are
taken to be not merely inferior modalities of production but deviations from
some obvious truth" (46). But in fact the humanistic tradition has valued in the
English novel the very qualities of sensibility, sensitivity, and even "extravagance"—if I understand the term correctly as implying idiosyncratic and excessive behavior that transgresses the norms. More than any single book in America, Dorothy Van Ghent's *The English Novel: Form and Function* defined the canon
of the English novel. In a prior generation, Virginia Woolf's *The Common Reader*
had much to do with shaping the traditional canon of English fiction; and, as
soon as the modern novel became a subject, Woolf's fiction was widely taught in
England and America. Q. D. Leavis and Muriel Bradbrook were vital parts of
Scrutiny, which up until recently set the canon in England.

Culler's equation of logocentricism and phallocentricism is simply the creation of a world of words based on little or no evidence. At times, "phallocentric"
is less a concept than a kind of name-calling in an academic version of the rhetoric of insult. One problem of textuality, of writing for its own sake rather than
with reference to an origin or a presence, is that it relieves writing of the responsibility of accuracy. Culler's assertions proceed on the simplistic equation of male
with Bad and female with Good: "[Feminist readings] demonstrate the limitations of male critical interpretations in terms that male critics would purport to
accept, and they seek, like all ambitious acts of criticism, to attain a generally
convincing understanding—an understanding that is feminist because it is a critique of male chauvinism. . . . Men have aligned the opposition male/female with
rational/emotional, serious/frivolous, or reflective/spontaneous: and feminist
criticism of the second moment works to prove itself more rational, serious, and
reflective than male readings that omit and distort" (1982, 58). While objecting to
simple oppositions, deconstruction in the above and following passages speaks
as if it requires a binary perspective and needs to propose ideas in terms of dichotomies: "The more convincing its critique of phallic criticism, the more femi-

nist criticism comes to provide the broad and comprehensive vision, analyzing and situating the limited and interested interpretations of male critics. Indeed, at this level one can say that feminist criticism is the name that should be applied to all criticism alert to the critical ramifications of sexual oppression, just as in politics 'women's issues' is the name now applied to many fundamental questions of personal freedom and social justice" (1982, 56). But the question of arms control, of support for humane regimes in South America, opposition to apartheid, the plight of the homeless, the reverse Robinhoodism of the Reagan government, are not "women's issues" but human issues requiring the energy and engagement of both genders. What Judith Fetterley, focusing on the woman reader, writes of feminist criticism is true of homosexual, black, Third World, Jewish, Marxist, deconstructive, psychoanalytic criticism—or, indeed, of my apologia for humanistic formalism: "Feminist criticism is a political act whose aim is not simply to interpret the world but to change it by changing the consciousness of those who read and their relation to what they read" (Fetterley, vii).

Feminist criticism performs a valuable function in reminding us of the biological, cultural, and historical reasons that women read differently. But to propose a dichotomy in which half the world reads as women and the other half as men is reductive. We all belong to several groups that shape our responses. For the most part women, like men, write and read as part of multiple intersecting and constantly evolving identities. Men and women from similar cultural backgrounds reading an Ann Beattie or a John Updike story in *The New Yorker* have far more in common than readers of the same sex who have a different cultural background. Jews who have suffered through the Holocaust, blacks who have lived through the era of Jim Crow laws and customs, those who were raised in the Mississippi Delta, Japanese-Americans who were (dis)placed in camps in World War II, have common bonds that transcend gender differences. For how many people outside the academy is the gender difference the dominant factor—as opposed to one of several important factors—in the way they read and experience?

My own reading is an intersection of my experience and personality. Major factors in my responses include my teaching and writing about the novel for the past eighteen years. But this professional self at times gives way to a self defined by my Jewish heritage; by my growing up in a middle-class community on Long Island and my access to theater and museums; by parental influences; by my relatively cosmopolitan background, including travel experiences; by my relatively provincial life in Eastern university English departments for more than two decades as a graduate student and teacher; by my life in rural Ithaca these past seventeen years; by my marriage to a school administrator of a quite different background with whom I shared twenty-two often satisfying and at times tumultuous years trying to define a relationship in which each of us (at best) helped the other grow but (at worst) bogged the other down in carping and failed to provide an adequate support system; by my complex relation with my adolescent children, particularly my independent and iconoclastic elder son, who says "no" before doing "yes." (The above sentence, it will be noted, not only gives some clues as to what it is like to read as Dan Schwarz, but enacts my credo by giving the author a human voice to which the reader must respond; it is meant to be in striking contrast to critics whose polemical abstractions, even when they ritually define their own subjective stances, are themselves an attack on reading and writing as a living experience.)

V. The Humanistic Critical Legacy

While Anglo-American critics have not articulated a philosophic basis for their criticism, they have developed a methodology and principles—even, indeed, an implicit theory—that interprets, analyzes, and judges novels effectively. I have spoken at length about this tradition in my *The Humanistic Heritage: Critical Theories of the English Novel from James to Hillis Miller*. I have called this tradition humanistic formalism and have cast a wide net to include critics as diverse as Forster, Booth, Van Ghent, Watt, and Kermode, and have even appropriated Auerbach, Raymond Williams, and some aspects of the work of Hillis Miller. Despite some failures, this tradition has explicated the texts of major novelists of the past three centuries and has made these texts more accessible to readers. That complicated and problematic novels, like *Lord Jim*, *The Golden Bowl*, *The Sound and The Fury*, and *Ulysses*, have become part of the consciousness of educated people and that major English and American eighteenth- and nineteenth-century novels have been better understood—more subtly and fully read—is a tribute to the efficacy of this criticism.

The concerns of this tradition have been accuracy, inclusiveness, and the quality—the maturity and sincerity—of its mimesis, and its mimesis represents how people live in a social community. Perhaps from an historical perspective this criticism should be seen as a response to the British novel's interest in content and its moral effects on readers. For this body of criticism would usually subscribe to what Gene Thornton wrote in another context, "[A]rt is about something other than art, and subject matter is important precisely because it distracts the viewer's attention from art and focuses it on something outside the picture—life, the world, God—that is more important than art" (25–26). Humanistic novel criticism also takes seriously the importance of subject matter, and believes that the doing—technique, structure, and style—is *important* because it reveals or discusses the meaning inherent in the subject.

The differences that separate various strands of Anglo-American criticism seem less significant than they once did. Now we are able to see that the New Critics, Aristotelians, the *Partisan Review* group, contextualists, and literary historians share a number of important assumptions: authors write to express their ideas and emotions; the way people live and the values for which they live are of fundamental interest to authors and readers; literature expresses insights about human life and responses to human situations, and that is the main reason why we read, teach, and think about literature. While the emphasis varies from critic to critic, we can identify several concepts that define this criticism:

1. The form of the novel—style, structure, narrative techniques—expresses its value system. Put another way: form discovers the meaning of content.
2. A work of literature is also a creative gesture of the author and the result of historical context. Understanding the process of imitating the external world gives us an insight into the artistry and meaning of the work.
3. The work of fiction imitates a world that precedes the text, and critics should recapture that world primarily by formal analysis of the text, although knowledge of the historical context and author are often important. Such critics believe that there is an original meaning, a center, which can be approached, and at times reached, by perceptive reading. The goal is to discover what the author said to his/her intended audience *then* as well as what he/she says to us now. Acts of interpretation at their best—subtle, lucid, inclusive, perceptive—can bring that goal into sight.
4. Human behavior is central to most works, and should be the major concern of analysis. In particular, these critics are, with the notable exception of Northrop Frye, interested in how people behave—what they fear, desire, doubt, need. Although modes of characterization differ, the psychology and morality of characters must be understood as if they were real people; for understanding others like ourselves helps us to understand ourselves.
5. The inclusiveness of the novel's vision in terms of depth and range is a measure of the work's quality.

In the last several years, humanistic criticism has made several advances; specifically, it has become more attentive to the role of the reader and of the temporality of the structure of literary works. By seeing the structure as an evolving process, rather than as a static and spatial architectonic shape, and by conceiving of the reader as an active figure who is constantly testing, discarding, and modifying his or her impressions, the dialogue between reader and work has taken on another dimension. It should be noted that well before deconstruction, humanistic formalism was moving in similar directions in its stress on the process of reading—in the work of Burke, Booth, and Kermode—and in its close analysis of the tensions and ambiguities within novels—in the work of Van Ghent, Schorer, Watt, and Guerard as well as in a host of their successors. The idea that works are not seamless organic wholes and that works have fissures and tensions which undermine unity is not new. Critics working in the tradition of humanistic formalism have taught us that Esther Summerson is a different kind of narrator than the omniscient narrator; that Father Time as an allegorical figure depends on a different kind of mimesis than either the representative Jude or idiosyncratic Sue, and that the catalogues in "Cyclops" do not occupy the same status in the imagined world as Bloom's reveries.

Humanistic formalism calls into question deconstruction's insistence on the arbitrariness of signs in the only sense that such a concept matters to literary criticism. It assumes that in specific circumstances readers share similar recognition of signs and thus respond in approximately similar ways. Of course, the more readers share the same cultural background as the author, the more they will share her/his experience and the less arbitrary will appear the author's signs. Readers who have been reading similar works and studying in the same field will share a greater recognition of the signs I am now writing on this page. Thus the arbitrariness of signs is not absolute but rather a function of the reader's experience, the author's intent, and, of course, historical circumstances, which render some signs far more arbitrary to a contemporary audience than they were for the original reader. For example, Conrad would have expected contemporary readers of "The Secret Sharer" to understand the British maritime code; he could not have expected them—as many of his readers today do—to extenuate Leggatt or to be reluctant to pass judgment about the captain's providing refuge for an escaped murderer. Nor would he have expected us to be taken in by Marlow's empathetic reading of Jim's abandonment of the native passengers and crew in *Lord Jim*.

In terms of my own personal aesthetic, let me propose directions that a revised humanistic novel criticism—a criticism that builds upon the above concepts—might take. I assume that the author has created an imagined world, an ontology separate and distinct from the real one, and that the created world of a good novel is organized according to orderly principles and is apprehensible by orderly principles, although the reader's concepts of order may be different from those of the author. The structure of a novel is an evolving process in which the reader participates with the author. After all, the author embodies in his or her work a structure of effects that arouse expectations and subsequently fulfill, modify, transform, postpone, or deflate them. Since each novel generates its own aesthetic, we need to inquire into how a particular novel signifies. We must define the voice of the novel by continually asking, "Who is speaking to what implied audience and with what intended effects?"

Finally, the language of a novel presents a concatenation of events or episodes that constitute a narrative. Notwithstanding the deliberate efforts to subvert the expectations of traditional narrative by disrupting chronology and doubling every action (a technique that paradoxically calls attention to the fictionality of the text and the inevitability of the events within the imagined world), the narrative that we find in a novel like *Lord Jim* makes a coherent statement about the way life is lived in the imagined world within the text. Just as we value the integrity of literary works that account for the complexity of life and language, we should value the integrity of readings that provide coherent explanations of the infinite variety of the multiple dimensions of a complex work. Moreover, our interest in imagined worlds relates to their relation to real ones; although that relation may be oblique, we do look for kinds of representation in our fictions, and we do understand events in fiction in terms of signification beyond as well as within the imagined world of the novel. Thus it is not only appropriate but necessary to inquire into the relationship between the presence embodied in the form of the novel and the real author. Reading is a mode of perception, a mode of construing, and reading about characters within an imagined world appeals to us because such reading is an extension of how we perceive and understand the events in our own lives. Of course, we must understand that characters in fiction are functions of the formal properties of a novel's imagined world. But, despite some recent attacks on the "metaphysics of presence," we should not be apologetic for or embarrassed by thinking of characters in literature as if they were human within the "hypothesis" of their imagined worlds, or as reflections, distortions, or parodies of their creators.

Without abandoning interpretation of literary works, a revised humanistic criticism should develop concepts about how novels behave and how readers respond. It should perceive reading as an active quest to discover what words mean and signify within the imagined world. It should seek to understand how these words function within their own ontology and how the rhetorical effects— usually, but by no means always, consciously built into the world by the author—affect the reader in her or his world.

Works Cited

Culler, Jonathan. *On Deconstruction*. Ithaca: Cornell University Press, 1982.

———. *The Pursuit of Signs*. Ithaca: Cornell University Press, 1981.

———. *Structuralist Poetics*. Ithaca: Cornell University Press, 1978.

Eco, Umberto. *The Name of the Rose*. Trans. William Weaver. New York: Warner Books, 1983.

Fetterley, Judith. *The Resisting Reader: A Feminist Approach to American Fiction*. Bloomington: Indiana University Press, 1978.

Frye, Joanne. *Living Stories, Telling Lives*. Ann Arbor: University of Michigan Press, 1986.

Hartman, Geoffrey. *Saving the Text: Literature / Derrida / Philosophy*. Baltimore: Johns Hopkins University Press, 1981.

Gilbert, Sandra M. and Susan Gubar. *The Mad Woman in the Attic: The Woman Writer and the Nineteenth-Century Literary Imagination*. New Haven: Yale University Press, 1979.

Hirsch, E. D. *Validity in Interpretation*. New Haven and London: Yale University Press, 1967.

———. *The Aims of Interpretation*. Chicago: University of Chicago Press, 1976.

Miller, Nancy K. "Emphasis Added: Plots and Plausibilities in Women's Fiction." *PMLA* 96:1 (January 1981).

Nuttall, A. D. *A New Mimesis: Shakespeare and the Representation of Reality.* New York: Methuen, 1983.

Riffaterre, Michael. "Interpretive and Descriptive Poetry: A Reading of Wordsworth's 'Yew-Trees.'" *New Literary History* 4 (Winter 1973). Quoted by Wayne Booth. *Critical Inquiry* 3:3 (Spring 1977).

Schwarz, Daniel R. *The Humanistic Heritage: Critical Theories of the English Novel from James to Hillis Miller.* Philadelphia: University of Pennsylvania Press, 1986.

Spacks, Patricia. Introduction to *The Author in his Work.* Ed. Louis L. Martz and Aubrey Williams. New Haven and London: Yale University Press, 1978.

Thornton, Gene. "P. H. Polk's Genius Versus Modernism." *New York Times,* February 12, 1982, Leisure section.

II

✤ ✤ ✤

Four Precursors

Narrative Fictions and Reality:
A Comment on Frank Kermode's
The Sense of an Ending

ROY PASCAL

The discussion of the nature of the structural fictions of narrative seems scarcely to have been taken further since Frank Kermode's brilliant book, *The Sense of an Ending,* that appeared in 1967. It is disappointing that the essays in *The Theory of the Novel* (1974), edited by John Halperin, do not investigate this problem, and Kermode's own contribution to this volume, though it is largely concerned with Roland Barthes, occupies itself with the later structuralist and not the radical questioner of *Le degré zéro de l'écriture.* Here I want to take up a question concerning the general conception of the nature and function of fictions, primarily of novelistic fictions, though it might include other fictions too, logical or legal for instance. In one respect Kermode's wide-ranging, imaginative, and acute exposition comes to conclusions that are in my opinion unsound and that, if they were true, would suggest that the narrative fictions are arbitrary or purely subjective. The book must, I think, leave such an impression; for instance, the perceptive review of it by Ruth apRoberts in the first Number of NOVEL, properly appreciative of Kermode's justification of fictions as a means to "make sense of the world," also accepts the book's thesis that they are "untrue" or "false."

I must first briefly sketch Kermode's argument, reducing its richness to the bare theoretical points that are at issue. It starts from Sartre's critique of the traditional form of the novel, the chief falsity of which lies for him in the narrator (personal or impersonal), who writes from the standpoint of the outcome of the events related, and who thereby profoundly distorts the nature of real experience. The whole pattern of a story, the coherence of its events, is built on this false premise of retrospection, for it is only in retrospect that we can recognize events to be significant or irrelevant and contingent. The nature of living, which Sartre powerfully illustrates from the experience of participating in the Resistance during the war, is quite opposite to that of fiction, since when acting we never know the outcome, we are unsure of effects, and we ignore what is happening elsewhere and in the minds of the people around us. Sartre considers this falsification of life to be a subtle form of self-assertion on the part of the bourgeois class.[1] In his novel *La Nausée* of 1938 he had already tried to incorporate the pure contingency and "opacity" of life as it really is. Roland Barthes' *Le degré zéro de l'écriture* (1953) extends and systematises Sartre's criticism of the narrative fictions, though this book is not discussed by Kermode in *The Sense of an Ending.*

[1] J. P. Sartre, *Qu'est-ce que la littérature?,* in *Situations* 2 (1948).

In *The Sense of an Ending* Kermode acknowledges the force of Sartre's criticism of the fictional nature of retrospective narrative. The "ending," as he understands it, is representative of the narrative fictions, since it is the postulate of an ending that makes a beginning possible, that makes a meaningful pattern out of the varied items of the story, that fulfils the story. But his theme is totally contrary to Sartre's, for he argues not only that no novel, no story is possible unless some fictional structures are used, but also that, as in other activities of the mind, understanding depends on the invention of fictions (of which language itself is an all-pervading one). He refutes the concept of a fixed "bourgeois" or traditional novel, showing how the history of the novel is from the beginning the history of successive modifications of established fictional forms. Since formal resistance and experimentation are not peculiar to modern times, Kermode looks for a more general source of the modification of fictions, which he defines roughly as the search to "make sense of the world." In the course of his exposition he shows, in a masterly piece of concrete criticism, how Sartre was forced, in *La Nausée*, to have recourse to novelistic fictions, though here as elsewhere Kermode also acknowledges the significance of the modifications Sartre introduced and the validity of his search for the authentic expression of experience.

All this is illuminating and needs no comment here. It is also much to be welcomed that Kermode does not stop at this point, but also ventures a theory of novelistic fictions within a general theory of fictions, pointing out that philosophers who have written on logical and similar fictions have not recognised literary fictions. Much of what he writes in this connexion is admirable; but it is in this area that my doubts arise. For this general theory, Kermode relies greatly on Vaihinger's work, and since my criticism attaches to Vaihinger also, I must first say something about his theory.[2]

Vaihinger analyses the fictions used in mathematics, logic, law, sociology etc., such as zero and infinity, moral responsibility, "economic man," the absolute, abstract or collective concepts like "tree." His main argument is that while all these concepts do not refer to anything real, at the same time they are not false or misleading. The reason is, that they do not claim to be true, but are tools that the mind invents in order to understand and master the problems of our world. Thus zero or infinity do not indicate any real number, but their invention allows us complicated calculations about reality and practical operations. There is no such thing as "economic man" or pure moral responsibility, but social science and the law require these concepts. Fictions are essentially different from theories or hypotheses, Vaihinger reiterates; they are not would-be descriptions of reality, but only instruments of thought. He points out what grievous errors have resulted when men have taken them to be descriptions of reality, for instance when "tree" has been understood to mean a reality beyond that of empirical experience. So Vaihinger frequently repeats that fictions are "contrary to

---

[2] H. Vaihinger, *Die Philosophie des Als-Ob*, 1911, translated by C. K. Ogden as *The Philosophy of As If*, 1924 (London: Routledge & Kegan, 1968). Chapters 2 and 5 of Kermode's *The Sense of an Ending* are devoted to the theory of fictions, and he acknowledges his debt to Vaihinger.

reality," "arbitrary deviations from reality," but without therefore being delusions or lies.[3]

Kermode seizes on Vaihinger's argument and applies it to the fictions of the novel. These fictions—the perspective of the narrator, coherence of events, the ending that fulfils the story, creates its coherence, and rounds off everything—do not suggest that life itself has such endings, such coherence, such transparency, but are simply means to investigate human life and relationships. Their functioning is heuristic. From the beginning, from Cervantes onwards, novelists have pointed to the disparity between their invented world and the real world. This disparity leads to a continuing modification of fictions, in order to mitigate their inadequacies; but however modified, they remain fictions and do not mislead so long as we are aware that they are fictional—just as we would not be likely to confuse the world on the stage with the world outside the theatre. Thus Kermode, in his richly suggestive exposition, can justify the role of the imagination in understanding our world and communicating this understanding to others, without confusing the fictional with the real.

But in one respect, the relationship of these invented fictions to the real world, his theory is perplexing and somewhat unclear. Vaihinger repeatedly insists that the fictions are "contrary to reality"; it is not clear whether Kermode adopts this view, or even has a consistent view. Sometimes he seems to think of them as unreal and arbitrary in Vaihinger's sense, "arbitrary" here meaning above all "subjective," "anthropocentric,"[4] in the Kantian sense categories of understanding that arise from man's "basic need" to understand (44); thus he can use such a phrase as the right, in modern times, to "an arbitrary and private choice of fictional norms" (36). The historical modification of fictions seems sometimes to be ascribed to the growing sophistication of the mind, which requires more subtle and complex fictions in the place of the inadequate old ones (45), almost as if the world were always the same and the fictional developments recorded in the novel form were the result only of developments in the writers' consciousness. On the other hand, when Professor Kermode pursues his illuminating discussion of the difference between the fictional duration of the novel and the "chronicity" of experienced time, he writes that these "fictive models of the temporal world" will be "humanly serviceable" only "if they pay adequate respect to what we think of as 'real' time, the chronicity of the waking moment" (54). Here, it will be observed that a condition of the effectiveness of the fiction is that it embodies in some degree ('pays adequate respect to') the reality it seeks to illuminate. When Kermode writes that fictions change "because times change" (64), it seems again likely that he refers their change to changes in the actual world of human activities and relationships, not only to changes in consciousness. But such a theme is not made explicit or emphatic,

---

[3] See particularly Chapter 24, "The Main Characteristics of Fictions" in *The Philosophy of As If*.

[4] Figures in brackets refer to *The Sense of an Ending* (London: Oxford University Press, 1967), p. 56. Citations to this edition hereafter appear in parentheses in the text.

and when, in discussing "ending," he writes that "the End is a fact of life and a fact of the imagination" (57–8), the remark occurs in the context of an argument that asserts the primacy of the mind's fiction of an ending. If I am right that there is some inconsistency on this matter in Professor Kermode's book, I think I may also be right in thinking that it occurs because some of his insights contradict the theory of Vaihinger in this respect, without leading him to a critical reexamination of this theory. My purpose here is to explore this possibility.

But before getting down to this, I must mention a subsidiary problem. Both Vaihinger and Kermode complicate the problem greatly by producing Nietzsche as a witness in their cause. Vaihinger's long last chapter is an extensive review of the evidence in Nietzsche's writings for his theory of fictions, and it is certainly true that, from the early essays onwards, Nietzsche continuously attacked both positivism and idealism with his view that our mental tools—language, numbers, causality etc.—are fictions that do not describe an objective reality but are merely means of mastering nature. Their quality is subjective, anthropomorphic, and we know not things but "metaphors of things." Thus Nietzsche rejoices to provoke us by calling our notions "lies" and "delusions."

Now, it is rather surprising that Vaihinger (who had earlier written a full study of Nietzsche) should have found in this type of statement support for his doctrine, since he demonstrates that such terms as "lies" and "delusions" are quite inappropriate for fictions that do not claim to be true. Still more surprisingly, he does not seem to notice that Nietzsche's intentions are the very opposite of his own. For Nietzsche's defense of fictions is part of a general onslaught on rational thought and the moral values usually associated with it, in favour of an irrationalism that serves creativity and the will to power. While Vaihinger defends the "untruth" of fictions because of the service they render to rational understanding, Nietzsche rejoices in it because it is one of the many forms of illusion that outstrip the reason. Consequently, Nietzsche associates fictions with irrational theories and ideologies, as expressions of the "will to illusion" that he advocates. The curious thing is that Vaihinger, who makes the difference from hypotheses so fundamental a characteristic of fictions, does not seem to notice that many of the "illusions" that Nietzsche glories in are not fictions, but actual doctrines, ideologies, hypotheses.

Kermode, I think unfortunately, takes over this championship of Nietzsche's conception of fictions, though not without some justifiable moral scruple. He quotes (37) a little of the famous passage from Paragraph 4 of *Beyond Good and Evil* which most directly claims to be about logical fictions[5]:—"The falsity of an opinion is not any objection to it. . . . The question [Kermode says, the "only relevant question"] is how far the opinion is life-furthering, life-preserving, species-preserving" (Nietzsche adds "perhaps even species-breeding"). Though

---

[5] Trans. by Walter Kaufmann (New York: Random House, 1966), pp. 11–12. The paragraph opens: "The falseness of a judgment is for us not necessarily an objection to a judgment; in this respect our new language may sound strangest. The question is to what extent it is life-promoting, life-preserving, species-preserving, perhaps even species-cultivating. And we are fundamentally inclined to claim that the falsest judgments . . . are the most indispensable for us; that without accepting the fictions of logic, without measuring reality against the purely invented world of the unconditional and self-identical, without a constant falsification of the world by means of numbers, man could not live. . . ."

Nietzsche in the following sentences (not referred to by Kermode) goes on to speak of these "false opinions" as "logical fictions," it is clear that here, as elsewhere, what he is thinking of includes the postulates of his whole irrationalistic, individualistic ethic. His use of the phrase "the falsest opinions" itself indicates that he is thinking of theories or faiths, as indeed when he calls them "lies" and "delusions." Now, Kermode immediately observes that the above quotation from Nietzsche contains an immense moral danger, since success becomes the sole criterion of the value of a notion or judgment. He therefore tries to fend off the danger by saying that the danger arises when the fiction is taken to be a statement about reality, when it consequently degenerates into a myth. The danger lies, then, in how we understand Nietzsche's contention, not in the contention itself. Kermode himself gives as an example the doctrine of anti-semitism, but this only deepens the confusion. Anti-semitism cannot be called a fiction in Vaihinger's sense, for it is a cultural and biological doctrine, theory, or if you like hypothesis, claiming to be a truth. The fault in assertions like those of Nietzsche's quoted by Kermode above is not that they have been falsely considered to be theories or myths, but that they are in fact theoretical, ideological assertions, totally different in kind from logical and other fictions.

I could (and should have liked to) have ignored the issue of Nietzsche were it not that Kermode, embracing Vaihinger's ascription of fictions to the category of "the consciously false," concludes: "They [the literary fictions] are not subject, like hypotheses, to proof or disconfirmation; only, if they come to lose their operational effectiveness, to neglect" (40). This has precisely the pragmatic Nietzschean ring that causes him, in the ethical sphere, alarm, since it suggests that there can be no test of truth or reality for fictions, only that of effectiveness. At the same time, this term is not easily applicable to literature; and, more importantly, perhaps this is no true alternative, since one of the conditions of "effectiveness" might well be truth.

From these critical considerations there arise three main groups of questions, to which I would suggest an approach, if not an answer. They are: Does not the campaign led by Sartre and Barthes against the fictions of the "bourgeois" novel aim at the foundations of "story" of all types? Is the coherence found in every story, the pattern, alien to reality? And finally: Have the narrative fictions only a subjective or arbitrary source? and, what hangs on our answer?

Story and Novel

Throughout the criticism of Sartre and Barthes, in Adorno's aesthetics too,[6] the novel is defined as a *bourgeois* art form, and the narrative fictions are considered to be powerful instruments of the bourgeois class in asserting its ideological predominance. By "bourgeois" is meant the middle class of western European civilisation, in the period opening roughly in the 17th century; Cervantes and Defoe

---

[6] See particularly the essay "Standort des Erzählers im zeitgenössischen Roman" (1954), reprinted in Theodor W. Adorno, *Noten zur Literatur* i, (Bibliothek Suhrkamp: 1965).

are the great initiators of its fiction. The fictions that these critics indict exist in all essentials of every type of story—the retrospective narrative, the narrator who can tell his readers the thoughts and feelings of his characters, the creation of coherence out of accidents, the fulfilling ending. Stories constructed upon these fictions have been and are narrated in all cultures; we know them best, outside the novel, in Greek epic, the Biblical stories, in myth generally, in folktale, as well as in historical narrative. It is absurd to claim that the narrative fictions serve merely bourgeois interests; they are a universal means of understanding.

What sort of understanding, and understanding of what? L. O. Mink has done us a service by calling our attention to the book of W. B. Gallie, *Philosophy and the Historical Understanding*.[7] Professor Gallie is here concerned with the function of historical narrative, but he sees its connexion with fictional story, and indeed uses a simple model of the latter to begin his investigation (it is a pity that he seems to be unaware of the controversy over literary fictions and hence does not discuss more sophisticated story-models). Professor Gallie takes a story not as a completed object, whose meaning is to be summed up in its conclusion, but as something that is read or listened to, whose meaning lies in the cumulative experiences of the reading process. As we read, we are led to form a series of anticipations, of provisional conclusions, which are continually corrected by later events. While the ending is of supreme importance, since it alone establishes the unity of all items of the story, it also is never final, for we always find more in a story on re-reading, and our understanding of the story is thereby modified. A story is inexhaustible. Gallie lays stress upon the interplay of accident and coherence. If it is a story, the events and final outcome must be impredictable until they occur. That is, the ending, the coherence do not deny the contingent, they are indeed composed out of contingencies; "the factor of contingency," Gallie writes, "that matches that in everyday life," is embodied in the very nature of story. The main task of the story-teller is, not to eliminate the accidental and contingent, but to show how some elements in the contingent can be turned, in the process of the story, into meaning.[8]

For Gallie, narrative (and he is chiefly concerned with narrative in historiography) is an essential instrument for understanding human relationships, the relations between thought, will, and behaviour, and especially between accident and coherence, *i.e.*, the understanding of the relationship between the manageable and the unmanageable. There is no other means than narrative by which we can project a model that will illuminate these relationships and allow us to contemplate them. H. R. Jauss comes to similar conclusions when he refutes Droysen's wish to abolish narrative from historiography in the interests of truth. Professor Jauss, a literary scholar, is well aware of the fictions that historical nar-

---

[7] W. B. Gallie, *Philosophy and the Historical Understanding* (New York: Schocken Books, 1964). L. O. Mink's essay, "History and Fiction as Modes of Comprehension," appeared in *New Directions in Literary History*, ed. Ralph Cohen (Baltimore: Johns Hopkins, 1974). Mink makes some criticisms of Gallie's work, but these are not important in the present context.

[8] It might have been shown how brilliantly the two aspects are illustrated in the narrative form of Dickens's *Bleak House*. In "Esther's Narrative" the perspective is the conquest of the contingent, the establishment of order, coherence, harmony, justice; in the authorial third-person narrative, the accidental, contingent, unmanageable predominate. For the former, the past tense is used; for the other, the present tense of narration marvellously enhances the sense of the unforeseeable and uncontrollable.

rative depends upon, but in spite of (or rather because of) the fictions of narrative, it is what he calls "a basic category of historical apprehension (Wahrnehmung)," without which we cannot understand human relationships.[9] He links fictional and historical narrative more explicitly than Gallie, for he boldly claims that the structure of nineteenth-century historical narrative was first established by the historical novel, just as he considers the great modifications of novel-structure in this century are influencing modern historical narrative.

Both Gallie and Jauss recognise that "story" is much wider than the novel, and imply that any such sub-group as the "bourgeois novel" must be distinguished by other factors than those generally required for story. They justify story as a category of the understanding, the understanding of human, social relationships. But by understanding they do not mean the reduction of these relationships to a theorem, nor even to a conclusion. The essence of the story is the process, the reader's experience of a process that is a model of some aspect of human relationships, during which he is constantly engaged in anticipations and surprises, wishes and setbacks, judgments that require correction, a series that is somewhat altered with every new reading and involves, like life, alternations of expectations and revisions until the ending. Its stuff is the contingent, its purpose the discovery of some coherence within the great mass of the contingent. The sort of understanding it conveys may, like life itself, be reduced to formulated conclusions, but these can never cover the whole complexity of the experienced events and thoughts, so that the "understanding" is essentially that of experiencing through a model and imaginatively various connected human situations.

I do not think this approach is contrary to that of Professor Kermode, but rather complementary; however, consideration of it might have led him to a rather different handling of the notion of "pure contingency" in his own argument. This can best be considered under a separate heading.

Coherence and Incoherence

It is Sartre's main theme, formulated in a more systematic and dogmatic form by Barthes (in *Le degré zéro*), that the formal structure of the novel, like that of historical narrative, falsifies the very essence of reality as we experience it, since it establishes connexion and coherence whereas in reality events, even psychological events, are random and inscrutable. Living always in the present, we live in a jumble of pure contingency. As we have seen, Kermode defends the novel and its fiction against the imputation of falsification, but he does not seem to take exception to such definitions of life as "pure contingency," and adopts them himself—*e.g.* he asks "How to do justice to a chaotic, viscously contingent reality?" (p. 145) Can one be content with such statements, and with the resulting contrast established between life and art?

Such statements are not meant to arise from the lack of a metaphysical mean-

---

[9] H. R. Jauss, *Literaturgeschichte als Provokation* (Suhrkamp: 1970), p. 228.

ingfulness in the universe; throughout this argument we are only concerned with the secular human and physical world (even though we can suspect that the bitter indictment of the incoherence of the world arises originally from a religious disillusionment). As a statement regarding the physical and human world, we can only answer that in it there are evidently vast coherences, formulated in a series of laws, that constitute our environment and make life possible. There are also anomalies, incoherences and obscurities in the physical universe, but our failure to create a fully coherent order does not negate the coherences observed. In organic life, to the physical laws are added biological, which establish not only the conditions governing the existence of organic forms, but also introduce teleological laws, since here certain individual characteristics are functions of a biological purpose, notably the maturing of the individual and the preservation of the species. In human beings, to these physical and biological patterns are added complex relationships between biological, psychological, and social systems and events. If it is extremely difficult to formulate what laws govern such coherences, that they exist is attested by our behaviour, for we found our daily lives and expectations on the assumption of such coherences. If we did not know that certain results are likely to follow from certain types of circumstances, attitudes, and behaviour, we could not exist, as individuals or families or societies.

Why repeat such clichés? Much hangs upon their acceptance or rejection, and because of this Michael Frayn, an ingenious and intelligent novelist, devotes to such considerations and their implications a number of the reflexions in his book *Constructions*.[10] On several occasions he comments on the contrast between the orderliness of the novel and the disorderliness of reality. The world of the novel, he writes, "is enclosed . . . not open to the incomprehensibility of the real present and the uncertainty of the real future" (No. 214). But when he considers not just our immediate experience, but the whole context in which it stands, he is not content with this simple contrast. He recognises that the universe as a whole, like its parts, exhibits both coherence and incoherence. "Is there an order in the universe?" he asks, to give the disarming answer, "There are orders. And disorders" (No. 233).

However, such a statement is far too general and abstract to be of immediate help, and it only sets the framework for what most interests Frayn. This is the inherent need of all living organisms to impose an order, as it were, on their universe, that is, to filter out of the chaotic complexity of their environment and of change that which promotes their own growth and survival. "We are significance-seeking organisms. We seek out significance from our environment as we seek out food" (No. 6). From the simplest perceptions and actions to the most complicated mental operations, we construct some coherence, some pattern, that enables us to register experience in a form we can put to use. Language itself is the means to such an ordering, for by language we impose connexions and

[10] Michael Frayn, *Constructions* (New York: British Book Center, 1974). This book has no pagination. It consists of a collection of separate reflexions, each numbered. I give in my text the numbers of the reflexions referred to.

coherence for the sake of securing purposeful communication (Nos. 185–6, 290).

Now, this might ring a little like Barthes, and indeed in a preface to Bruce Morrissette's *Les romans de Robbe-Grillet* (1963) Barthes did write that it is a fault to believe that, in life, things remain "mute," by which he means detached from us, unrelated, contingent, for "anthropologiquement les choses signifient tout-de-suite." But Frayn differs from Barthes—the Barthes of *Le degré zéro*—in two essentials. First, this imposition of patterns, of coherence is not contrary to reality, it is a condition of existence altogether; it is not a fraud, since there is no contrasting way of truth or honesty, there is no other way of being and thinking. Second, the imposition of patterns in art corresponds to that in life, and therefore it cannot be called "bourgeois," since it is required for all forms of social life. Therefore, when Frayn considers the patterning that narrative requires, his theme is that it may in some respects come into collision with our sense of life, when new types of narrative structure have to be invented (Mr. Frayn himself has essayed a novel written in the future tense).[11] But a novel would be untrue to the reality of living were it without coherences, just as it would be so were it without contingencies.

Fictions and Reality

The lines of approach illustrated by the work of Gallie and Frayn reveal the inadequacy and fragility of some of the assumptions and arguments of Sartre and Barthes, but do not reach as far as the more general theory of fictions with which Professor Kermode refuted their claims. In this more general field, the most pertinent contribution that I have come across is that in Moritz R. Cohen's manual, *A Preface to Logic*, a short section of which is devoted to a criticism of Vaihinger's *The Philosophy of As-If*.[12] Cohen does not reject the concept of fictions, but criticises Vaihinger's interpretation, in particular his failure to recognise their connexion with reality. With all aspects of his criticism I am not concerned in our context, only with those that clarify my own criticisms (unfortunately Cohen, like other philosophers, does not deal explicitly with literary fictions). Vaihinger, like a typical positivist, Cohen writes, accepts only the concrete and individual as real, and therefore characterises the abstract as unreal. His error is to have failed to understand that reality is not made up of separate, unrelated things, but of "things-in-relation"; "propositions about abstractions and abstract relations no more falsify reality than do propositions about particulars." Fictions tacitly entail such propositions, but what, in many of them, seems to Vaihinger a puzzle is resolved when we understand that they refer to relationships, not things. Thus the mathematical zero or infinity do not stand for a particular identity, but indicate a mathematical relationship, as real as a finite number. Vaihinger's error led him to claim that fictions were "contrary to reality," but this is not so. These

---

[11] Michael Frayn, *A Very Private Life* (London: Collins, 1968).

[12] Moritz R. Cohen, *A Preface to Logic* (New York: Meridian Books, 1960), pp. 103–112. The substance of this Chapter was first published in *The Journal of Philosophy*, 20 (1923). The author is "the great Morris Cohen" referred to in Saul Bellow's *Humboldt's Gift*, from whom Humboldt "had gotten A's in philosophy."

fictions—Cohen speaks like Vaihinger about mathematical, logical, legal and sociological concepts—indicate "real parts, phases, or elements of things or their relations." They are helpful to understanding precisely because they *do* "rest on a real basis." There is, for example, nothing in reality that can be called an "economic man," there is no such political form as "pure democracy." But there are economic motives and democratic forms, and the fictional concept comes into being when we abstract these elements from the real man and real society, in which they exist in combination with many other elements. Because such concepts are not arbitrary and are related to reality, they can enable the economist to understand the economic process. "The fact that certain elements always occur in conjunction with others and never in isolation is no more an argument against their reality than the fact that no one can be a brother or a creditor without being other things is an argument against the possibility of having these abstract characteristics. Science must abstract some elements and neglect others because not all things that exist together are relevant to each other."

How gladly might an imaginative writer, if considering his procedures, appropriate the last sentence for his own art, substituting "art" or "the understanding" for "science"! Cohen's observations are indeed helpful when we are discussing the structural fictions of the novel. Coherence, retrospective perspective, insight into feelings and thoughts, endings, etc. embody features of real life and experience, though these features may not exist in isolation from other elements, and may never have the pure form they have in art. Thus, the fulfilment ending is not contrary to life; we know innumerable partial and provisional endings, in personal and social life, which constitute the closure of a series of outer and inner events; the coherence between the events of a novel or in the behaviour of persons reflects the much more imperfect coherences that we encounter or try to establish in life; the role of the narrator, his insight into his characters, has its models in actual life, where we do know quite a lot about what is going on within other people, where we can often anticipate consequences, and where retrospection is a constantly used instrument of understanding. The novelistic fictions are not, as Vaihinger says and Kermode seems to re-affirm, "contrary to reality" or "arbitrary deviations from reality," they are abstractions, projections of actual relationships isolated from some of the associations with which in real life they are bound, and which are thought by the novelist to be irrelevant to his immediate object. Thus there is no antithesis of "truth" and "effectiveness" in regard to fictions; their effectiveness, usefulness, depends on the fact that they embody an aspect of reality.

That fictions also have a subjective source is of course clear, and I need add nothing on this aspect of them to what Vaihinger and Kermode have written. A simple example of this dual nature, objective and subjective, of fictions can be found in the practical tools that man invents and uses. A wood-plane reflects the character of the hand and body of the workman, the physical situation in which it is to be used, and the purposes of the worker. But it also reflects, embodies, the nature of the material it is intended for, wood, in the character of the cutting edge, and perhaps the plane's whole shape is modified according, for instance, to whether it is to be used with the grain or across it.

If we understand that fictions possess an attachment to reality as well as to the subjective purpose, we can more readily see that it is as erroneous to believe that fictions can be dispensed with as to believe they are misleading. Sartre and Barthes express great admiration for the works of Kafka, in which an "opaque" hero moves in an inscrutable, uninterpretable world of pure contingency. They have of course every right to admire Kafka. But they are wrong to believe that in his novels the narrative fictions are dispensed with; for the Kafka-type hero, with his lack of "character," obscurity of purpose, and extreme alienation, and his dislocated, incoherent world, are no less fictional, distinct from real life, than, say, the characters and world of Thomas Mann's *Death in Venice* or *The Magic Mountain*. Like all other novels, both types are built upon fictional constructs, themselves related to features of real existence. As such, one can appreciate both, though anyone may well prefer one to the other as corresponding to a more urgent and relevant feature of the modern situation.

Cohen's criticism of Vaihinger provides a basis for my own dissatisfaction with Kermode's theory of the narrative fictions. It does not affect Kermode's main purpose and argument, especially his criticism of the modernist rejection of fictions, and his definition of fictions as instruments, as distinct from interpretations. This justification of the fictitious nature of narrative structure remains extremely valuable. Also valuable is Kermode's insistence that the history of the novel from the beginning is an unremitting process of modification of fictional forms, and his ascription of these changes to the artist's urge to "make sense of the world," an urge known to his own generation as the search for authenticity. But my criticism of his rather indecisive views on the relation of the fictions to reality, if it does not challenge these important insights, is itself not a mere pedantic cavil.

First, if we understand that the narrative fictions are shaped out of real features of reality, it helps us to understand why they can be used from generation to generation, for centuries, as a means to illuminate and discuss real life; like the great literary genres, epic, drama, lyric, they are rooted in our existence. Second, it helps us to understand how modifications of the fictions come about. For we should look for their source not merely in a rather tautological changed sense of life, but ultimately in the changing world that men create, the changing human relations and values that accompany changes in economic forms, in thought, in social structure and political relationships. The investigation of the changing sense of what constitutes an ending to a novel, or of Sartre's sharpened awareness of contingency, would have to reach into the whole world in which the novel functions, and would properly have something of the complexity that so complex a question requires. And lastly, it might restrain some of the more extravagant and arbitrary attempts at replacing older fictions with more authentic—or at least would provide the readers with some defence against arbitrary innovations.

Don Quixote, Ulysses, *and the Idea of Realism*

TERRENCE DOODY

Eat from my plate and drink from the vessel I drink from; for it can be said of knight errantry as of love: that it puts all things on the same level.

Don Quixote, *I:xi*

Extremes meet.

Ulysses, *Circe*

I

—Maybe, but in realism you are down to facts on which the world is based: that sudden reality which smashes romanticism into a pulp. What makes most people's lives unhappy is some disappointed romanticism, some unrealizable or misconceived ideal. In fact you may say that idealism is the ruin of man, and if we lived down to fact, as primitive man had to do, we would be better off. That is what we are made for. Nature is quite unromantic. It is we who put romance into her, which is a false attitude, an egotism, absurd like all egotisms. In Ulysses *I tried to keep close to fact.*

But a writer must maintain a continual struggle against the objective: that is his function. The eternal qualities are the imagination and the sexual instinct, and the formal life tries to suppress both. Out of this present conflict rise the phenomena of modern life.—In my Mabbot Street scene I approached reality closer in my opinion than anywhere else in the book except perhaps for moments in the last chapter.

These remarks, which are quoted from Arthur Power's *Conversations with James Joyce,* illustrate how difficult it is for anyone, even himself, to define realism both precisely and comprehensively.[1] In the first passage, Joyce is the Catholic, classically-tempered writer who developed the theory of impersonality that Stephen Dedalus pronounces in *A Portrait of the Artist;* in the second passage, he is the intensely private, openly defiant writer of a book that managed to be both obscure and obscene. And in this passage, he confuses the issue further by apparently contradicting himself, for nothing in Circe seems to be like anything in Penelope. The Bunyan-like voice of Oxen of the Sun calls Circe "the land of Phenomenon."[2] There everything is reduced to a single level of being: the self and the world interpenetrate with no distinction between the inner and the outer, the past and the future, the living and the dead; clothing is costume; fantasies are immediately realized and embodied; buttons, among other things, talk; and

---

[1] *Conversations with James Joyce,* ed. Clive Hart (London: Millington, Ltd., 1974), pp. 98 and 74–75.

[2] *Ulysses* (New York: Random House–Vintage Books, 1961), p. 395. All further citations in the text.

Joyce's style eschews characterization and narrative in order to imitate the cinema's speed and montage.[3] Circe doesn't seem "down to fact" in any way. Penelope, by contrast, in its artless, unmediated representation of character has the primitive realism of *Moll Flanders;* and by the time we get to it, after chapters like Oxen of the Sun, Circe, and Ithaca, Penelope seems conventional.

Joyce's contradictions could be resolved, perhaps, if we knew exactly what "moments" in Circe he refers to, but the ambivalence of his remarks is valuable because it expresses unself-consciously the polarity that has always been intrinsic to the idea of realism, the conflict between the world and self that he expresses in his desire to stay "down to fact" *and* to resist the "objective." This polarity, I think, is a fairly direct, traditional expression of the dualism in human nature. And in English, Raymond Williams explains, this polarity has meant that the word "real" itself, which is derived from *res,* has always signified both the physical entity of a thing and the immaterial principle which lies beneath or beyond mere appearances—what the thing really is.[4] So, the history of realism has been the history of those ideas of what *the thing* really is, those essential principles which are the norms of being and meaning and which have changed throughout time. The course of their change is recorded in Erich Auerbach's *Mimesis,*[5] and Auerbach's own great sympathy for so many of these ideas allows us to accept as uncontradictory Nietzsche's scorn for the ideal of realism—"Realism in art is an illusion, all the writers of all the ages were convinced they were realistic"—and Harry Levin's praise for its practice and moral purpose—"for all great writers, in so far as they are committed to a searching and scrupulous critique of life as they know it, may be reckoned among the realists."[6]

The novel has flourished in this ambivalence, at least since *Don Quixote,* because it is the fox, not the hedgehog, who wants to write a novel.[7] In *Don Quixote,* at the end of Part I, the Canon makes two long statements which pose in Renaissance terms a parallel to the remarks about realism Joyce made to Power. The first passage is the Canon's own injunction against the egotism of the writer which produces distortions and romance. Like Joyce, the Canon invokes the norm of nature; unlike Joyce, however, he can still invoke a community of taste which makes the reader's own experience a standard of realism as well.

---

[3] A thorough discussion of Circe's anti-realism is contained in Marilyn French, *The Book as World: James Joyce's* Ulysses (Cambridge, Massachusetts, and London, England: Harvard University Press, 1976), pp. 185–206. See also Hugh Kenner, "Circe," *James Joyce's* Ulysses, ed. Clive Hart and David Hayman (Berkeley, Los Angeles, London: University of California Press, 1974), pp. 341–362, for a very discriminating study of the chapter's styles and what actually happens. Also interesting are Alain Robbe-Grillet's remarks about the cinema's influence on prose fiction, in "Time and Description in Fiction Today," *For a New Novel: Essays on Fiction,* trans. Richard Howard (New York: Grove Press, Inc., 1965), pp. 149 and 151.

[4] *Keywords: A Vocabulary of Culture and Society* (New York: Oxford University Press, 1976), pp. 216–220.

[5] *Mimesis,* trans. Willard Trask (Garden City, N.Y.: Doubleday–Anchor, Inc., 1957). See pp. 484 and 490–491 for Auerbach's explanation of his exemplary method.

[6] Nietzsche is quoted in Erich Heller, "The Realistic Fallacy," *Documents of Modern Literary Realism,* ed. George J. Becker (Princeton, N.J.: Princeton University Press, 1963), p. 595. And Harry Levin, *The Gates of Horn: A Study of Five French Realists* (New York: Oxford University Press–Galaxy Books, 1966), p. 83.

[7] See Isaiah Berlin, *The Hedgehog and the Fox: An Essay on Tolstoy's View of History* (London: Weidenfeld and Nicolson, 1953). This essay can be construed as a definition of Tolstoy's idea of realism, which is not incongruent with the argument I make here. In a longer essay, Tolstoy could be placed between Cervantes and Joyce to make the case more complete.

"If you reply that the men who compose such books write them as fiction, and so are not obliged to look into fine points or truths, I should reply that the more it resembles the truth the better the fiction, and the more probable and possible it is, the better it pleases. Fictions have to match the minds of their readers, and to be written in such a way that, by tempering the impossibilities, moderating excesses, and keeping judgement in the balance, they may so astonish, hold, excite, and entertain, that wonder and pleasure go hand in hand. None of this can be achieved by anyone departing from verisimilitude or from that imitation of nature in which lies the perfection of all that is written. I have never seen a book of chivalry with a whole body for a plot, with all its limbs complete. . . ."[8]

This corporeal metaphor for a book's integrity is important because it affirms the physical norm of reality that Sancho uses to oppose the Don's romantic ascesis; and it looks toward one of Joyce's designs for keeping *Ulysses* "down to fact" by organizing the themes of each chapter according to a part of the body. The Canon also anticipates Joyce by apparently contradicting himself and defending the epic for the expressive latitude it gives the writer.

Yet he continued that, for all that he had said against such books, he found one good thing in them: the fact that they offered a good intellect a chance to display itself. For they presented a broad and spacious field through which the pen could run without let or hindrance, describing shipwrecks, tempests, encounters and battles; painting a brave captain with all the features necessary for the part; . . . now depicting a tragic and lamentable incident, now a joyful and unexpected event; here a most beautiful lady, chaste, intelligent, and modest; there a Christian knight, valiant and gentle; in one place a monstrous, barbarous braggart; . . . Sometimes the writer might show his knowledge of astrology, or his excellence at cosmography or as a musician, . . . and he might even have an opportunity of showing his skill in necromancy. He could portray the subtlety of Ulysses, the piety of Aeneas, the valour of Achilles, . . . and, in fact, all those attributes which constitute the perfect hero, sometimes placing them in one single man, at other times dividing them amongst many. . . . the loose plan of these books gives the author an opportunity of showing his talent for the epic, the lyric, the tragic and the comic, and all the qualities contained in the most sweet and pleasing sciences of poetry and rhetoric; for the epic may be written in prose as well as in verse. (426)

This is a more generic, more modern theory, and even a description of many aspects of *Ulysses*. But this is only an accidental connection between two novels which are connected in so many other, more essential ways that they can stand as a beginning and an end of the realistic tradition of the novel. They share what all novels have: a definitive interest in the experience of the individual in a particular time and place; but they also share an unusual self-consciousness of their

---

[8] *Don Quixote*, trans. J. M. Cohen (Harmondsworth, Middlesex, England: Penguin Books, Ltd., 1976), p. 425. All further citations in the text.

own relation to literature, a variety of styles that establishes a complicated satire, and a concern for the semantic distance between the word and the thing it names.[9] Moreover, they suggest a general definition of realism, a generic idea, that is pertinent to explore because it contains three propositions about the novel which we must continue to acknowledge in our effort to establish the novel's poetics.[10] These propositions are that the novel is a thing—not the author's self expression so much as it is an object in its own right; that this kind of objective artifact entails the notion of an impersonal artist; and, most important, that the novelist who wants to create a thing and remain impersonal will necessarily be willing to undermine, distribute, or share his own authority in order to define his meaning by the proposal of a consensus rather than by an appeal to some superior or antecedent norm. This last proposition also implies that the author will not even try to rely on the authority of the genre he uses, that he will try to say this thing is not merely a novel.

Not every realistic novel will embody all of these propositions as clearly as *Don Quixote* and *Ulysses* do; and, in fact, not even *Don Quixote* and *Ulysses* embody all of them in the same way. In making the case I want to make about the idea of realism, it is not necessary to argue that *Ulysses* was intended as a thing because this is an idea about it we have acknowledged for some time. It is interesting and necessary, however, to show the reason *Don Quixote* is intended as a thing, just as it is to define the kind of realism in Joyce that can be taken for granted in Cervantes. The incongruity of even these two novels, moreover, is perfectly fitting, for the idea of realism that I want to define has to do with a novel's internal relationships and does not point to any particular consensus that all novels seek—not to the pastoral idea of harmony that John Loofbourow sees as the ground of the Anglo-American novel, and not merely to the rhetorical consensus that Wayne C. Booth recognizes in the meeting of every implied author and his reader.[11] The consensus the realistic novel looks to is broader because it is one that tries to acknowledge the world's plurality and to give everything its due.

Another way of saying this, which does apply to every novel, is that realism achieves its objectivity by recognizing the inviolable subjectivity of all its human characters, the potentially equal value and authority of every individual, the

---

[9] These are the general criteria proposed by Ian Watt in *The Rise of the Novel* (Berkeley and Los Angeles: University of California Press, 1964) and by Levin in *The Gates of Horn.* I am also indebted to Robert Scholes' and Robert Kellogg's *The Nature of Narrative* (London, Oxford, New York: Oxford University Press, 1966), especially for the way in which they see *Ulysses* as an end; and to David Goldknopf's *The Life of the Novel* (Chicago and London: The University of Chicago Press, 1972), especially for his fine first chapter.

[10] It is interesting that no essay specifically on realism appears in the collection from *Novel,* which is entitled *Towards a Poetics of Fiction* (ed. Mark Spilka, Bloomington and London: Indiana University Press, 1977). Realism is not an issue in Jonathan Culler's *Structuralist Poetics* (Ithaca, N.Y.: Cornell University Press, 1975).

[11] John W. Loofbourow, "Realism in the Anglo-American Novel: The Pastoral Myth," in *The Theory of the Novel: New Essays,* ed. John Halperin (New York: Oxford University Press, 1974), pp. 257–270. Wayne C. Booth, *The Rhetoric of Fiction* (Chicago and London: The University of Chicago Press, 1961). Booth, of course, is a great opponent of "objectivity," but his notion of fiction's rhetoric is basically an idea of realism that encourages a consensus. And *The Rhetoric of Fiction* contains a great deal of thinking on the nature and origin of objectivity. See also the section on "The Objective Artifact," in *The Modern Tradition,* ed. Richard Ellmann and Charles Feidelson, Jr. (New York: Oxford University Press, 1965), for additional statements.

possibility of another point of view. Cervantes himself establishes a model of this attitude by giving his protagonist a partner who is quite different but ambiguously equal and not a mate.[12] The fact that the Don and Sancho (like Stephen and Bloom) cannot resolve their differences sexually is important. For sexual couples like Elizabeth Bennet and Darcy, or Mr. and Mrs. Ramsay, can embody the problem of knowledge at the heart of realism, but pairs of partners can keep these epistemological issues open and unaccommodated by emotional and institutional resolutions like marriage. So, the general narrator of *Bleak House* is a more equal and interesting partner to Esther Summerson than Allan Woodcourt or even Inspector Bucket is; and the tragedy of Anna Karenina seems harsher or more significant than Emma Bovary's because Anna is paired with Levin and set against his reasonably successful, open quest for life's meaning. Pairs of partners keep a balance, an open equilibrium, that resists both identification and an absolute.

This equilibrium is at the center of the generic idea of realism that *Don Quixote* and *Ulysses* together suggest: realism is the idea that man and the world exist in a relationship of intelligibility. Under this idea, things are meaningful in themselves; they do not refer for their significance to some higher or ulterior principle; they are, rather, immediately accessible to man's intelligence and amenable to the meaning he discovers and creates. The idea of realism does not depend upon a particular ontological program, and it does not assume any particular theory of human character or knowledge. What this idea of realism does demand, though, is that the concept of character be commensurate with the theory of things. An imbalance in this relationship means that it is no longer realistic, that the literary situation is something else. For things which are not meaningful in themselves, or are not fully intelligible to man, but which embody some superior force or principle, such things are part of a relationship that is deterministic. There are deterministic principles that are religious and there are those that are secular, and the difference between them can be illustrated by Kafka's "The Metamorphosis." This story maintains all of the surface decorum we expect of realistic narrative, but the principle of Gregor Samsa's transformation is never defined. If the reader decides the principle is religious in any way, then "The Metamorphosis" can be read as an allegory; if, however, the principle is secular, then things have the opacity or hostility we call naturalistic or absurd. Perhaps the most terrifying way of taking the story is in insisting that it is realistic and that there is no ulterior principle which explains it at all.

On the other hand, things which are not meaningful in themselves because they are empty of intrinsic significance, or which have meaning only in man's presence and by his agency, and which offer no limits to his freedom, these things are the props of romance: like the moon in most lyric poems or the paper money

---

[12] See Lowry Nelson, Jr., "Introduction," *Cervantes: A Collection of Critical Essays*, ed. Lowry Nelson, Jr. (Englewood Cliffs, N.J.: Prentice–Hall, Inc., 1969), p. 4. See also Edward Mendelson, "Gravity's Encyclopedia," in *Mindful Pleasures: Essays on Thomas Pynchon*, ed. George Levine and David Leverenz (Boston, Toronto: Little, Brown and Company, 1976). He compares *Don Quixote* to *Ulysses*, as well as to other encyclopedic novels, in a number of very interesting ways; for his remarks about partners, see pp. 165–166.

is printed on. These things often figure in mythic narratives and in allegories of another kind, and they usually have a different relationship to time than the constituents of realism do. For the fact that things and men exist through time is also definitive of realism. Because things grow, change, decay, they can never be completely known because they can never be known at once; nor can man's intelligence claim any absolute authority when it is changing as the world is. So time itself, under this idea of realism, is the only absolute in so far as it is the ultimate limit of both knowledge and freedom: within time are the "imprevidibilities" of change,[13] beyond it the mystery of death.

The advantage of this idea of realism is that it is not limited to any particular metaphysics, nor to the *style* of realism of any particular nation or era; and it does not posit any single organizing idea of its own except that of the world's intelligibility to man's cognate intelligence, so it tries not to harbor any hierarchies. (And it is not perfect.) Harry Levin's elegant formulations clearly apply to the French novel more aptly than to the English; and Ian Watt's ideas of the eighteenth-century British novel work for much of the nineteenth-century British novel too, but the empiricism and rational psychology he uses to define Defoe and Richardson do not apply to Fielding exactly, much less to Dickens, and not at all to their modern heirs like Joyce and Lawrence who must include in their conception of character the unconscious. Yet Joyce and Lawrence, like Woolf and Faulkner, all now seem to us to be realistic, in at least the honorific sense in which we use that word, and it is important to realize that what once seemed strange, now seems true. And it does seem true because our sense of the world has changed with the changes in our sense of human nature. So, Lawrence's famous letter to Edward Garnett is an important example of the way in which character, the "old stable ego," can be redefined in a realistic way according to principles the author sees in the natural world, in things; as part of the world, the ego can have its deeper, allotropic states just as carbon can.[14] It has become a truism to remark that a scientific theory of the unconscious was developed in the same generation that physicists developed theories of relativity and quantum mechanics. But it is important to remark as well that as man has displaced more and more of the external world into himself, as he has seen more deeply into his own mind and nature, he has also discovered a greater depth and complexity in matter; and in both places, the center of the atom and the center of the unconscious, the laws of time are the same. Neither one is subject to the traditional, "realistic" sense that time is linear and mechanical, and in neither place is the *field* of time eternal.

The literary history of this appropriation of the world by the mind Erich Kahler has called "the inward turn of narrative," but this inward turn can also be figured as a fall. In Northrop Frye's scheme, it is the descent from the mythic and romantic through the high and low mimetic to the ironic; for John Loofbourow, the shift is described in our belief that now the natural man is more authentic

[13] See *Ulysses*, p. 696. "Imprevidibility" was coined by Joyce.

[14] A fine discussion of this letter is Garrett Stewart, "Lawrence, 'Being,' and the Allotropic Style," in *Towards a Poetics of Fiction.*

than the god or king.[15] Yet whatever nostalgia we may feel for what we have supposedly lost, the idea of realism tried to compensate in the sense that we are also
growing less estranged from the world we really occupy. In Stevens' words, we
may be descending "downward to darkness, on extended wings," but

> The sky will be much friendlier then than now,
> A part of labor and a part of pain,
> And next in glory to enduring love,
> Not this dividing and indifferent blue.

II

Ulysses is at first hard to read because it is so thoroughly realistic; we are not
prepared for an ordinary mind like Bloom's to be so spacious, nor for a world as
small as DEAR DIRTY DUBLIN to be so rich in significant detail. Telemachus is a
relatively easy, naturalistic beginning; the difficulties in Nestor are the ironic result of the characters' self-involvement; in Proteus, however, we begin to see the
essence of the equilibrium that Joyce wants to maintain, his position that a human character is most himself not in any social relationship, but alone with his
thoughts of the world. Stephen is the most alert and articulate exponent of this
position because he is himself in the process of figuring it out, and his most dramatic attention to the world's readiness comes in the opening paragraphs of Proteus, when he is fully alone for the first time.

> *Ineluctable modality of the visible: at least that if no more, thought through my*
> *eyes. Signatures of all things I am here to read, seaspawn and seawrack, the nearing*
> *tide, that rusty boot. . . .*
> *Open your eyes now. I will. One moment. Has all vanished since? If I open and*
> *am forever in the black adiaphane. Basta! I will see if I can see.*
> *See now. There all the time without you: and ever shall be, world without end.*
> (37)

The facts that must be "lived down to" here are both elemental and trivial, "the
nearing tide, that rusty boot"; but the incomplete, unaffirmed allusion to the lit-
urgy, "and ever shall be, world without end," suggests that a world endless in
time is not finally determined in meaning, that the signatures he is here to read
are not a holy code.

In fact, the only other determinant of meaning, balanced against a world meaningful in itself, is what we might call the ineluctable modality of the individual
which Stephen formulates later in Scylla and Charybdis. This is the subjective
complement of knowledge, the way in which the self imposes the meaning it

---

[15] Kahler, *The Inward Turn of Narrative*, trans. Richard and Clara Winston (Princeton, N.J.: Princeton University Press, 1973). Frye,
Anatomy of Criticism (Princeton, N.J.: Princeton University Press, Bollingen Series LXXXVIII, 1957), pp. 33–35. Loofbourow,
"Literary Realism Redefined," *Thought*, 45, 178 (Autumn, 1970); this is a fine brief survey of many ideas of realism—see espe-
cially p. 437.

may otherwise think it discovers, and also a principle which explains the individual self's variety, its own complement to the world's endless detail.

> *He found in the world without as actual what was in his world within as possible. Maeterlinck says:* If Socrates leave his house today he will find the sage seated on his doorstep. If Judas go forth tonight it is to Judas his steps will tend. *Every life is many days, day after day. We walk through ourselves, meeting robbers, ghosts, giants, old men, young men, wives, widows, brothers-in-love. But always meeting ourselves.* (213)

Scylla and Charybdis, in its examination of theories of art, contains a number of ideas about the nature of *Ulysses*—explicitly in Stephen's theory of Shakespeare, implicitly in his theory of the incertitude of paternity and its relation to artistic creation (207), and offhandedly in such remarks as: "They remind one of don Quixote and Sancho Panza. Our national epic has yet to be written, Dr. Sigerson says" (192). Moreover, it contains even more explicitly than Proteus does Stephen's realization that the equilibrium he must maintain between the self and world is a relationship that exists in time. His opponents, like AE, insist that we are eternal essences and that the truth is too; against such an idealism, Stephen has to assert that his personal identity is temporal, that it is continuous despite its changes, and that it is not totally subject to mere circumstance. He says:

> Wait. Five months. Molecules all change. I am other I now. Other I got pound.
> Buzz. Buzz.
> But I, entelechy, form of forms, am I by memory because under everchanging forms. (189)

And later he adds: "As we, or mother Dana, weave or unweave our bodies, . . . so does the artist weave or unweave his image. . . . that which I was is that which I am and that which in possibility I may come to be" (194). As part of this intuition Stephen also realizes he is both the agent and the patient of his own life, and he says: "Act. Be acted on" (211), which on this day in particular is an important and complicated pair of imperatives. As W. J. Harvey says: "Novels which portray roughly the same equipoise between Self and World, which achieve the effect of conditional freedom that I have described, we may call *realistic.*"[16]

Bloom states his own version of these fundamental principles of the idea of realism more laconically. He is less abstract than Stephen and more accommodated to the conditions of life, and much of what Stephen comes to formulate in a debate in the library Bloom arrives at on his way to lunch in Lestrygonians. The realistic relationship of intelligibility, which is subject to the changes of both man and the world in time, Bloom almost sums up in the word "Parallax" (154). His sense of his own identity he debates with: "I was happier then. Or was that I? Or am I now I? . . . Am I like that? See ourselves as others see us" (168, 169). This

---

[16] *Character and the Novel* (Ithaca, N.Y.: Cornell University Press, 1965), p. 133.

kind of distance on himself is a maturity or discipline that Stephen is not quite capable of, for he feels himself this day in too much pain, and he thinks, later in Wandering Rocks: "Stop! Throb always without you and the throb always within. Your heart you sing of. I between them. Where? Between two roaring worlds where they swirl, I. Shatter them, one and both. But stun myself too in the blow. Shatter me you who can. Bawd and butcher, were the words. I say! Not yet awhile" (242). Stephen's reversion to religious belief for an Apocalyptic solution to his problem is not in keeping with the realism of *Ulysses'* first half, but it is appropriate to Wandering Rocks' overture to the second half and a clear foreshadowing of the moment in Circe when he smashes the chandelier with his ashplant and screams *"Nothung!"* (583). Bloom keeps a better balance between the human and the divine when he brackets his very poignant realization, "Me. And me now" (176), between his memory of the moment on Howth when he and Molly passed the seedcake to each other, a moment she will remember in Penelope, and his resolution to investigate later at the library whether or not goddesses have anuses.[17]

The first half of *Ulysses* ends with the meeting of Bloom and Stephen on the library steps. Bloom has seen Stephen from the carriage in the Hades chapter, which is appropriate to the epic convention by which the hero foresees his future in his trip to the underworld.[18] But their actual meeting here is more important because it establishes them consciously in each other's world and predicts their common future. The scene begins in Stephen's mind as he is trying once again to get away from Mulligan:

> *Part. The moment is now. Where then? If Socrates leave his house today, if Judas go forth tonight. Why? That lies in space which I in time must come to, ineluctably.*
> *My will: his will that fronts me. Seas between.*
> *A man passed out between them, bowing, greeting.*
> *—Good day again, Buck Mulligan said.*
> *The portico.*
> *Here I have watched the birds for augury. Aengus of the birds. They go, they come. Last night I flew. Easily flew. Men wondered. Street of harlots after. A cream-fruit melon he held to me. In. You will see.*
> *—The wandering jew, Buck Mulligan whispered. . . . (217)*

Stephen's ironic prophecy that in meeting himself that night he will meet Bloom, "ineluctably," anticipates the narrative that will join them in Oxen of the Sun and keep them together until Stephen leaves from 7 Eccles Street in Ithaca. It also anticipates the elaborate rapprochement in Ithaca, where they become Stoom and Blephen (682), which parodies in the style of the catechism all of the realistic balances the novel sets up, all the symmetries between the mind and the world

---

[17] On this point, as on many others, I am most indebted for my understanding of *Ulysses* to Richard Ellmann's *Ulysses on the Liffey* (New York: Oxford University Press, 1972).

[18] See R. M. Adams, "Hades," in *James Joyce's* Ulysses, p. 92, for a different opinion.

that the second half of the novel questions by its variety of styles. But most important here is the manifestation that Bloom and Stephen have had the same dream about an encounter in the street of harlots (see also 57 and 381). Molly will participate in this dream herself, both in the fantasia of Circe (439) and also in her monologue in Penelope (780). Now, the fact they have all had this dream seems to be more significant than the coincidence of Throwaway's victory that makes Bloom seem a prophet, and it also seems to be of another order of being than the interpenetrations of Circe. In fact, their common dream suggests that the isolation each one of them feels in Proteus, Lestrygonians, and Penelope is not inescapable. While this isolation is fostered and reinforced by the stream-of-consciousness style that works best in a character's solitude, it is a style that also recognizes the independence of the world. And since the world itself contains other minds, its complete meaning has to come from a consensus in which others are acknowledged as equals and then joined. In *Ulysses*, not even in dreams can the individual alone claim authority, even for himself.

In *Don Quixote*, dreams are equally important, but in a different way. *Don Quixote* is a book about books, so Cervantes assumes a stability about the world in order to measure certain questions of perception, which Joyce treats as resolved so that he, in turn, can use them to look back at the world. There is nothing in *Don Quixote* like the opening of Proteus because there does not have to be, and there is no book in *Ulysses* like Amadis de Gaul's or the texts of chivalry. When Don Quixote reads the windmills as giants, there is no question about his mistake; when Bloom walks through the meticulously recorded Dublin of 1904, there is no question he is also *lisant au livre de lui-meme* (187). Bloom, therefore, would never have the kind of problem the Don has with the dream he has had in the Cave of Montesinos.

This experience is a singular adventure for the Don because it is not an illusion or "enchantment," but the one experience he has by himself which no one else witnesses and he cannot rationalize. Yet he is bothered by it so much that he seeks a confirmation for it later, a kind of consensus, when he tries to get Sancho to equate his experience in the cave with Sancho's own experience on the wooden horse Clavileno: "Sancho, if you want me to believe what you saw in the sky, I wish you to accept my account of what I saw in the Cave of Montesinos. I say no more" (735). The modesty of the favor the Don requests makes Sancho's refusal even more painful; for Sancho's story of what he saw in the sky, which plays the height of vision off the depth of dream here, is an elaborate, obsequious fabrication, designed to appeal to the Duke and Duchess who are toying with Don Quixote. Sancho could only have learned to make up a story like this from the Don himself, and telling it makes him a fool in the eyes of the Court. The Don, however, is as simple and abashed as Sancho usually is, with no realization that his real dream is very different from Sancho's fake apology. And the dream remains so important to him that it is the only experience of his life that he repudiates on his deathbed (624), where it still seems to him a perversion because it was so authentically private and so unaccommodated by the conventions of chivalry under which he had organized the meaning of his life. His dream is a real experience, but Don Quixote has no idea by which he can "naturalize" it. It is his great irony that he always prefers the apparently realistic, as the convention of chivalry would define it, to the actually real.

Don Quixote makes its essential propositions about the idea of realism by making a continual inquiry into the differences between the real and the realistic, the thing itself and the ideas by which any thing is given meaning, value, or representation. The barber's basin which becomes the helmet of Mambrino is an obvious counterpoint to the adventure in the Cave of Montesinos, for it is an example of a consensus too easily arrived at, a convention too obviously discrepant with individual perception.[19] In order to gull the Don and have some fun with the barber whose basin it is, the priest and the barber from La Mancha, Don Cardenio, Don Ferdinand, and his companions all agree that the basin is Mambrino's helmet. The incredulous barber says:

> 'Well, if this basin is a helmet, then, this pack-saddle must be a horse's harness, as this gentleman said.'
> 'It looks like a pack-saddle to me,' said Don Quixote, 'but, as I have already said, I am not interfering in that.'
> 'Whether it is a pack-saddle or a harness,' said the priest, 'Don Quixote has only to say; for in these matters of chivalry, all these gentlemen and myself defer to him.' (404)

This scene shows the way in which a false consensus or a merely social consensus can become tyranny. It shows too what the Don loses when he does not have his usual passionate belief in what he is doing. When he has discussed the helmet of Mambrino earlier, on his own initiative and according to his own principles, he offers an explanation of its mysterious variety that does not denigrate the potential good faith of anyone involved.

> "Is it possible that all this while you have been with me you have not discovered that everything to do with knights errant appears to be chimaera, folly and nonsense, and to all go contrariwise? This is not really the case, but there is a crew of enchanters always amongst us who change and alter all our deeds, and transform them according to their pleasure and their desire either to favour us or to injure us. So what seems to you to be a barber's basin appears to me to be Mambrino's helmet, and to another as something else. It shows a rare foresight in the sage who is on my side to make what is really and truly Mambrino's helmet seem to everyone a basin" (204).

The Don's explanation of the sage's foresight is not only one of the ways in which viewpoints other than his own are acknowledged, it is also one of those moments when the characters inside the book talk about the book itself, as though they

---

[19] See Leo Spitzer, *Linguistics and Literary History: Essays in Stylistics* (Princeton, N.J.: Princeton University Press, 1948), pp. 41–86, for a different approach to Don Quixote's realism and a different evaluation of Cervantes' impersonality.

actually are antecedent to it and independent: historical persons before they have become realistic characters.

This trespass across ontological frontiers first occurs when Sancho calls Don Quixote the Knight of the Sad Countenance. He explains that "your worship has lately got the most dismal face I have ever seen. It must be either from weariness after the battle or from your worship's losing his teeth."

> *'It is from neither,' replied Don Quixote, 'but because the sage whose task it is to write the history of my deeds must have thought it right for me to take some title, as all knights did in the olden days. . . . That is why I say that the sage I mentioned has put it into your thoughts and into your mouth to call me now* The Knight of the Sad Countenance. (147)

What is wonderful about this preposterous explanation is that it is true.[20] It does not obviate Sancho's explanation, which is also true in another way. And these complementary truths promote, even comically, the claim that the full truth of *Don Quixote* resides in its proposal of a consensus that does not violate anyone's individual perception or refer to only one source of authority. Not even to Cervantes himself, who is and is not the sage, for he treats the book as Don Quixote treats the book—as a thing apart from himself, an object.

For the Don, the history the sage writes is an objectification of his most fantastic ideas of himself, his most subjective longings; and this reification that confirms the meaning of his life as a knight errant is the necessary premise on which Part II becomes possible. Part I is picaresque and centrifugal: Don Quixote wanders out to encounter the world. Part II is centripetal and more realistic: it criticizes the false history written as a sequel to Part I, and it presents the Don as a celebrity whom others now seek out. Although he has an itinerary, which includes the Cave of Montesinos, in Part II the world comes to Don Quixote to enter the circle of enchantment that he has created by the intensity of his own idea of himself. And however ironic or condescending they are about their motives to be included in the next installment of the history, figures like the Duke and Duchess confirm the Don's idea of himself by playing his game on his field. Their court is not the Cave.

By the same token, the *thingness* of *Don Quixote* itself, its existence as a text or object, guarantees Cervantes that his fiction is not like the Don's self-delusions and uncertifiable dreams, and Cervantes goes to some lengths to reify his book in order to distance himself from creatures he does not claim. Cide Hamete Benengeli is always presented as the author of this history; and between Cide Hamete and Cervantes, who says he is its "step-father" (and who acts like its "stylist"), there are at least two translators, one of whom is hired on the spot when Cervantes finds a part of the manuscript in the Alacana at Toledo (76). This fragment

---

[20] See also Cardenio's remark on p. 267: "It is so strange and rare that I do not know whether anyone trying to invent such a character in fiction would have the genius to succeed."

contains pictures of Don Quixote and Rosinante (77), and Cervantes gives the manuscript even greater historicity by including himself within it as the author of *Galatea* (62) and as the almost unidentified heroic rebel of "The Captive's Tale" (355). In this way, Don Quixote is given the same ontological status Cervantes has as an historical figure, and the various narrators of the interpolated tales, the translators and commentators Cervantes is always referring to as his sources, are treated as his equals too, for they have become his collaborators. They are to Cervantes what the Duke and Duchess are to the Don: confirmation that *Don Quixote* is more like a windmill than a giant, a thing rather than a romance.

In *Cervantes's Theory of the Novel*, E. C. Riley says: "Cervantes handles his work in such a way as to show his complete control over the creation he tries so hard to make seem independent."[21] But Cervantes' control is not what is most interesting here: it is exactly what we expect from art. What is interesting is his effort to make it seem not *his*, to resolve his artistry away and make his book seem life's. This is the effect, I think, of reading Penelope after the self-conscious *literature* of the preceding chapters: in Molly's artless words, Joyce gives his book back to life. And the attitude he shares with Cervantes, that a univocal authority is less valuable and true than the experience of multiplicity, is at the heart of their common idea of realism.

III

In *The Situation of Poetry*, Robert Pinsky claims that the tradition of the "persona," "a borrowed voice or alter-identity, as speaker or central character partly distinct from the poet, constitutes one of the most widely-noted, perhaps overemphasized, critically chewed, and fundamental aspects of modernism. . . . And 'the speaker' as a method stands in clear logical relation to the modernist goal of moving the poem away from the abstraction of statement, toward the being of an object."[22] It seems, however, that this idea of impersonality is, generally, a *modern* idea, which is not limited merely to modernism and which has been a natural resource and goal of realistic novelists since the time of Cervantes. Yet I don't think it is over-emphasized because it is an idea that has had so many different intentions. Joyce, for instance, seems to have wanted the pervasive, invisible, God-like presence of the dramatist, whereas Eliot wanted both an escape from emotion and a discipline before he got religion. But Yeats wanted to complete or fulfill his identity in the "double" or "anti-self" he defines in "Ego Dominus Tuus," and Wallace Stevens, in poems like "The Snow Man," wanted to keep himself from solipsism and anthropomorphic distortions by maintaining a perfect metonymic balance with the landscape.[23] One of the most interesting ver-

---

[21] *Cervantes's Theory of the Novel* (Oxford: Oxford University Press, 1962), p. 41.

[22] *The Situation of Poetry* (Princeton, N.J.: Princeton University Press, 1976), p. 14.

[23] Metonymy as a principle of realism is the insight of Roman Jakobson's "The Metaphoric and Metonymic Poles," in *Critical Theory Since Plato*, ed. Hazard Adams (New York, Chicago, San Francisco, Atlanta: Harcourt Brace Jovanovich, Inc., 1971), pp. 1113–1116. The complete essay is contained in Jakobson, *Selected Writings*, II *Word and Language* (The Hague, Paris: Mouton, 1971), under the title "Two Aspects of Language and Two Types of Aphasic Disturbances," pp. 239–259. It is also widely discussed in places like Robert Scholes' *Structuralism in Literature* (New Haven and London: Yale University Press, 1974), pp. 19–22.

sions of the idea was Brecht's, who had the impersonality of the ideologue to add to that of the dramatist, but who also wanted to impose it as a condition on the audience. Still, Wayne C. Booth's objections to the idea of impersonality are given an unintended ratification in the claim Hugh Kenner makes that Pound practiced translation to purge "the contingencies of a personality partly private (Hailey, Idaho; Hamilton College), partly public (the legacy of Rossetti, the emotional climate of 1900–12) but in any case irrelevant to the fulness of poetic achievement." [24] This is a fairly ruthless formulation that suggests a personality purged of its contingencies and therefore reduced to its *necessary* reality may be capable of authenticity and objectivity only at the physiological level. [25] A much more humane defense of the ideal comes from Marx, in the "Economic and Philosophical Manuscripts," when he explains how the objectification of the self in a piece of work not only confirms the self, but affirms as well its essentially communal nature.

> *Supposing that we had produced in a human manner; each of us would in his pro-duction have doubly affirmed himself and his fellow men. I would have: (1) objec-tified in my production my individuality and its peculiarity and thus both in my activity enjoyed an individual expression of my life and also in looking at the object have had the individual pleasure of realizing that my personality was objective, visible to the senses and thus a power raised beyond all doubt. (2) In your enjoyment of use of my product I would have had the direct enjoyment of realizing that I had both satisfied a human need by my work and also objectified the human essence and therefore fashioned for another human being the object that met his need. (3) I would have been for you the mediator between you and the species and thus been acknowl-edged and felt by you as a completion of your own essence and a necessary part of yourself and have thus realized that I am confirmed both in your thought and in your love. (4) In my expression of my life I would have fashioned your expression of your life, and thus in my own activity have realized my own essence, my human, my communal essence.* [26]

We do not have to claim for this passage that it contains a theory of reading in order to say that it implies a condition of the novel that we often ignore: whereas poems are often songs, and plays are performances, novels are things we must hold in our hands to read. And in such a thing, Marx argues, is objectified not only the individual being of the writer and reader, but also what Marx calls the "species-being" of each: not only the singularity of an individual identity, but its intrinsic multiplicity as well. This notion of the self's variety is important to the idea of realism and its proposal of a consensus because it means that the writer who does not want to speak *in propria persona* is not confined to a single other

---

[24] *The Poetry of Ezra Pound* (Norfolk, Connecticut: New Directions, 1951), p. 134.

[25] See Stanley Burnshaw, *The Seamless Web* (New York: George Braziller, 1970), for a physiological theory of art.

[26] Quoted in David McLellan, *Karl Marx* (New York: The Viking Press, 1975), pp. 31–32.

voice and that the voices he does use are not merely prosthetic devices, but real extensions of himself, part of his human nature. When Don Quixote says:

> 'I know who I am, . . . and I know, too, that I am capable of being not only the characters I have named, but all the Twelve Peers of France and all the Nine Worthies as well, for my exploits are far greater than all the deeds they have done, all together and each by himself,' (54)

he gives a comic correlative to Cervantes' use of so many different translators, commentators, and narrators; and he emphasizes that both he and his author are distributing themselves throughout their various roles quite deliberately and responsibly. Not all the role-playing in *Don Quixote* is so responsible; in fact, the moral lesson of one of the longest and best of the interpolated tales, "The Tale of Foolish Curiosity," is that the actor must guard against being overtaken by his act, that he must not lose himself.

This moral aspect of role-playing is not a problem for Joyce. The variety of his obvious presence throughout the second half of *Ulysses*, after his magisterial invisibility throughout all the first half but Aeolus, is an easy demonstration of one of the principles of modernism Stevens epitomizes in the "Adagia": "A change of style is a change of subject."[27] The pun on subject is important, of course, but it should not distract us from the fact that Joyce's virtuosity expresses quite directly his sense of what it means to be human. When he discussed the Ulysses theme with Frank Budgen and George Borach, he emphasized both Ulysses' *humanity* and his *fullness*, the variety of his roles, until the two seemed to mean the same thing. This long passage, which Richard Ellmann quotes from Borach's journal, should recall to us both the Canon's remarks in *Don Quixote* about the expressive latitude the epic offers a writer and Stephen's remarks in Scylla and Charybdis that "We walk through ourselves, meeting robbers, ghosts, giants, old men, young men, wives, widows, brothers-in-love. But always meeting ourselves."

J. J. thinks:
'The most beautiful, all-embracing theme is that of the Odyssey. It is greater, more human, than that of Hamlet, Don Quixote, Dante, Faust. The rejuvenation of old Faust has an unpleasant effect upon me. Dante tires one quickly, it is like looking at the sun. The most beautiful, most human traits are contained in the Odyssey. I was twelve years old when we took up the Trojan War at school; only the Odyssey stuck in my memory. I want to be frank; at twelve I liked the supernaturalism in Ulysses. When I was writing Dubliners I intended at first to choose the title Ulysses

---

[27] *Opus Posthumous*, ed. Samuel French Morse (New York: Alfred A. Knopf, 1966), p. 171. In "The Noble Rider and the Sound of Words," Stevens also briefly adumbrates a theory of realism like the one I have proposed here; in the remarks he makes about the pressure of reality and the resistance offered by the imagination, he also sounds like Stephen Dedalus, in Wandering Rocks, between two roaring worlds. See *The Necessary Angel* (New York: Random House–Vintage Books, 1965), pp. 22–23, especially.

in Dublin, *but gave up the idea. In Rome, when I had finished about half the Por-trait, I realized that the Odyssey had to be the sequel, and I began to write* Ulysses.

'*Why was I always returning to this theme? Now* in mezzo del cammin *I find the subject of* Ulysses *the most human in world literature.* Ulysses *didn't want to go off to Troy; he knew that the official reason for the war, the dissemination of the culture of Hellas, was only a pretext for the Greek merchants, who were seeking new markets. When the recruiting officers arrived, he happened to be plowing. He pre-tended to be mad. Thereupon they placed his little two-year-old son in the furrow. Observe the beauty of the motifs: the only man in Hellas who is against the war, and the father. Before Troy the heroes shed their life-blood in vain. They want to raise the siege.* Ulysses *opposes the idea. [He thinks up] the strategem of the wooden horse. After Troy there is no further talk of Achilles, Menelaus, Agamemnon. Only one man is not done with; his heroic career has hardly begun: Ulysses.*

'*Then the motif of wandering. Scylla and Charybdis—what a splendid parable.* Ulysses *is also a great musician; he wishes to and must listen; he has himself tied to the mast. The motif of the artist, who will lay down his life rather than renounce his interest. Then the delicious humor of Polyphemus. "Outis is my name." On Naxos, the oldster of fifty, perhaps baldheaded, with Nausicaa, a girl who is barely seven-teen. What a fine theme! And the return, how profoundly human! Don't forget the trait of generosity at the interview with Ajax in the nether world, and many other beautiful touches. I am almost afraid to treat such a theme; it's overwhelming.*'

"It is not surprising," Ellmann comments, "that Joyce's description of Ulysses as pacifist, father, wanderer, musician, and artist, ties the hero's life closely to his own." [28] I think it is no coincidence, either, that a writer so noted for his im-personality would appreciate in a character so favored for his multiplicity the statement, "Outis is my name." For the tie between Joyce and Ulysses that is most important is the one between Ulysses as a model and Joyce as the creator of Bloom. It is obvious we are supposed to see Bloom as a father and a son, hus-band and lover, pacifist, wanderer, inventor, companion, figure of the artist, and good gentle man. It is also important we see him eating and sleeping, going in Calypso and coming in Nausicaa, at work and at large, through his own eyes and through the eyes of other Dubliners. For in seeing him through Joyce's eyes, we often see him as he cannot see himself, in Sirens and Oxen of the Sun, for instance, as well as in Circe and Ithaca. These seem not to be realistic chapters in the way Nausicaa and Penelope are because there is in them no more equilib-rium between Bloom's intelligence and the intelligibility of the world he is in. He "contains" Lestrygonians beautifully; it is, in fact, one of the novel's great chap-ters because so much is said so artlessly. But there is no way he can be said to contain even his own identity in Oxen of the Sun, nor that even his unconscious can hold all the phenomena of Circe. And were he allowed somehow to read

---

[28] *James Joyce* (New York, London, Toronto: Oxford University Press, 1959), p. 430. See *Ulysses on the Liffey* for similar remarks made to Frank Budgen, pp. 29–30.

Ulysses, there are parts he would not be able to recognize as his own experience as well as even more parts, probably, that he simply wouldn't get.[29]

This same lack of comprehension can be attributed to many other characters central to the modern novel, yet these characters, like Lawrence's Brangwens or Faulkner's Bundren family, do not now seem unrealistic to us. We have grown to accept them, and other characters like them, as we have grown to accept ideas about human nature that exclude parts of our being from our own self-consciousness or aspects of our most basic experience from the reach of language. In doing so, we have also come to accept the necessity of omniscient authors who make no final claims for their omniscience, who in fact try to disguise or deny it by dealing it away. No one has done this more adamantly than Faulkner has, except Joyce, perhaps, throughout the chapters of *Ulysses'* second half. Whether we want to say that the different styles of Sirens and Circe amount to different "characters" of the narrative (as the narrator of Cyclops in particular seems to be), or that they are rather different aspects of Joyce himself, which I think is simpler and makes more sense, the fact remains that no one of them is given a superior claim. The style of Sirens is not truer than the style of Cyclops; the prose of Nausicaa is not less "Joycean" than that of his favorite chapter, Ithaca. Joyce does not distribute himself throughout Moorish historians and interpolated raconteurs, but he achieves the same value by adopting for himself a series of identities in *Ulysses* as easily, as fluently, as Stephen adopts new identities for himself in Proteus, with little more but with nothing less than the change of style that amounts to a change of subject.[30] Not every one of these last nine chapters of *Ulysses* is realistic by any definition, but all the chapters together are faithful to realism's commitment to the truth based upon a consensus of equal individual principles. And while it would be hard to draw a simple consensus from what these last nine chapters say about the self and the world, it is easier now to grant that when Joyce said, "In my Mabbot Street scene, I approached reality closer in my opinion than anywhere else in the book except perhaps for moments in the last chapter," he was defining his idea of realism quite exactly: posing his opinion at the moment against the objectified body of his work and one of his styles against another, claiming nothing absolute for any of them, and leaving an exact definition of "reality" just out of reach.

IV

The polarity intrinsic to the idea of realism, the equilibrium that realistic novels try to maintain, is a recognition of the essentially equal but contending claims that issue from, and yet also bind together, the self and the world, the author

---

[29] See Richard Poirier, "The Importance of Thomas Pynchon," in *Mindful Pleasures*, p. 21, for more on who is fit in modern literature to read the books they appear in. There are no more Don Quixotes, who may be the father of the novel because he was so great a reader.

[30] See J. Mitchell Morse, "Proteus," in *James Joyce's* Ulysses, pp. 29–50, who has many important things to say about the ideas of identity and time and about the connections between Proteus and the last nine chapters. I also want to remark on behalf of my conclusions about *Ulysses* that the very existence of a book like this, with one critic for each chapter of the novel, also argues for the principle of consensus.

and his work, one character and another, the narrator and the reader, readers and their experience. In order to acknowledge all of these relationships and to give them a form, Cervantes and Joyce, who represent a beginning and an end of the novel's most self-conscious tradition, each tried to present his novel as a thing; and then from this thing, each also tried to efface himself in order not to impose a single standard of authoritative meaning. In doing so, each has distributed himself among many different points of view, which is the literary strategy by which they recognize both the great variety of human experience and the possible multiplicity within each individual self. Meaning, they propose, arises from a consensus; identity, they imply, is actually legion. In doing this, they demonstrate how important the anti-authoritarian nature of realism has been to the modern world, and they explain why the correlative of narrative impersonality has been the idea of selflessness that moved Lionel Trilling to call the novel "the literary form to which the emotions of understanding and forgiveness were indigenous, as if by definition of the form."[31] Realism evokes selflessness as an ideal because it is so essentially committed to the value of individuality, to the fullness and freedom of every individual, that it can also comprehend its own limit. For this reason, if for no other, the idea of realism is still necessary to maintain and defend in a world where things and other ideas proliferate so rapidly that a single governing idea, a univocal system of any kind, is seductively restful, reductive, annihilating. There is about the idea of realism a modesty that characterizes Bloom's deference to Stephen and Sancho's to the Don, but this same modesty promotes their survival and suggests that these two shall inherit the world where, as William Carlos Williams says,

> *so much depends*
> *upon*
>
> *a red wheel*
> *barrow*
>
> *glazed with rain*
> *water*
>
> *beside the white*
> *chickens.*

[31] "Manners, Morals, and the Novel," *The Liberal Imagination* (Garden City, N.Y.: Doubleday–Anchor Inc., 1953), p. 215.

The Rise of Feminine Authority in the Novel

NANCY ARMSTRONG

I

At some point during the eighteenth century, the cultural climate in England was right for the novel to begin its rise to a prominent position in the hierarchy of genres. The same conditions also made it possible for women's lore, taste, judgement, feeling and words to become, for the first time in history, the fit matter for literature. Despite the scholarly attention that has been devoted to each of these groundbreaking events, there remains the obvious question of what the one literary phenomenon had to do with the other, or how together they participated in a larger cultural change. It is Ian Watt's well-known contention that the popularity of such writers as Defoe and Richardson—and the subsequent rise of the novel—depended on the economic individualism and the Puritan ethic they shared with a substantial portion of the new reading public. But as his study of the eighteenth-century novel comes to a close, Watt seems to realize that a notion of literary production based on shared social values and inside knowledge of commercial life fails to explain "the majority of eighteenth-century novels," namely, those written by women.[1] To account for the conspicuous appearance of a woman writer on the literary scene, he falls back on a nineteenth-century commonplace and, speaking of Jane Austen, claims, "the feminine sensibility was in some ways better equipped to reveal the intricacies of personal relationships and was therefore at a real advantage in the realm of the novel."[2] Surely this will not do as the explanation for why women gained the authority to write literature and have it received as both female and literary, nor does it indicate why female literary authority coincided with the emergence of the novel as a literary form.

Lest we dismiss Watt's theory too quickly, we should note that feminist critics also have difficulty in correlating the social and literary changes that occurred during the late eighteenth and early nineteenth centuries. Watt's theory of the text as a reflection of socio-economic interests on the part of the new middle classes derives from his study of the readership and the conditions for literary reception. In contrast, Sandra Gilbert and Susan Gubar's definitive study of nineteenth-century women novelists concentrates on the authors and the conditions in which their works were produced. On this basis, they argue that the author's sex is far more important than class affiliation, nationality, or matters of personality.[3] Since so many novelists were women by fact of nature, and since

---

[1] Ian Watt, *The Rise of the Novel* (Berkeley: University of California Press, 1957), p. 39.

[2] Watt, p. 298.

[3] Sandra Gilbert and Susan Gubar, *The Madwoman in the Attic* (New Haven: Yale University Press, 1979), p. xi.

their social position was invariably inferior to that of men, Gilbert and Gubar see sexual conflict as the crucial factor shaping the form and content of novel writing. Unlike their male counterparts, women authors had to manage "the difficult task of simultaneously conforming to and subverting patriarchal literary standards."[4] If we carry this theory through to its logical conclusion, however, women should not have become authors at all, nor, for that matter, should male-authored fiction employing female personae and feminine subject matter have had such an immense appeal for a readership composed largely of men.[5] Neither of these ambitious attempts to describe what is essentially the same phenomenon really accounts for these facts: that women did start writing as women and that fiction dealing primarily with courtship and domestic life was occasionally recognized as possessing true literary merit. This, at precisely the time when British society, in making the shift to a growth economy, seemed to want women confined to the home, their labor devalued, and their political rights perpetually denied to them.

This apparent contradiction between the literary and political fortunes of women in history reappears, significantly, in the apparent contradiction between a socio-historical approach to the novel such as Watt's and the feminist viewpoint adopted by Gilbert and Gubar. Together these divergent conceptions of literary history confirm the assumption that the two spheres of middle-class culture require two radically different modes of interpretation and yield two mutually exclusive bodies of data. But it is characteristic of nineteenth-century thinking itself to divide the economic from the domestic and remove family life from history. So long as this distinction is mistaken for a fact of nature rather than culture, as was the case during the nineteenth century, then the relationship between the modes of conducting courtship and commerce will appear inaccessible to rational investigation. In turn, we are unable to see how the sexual and social dimensions of human experience serve as interdependent parts of an

---

[4] Governed by the assumption that oedipal rivalry underlies all productivity, a nineteenth-century notion at heart, the model Gilbert and Gubar have adopted to explain literary production leaves no reason for women to write. Since the female is conceived as the absence of maleness, what she writes will necessarily be viewed as trivial or written in bad faith in imitation of men. Arriving at this logical impasse, Gilbert and Gubar themselves have no choice but to see women writers as cultural anomalies. Given the relative success of women writers from the eighteenth century on, however, as well as the general economy of culture that keeps exceptions in check, it seems more likely that a tradition of women writers emerged when it did, not in spite of their sex, but because a female author could say something important in feminine terms that masculine writing could not accomplish.

[5] I am of course aware of the commonplace voiced, for example, in Richard D. Altick's *The English Common Reader* (Chicago: University of Chicago Press, 1957), p. 45, that the domestic novel came into favor chiefly because there was a growing number of literate women with leisure time that could not be otherwise occupied. But the ongoing debate over literacy in England— whether it rose or diminished with urbanization, preceded or followed the industrial revolution—does not seem to indicate a factual basis for this commonplace. In this debate over literacy, that of women is never a major issue; the question is simply a matter of whether the ratio of literate men to women is seven or eight to one (see, for example, Lawrence Stone's "Literacy and Education in England, 1640–1900," *Past and Present*, 42 [1969], 69–139, and E. G. West's "Literacy and the Industrial Revolution," *Economic History Review*, 31 [1978], 369–78). Nor is there any question of women achieving literacy at a faster pace than men during the late eighteenth century (see Carlo Cipolla, *Literacy and Development in the West* [Baltimore: Penguin Books, 1969], p. 56), nor any basis for assuming that they acquired leisure hours more rapidly than men, or read more novels because such hours were generally spent within the home. But we should perhaps take our cue from a novelist who purportedly wrote for this class of idle women. In *Northanger Abbey*, Jane Austen makes it clear that only the naive Catherine Morland could actually believe that chiefly women read novels such as those by Anne Radcliffe, while "gentlemen read better books" (London: Oxford University Press, 1975, p. 95).

ongoing cultural discourse. If, on the other hand, we think of sexuality not as a biological fact, but as a cultural phenomenon whose meaning and function change from one period in history to another, the way is opened for investigating how the rise of the novel and the emergence of female authority were actually elements of a single historical event. As such an event, any major change in the idea of who could write literature is just one part of a much larger revision in the culture's conception of social authority. In order for female literary authority to come into being, this revision obviously must have included a redefinition of gender as well as of the powers considered appropriate for each of the sexes.

Throughout the nineteenth century, indeed, it appears that men and women of the literate classes thought of sexuality in a way peculiarly adapted to the dynamics of social life as shaped by the British economy. It can hardly be accidental, I believe, that novels dealing primarily with sexual relations—with the vicissitudes of courtship and domestic life—should become a major literary genre at precisely the time in history when the work unit and the family unit could no longer be considered identical. The world of work was detaching itself from domestic affairs to create the all too familiar gulf between public and private life. By presenting this split in the social world as one of the sexual differences, or of male and female spheres of experience, the domestic novels of the period were able to describe a fractured and rapidly changing social world as if it were nothing else but a natural order that had maintained its shape down through the generations. Not only did these fictions make the social world of the late eighteenth and early nineteenth centuries seem coherent in its own right, they also provided a language for resolving the obvious contradictions between a competitive society and the old patriarchal traditions of pre-industrial England, thus sanctifying the new middle-class order.

So thoroughly confused with nature itself was this cultural model that even John Stuart Mill, while arguing for women's right to suffrage, draws upon the very principle that ratified their political subjection. No harm can come of giving them political privileges, he assures the recalcitrant reader, "for the law already gives it to women in the most important of all cases to themselves: for the choice of the man who is to govern a woman to the end of her life, is always supposed to be voluntarily made by herself."[6] Given that her power chiefly derives from emotional preference in a mate, in return for which she relinquishes all direct political power, Mill concludes that "the majority of women of any class are not likely to differ in political opinion from the majority of men. . . ."[7] In the name of science, Charles Darwin, too, found it necessary to grant women power with one hand while taking it away with the other. He felt strangely compelled to supplement his *Origin of the Species* with the companion piece, *The Descent of Man and Selection in Relation to Sex,* where he specifies the female's contribution to the general triumph of the species:

[6] John Stuart Mill, "The Subjection of Women," *Women's Liberation and Literature,* ed. Elaine Showalter (New York: Harcourt Brace Jovanovich, 1971), p. 36.

[7] Mill, p. 37.

The sexual struggle is of two kinds; in the one it is between individuals of the same sex, generally the males, in order to drive away or kill their rivals, the females remaining passive, whilst in the other, the struggle is likewise between individuals of the same sex, in order to excite or charm those of the opposite sex, generally the females, which no longer remain passive, but select the more agreeable partners.[8]

Thus it is by a curious twist in the law of heredity that competitive features are virtually absent in the female, her survival depending upon the mate she selects. Darwin, like Mill, insists that each sex furthers the competitive effort of the species, but that the female does this strictly by means of a passive form of aggression when she grants approval to the most domesticable male. Both of these prominent Victorian spokesmen therefore exempt women from political activities and detach the domestic world from the competitive interaction prevailing among men. It is not difficult to imagine how women came out on the short end of things in social applications of the model. What remains a far more interesting question is how these particular limitations on female power might have served the interests of a readership composed of both sexes and, in so doing, authorized women writers.

Fredric Rowton's preface to his anthology of women's poetry, appearing in 1848, offers a clear example of the cultural sleight of hand whereby women were both granted literary authority and denied political power. To justify his selection of poetry exclusively written by women, Rowton obviously draws on the same notion of sexuality that Mill tried unsuccessfully to challenge and that Darwin would later make into science:

I am quite prepared to grant that the mental constitutions of the sexes is different; but I am not at all prepared to say that "difference" means "inferiority." It is easy enough to understand that the sphere of woman's duty requires powers altogether dissimilar from those which are needed by the male; but that this is any proof of a smaller development of mind, I beg leave to deny. Woman's qualities may be less conspicuous, but they are quite as influential. Man has to bear outward, tangible rule; and his faculties are necessarily of an authoritative, evident, external commanding order. Woman has to bear invisible sway over the hidden mechanism of the heart; and her endowments are of a meek, persuasive, quiet, and subjective kind. Man rules the mind of the world; woman its heart.[9]

Two points are to be drawn from this statement. Rowton's characterization of the sexes and his designation of power as either feminine or masculine in nature are anything but original, of course. The virtue of his statement is that it is composed entirely of middle-class commonplaces which were formulated and tested

---

[8] Charles Darwin, *The Descent of Man and Selection in Relation to Sex* (New York: Random House, n.d.), p. 916.

[9] Fredric Rowton, "Introductory Chapter," *The Female Poets of Great Britain* (Philadelphia: Henry C. Baird, 1853), p. xiv. I would like to thank Marilyn Williamson for access to this material. Her edition of this anthology was published in 1981 by Wayne State University Press.

during the previous century of publishing history.[10] It therefore reveals the cultural machinery that generated such statements, an elaborate model of sexual exchange peculiar to the culture as it was undergoing industrialization. According to this bourgeois idea of love, or what Lawrence Stone has called "the companionate marriage," the female relinquishes political and economic control to the male in order to acquire exclusive authority over domestic life, the emotions, taste, and morality.[11] This exchange does not reduce women to an inferior position, supposedly, nor does it keep them there. To the contrary, the reasoning goes that women have only to gain authority when their power is distinct from and complementary to that of the male. In either case, however, the main point of the model is not to usher in a new social status for women or to maintain their existing role, but to register a shift of cultural categories by symbolically breaking down the prerogatives once belonging entirely to a male aristocracy into masculine and feminine powers. This revised conception of social power indicates a change in the rules for symbol-making activities, for those, at least, among the literate classes.

The other point to be made regarding Rowton's preface is the derivation of a feminine perspective from this distribution of social authority. Central to his rationale for publishing *Female Poets of Great Britain* is the unquestioned belief in the female's inferiority that is merely denied by the notion of difference. Since, as he reminds us, women write, "not as the rivals" but as the "partners" of men, it simply follows that feminine discourse will be personal and subjective rather than political or philosophical in character. By way of proof he would have the reader observe, "In all the Poems in this volume, it would be difficult to find a passage written to accelerate man's political advancement; whilst every page will display some effort to stimulate his moral progress."[12] Thus it is, ironically enough, that the female's lack of competitive features, her consequent lack of access to economic and political power, came to serve as a basis for moral authority in nineteenth-century literature. Irrespective of the author's biological gender, moreover, language itself was thought of as essentially feminine in nature when detached from the competitive ways of the marketplace and rooted instead in the emotions and values of the home.

Not accidentally, novels by such major authors as Jane Austen, the Brontës, Mrs. Gaskell, and even Dickens and Thackeray move toward just this distribution of power, and it is such a division and balance of authority that consti-

---

[10] See, for example, Eli Zaretsky's *Capitalism, The Family & Personal Life* (New York: Harper & Row, 1976) and Anne Foreman's *Femininity as Alienation* (London: Pluto Press, 1977) for sociological explanations of the change in sex roles accompanying the growth of an industrial society in England. Anne Douglas's *The Feminization of American Culture* (New York: Avon Books, 1977) describes a similar phenomenon in nineteenth-century America. Elaine Showalter's *A Literature of Their Own* (Princeton: Princeton University Press, 1977) provides an invaluable description of how these changes influenced the policy of the publishing industry with respect to women writers.

[11] Lawrence Stone, *The Family, Sex and Marriage in England: 1500–1800* (New York: Harper & Row, 1977), pp. 390–405.

[12] Rowton, p. xvii. It should be noted that the same logic can be found in the more sophisticated critics of the age. Consider, for example, the close parallels between Rowton's poetics and this statement by George Henry Lewes: "Woman, by her greater affectionateness, her greater range and depth of emotional experience, is well fitted to give expression to the emotional facts of life, and demands a place in literature corresponding with that she occupies in society," in "The Lady Novelists," *Women's Liberation and Literature*, p. 174.

tutes the happy ending of a conventional plot. Particularly when enacted by a female protagonist, the successful conclusion to competitive enterprises could be only one thing, a life of aristocratic leisure secured through the patronage of a good man. The fiction that one could indeed gain authority through this kind of dependency undoubtedly served manifold political interests while it justified the exclusion of women from the economic activities of men. But the belief that domestic life and moral sensibility were the female's provenance was much more than a cultural sop. In being neither political nor economic at base, female authority was nonetheless real. The language of sexual relations itself, after all, fell squarely within the provenance of feminine letters. Because of its apparent innocence, a seeming fidelity only to the natural and moral verities of human experience, the language of sexual relations was, as it is for any culture, one of the single most powerful means for engaging social and economic issues and imposing an ideology on them.[13]

If their traditional lack of literary authority sometimes prompted women to write under male pseudonyms, then it may also be true that male authors sometimes adopted female personae so as to enhance their authority as men, if only by way of denying it. Such authors as Defoe and Richardson were indeed renouncing what Walter Ong has called "a sexually specialized language used almost exclusively for communication between male and male." Until well into the nineteenth century, he points out, "learning Latin took on the characteristics of a puberty rite, a *rite de passage*, or initiation rite: it involved the isolation from the family, the achievement of an identity in a totally male group (the social), the learning of a body of relatively abstract tribal lore inaccessible to those outside the group."[14] In turn, the absence of this specialized language automatically established an author's position outside the elite social group and his lack of access to the languages of power. Fielding's uncouth heroes generate a sense of political innocence by indicating the gap between their kind of education and that of the urbane narrator, but the explicitly female voices one encounters in such novels as *Moll Flanders*, *Pamela*, or *The Mysteries of Udolpho*, for instance, would more certainly indicate the same thing. These narrators experience mainly sexual encounters, and their responses are characteristically naive. Yet they are far from simplistic in a literary sense. They allow for a sophisticated range of sensations,

---

[13] In *S/Z*, trans. Richard Miller (New York: Hill and Wang, 1974), Roland Barthes isolates what he calls "the major voice of a minor science," by which is meant the middle-class commonplaces mobilized in the nineteenth-century novel. While appearing to be principles of nature, these commonplaces are actually "derived from books," he maintains (p. 206). In *The History of Sexuality*, trans. Robert Hurley (New York: Pantheon Books, 1978), Michel Foucault argues that sexuality is primary among such commonplaces, that it is always a function of culture aimed at rationalizing the distribution of social power because sexual relations themselves serve "as an especially dense transfer point for relations of power" (p. 103). In *The Elementary Structures of Kinship*, trans. James Harle Bell, John Richard von Sturmer, and Rodney Needham (Boston: Beacon Press, 1969), Claude Lévi-Strauss similarly maintains that marriage comes into being as a concept and set of rules to fill the gap between a sexual union that requires merely a male and a female, and the complex requirements for the possible contents of this form specified by various cultures and necessary for maintaining a social order. "Culture yields to the inevitability of biographical heredity," he contends. "But culture, although it is powerless before descent, becomes aware of its rights, and of itself, with the completely different phenomenon of marriage, in which nature for once has not already had the last word. There only, but there finally culture can and must, under pain of not existing, firmly declare 'Me first,' and tell nature, 'You go no further'" (p. 31).

[14] Cited in Irene Tayler and Gina Luria, "Gender and Genre: Women in British Romantic Literature," *What Manner of Woman*, ed. Marlene Springer (New York: New York University Press, 1977), p. 100.

emotional nuances, and moral judgements. More importantly, stories that revolve around courtship and marriage offered a way of indulging in fantasies of political power with a kind of impunity, so long as these were played out within a domestic frame of reference, and so long as the traditional relationship between husband and wife was ultimately affirmed. Domestic fiction, in other words, provided a way of talking about conflict and contradictions within the socio-economic sphere while remaining remote from that world. To this special connotative power of the feminine voice and subject matter, we can probably attribute the development of a distinctively feminine mode of literature. For despite assaults on what they called romance and sentimentality by male critics and reviewers and attempts like Fielding's to place the novel within established and exclusively masculine categories, the novel early on assumed many of the distinctive features of a specialized language for women. As often as not it might have an explicitly female source, concentrate on a woman's experiences, address an audience of young middle-class ladies, or find itself censored by female reviewers.[15]

II

When Jane Austen opens *Pride and Prejudice* she identifies herself as an author by citing a model of sexual exchange to which she obviously did not personally subscribe: "It is a truth universally acknowledged that a single man in possession of a good fortune must be in want of a wife." By means of this asseveration the concept of sexuality governing the internal structure of her fiction, whether ironically or not, is reproduced outside in the author's relationship to the discourse of her society. Thirty years later, however, Charlotte Brontë begins a fictional autobiography, *Jane Eyre*, in the voice of a woman who seems to be empowered by her speech alone. Presumably Brontë can assume a common ground with her readership where Austen felt it necessary to stake out claims to one. The speaking presence of the female is sufficient to place her work within that system of belief which authorized feminine discourse. George Eliot, writing in the seventies, begins *Middlemarch* by insisting that any competent reader must be well aware of at least one heroic instance of a woman's self-sacrifice: "Who that cares much to know the history of man, and how the mysterious mixture behaves under the varying experiments of Time, has not dwelt, at least briefly, on the life of Saint Theresa. . . ." But the author calls attention to this event mainly to show that a more important contribution on the part of women goes unrecognized in the annals of history. In concluding the novel, furthermore, she asks us to concede that human experience is profoundly affected by those who

---

[15] In *A Literature of Their Own*, Elaine Showalter explains how, by the sixties, a number of prominent women authors had worked their way into editorial positions that, "like the ones Dickens and Thackeray occupied at *Household Words* and the *Cornhill*, provided innumerable opportunities for the exercise of influence and power" (p. 156). But the role of critic-reviewer was not completely unknown to women even during the eighteenth century. See, for example, Elizabeth Montagu's *Dialogues of the Dead* (1760) and Anna Seward's critical essays in *Variety* (1787–88), in Ioan Williams, *Novel and Romance: 1700–1800, A Documentary Record* (New York: Barnes and Noble, 1970), pp. 222–29, 357–66.

exert their influence passively from outside the political sphere. What is true of the woman obviously now holds true of the artist and intellectual as well: that "the growing good of the world is partly dependent on unhistoric acts; and that things are not so ill with you and me as they might have been, is half owing to the number who lived faithfully a hidden life, and rest in unvisited tombs."

While these few examples should suggest the degree to which the sexual code both authorized women writers and governed the form and content of their fiction, Emily Brontë's *Wuthering Heights* demonstrates the basis on which feminine authority assumed precedence over that of the male in the production of a story. In this novel the Earnshaw family history is transcribed by a gentleman. Lockwood's classical education and worldly experience qualify him to serve in this capacity, but it is the family retainer, Nelly Dean, who has access to the language that can make sense of family affairs. It is she who combines the learning of the "master's library" with lore garnered from "country folk," as well as a confidant's earful of the private events in the household and a range of emotional experiences of her own. The radical changes in the distribution of authority within the family make little sense without Nelly's explanations for the emotional undercurrents instigating them. And though it falls to Lockwood to solicit the tale and put it in writing, his language is not what provides the source of meaning. This male point of view proves both ignorant and inauthentic for all its worldliness.

We might even go so far as to see the "Puppet Master" in *Vanity Fair* or the "story-weaver at his loom" in the afterword to *Our Mutual Friend* as acknowledgements of the fact that the viewpoint of male novelists was similarly bound to be personal, domestic, and hence essentially feminine. Thackeray's concern for Napoleonic history notwithstanding, the author's perspective in *Vanity Fair* is certainly neither the grand scope of political events on the Continent nor the fortunes of Englishmen in love and war. His is the record of small shockwaves felt on the homefront by two women as they endeavor to keep themselves well supported by men. Nor was Dickens completely exempt from the rules of a discourse that opposed morality to politics on the basis that the one was feminine and the other masculine in nature. George Ford's informative investigation of Dickens's relationship with his readers indicates just how his failure to observe these rules caused Dickens to lose approbation where it counted. "According to the reviewer in the *Westminster*: 'In all his tales there is a latent desire to improve and strengthen the charities of life, raise the trampled upon, soften intolerance, diffuse knowledge, promote happiness.'" Yet, Ford notes, "Oddly enough, twenty-two years later, in 1864, the *Westminster* reversed its verdict. 'We believe him to have been the main instrument in the change which has perverted the novel from a work of art to a platform for discussion and argument.'"[16] In a genre

---

[16] George H. Ford, *Dickens and His Readers* (New York: Norton, 1977), p. 81. It is worth noting that these very constraints could work in the other direction and brand a woman's writing as masculine, as when the reviewer for *Fraser's* decided, no doubt on the basis of her socio-economic focus, that "Miss Edgeworth *never* wrote the Edgeworth novels . . . all that, as we have long had a suspicion, was the work of her father," cited in Elaine Showalter, *A Literature of Their Own*, p. 74.

that was supposed to influence the moral sentiments by means of feminine strategies ("improve and strengthen the charities of life, raise the trampled upon,
soften intolerance, diffuse knowledge, and promote happiness"), Dickens had
entered into political debate. This was conceived as an intrusion of the masculine
into feminine discourse, and, as such, it threatened his authority as a novelist.

More telling perhaps than such transgression of the sexual boundaries of discourse is the insistence on the part of women writers that difference should be
maintained. Mary Shelley's 1831 preface was written as testimony to the fact that
Frankenstein was nothing other than "my waking dream." She claims for her
novel an unmediated source in the female imagination, her own. And as for her
husband's tinkering with the manuscript, that, she assures us, extended only to
superficial matters of style. The worldly-wise Mrs. Gaskell introduced *Mary Barton*, her "tale of Manchester life," to the readership of the turbulent forties by
insisting, "I know nothing of Political Economy, or the theories of trade." [17] Her
claim to possess only feminine authority as a writer, the knowledge of the heart,
is hardly a humble one, however, for her account of savage class conflict proves
that love, rather than political economy, is the most powerful "regulating law
between two parties." [18] Charlotte Brontë makes the demonstration of emotional
power into an aesthetic imperative when she chides Jane Austen for failing to
plumb the depths of her characters. Austen strikes Charlotte as "a lady, but certainly no woman," one whose main "business is not half so much with the human heart as with the human eyes, mouth, hands, and feet." [19] From this we
might infer that Emily Brontë won her sister's unqualified praise for writing a
novel in which passion overturns domestic conventions and runs roughshod
over the well-polished style established by Austen. Instead, Charlotte takes her
sister's work to task for a deficiency quite antithetical in character to Austen's. It
seems that Emily's "will was not very flexible, and it generally opposed her interest. Her temper was magnanimous, but warm and sudden; her spirit altogether
unbending." [20] These imperious qualities manifest themselves in writing that
Charlotte, intentionally or not, conceives in terms of masculine features, "the
rough, strong utterance, the harshly manifested passions, the unbridled aversions, and headlong partialities of unlettered moorland hinds and rugged moorland squires. . ." (9). In its aggression, her sister's fiction is honest but terribly
"unlettered," to Charlotte's mind, and undermines its authority by going to this
other extreme.

While conceding these points in response to the rather negative reviews
received by the first edition, Charlotte's chief purpose is to demonstrate that
Wuthering Heights was not in fact "strange," "coarse and loathsome," the result

---

[17] Elizabeth Gaskell, *Mary Barton* (New York: Penguin Books, 1970), p. 38.

[18] Gaskell, p. 460.

[19] From a letter to W. A. Williams in 1859, *The Brontës: Their Friendships, Lives and Correspondence*, ed. T. J. Wise and J. A. Symington (London: Oxford University Press, 1932), III, p. 99.

[20] Charlotte Brontë, "Biographical Notice of Ellis and Acton Bell," *Wuthering Heights*, ed. William M. Sale, Jr. (New York: Norton, 1972), p. 8. Further references to *Wuthering Heights* and to its prefatory materials are to this edition and have been included in the text.

of artistic "power thrown away." [21] In the preface to the 1850 edition and an additional biographical notice, she devises a strategy for undermining these charges by characterizing the author as someone who possessed the genius of a Romantic artist, a masculine figure, but was in essence and by circumstances actually an ingenue: In place of the masculine pseudonym under which the first edition of *Wuthering Heights* had appeared, the novel subsequently came to the reader as the product of a remote and ailing woman. "Under an unsophisticated culture, inartificial tastes, and an unpretending outside," Charlotte tells us, "lay a secret power and fire that might have informed the brain and kindled the veins of a hero; but she had no worldly wisdom" (8). This description of the author clearly seeks to explain away the apparent lapses in literary decorum and taste by making them signs of her innocence and femininity. More importantly, it removes the text from the contemporary social world in reference to which its presentation of sexual relationships would have to be viewed as subversive. Readers are encouraged to locate the meaning of Emily Brontë's fiction in the secret recesses of her personality, as J. Hillis Miller indeed finds is the case: "The validity of Emily Brontë's visions depends," in his view, "upon their being kept private. Their purpose is to create an inner world excluding other people and the real world. . . ." [22]

We are led to assume, from Charlotte's argument, that somewhere between the excesses of Austen's inauthentically feminine prose and Emily's authentically masculine style, the ideal feminine writing finds a form. This she anticipates in Emily's work had her imagination been allowed to develop. "Had she but lived," Charlotte claims, "her mind would of itself have grown like a strong tree, loftier, straighter, wider-spreading, and its matured fruits would have attained a mellower ripeness and sunnier bloom. . ." (11). The lofty fruit-bearing tree is Charlotte's metaphor for a positive feminine style that is neither aggressive nor withholding in the manner of her sister and Jane Austen. We can regard *Jane Eyre* as Charlotte's dramatization of the limits and privileges of such an authority. In developing the character of a heroine who gains the power to author her own history, Brontë identifies the source of her own literary authority as well. To achieve the position from which publishable utterances issue forth, namely, the words that we read, Jane must abdicate her roles within the economic, religious, and educational institutions of her society. These operate as cul-de-sacs in the novel that limit the heroine's power and mobility, and she has only to gain, as it turns out, by relinquishing her positions within them. Once outside the world of work, Jane's emotions can flower without threatening her virtue or reason, and by mitigating the conflict among the various aspects of her character, the role of wife provides for her the full realization of identity. As if to

---

[21] William Sale prefaces his selection of the early reviews of *Wuthering Heights* with this general assessment of the evidence to follow: "The critical reception of *Wuthering Heights* has been generally assumed to have been unsympathetic, and so of course it seems in the light of the extraordinary tributes that have later been paid to the novel. But if we compare what Charlotte herself said of the novel in her 'Preface' with what many of the early critics said, we should perhaps conclude that both Charlotte and the critics were finding it difficult to come to terms with a strangely different piece of fiction" (p. 277).

[22] J. Hillis Miller, *The Disappearance of God* (New York: Schocken, 1965), p. 157.

serve as evidence of the authority she has gained by this exchange, Jane's character bears fruit in the production of an autobiography as well as in the birth of a son.

This novel has understandably prompted debate over which matters more in shaping Jane's character, her desire or self-restraint. By focusing on this issue, however, the novel allows us to neglect the crucial point that an endowment from Jane's wealthy uncle, more so perhaps than her virtue, passion, or intellect, is what makes happiness possible. Money of course serves as the link in the causal chain of events by which she moves from orphanhood into social prominence, but Jane's inheritance plays a still more necessary role in that it fulfills the cultural formula, the symbolic exchange of masculine power for feminine authority. First, it allows Jane to get out from under an obligation to her impoverished relatives, whereupon she suddenly gains in return the power to create a private world of her own: "I broke from St. John, who had followed, and would have detained me. It was *my* time to assume ascendancy. *My* powers were in play, and in force."[23] It is clear that Jane breaks off the impending alliance with her cousin, not because he offers her a life of poverty and self-denial, but because he refuses to give her authority over his heart. Earlier on in the novel, on the other hand, Jane's alliance with Rochester was disallowed on quite different grounds, not simply because he is married to Bertha Mason (for all Jane knows when she returns to him, that contract is still in existence), but because Jane has no economic power to relinquish. The novel seems to insist that only when an exchange of economic for emotional power has been fully and freely transacted, can the female achieve her proper dominion over the home. As Rochester's wife, furthermore, Jane's function becomes primarily linguistic in nature. "He saw nature—he saw books through me," she explains, "and never did I weary of gazing for his behalf, and of putting into words the effect of field, tree, town, river, cloud, sunbeam . . . and impressing by sound on his ear what light could no longer stamp on his eye" (397).

By presenting this transaction as either a moral or an emotional imperative, primarily, rather than a matter of economic necessity, *Jane Eyre* partakes of a larger cultural strategy, that underlying the middle-class notion of sexuality itself. The detachment of personal motivations like love and morality from the imperatives governing the economic aspects of experience sustains the illusion of the individual's autonomy, hence his or her control over personal life. The good marriage concluding fiction of this sort, where characters succeed in achieving middle-class goals, therefore appears to resolve problems much more encompassing than those troubling only the domestic world, the conflict between labor and property, for instance, that between an agrarian gentry and urban capitalists, or, at a more abstract level, that between self and society. Resolutions within the domestic sphere could provide demonstration that, despite the vast social and economic inequities of the age, emotional gratification was equally

---

[23] *Jane Eyre*, ed. Richard J. Dunn (New York: Norton, 1971), p. 370. Further references to *Jane Eyre* are to this edition and have been included in the text.

available to everyone in private life and moral order could be realized by each individual from within. What is perhaps still more important for understanding the appeal of these fictions, however, are the contradictions within the political thinking of the time that were allowed to remain unacknowledged, chief among them being the inherent conflict between open competition and paternalism. By offering solutions to political problems on a personal and emotional scale (Mrs. Gaskell's fiction being one of the most obvious cases in point), stories of courtship and marriage did away with certain contradictions within middle-class thinking and did so without forcing a confrontation of differing views. This was possible because the feminine sphere itself was in the world but not of it. As the other half of the masculine sphere, the domestic world replicated the new social order. But domestic life was also thought to be detached from that order by definition and, in replicating it, was therefore capable of transforming the world of practical necessity into what Marcuse has called its "counterimage," an idealized object.[24]

III

This apparent detachment from the social issues of the day, ironically enough, is what prompts us to see domestically-oriented fiction as "limited," the word both her detractors and loyalists so often apply to Jane Austen's work. What we have implicitly done by making a separate tradition of such relatively homebound authors as Anne Radcliffe, Austen, the Brontës, Mrs. Gaskell, Elizabeth Barrett Browning, George Eliot, and Virginia Woolf is to make men the participants and engineers of history, the creators of ideology and forgers of political conscience, as Rowton, the Victorian editor, did. This is not to say we should disregard the information these women writers provide concerning the female imagination, personality, or social condition. One may argue that, indeed, many of their novels signal the reader to regard the fiction as just this. The more closely nineteenth-century fiction focuses on domestic life and emotional experience, however, the more it insists that the truths being communicated are natural and thus universal, or exempt from the vicissitudes of political history. Unless the depiction of personal life and domestic relations is conceived as a cultural strategy arising from specific historical conditions and serving political ends, we fall into the trap of reifying a nineteenth-century model of sexual exchange. The information we receive in this event is not female nature nor even female culture, strictly speaking, but ideology and cultural myth. To determine what is specifically female about women's literature would require comparative work beyond the scope of this essay, but by establishing what information in this fiction is definitely code and convention, or the vehicle for ideology, we can, on the other hand, prepare some of the ground for this kind of work. We can evade the trap of seeing sexual differences as a universal condition—a static paradigm—simply by considering how, in a few important examples, the concept develops along with the changing conditions for literary reception.

[24] Herbert Marcuse, "The Affirmative Character of Culture," *Negations* (Boston: Beacon Press, 1968), pp. 88–133.

The degree to which the gender of literary language is not in fact bound to the sex of the writer but to the rules of genre and the changing values of the readership will become evident the minute we draw some comparisons between major women novelists of a period and one or two of their illustrious male contemporaries. For men, too, the model of sexual exchange provided a language for talking about power relationships while denying the politics of one's pleasure. Acted out through a female, for instance, aggressive individualism inevitably buckled under to paternalism by way of her marriage into a superior class. Moll Flanders is an obvious case in point, for after surmounting social barriers to win her place among the leisure classes chiefly by pretending to be a gentlewoman, she explicitly advocates class distinctions. By taking on a new name and viewing her most advantageous moves up the ladder as crimes, she assumes, in effect, an adversarial relationship to her former social identity.[25] We are finally as disturbed by Moll's disingenuous morality as we are by her flagrant opportunism, perhaps even more so. All the same, Defoe's female protagonists can fulfill a fantasy of upward mobility within a social frame of reference, while Robinson Crusoe acts out essentially the same kind of fantasy "all alone in an un-inhabited island." The rhetorical differences between them notwithstanding, Richardson's *Pamela* uses a female character in much the same way. Also couched as the personal record of a servant girl, its story of her abuse by the unscrupulous Mr. B makes his overthrow seem only justified. In the face of relentless persecution, Pamela's passivity becomes almost as aggravating as it is praiseworthy. When her persecutor undergoes a moral conversion and asks her to marry him, we can therefore regard Pamela's sudden elevation in social position as personal salvation on his part rather than presumption on hers. As Ian Watt has observed, "these struggles . . . mirror larger contemporary conflicts between the two classes and their way of life."[26] At the same time, however, competition can be allowed much freer rein through a female protagonist on the assumption that her power is ultimately subject to the authority of a man. What appear to be competing social interests can in turn be reconciled by reference to sexual relationships, for example, by the conversion of prostitution or rape into marriage.

If we pursue this line of thinking we have to consider that a novel like *Pride and Prejudice* operates according to a broadly-based political strategy simply because it seems to be concerned exclusively with the domestic problem of marrying off five daughters. As established by such novelists as Richardson and Defoe, the literary tradition had already charged this situation with meaning. Austen could not choose to depoliticize sexual relationships, but she could modify the existing strategies for resolving the conflict among competing social

---

[25] Watt sees this self-alienation on Moll's part as a sign of bad writing on the part of Defoe. Because of her tendency to do one thing and espouse another, he argues, "confusion about point of view becomes apparent: we notice that to Moll Flanders other pickpockets, and the criminal fraternity in general, are a 'they,' not a 'we' " (p. 98).

[26] Watt, I should add, sees the novel as a "mirror" of class conflict rather than as a middle-class fantasy in which social identities are the components in a game of power in which the denial of the game is a large part of the pleasure. For this reason, he has trouble explaining not only the phenomenon of Austen's fiction, but also Richardson's success. That is, he cannot account for the fact that Richardson, Puritanical as he was, "should have signalized his entry into the history of literature by a work which gave a more detailed account of a single amorous intrigue than had ever been produced before" (p. 172).

groups. Her strategies are notably subtle. *Pride and Prejudice* presents the reader with a group of women competing only among themselves in a matchmaking game whose goal is implicitly economic power, and explicitly, the rescue of the family from imminent poverty and shame. The female position relative to society and to men in particular is thus presented as an essentially defensive one. In this game, such traditional feminine attributes as chastity, wit, pragmatism, manners, imagination, beauty, generosity, kindness, and desire are faced off and evaluated in terms of which are the most advantageous for a woman aspiring to gentry life to possess. Jane, the Richardsonian sister, languishes for want of a husband until the end of the novel, but it is also the case that the picaresque adventuress, Lydia, jeopardizes the family's survival. What then enables the heroine, Elizabeth Bennet, to make the marriage contract which not only saves the day economically but brings her family into respectability and prominence? While excelling in none of the traditionally feminine qualities represented by her competitors, Elizabeth surpasses them on another basis altogether. She possesses additional assets of character, traditionally masculine qualities of rational intelligence, integrity, self-possession, and particularly a command of words, all of which at first seem to operate as deterrents to marriage.

In the beginning, her father distinguishes Elizabeth from his other daughters, even though, as Mrs. Bennet puts it, "she is not half so handsome as Jane, nor half so good humored as Lydia": "'They have none of them much to recommend them,' replied he; 'they are all silly and ignorant like other girls; but Lizzy has something more of quickness than her sisters.'"[27] In the end, Darcy confirms this alternative basis for female merit when asked why he chose Elizabeth: "For the liveliness of your mind, I did." In a characteristic act of verbal aggression, Elizabeth then answers her own question for him more precisely: "The fact is, that you were sick of civility, of deference, of officious attention. You were disgusted with women who were always speaking and looking, and thinking for *your* approbation alone. I roused, and interested you, because I was so unlike *them*" (262). Though winning his heart on this basis, what amounts to deviance from the feminine ideal, Elizabeth seems to lose most of this pertness in establishing a permanent relationship with Darcy, her masculine attributes conveniently dissolving into more typically feminine ones. Her "liveliness of mind" loses its cutting edge, significantly, and comes to exert a softening and passive, or purely feminine, influence within the domestic world. But what might appear to be a discontinuity within her character actually demonstrates its compliance to a fundamental cultural code. For through the redistribution of sexual features between Elizabeth and Darcy, a nineteenth-century model for sexual exchange takes shape as the means for representing the ideal distribution of authority:

> It was a union that must have been to the advantage of both; by her ease and liveliness, his mind might have been softened, his manners improved, and from his

---

[27] *Pride and Prejudice*, ed. Donald J. Gray (New York: Norton, 1966), p. 2. Further references to *Pride and Prejudice* are to this edition and have been included in the text.

judgement, information, and knowledge of the world, she must have received benefit of greater importance. (214)

This realignment of sexual features is what makes it possible for the novel to imply that such a marriage actually democratizes social relationships while it also reestablishes the traditional patriarchy.

Novels rewarding self-assertion on the part of those in an inferior position undoubtedly provided the middle-class readership with a fable for their own emergence. Especially when acted out through the options of a female character, social competition could be denied even while it was entertained because the competition was feminized. Once the proverbial ills of industrialism made middle-class supremacy seem less of a utopian fantasy and more of a fact to be justified and defended, it stands to reason that individualism itself should change value. This is particularly evident in the difference between Austen's characteristic strategy for resolving social conflict and that more typical of the thirties and forties. Like Dickens's *Oliver Twist* and Thackeray's *Vanity Fair*, for example, *Wuthering Heights* and *Jane Eyre* were composed during the turbulent period between the reform bill of 1832 and the onset of midcentury prosperity. They all enact a fantasy of upward mobility in which a protagonist of inferior status enters the elite classes. In this respect, they demonstrate a common ancestry of eighteenth- and nineteenth-century fiction, but like the novels of Dickens and Thackeray, those of the Brontës modify the political fantasy in a significant way. In contrast with Austen's Elizabeth Bennet, for instance, neither Jane Eyre nor Heathcliff can penetrate the old squirearchy without dismantling it. The same can be said of Becky Sharp of course, and less obviously of Oliver, who ruptures the bonds among his distinguished forefathers merely by coming into the world. These social climbers of the thirties and forties threaten to become intruders or tyrants in their own right by pursuing individualistic goals. Rather than justifying the social authority that comes into being on this basis, competition comes to be seen as more of a disruptive force and threat to paternalism, as one might expect, in novels which were written against the ominous background of swelling industrial centers and Chartist rebellions.

An intense ambivalence towards social authority indeed manifests itself in conflicts between the masculine and feminine features within and among social types, conflicts which Austen's fiction could finesse without apparent difficulty. In *Oliver Twist*, it is worth recalling that Fagin's villainous nature is initially cloaked by a maternal exterior, his sizzling sausages, schoolroom games, and endearing turns of phrase, for example. But the competitive life of the city understandably fails to sustain Oliver when the profit motive emerges in conflict with Fagin's softer virtues and cancels them out. Together with the evil stepbrother, Fagin obstructs the search for Oliver's true mother, and through Sikes, he instigates Nancy's murder, the deed which requires his execution in turn. In *Wuthering Heights*, an unlikely comparison on the surface of it perhaps, Heathcliff's features change in a remarkably similar way, his positive emotional qualities giving way to the "besetting sin" of avarice in the second half of the novel. Here, too, aggression towards the established form of authority proves ultimately self-defeating, and value comes to be located in a feminine power that preserves the system of primogeniture, excludes intruders from the city, and thus eliminates the competition otherwise prevailing among men. A second generation of characters—notably domesticated in comparison with the original set—comes into dominance by passive means, through inherited rights rather than competition. Similar ambivalence makes itself felt in the dual heroines of *Vanity Fair*, one trusting in emotional constancy and moral restraint, the other relying on unscrupulous instincts and economic opportunism. The reader discovers soon enough that the prosperity of either invariably means deprivation for the other. Thus it is that with Becky's ascendancy one shifts allegiance to the sentimental heroine, Amelia, only to find that her passivity is a humiliation and a bore. At the end of the novel Thackeray leaves us, by way of a resolution, in a world generated out of this conflict, one with no more Napoleons in it, where there is less to be gained than lost, and where marriage provides a comfortless form of security rather like that of a prison.

There are parallels to be drawn between the ambivalence towards competition characterizing these novels and that manifesting itself in Jane's two liaisons with Mr. Rochester. Despite the symbolic machinery of marriage that supposedly signals a proper distribution of power, something obviously gets out of hand in this novel. Too many readers have seen Jane's ascendancy in the final chapters, not as a mutually enhancing exchange, but as the symbolic castration of the bridegroom. This, even though his rank and fortune—the signs of masculine authority—remain intact. This sense of imbalance is at least in part due to a decentering, as it were, of the patriarchal system, a disruption having its counterpart in other fiction of the forties. It is not only in the novels of the Brontës that the shift to matrilineage, as well as the suppression of feminine power, is generally accompanied by violence. The executions in *Oliver Twist* and the plunge of Clytemnestra's knife in *Vanity Fair* enable feminine power to come into being, as do the intrusions of Catherine Earnshaw's ghost and the maiming and blinding of Rochester.

Pride and Prejudice closes by recentering social authority at Pemberley, Darcy's ancestral home and the point at greatest distance from the town where the Bennets' irredeemably middle-class relatives live. By means of this geographical shift, the novel maintains the continuity of traditional power even while seeming to broaden its social base. In contrast, novels of the later period stress the disruptive effects entailed in redistributing authority. We see the social gap between male and female widen in *Wuthering Heights* and *Jane Eyre*, as well as in *Vanity Fair*, and the distance closes, it seems, only when one of the contending parties has been, in effect, eliminated. It would seem, then, that with the entrenchment of middle-class power occurring during this period, the political investment of sex roles changed, as did the dynamics of exchange between them. In converting male into female authority, fiction presents the female in a menacing light and creates discontinuities that are never quite resolved in spite of the novelists' gestures towards traditional closure.

We are certainly relieved when Heathcliff's power is subdued and feminized under Catherine Earnshaw's supernatural spell, but as he explains this process to Nelly, the loss of his destructive energy itself takes on sinister implications: "Nelly, there is a strange change approaching—I'm in its shadow at present. I take so little interest in my daily life, that I hardly remember to eat, and drink" (255). Only because of this change is the ancestral home restored to the "ancient stock and lawful master," but again this is achieved through feminine influence, that of Catherine Earnshaw's daughter. In raising the heir apparent from his servile position, she takes on the overbearing features of her mother: ". . . she changed her behavior, and became incapable of letting him alone: talking at him; commenting on his stupidity and idleness; expressing her wonder how he could endure the life he lived—how he could sit a whole evening staring into the fire, and dozing" (245). Brontë provides us with a figurative analogue to the civilizing of Hareton when Catherine has him devastate the wild foliage of Wuthering Heights in order to fix "her choice of a flower bed in the midst of them" (250). The disruptive effect of feminization is finally driven home when the household abandons the Heights for Thrushcross Grange, the more modern and decidedly effeminate of the two seats of power. A similar dislocation occurs in *Jane Eyre* where it is possible for the lovers to unite only after Thornfield Hall has been burnt to the ground and the center of family life transferred to feminine turf, a villa at the outskirts of the feudal estate. As Jane approaches this location, it resembles nothing quite so much as the somnambulant castle in stories on the order of "Briar Rose," this one, however, entombing the prince who must be kissed back to life by the princess (379). Rather than interacting as complementary or mutually authorizing concepts, masculine and feminine authority are so clearly competitive in these novels that the traditional exchange between the sexes seems to exhaust the male and render him passive.

To close a description of what is in actuality a continuing process, a few examples of how this exchange appears in later novels are certainly in order. It is worth noting, first of all, that while Charlotte Brontë could allow Jane Eyre a degree of sexual freedom and social mobility beyond the author's own reach, the same does not hold true for Lucy Snowe, the radically constrained heroine of Brontë's later novel, *Villette*. Nor does George Eliot, also writing after midcentury, grant her protagonists nearly so much room to exercise their individualism as Eliot herself enjoyed in real life. It is remarkable, furthermore, that the mere thought of sexual initiative on the part of Louisa Gradgrind, an otherwise unnoteworthy bourgeoise, overshadows the more momentous issues raised by Dickens's novel *Hard Times*. In a novel rumbling with labor unrest and crises within the educational system, Dickens pursues the sexual theme with perfect aplomb, as if he knew that in fiction at least these volatile issues could be resolved by subjugating the female. This does not entail her submission to the authority of a Darcy or Mr. Rochester, the patriarchs of earlier fiction, for Dickens returns the wayward daughter to her father and a state of infantile dependency that mitigates female power altogether. The central transformation scene in the novel does not entail submission to a male figure at all, but to that of a superior woman, Sissy Jupe, who has proved to be conspicuously lacking in competitive features. Dickens's novel clearly breaks down the character of the self-possessed woman into those two familiar Victorian stereotypes, the passive virgin and permissive adventuress. His resolution is not a mediation of the two, furthermore, for it depends upon exalting passivity and expurgating aggression. In Eliot's *Mill on the Floss*, the *locus classicus* for Maggie Tulliver's dilemma, appropriately enough, is the medieval trial for witchcraft where the woman is condemned for having demonic powers if she swims and hailed as a saint if she drowns. The dynamics of sexual relations are such that the female gains power only by redeeming the male, not by directly pursuing her own salvation. In fiction written after midcentury, more often than not, female characters are struck low if they oppose established forms of authority and succeed if they steadfastly oppose competitive behavior which has come to smack of the heartless warfare mapped out in Darwin's biology.

Rowton's anthology of female poetry and his proscriptive feminine poetics thus appear at the moment of transition when the dynamics of sexual exchange are most problematic. At this point, the strategy behind the symbolic exchange between the two sexes can no longer be to inject competition benignly into the system by way of the female, but rather to transform the male from a competitive beast into a benevolent father and produce a stable hierarchy reminiscent of an earlier and largely imaginary form of paternalism. Both of Rowton's gestures assert the mutually exclusive natures of sexual character, and both attempt to circumscribe female authority. But given the fact that, thanks in part to the labor reforms they themselves had endorsed, middle-class women had little direct access to economic or political power, we must consider why it was that the Victorians suddenly felt it was necessary for literature to render the female passive and exclude her from the competitive sphere.

It must be emphasized again that the Victorian obsession with sexual purity was, as much as anything else, an attempt to revise the language in which people talked, wrote and thought about the way that social power was distributed, an effort which was part of a much wider revision of cultural categories extending from those of economics, politics and science, to those of theology and literature, and entailing a general revaluation of tradition, or the claims of community, over and above competition, or the claims of the individual. Given the altered context that developed around midcentury, it would no longer do for the ideal woman to represent an emergent form of social power. She is conceived as being completely outside a now openly competitive system, or "different," rather than on the inside where she might clamber up. Once cultural territory has been mapped out as meaningful in some way, however, this meaning cannot simply be recalled and relegated to nature once again. It can only be revised and transformed. From the position of difference, feminine authority therefore continued to extend well beyond the domestic sphere. The voices we hear in Hardy and Conrad, for example, gain their moral authority from detachment, by coming from outside society and not from its center. To this separation of powers within middle-class culture we can also attribute the appearance of reviewers, censors, and such conscientiously liberal editors as Mr. Rowton, as well as the early feminists for whom, as Elaine Showalter explains, the Victorian ideal of womanhood served as the basis for the politics of a feminine subculture.[28]

As if to demonstrate that no component of culture—not even sexuality—remains stable in meaning and function through time and repeated usage, these various attempts to define femininity in rigid opposition to masculinity necessarily fail. They fail because sexuality ultimately proves to be nothing less than a language. Such modernists as Virginia Woolf and Jean Rhys seem to abandon the feminine aesthetic deliberately. Post-Freudian culture apparently gave them what their predecessors lacked, a language for articulating the gaps and silences of earlier domestic fiction. Or, perhaps, it is more accurate to say that the new language of the self provided by psychoanalysis, as well as advances in the other sciences, philosophy, and the sister arts, including literary criticism, allowed them to invent depths of female nature that had previously been beyond the limits of feminine discourse. In *Mrs. Dalloway*, for example, Woolf demonstrates that the polite exchanges which had, in earlier fiction, provided the terms for emotional, social and economic relationships are now conceived as merely a language of women, an empty ritual bespeaking the absence of meaningful communication, as well as community, among individuals.[29] The "true" self is multiple, even duplicitous, according to this novel, neither masculine nor feminine, neither one class nor another, neither unified nor incoherent, but fluid and unconstrained by the categories of any discourse other than its own, including that of psychoanalysis. Jean Rhys's *Wide Sargasso Sea* is another instance of rewriting the domestic novel. It retells the story of *Jane Eyre* from the perspective of the madwoman in the attic, this time revealing the psychological and cultural otherness of the female, and constituting a female fantasy that designates the femininity of an earlier age as the fantasy of the male. Again we find that the male author, someone like D. H. Lawrence, for instance, shares a notion of sexuality with women that similarly breaks down the distinctions between masculine and feminine discourse maintained in novels throughout the nineteenth century. The point to be made is that such transgression of sexual boundaries became not so much a specifically female or feminist response to the constraints of sex roles in life and in literature. It became a standard technique by which the modernists placed themselves outside the classification system of middle-class culture and created the fiction of an elite intellectual community.

[28] See, for example, Elaine Showalter's account of the rise of feminism out of the feminine aesthetic in *A Literature of Their Own*, pp. 182 ff.

[29] In *Mrs. Dalloway* (New York: Harcourt Brace Jovanovich, 1925), Peter Walsh, a reliable source for this particular observation, refers to Mrs. Dalloway's party, and "that network of visiting, leaving cards, being kind to people; running about with bunches of flowers, little presents," as the "interminable traffic that women of her sort keep up" (p. 117). In contrast with this ossified and ossifying language is that of the "solitary traveller" which, uniquely, in terms of this novel, is neither damaged nor mad, but both full and communicative, a language that conveys the illusion of its being a language of art independent of social interests and unencumbered by cultural necessity.

Figures beyond the Text:
A Theory of Readable Character in the Novel

STEVEN COHAN

I

What do we mean when we expect a character to be readable enough to stimulate an interaction of some kind between the text of a novel and its reader? Most
efforts to define "readable character" turn to the novel's realist tradition of psychological representation, but I want to propose a different and more flexible approach to this important question. I want to argue that character is readable
when the text and its reader work together to promote the representational figure's transformation into a virtual existent. In the text itself character is embedded in a discourse which presents the human figure as a subject in its own right.
Thus the strong appeal of character as a psychological representation. But
through the reader's active participation in the text he collaborates with it to experience character as something more: an object of his perception. The virtual
existence of character results from the construction of the figure as subject-as-
object in the reader's own imaginative space. Regardless of the referential identity the figure means to signify in the discourse, character is actually readable
because of its virtual identity, which in effect promotes an imaginative gestalt for
the figure, "a unitary whole of varying degrees of richness of detail, which, by
virtue of its intrinsic articulation and structure, possesses coherence and consolidation and, thus, detaches itself as an organized and closed unit from the surrounding field."[1] Character is therefore readable, not as a representation, but as
a coherently perceived figure existing, during the reading act, in the imaginative
space produced in the reader's mind by the transmission of that figure (the text's
coded instructions for perceiving it as a figure) and its reception (the reader's
acting upon those instructions to imagine it as a figure).

A perspective of the sort I have in mind is necessary if we are to understand
what we require of character in our effort to read it, but this orientation is one
which criticism has only begun to delineate. Seymour Chatman recognizes the
need for "an open theory of character" which can push our concerns beyond the
matter of "plot functions" to "argue that character is reconstructed by the audience from evidence announced or implicit in an original construction and communicated by the discourse. . . ."[2] We cannot arrive at such a desirable "open
theory," however, until we put into place the representationalism implied by the
conventional function of the human figure. Chatman himself, in response to his
important question, "What is it that we reconstruct," finally resorts to a psychological model, defining "character" as "a paradigm of traits." These traits, for

[1] Aron Gurwitsch, *The Field of Consciousness* (Pittsburgh: Duquesne University Press, 1964), p. 115.

[2] Seymour Chatman, *Story and Discourse: Narrative Structure in Fiction and Film* (Ithaca: Cornell University Press, 1978), p. 119.

Chatman, imply the psychology of the figure, one organized around the revelation of behavior.[3] Likewise, Tzvetan Todorov attempts to define "character" as
more than a cipher, as more than the product of "referential linguistic forms" or
"the agent of a series of actions." But he too can do so only by equating the human sign with the psychological reality it signifies. "[While] not every character
has a character, so to speak," Todorov explains, ". . . as soon as psychological
determinism appears in the text, the fictional character becomes endowed with
character: he acts in a certain way, *because* he is shy, weak, courageous, etc.
There is no such thing as character without determinism of this type."[4]

Why is it so difficult for narratologists like Chatman and Todorov to define
"character" from a perspective that respects the convention of "psychological
determinism" without requiring it or, and this is usually the case, becoming synonymous with it? Surely we all nod our heads in agreement at the familiar observation that character is a character with character; but in doing so we end where
we began and, like the tramps waiting for Godot, stand still in the process of
getting there. So why can't we avoid this snare of tautology when it comes to a
theory of character?

Much of what we customarily attribute to the significance of character as the
primary human referent in a novel's text—the point of instigation for the
reader's own construction of the text as a fictive world—has become equated
with the example of nineteenth-century realism, which orients its representation
of experience around character as an intelligible psychology. Though George
Levine argues that the disruptive texts of realism actually predict modernism,
about character he sees a departure: "The Victorian realist . . . puts primary emphasis on character; and the shift of emphasis from character is part of the whole
transformation away from realism."[5] If we associate the function of character
with the program of realism, as Levine does, then we place our emphasis on too
limited an area of inquiry and remain with Chatman and Todorov, defining character as a "paradigm of traits."

Most critics seem unwilling to move any further, however, so character and
psychological representation stay joined together as the Siamese twins of novel
theory. Realism in particular seems to epitomize the "psychological determinism" of character because it shouts its "insistence," to quote Leo Bersani, "on the
readability of personality."[6] As a result of this assumption, Bersani argues, "Behavior in realistic fiction is continuously expressive of character. Apparently random incidents neatly carry messages about personality; and the world is thus at
least structurally congenial to character, in the sense that it is constantly proposing to our intelligence objects and events which contain human desires, which

[3] Chatman, pp. 119, 126.

[4] Tzvetan Todorov, "Reading as Construction," trans. Marilyn A. August, *The Reader in the Text: Essays on Audience and Interpretation*, ed. Susan R. Suleiman and Inge Crosman (Princeton: Princeton University Press, 1980), pp. 76–77.

[5] George Levine, *The Realistic Imagination: English Fiction from Frankenstein to Lady Chatterley* (Chicago: University of Chicago Press,
1981), p. 271.

[6] Leo Bersani, *A Future for Astyanax: Character and Desire in Literature* (Boston: Little, Brown, 1976), p. 69.

give to them an intelligible form."[7] Cast in this light, "readable character" translates into "the readability of the human personality,"[8] meaning the *representation* in narrative of "a coherent, unified, describable self."[9] In effect, Bersani argues that realism not only relies on character to make experience intelligible; more to the point, he, too, makes inseparable from the concept of character the specific psychological value of "predictable continuities."[10]

The conventional assumption that character is readable only when grounded in the specific ideology of psychological coherence equates "character" with the principle of intelligible behavior it traditionally illustrates, whether we refer to such representation as "a paradigm of traits," "psychological determinism," or "predictable continuities." But this conservative line of reasoning, typical of critics when they approach the question of character in the novel no matter what radical theory of fiction they may otherwise advance, obscures the imaginative function of character by making it a primary avenue of entrance into the debate over the merits of realism as a mode of representation and, hence, as a psychological ideology. Responses of this sort to the problem of character generally fall into one of three camps. The first includes humanists such as W. J. Harvey, Christopher Gillie, John Bayley, and Martin Price, who defend the importance of character by appealing to the mimetic values of realist fiction.[11] The second includes structuralists such as Chatman and Todorov, who describe these values as "components" of narrative while not responding to them as values at all. The third includes post-structuralists such as Bersani and Hélène Cixous, who follow the models of Barthes and Lacan to claim, in Cixous's words, that "'character' is the product of a repression of subjectivity."[12] By thus challenging realism as a bogus ideology, this third camp calls into question the identifying function of character as something "to be *figured out*, understood, read," since "The ideology underlying this fetishization of 'character'" works only to produce a "marketable" text for consumption by a conservative, bourgeois audience, one so committed to the values of stability and coherence in reality that it seeks confirmation of these values in its fiction.[13] When placed in this critical arena, character functions—comfortably, indifferently, or deviously—as a psychological microcosm of the text itself as a representation, and a debate of this sort only misdirects our attention. From whichever side of the arena we look, the readability of character still seems to require, for good or ill, that the figure be a transparent grid—a personality for the first group, a paradigm for the second, a *per*-

---

[7] Bersani, p. 53.

[8] Bersani, p. 69.

[9] Bersani, p. 214.

[10] Bersani, p. 69.

[11] W. J. Harvey, *Character and the Novel* (Ithaca: Cornell University Press, 1965); Christopher Gillie, *Character in English Literature* (London: Chatto and Windus, 1965); Martin Price, "The Other Self: Thoughts About Character in the Novel," *Imagined Worlds*, ed. Maynard Mack and Ian Gregor (London: Methuen, 1968), pp. 279–99; John Bayley, "Character and Consciousness," *New Literary History* 5 (1974), 225–35.

[12] Hélène Cixous, "The Character of 'Character,'" trans. Keith Cohen, *New Literary History* 5 (1974), 384.

[13] Cixous, p. 385.

sonage for the third—that overlays the world of the text upon the world of its audience, or vice-versa, to equate the figure with the material reality it seems programmed to represent.

Although we do need to recognize the limitation of this critical orientation towards character, we still cannot ignore the figure's referentiality altogether, and I am not proposing that we do so. Character does point to a human referent, for as readers we rely on the figure's being more than a series of linguistic signals encoding it in the text so that we can respond to it as an imaginative construction of human reality; and this is the case even with characters in novels that openly defy realist conventions regarding intelligible personality. Granted, the modernist reaction to realism often focused on the representation of character, as in Virginia Woolf's celebrated attack on Arnold Bennett.[14] Prodding of this sort, however, which encourages Levine to exclude character when it comes to charting realism's evolution into modernism, does not necessarily lead to Jonathan Culler's explanation of why characters in novels by writers such as Woolf "cannot be treated according to nineteenth-century models; they are nodes in the verbal structure of the work, whose identity is relatively precarious."[15] To understand character as "nodes in the verbal structure of the work" assigns to it the same textual status as rhetoric, and this designation claims to eliminate from the human figure its representational *human* status entirely. Now character becomes, in Martin Price's words, "at most the constelled form of image patterns, historical allusions, philosophic themes."[16] Yet Price, like Culler, overstates the case. Even the rhetoric of a modernist text must somehow be leading us beyond the text, past its verbal nodes to an imaginary space in the reader's mind. Otherwise how could Culler put forth his claim that the "identity" of character in modernist fiction "is relatively precarious"? In other words, if we follow Culler, first to conceive of character as a verbal node, then as an identity, however precarious its representation, we find ourselves once again moving away from the text—the discourse—to imagine the human referent of the text—the character whose identity is somehow created by that discourse. However we approach it, character sustains an imaginative position superior to and yet not detached from the text's discourse, because of the figure's claim of referentiality, whatever stylized form that claim may take. So the question remains, especially when prompted by contemporary fiction and its challenge to "psychological determinism": can we examine character as a figure projecting an identity without necessarily relying upon realism's psychological model to define the imaginary dimensions of that identity as the text both promotes and grounds it?

Todorov, I think, isolates our problem somewhat when he observes that a character may actually lack a character in the psychological sense of the word. To begin with, he points out, "In and of itself the fictional character [at first evoked

[14] Virginia Woolf, "Mr. Bennett and Mrs. Brown" (1924), rpt. *The Captain's Death Bed and Other Essays* (New York: Harcourt, 1950), pp. 94–119.

[15] Jonathan Culler, *Structuralist Poetics: Structuralism, Linguistics, and the Study of Literature* (Ithaca: Cornell University Press, 1975), p. 231.

[16] Price, p. 291.

by a text's linguistic reference to an anthropomorphic being] has no content: someone is identified without being described."[17] That a text must then "describe" something in order to give the character "content" or, more precisely, that the text must instruct us how to imagine the character as a character, as more than a "linguistic reference" to the human, this is the central issue we must explore if we are to posit a theory of readable character "open" enough to move beyond a definition of the human figure solely as a "paradigm of traits" or "constellation of images." To examine the inherent readability of character, then, we need to locate our orientation not in the psychological grounding of realism (representationalism) or in the aesthetic grounding of modernism (self-reflexivity), but in that crucial space between the text and its reader. For it is here that the coherence of character as a virtual existent comes into play.

II

Wolfgang Iser's explanation of the reading process in phenomenological terms has begun to map out clear directions leading us to that space between text and reader, which I see as the location where we can understand character as an imaginative construction that does not necessarily depend upon the requirement of intelligible psychological representation. Iser approaches reading as an act of ideation, a concept he derives from Husserl. According to Iser the text itself relies on its own indeterminacy—those implicit areas in the discourse he identifies as "gaps" or "blanks," as well as the more explicit areas he calls "negations"—to force the reader's active participation, so that he can experience the aesthetic dimension of the text by ideating its content.

> *Communication in literature, then, is a process set in motion and regulated not by a given code but by a mutually restrictive and magnifying interaction between the explicit and the impicit, between revelation and concealment. . . . Blanks and negations both control the process of communication in their own different ways: the blanks leave open the connections between perspectives in the text, and so spur the reader into coordinating these perspectives—in other words, they induce the reader to perform basic operations within the text. The various types of negation invoke familiar or determinate elements only to cancel them out. What is canceled, however, remains in view, and thus brings about modifications in the reader's attitude toward what is familiar or determinate—in other words, he is guided to adopt a position in relation to the text.*[18]

From this engagement the reader produces his sense of the work's coherence, to see it emerging from beneath the textual manifestations of indeterminacy.

Ultimately Iser has in mind a distinction between the interpretation and the reception of the text regarding its coherence, and I will be referring to that part of

---

[17] Todorov, p. 77.

[18] Wolfgang Iser, *The Act of Reading: A Theory of Aesthetic Response* (Baltimore: Johns Hopkins, 1978), pp. 168–69.

his theory later. But first I want to emphasize what he explains about a text's appeal to its reader to construct a virtual world out of the discourse, which itself embeds that world—along with its potential for readerly ideation—entirely in words. The text stimulates the reader's imagination by heightening blank or negational spaces to interrupt the discourse's appearance of straightforward semantic content. Blanks and negations draw the reader into the virtual world encoded within the text, because the discordances they generate appeal to his imagination to smooth the sudden ruptures or to fill the unexpected gaps. The reader himself provides the missing connections or accounts for the reversals of conventional strategies in the text's "repertoire," which can include character as a representational figure. Once he constructs this virtual space in his mind and enters it imaginatively, the reader "makes conceivable that which has not been formulated" in the text itself,[19] and this activity includes not only the assemblage of "meaning" but also the construction of a character's identity as a virtual existent. Consequently, since the reader experiences a virtual reality that exists only so long as it is perceived as a coherent structure in his imagination, the act of reading, according to Iser, stimulates an experience of "irrealization, in the sense that we are preoccupied with something that takes us out of our own given reality."[20]

This latter point I want to emphasize in particular. Iser's explanation of the reading process as an act of irrealization provides us with a useful framework for understanding character as an imaginative construction, what I have been calling a "virtual existent." But at the same time some redirection of Iser's theory is in order, for in the long run his discussion works to minimize the imaginative dynamic of irrealization occurring through the reader's contact with the text. Although his model of the reading act begins with the text's indeterminacy stimulating mental images in the reader's mind, Iser tends to equate such images with ideas, thereby emphasizing the text's appeal to the reader's intellect above all else. Whenever he applies his model to a particular text he ends up subordinating the reader's experience of irrealization to the achievement of intellectual comprehension, so the illustrations he cites to demonstrate his theory of reading do not fully sample its imaginative dimensions as a virtualizing activity. Yet the advantage of Iser's model for our purposes is that it does move us beyond an exclusive concern with comprehension, even though he himself does not make full use of this potential.

To build a theory of character from Iser's model we therefore need to extend its application and its emphasis beyond his own concern with intellectual comprehension as the goal of reading. The intellect certainly does not remain passive while reading, but that is not the sole area of the reader's mind stimulated by the text. Reading fiction is, finally, an act of imaginative perception that calls into play more than the reader's intellect to serve more interests than that of comprehension alone, because the reader's engagement with the human figure re-

[19] Iser, p. 139.
[20] Iser, p. 140.

quires that he bring to bear upon the text a variety of imaginative resources: only then can he experience the fictive world as a virtual reality while reading. The reader's construction of the text as a virtual reality transports the figure and its world from the text to that "irrealized" space in his own mind, which exists beyond the realm of discourse. The value of Iser's model, then, is that it asks us to recognize how the process of constructing the figure's virtual existence, while grounded by the text and performed by the reader, actually occurs neither in the text, though the conventions of narrative make it appear otherwise, nor in the reader's own "given reality," for any stimulus from outside the text will intrude upon the activity of irrealization to disrupt it, but rather in what I have called the imaginative space between the two, which materializes in the reader's mind.

Let me begin to illustrate the orientation I am proposing for our understanding of character as a readable figure by looking at a few examples of my own. One of the most self-conscious, not to say outrageous, instances of a text's appeal to its reader to enter that imaginative space beyond the text occurs in *Tristram Shandy*. Tristram announces that he will describe the Widow Wadman (to give her a content, so to speak), but then provides instead two blank pages with these instructions: "Sit down, Sir, paint her to your own mind—as like your mistress as you can—as unlike your wife as your conscience will let you— 'tis all one to me—please but your own fancy to it." [21] Even though Tristram confesses that what his reader may choose as filler for this quite literal blank may be "all one" to him, since he equates the two blank pages with a transparency, elsewhere Sterne's text does implicitly direct our ideation of the Widow's character, as later revealed by her vigorous pursuit of innocent Uncle Toby, to determine what we, as collaborating readers, may put down upon those two blank pages without ignoring the text altogether. Their context in the entire work, then, already starts to fill those pages with invisible script, despite Tristram's claim that we have our own fancy—not to say our own lived experience—at our disposal to make the text itself, in essence, disappear from view as a text.

Now we should not take Sterne's joke lightly. First of all, it reminds us how much the creation of character in a novel seems to depend upon the text's discourse and its representationality, which fill that empty space with a content for the Widow's otherwise blank figure. If character were just a blank page we would be at a loss, for we would literally have nothing to read. But too, this joke makes us realize that a reader does indeed bring something of his own experience—his imagination—to a novel: the character is actually a blank space in that the figure exists solely in the reader's imagination, not in the text, so these two pages in *Tristram Shandy* invite us as readers to enter an extra-textual space in our own heads.

Just how do we get there? It is not the description or explanation of behavior, that "paradigm of traits" exhibited by the figure, which necessarily transforms the Widow into an imaginative gestalt, a figure whose identity we can imagine. Rather, her behavior with Uncle Toby instigates a coded set of instructions that

---

[21] Laurence Sterne, *Tristram Shandy*, ed. James Aiken Work (New York: Odyssey Press, 1940), p. 470.

determine our options for what we see her as, by foregrounding some "traits," precluding others, in the process supplying us with enough clues so as to distinguish figure from narrative background. "If what we call 'identity' were not anchored in a constant relationship with environment," Gombrich claims in *Art and Illusion*, "it would be lost in the chaos of swirling impressions that never repeat themselves."[22] In this example the Widow's behavior, set in contrast to that of the other characters, provides us with such an environment for singling out her figure (and for laughing, too, at what we discover). "Character," Todorov asks us to remember, "is a compromise between difference and repetition,"[23] so our construction of the Widow as a virtual existent depends on both. We need to find an attribute of difference in her figure, in order to identify it *as* a distinct figure (the Widow as opposed to Mrs. Shandy, say), and one of repetition, in order to keep locating that distinct figure in the imaginative field whenever we come upon references to her in the narrative.

These two attributes, however, need not necessarily be translated into the psychological discourse of behavior. Rhetoric, of the sort Dickens's novels rely upon, works just as well. There the textual assertion of a peculiar rhetorical description proceeds, in one breath, to define the sameness identifiable with the figure and to establish its difference from other figures, for the specific trope becomes so vivid in our minds that it seems inseparable from the figure it supposedly means only to describe as a piece of discourse. Recall, for instance, Mrs. Snagsby in *Bleak House*. She is not a very important character in the novel. E. M. Forster would have called her a "flat" character, one who does not surprise us because her behavior follows a predictable, unvarying pattern. In this respect, she lacks a character as Todorov defines the word: there is little "psychological determinism" operating upon her figure. But while Mrs. Snagsby may lack dimension as a psychological representation, she is still quite vivid as an imaginative figure.

Dickens's text establishes Mrs. Snagsby's potential for a virtual existence from the moment it first introduces her. She is "short," we are told, with a "compressed" waist, but most of all it is her nose that should command our attention. She has "a sharp nose like a sharp autumn evening, inclined to be frosty towards the end."[24] Here Mrs. Snagsby's nose stands in for her entire personality. The discourse renders her as little more than a rhetorical device, synecdoche, in much the same way that the luminous reflection of something on water is suggested on a canvas of Monet's by brush strokes and dabs of colors: bits and pieces produce the optical (or virtual) illusion of a representational whole. Dickens's rhetoric similarly invites us to collaborate with it to complete the image, to make of Mrs. Snagsby something more than the sum of the few words affixing her to the text. The sharpness of a frosty autumn evening connotes a range of sensation larger than the actual subject matter of this descriptive state-

[22] E. H. Gombrich, *Art and Illusion: A Study in the Psychology of Pictorial Representation*, rev. ed. (New York: Pantheon, 1961), p. 50.

[23] Todorov, p. 77.

[24] Charles Dickens, *Bleak House*, ed. George Ford and Sylvère Monod (New York: Norton, 1977), p. 116.

ment—her nose—would suggest, releasing for our imaginations a sense of the shrillness of her "sharp" personality so that we experience her figure as more than just the rhetoric it is in the text. Evoking a concrete visual image of the woman's nose through the simile of an autumn evening, the discourse first encourages us to use observations from our own experience to see Mrs. Snagsby as something physical—an imaginatively visual figure, in possession of a face and a body as well as a nose—and then as something more intangible as well—the shrill-tempered woman sporting this sharp and frosty nose.

In other words, as we read we follow a direction encoded in the text to see the character, not as words, but as an eidetic image, "Mrs. Snagsby," and the words have led us into filling in the blank established by the synecdoche, so we supply the visual pieces that the discourse itself does not explicitly provide. Since discourse, even as a spur towards representation, can only offer us a metonymic exposition of a figure, we *have* to participate in the character's construction, much as Tristram invites us to do with the Widow Wadman, by completing the instruction encoded in the partial description to achieve a more complete actualization of the figure's virtual presence in our minds. Indeed, the inability to do just that, to construct a virtual existence—an *eidos*—for the figure, may well discourage a reader from turning to novels for pleasure, as a student confessed to me, when he explained that he could not respond to characters in a novel as more than "words," unless he had originally seen a film version of it.[25]

Mrs. Snagsby's existence therefore depends upon our constructing her as a virtual presence according to the direction encoded in the text's condensation of her figure into metonymic and metaphoric discourse. Throughout our reading of *Bleak House* we continue to think of her as a "flat" character only because Dickens's text does not change or extend the coding for our construction of her virtual existence. As an imaginative figure she is not "flat" at all; she just remains limited to the same "sharp" note trumpeted every time she appears. Our sense of her as a virtual existent distinguished from other such figures in *Bleak House* consequently develops without further variation because of the text's repetition of its initial direction. Grounded by a discourse which keeps her potential for virtual existence couched in a recurring type of rhetorical description, our ideation of her figure now remains consistent; it is continually reinforced by Dickens's narration (and her own dialogue) but not extended any further. If this were to remain the only type of direction for our construction of the figures in Dickens's text, we would not be able to sustain our interest in them for long, and *Bleak House* is very long.

For an extension of our engagement with the figures in Dickens's novel we can, of course, turn to Esther. The text provides us with a more dimensional (and more psychologically representational) range of direction for Esther's figure. This is a rather conventional means of readerly engagement with a figure's

---

[25] Iser argues how such passivity on my student's part would work against his imaginative engagement with a novel's text. In his case the supposed "optical enrichment" of a filmic treatment, whose actors make the figures visually determinate, actually excludes him from an active role in the production of the figures as mental images, so that the figures are perceived entirely within their own space, inhibiting an effort on his part to collaborate in their construction (see Iser, pp. 138–39).

virtual existence. More revealing for our purposes, and more crucial to Dickens's text itself, is Lady Dedlock. The text seems to provide very little helpful direction when it comes to Lady Dedlock, especially in contrast to the more complete psychological representation of her daughter. This contrast in and of itself establishes a blank that draws us towards Lady Dedlock's figure, and the discourse encourages our interest because it instructs us to envision her not in a "melting" but in a "freezing" mood of inanimation and indolence,[26] as a further pointed contrast to the obsessive, manic energy of the other characters, such as Mrs. Snagsby.

Lady Dedlock is not a cipher, yet neither is she "round" in Forster's psychological definition of that term. Because she is not explained psychologically by the text's discourse, we construct her figure much in the way we do Mrs. Snagsby's. In this case, however, the discourse as a whole supplies the metonymic reference that stimulates our imaginative construction of her virtual existence. In contrast to Esther, whose history the text documents to encourage our understanding of her figure as it was psychologically determined by her childhood, Lady Dedlock shows how little character need depend upon psychological discourse of that sort to activate our imaginative construction of the figure as a virtual existent. Lady Dedlock, the most psychologically elusive of the characters in *Bleak House*, is, along with Tulkinghorn, actually the most imaginatively compelling, precisely because she seems so blank a page as a "person." To read her character we need to look between the lines of the text with greater penetration and more imaginative engagement than we need to use in order to ideate an existence for Esther or Mrs. Snagsby.

For much of *Bleak House* Lady Dedlock seems opaque, masked, her face not a mirror of her personality, as it is for Mrs. Snagsby. The text presents Lady Dedlock to us through a series of aristocratic poses ruptured infrequently by an emotional outburst. Whenever the narration allows us to glimpse the heat smoldering beneath the icy exterior it only draws us further into the text in an attempt to penetrate her usual indifference to account for that volatile contrast of "freezing" and "melting" moods. In other words, we try to interpret her as a character in the psychological sense by completing the missing psychological discourse ourselves. The plot, it would seem, provides us with some explanation of her behavior; but when all is said and done it actually gives us very little to go on, since her relationship with Hawdon remains shrouded in unanswered questions about her past. All we have to rely on for our knowledge of her history is what Tulkinghorn reports, and the sinister tone of his veiled explanation in Chapter 40 makes what he says suspect. So with this the case we go beyond the discourse about her to find our way, to coordinate her lack of animation to the recurring images of disease, or to the problem of sexual repression, or to the spiritual bankruptcy of a moneyed class, all three very standard explanations of her "character."

No matter how we do try to account for her presence in the novel, however, Lady Dedlock remains a puzzle, a blank, psychologically indeterminate, but nevertheless very readable. Whatever psychological content we try to imagine

[26] Dickens, p. 13.

for her out of the text's grounding of her figure in a representational world traumatized by sex, class, and money, Lady Dedlock's "frozen" personality makes
her anything but a statue in our minds, as the variety of explanations for her
behavior testifies. Because her figure is grounded by ellipses it pulls us through
the text, first to focus the emotional tensions that make the text itself so imaginatively compelling, and then to draw these tensions into our own readerly space.
Thus she well serves her text's reception, not as a psychological representation,
but as a virtual existent; for what we end up doing for her figure is to supply
ourselves the passionate energy which the text implicitly directs us to see there
in her figure but which it resists addressing in the discourse about her except in
the most conditional of phrasing to emphasize how masked she is even to the
omnipresent narrative voice. When we do finally watch her passions erupt in
Chapters 41 and 55, we find confirmation of the volatile energy we have been
imagining between the lines of the elusive discourse about her, and more encouragement to continue doing so. For even in these two scenes, while the narration observes her in a display of passion, it relies mainly on the image of her
unkempt hair "wildly thrown" and "wildly scattered" as a metaphoric reference
to her mental disorder.[27]

We can conclude, then, that Lady Dedlock exists for our imaginations solely
as the product of an incomplete discourse about her repressed energy; and for
her figure to radiate that energy which she strains against, as her figure seems to
do, we provide it in our imaginative conception of her, although we tend to attribute its presence to the text itself.[28] In fact, however, the text only stimulates
our imaginative production of her as a virtual figure suspended between those
two extreme points of "freezing" and "melting."

III

The Widow Wadman, Mrs. Snagsby, Lady Dedlock, each figure lacks the degree
of coherent psychological content we readily find in Emma Woodhouse, say, or
Dorothea Brooke; and I have chosen these three "incomplete" characters as my
initial examples for that very reason. Their resonance as human figures does not
depend upon their being framed by a specific psychological discourse—whether
articulated through an evolving sequence of actions to promote growth or a narrational account of growth—to make them imaginatively credible or readable.
What I have wanted to emphasize through their example is that to understand
character as a readable figure we need to distinguish between its psychological
attributes as a representational figure and its phenomenological identity as an
imagined figure.

I have in mind when I stress this point the line drawn by phenomenologists

---

[27] Dickens, pp. 513, 666.

[28] Susan R. Horton agrees with what I am saying, although she concentrates on the text as a representation which affords the
reader access to Dickens's imagination. "The great amount of energy that radiates from Dickens's novels is actually in part our
own," Horton concludes. "Reading Dickens, finally, is a participatory sport." *The Reader in the Dickens World: Style and Response*
(Pittsburgh: University of Pittsburgh Press, 1981), p. 13.

between "the [perceived] thing as it really is," which we can roughly call the psychological reality character represents, and "the [perceived] thing as it appears and is experienced through the given act, and through that act alone," which we can similarly call the virtual identity a reader constructs for the character during the reading experience.[29] This sharp distinction allows us to put the human figure's representationality in a perspective subordinate to the space between the text and its reader. When we conceive of the perceived figure's identity in this context—to comprehend what makes the figure identifiable enough to be perceived and experienced by the reader as a figure with a "content" that distinguishes it from other figures or grounds—we can then move beyond the matter of identity as a psychological content, for we are now conceiving of the figure as an imagined object as well as an imagined subject.

Ordinarily the discourse of a novel seems to obscure this perspective. As a representational mode narration tends to blur a distinction between character as object and subject, because of the genre's particular richness in representing character as a bearer of consciousness. In the text as a representational mode character appears in the discourse as the *subject* of consciousness. As Dorrit Cohn quite rightly observes, "narrative fiction is the only literary genre, as well as the only kind of narrative, in which the unspoken thoughts, feelings, perceptions of a person other than the speaker can be portrayed."[30] Nevertheless, while that feeling of sharing another's consciousness seems very real in many novels, while it greatly contributes to the power such fictions have for readers, just as it activates, as well, the text's own claim as an intelligible psychological discourse—while the narration seems to do all of this, it actually deflects the imaginative reality of character as a figure experienced by the reader in a space beyond the text. Despite the discourse's encouragement, we are not intruders upon another's consciousness. That consciousness does not exist materially as consciousness, only as a discourse about consciousness. It therefore follows that the figure identified by the text's discourse as a subject of consciousness is also the *object* of our consciousness as readers of that discourse. Reading, after all, involves us in an act of consciousness that is stimulated by the text. As Iser puts it, "The ability to perceive oneself during the process of participation is an essential quality of the aesthetic experience; the observer finds himself in a strange, halfway position: he is involved and he watches himself being involved."[31] Like all acts of consciousness, this one too produces for the perceiver (the reader) a gestalt, "a universal, formal pattern of organization [for the perceived object as it appears to the perceiver], realized in every field of consciousness, regardless of content."[32]

The text's narration of the figure's representational existence as a subject

---

[29] Gurwitsch, p. 170.

[30] Dorrit Cohn, *Transparent Minds: Narrative Modes for Presenting Consciousness in Fiction* (Princeton: Princeton University Press, 1978), p. 7.

[31] Iser, p. 134.

[32] Gurwitsch, p. 55.

works with the reader's imaginative perception of the figure as an object to stimulate the reader's own double consciousness as subject (becoming involved in the representation) and object (watching that involvement occur). Out of this double engagement the reader builds a similar double construction of character, the imagined figure as subject-as-object, which we can understand as two concurrent fields of readerly perception.

For an illustration of this double construction consider *Mrs. Dalloway*. As a psychological representation Woolf's novel records, in James Naremore's phrase, "a world without a self."[33] Clarissa Dalloway's character seems to resist the conventional equation of identity with predictable continuities, for she appears to be a bundle of competing impressions. At times she sees herself as young or old, as female or male, as wife or virgin, as corporeal or ethereal. When we think of Clarissa as a representational figure, the subject of consciousness, her identity seems fluid, without shape. We do not ignore her feeling of "being laid out like a mist between the people she knew best, who lifted her on their branches as she had seen the trees lift the mist."[34] Nor do we minimize her belief that "our apparitions, the part of us which appears, are so momentary, compared with the other, the unseen part of us, which spreads wide" (p. 232). Although the self she assembles for presentation to her world must be "pointed; dartlike; definite" (p. 55), at bottom she senses something amorphous within her consciousness, something "invisible; unseen; unknown" (p. 14).

The text of Woolf's novel renders Clarissa's sensation of fluidity and shapelessness through its discourse about her. Here, for example, is the narration recounting one of those moments during which Clarissa feels her self spreading wide:

> *Only for a moment; but it was enough. It was a sudden revelation, a tinge like a blush which one tried to check and then, as it spread, one yielded to its expansion, and rushed to the farthest verge and there quivered and felt the world come closer, swollen with some astonishing significance, some pressure of rapture, which split its thin skin and gushed and poured with an extraordinary alleviation over the cracks and sores! Then, for that moment, she had seen an illumination; a match burning in a crocus; an inner meaning almost expressed. But the close withdrew; the hard softened. It was over—the moment. (p. 47)*

This passage describing Clarissa's "sudden revelation" occurs in a paragraph that runs over two pages, but these five sentences stylistically enclose her moment of consciousness as a self-contained unit to draw us towards her figural space so that we experience the emotional intensity of her "illumination." The relatively brief first sentence, two independent clauses linked by a semi-colon, stands out in contrast to the lengthy sentences that precede it in the paragraph. The cadence of this sentence, a recurring syntactic structure in Woolf's prose,

---

[33] James Naremore, *The World without a Self: Virginia Woolf and the Novel* (New Haven: Yale University Press, 1973).

[34] Virginia Woolf, *Mrs. Dalloway* (New York: Harcourt, 1925), p. 12. Further page references will be included in my text.

thus signals the opening of Clarissa's epiphany. The second sentence expands syntactically in contrapuntal rhythm to the first to reflect Clarissa's own sensation of expansion; and as this sentence builds through the accumulation of clauses, punctuated only by commas to quicken the speed, it seems about to burst as syntax when it ends in an exclamation, much as Clarissa herself feels "swollen" from "the pressure of rapture" she experiences. The third sentence then slows down the intensity of expression to relieve the tempo of the previous sentence; here the linking of three phrases with semi-colons makes the cadence somewhat weightier as a reflection of the waning of intensity and as a preparation for the moment's termination. The fourth sentence now repeats the syntax of the first to frame the epiphany, and the moment's closure is itself announced in the last and shortest, most straightforward sentence of the five: "It was over— the moment."

The style of this passage renders the intensity of Clarissa's revelation so that we imagine her as a figural subject, for it makes her consciousness known to us through a piece of discourse whose semantic content visibly manifests itself in a syntactic pattern. When the rhythm of Woolf's syntax reflects Clarissa's epiphany as sensation, we seem to penetrate her consciousness even though she herself assumes it is "invisible; unseen; unknown." In doing so, we imagine what she experiences as a subject of consciousness, but we also experience a continuity heightening our sense of her as a figural object. The rhythm of expansion/contraction, which Clarissa feels as a moment of discontinuity and dissolution, is actually narrated in a style that carries us into the density of the moment while moving us beyond its specific psychological content because of its peculiar stylistic rendering. The syntactic reinforcement of Clarissa's consciousness in this passage does render the single moment quite vividly, but the style is also representative of the text's prose throughout. The passage, taken as discourse, actually makes us perceive both the difference (this single moment) and the repetition (the recurring style) of Clarissa's experience. Woolf's prose consequently informs each isolated moment of psychological fragmentation with a principle of repetition and, hence, of continuity, for it gives to all such moments a similar stylistic identity in the discourse. The narration itself thus encourages us to see Clarissa's consciousness radiating from a continuous identity, what she thinks of as "one centre, one diamond . . . that diamond shape, that single person" (pp. 55–56), even though she herself fragments that center. The text of *Mrs. Dalloway*, then, as opposed to the reality represented by the text, directs us to imagine Clarissa's figure as an object, so to construct an identity for her figure, we respect her own discontinuous psychological content but also go beyond it. In this sense do we construct her as subject-as-object to imagine her as a continuously identifiable virtual existent throughout our reading.

We receive Clarissa's momentary selves as variations of a single virtual identity that seems continuous to our imaginations only because the text embeds the figural consciousness in discourse, in language, to encourage our perceiving the figure as subject-as-object. Clarissa's discontinuity as a figural subject is further balanced by her continuity as a figural object through the narrative's chronological sequence of a single day and its shifting viewpoint. Both the structure and the narration of the text direct our reading of Clarissa's figure so that she becomes imaginatively visible in our minds as an existent. As a figural subject Clarissa sustains a discontinuous psychological content, but the rhythm of variation in her consciousness, we discover as we proceed serially through the narrative, is itself the repetition of states of self-consciousness and self-effacement, of expansion and contraction, so the passage I cited offers us an example of the type of revelation she repeatedly experiences throughout the day. Within this pattern of expansion/contraction is her figure's own subjective (and representational) consciousness, which we construct as the object of our perception, because the text instructs us to look beyond the individual moments which define her as a discontinuous subject.

Being Clarissa's readers, we respond to such textual signals to move her figure beyond the temporal, psychological dimensions that otherwise restrict her to a representational human world. Only then can we take notice of her experiencing both difference and repetition to imagine her as subject and object. Since the narration's shifting viewpoint presents Clarissa as she sees her self, as she thinks others see her, and as others see her, the text continually directs us to imagine her figure from this double perspective. Clarissa herself can momentarily experience the same degree of irrealization: "She sliced like a knife through everything; at the same time was outside, looking on" (p. 11). But whereas this double consciousness of her self as both subject and object lasts only a moment for Clarissa, we sustain it for the duration of our reading, because Woolf's viewpoint, which can even shift between authorial and figural perspectives in midsentence, insures our continual reception of Clarissa as subject-as-object, just as the prose style and the structure invite us to imagine the continuity and repetition underlying the discontinuity and difference that Clarissa experiences.

In *Mrs. Dalloway* we achieve a type of readerly engagement that I want to offer as a model for our construction of character as a readable figure. The reader's own imaginative centralization of the character as a virtual existent overcomes without denying the fragmentation which the character herself may experience as a representation of reality. The reader consequently imagines the figure from two concurrent perspectives in relation to the text and its fictive impression of reality: the character as subject-as-object. Affixed to the discourse as the subject of consciousness, character renders the text as a representational world; whereas, at the same time, provoked by that discourse into becoming the object of the reader's perception, character stimulates the reader to transform the representational world into a virtual world, whose coherence he can perceive because the text instructs him to imagine virtually what it can only shape through words.

When identifying this pattern as a model of readable character, however, we must also recognize that it works inversely just as well. The reticence of narration to penetrate consciousness in a novel, like the absence of narration in film or drama, does not necessarily impoverish our response. Far from it, as Lady Dedlock shows, since Dickens's narration treats her as a minimal subject. The more the discourse presents the figure as an object by not presenting its inner space as a subject through narration, the more it draws the figure into our space where we construct its identity as a subject, by and large just reversing the procedure I've described occurring through the narration of *Mrs. Dalloway*. In either case, the figure imagined as subject-as-object or as object-as-subject, we are working with the same dynamic that "enables us to produce an image of the imaginary object [the figure as a virtual existent], which otherwise has no existence of its own. . . . and because we are imagining and producing it, we are actually in its presence and it is in ours." [35] I am concentrating on narration as the spur for our construction of the figure as a virtual existent because it is the mode of presenting character peculiar to the novel as a text; and since character in the novel so depends upon narration for its ground, the discourse can facilitate the ease with which we move the figure into our space, as in the examples of both Clarissa Dalloway and Lady Dedlock, or it can seem to thwart our imaginative possession of the figure, to underscore the pressures we exert upon the text. Consequently, the text's invitation to coordinate or separate these two perspectives—the figure as subject-as-object—works to determine our particular reception of the figure as a virtual existent.

IV

One might counter what I have been proposing by arguing that I can make my claim about the figure as subject-as-object in *Mrs. Dalloway* only because, in this particular instance, the text as Woolf constructed it assents to my readerly organization of its pieces of representation into an imaginative whole. For one thing, her style, I said, instructs us to do just that. To be sure, critics vary in the degree to which they are willing to accept fiction, in Iser's phrase, "as the gestalt of the imaginary," [36] what for our purposes we might term the imaginative ground encoded within the text that outlines character as a perceived figure (subject-as-object) and then promotes that figure's virtual existence for the reader. Chatman does believe that by definition a narrative manifests "discernible organization" or it would not be a narrative. [37] Bersani, on the other hand, disagrees. He maintains that such manifestations of organization (he calls them "significant design" [38]) work, especially when they concern character, to repress expressions of desire because they correlate the narrative field to a stable representation of the self. Thus he interprets the readability of character in the context of his dissatisfaction with representations of a structured self. "For what we call character," he concludes, "is also a partial self. Its appearance of completeness, of wholeness, may be nothing more than the illusion created by the *centralizing* of a partial self.

[35] Iser, p. 139.

[36] Wolfgang Iser, "The Current Situation of Literary Theory: Key Concepts and the Imaginary," *New Literary History* 11 (1979), 17.

[37] Chatman, p. 21.

[38] Bersani, p. 52.

Such centralization involves both the organization of our desires into psychic structures and the expulsion of nonstructurable desires. Character, in short, is also a piece of a person; it has the factitious coherence of all obsessions."[39] Bersani, in other words, would argue, first, that the degree of coherence I claimed for the reader of *Mrs. Dalloway* depends upon an illusion of centrality asserted by the text itself, which ends up falsifying what the character herself experiences; and second, that the reader should only imagine this illusion of coherence if instructed to do so by the text's explicit narrative "design," its organization of experience as a discourse (here, in Woolf's text, through its style, structure, and viewpoint) advocating psychological coherence.

I find that Bersani's explanation actually confuses the problem of "character" as a "centralized" figure. To begin with, he does not consider the important distinction between character as an object and as a subject of perception, which in the case of *Mrs. Dalloway* allows us to confront the fragmentation of self as a character experiences it and, at the same time, to move beyond what we normally consider to be the psychologically "real" (the self as a single self, as a subject) through the "irrealization" demanded of reading. In fact, this imaginative activity allows us to experience what Cixous, who responds to character much as Bersani does, wants from a radical literature: "space enough for everyone, for each more-than-one, and for each one of me."[40]

In contrast to what I am claiming, Bersani lodges the question of the figure's coherence entirely inside the text's representationality, rather than beyond it, so his reasoning, like Cixous's, only encourages him to read character as a psychological print-out and not as an imaginative configuration produced by the collusion of text and reader to coordinate objective and subjective fields into a virtual existence. Consequently, while he advocates an exciting, subversive "incoherent" literature that deconstructs what he calls realism's production of "readable personality" to expand the scope of character, he treats the reader's role in that production—or, for that matter, in that deconstruction—much too lightly, attributing the pursuit of coherence, as far as the reader is concerned, to previous experiences of realistic fiction, and defining coherence only on psychological grounds: how a text represents consciousness through its characterization of the figure as a stable representation of the self. So however he cuts his cake, Bersani still conceives of the text as a psychological discourse, whereas the interaction between the text and its reader, which actually produces that "appearance of completeness" for character in the reader's imagination, is more complex and versatile than Bersani allows.

What needs to be explained here is the imaginative coherence we as readers strive for while reading character in order to construct the figure as a virtual existent distinct enough from its ground so that it can be experienced as subject and object. "Perception," Rudolf Arnheim explains, "can abstract objects from

<hr>

[39] Bersani, p. 313.

[40] Cixous, p. 402.

their context only because it grasps shape as organized structure, rather than recording it as a mosaic of elements."[41] With this in mind, then, we need to consider the degree to which the text must prompt such abstraction by embedding within its own discourse a reflection of what the reader himself constructs in his imagination.

Stanley Fish goes so far as to dislocate the reader's sense of coherence from the text's discourse entirely: "the place where sense is made or not made," he maintains, "is the reader's mind rather than the printed page or the space between the covers of a book."[42] This is indeed the case, as Iser's model proposes, but we still need to account for the stimulus which encourages the reader to make sense, to abstract shape as an organized structure, or which frustrates his attempt to do so. James Kincaid wonders if we attribute coherence as a principal inseparable from narrative, as Chatman does, because we fear "logical contradiction." To assuage this implicit threat of a text's potential for contradiction, Kincaid believes that we hunt for "organizing patterns." Thus he postulates that a text, far from being a highly patterned or randomly arranged sequence, actually presents its reader with "a structure of mutually competing coherences," which he then tries to sort out, to organize, to totalize or centralize because of the very demands of reading as an act of perception and cognition.[43]

All this may be rather thorny brush to try to part, but once again Iser's model of the reading act may perhaps help clear our way. In addressing the matter of a reader's construction of "totality" from the text's own indeterminacy, Iser delineates two areas of comprehension in the reading process, following Paul Ricoeur to distinguish the enterprise of achieving "meaning" from that of finding "significance." "Meaning," Iser explains, "is the referential totality which is implied by the aspects contained in the text and which must be assembled in the course of reading. Significance is the reader's absorption of the meaning into his own existence. Only the two together can guarantee the effectiveness of an experience which entails the reader constituting himself by constituting a reality hitherto unfamiliar to himself."[44] This distinction points to the reader's need to interpret (to comprehend significance in) the meaning (the assemblage of blanks and negations into a gestalt) which he experiences while reading. Or as Rudolf E. Kuenzli summarizes Iser's intention: "Significance then is the reader's interpretation of his aesthetic experience; he explains the meaning by relating it to familiar codes."[45]

Nevertheless, in conventional use "meaning" and "significance" do not seem to fall into such different streams, however much Iser tries to part the waters; and as Kuenzli notes, since publishing *The Act of Reading* Iser has changed his

---

[41] Rudolf Arnheim, *Visual Thinking* (Berkeley: University of California Press, 1969), p. 41.

[42] Stanley E. Fish, "Literature in the Reader: Affective Stylistics," *New Literary History* 2 (1970); rpt. *Reader-Response Criticism: From Formalism to Post Structuralism*, ed. Jane P. Tompkins (Baltimore: Johns Hopkins, 1980), p. 81.

[43] James R. Kincaid, "Coherent Readers, Incoherent Texts," *Critical Inquiry* 3 (1977), 783.

[44] Iser, *Reading*, p. 151.

[45] Rudolf E. Kuenzli, "The Intersubjective Structure of the Reading Process: A Communication-Oriented Theory of Literature," *Diacritics*, 10 (Summer 1980), 52.

terminology in order to clarify his point: semantic interpretation ("significance" or concretely verbalized meaning) as distinct from imaginative reception (the experience of the text or ideated "meaning" in the sense of perceiving an aesthetic gestalt). In this clearer light, both "meaning" and "significance" as conventional terms address the semantic interpretation of the text. Interpretation necessarily domesticates the more "ultimate" dimension of the "imaginary," the irreal and the non- or pre-verbal dimensions of the text's linguistic codes, which lead us to comprehend a semantic content and then to interpret the import of what we have read to find significant meaning. "Meaning as such," Iser now points out, "is not the ultimate dimension of the literary text, but of literary theory, whose discourse is aimed at making the text translatable into terms of understanding." The reader's act of interpretation strains "to assemble meaning," to coordinate "what is represented and what the representation stands for," in order to heal the unavoidable split between the two by understanding representation *as* semantic content. The reader's act of reception, on the other hand, "is a process of experiencing the imaginative gestalt brought forth by the text."[46] Reception, in other words, leads to the imaginative production of virtual perception, that phenomenological irrealization of the reader's to produce an ideation—the construction of both virtual existence and virtual meaning—of what the text represents verbally—and incompletely—in its own language: "The aesthetic object is produced in the recipient's mind as a correlate of the text, and as such it is open to inspection by acts of comprehension; hence the business of interpretation, which translates the aesthetic object into a concrete meaning."[47]

I want to emphasize Iser's point of contrast between "interpretation" and "reception," because it articulates in critical terminology the distinction I referred to earlier between our sense of character as the representational subject the text means it to be (our interpretation of what the figure represents as a subject) and our sense of what it appears as virtually (our reception, our absorption of the figure as subject-as-object into our own imaginative fields). Character, then, is very much what Bersani says it is, though for different reasons and with different implications: the figure is "a piece of a person" masquerading as "the appearance of completeness" only in that the text stimulates in our imaginations certain impressions of the human figure and persuades us, through its unavoidable indeterminacy, to imagine some kind of coherent package, a gestalt, for these impressions, so that we can, in essence, complete the text by following its coded instructions to construct the virtual existence of the figure; and in doing that, we can experience its fragmentation as a representation, or its stability, or even both.

Consequently, as Kincaid suggests, we do seek implications of coherence while reading the text; but to admit this is not to agree with Bersani that the direction to organize the represented experience into a coherent imaginative gestalt necessarily translates back into a confirmation either of semantic or psycho-

---

[46] Iser, "Current Situation," pp. 17–19.

[47] Iser, "Current Situation," p. 19.

logical intelligibility. In this regard, semantic coherence, achieved through the act of interpretation, requires some kind of violation of the text's inherent richness as a tension between rupture and containment, harmony and discord, whereas imaginative coherence, achieved through the act of reading, allows us to experience both possibilities concurrently. To ask whether we understand the self in *Mrs. Dalloway* as either object or subject so as to decide, once and for all, whether or not there *is* a self in Woolf's fictive world, this question, like the concern with a coherent psychological discourse in general, demands an answer only to stabilize an interpretative choice as an argument about the narrative's content, thereby translating "the aesthetic object into a concrete meaning."

The text itself is actually built out of a potential for semantic incoherence, which can lead to interpretive difference, but which above all else engages the reader in the construction of the work as an imaginative coherence. This activity involves the reader in both imaginative and interpretative acts. The potential breach between these two activities is very much the concern of fiction when its discourse openly frustrates our effort to read character as an intelligible psychological representation. In *The French Lieutenant's Woman*, for example, the text's discourse does not assent to our construction of Sarah Woodruff as a virtual existent in the manner by which Woolf's discourse seems to encourage our reading of Clarissa's figure as subject and object. Indeed, in contrast to Woolf's, Fowles's novel seems to be an active demonstration of Kincaid's claim that texts present their readers with structures of mutually competing coherences. When we turn to Sarah in particular, all our attempts to read her figure as subject-as-object seem to short-circuit if we are not to violate the text's overt declaration of indeterminacy. Sarah's figure ends up seeming as blank a page as Lady Dedlock's, but whereas Dickens's text appears willing to aid our reception by dwelling upon the figure as object and blanking it out as subject, Fowles's text continually negates and reverses the figure as *both* object and subject. Sarah's grounding in indeterminacy therefore appears in a text that seems openly hostile to our receiving her figure at all. We are consistently made to see her in two competing lights, neither one clearly focused, neither one complementing the other, as they do in *Mrs. Dalloway*. At times Sarah emerges in the text as a representation, a figural subject with motives for her behavior and thus a psychological content to which we as readers have access; but at other times she stands out as the text's own invention, a figural object which the narrator manipulates at will in his chess game with the reader. The indeterminacy of Sarah's figure is thus established by the lack of coordination between subject and object in the discourse: the figure is either one or the other at any given moment in the narration, often in a single paragraph. Any attempt to conjoin her figure as both subject and object only seems to instigate more gaps and ruptures, serving to place all responsibility for understanding her behavior (or her moves as a chess piece, queen to our unknowing pawn) onto *our* shoulders.

Sarah's figure seems unreadable, then, because the text's discourse claims to be representational when at the same time it sends us a competing signal to cancel its earlier instruction to centralize her character as a psychological representation. The narrator explains that Sarah "*was* intelligent . . . [able] to classify other people's worth: to understand them, in the fullest sense of the word."[48] Likewise, he informs us about her behavior as the French Lieutenant's Woman, that "she was far less mad than she seemed. . . . Her exhibitions of her shame had a kind of purpose" (pp. 56–57). (And Sarah later confirms this reading when she explains to Charles her motive for making her history public.) Yet all the while he encourages his reader to pursue this line of reception, to understand Sarah as a credible subject, the narrator simultaneously repels such an effort. "Who is Sarah?" he asks. "I do not know. This story I am telling is all my imagination. These characters I create never existed outside my own mind. . . . Modern women like Sarah exist, and I have never understood them" (p. 80). The narrator ends up contradicting himself. After denying any referent for Sarah's figure other than his own imagination (and yet supplying one, too—"modern women"—at the same time), he claims to be unable to penetrate her figure as a subject, whereas previously he has done so. All he can do as her narrator, he explains, is "report" (p. 81), that is, present her as a figural object. But even then he proceeds, not to report, but to penetrate her once again as a figural subject. Why does she emerge from the woods to expose herself? "The reason was simple. She had overslept, and she knew she was late. . . . Also, Charles' down-staring face had shocked her" (p. 83). To make matters even more confusing, in the light of later revelations everything the narrator has so far explained or reported about Sarah seems suspect, since we cannot help inferring from each sudden twist of the plot that her role-playing has always been working to entrap Charles, for whatever reasons she has in mind, and the narration suggests several. Our minds cannot help spinning in the face of such negation and contradiction, as we realize that the text seems unwilling to help us when it comes to interpreting her figure as either a psychological representation or an authorial tool. Nonetheless, our imaginations go to work all the more, since the indeterminacy of the narration only draws us closer to her figure, inviting us—daring us—to imagine her existence as a virtual figure.

Because Sarah's indeterminate figure does seem to frustrate our efforts at both interpretation and reception, it actually stimulates our readerly engagement to make us appreciate how the text does work to center, not our interpretation, but our reception of her figure. The difficulty we face in reading Sarah arises only if we assume that interpretation and reception, representation and imagination, work together here, as they do in *Bleak House* or *Mrs. Dalloway*. This is the readerly expectation that Fowles's text evokes through its many allusions to traditional fiction and then cancels out to seem hostile to our efforts at reception. Part of what we must experience as readers in order to construct Sarah's virtual existence is her very lack of focus as an instrument of representation and, hence, of interpretation.

As a result, even though the narrator's discourse retreats as much as it ad-

---

[48] John Fowles, *The French Lieutenant's Woman* (New York: New American Library, 1970), p. 47. Further page references will be included in my text.

vances every time he tries to get a fix on Sarah, the text does signal an instruction for our construction of her figure as a virtual existent. The narrator himself,
remember, says that "Modern women like Sarah exist, and I have never understood them." Her essential mystery, her inability to be understood, undermines
her as a representation with a stable psychological content, but it also provides
the clue to her identity as a virtual existent. For by the same token, the narrator's
confession that he can indeed *imagine* her and *create* her without understanding
her suggests that we can well do the same, though we must construct her on her
own terms: "I am not to be understood even by myself" (p. 354).

We can therefore find a point of centrality for Sarah's figure that can accommodate the text's indeterminacy without having to make it a determinate content. That is, the more opaque Sarah becomes in the text as an unreadable psychological content, the more determinate her figure becomes in our imaginative
fields so long as we construct her virtual existence according to the dimensions
of mystery she herself continually establishes by virtue of her indeterminacy as a
subject. These dimensions do set her apart from the narrative ground because
her figure deflects penetration by that ground. Through her opacity Sarah
emerges in our minds as a figural object which we try to imagine as a figural
subject, first by pursuing her motives, perhaps, but ultimately by reversing the
procedure I outlined in *Mrs. Dalloway* to construct her figure as object-as-
subject. By concentrating on her inherent opacity as an object we confront and
absorb her inescapable mystery as subject.

When Sarah smiles at Charles, for instance, we get a clue for such figural construction from the text. To Charles her smile becomes a "revelation of her humor, that her sadness was not total. And in those wide eyes, so somber, sad and
direct, was revealed an irony, a new dimension of herself" (p. 150). This new
dimension, I want to stress, is non-verbal, even in the features being described;
it emerges from a facial gesture, so it resists semantic translation, although
Charles himself tries to interpret it. By understanding her humor as an alternative to her sadness, he wants to coordinate this new view of her to his previous view, but he does so in terms of her local history, The French Lieutenant's
Woman, for that is the only way he knows how to read her. The narration denies
for us that type of reading, since it makes her history too indeterminate to understand unless we engage in an act of interpretation ourselves, which requires us
to select one pattern of coherence from the many that compete for our attention.

By so frustrating our initial attempts to construct Sarah as a representation of
an intelligible personality, the text actually highlights for us the importance of
her ironic look, which is a mode of expression, particularly in the specific instance I just cited, that works by indirection, by meaning what it cannot say to
remain beyond our ken semantically. Sarah is, finally, unintelligible in that her
figural content is imaginative, not semantic, so it always seems able to repel any
attempt to understand it fully through the discourse of representation and interpretation, the conventional mode of narration. But if we receive her imaginatively as a figure who is not to be understood in the conventional manner by
which novelistic characters are assumed to be understood, then she does project

a virtual existence. As we construct her figure, she then begins to centralize for our readerly space the mystery and tension that the narration itself articulates through its indeterminate discourse about her. Whether viewed as Victorian woman, modern woman, or the text's invention, Sarah's figure works upon us to imagine, and consequently to experience in our own space, the energy of desire (fiction) subverting the restraints of culture (determinate form). This imaginative content the discourse can only render incompletely through its language; and the text's own indeterminacy embodies the inability of discourse to achieve its end, semantic content, without first domesticating its imaginative content through an act of interpretation.

With Sarah we come back full circle to the Widow Wadman and Tristram's two blank pages. Like Sterne's novel, *The French Lieutenant's Woman* orchestrates the negations and blanks in its discourse to increase our self-consciousness of the reading act itself. The textual discourse explaining the representational figure is no more than an unactualized field of imaginative existence for that figure. What the text actually does is to present its reader with discourse, relying on him to use it to construct the figure as a virtual existent with an imaginary content. So when we read we do need some encoded direction, however enigmatic, some encouragement, however devious, from the text to learn how it informs its discourse with the potential for stimulating in our imaginations a perception of the figure as distinct from its narrative ground. Fowles's text works through its competing instructions about Sarah's character as a representation to make us aware of our very need to centralize what we receive from a text through both interpretative and imaginative acts; and, like Tristram's two blank pages, it intensifies our realization that such activities take place in our space alone, not in the text's, even though more straight-forward, representational novels may claim otherwise when they work to superimpose their own textual space onto their reader's imaginative space.

Character is readable, Sarah being no exception, when it helps stimulate our construction of that imaginative space in our minds as we read. Character, after all, only creates the illusion of being a reference to the real world. In truth, the figure is an imaginative construction, a virtual existent that leads us beyond a concern with psychological intelligibility, with the figure's semantic content. Our construction of the figure, like the text's encoded directions, may build out of referential material, just as it builds out of discourse; but it always pushes us beyond the text into an imaginative space located in our own heads. The act of interpretation effects to bridge our way back into the text, or even outward to the real world, in order to account for our reception, to explain its import, and, most of all, to communicate to other readers what we have experienced while reading.

While we should not minimize this activity, we should also put it into perspective, for it necessarily conceives of character's readability in the light of semantic coherence. Our reception of the figure may encourage that semantic translation, it may not. In any event, the act of reading itself, if understood as an imaginative rather than an interpretative activity, does not require, finally, that we coordinate what we receive to what the text represents in order to achieve a coherent semantic content. In fact, as Iser explains, any text must produce some semantic rupture, some discordance, for it to be received imaginatively. This is particularly important when it comes to reading character. Our construction depends, not on psychological delineation as the primary impetus, but on our absorbing the figure into that space beyond the text, where it can be transformed from a series of linguistic signals and semantic referents into a virtual existent. This capacity for transformation is what draws us towards novels, and makes us focus our attention on their characters, in the first place.

III
✛ ✛ ✛
The Conference

Why the Novel Matters:
A Postmodern Perplex

THE EDITORS

Late in April 1987 our still thriving journal celebrated its twentieth anniversary with a three-day conference on "Why the Novel Matters: A Postmodern Perplex." Held at Brown University, funded by a grant from the National Endowment for the Humanities, by Marshall Woods and Wetmore lectureships from Brown, and by modest contributions from local departments and from NOVEL itself, the conference featured twenty-one speakers and panelists from England, South Africa, and Canada as well as the United States plus a dozen guest respondents from a wide range of American universities. A keynote speech, four panels, and a reading were held on the first day of the conference; three panels and a reading on the second day; and a windup discussion between presenting and responding participants on the third. One panel session, on "The Novel as Prophetic Mode," featuring Nadine Gordimer and Paule Marshall answering prepared questions, proved unretrievable through mechanical failure—*i.e.*, tape recorders that picked up only a blurred rendition of their impromptu remarks. What follows, in this conference issue, is a collection of revised and amended papers from the six remaining panels, plus the keynote speech and two of the more spirited discussions.

Meanwhile more words of explanation seem in order. The main conference title, "Why the Novel Matters," came initially from a famous 1920s essay by D. H. Lawrence in which the novel figures as "the one bright book of life." In Spring 1985 the journal launched a new series under Lawrence's rubric, "Why the Novel Matters," beginning with an MLA Colloquium (December 1984) originally entitled "Still Towards a Poetics of Fiction?" after our own earlier series (1967–76) called "Towards a Poetics of Fiction." For polemical purposes which bear on the conference we retitled that Colloquium "Still Towards a Humanist Poetics?" At stake in our retitling was the question of bridging the differences between old humanist approaches to fiction, which NOVEL itself had advanced during the first decade of its publication through the "Poetics" series and others like it, and the new semiotic and poststructural approaches that have more or less taken over the field of fiction theory in the last decade–approaches which are often deliberately anti-humanistic and/or anti-aesthetic in nature, and which accordingly raise the question as to why novels matter if they are no longer seen as performing their traditional moral, social, and aesthetic functions.

This is in brief the postmodern perplex–we continue to study novels in literature departments, using old and new approaches, but the evaluative bases on which we proceed are very much in question. As with other literary works, novels are now seen by many theorists as intertextual documents of no special "privilege" or merit and are often approached negatively as culturally coded texts of dubious merit indeed. On the other hand they are no longer sacralized as "verbal icons" and are forced to compete for attention on a more democratic basis with other cultural texts, whose languages they often reflect. What D. H. Lawrence once called "the one bright book of life" has become a dimmer affair in our time, though we continue to deal with it as if our academic lives still depend upon its brightness. Our journal was in fact established with that vital dependence in mind as a humanistic and not merely a vocational condition, and our "bridging" conference proceeded also from that vital assumption.

We began to raise these issues at our tenth anniversary conference, back in April 1977, when the terms of conflict were still unclear. Our panel discussions were then addressed to such conflictual topics as the new structuralism versus the old formalism and the new reader psychologies versus the old interpretive study of verbal icons. Ten years later, much older and a trifle wiser, we saw no point in head-on confrontations that often generate more heat than light. We proposed instead to focus on assumptions about the nature of the novel, what it is customarily credited with doing, and to engage our different approaches, old and new, in determining how those assumptions were in question. By examining the premises of the novel, its traditional sources of meaning and function, we hoped to address the genre itself and to direct our various approaches toward issues rather than warring theories. In this way, with any luck, we might well find bridges between our approaches that have so far gone unnoticed or unbuilt.

It may be that the great value of the conference was to articulate the fact that bridges are a-building, that in modest and sophisticated ways new and old theories are adapting to each other, that a subtle yet demonstrably synthetic process is under way. Certainly the papers offered by Professors Lodge, Spacks, Scholes, Levine, Suleiman and Ermarth were marked by an accommodating sympathy, or by an openness to dialogue, that seems promising and refreshing; and though others were confrontational—*e.g.*, those by Professors Gold, Miller, and Schwarz—still others were receptive and often positively engaged. All of which jibes with our own observation, over the last decade, of a marked change in types of critical contributions to our journal, a blending of old and new views that has not been publicly assessed and amplified; and with our own impulse, as *a forum on fiction,* to sort out and clarify such practices, as with our past treatment of the feisty trends in humanistic theory in the 1960s and 1970s. So too our new series and our recent conference were designed to sort out and clarify the confused amalgam of blending and conflictual theories in the 1980s.

Whether they have succeeded in that aim, or will succeed, is another matter. The conference itself, though exhilarating and enjoyable, was neither blandly harmonious nor ideally conceived. Our basic premises as to the existence of a conflict in the academies between humanist and anti-humanist approaches to fiction, and to the applicability of traditional assumptions about the nature and function of the novel, were sharply questioned. Even our desire to go beyond traditional categories was thwarted when three panel departures from that scheme—the novel as carnivalistic dialogue à la Bakhtin, the novel as cosmic outlook à la García Márquez, the novel as contemporary perplex à la Newman—had to be collapsed for lack of funds and/or the right participants. But the conference did take place, the dialogue did begin, and the results are herewith presented as a step, however tentative, toward determining how fiction will be taught and assessed over the remaining years in this century.

Keynote Address

Keynote speaker David Lodge was introduced by Novel*'s chief editor, Mark Spilka, who knew him when–when being 1964 when Professor Lodge first came to Brown for a sabbatical semester before leaving for further academic adventures on the west coast, there and perhaps here also to meet with prototypes for the infamous Morris Zapp, his American counterpart and a prominent figure in both* Changing Places *(1975) and* Small World *(1984), two of novelist Lodge's most famous comic romances. As Professor Lodge also reminded us, it was then that he had sat in on discussions leading to the founding of* Novel*, for which he has served for many years as an advisory British editor. Fellow founder and present American editor Spilka had meanwhile launched the conference by characterizing it as one "that dares to ask the question as to why the novel matters, and to pose that question as a postmodern perplex":*

> We live in a time when the novel, like other literary forms, seems to have lost something of its former glory, its moral and aesthetic functions, particularly; at a time also when works have lost their former status as literary icons and are often seen as texts, or as intertextual or coded or loaded documents with dubious cultural effects. It's a time too of resisting readers and of seekers after textual powers by which to counter the ill effects of these seemingly dangerous fictions, as of course they are and always have been. It is also ... an exciting time, a time when new theories abound and therefore a time much in keeping with the journal's subtitle, "A Forum on Fiction"– a time then to discuss approaches old and new as they apply to traditional functions of the novel, so that differences might be defined and if possible bridges built between them, a time then for sorting things out, for building bridges, or for seeing if after all such bridges are actually in the process of being built even as we speak....

After striking the official conference keynote in this fulsome manner, Spilka had then introduced Lodge by way of his own fictive view of the essence of all such ventures:

> There is a moment toward the end of Professor Lodge's recent academic romance called *Small World* in which the questing hero attends an MLA panel in New York on the function of criticism and poses an unusual question to each of the warring panelists, ... namely, "What follows if everybody agrees with you? What do you do if everybody agrees with you?" When none of the panelists seems able to field that question, the moderator leans forward with a helpful gloss: "You imply," he says, "... that what matters in the field of critical practice is not truth but difference. If everybody were convinced by your arguments they would have to do the same as you, and then there would be no satisfaction in doing it. To win is to lose the game. Am I right?"

Although our hero neither accepts nor refuses this tribute to literary one-upmanship as our common motive, the driving force behind our differences–perhaps one can also see a Trillingesque tribute here to our own "variety and recalcitrance"–his question does in fact evoke a rather mellow atmosphere in which it seems possible to preserve those saving differences while at the same time creating modifying dialogues between them–which is to us the best formula we've ever seen for a good literary conference. This is at any rate the best reason we at Novel have ... for asking David to be our keynote speaker. He seems to us, that is, a moderator of saving differences. . . .

The speaker then went on to delineate and praise Lodge's dual role as critic and novelist, "his ability to write mellow satires and romances, which like Small World *are themselves a kind of gloss on contemporary theories and practices, and his ability to discuss, assemble, and contribute to those theories and practices with his own critical texts."*

The Novel Now:
Theories and Practices

DAVID LODGE

When the journal Novel was founded some twenty years ago, the relationship between fiction and criticism was comparatively unproblematical. Criticism was conceived of as a second-order discourse dependent on the first-order discourse of fiction. Novelists wrote novels and critics criticized them. This latter activity was usually described as a combination of description, interpretation, and evaluation of texts, with different schools striking a different balance between the terms of this formula. The function of theory was to provide a more and more comprehensive and refined methodology for carrying out this work, and in the mid-1960s in England and America this task was seen as very much a matter of bringing novel criticism up to a level of formal sophistication comparable to that achieved by the New Criticism in relation to poetry.

This critical activity also had an ideological function, seldom overtly acknowledged, namely, the maintenance of a canon. The storehouse of fiction has many floors, but it is shaped like a ziggurat, or pyramid. There is a lot of space on the ground floor for contemporary work, but much of it is speedily dumped in the trash cans outside the back door, without ever having been shelved upstairs in the storeys reserved for "serious" writing. As authors are

promoted higher and higher up the scale of value, and recede into the historical past, their number becomes fewer and fewer, the accommodation for
them more limited. The top floor, reserved for the classics, is very small indeed. The English Victorian novel, for instance, is represented by the work of
perhaps a dozen novelists, out of the thousand or more who actually wrote
novels in that period. This is inevitable: the collective consciousness can store
only a finite number of texts; when one is added, another must drop out to
make room for it.

The higher you go up the storeys of the ziggurat, the more evident it is
that the process of selection and exclusion is controlled by academic critics,
rather than by reviewers, literary journalists and writers themselves. This is
because the academic study of literature depends crucially on the existence of
a canon. Without a common body of texts to refer to and compare the subject
would become impossible to teach or learn. Teachers who set out to subvert
the idea of the literary canon are obliged to provide an alternative one,
usually of theoretical texts. And if critics need a canon, novelists need a tradition. You cannot begin to write novels without having read at least one, and
probably hundreds; without defining yourself in relationships of apprentice-
ship, discipleship, rivalry, antagonism with precursors and peers. Sometimes,
for instance in the hey-day of Modernism, a re-alignment of writers in
relation to tradition is carried over into a revision of the academic canon,
which in turn affects the reading of the next generation of aspirant writers.
The comparative rarity of such cross-fertilization in today's literary culture is
one of its more worrisome symptoms.

I.

The traditional model of the relationship between fiction and criticism is not,
then, entirely disinterested. It privileges the novelist in the sense that he or
she is seen as the creative source without whom the critic would have
nothing to criticize, but it is used to police the work of contemporary writing
in a way that can be oppressive. It is an author-centered model–the history of
the English or American novel is seen as the story of exceptionally gifted
writers who handed on the great tradition of fiction, each adding some distinctive contribution of their own. But it is also self-centered, since the
process of sifting and evaluating and interpreting the classic or potentially
classic texts serves the purpose of the academic institution. Academic critics
have great respect for the canonical novelists, but not much for novelists who
don't seem to be interested in getting into the canon. One gets the
impression from a good deal of traditional academic criticism, certainly that
associated with the name of F.R. Leavis, that it is a finer thing to be a critic
working on a major novelist than to be oneself a good minor novelist. This is
not generally true of reviewers, who are more generous in their reception of
new fiction. Indeed, one of the functions academic critics have often seen
themselves as performing is to counteract the inflated currency of journalistic

reviewing. But both kinds of critic have, until recently, shared the same implied aesthetic, which a contemporary academic theorist, Catherine Belsey, has labelled "expressive realism."[1] That is to say, they have interpreted and evaluated novels as more or less powerful expressions of a unique sensibility or world-view–the author's–and as more or less truthful representations of reality.

This traditional, or as it is sometimes called, humanist model of the relationship between fiction and criticism is still widely subscribed to. However, in the last twenty years or so it has sustained a number of attacks from within the academic institution as the latter has become increasingly dominated by structuralist and poststructuralist theory. The effect has been to throw academic literary studies into a state of exciting intellectual ferment or terminal crisis, according to your point of view. But as far as I can see it has had little effect on the ground floor of the ziggurat, that is to say on the reception of new writing, at least in England and America. Whether it has had any effect on novelists themselves, and whether such an effect is or might be either liberating or inhibiting are questions that we might discuss in the course of this conference.

It all started, of course, with the impact of structuralism on literary criticism in the 1960s. In its classic form, structuralism seeks to understand culture in terms of the systems of signification that underlie it: the emphasis is on the system, not individual realizations of the system. In this respect it modelled itself on the linguistics of Saussure, who maintained that linguistic science should concern itself with the finite system of *langue*, not the infinite variety of *parole*. Another of Saussure's seminal ideas, much misunderstood, and often vulgarized, was that the relationship between the two aspects of the verbal sign, the signifier and the signified, is arbitrary. It is not the relationship between words and things that allows language to signify, but the differences between elements of the linguistic system. Language, in the famous phrase, is a system of differences.

It is easy to see why this way of thinking, when applied to literature, diverted attention away from what was unique to texts and towards what they have in common: codes, conventions, rules; why it reduced the originating power of the author, and elevated the importance of the reader, in the production of meaning; why it subverted the privileged status of the literary canon, since the beauty of semiotic systems could be demonstrated as well, or better, by reference to anonymous folk tales and myths, or the products of popular culture like thrillers, advertising and fashion; why it subverted the notion of realism, exposing it as an art of bad faith because it seeks to disguise or deny its own conventionality. In short, although structuralism in its classical form was a rather conservative methodology, seeking to interpret rather than change the world (to invoke Marx's formula), it was capable of being co-opted, in the revolutionary atmosphere of the 1960s, to a radical intellectual critique of traditional humanistic ideas about literature and culture.

---

[1] Catherine Belsey, *Critical Practice* (London: Methuen, 1980), p. 7 ff.

At the time there *was* some creative interaction between the new structuralist-influenced criticism and the production and reception of new writing. In France the *nouvelle critique* provided a basis for defending and interpreting the *nouveau roman*. In America and to a lesser extent in Britain, various kinds of postmodernist experiments in fiction seemed to derive from or at least could be explained in terms of the new critical attacks upon realism. But, as structuralism pursued its own premises and problematics into a second phase of debate and speculation generally called "poststructuralism," it became more and more scholastic, esoteric and inward-looking in its concerns, and had less and less to do with the encouragement or criticism of new imaginative writing–unless you regard it as a form of avant-garde literature in its own right. The tendency of poststructuralist theory has certainly been to abolish the conceptual boundary between creative and critical discourse which was one of the basic assumptions of the traditional humanist model. The most influential figures in this poststructuralist phase–Lacan, Derrida, Althusser, Foucault–were not literary critics by discipline. And although their theories have had a profound effect upon academic literary studies, it is not one which, at first glance, seems likely to inspire or encourage the writer who practices his art outside the academy.

Unfortunately, this discourse is so opaque and technical in its language that the first glance–baffled, angry, or derisive–is likely to be the last one. One unhappy consequence of recent developments has certainly been the loss of a common language of critical discourse which used to be shared between academic critics, practicing writers, literary journalists and the educated common reader. Thirty or forty years ago, a reader of the book pages of the London *Observer* or the *New York Times Book Review* could pick up a copy of *Scrutiny* or the *Sewanee Review* and be able to take an intelligent interest in most of what he found in those university-based journals. If such a reader were to pick up their equivalents today–*Critical Inquiry*, say, or the *Oxford Review*–he would in all probability be totally baffled and bewildered, unable to make any sense at all of what purports to be literary criticism. Nor would he find there much comment on contemporary imaginative writing. Critics these days are too busy keeping up with each other's work.

Perhaps this discontinuity between the most advanced and innovative discourse about literature and the production and reception of new writing matters more to someone like me, who has a foot in both worlds, than it does to writers who have no connection with the academic world and are free to ignore its abstruse debates, or to academics who take for granted that the high ground of aesthetics will always be accessible only to a small minority. But I can't believe that this is a healthy situation, and I do believe that contemporary theory has something useful and important to say about what Poe called the philosophy of composition, alien as it may seem to the creative writer at first sight.

Let me try and illustrate the point by citing two statements by two eminent modern theorists, Roland Barthes and Paul de Man, on two issues, the idea of the author, and the relationship between fiction and reality, which have been central both to the practice of fiction writing and the reception and criticism of fiction in modern culture. The idea of the author as a uniquely constituted individual subject, the originator and in some sense owner of his work, is deeply implicated in the novel as a literary form and historically coincident with the rise of the novel; so is an emphasis on the mimetic function of verbal art, its ability to reflect or represent the world truthfully and in detail. Both these principles are called into question in the statements I wish to cite.

The first is from Roland Barthes' essay, "The Death of the Author" (1968). He seeks to replace "author" with the term "scriptor":

> *The Author, when believed in, is always conceived of as the past of his own book: book and author stand automatically on a single line divided into a* before *and an* after. *The Author is thought to* nourish *the book, which is to say that he exists before it, thinks, suffers, lives for it, is in the same relation of antecedence to his work as a father to his child. In complete contrast, the modern scriptor is born simultaneously with the text, is in no way equipped with a being preceding or exceeding the writing, is not the subject with the book as predicate; there is no other time than that of the enunciation and every text is eternally written* here and now. . . .
>
> *We know now that a text is not a line of words releasing a single "theological" meaning (the "message" of the Author-God) but a multidimensional space in which a variety of writings, none of them original, blend and clash.*[2]

The second quotation is from Paul de Man's essay, "Criticism and Crisis," in *Blindness and Insight* (1971):

> *That sign and meaning can never coincide is what is precisely taken for granted in the kind of language we call literary. Literature, unlike everyday language, begins on the far side of this knowledge; it is the only form of language free from the fallacy of unmediated expression. . . . The self-reflecting mirror effect by means of which a work of fiction asserts, by its very existence, its separation from empirical reality, its divergence, as a sign, from a meaning that depends for its existence on the constitutive activity of this sign, characterises the work of literature in its essence. It is always against the explicit assertion of the writer that readers degrade the fiction by confusing it with a reality from which it has forever taken leave.*[3]

Now my first reaction as a novelist is to contest these remarks—to say to Barthes that I *do* feel a kind of parental responsibility for the novels I write, that the composition of them *is*, in an important sense, my past, that I do think, suffer, live for a book while it is in progress; and to say to de Man that

[2] Roland Barthes, *Image–Music–Text* (London: Fontana, 1977), pp. 145–46.

[3] Paul de Man, *Blindness and Insight* (London: Methuen, 1983), p. 17.

my fiction has not "for ever taken leave of reality" but is in some significant sense a representation of the real world, and that if my readers did not recognise in my novels some truths about the real behavior of, say, academics or Roman Catholics, I should feel I had failed, and so would my readers.

Certainly the way in which fiction is produced and circulated and received in our culture is totally at odds with the assertions of Barthes and de Man. The reception of new writing has in fact probably never been more obsessively author-centered than it is today, not only in reviewing, but in supplementary forms of exposure through the media—interviews and profiles in the press and on TV, prizes, public readings and book launches and so on. All this attention is focussed on the author as a unique creative self, the mysterious, glamorous origin of the text; and the questions one is asked on these occasions invariably emphasize the mimetic connection between fiction and reality which de Man denies exists: What is your book *about*? Is it autobiographical? Is such and such a character based on a real person? Do academics/Catholics really behave like that? and so on. Let it not be supposed that such questions come only from naive or uneducated readers. Some of the most committed poststructuralists among my acquaintances are also the most determined to read my novels as *romans à clef*.

I suppose all of us who are novelists here have had this experience, and found it an uncomfortable one. Then the extreme formulations of Barthes and de Man about the impersonality and fictiveness of literary discourse begin to look rather attractive, and one may appeal to something like them in order to discourage a reductively empiricist reading of one's work. For what is objectionable about such a reading is that it seems to treat the text as a sign of something more concrete, more authentic, more real, which the writer could, if he or she cared to, hand over in its raw and naked truth. Even much more sophisticated criticism based on the same assumptions can seem oppressive to the author, delving into the biographical origins of one's fiction, seeking to establish a perfect fit between the novelist's personal identity and his *oeuvre*. Graham Greene has a nice passage in *Ways of Escape* where he says that there comes a time when the established writer

> is more afraid to read his favourable critics than his unfavourable, for with terrible patience they unroll before his eyes the unchanging pattern of the carpet. If he has depended a great deal on his unconscious, and his ability to forget even his own books when they are once on the public shelves, his critics remind him—this theme originated ten years ago, that simile which came so unthinkingly to his pen a few weeks back was used nearly twenty years ago. . . . [4]

Greene's insistence on the need of the novelist to forget his own books, and in a sense his own past, sounds surprisingly close to Barthes' concept of the modern scriptor who only exists at the moment of composition. But in the

---

[4] Graham Greene, *Ways of Escape* (London: The Bodley Head, 1980), p. 134.

same book Greene claims a documentary truthfulness for his fiction that neither Barthes nor de Man would allow:

> *Some critics have referred to a strange violent "seedy" region of the mind . . .*
> *which they call Greeneland, and I have sometimes wondered whether they go*
> *round the world blinkered. "This is Indo-China," I want to exclaim, "this is*
> *Mexico, this is Sierra Leone carefully and accurately described."*[5]

The closer we come to the actual experience of writing, the more we encounter paradox and contradiction. Are books made out of the writer's observation
and experience, or out of other books? Does the writer write his novel or
does the novel "write" the writer? Is the implied author of a novel–the creative mind to whom we attribute its existence, and whom we praise or blame
for its successes and failures–the "same" as the actual historical individual
who sat at his desk and wrote it, and who has his own life before and after
that activity, or an identity who exists only at the moment of composition?
Can a novel be "true to life" or does it merely create a "reality effect"? Is reality itself such an effect? Is the absence of the writer from his own text that
which spurs him to refine and polish his language so that his meaning will be
effectively communicated without the supplementary aids of voice, gesture,
physical presence, *etc.*, which assist communication in ordinary speech? Or is
the association of meaning with presence a fallacy which writing, through its
inherent ambiguity and openness to a variety of interpretations, helps to expose?

Structuralists and poststructuralists will give one set of answers to these
questions and humanist or expressive realist critics another set. Most writers,
I suspect–certainly I myself–would be inclined to say in each case, "Yes and
no," or "both alternatives are true." But the expressive realist theses (that
novels arise out of their authors' experience and observation of life, that they
are works of verbal mimesis, and so on) are based on common-sense, the
grounds for believing them are self-evident. The grounds for believing the antithetical propositions are not self-evident, and the value of contemporary literary theory may be that by articulating them it prevents–or would prevent if
it were more accessible–the total dominance of our literary culture by expressive realism.

It is not fortuitous, I think, that the anxieties generated by modern critical
theory weigh more heavily, or press more sharply, upon writers and critics of
prose fiction than upon poets and dramatists and their critics. The novel came
into existence under the sign of contradiction, as Lennard J. Davis has argued
in his stimulating book, *Factual Fictions: the origins of the English novel.*[6] It
emerged, he argued, from a new kind of writing which he calls "news/novels
discourse," the earliest manifestations of that journalistic, documentary reporting of recent or current events which we take for granted in the modern

---

[5] Greene, p. 77.

[6] Lennard J. Davis, *Factual Fictions: the origins of the English novel* (New York: Columbia University Press, 1983), p. 42 ff.

era, but which was virtually unknown before the Renaissance because it depended upon the invention of the printing press. As Davis points out (he is
not of course the first to do so, but he gets more mileage out of the idea than
earlier critics), most of the early English novelists had close connections with
the world of printing and/or journalism, and framed their fictitious narratives
with avowals that these were factual documents (letters, confessions *etc.*) of
which they were merely the editors. Novelists perceived that by imitating the
form of documentary or historical writing they could exert an exciting new
power over their readers, obtaining total faith in the reality of fictitious characters and events. (There was no way, Davis plausibly argues, by which an
eighteenth-century reader could be sure whether *Robinson Crusoe* or *Pamela*
were true stories or not.) By the same means they threw a defensive smoke
screen around the contradictory demands made upon them as storytellers–on
the one hand the traditional aesthetic imperative that literature should embody general truths about human nature, and on the other hand the audience's appetite for the truth-is-stranger-than-fiction particularity of journalistic
reportage.

Like Ian Watt's, Davis's theory of the rise of the novel applies more obviously to Defoe and Richardson than it does to Fielding, who mocked the
technique of pseudo-documentary reporting in *Shamela* and *Joseph Andrews*.
But Davis points out that Fielding was a journalist before he was a novelist
and that he integrated the facts of a real historical event (the Jacobite Rising
of 1745) into his fictional *History of Tom Jones* with unprecedented care and attention to detail. He was also attacked (ironically enough by Richardson
among others) for basing his characters transparently upon real people.

Davis's thesis may be overstated, but he is certainly on to something. The
ambivalent and sometimes contradictory relationship between fact and fiction
in the early novel persists into its classic and modern phases. Think for instance of Dickens's Preface to *Bleak House*, where he insists that "everything
set forth in these pages concerning the Court of Chancery is substantially true
and within the truth," and assures his readers that there are "about thirty
cases on record" of spontaneous combustion, while at the same time saying,
"I have purposely dwelt on the romantic side of familiar things." Or consider
the work of James Joyce. Almost every incident and character in his novels
and stories can be traced back to some fact of his own life and experience,
and he boasted that if the city of Dublin were to be destroyed it could be reconstructed from his books, yet at the same time he made large implicit and
explicit claims for the timeless and universal significance of those narratives.
Novelists are and always have been split between, on the one hand, the desire to claim an imaginative and representative truth for their stories, and on
the other the wish to guarantee and defend that truth-claim by reference to
empirical facts: a contradiction they seek to disguise by elaborate mystifica-
tions and metafictional ploys such as framing narratives, parody and other
kinds of intertextuality and self-reflexivity or what the Russian Formalists
called "baring of the device." These ploys are not, as is sometimes thought,
absent from the classic realist novel–one finds examples in for instance, *The*

Heart of Midlothian, Northanger Abbey and *Vanity Fair;* but they do seem to be particularly marked in contemporary fiction, as if in response to or defense against the epistemological skepticism of contemporary critical theory.

I recently taught, at the University of Birmingham in England, a short course on contemporary British fiction. Taking Kingsley Amis's *Lucky Jim* as a benchmark to represent the kind of social realism typical of British fiction in the fifties, I selected seven texts to illustrate subsequent developments: *A Clockwork Orange* by Anthony Burgess, *The French Lieutenant's Woman* by John Fowles, *Not to Disturb* by Muriel Spark, *Briefing for a Descent into Hell* by Doris Lessing, *The White Hotel* by D. M. Thomas, *The History Man* by Malcolm Bradbury, and *Money* by Martin Amis. Five of these texts introduce their author, or a thinly disguised surrogate for him or her, into the text itself in order to raise questions about the ethics and aesthetics of the novel form; and the other two (the Lessing and the Thomas) incorporate documentary sources into their fictional stories in ways which transgress the conventional distinction between factual and fictional narrative. Martin Amis actually has his hero, or anti-hero, who is called John Self meet *him*self, that is to say, a character called Martin Amis, a novelist. John Self asks the question that everybody asks novelists. "'Hey,' I said, 'When you [write], do you sort of make it up, or is it just, you know, like what happens?'" The Martin Amis character answers: "'Neither.'"[7]

In the passage I quoted earlier, Paul de Man referred to "the self-reflecting mirror-effect by means of which a work of fiction asserts, by its very existence, its separation from empirical reality, its divergence as a sign from a meaning that depends for its existence on the constitutive activity of [that] sign." What is self-evident to the deconstructionist critic is, in fact, by no means obvious to the average novel reader. But by arranging an encounter—indeed, several encounters—between himself and his character within the story he is writing, Martin Amis makes that "self-reflecting mirror effect" concrete and explicit. So do, in different ways, the other writers I mentioned.

I do not mean to suggest that such metafictional devices are mandatory for the contemporary novelist. The vitality and viability of the realist tradition in fiction continues to surprise those who have pronounced obsequies over it. The work of Raymond Carver is one example that comes to mind. Another is the work of Nadine Gordimer, who honors this conference with her presence. Indeed it would be false to oppose metafiction to realism; rather, metafiction makes explicit the implicit problematic of realism. The foregrounding of the act of authorship within the boundaries of the text which is such a common feature of contemporary fiction, is a defensive response, either conscious or intuitive, to the questioning of the idea of the author and of the mimetic function of fiction by modern critical theory.

Having mentioned Lennard Davis's *Factual Fictions,* I must take note of his latest book, *Resisting Novels,* which articulates a critique of the traditional humanist conception of the novel that comes from the ideological rather than

---

[7] Martin Amis, *Money* (Harmondsworth: Penguin, 1985), pp. 87–88.

the semiotic wing of poststructuralist theory. The book is in a sense the confessions of a justified sinner. Davis writes as a long-term addict of fiction who
has come to the conclusion that novel reading is bad for us. "We can no
longer smugly think of the novel as the culmination of the human spirit or
the height of mimetic accomplishment," he says.[8] "Novels are not life, their
situation of telling their stories is alienated from lived experience, their subject matter is heavily oriented towards the ideological, and their function is to
help humans adapt to the fragmentation and isolation of the modern world"
(12). "Novel reading as a social behaviour helps prevent change" (17).

What Davis does is to draw out the ideological implications of the formal
conventions of the novel. The novelistic handling of space encouraged the fetishization of objects and personal property. The complexity of characters in
the classic novel is actually an illusion made possible by the very *few* traits of
which they are composed and the codes of consistency and relevancy which
bind them together. This novelistic concept of character has the ideological
function of reconciling us to the alienation of modern existence. The novel
cannot deal easily with group action, on which political change depends–or
even group discussion. Dialogue in novels bears very little resemblance to
real speech not only because it is grammatically well-formed but because it
lacks the negotiated turn-taking of real conversation. And so on.

Davis's polemic in many ways resembles the critique of the classic realist
text initiated by Roland Barthes and carried on by British critics of a left-wing
political persuasion, for example Terry Eagleton, Catherine Belsey and Colin
MacCabe. But whereas these critics usually bring forward the modernist or
postmodernist text as a kind of fiction which avoids complicity with the ideology of bourgeois capitalism, Davis will make no such exceptions. His comment on modern fiction is that "change is now removed even from the realm
of the personal and psychological, as it had already been from the historical.
Change becomes valenced by purely aesthetic categories–an aestheticism approved and promulgated by much of modern criticism" (221).

I have dwelt on Davis's book because it expresses a view antithetical to
that put forward by D. H. Lawrence in the essay whose title flies like a ban-
ner over our conference: "Why the Novel Matters." To Lawrence the novel
mattered because of all forms of human discourse and cognition it was the
only one which could embrace the totality of human experience, the whole of
man alive:

> . . . *being a novelist, I consider myself superior to the saint, the scientist, the
> philosopher, and the poet, who are all great masters of different bits of man
> alive, but never get the whole hog.*
>
> *The novel is the one bright book of life. Books are not life. They are only tre-
> mulations on the ether. But the novel as a tremulation can make the whole man
> alive tremble. Which is more than poetry, philosophy, science, or any other book-
> tremulation can do.*[9]

[8] Lennard J. Davis, *Resisting Novels: Ideology and Fiction* (New York: Methuen, 1987), p. 5. Subsequent page references are
given in parentheses.

Notice that Lawrence emphasizes that "books are not life." This is something Davis cannot forgive them for. He yearns nostalgically for a more primitive or organic culture in which narrative was not commodified in the form of a printed book, and consumed in silence and privacy, but exchanged orally in a real social encounter. The metaphysics of presence returns with a vengeance, not to bolster up the novel, but to sweep it away.

In one sense there is no answer to Davis's polemic. If you oppose life to art, acting to reading, rather than including the second term of these pairs in the first, if you think that the important thing is not to interpret the world but to change it, then the novel will seem at best an irrelevance, at worst an obstacle. But the logical conclusion of Davis's argument is that he should stop being a literary critic and become a political activist. His reluctance to do so leaves him floundering in his last chapter, hoping rather lamely that "resisting the novel may in fact be a way of reforming the novel ... " (239). One might argue that this is precisely what novelists themselves have always done, from Cervantes to Martin Amis: re-formed the novel by building resistance to fictional stereotypes and conventions into the novel itself.

II.

If we are looking for a theory of the novel that will transcend the opposition of humanist and poststructuralist viewpoints and provide an ideological justification for the novel throughout its history that will apply to its entire history, the most likely candidate is the work of Mikhail Bakhtin. In their recent study of his life and work, Katerina Clark and Michael Holquist observe:

> Bakhtin's view of language differs from two other current conceptions of language.... Personalists [i.e., humanists] maintain that the source of meaning is the unique individual. Deconstructionists locate meaning in the structure of the general possibility of difference underlying all particular differences. Bakhtin roots meaning in the social, though the social is conceived in a special way.[10]

The special way is of course Bakhtin's concept of language as essentially dialogic: that is, the word is not as in Saussure a two-sided sign–signifier and signified–but a two-sided *act*. Bakhtin's linguistics is a linguistics of *parole*. The words we use come to us already imprinted with the meanings, intentions and accents of previous users, and any utterance we make is directed towards some real or hypothetical Other. "The word in living conversations is directly, blatantly, oriented toward a future answer word," says Bakhtin. "It provokes an answer, anticipates it and structures itself in the answer's direction."[11] According to Bakhtin, the canonic genres–tragedy, epic, lyric– suppressed this inherently dialogic quality of language in the interests of expressing a unified

---

[9] D. H. Lawrence, *Selected Literary Criticism*, ed. Anthony Beal, (London: Heinemann, 1956), p. 105.

[10] Katerina Clark and Michael Holquist, *Mikhail Bakhtin* (Cambridge, Mass.: Harvard University Press, 1984), pp. 11–12.

[11] Mikahil Bakhtin, *The Dialogic Imagination: Four Essays* (Austin: University of Texas, 1981), p. 280.

world-view. These genres, at least before they were "novelized," are monologic. It was the destiny of the novel as a literary form to do justice to the inherent dialogism of language and culture by means of its discursive polyphony, its subtle and complex interweaving of various types of speech–direct, indirect and doubly-oriented (stylization, parody, *skaz, etc.*)–and its carnivalesque irreverence towards all kinds of authoritarian, repressive, monologic ideologies.

Davis is aware of the Bakhtinian defense of the novel, and tries to combat it in his chapter on "Conversation and Dialogue":

> ... *conversation is truly "dialogic," to use Bakhtin's phrase–that is, including all voices. However, and here I would disagree with Bakhtin, dialogue in novels lacks this crucial and democratic strand–everything that comes from the author is autocratically determined. The very basis of conversation–mutually negotiated turntaking–is replaced by order determined unilaterally by the author.* (177–78)

This, however, is based on a misunderstanding, or misrepresentation of what Bakhtin means by the dialogic in fiction. The dialogic includes, but is not restricted to, the quoted verbal speech of characters. It also includes the relationship between the characters' discourses and the author's discourse (if represented in the text) and between all these discourses and other discourses outside the text, which are imitated or evoked or alluded to by means of doubly-oriented speech. It is of course true that everything in a novel is put there by the novelist–in this sense the literary text is not, like a real conversation, a totally open system. But it is Bakhtin's point that the variety of discourses in the novel prevents the novelist from imposing a single world view upon his readers even if he wanted to.

Bakhtin first formulated the idea of the polyphonic novel in his early monograph, *Problems of Dostoevsky's Art.*[12] What then seemed to him to be a unique innovation of Dostoevsky's–the way in which the Russian novelist allowed different characters to articulate different ideological positions in a text without subordinating them to his own authorial speeeh–he later came to think was inherent in the novel as a literary form. In the revised and much expanded version of the Dostoevsky book, *Problems of Dostoevsky's Poetics* (1963) and in the essays collected in English under the title *The Dialogic Imagination,* he traced its genealogy back to the parodying-travestying genres of classical literature–the satyr play, the Socratic dialogue and the Menippean satire–and to that carnival folk-culture which kept the tradition alive through the Middle Ages and up to the Renaissance.

There is an indissoluable link in Bakhtin's theory between the linguistic variety of prose fiction, which he called heteroglossia, and its cultural function as the continuous critique of all repressive, authoritarian, one-eyed ideologies. As soon as you allow a variety of discourses into a textual space–vulgar discourses as well as polite ones, vernacular as well as literary, oral as well as

---

[12] Mikhail Bakhtin, *Problemy tvorčestva Dostoevskogo* (Leningrad: Priboj, 1929).

written–you establish a resistance (to use Davis's word) to the dominance of any one discourse. Even in the classic realist novel and its modern descendants, in which, we are so often told by poststructuralist critics, the author's discourse is privileged and controls the proliferation of meaning by judging and interpreting the discourses of the characters–even there this control is only relative, and largely illusory. "The possibility of employing on the plane of a single work discourses of various types, with all their expressive capacities intact, without reducing them to a common denominator–this is one of the most characteristic features of prose," says Bakhtin.[13] To allow characters to speak with their own social, regional and individual accents, whether in quoted direct speech ("dialogue" in the ordinary sense of the term) or by alloting them the task of narrating itself, as in the epistolary novel, the confessional novel, and the colloquial vernacular narrative known to the Russians as *skaz*; or by means of free indirect style, a rhetorical technique discovered by novelists in the late eighteenth century and developed to stunning effect in the nineteenth and twentieth–to do all or any of these things in narrative is to make interpretive closure in the absolute sense impossible.

"The one grand literary form that is for Bakhtin capable of a kind of justice to the inherent polyphonies of life is the 'novel,'" says Wayne Booth, introducing the latest translation of *Problems in Dostoevsky's Poetics*, and echoing, consciously or unconsciously, Lawrence's definition of the novel as "the one bright book of life."[14] In another essay, called simply "The Novel," first published in *Reflections on the Death of a Porcupine* (1925), Lawrence wrote:

> You can fool pretty nearly every other medium. You can make a poem pietistic, and still it will be a poem. You can write Hamlet in drama: if you wrote him in a novel, he'd be half comic, or a trifle suspicious; a suspicious character, like Dostoevsky's Idiot. Somehow, you sweep the ground a bit too clear in the poem or the drama, and you let the human Word fly a bit too freely. Now in a novel there's always a tom-cat, a black tom-cat that pounces on the white dove of the Word, if the dove doesn't watch it; and there is a banana-skin to trip on; and you know there is a water-closet on the premises. All these things help to keep the balance.[15]

This apologia for the novel was hardly likely to have been known to Bakhtin, yet it anticipates his theory in a remarkable way, especially in the polemical opposition it sets up between the novel and the canonized genres of tragedy and lyric poetry in its invocation of Dostoevsky, and in the way it relates the novel's treatment of the human Word to its carnivalesque elements–represented here by the black tom-cat, the banana-skin and the water-closet. I have commented elsewhere on the carnivalesque in Lawrence's fiction, especially in *Mr. Noon* and *The Lost Girl*, and on Dostoevskyean

---

[13] Mikahil Bakhtin, *Problems in Dostoevsky's Poetics* (Manchester: Manchester University Press, 1984), p. 200.

[14] *Problems*, p. xxii.

[15] D. H. Lawrence, *Reflections on the Death of a Porcupine* (Philadelphia: Centaur Press, 1925), pp. 106–107.

polyphony in *Women in Love*.[16] But the fact is that Bakhtin's theory of the novel applies equally well to all the other novelists I have mentioned in the course of this lecture.

To demonstrate this claim exhaustively would obviously take too long. In some cases–Cervantes and Dickens, for example–Bakhtin has already done the job himself; in others–notably James Joyce–it has been done by latter-day Bakhtinians.[17] But to conclude: cast your minds briefly over that list of set texts I mentioned earlier, chosen to represent recent developments in British fiction, and consider how well they also answer to Bakhtin's theory of the novel: the carnival face-pulling, the parodying and travestying of academic discourse by *Lucky Jim*; the invented polyglossia, the *skaz* energy and vitality, the *Notes-from-Underground* subversiveness of *A Clockwork Orange*; the disconcerting hybridization of *The French Lieutenant's Woman*, its deliberately unresolved juxtaposition of nineteenth-century discourse with twentieth, of two antithetical types of fiction categorized by Bakhtin as the existential adventure story and the social-psychological novel of everyday life; the parodying and travestying of literary genres in *Not to Disturb*–the whodunnit, the gothic novel, the Jacobean revenge tragedy; the violent clash of discourses–visionary, parodic, clinical, pornographic, documentary–in *Briefing for a Descent into Hell* and *The White Hotel*; the elaborate exploitation in *The History Man* of the social speech acts Bakhtin studied and classified under the heading of *"causerie,"* especially the "rejoinder" and the "glance at someone else's word"–a feature of that particular text foregrounded by the author's refusal to make any authoritative judgment or interpretation of his characters, or to make us privy to their thoughts. Finally, *Money* is another *skaz* narrative in the *Notes-from-Underground* tradition, a demonic carnival, a suicide note from a character who indulges in every excess of the lower body, sexual and gastronomic, that the modern urban culture can provide, a repulsive character in many ways, yet one who retains an undeniable vitality by the sheer punk brilliance of his rhetoric; a hero or anti-hero who not only answers the author back, as Bakhtin said of Dostoevsky's heroes, but actually throws a punch at him.

As for my own contribution to contemporary British fiction, I must leave the Bakhtinian reading of that to others; but, having written a distinctly carnivalesque novel about academic literary conferences, I should hardly venture to address this one without the reassuring protection of Mikhail Bakhtin's theorization of why the novel matters.

[16] David Lodge, "Lawrence, Dostoevsky, Bakhtin: D. H. Lawrence and Dialogic Fiction," *Renaissance & Modern Studies* 29 (1985), 16–32.

[17] See, for example, my "Joyce and Bakhtin: *Ulysses* and the Typology of Literary Discourse," *James Joyce Broadsheet* 11 (June 1983), 1–2.

The Novel as Subjective Mode

The first panel, "The Novel as Subjective Mode (as traditional definer or constituter of subjectivity, of the terms of character and selfhood)," was also introduced by Mark Spilka. He began by citing the defensive approach to such matters in NOVEL's *tenth anniversary conference back in 1977, the sense of opposition between the inrush of largely European theories, such as structuralism, Russian formalism, and hermeneutics, into British and American academies, and the ongoing attempt to reclaim from the New Criticism its implicit humanism by restoring the importance of authors, readers, and characters to the study of verbal icons, and therefore restoring the importance of things relative and mimetic rather than absolute and autonomous. He pointed out how the panel titles of that conference–In Defense of Authors, In Defense of Readers, Character as a Lost Cause–were unmistakably biased toward eclectic humanism, and how the conference title itself–Towards a Poetics of Fiction–was in this respect a kind of academic swansong for the going humanistic theories of fiction and for the journal's attempt to bring them together into some kind of serviceable package in the interest of more and better criticism of the novel; whereas from that time forward the ferment of new anti- or posthumanistic theories would remarkably increase and flourish. Yet if the new eclecticism which the journal had helped to crystallize would meanwhile overtly subside, "in some sense," Spilka argued, "our profession may still be said to be divided between these active and quiescent views, or to put it more hopefully, may still be said not to recognize the ways in which bridges between them may be in the making":*

> Today we want to begin to be more articulate, if we can, about those bridging possibilities by avoiding a contest of warring theories and concentrating instead on new kinds of humane enterprises within our midst and their possible affinities with old kinds. We may say then that character and selfhood are not so much lost causes as radically redefined aspects of both life and the novel as we now see them, and that our speakers today will address at least some of those radical redefinitions–the most obvious being the new sense of polymorphous diversity if not perversity and of discontinuity rather than unity of selfhood, seen as a happier prospect than it once seemed, and the new sense of gender difference in the nature of subjectivity, of human consciousness; and perhaps also the new sense of cultural complexity and diversity, and of historical differences, in even beginning to talk about the novel's traditional function in simulating human consciousness and interiority.

Editor Spilka then mistakenly supposed that he had "just described the emphases that [would] now be brought to bear by our three speakers." He had not seen their papers, and could not predict their very different angles of approach to bridging possibilities. Thus, instead of making further pronouncements on discontinuous character, Leo Bersani would concentrate instead on ontology and politics in Bouvard et Pécuchet

as they help us to resist the pressures and aversions of our encyclopedic culture; Kaja
Silverman would concentrate on male rather than female subjectivity "at the margins";
and Alan Singer would amend Bakhtin by introducing history into his treatment of
those oblique aspects of subjectivity–voice, parody, and dialogue.

Flaubert's Encyclopedism

LEO BERSANI

Unable to agree on either the subject or the compositional principles of the
novel they have decided to write, Flaubert's Bouvard and Pécuchet turn to
"the science called aesthetics." After receiving a list of books on the subject,
the two friends go to work. First, they study the nature of the Beautiful; then,
Flaubert reports,

> *They tackled the question of the sublime.*
> *Certain objects are sublime in themselves, the thunder of a torrent, deep dark-*
> *ness, a tree struck by a storm. A character is beautiful when it triumphs, and*
> *sublime when it struggles.*
> *'I understand,' said Bouvard, 'the Beautiful is the Beautiful, and the Sublime*
> *the very Beautiful.' How can they be distinguished?*
> *'By intuition,' answered Pécuchet.*
> *'And where does that come from?'*
> *'From taste!'*
> *'What is taste?'*
> *It is defined as special discernment, rapid judgement, the ability to*
> *distinguish certain relationships.*
> *'What it comes to is that taste is taste, and none of that tells you how you get*
> *it.'*
> *Conventions must be observed, but they vary, and however perfect a work*
> *may be it will not always be above reproach. Yet there is an indestructible Beau-*
> *tiful, whose laws we do not know, because its origin is mysterious.*
> *Since an idea cannot be translated by every form, we must recognize limits*
> *between the arts and, in each of the arts, several genres; but combinations arise*
> *in which the style of one will enter into another, or else miss the target, fail to*
> *be true.*
> *The Truth too slavishly applied impairs Beauty, and preoccupation with*
> *Beauty impedes Truth; however, without an ideal there is no truth; which is*
> *why the reality of types is more continuous than that of portraits. Besides, art*

only deals with verisimilitude, but that depends on the observer, is something
relative, transitory.[1]

Read referentially, this passage leads to certain attributive questions: does
Flaubert mean to be satirical, and of what and of whom? It may be of
Bouvard and Pécuchet's deficient intellectual method or habits of reading, or
it may be of the books they read–but what are those books? Flaubert usually
names some of the authors his protagonists consult in their studies (just before the lines quoted he mentions five writers on esthetics) without, however,
mentioning the particular source of each theory or set of facts. The passage
on esthetic theory is typical in this respect: it condenses a mass of quite different theories into a single page of theoretical pronouncements with no attri-
butions whatsoever. And yet stylistically that page could be a direct quote
from a single author, for in this version of free indirect discourse Flaubert has
reduced the distance between the narrator and his nearly quoted referent by
using the present tense instead of a past tense. It is, in other words, as if
esthetic theory were speaking directly–not a particular theorist of esthetics,
but the sourceless theory itself.

The passage is, however, distinguished by a certain type of stylistic performance which, far from speaking the truth of esthetic theory or of the characters immersed in that theory, is repeated throughout the novel regardless of
the changes in epistemological reference. In the quoted passage, there are numerous examples of Flaubert's rhythmical "signature." I'm thinking, for example, of the ternary construction: in the first paragraph, "the thunder of a
torrent, deep darkness, a tree struck by a storm," then the one-sentence paragraph on definitions of taste, and, in what might be considered a variation on
that construction in which the second and third syntactic units decrease in
size (the third is a single word), "but that depends on the observer, is something relative, transitory." There is also a prodigious use of directional shifts:
note the interruptive nature of "But," "Yet," and, peculiarly enough, "and" in
the paragraph on the Conventions and the Beautiful, and, especially, the zig-
zagging effect in the final paragraph of the first sentence's two clauses and of
the subsequent "however," "besides," and "but." All these swerves and negations are of course swerves and negations of thought; but given the
rapidity with which we pass from one thought to the next (each originally
complex theory gets only a few words), we tend to experience intellectual inconsistency and confusion here as an almost purely rhythmical agitation, as a
linguistic approximation of musical repetitions, variations, and abrupt shifts
in thematic lines. In other words, the passage–and the novel as a whole–is
really not "about" the deficiencies of either Bouvard and Pécuchet's understanding or of the state of human knowledge in a particular area; rather, Flaubert's work performs an erasure of the very ontology which would allow for
such critical intentions in the first place. Human knowledge is cut off from
both its sources and its reception; it is reduced–or elevated (such oppositions

[1] Gustave Flaubert, *Bouvard and Pécuchet*, tr. A. J. Krailsheimer (New York: Penguin Books, 1976), pp. 143–44.

are meaningless applied to ontological mutations)–to intellectually and psychologically insignificant rhythms.

Bouvard and Pécuchet themselves undergo the same mutation as the books
they devour. If, in the course of the novel, Flaubert nearly eliminates the distance between himself and his *bonhommes,* it is not, as some critics have said,
because they become more intelligent or that Flaubert comes to feel more
sympathy for them, but rather in order to eliminate them. Consider the following account of Pécuchet's ideas for religious reform:

> 'The world has expanded, the earth is not the centre any more. It turns
> among the infinite multitude of worlds like it. Many exceed it in size, and this
> shrinking of our globe brings about a more sublime ideal of God.'
> So, religion had to change. Paradise is something childish with its blessed
> ones always rapt in contemplation, always singing and looking down on the tor-
> tures of the damned. When you think that the basis of Christianity is an apple![2]

Our first impression is that Flaubert stops quoting Pécuchet in order to continue quoting him. Except for the dropping of quotation marks, the change
from direct discourse to free indirect discourse is indicated by a single tense
shift: *"Donc la religion devait changer"* transposes Pécuchet's saying: *"Donc la religion doit changer,"* The rest of the paragraph continues in the present, and if
the whole passage were put in quotes and *"devait"* became *"doit,"* we would
certainly not feel that Pécuchet is speaking "out of character." Having made
Pécuchet's speech nearly indistinguishable from his own, the narrator's move
into free indirect discourse is therefore primarily experienced not as a strategy
of point of view (which such moves largely are in *Madame Bovary*) but rather
as the expression of an ontological preference. The narrator continues Pécuchet's speech by eliminating him as its source; Pécuchet as a thinking subject
merely provides the anecdotal term for an anonymous performance of the imaginary. Nothing subsists of Pécuchet except his speech as sourceless
style–that is, speech which, by virtue of its essence, can no longer be considered as quotation.

Human knowledge and human character are neither evaluated nor performed in their essential being in *Bouvard et Pécuchet*; rather, they undergo a
change in ontological status. This operation is the same throughout the novel;
what happens to horticultural or jam-making expertise is identical to what
happens to theological doctrine. What we might be inclined to consider as the
tics of Flaubert's style are perhaps the excessively visible signposts of the mutation I am discussing; the stylistic sameness which they produce suggests–in
a way which contradicts Flaubert's own notions of style, at least as he expressed them in the letters written during the composition of *Madame Bovary*–the epistemological indifference of art to its objects. Furthermore, once
the model of these mutations is given, their repetition is, in a sense, unnecessary. The encyclopedism of *Bouvard et Pécuchet*–Flaubert's massive reading for

[2] *Bouvard and Pécuchet,* p. 249.

the novel notwithstanding–is, then, somewhat illusory. What we have is the appearance of an encyclopedic novel, an accumulation of facts and theories from the most diverse fields of knowledge in order to discredit the claims of art to any epistemological validity whatsoever.

In *Bouvard et Pécuchet* Flaubert makes, then, a perhaps unexpectedly modest claim for the authority of art. If the novel ceaselessly repeats an operation which could be thought of as requiring a single demonstration (since the effect of the operation will not be changed by the use of new material), this is because Bouvard and Pécuchet are themselves in a tensely frictional opposition to the narrator's mutational work. By resisting their total absorption into the Flaubertian free indirect discourse, Bouvard and Pécuchet keep open another option: that of consciousness at work in the world. If they lack both the believability and the psychological density which we associate with the characters of realist fiction, they nonetheless have a very marked specificity as characters–more precisely, as philosophical characters. The relation of Bouvard and Pécuchet to knowledge is highly practical; if Flaubert has satirical intentions towards them, it is not because they are intellectually mediocre, but because they would put knowledge *to use*. As their studies proceed, they develop, Flaubert tells us, *"le besoin de la vérité pour elle-même,"* but their philosophy always takes the form of *applied* philosophy, of innumerable experiments (on themselves and on others) and of tireless attempts to enlighten themselves and their neighbors. These inveterate lecturers are extraordinarily restless; they always have to do something with knowledge, and they must have an audience. A suitable climax to the careers of such eminently practical and public philosophers, Flaubert suggests, might have been in urban planning and adult education. But by their very excesses, Bouvard and Pécuchet come to figure the sublimity of a civilization without art, of a civilization devoted exclusively to the use of knowledge to bridge the gap between human consciousness and its environment. At this level of emblematic significance, the quality of Bouvard and Pécuchet's learning is irrelevant; intelligence itself is finally irrelevant to the boundlessly energetic will to make the human mind ideally consequential, to *realize representation*.

Against this temptation, Flaubert's narrative performs a highly seductive de-realization: the mere *representation of representation*. Bouvard and Pécuchet rush into the world with their representations of it; Flaubert, by severing their knowledge from its sources, its reception, and its possible uses, simply repeats it as nothing more than a series of moments in the life of an errant, unidentifiable, unusable consciousness. Bouvard and Pécuchet ceaselessly militate against the imaginary nature of the mind's representations; Flaubert just as ceaselessly emphasizes the autonomy of representations, thus suggesting that the effect of our inclination to represent the real is, by virtue of an ontological necessity, to alienate us from objects of representation. The comedy of *Bouvard et Pécuchet* depends, precisely, on the two friends being defeated by this opposition to their projects; they are, that is to say, saved from the world's persecution by the ontological erasure of their projects *as* projects. But

it is of course impossible to speak of them as if they themselves merely opposed such erasure. The energetic will to live with knowledge in the world
has already been invalidated by what might be called the primary representation of that will–that is, by the very pre-condition of our being able to recognize it, the writing of *Bouvard et Pécuchet*. Before the quotation marks of their
speech have been removed, they are already not there, although it is of
course one of the tricks of literature–and especially of realistic fiction–to make
us believe in its multiple contacts with the world. Art is the luxury form of
ontological alienation. In art, the price of comic relief is always the inconsequential nature of both catastrophe and salvation. Nothing is more ordinary–or astonishing–than the power of language to create the illusion of tensions; the frictions of our words are, after all, only verbal fictions.

And yet the Flaubertian move into the imaginary–which Sartre saw as a rejection of history and politics–should, I think, also be seen as a political strategy. The alienation I have been describing is a form of resistance, and this in
two ways. First of all, the practice of an *inapplicable discourse* could be thought
of as a defense against the manipulative seductions of political language. In
the famous *Comices agricoles* scene in *Madame Bovary*, Flaubert renders the sexually and politically pornographic language of Rodolphe and Lieuvain impotent merely by juxtaposing their two discourses, by letting each of them cut
into or interrupt the other. The juxtaposition of Rodolphe's amorous
rhapsody with the *sous-préfet's* praise of agriculture and civil obedience reveals
important rhetorical similarities between the two. Each speech is designed to
seduce its audience, and the superficial differences of content (the spiritual
opposed to the basely material, passion against manure) hide a common intention: that of making the listeners passive and obedient (sexually and politically). This intention is realized through certain "literary" means, through
metaphor, antitheses, rhetorical questions, and, more generally, a pleasantly
numbing musicalizing of the brutal message. I have spoken of a certain dominance of rhythms in Flaubert's writing as the sign of language being severed
from any such intentions, of its participating in the disinterested, purposeless
activity of the imaginary. We should, however, see that Flaubert recognizes
the potential *uses* of verbal musicality, and, more generally, that he implicitly
distinguishes–in, we might say, an absolute way–between art and the persuasive potentialities of rhetoric. Art occurs only as a kind of rhetorical ascesis,
that is, when rhetoric itself renounces its persuasive or seductive powers.
And this seems to occur principally through a kind of self-reflexiveness or
what we might call an ontologically ironic move. Rodolphe's and Lieuvain's
representations of love and of the nation are neutralized–and, it is implied,
authentically estheticized–simply by being themselves represented, repeated
within a *different* musical structure–one of alternating blocks of discourse–which preempts the shorter persuasive rhythms and reduces–or ele-
vates–both discourses to the status of artistic display.

The representation of representation can therefore be a politically defensive
move. The estheticizing repetition of Rodolphe and Lieuvain operates almost

as a pedagogical model of how to elude the manipulative immediacy of seductive speech. It is not exactly a question of a critical analysis of such
speech, but of a perhaps more potent invalidating strategy: a kind of distanc-
ing repetition or reenactment of it in which the manipulative agent's
discourse is deprived of any subject who might profit from its effectiveness.
Flaubert's art suggests ways in which the estheticizing of discourse can operate *outside art* if only as "moments" of resistance within networks of political
or sexual power. It is of course true that neither Emma nor Lieuvain's peasant
listeners nor finally–but this is more ambiguous–the protagonists of *Bouvard et
Pécuchet* profit from such ironic repetitions. They are nonetheless models of
how a certain type of appropriation of language can, at least momentarily,
protect us from its coercive designs. In *Bouvard et Pécuchet*, however, Flaubert
goes so far as to save the realistic novel itself from its collaborative participation in such designs. The instability of Bouvard and Pécuchet as characters–the process by which they are "re-played" as the subjectless rhythms of a
depersonalized narrative–points to a kind of resistance to strategies of power
that would no longer be dependent on the spectacle of defeated (if heroic)
characters. As long as the novelist acquiesces in, say, the very possibility of
Emma Bovary as a psychological subject, the novel which presents itself as an
ironic repetition of her fate can resist that fate only if it presents art as a *retreat* from the phenomenal to the imaginary. *Bouvard et Pécuchet* raises the
more exciting possibility of the imaginary as *politically aggressive*. The incoherence of Flaubert's *bonhommes* is perhaps the novel's most precious achievement, for it suggests that the *errance* of the imaginary dissolves the identities
which coercive strategies must at least assume in order to be effective. On the
one hand, Bouvard and Pécuchet are so uncompromisingly definite in their
projects that they become easy targets for an antagonistic community; on the
other, the very excess of their philosophical and proselytizing energy is constantly undoing their projects, giving them a kind of crazy mobility which
may, had Flaubert completed the novel, have allowed them to escape their
countrymen's wrath and enjoy the ambiguous freedom of harmless madmen.
This may not seem like much in the way of political aggressiveness, and yet it
is potentially more radical than any reformist projects. For it proposes the
esthetic as a strategy for eluding definitions and identifications, and in so doing it suggests, paradoxically, the political uses of art's uselessness in any
struggle for a free society.

Flaubert's brief mutational résumés of vast areas of knowledge suggest
that, far from being condemned to cultural insignificance if it does not somehow account for the encyclopedic knowledge of its time, art is, by definition,
an ontological relocation of the materials of philosophy and science. *Bouvard
et Pécuchet* does not imply–as, say, *Ulysses* does–that its own performance can
redemptively replace all those materials, but it does propose what we might
think of as *a salutary de-acceleration of the processing of knowledge as power*. At the
price of a certain indifference to the beneficial effects of thought's mastery
over nature (as well as over its own nature ...), art cultivates a deliberately
fragmentary, unusable, even ignorant relational play with the entries of its

culture's encyclopedia. Flaubert's treatment of all the books devoured with such anxiety by his heroes is to convert the vast matter which those books treat into a few occasions of purposeless pleasure. For the Flaubertian writer that pleasure involves certain rhythmical preferences. He sensually repeats the knowledge of his time in the form of his narcissistically musical prose, a prose continuously returning to, and playing with, its preferred rests and measures. Bouvard and Pécuchet–not to speak of the hostile world of Chavig-nolles–retain just enough resistant presence to remind us, metaphorically, that the world is still there, that the narcissistic luxury of art is always a momentary delay in the necessary, or at least inevitable, work of civilization.

Flaubert, for all his presumed idolatry of art, therefore reminds us that, far from having a secure place, or a central role, in that accumulation of knowledge by which civilizations achieve historical mastery, the artist is content to repeat himself in the margins of such work. The language of every page of *Bouvard et Pécuchet* quite obtrusively reenacts that turning away from objects (and by objects I mean here the entire fictional world of the novel: the two friends, the books they read, the community they live in), that solipsistic play, which, as I have suggested elsewhere, psychoanalysis invites us to see as intrinsic to sexuality and to art. Indeed, art could be put on the side of sexuality in the Freudian opposition between civilization and pleasure. But if the narcissistic estheticizing of Bouvard and Pécuchet's studies suggests that art transforms discursive communications into the privacy of a verbal *jouissance*, the very blocking of the message in art affects and limits the political uses of knowledge. Flaubert implicitly defines both the limitations and the necessity of art. In *Bouvard et Pécuchet* style caresses an encyclopedic culture out of its projects of mastery and into a liberalizing impotence.

Too Early/Too Late:
Subjectivity and the Primal Scene
in Henry James

KAJA SILVERMAN

*"You've all of you here so much visual sense that you've somehow all 'run' to it.
There are moments when it strikes one that you haven't any other."*
                                        Lambert Strether in *The Ambassadors*.[1]

At first glance, there is no novelist who seems to deploy the novel more insistently as a "subjective mode" than Henry James. His fictions are, after all, about nothing so much as "seeing" and "feeling," or to phrase it slightly differently, about the psychic registration of sexual, social and aesthetic nuance and complexity. In *The Art of the Novel* James talks about giving Lambert Strether all the "subjective 'say'" in *The Ambassadors*, and he describes *The Spoils of Poynton* as the story of Fleda Vetch's "appreciation."[2] But do James's novels or critical writings in fact have anything whatever to do with what has been recently theorized as subjectivity?

Let us consider for a moment that famous passage from the "Preface to *The Portrait of a Lady*" where James compares fiction to a house of many windows. Each of those windows, he explains, "has been pierced, or is still pierceable, in its vast front, by the need of the individual vision and by the pressure of the individual will." Behind each one stands "a figure with a pair of eyes, or at least with a field-glass, which forms, again and again, for observation, a unique instrument, insuring to the person making use of it an impression distinct from every other." This pair of eyes or field-glass is an image of the artist, or as James insists, of "the consciousness of the artist." "Tell me what the artist is," he concludes, "and I will tell you of what he has been conscious. Thereby I shall express to you at once his boundless freedom and his 'moral' reference."[3]

Consciousness, individuality, boundless freedom, moral reference: what do any of these concepts have to do with subjectivity? Psychoanalysis comes as a veritable refutation of this catalogue, displacing individuality with intersubjectivity, boundless freedom with psychic and social determination, and moral reference with desire. The concept of consciousness undergoes perhaps the most drastic diminution of all within the confines of psychoanalysis. Essays like "Dostoevsky and Parricide," and "Leonardo da Vinci and a Memory of His Childhood," which constitute Freud's two most extended discussions of the artistic psyche, could be glossed by an epigraph the very obverse of James's. "Tell me what the artist is," Freud seems to say, "and I will tell you of what he or she has been *unconscious*."

---

[1] Henry James, *The Ambassadors*, ed. S.P. Rosenbaum (New York: W.W. Norton and Co., 1964), p. 126. All future quotations will be from this edition.

[2] *The Art of the Novel*, ed. Richard P. Blackmur (New York: Scribner's, 1934), pp. 320, 129.

[3] Blackmur, pp. 46–47.

But what have other critics had to say about subjectivity in James's fiction? I want to glance briefly at two books, both published in 1976, which offer what are apparently diametrically opposed readings of Jamesian interiority, but which nonetheless converge on one crucial point–Leo Bersani's *A Future for Astyanax*, and Peter Brooks's *The Melodramatic Imagination*. Bersani argues that James's fiction offers psychological detail without psychological depth, and that it works to complicate surfaces rather than to disclose a hidden "truth":

> *Complexity consists not in mutually subversive motives but rather in the expanding surface itself which, when most successful, finds a place in its intricate design for all the motives imaginable. We can easily be misled by the numerous passages where James's characters, burdened by their sense of the portentous, retreat into exclamation or expressive groans. What they renounce trying to express is generally not an intuition that would expose the ambiguity of all efforts to understand, but rather a richness of understanding which would expand the dialogue to monstrous proportions.*[4]

Brooks, on the other hand, accounts for these same exclamations and expressive groans as the failure of language in the face of an inexpressible or unspeakable hidden reality, a reality which he comes close to equating with the unconscious. Interestingly, however, when he attempts to conceptualize this hidden reality he hesitates between two spatial images, one implying surface and depth, and the other implying forward and rear movement. The result is a tellingly mixed metaphor:

> *The need for melodrama, on this basis, is the need for a form of statement and dramatization that will make the plane of representation yield the content of the plane of signification. This means in practice a pressure on the surface–the surface of social forms, manners; and the surface of literary forms, style–in order to make surface release the vision of the* behind *[my emphasis]: as Strether's pressure of imagination applied to Mme de Vionnet's hôtel conjures forth "the smell of revolution, the smell of the public temper–or perhaps simply the smell of blood." . . . The technique is expressionistic in that surface forms are treated, not for themselves, in their interrelation and as ultimate integers, but as signs of what lies* behind *them [my emphasis] and charges them.*[5]

This passage thus rests upon a false opposition. In it, Brooks twice creates the impression that he is about to contrast surface to depth, but both times he defeats that expectation by opposing surface to what lies "behind," *i.e.* to a different point on the same plane. Thus, although he insists upon the importance of unconscious meaning within James's novels–although he is firm in

[4] Leo Bersani, *A Future for Astyanax: Character and Desire in Literature* (Boston: Little, Brown and Company, 1976), p. 131.

[5] Peter Brooks, *The Melodramatic Imagination: Balzac, Henry James, Melodrama, and the Mode of Excess* (New Haven: Yale University Press, 1976), p. 171.

maintaining that those novels project another psychic scene than the one within which the characters move and speak–he is no more prepared than is Bersani to impute psychological depth to them. What are we to make of this emphasis in both *A Future for Astyanax* and *The Melodramatic Imagination* on surface? And what is the force of Brooks's mixed metaphor?

The false opposition of surface to what "lies behind" recalls a phrase which recurs again and again in the "Prefaces" to the New York Edition, a phrase with distinct pederastic resonances of which James remains sublimely oblivious, and which is absolutely central to his theory of the novel. James repeatedly speaks of "going behind" a particular character, by which he means us to understand that he adopts that character's point of view. Several writers have already persuasively demonstrated that James constructs his authorial persona through this organizing consciousness–that it is given as somehow representing him, and that he in turn authorizes it. As David Carroll puts it, "Essential to James's theory of the novel ... is the presence of the author at its source–the fictional universe has its center in the consciousness of a fictional subject behind which stands the 'true origin' and subject of the novel: the author and his consciousness."[6] But what if behind this phenomenological sleight-of-hand the authorial subject sustains a very different relationship with his fictional surrogates–one predicated upon unconscious desire rather than an organizing consciousness? (I say "behind" rather than "beneath" because the psychic model upon which I am drawing is that provided in *The Interpretation of Dreams* rather than the one outlined in *The Ego and the Id*, and that model rests precisely upon the possibility of forward and backward movement between the unconscious and the preconscious/conscious system.)

James's defenses are securely in place against such an unwelcome discovery. One can scarcely help remarking that the artist who stands at the window of the house of fiction has no intention of turning around to see what lies within, but looks resolutely outward. James shows himself even more armored against unwanted self-knowledge in the "Preface to 'Lady Barbarina'," in which he first makes the uncharacteristic admission that his work is determined by forces beyond his conscious control, and then voices his firm determination not to consider what those forces might be. Significantly, he declines self-knowledge through the very phrase with which he habitually describes his assumption of a particular point of view–*i.e.* through the phrase "to go behind." James in effect refuses to "go behind" his desire to "go behind" certain fictional characters:

---

[6] David Carroll, *The Subject in Question: The Languages of Theory and the Strategies of Fiction* (Chicago: University of Chicago Press, 1982), p. 56. Carroll goes on to say that "the fictional-subject as center and origin is not solid enough ground for the [Jamesian] novel, not sufficiently substantial or autonomous. The author-subject will provide the definitive origin and center of the novel outside or *behind* [my emphasis] the novel...." (56). Carroll is of course referring here to the terms through which the Jamesian fictional system presents itself, not to a theoretical model which he himself endorses. For a further discussion of the central consciousness within James's novels as a "metonym" for the author, see John Carlos Rowe, *The Theoretical Dimensions of Henry James* (Madison: University of Wisconsin Press, 1984), p. 240.

[O]ne never really chooses one's general range of vision–the experience from which ideas and themes and suggestions spring: this proves ever what it has had to be, this is one with the very turn one's life has taken; so that whatever it "gives," whatever it makes us feel and think of, we regard very much as imposed and inevitable. The subject thus pressed upon the artist is the necessity of his case and the fruit of his consciousness; which truth makes and has ever made of any quarrel with his subject, any stupid attempt to go behind that, the true stultification of criticism. The author of these remarks has in any case felt it, from far back, quite his least stupid course to meet halfway, as it were, the turn taken and the perceptions engendered by the tenor of his days. Here it is that he has never pretended to "go behind"–which would have been for him a deplorable waste of time.[7]

We will have occasion to return more than once over the course of this essay to James's predilection for rear subject-positions. First, however, let us consider what it would mean to "go behind" this (or for that matter any other) authorial desire.

I.

In considering James's authorial relation to characters like Isabel Archer, Fleda Vetch and Lambert Strether, at least one critic has felt impelled to invoke the essay in which Freud elaborates his *ars poetica*, "Creative Writers and Day-Dreaming."[8] That essay, we recall, presents the fiction writer as someone who is able to disguise and generalize his or her daydreams in such a way that they are able to gratify the reader's own unconscious desires without inducing guilt. What is it about this aesthetic paradigm which fails to satisfy, particularly in the case of a writer like James? It is not that there are no points of coincidence between his work and the pulp novels upon which Freud bases his theoretical model; as James himself acknowledges, there is often an element of the pot boiler about his stories. However, the psychic drama which those novels and stories play out has little to do with the one described in "Creative Writers and Day-Dreaming":

One feature above all cannot fail to strike us about the creations of these story-writers: each of them has a hero who is the centre of interest, for whom the writer tries to win our sympathy by every possible means and whom he seems to place under the protection of a special Providence. If, at the end of one chapter of my story, I leave the hero unconscious and bleeding from severe wounds, I am sure to find him at the beginning of the next being carefully nursed and on the way to recovery; and if the first volume closes with the ship he is in going down in a storm at sea, I am certain, at the opening of the second volume, to read of his miraculous rescue . . . . through this revealing characteristic of invulnerability

---

[7] *The Art of the Novel*, p. 201.

[8] See Rowe, p. 241. Rowe cites the article as "The Poet and Day-Dreaming," n. 37.

we can immediately recognize His Majesty the Ego, the hero alike of every day-dream and of every story.[9]

Far from being under the protection of a special providence, the prototypical Jamesian character is the one who, like Lambert Strether, gets nothing for him or herself "out of the whole affair"[10]–the one who is marked, moreover, precisely by vulnerability. That character also bears scant resemblance to the exuberantly active hero described by Freud; he or she often stands to one side of the "action," watching rather than participating in the flow of events. Indeed, the paradigmatic Jamesian character bears an uncanny resemblance to the artist evoked by James himself in the "Preface to *A Portrait of a Lady*," the artist who looks onto a scene from which he or she is somehow excluded.

But what is least satisfying for me about Freud's *ars poetica*, especially when it is juxtaposed with James's work, is its crude notion of wish-fulfill-ment–its assumption that what manifests itself in daydreams and novels will always be what in the final analysis serves to "crown" or aggrandize the ego. A theoretical abyss separates "Creative Writers and Day-Dreaming" from later essays like "A Child Is Being Beaten" or "The Economic Problem of Maso-chism," with their much more complex understanding both of pleasure and fantasy.

"The Economic Problem of Masochism" is corrective primarily with respect to the issue of pleasure, elaborating as it does three categories of voluptuous or exquisite pain.[11] The first of these categories, "erotogenic masochism" (161), underlies the other two, and designates that pleasure which attaches it-self to the traumatic infraction of an organ, whether that organ be physical or psychic, as in the case of the ego. Freud associates the second of these cat-egories with fantasies and sexual practices involving bondage and ritual pun-ishment. It is so named because it enacts a hyperbolic dramatization of female subjectivity, although the patients upon which Freud bases his account are all men. As I have argued at length elsewhere, this form of masochism can be read as a phallic divestiture.[12] The last of Freud's categories, moral maso-chism, poses perhaps the most direct challenge to "Creative Writers and Day-Dreaming" in that it turns upon the abasement and castigation of the ego. Moral masochism occurs when the ego begins to enjoy and indeed to provoke the super-ego's severity. Any artistic text functioning as even the indirect "trace" of masochistic desire, whether it be "feminine" or "moral," would put certain obstacles in the way of an easy transition from injury and humiliation to recovery and exaltation.

---

[9] James Strachey, trans., *The Standard Edition of the Complete Psychological Works of Sigmund Freud*, Vol. 9 *(London: Hogarth Press, 1959), pp. 149–50.*

[10] *The Ambassadors*, p. 344.

[11] "The Economic Problem of Masochism," in Vol. 19 of *The Standard Edition*, pp. 157–170.

[12] See Kaja Silverman, "Masochism and Male Subjectivity," in *Camera Obscura* 17 (1988) or *Male Subjectivity at the Margins* (forthcoming), for an extended discussion of male masochism as phallic divestiture and for a much fuller analysis of "The Economic Problem of Masochism" and "A Child Is Being Beaten."

"A Child Is Being Beaten" not only delves more deeply into what Freud would later call "feminine" masochism, but theorizes phantasy in ways which enormously complicate the 1908 formulation.[13] It insists much more strenuously than "Creative Writers and Day-Dreaming" on the link between daydreams and unconscious phantasies. Indeed, whereas the earlier essay is prepared only to connect daydreams to infantile memories (148), "A Child Is Being Beaten" insists that conscious phantasies are nothing more than another phase of unconscious ones. It also indicates that the pleasure towards which unconscious phantasy aims may depend in some very profound way upon passivity, punishment, loss or pain. Finally, whereas "Creative Writers and Day-Dreaming" focuses primarily upon narrative reversal in its attempt to uncover authorial desire, "A Child is Being Beaten" places its emphasis rather upon the scene. It suggests that unconscious desire generally assumes the form of a visual tableau or narrateme like the one indicated by the repressed beating phantasy, which Freud transcribes with the sentence "I am being beaten by my father" (179). (Even the two conscious versions of the beating phantasy have this same scenic quality. The female version, for instance, has the girl watching while a group of boys are whipped.)

But no summary of Freud's views on the relation of phantasy to art would be complete without some reference to "Leonardo da Vinci and a Memory of His Childhood," an essay whose focus is much more explicitly visual, and whose pursuit of authorial desire in assorted texts by Leonardo leads him to two privileged scenes. The first of these scenes, which was consciously "remembered" by the artist, but which Freud insists was a phantasy transposed onto infancy, is recounted by Leonardo in his scientific notebooks, and misquoted in several key details in *The Standard Edition*:

> "*It seems that I was always destined to be so deeply concerned with vultures [kites]: for I recall as one of my very earliest memories that while I was in my cradle a vulture [kite] came down to me, and opened my mouth with its tail, and struck me many times with its tail against [inside] my lips.*"[14]

The second scene is constructed by Freud in the course of analysis, and is posited as the unconscious phantasy hidden behind the conscious phantasy of the kite. In it the infant Leonardo sucks upon the breast/penis of a phallic and self-sufficient mother. Freud finds in this second scene the structuring psychic principle behind not only Leonardo's sexuality–his repressed homosexuality–but the *Mona Lisa, Saint Anne with Two Others*, and an anatomical drawing of the sexual act. Leonardo's libidinal apparatus, according to Freud, sustained two erotic objects, both of which were present within the unconscious phantasy: the noncastrated mother of his infancy, and the male youth capable in some way of mirroring or replicating the child he himself once was.

[13] "A Child Is Being Beaten," in *Collected Papers of Sigmund Freud* (London: Hogarth Press, 1924), pp. 172–201.

[14] "Leonardo da Vinci and a Memory of his Childhood," in Vol. 11 of *The Standard Edition*, pp. 63–137. See especially p. 82.

At issue here is what Freud was in an essay written two years after "Leonardo da Vinci and a Memory of His Childhood" to call a "stereotype plate... which is constantly repeated–constantly reprinted afresh–in the course of the person's life, so far as external circumstances and the nature of the love-objects accessible to him permit...."[15] This concept has been suggestively elaborated and refined by Laplanche and Pontalis under the more appropriate rubric of the "phantasmatic" or "structuring action" which shapes and orders the whole of psychic life.[16] A phantasmatic is an unconscious phantasy or group of related phantasies which underlie dreams, symptoms, acting out, repetitive behavior, and daydreams. As I have already proposed with respect to cinema, it can also be seen to organize artistic production, and indeed to be the best way into the whole question of authorship.[17] Authorial subjectivity, in other words, is constituted at least in part through the repeated inscription of a particular phantasy or group of interconnected phantasies within a textual corpus.

I want to stress that the project which I have briefly outlined here deviates from Freud's in at least one crucial respect, which is that it distinguishes rigorously between the author "outside" the text and the author "inside" the text. The author "outside" the text can perhaps best be described as an "origin under erasure"–as a site which is simultaneously productive of desire and devoid of authorial "substance" or presence. He or she in some sense "gives rise" to the author "inside" the text, but is at the same time constituted as authorial subject only through that textual citation, one of whose forms is what I have been theorizing here as the phantasmatic. Since it is, then, in large part the shadow cast "outside" the text by the author "inside" the text which constitutes what we conventionally think of as the author, it is with the latter that we should begin our interrogation of authorship, rather than within the wealth of biographical detail that supports most traditional archaeologies, including Freud's. This is not to say that the theorist should bracket the biographical author's race, class, historical moment or socially-assigned gender; on the contrary, authorial subjectivity assumes much of its political force and meaning from its relation to these crucial elements. However, rather than automatically assuming, as Freud does, that there will be a direct match between the biographical author and the authorial phantasmatic, we should be prepared to see elements within the latter which are excessive, transgressive or reactionary with respect to the former–to read the authorial phantasmatic, when it is appropriate to do so, against the class, race, gender or historical moment of the biographical author, and the class, race, gender or historical moment of the biographical author *against* the phantasmatic. (I will attempt to show, for instance, that James's authorial subjectivity is radically subversive of his assigned sexual position.)

---

[15] "The Dynamics of Transference," in *The Standard Edition*, Vol. 12, p. 100.

[16] J. Laplanche and J.-B. Pontalis, *The Language of Psycho-Analysis*, trans. Donald Nicholson-Smith (New York: W.W. Norton and Co., 1973), p. 317.

[17] See Kaja Silverman, "The Female Authorial Voice," in *The Acoustic Mirror: The Female Voice in Psychoanalysis and Cinema* (Bloomington: Indiana University Press, 1988), pp. 187–234.

Before attempting to determine what phantasmatic structures James's work, I want to stress with Laplanche and Pontalis that more is involved here than a "thematic." The phantasmatic is what *The Language of Psycho-Analysis* calls a *"mise-en-scène* of desire," a dramatization of a scene or scenario in which the subject always has a part to play. It can undergo syntactical changes, as it does from one phase to another of "A Child Is Being Beaten," and roles can be reassigned within it. It also facilitates "the most primitive of defence processes, such as turning round upon the subject's own self, reversal into the opposite, negation and projection."[18]

II.

It is almost as though that prying, peeping child, who is at the psychological core of all these morbidly and sexually curious observers during this period of Henry James's work, had at long last gained entrance to what has been called "the primal scene" of his parents' sexual intercourse.[19]

Since Foucault, the signifiers "knowledge" and "power" have been frequently linked as a compound noun. In James's fiction, however, they are often placed in stark opposition. Nothing could speak more eloquently to the inadequacy of an intractably Foucauldian reading of that fiction[20] than the climactic scene in *The Ambassadors*, where Lambert Strether, spending a quiet day in the French countryside, catches a glimpse of Mme de Vionnet and Chad Newman boating alone together on the river, and has forced upon him an unwanted and incapacitating knowledge. He responds with a social version of that most classic of all psychic defenses—disavowal; he pretends, or as the novel puts it, he "make[s]-believe,"[21] that he hasn't understood what he has seen. Only later, in a deferred action, does he acknowledge to himself what he is unable to face at the time.

What is it that Lambert Strether so unpleasurably discovers during his day in the country? He learns that the relationship between Chad and Mme de Vionnet isn't, as he has hitherto assured himself, virtuous—he learns, as James puts it, that those two figures are "expert, familiar, frequent"—that "they [know] how to do it," and that "this wouldn't at all events be the first time" (307). I do not think I am stretching a point in suggesting that what is enacted here is in effect a primal scene, albeit one in which the generations are strangely confused. Strether, as he tells us in his celebrated speech to Little Bilham at Gloriani's house, after meeting Mme de Vionnet for the first time, is out of synchronization with what he sees, much like the child who "sees" his or her parents having coitus. However, whereas the child is "too early" with respect to sexual knowledge, Strether is "too late." "Live all you can," he tells Little Bilham,

[18] Laplanche and Pontalis, p. 318.

[19] Maxwell Geismar, *Henry James and the Jacobites* (Boston: Houghton Mifflin, 1963), p. 207.

[20] For a Foucauldian reading of James which I would in no way characterize as "intractable," see Mark Seltzer, *Henry James and the Art of Power* (Ithaca: Cornell University Press, 1984).

[21] *The Ambassadors*, p. 313.

[I]t's a mistake not to. It doesn't so much matter what you do in particular, so long as you have your life. If you haven't had that what have you had? This place and these impressions ... of Chad and of people I've seen at his place—well, have had their abundant message for me.... I see it now. I haven't done so enough before—and now I'm old; too old at any rate for what I see. Oh I do see, at least. ... It's too late. And it's as if the train had fairly waited at the station for me without my having had the gumption to know it was there. (132)

As we learn in *The Notebooks*, this speech, with its insistence upon Strether's status as a spectator, and his marked isolation from what he sees, was the "germ" of the entire novel.[22]

Like the primal scene, moreover, what Strether sees on the river is strongly marked precisely *as a scene*. Interestingly, he is himself "in the picture," albeit at the edges, much like the watching child in the larger context of the primal fantasy; indeed, James has recourse to a very insistent representational metaphor in describing Strether's sense of himself as he wanders around the village. Not once, we learn, does he "[overstep] the oblong gilt frame," which "[draws] itself out for him, as much as you please" (305):

> *For this had been all day at bottom the spell of the picture—that it was essentially more than anything else a scene and a stage, that the very air of the play was in the rustle of the willows and the tone of the sky. The play and the characters had, without his knowing it till now, peopled all his space for him, and it seemed somehow quite happy that they should offer themselves, in the conditions so supplied, with a kind of inevitability.* (306)

Eventually Strether sits down in a small pavilion by the water—a space clearly differentiated from the river tableau—and awaits the play to unfold within the picture frame.

This is one of the moments of intensest subjectivity (at least in the Lacanian sense of that word) in all of James's novels, and it does much to clarify a point of earlier puzzlement—to clarify, that is, why not only Bersani, but Brooks as well should ultimately privilege surface over depth in their account of Jamesian character. Strether sees himself as he might be seen by the Other, experiences himself precisely as a representation. The pictorial metaphor through which this heightened sense of self is communicated to us is startlingly close to the image through which *The Four Fundamental Concepts of Psycho-Analysis* "visualizes" subjectivity,[23] adding as it does the notion of what I have elsewhere called "the photo session" to that of the mirror stage as "formative of the I."[24] Significantly, this exaggerated self-awareness coincides with the primal scene. Strether in effect sees himself (over) seeing the

22 *The Notebooks of Henry James*, eds. F.O. Matthiessen and Kenneth B. Murdock (New York: Oxford University Press, 1947), p. 226.

23 See Jacques Lacan, *The Four Fundamental Concepts of Psycho-Analysis*, trans. Alan Sheridan (New York: Norton, 1978), pp. 105–108.

24 See Silverman, *The Acoustic Mirror*, pp. 161–62.

scene from which he is so markedly excluded. Subjectivity is thus put in place here through the pictorial (or as Lacan would have it, the photographic) surface, rather than through the projection of psychological depth. It is the consequence of a *mise-en-scène*–of the deployment of bodies within a spatial logic–and of the play of the gaze across that *mise-en-scène*.

The pictorial inflection which James gives to the scene in the French countryside also makes a special kind of sense when we recall that the primal scene occurs not so much in "reality" as in phantasy–that it is a construction after the fact, subsequent to an event with which it is by no means commensurate. The primal scene, in other words, never actually "happens" as such, but is either constituted through a deferred action much like that through which Strether reacts to what he has seen on the river, or constructed as a phantasy on the basis of some remembered detail.

But what precisely is the primal scene, and what range of possible desires and identifications does it sustain? In "Some Psychical Consequences of the Anatomical Distinction Between the Sexes" Freud describes it as a "primal phantasy" which is activated by the sounds of parental copulation, and which is capable of producing sexuality within the child (". . . analysis shows us in a shadowy way how the fact of a child at a very early age listening to his parents copulating may set up his first sexual excitation, and how that event may, owing to its after-effects, act as a starting-point for the child's whole sexual development").[25] In his much more extensive treatment of the primal scene in *From the History of an Infantile Neurosis*, Freud focuses upon it initially as a literal spectacle whose significance is only subsequently understood, but later suggests that it is a phantasy loosely based upon the observation of animal coitus.[26] The primal scene thus routes sexuality along the axes of vision and hearing, privileging image and sound over smell, touch or taste.

The watching/listening child is separated from the parental embrace by more than age. As Christian Metz suggests, voyeurism always "*concretely represents the absence of its object* in the distance at which it maintains it and which is part of its very definition: distance of the look, distance of listening."[27] Within the primal scene this distance implies an isolation both from genitality and from the tumult of passion, except–and this is a crucial qualification–at the level of identification. I will return to this last point in a moment, but first I want to note that whereas within the Metzian definition voyeurism always implies mastery and sadism,[28] here it is characterized instead by passivity

[25] "Some Psychical Consequences of the Anatomical Distinction Between the Sexes," in Vol. 19 of *The Standard Edition*, pp. 248–58. See pp. 251, 250.

[26] See *From the History of an Infantile Neurosis*, in Vol. 17 of *The Standard Edition*, pp. 48–60, for an extended discussion of the status of the Wolfman's primal scene. Building on this case history, Ned Lukacher has defined the primal scene as "an ontologically undecidable intertextual event that is situated in the differential space between historical memory and imaginative construction, between archival verification and interpretive free play," in *Primal Scenes: Literature, Philosophy, Psychoanalysis* (Ithaca: Cornell University Press, 1986), p. 24.

[27] Christian Metz, *The Imaginary Signifier: Psychoanalysis and the Cinema*, trans. Celia Britton, *et al.* (Boomington: Indiana University Press, 1982), p. 59.

[28] Metz, pp. 59–63.

and masochism. Far from controlling the sounds and images of parental sexuality, the child held captive within the crib is controlled–indeed, overwhelmed–by them. Adult sexuality invades him or her through the eyes and ears, puncturing, as it were, those vital organs.[29] The mastering, sadistic variety of voyeurism discussed by Metz can perhaps best be understood as a psychic formation calculated to reverse the power relations of the primal scene–as a compensatory drama whereby passivity yields to activity through an instinctual "turning around" and reversal.

Like the distance separating the viewer from the cinematic screen, the distance separating the child from the scene of passion paradoxically promotes identification with its actants. Freud's account of the primal scene phantasy both in "Some Psychical Consequences of the Anatomical Distinction Between the Sexes" and the Wolfman case history suggests that this identification can take some startling forms, forms which pose a serious challenge to traditional gender alignments. He notes in the first of those essays that the primal scene phantasy opens onto both the positive and the negative versions of the Oedipus complex, promoting desire for the father and identification with the mother as well as desire for the mother and identification with the father.[30] *From the History of an Infantile Neurosis* goes even further, asserting at one point that "it was not only a single sexual current that started from the primal scene but a whole series of them," and that the Wolfman's sexual life "was positively splintered up by it" (43–44). It falls outside the scope of this essay to track each element within this series, but I want to stress that Freud returns again and again to the Wolfman's identification with his mother, an identification which gave rise to complex intestinal symptoms as well as to the desire to be used by his father as she was used within the phantasmatic primal scene.[31]

But the primal scene is perhaps most profoundly disruptive of conventional masculinity in the way it articulates knowledge. Knowledge, within the Freudian paradigm, is usually insistently anchored to sexual difference, in the sense that to know is to recognize woman's "castration." Insofar as he is capable of accepting this "knowledge," which generally exercises a delayed effectivity, the male subject places a maximum psychic and moral distance between himself and his female counterpart,[32] and fortifies himself within a paternal identification by renouncing his Oedipal desires. Male "knowledge," in other words, is synonymous with phallic rectitude.

---

[29] Jean Laplanche has also commented in passing on the helplessness and masochism of the child within the primal scene: "the child, impotent in his crib, is Ulysses tied to the mast or Tantalus, on whom is imposed the spectacle of parental intercourse. Corresponding to the perturbation of pain is the 'sympathetic excitation' which can only be translated regressively through the emission of feces: the passive position of the child in relation to the adult is not simply a passivity in relation to adult activity, but passivity in relation to the adult fantasy intruding within him." See *Life and Death in Psychoanalysis*, trans. Jeffrey Mehlman (Baltimore: Johns Hopkins University Press, 1976), p. 102.

[30] "Some Psychical Consequences of the Anatomical Distinction Between the Sexes," p. 250.

[31] *From the History of an Infantile Neurosis*, pp. 77–79.

[32] In "Some Psychical Consequences of the Anatomical Distinction Between the Sexes," for instance, Freud writes that the sight of a girl's genitals eventually elicits from the boy either a "horror of the mutilated creature" or a "triumphant contempt" for her (252).

From the History of an Infantile Neurosis tells a different story. Freud writes that the Wolfman in effect "refused" the "knowledge" which would permit him to distinguish clearly between himself and his mother. Although he suffered from castration anxiety which, according to Freud, could only have derived from a recognition of woman's anatomical "lack," his unconscious sexuality was entirely organized around an erotogenic zone which is undecidable with respect to gender, *i.e.* the anus. Even his conscious sexual phantasies and practices turned upon a blurring of the distinction between the vagina and the anus–upon the possibility of the former standing in for the latter (hence his intense excitement when glimpsing the female form from behind, in a floor-scrubbing attitude). Because of the privileged status given by the Wolfman to various anally coded memories of servant women, his obsessive preoccupation with Christ's anus during a childhood period of deep identification with him, and various symptoms relating to disorders of the bowels, Freud deduces that his patient's primal scene phantasy revolved around *coitus a tergo*. At the level of the unconscious, the Wolfman identified strongly with the imaginary position of his mother, on all fours like an animal, and dreamed of being anally used by his father in a similar way. At the level of conscious phantasy and practice, he himself assumed the imaginary position occupied by his father, and used women sexually from behind. However, this second identification was never very strong, and was radically undermined by the maternal identification revealed by his psychosomatic difficulties. Freud writes that "from the time of his dream onwards, in his unconscious he was homosexual, and in his neurosis he was at the level of cannibalism [his neurosis included the fear of being eaten by the wolf/father]; while the earlier masochistic attitude remained the dominant one. All three currents had passive sexual aims; there was the same object [*i.e.* the father], and the same sexual impulse, but they had become split up at three different levels" (252–53). The "fact" of woman's anatomical "castration" was thus something in excess of the Wolfman's psychic economy, something which threatened to capsize him by distinguishing him from her. It may very well be that knowledge always has this disruptive force within the primal scene, even when it does not assume such a classically Freudian form as recognition of a penile lack.

Masculinity is thus perhaps never as fully troubled as it is within the primal scene. It is not merely that knowledge fails there to provide power, or to shore up sexual difference, but that vision, which is culturally coded as a phallic function, and which indeed helps to constitute masculinity, turns back against the child, inducing a sense of inadequacy and exclusion. If that child is male, he is what Freud in his case history of *Dora* calls "a man without means,"[33] and that–as Luce Irigaray argues in *Speculum*–is precisely how psychoanalysis defines woman.[34] Finally subjectivity within the primal scene is enormously complicated by the possibility of the watching child identifying either with the mother or with the father–of putting himself or herself psychi-

---

[33] *Fragment of an Analysis of a Case of Hysteria*, in *The Standard Edition*, Vol. 7, p. 47.

[34] Luce Irigaray, *Speculum of the Other Woman*, trans. Gillian C. Gill (Ithaca: Cornell University Press, 1985), pp. 25–33.

cally in the place of both parents. What would seem to facilitate this easy slip-page from masculinity to femininity, at least within *From the History of an Infantile Neurosis,* is the child's belief that the father is penetrating the mother anally–that he is "going behind" her. The primal scene, Freud suggests, is not only voyeuristic, but potentially pederastic.

III.

Who can fail to remember, in this context, that Strether is preeminently a man without (economic) means, who must be financed by Mrs. Newsome? That he feels himself to be at home in Wollett's "society of women," something which he himself acknowledges to be "an odd situation for a man" (213)? That he is given to sudden sharp identifications with Mme de Vionnet, who occupies the place of the mother within his primal scene, identifications which are described by the novel as "queer displacement[s] of his point of view" (235)? That even before the scene by the river he has crept up on some-one who didn't know he was watching, someone–Mamie Pocock–who was holding herself in an attitude of readiness for the visit of Little Bilham? Or that he shrinks from the position of "hero" (265), preferring to be "behind the scenes" (262)? Finally, who can forget the facility with which James-as-narrator or speaking subject establishes imaginary alignments with feminine characters–Fleda Vetch, the governess in *Turn of the Screw,* Isabel Archer, or Maisie, to name but a few?

It seems to me that subjectivity in James's corpus is bound up in some very fundamental way with the primal scene–that that scene indeed consti-tutes one of his authorial phantasmatics, if not indeed the primary one. There is, first of all, James's extraordinary obsession with the scenic principle, an obsession which reaches its apotheosis in *The Awkward Age,* but which also surfaces quite explicitly in his constant self-exhortations to "dramatize, drama-tize," and in the organization of *The Tragic Muse.* "The whole thing has visi-bly, from the first, to get itself done in dramatic, or at least scenic conditions," writes James in the "Preface" to that last novel,

> –though scenic conditions which are as near an approach to the dramatic as the novel may permit itself and which have this in common with the latter, that they move in the light of alternation. This imposes a consistency other than that of the novel at its loosest, and, for one's subject, a different view and a different placing of the centre. The charm of the scenic consistency, the consistency of the multiplication of aspects, that of making them amusingly various, had haunted the author of "The Tragic Muse" from far back, and he was in due course to yield to it all luxuriously, too luxuriously perhaps, in "The Awkward Age."[35]

---

[35] *The Art of the Novel,* p. 90.

The effect of conceiving the novel as a series of "scenes" is to position the narrator emphatically as an onlooker, even when he is not closely identified with a fictional "perceiver."

James's novels and short stories also return again and again to situations which, like Strether's visit to the French countryside, somehow reprise that phantasmatic moment where the child is first made aware of adult sexuality. The most crucial scene in *The Portrait of a Lady*, for instance–at least insofar as Isabel's consciousness is concerned–is surely the one in which, hesitating on the threshold of her Italian drawing room, she catches sight of Madame Merle and Gilbert Osmond immersed in an intimate colloquy. As in *The Ambassadors*, there is nothing explicitly carnal in what she sees, but the glimpsed tableau bristles with an assumed privacy whose effect is to make the spectator suddenly aware of a sexual secret from which she has been barred:

> What struck Isabel first was that he was sitting while Madame Merle stood; there was an anomaly in this that arrested her. Then she perceived that they had arrived at a desultory pause in their exchange of ideas and were musing, face to face, with the freedom of old friends who sometimes exchange ideas without uttering them. There was nothing to shock in this; they were old friends in fact. But the thing made an image, lasting only a moment, like a sudden flicker of light. Their relative positions, their absorbed mutual gaze, struck her as something detected.[36]

Here, too, the spectacle assumes its full force only later, after it has been internalized as representation. Isabel sits up late the same night, thinking about her husband, and gazing at the "remembered vision" of him and Madame Merle "unconsciously and familiarly associated" (434).

The Princess Casamassima builds toward a structurally identical scene, to which Hyacinth Robinson has a more classically readable response. Furtively watching the Princess get out of a cab and go into her house with Paul Muniment, he has "a very exact revelation of the state of feeling of those who love in the rage of jealousy. If he had been told half an hour before that he was capable of surreptitious peepings in the interest of that passion he would have resented the insult; yet he allowed himself to be checked by his companion just at the nearest point at which they might safely consider the proceedings of the couple who alighted."[37] This is perhaps the earliest example of an interesting variation on the usual primal scene, a variation to which James was to return more than once in his later work. Hyacinth is joined in his lookout point–indeed brought there–by Prince Casamassima, so that the cast of characters includes four rather than the usual three. This doubling up of the figure of the spectator foregrounds the voyeurism of the scene. It also places Hyacinth and the Prince emphatically onstage, albeit at the margins rather than at the center of the spectacle:

[36] Henry James, *The Portrait of a Lady* (New York: Modern Library, 1966), p. 407.

[37] Henry James, *The Princess Casamassima* (New York: Harper and Brothers, 1959), p. 445. Future quotations will be from this edition.

"What does he say? What does she say?" hissed the Prince; and when he went on the next moment, "Will he go in again or will he go away?" our stricken youth felt a voice given to his own sharpest thought. The pair were talking together with rapid sequences, and as the door had not yet been opened it was clear that, to prolong the conversation on the steps, the Princess delayed to ring. "It will make three, four hours he has been with her," moaned the Prince.

"He may be with her fifty hours!" Hyacinth laughed as he turned away ashamed of himself. (445–46)

The last chapter of the novel contains a matching tableau, except that its spectator is solitary. Rejected by the Princess Casamassima, and confronted with the painful obligation to perform an assassination for a political cause in which he no longer believes, Hyacinth goes in search of Millicent at the shop where she works. When he at last finds her, she is standing with her back to him, but with her face to Captain Sholto, ostensibly modelling a fashionable dress for the latter's inspection, but in fact offering up her body to his visual delectation:

In spite of her averted face he instantly "spotted" Millicent; he knew her shop-attitude, the dressing of her hair behind and the long grand lines of her figure draped in the last new thing. She was showing off this treasure to the Captain, who was lost in contemplation. . . . his eyes travelling up and down the front of their beautiful friend's person. . . . (506)

Sholto catches sight of Hyacinth, but fails to acknowledge him; he only gives the young man a "hard" look, intimating the privacy of his negotiations with Millicent.

And then there is *The Golden Bowl*, which is in many ways an extended primal scene, and which does not fail to conjure forth an image which brings home with particular force to Maggie Verver that, as James puts it elsewhere in the novel, "Amerigo and Charlotte [are] arranged together," whereas she "[is] arranged apart." That image, which is curiously displaced with respect to the moment at which Maggie learns of her husband's adultery, is produced for her one day as she returns home. Waiting for her on the balcony are Charlotte and Amerigo, in a display whose calculated publicity is unable to conceal their private understanding–a display that "might have shocked the decency of Portland Place":

. . . the pair were perched together in the balcony, he bare-headed, she divested of her jacket, her mantle, or whatever, but crowned with a brilliant brave hat, responsive to the balmy day. . . . They were gay, they were amused, in the pleasant morning. . . . The group on the pavement stared up as at the peopled battlements of a castle. . . . Maggie's individual gape was inevitably again for the thought of how the pair would be at work.[38]

---

[38] Henry James, *The Golden Bowl* in 2 vols. (New York: Grove, 1952), 2:102–103 358–59. Bersani has commented on the "scenic" quality of this and several of the other passages I have cited here, and in terms which very much anticipate the

I must not omit from this brief catalogue three James texts which turn the spotlight away from the primal scene itself to its spectator–*The Turn of the Screw*, *What Maisie Knew*, and *The Awkward Age*. The governess in the first of those works manifests a veritable obsession with the question of what the children know and what they have seen of the compromised (and compromising) Peter Quint and Miss Jessel. What she *herself* knows and sees has of course become the crux of the critical controversy about the *nouvelle*.[39] What *Maisie Knew* and *The Awkward Age* similarly focus on girls who are "exposed" to adult sexuality, and in each case the interrogation of that personage's knowledge forms the central drama of the book. In all three instances, knowledge leads not to power and social integration, but to loss and isolation. Nanda is obliged to leave her parents' world for the celibacy of Longdon's country estate at the end of *The Awkward Age*, and the eponymous heroine of *What Maisie Knew* is ejected from all of her various family circles and left to the devices of Mrs. Wix at the end of that novel. The consequences are even more severe in *The Turn of the Screw*; when Miles is finally brought to the point of uttering Peter Quint's name, his heart stops.

A surprising number of Jamesian characters, moreover, are–like the infantile voyeur–conspicuously either too early or too late with respect to sexuality. Miles, Flora, Nanda and Maisie are all out of temporal alignment with the sexuality they somehow hear or see. Like Lambert Strether, Mr. Longdon of *The Awkward Age* comes to sexual awareness only when he is too old for that awareness to be implemented. Even Isabel Archer encounters sexuality in the form of Caspar Goodwood's "white lightning" kiss only after she has married the passionless Gilbert Osmond.

But the most explicit and complex dramatization of the temporality specific to the primal scene is surely "The Beast in the Jungle." John Marcher has all the curiosity and scopic urgency of the spectating child, and his voyeurism is reinforced by May Bartram's; for decades they wait and watch together, both of them "peeping," as James puts it, through the same "apertures at Marcher's life."[40] They both live "to see what would *be* to be seen," but their joint gaze meets a specular void. At first glance it seems as though the heterosexual couple–the protagonists of the primal scene–have repositioned themselves as the onlookers, leaving an empty space at center stage. However, Marcher is very emphatically coded as the man apart, the man "to whom nothing on earth [is] to [happen]" (535).

present discussion: "Each of these scenes is interpreted as a betrayal, and the betrayal takes the form of an intimacy which excludes its witness. The violent, traumatic nature of these sights is not always immediately explicit ... but they haunt the consciousness of the Jamesian hero as images of a hidden and threatening truth from which, for what usually turn out to be sinister reasons, he has been excluded" (133–34).

[39] Lukacher also relates *Turn of the Screw* to the primal scene, although his project is very different from mine. He is primarily concerned with establishing what, with respect to the events related within that story, might be said to be "real." (See *Primal Scenes*, pp. 115–32.)

[40] "The Beast in the Jungle," in *Henry James: Selected Fiction*, ed. Leon Edel (New York: Dutton, 1964), p. 500. All future quotations will be from this edition.

Eve Sedgwick has recently suggested that the "real truth" of Marcher's "predicament" is repressed homosexuality, and that this is why he is unable to marry May Bartram.[41] Her reading is very elegant and persuasive, but she is obliged to discount the ending in order to secure it. (She asks us to "imagine" the story without the "enforcing symmetry" of Marcher's revelation that heterosexuality would have provided both Bartram and himself with an "escape" from aridity and lifelessness [168]). Within Sedgwick's reading, moreover, the figure of Bartram is a structural excrescence, at least with respect to the operations of male homosexual desire; she is the prototype of "the woman ... who has not only the most delicate nose for but the most potent attraction toward men who are at crises of homosexual panic" (179), but she has herself no place within Marcher's–or James's–libidinal economy.

It seems to me important to find a way of reading the many signifiers of homosexuality within this story without at the same time refusing its conclusion, and I would argue that the only way to do that is through locating the primal scene within it–that scene which is at first glance so curiously absent. Before attempting to do that, I want to emphasize once again that Marcher is in every important sense comparable to the watching child within the Freudian account. Not only is he strongly marked precisely as a spectator, but the spectacle for which he waits is something "rare and strange, possibly prodigious and terrible"–something that will "overwhelm" or even "annihilate" him (490–91). Here again is voyeurism with a difference, voyeurism which bears no relation to that mastering vision which has been so exhaustively interrogated within film theory.[42] Marcher is also a man without sexual means, foreclosed from start to finish from the scene of passion, *except through identification*. Finally, at the point that knowledge comes to him–knowledge, that is, of his own libidinal isolation–it frightens and sickens him:

> *This horror of waking*–this *was knowledge, knowledge under the breath of which the very tears in his eyes seemed to freeze. Through them, none the less, he tried to fix it and hold it; he kept it there before him so that he might feel the pain. That at least, belated and bitter, had something of the taste of life. But the bitterness sickened him, and it was as if, horribly, he saw, in the truth, in the cruelty of his image, what had been appointed and done. He saw the Jungle of his life and he saw the lurking beast. . . .* (536)

The same cannot be said of the only other two characters in the story, May Bartram and the stranger Marcher encounters in the graveyard. Although it is only retrospectively that the image of Bartram's sick face speaks to Marcher of wasted desire, that meaning is available to the attentive reader much earlier, and is made almost explicit on the occasion of the visit Marcher later

41 Eve Kosofsky Sedgwick, "The Beast in the Closet: James and the Writing of Homosexual Panic," in *Sex, Politics, and Science in the Nineteenth-Century Novel*, ed. Ruth Bernard Yeazell (Baltimore: Johns Hopkins University Press, 1985), pp. 148–186.

42 See, for instance, Metz, *The Imaginary Signifier*; Laura Mulvey, "Visual Pleasure and Narrative Cinema," *Screen*, vol. 16, no. 3 (1975), 6–18; Stephen Heath, "Difference," *Screen*, vol. 19, no. 3 (1978), 51–112; and Teresa de Lauretis, *Alice Doesn't: Feminism, Semiotics, Cinema* (Bloomington: Indiana University Press, 1984), pp. 12–36.

remembers. James writes that on the afternoon of a cold April day shortly before her death it became "suddenly, from her movement and attitude, beautiful and vivid to [Marcher] that she had something more to give him.... they
continued for some minutes silent, her face shining at him, her contact im-
ponderably pressing" (519). The face of the stranger is even more expressive;
there is "a kind of hunger in his look," which even after he has passed continues to "flare" for Marcher like a "smoky torch" (533, 534).

It occurs to me that what we have here is a curiously fragmented and dispersed primal scene, recuperable primarily from the graveyard encounter,
with its insistence on specularity, and its curious evocation of sexuality. It is
not only that the stranger is "scarred" with "passion," but that he is twice described as "showing" (and James italicizes this word the second time) his
deeply ravaged features (534). Something in this spectacle "profane[s] the
air," "rouse[s], startle[s]" and "shock[s]" Marcher, and induces him to look
after it with the "envy" (535) of one excluded from a privileged transaction.

Because the dead lover for whom the stranger mourns is never represented
except through a strong structural parallel to May Bartram, the latter in effect
stands in for that figure. Together Bartram and the stranger comprise the passionate heterosexual couple of the classic primal scene, although they are in
no way present to each other; they designate, in other words, the passionate
man and the passionate woman. Lest this reading seem unduly strained, it
should be noted that Marcher imagines himself loving only through identification with the stranger's desire for the unknown woman who is herself a
projection of Bartram:

> No passion had ever touched him, for this was what passion meant; he had sur-
> vived and maundered and pined, but where had been his deep ravage? ... The
> sight that had just met his eyes named to him, as in letters of quick flame, some-
> thing he had utterly, insanely missed, and what he had missed made these
> things a train of fire, made them mark themselves in an anguish of inward
> throbs. He had seen outside his life, not learned it within, the way a woman
> was mourned when she had been loved for herself: such was the force of the con-
> viction of the meaning of the stranger's face. (534)

Like the child in the primal scene, sexual consciousness is implanted in
Marcher only through what is in effect Oedipal triangulation.

As I indicated earlier in this essay, that scene opens onto the negative as
well as the positive Oedipus complex, and it may at times be said to superimpose one of those triangles on top of the other. The Jamesian phantasmatic
effects just such a superimposition, as a result of which there are two imaginary points of entry into it. One of these points of entry is that designated by
Freud in From a History of an Infantile Neurosis, i.e. identification with the
"mother," and the desire to be used by the "father" as she is. This imaginary
access implies, once again, a blurring of the distinction between anus and vagina. It also constitutes a classic rendition of the negative or inverted Oedipus

complex. The second point of entry into James's primal scene is constituted through what can perhaps best be described as a "pederastic identification" with the "father," an identification which permits the phantasizing subject to look through that figure's eyes and to participate in his sexuality by going "behind" him. This convergence of desire for and identification with the father attests to something which psychoanalysis has not yet prepared us to conceptualize, *i.e.* the possibility of assuming a subject position at the intersection of the positive and negative Oedipus complexes. In neither the classic working out of the negative Oedipus complex nor in this second, more complex situation, is the "mother" dispensable. In the first instance she designates the point of interpellation, as Althusser would say,[43] and in the second she is the necessary third term within a relay which seems to begin with the phantasizing subject, who stands in phantasy "behind" the "father," but which in fact begins with the "father's" penetration of the "mother."

The Jamesian phantasmatic can thus be said to enclose homosexuality within heterosexuality, and heterosexuality within homosexuality. At the risk of violating a fundamental tenet of James criticism–the tenet that no matter how luridly suggestive the Master's language, it cannot have a sexual import–I would like to invoke at this point a passage from *The Art of the Novel* which locates the same relay within a much earlier text, and to insist that at least on this occasion we should take James at his word. "I never go behind Miriam," he writes of *The Tragic Muse*, "only poor Sherringham goes, a great deal, and Nick Dormer goes a little, and the author, while they so waste wonderment, goes behind *them*."[44]

But let us return to "The Beast in the Jungle." Sedgwick has already commented upon the "cruisiness" of the graveyard scene,[45] an observation with which I am in fundamental agreement. However, I also want to draw attention to a curious rhetorical reversal that occurs in that scene, and that attests to the two desires which the Jamesian phantasmatic sustains–the desire to be sodomized by the "father" while occupying the place of the "mother," and the desire to sodomize him while he is penetrating the "mother." When the stranger first appears to Marcher in the cemetery, he looks at the latter with "an expression like the cut of a knife" that goes "so deep down that [Marcher] wince[s] at the steady thrust" (532, 533). The second time the two men encounter each other, the wound has been displaced from Marcher to the stranger:

> *The most extraordinary thing that had happened to him ... took place, after his immediate vague stare, as a consequence of this impression. The stranger passed, but the raw glare of his grief remained, making our friend wonder in pity what wrong, what wound it expressed, what injury not to be healed. What had the man had, to make him by the loss of it so bleed, and yet live?* (534)

---

[43] This is a concept theorized by Louis Althusser in "Ideology and Ideological State Apparatuses: Notes towards an Investigation," in *Lenin and Philosophy*, trans. Ben Brewster (London: Monthly Review Press, 1971), pp. 127–86.

[44] *The Art of the Novel*, p. 91.

[45] Sedgwick, p. 180.

Whereas in the first passage the stranger is the one who penetrates Marcher with the knife of his vision, in the second passage he has become the one who is penetrated, and, in the process, feminized. The former marks the maternal point of entry into the Jamesian phantasmatic–that turning, in other words, upon identification with the "mother"–and the latter the point of entry which occurs through what I have called "pederastic identification" with the "father."

I cannot help but think, here, of two passages in Freud's *From the History of an Infantile Neurosis* where he remarks upon a "counter-current" working within the Wolfman's psyche, a "counter-current" which led the latter at times to see his own castration as the necessary condition of sexual satisfaction from his father (228), and at times to regard his father "as the person castrated and as calling, therefore, for his sympathy" (178). The castration of which Freud speaks closely resembles the displaceable wound in "The Beast in the Jungle." Is it possible that the Wolfman's primal scene phantasy, like the one which structures James's fiction, also posited the father as both penetrating and penetrable? If so–and I cannot see any other way to read Freud's statement–it would seem that to the degree to which the primal scene phantasy acknowledges castration it cannot help but generalize it by making it a consequence not of anatomy, but of subject position.

IV

I want by way of concluding this essay to turn to a novel which is seemingly the least "subjective" of James's major works, the one which is most fully realized according to dramatic principles, and which involves a minimum of "interiorization." I refer, of course, to *The Awkward Age*, a text which consists almost entirely of conversation; which is composed of a series of admirably constructed "scenes"; and which builds to a highly theatrical "climax." I propose to demonstrate that it is in fact one of the *most* "subjective" of James's novels in the sense in which I have been using that word–that it is a virtual showcase for his authorial phantasmatic.

The Awkward Age revolves around the issue of Nanda's sexual knowledge–around the question of what she has learned about all the illicit couplings that are a constant topic of adult conversation: Petherton and the Duchess, Aggie and Petherton, Harold and Lady Fanny, Lady Fanny and her other paramours, Mrs. Brook and Van. The other source of possible "corruption" is the racy reading material the adults are constantly exchanging, most particularly the French novel which is first mentioned in Book I and which resurfaces again in Book VIII. Given that Nanda is ultimately shown to know "everything," as she is fond of putting it, the whole of *The Awkward Age* could be said to be an extended primal scene, albeit one in which hearing is much more fully privileged than vision ("And yet to think that after all it has been mere *talk*!" is how Van describes the sexuality to which Nanda has been "exposed").[46]

Nanda's knowledge, as I have already mentioned, results in loss and isolation rather than in gain or social integration. It is the result, moreover, of adult sexuality and conversation rather than of Nanda's own intellectual efforts, so that it is difficult to conceptualize what she learns as mastery. She compares herself at one point to a drain pipe through which "everything" flows, an image suggestive of passivity as well as contamination. Mitchy counters with a more graceful metaphor, likening Nanda instead to "'a little aeolian harp set in the drawing-room window and vibrating in the breeze of conversation'" (243). However, the romantic tradition behind this metaphor does little to mitigate the impression created by the earlier image–the impression, that is, that Nanda is less acting than acted upon. Finally, although it is here the adults who are traumatized by the child's knowledge rather than the child herself, that knowledge continues to be generative of disruption and crisis.

The Awkward Age also contains a number of more compactly organized–albeit equally unconventional–primal scenes. One of these scenes occurs "off-stage," as it were, and is conveyed to us through a chorus of speculating voices. I refer to the occasion, late in Book VIII, when Petherton and Aggie engage in an erotic tussle over possession of the French novel in a room apart from the one in which everyone else is gathered, listening. The observing child has been replaced by a group of adult auditors, while the child herself has taken her "mother's" place within the primal scene.

As we will see, this is only one of the generational confusions which occurs in *The Awkward Age*. It is a result of the syntactic changes and defensive processes which Laplanche and Pontalis associate with phantasy. Rather than spying upon the "father" (Petherton) while he makes love to the "mother" (the Duchess), little Aggie–who must be understood at least in part as an authorial inscription in that she a) effects the movement from innocence to consciousness so central to the Jamesian system, and b) literalizes the dream of being used by the "father" as the "mother" was used–is observed by the latter while the former makes love to her. (Significantly, during his erotic struggle with Aggie, Petherton must literally "go behind" her since she sits on the French novel he seeks to secure.)

Once we have understood that those characters who are caught up in the primal scene phantasmatic are all citations of James's authorial subjectivity, with pride of place always given to the figure who enacts a coming-to-knowledge, we are able to see not only that Aggie acts out in a way which is usually denied to James's surrogates the desire to be in the mother's place, but that in the process scopophilia has given way to exhibitionism–a shift indicative of the "turning around" of the scopic drive upon the subject's own self. The active form of the verb "to watch" has also yielded to its passive equivalent, much as the phrase "my father is beating a child [whom I hate]" mutates into "a child is being beaten" in the essay of that name.

---

[46] Henry James, *The Awkward Age* (New York: Norton, 1969), p. 212. All future quotations will be taken from this edition.

The climax of the novel, moreover, is a veritable inversion of the primal scene. The adulterous grown-ups gather around Nanda to force out of her the confession that she has read the incriminating French novel and that she is consequently fully capable of understanding the libidinal intrigues that are going on all around her. It is of course Mrs. Brook who precipitates this crisis, and she does so to prevent a repetition of the Aggie/Petherton affair–to prevent the daughter from usurping the mother within a second erotic triangle. (Surely the most astonishing feature of this late Victorian novel, and the one pointing most unwaveringly to the primal scene, is the twice-repeated convergence of mother and daughter upon the same erotic object.) However, the end result of all this publicity is that Van turns away from both women, and that the social circle which has been predicated upon their "romance" disintegrates. The catastrophe which is usually circumscribed within the psyche of the watching child is generalized to the society as a whole, and the event is subsequently characterized as "that awful night" and "the smash."

Significantly, whereas Aggie flourishes in the social limelight (at the expense, moreover, of Mitchy and her mother), Nanda does not. Her "specularization" seems to work according to that all too familiar logic which decrees that insofar as woman is seen and heard she is found to be either lacking or in excess of the phallus. (Here, of course, what is located at the site of the female subject is a surplus of knowledge rather than, as is more customary, *jouissance*.) However, it seems to me that there is a better way of accounting for the different relation of Aggie and Nanda to the (adult) gaze. Whereas the first of these characters is situated within the scene of passion, the other is emphatically foreclosed from it at the moment that her "exposure" is revealed, and it is *this* which determines how she is looked at by the other characters in the novel. What the juxtaposition of these two primal scenes suggests is that it is the way in which the human look is imbricated with sexuality which determines power relations, and not that look *per se*. (I must add that the reader's "gaze" is orchestrated very differently from that of Mrs. Brook, the Duchess or Van–that, like Mr. Longdon, we are encouraged to validate Nanda's position of lack and exclusion more than Aggie's social and sexual integration.)

As if James's authorial phantasmatic were not already sufficiently encoded into *The Awkward Age*, the novel even goes so far as to equip Nanda with a primal scene "memory," a "memory" in which she functions once again as the watching and foreclosed child. "I verily believe she's in love with you," Nanda says of her mother to Van on the occasion of his final visit to her,

> "You're more to her, I verily believe, than any one ever was. I hate to have the appearance of plotting anything about her behind her back [my emphasis]; so I'll just say it once for all. She once said, in speaking of it to a person who repeated it to me, that you had done more for her than any one, because it was you who had really brought her out. It was–you did. I saw it at the time myself. I was very small, but I could see it." (342)

It should also be noted that Nanda's libidinal economy is itself explicable only in relation to the structure of the primal scene. She rejects the amorous Mitchy for the indifferent Van because she "positively like[s] to love in vain" (243)–because the subject-position which she occupies within the Jamesian phantasmatic is precisely the one which is always set apart from genital sexuality, forever out of synchronization with the passion it witnesses. Nanda, we recall, is never part of Mrs. Brook's inner circle, that society which is an extension of the latter's intimacy with Van. It is not surprising, then, that she can enter the circle within that circle (i.e. that space occupied by Van and Mrs. Brook) only through identification, and that her mother is the point of imaginary insertion. Nor is it surprising that she should herself be the agency whereby Van is returned to Mrs. Brook at the end of the novel, since only in that way will she have imaginary access once again to him.

There is yet another inscription of James's authorial phantasmatic in *The Awkward Age*, an inscription which includes the negative or homosexual Oedipus complex as well as its positive or heterosexual version. I refer here to the triangle which extends outward from Longdon, and which has at its other two points Nanda and Van. Like Lambert Strether in *The Ambassadors*, Longdon is out of temporal alignment with the world he enters at the beginning of the novel, and leaves at the end. Not only is he "too late" to be part of the sexual intrigues he witnesses, but–more remarkably–he is "too early" to be included in the erotic union which he never in fact sees, but which he might be said to "phantasize": the erotic union of Van and Nanda. Near the conclusion of *The Awkward Age* he is described as a much younger person than Nanda, and as much less "old-fashioned" than Van (368). He is psychically positioned, in other words, as their "child," and as he remarks at one point to the latter, "I've watched you both" (186).

As this remark would suggest, Longdon is another of James's "observers," manifesting the same hyperdevelopment of hearing and vision as Nanda, although his perceptual passions are more fully exercised upon an internal than an external scene. Interestingly, that internal scene intersects significantly with Nanda's childhood "memory"; indeed, it might be said to play out the desire which is at the very center of that "memory"–the desire that Van use Nanda as she "recalls" him using Mrs. Brook. Here is a virtual "group phantasy," although (as I will demonstrate in a moment) it speaks to a more complex libidinal economy in the older man's case than it does in that of the girl. Of course, Longdon is able to make Nanda's desires his own only because he identifies with her so fully–because he, in his own turn, imagines himself being used by Van as she wishes to be used. It is, after all, only after the Duchess has informed Longdon of Nanda's love for Van that he "conceives" (a signifier with unavoidably erotic connotations) the "desire" (181) to pair them up sexually. This desire eventually becomes so palpable that Van is prompted to exclaim: "How awfully you want it!" (186).

Longdon's "wants" are, it seems to me, extremely complex. His attraction to Nanda, like his identification with her, is frequently documented over the course of *The Awkward Age*; not only is she metonymically connected to the dead woman whose memory he cherishes, but he comes eventually to be "a man of her own." He sends her flowers and books, goes everywhere with her, and takes her off to live with himself at the end of the novel. As the girl herself remarks at several points, they are "one of the couples who are invited together" (153, 154).

Van also figures centrally within Longdon's libidinal economy. Mitchy declares at a key point that "[Longdon] likes [Van] not a whit less than he likes [Nanda]" (254), and this account of the elderly man's desires is borne out by other details in the text as well. It is not only Nanda, but Van, who benefits from what might be called a "libidinal legacy"; if she functions as a replacement for her grandmother, he does the same for his mother, who was also loved by Longdon in the past. There is even a moment of telling censorship when Nanda narrowly avoids confronting Longdon with his desire for Van, and that moment, interestingly enough, is precisely when she herself has been brought for the first time to acknowledge her own feelings for that character. "It would be good for me–by which I mean it would be easier for me–if you didn't quite so immensely care for him," Mr. Longdon says to her.

> *"Oh!" came from Nanda with an accent of attenuation at once so precipitate and so vague that it only made her attitude at first rather awkward. "Oh!" she immediately repeated, but with an increase of the same effect. After which, conscious, she made, as if to save herself, a quick addition. "Dear Mr. Longdon, isn't it rather yourself most–?" (365)*

Longdon's erotic investment in Van has, moreover, a monetary correlative, and money (as we have known from Freud) is never without anal significance. James's language underscores that significance when he has Longdon say of the fortune which he proposes to put at Van's disposal if the latter marries Nanda, "My dear boy, I *back* you" (182). It is not only that Longdon wishes to be used by Van as he phantasizes Nanda being used, but that he is bound to the young man through a pederastic identification analogous to that which binds Marcher to the stranger in "The Beast in the Jungle"; he wants, that is, to go "behind" the union of Van and Nanda, and in so doing to make imaginary love to her *through him*. Longdon's phantasmatic is structured both by his imaginary aspiration to occupy the place of the mother within the primal scene, and by his desire to become what he also wishes to possess, a desire which is at the same time homosexual and heterosexual, in that it encompasses the "mother" as well as the "father."

In the "Preface" to *The Awkward Age*, James writes that the "objectivity" of that novel comes "from the imposed absence of that 'going behind,' to compass explanations and amplifications, to drag out odds and ends from the 'mere' story-teller's great property-shop of aids to illusion: a resource under denial of which it was equally perplexing and delightful, for a change, to pro-

ceed."[47] However, this apparent refusal, for once, to look through a character's eyes, and experience the force of his or her desires, is belied by the photograph which serves as the frontispiece to the New York Edition of *The
Awkward Age*. That photograph represents Longdon's country home with an
image of James's own house in Rye.[48] It thus provides a startlingly frank acknowledgment that authorial subjectivity is concentrated at those sites
marked by the signifier "Longdon," and that the phantasmatic and desires
which I have attributed to the latter are in fact specific to the former.

The action of "going behind," with all of its pederastic ramifications, would
thus seem to have been displaced from the narrating voice to the figure of
Longdon. However, given that it is worked through the characters of Aggie
and Mrs. Brook, as well as Nanda and Longdon, the desire to be on the receiving end of that action would appear to exercise an even stronger force
within the psychic theater of *The Awkward Age*, and, by extension, James's authorial subjectivity. Either way, all libidinal roads seem to lead to Van. It is
not only Longdon and Nanda who desire that character, but Mrs. Brook.
Even Mitchy wants to help Longdon provide Van with financial "backing."
Mrs. Brook thus clearly speaks for the author as well as the others when she
says to her husband, at the end of *The Awkward Age*: "we were in love with
him" (311).

V.

What I have been calling "pederastic identification" is a variant of narcissistic
object-choice, the libidinal economy which Freud most frequently associates
with homosexuality.[49] Narcissistic object choice can assume a number of different forms, including love for what one once was, love for what one would
like to be, love for someone who was once part of oneself, or–quite simply–self-love.[50] It is primarily the third of these possibilities, where what one
would like to be coincides with what one would like to possess, that I would
associate with pederastic identification. The latter implies, in other words, the
convergence of identification and desire upon the same object, an object
which is in this case the "father." Pederastic identification also permits the
subject to participate at an imaginary level in the "father's" phallic
sexuality–to penetrate, in phantasy, and perhaps even in fact, through identifying with the one-who-penetrates. It is thereby a mechanism through which
a subject who is profoundly marked by passivity and lack can lay temporary
claim to an *active* sexual aim.

---

[47] *The Art of the Novel*, p. 111.

[48] For a reproduction of that photograph, see Ralph F. Bogardus, *Pictures and Texts: Henry James, A.L. Coburn, and New Ways of Seeing in Literary Culture* (Ann Arbor: U.M.I. Research Press, 1984), fig. 9.

[49] See, for instance, "Three Essays on the Theory of Sexuality," in Vol. 12, *The Standard Edition*, pp. 144f; "Leonardo Da Vinci and a Memory of His Childhood," in Vol. 11, *The Standard Edition*, pp. 99–102; and "On Narcissism: An Introduction," in Vol. 14, *The Standard Edition*, pp. 73–102. See especially pp. 88, 96, 101–02.

[50] Freud enumerates these narcissistic variants in "On Narcissism," p. 90.

However, pederastic identification is at the same time radically desubstan-
tializing, in that it is entirely subsumed within the conditional tenses of the
verbs "to be" and "to possess." The subject of whom I speak–the subject who
occupies a male position only through an imaginary conflation with the
"father" whom he also desires–would consequently seem incapable of effecting that *méconnaissance* so crucial to normative masculinity, *i.e.* of mistaking
his penis for the phallus. Nor, it would seem, could he unblushingly assume
himself to be the point of (sexual) origin. He would be only too alert to further syntagmatic possibilities, including that of being used as he imagines
himself using the father. The receptive position, in other words, is the overdetermined site of pleasure.

Pederastic identification with the phantasmatic father is, nonetheless, the
only means whereby the Jamesian "hero" can approximate a masculine position, and as we have seen, that position is only very briefly sustained in "The
Beast in the Jungle."[51] It represents an even more elusive goal in *The
Awkward Age* since the figure who occupies the position of the "father" in the
imagined primal scene is himself incapable of entertaining an active sexual
aim, at least with respect to Nanda. Van is at no point in the present tense of
the novel marked by any of the passion that "scars" the face of the stranger
in "The Beast in the Jungle," or that of Spencer Brydon's alter ego in "The
Jolly Corner." There is not even anything to validate Nanda's childhood
"memory" of Van "bringing out" her mother. *The Awkward Age* thus
ultimately attests as much to the impossibility of "actual" sexual penetration
as to the desire to be both on the "giving" and the "receiving" end. Appropriately, the novel concludes with the self-imposed exile from society of those
two characters–Longdon and Nanda–who have been most insistently coded
as watching children, their retreat from "real" sexuality to the world of Bec-
cles and phantasy.

James himself comments eloquently on the strangely marginal position occupied by many of the characters who function as the centers of
(un)consciousness in his novels. He speaks of a "particular *vice* of the artistic
spirit, against which vigilance had been destined from the first to exert itself
in vain" (and here, too, I would argue for a greater attentiveness to James's
language), "the effect of which was that again and again, perversely, incura-
bly, the center of my structure would insist on placing itself *not*, so to speak,
in the middle," but to one side.[52] The archness of James's "self-indictment"
does not prevent this passage from functioning simultaneously as a testimony
to the phantasmatic which organizes his work, and as an acknowledgement
of the radical heterogeneity of his authorial subjectivity to the proprieties of
sexual orthodoxy.

---

[51] Nancy Blake also comments on the limited erotic means of the Jamesian hero in *Henry James, Ecriture et Absence* (Petit-
Roeulx, Belgium: Cistre, 1985): "Object of desire, he does not have anything with which to satisfy the demand which is addressed to him" (p. 115).

[52] *The Art of the Novel*, p. 85.

Despite the ostensible gender of the biographical Henry James, the author "inside" his texts is never unequivocally male; situated at a complex intersection of the negative and positive Oedipus complexes, that author is definitively foreclosed from the scene of passion except through identifications which challenge the binarisms of sexual difference. "He" aspires to knowledge only under the sign of masochism, and is unable to grasp castration as a condition exclusive to woman. Finally, "his" recourse to vision is more generative of trauma than of power. The author "inside" James's stories and novels bears so little resemblance to what is popularly thought of as the "Master" that I can only think of that Jacobite specter as a compensatory construction.

The Voice of History/
The Subject of the Novel

ALAN SINGER

The Higher a genre develops and the more complex its form, the better and more fully it remembers its past.
                    M.M. Bakhtin

I. Introduction: Novelistic History

The novel is our most prescient invocation of the past, of history. In *The Sense of an Ending*, Frank Kermode reminds us of the truism that "novelty of itself implies the existence of what is not novel, a past."[1] Perhaps it follows that the novel is so inseparable from our experience of the past because, like history itself, the novel is formally a disjunctive moment expressed as a desire for conjunction. More conspicuously than other genres, the novel seeks its unity through heterogeneity. Consequently it speaks obliquely and nowhere more obliquely than in the convention of voice itself. Voice, the dominant metaphor for the totalizing power of novelistic form, is the genre's locus of subjectivity. But as such it is uniquely problematic, since novelistic voice is inherently and notoriously multiple: no *one* speaks in the novel. In its ineluctable multiplicity, novelistic voice subverts the unitary imperative of the very metaphor of human speech which otherwise endows its rhetorical aptitude.

Recent theorists of the novel who want to assert its perspicuous historicity, however, see the problematic of voice as precisely the touchstone of the genre's conceptual richness. According to this account, the paradox of voice in the novel is precisely what has made the genre a more rigorously

[1] Frank Kermode, *The Sense of an Ending: Studies in the Theory of Fiction* (New York: Oxford University Press, 1966), p. 117.

philosophical enterprise than, for example, lyric or epic. For the philosophical shadow cast longest on literary aesthetics in the twentieth century is Cartesian idealism. The idealist tradition has designated the subjective *cogito*, as a voice tragically divided from the world it speaks about, to be the insurmountable obstacle to its own historical self-realization. For post-Lukácsian theory this is the fate of the self which the novel has been bound to narrate by its formal complicity with such historical fatalism.

The recent currency of the theoretical writings of M.M. Bakhtin gives new urgency to the idea that the novel is a vital confluence of history and subjectivity. The force of Bakhtin's argument is carried in his assertion that the concept of voice is indistinguishable from the concept of dialogue. For Bakhtin, dialogical meaning in the novel is always articulated across the barrier of an intractable otherness: author versus character, character point of view versus character point of view. Speech gains intelligibility from neither the systematic integrity of the language nor the rhetorical fulcrum of authorial intention. Rather, this intelligibility is emergent in the ratio of perspectives which instantiates any social speech situation. In other words, novelistic dialogue conspicuously recapitulates the structural conflicts of the idealist *cogito* by virtue of its inescapable temporality. For time separates identity into otherness. Because novelistic voice mediates our knowledge through differential relations rather than through the tropes of identity, Bakhtin maintains that the novel expresses the struggle of historical existence in human subjects with a lucidity that is unavailable to traditional paradigms of subjectivity.

It is this problem of history's differentiating capacity which will be my focus in this paper. I want to examine the use of the concept of history as a strategy for grounding literary value in the uniquely "critical" structures of subjectivity endowed by the novel. In this way I might specify the genre's general usefulness as a tool of speculative inquiry into the nature of human subjectivity. While I will agree with Bakhtin that the category of history must be invoked to fend off the twin threats of formalist monism on the one hand and subjective relativism on the other, it will be necessary to specify the terms of dialogic history beyond the threshold of sheer otherness where Bakhtin leaves it. It will become clear that Bakhtin's history, articulated as unmediated difference, must be supplemented with a theory of contradiction and determinate negation (in T.W. Adorno's sense) if it is not to obscure the very process it is meant to reveal. Only in this way will history and subjectivity be brought into a conceptually productive relation. Only a theory of contradiction will constrain us from departicularizing history in the guise of an autonomous transcendental subject or rendering the subject a threshold of relativity across which history is dispersed into infinite particulars. I want to test the validity of Bakhtin's attempt to re-ground formal study of the novel in dialogue and history. But more importantly, I want to show how Bakhtin's history must entail a notion of the subject that is assimilable to the concepts of transformation and transition by which we elucidate contradiction without mitigating its disjunctive and therefore vital temporality. The dialectical path of the Bakhtinian novel, then, would lead us not to a reckless dismantling of subjectivity, but to a redefining of subjectivity under the valid materialist constraint which refuses to allow interpretation to rest outside the tumult of historical changes it gives voice to. By refusing interpretation any extra-locality in relation to historical change, the materialist subject irrepressibly parodies idealist notions of history. It is for this reason that Bakhtin himself specifically elides parody with history as a textual substrate of dialogue. Dialogic voice renders the individual voice indistinguishable from many voices insofar as it is specifically a function of social exchange–thus a counter of temporality. History, within the expressive scope of the Bakhtinian novel, is a kind of parodic ventriloquism, that speaks through the temporal contradictions it engenders.

II. The Subject of Dialogue

Of course, if we are to hear the dialogic voice of history in all its subtly audible multiples of self, Bakhtin admonishes us to listen for it under the deceptively peaceful murmurings of the dominant ideology. By contrast with Bakhtinian dialogue, ideological discourse enchants us into a stupor of uncritical reflection. It seduces us to the delusive harmonies of identity-based (rather than differentially based) language systems. Bakhtin judges ideological discourse to be too one-sided for the historical scope aspired to in dialogue because ideology is specifically not amenable to the exigencies of time.

With this proposition we can begin to appreciate the usefulness of the Bakhtinian aesthetic as a fulcrum of ideological critique. Nevertheless, we must realize that if Bakhtin's dialogue is (on the basis of his powerful historicity) to benefit from invidious comparison with ideological discourse, it must further enable us to conceptualize the subject of history as an agent of historical change better than ideology can. Above all, Bakhtinian dialogue must be able to specify the subject's mediational imperatives precisely as ideology does, but without reifying them in the modes of ideological production. If dialogue is to reveal a better grasp of change than ideological discourse, then the concept of dialogue must be reconciled with the perennial paradox of subject-object relations upon which every social or aesthetic totality produced within ideology rests. Yet it must be reconciled, I will insist, through a subjective agency comparable with what Julia Kristeva has called a "subject-in-process." That is to say, Bakhtin requires an agency which is not subsumed within the deductive imperatives of its own *telos*.

Indeed, Bakhtin takes parody as the most representative case of dialogue precisely because it so strongly intimates a subject-in-process. Parody is technically the appropriation of the voice of another twisted to new motives. But Bakhtin's exposition pre-empts our construing an overly facile Nietzschean will-to-power by this gesture. On the contrary, because dialogic voice is so exclusively constituted on the threshold of otherness, whether it is the voice of self or other, parody in Bakhtin's special context eschews the teleological traps of intentionality and univocal meaning.

The dialectical imperative of Bakhtinian utterance impels us all the more strongly toward embracing the concept of a subject-in-process when we consider the dynamics of the social scene out of which dialogue and parody arise. Though dialogue has its textual roots in the rhetorical forms of Menippean satire, Socratic irony, diatribe, and the serio-comic, its life spark is the social situation, the public space of carnival wherein one's (authorial) meaning is necessarily mediated by the intentions of others. The emphasis on movement, transformation, transition–which is intrinsic to the ritual of crowning and de-crowning in carnival–celebrates, as Bakhtin says, "the shift itself, the very process of replaceability."[2] In this regard, Bakhtin points out that the crowning/de-crowning rituals in medieval carnival are analogous to the key tropes of Menippean and Socratic irony: anacrisis and syncrisis (the rhetorical triggers of classical parody), which progress by disjuncture. These tropes, by proposing communication across a brazen contradiction of styles, require a unique agency of transition in order to mediate differences without nullifying the differential play, the parodic spirit which produces them.

With this preliminary understanding we see that the warrant for Bakhtin's privileging of dialogue/parody requires him to demonstrate how, in these genres, otherness articulates difference over time without losing its historical specificity. Otherness itself must be reconciled with subjective agency. As if to meet this demand head-on, Bakhtin, from his earliest "Architectonics of Answerability," elides dialogic/parodic meaning with the concept of action. Action definitively entails a change of state, a transitional moment. Dialogic discourse is deemed, above all else, to be an "activity" by virtue of its transitional recursiveness: that is, because the meaning of a word in dialogue is determined in the interpretation of "an other," the further dialectical entailment of intersubjective conflict is necessarily part of that interpretation. The transitional movement valorized in the crowning and de-crowning ritual of carnival is thus reflected under this principle in the implicit proviso that the resolution of "situations" in dialogue may never be abstracted from the conditions of their utterance.

Unfortunately, when Bakhtin attempts to indicate more precisely the terms of otherness which would elucidate the analogy of parody/dialogue to action, and thus render it a plausible site for historical specificity, his exposition attenuates to a set of conspicuously undialogical abstractions. Dialogue is profoundly mystified in the universalizing trajectory of Bakhtinian phrases like "joyful relativity" or "carnival sense of the world." Such characterizations imply that the only relevant "situation" of dialogue is the universality of difference or sheer alterity itself. Within the conceptual miasma of such abstraction, it appears as if the historical other were indistinguishable from an ontological "otherness." That is to say, Bakhtin appears to open a methodologically unbridgeable gap between dialogism and dialogue.

---

[2] *Problems of Dostoevsky's Poetics*, Caryl Emerson, ed. and trans. (Minneapolis: University of Minnesota Press, 1985), p. 125.

Furthermore, Bakhtin's attempts to clarify the meaning of dialogic "activity" by stipulating the relation of self to other, such that one is not lost or subsumed in the other, only result in an apparently irrational juxtaposition of contradictory motives: on the one hand, the threshold of otherness is deemed intentional so as to preserve its historical specificity; on the other, the threshold of otherness is deemed to be universal so as to transcend the teleological boundaries of intentionality and the subject-object dichotomy which imposes them.

To make matters worse, Bakhtin's most sympathetic commentators conspicuously founder on the contradictory coordinates of his theory by ignoring them. For example, in his enthusiastic preface to *Problems of Dostoevsky's Poetics*, Wayne Booth is driven to conflate intentional with differential imperatives in the concept of dialogue, in order to transcend the necessity of a logical transition between them. The result is that Booth confuses the dialogic moment with temporal immediacy. From that rhetorical springboard, Booth is obliged to make the dangerous leap into an airy–because conceptually empty–sublime, asserting that dialogue is unspecifiable except in terms of what Longinus called "a sublimity of freed perspectives."

Quite to the contrary, Bakhtin himself is adamant that sublimity, as a definitive measure of the mind's inability to particularize its experience, hence its inability to historicize, subsists exclusively in a monologic negation of nature. More importantly, the abstraction that obtains in sublimity, through the negation of historical immediacy, eschews the very subjective mobility which would give an ethical burden to carnival in the first place. Bakhtin, by contrast, wants to sustain subjective mobility as reciprocally a condition and an end of dialogic intelligibility. For this enterprise he must be able to specify the historical particulars of the dialogic situation dialectically, but without precipitously resolving the dialectic in that gesture. This, I believe, is the methodological demand that dialogue makes upon itself which it simultaneously denies itself the conceptual resources to satisfy.

III. Dialogue as Contradiction

We have arrived at an apparent impasse in Bakhtin's theory. We can see that the concept of dialogue is precisely what makes Bakhtin's theory of language transpersonal and therefore conducive to the critique of idealism so pervasive in contemporary theory. But now we must acknowledge that his novel concept also manifestly fails to account for the specific agency of its own unique mediation of difference through transition. For this reason, I want to propose that the most constructive way to follow Bakhtin's arguments to their desired conclusion–that dialogue is a basis of aesthetic form in the novel, that is to say, intentional, and a threshold of socio-linguistics which transcends literary form, that is to say relative–might be to construe Bakhtin's "otherness" as contradiction *per se*. That is, in order to transcend the contradiction between intentionalist and relativist imperatives at the heart of Bakhtin's theory of dialogue, we must construe contradiction itself as the methodological fulcrum of dialogic enterprise. Only by this means can we ascribe agency to the historical experience which Bakhtin is obliged to elucidate. Whereas in Bakhtin's lexicon, dialogue is sometimes definable as a variable of intention and sometimes as a variable of free relativity, contradiction reciprocally expresses both the universality of difference and the specificity or determinateness of temporality and plot. After all, contradiction requires a structure of resemblance which is temporally prior to its articulations.

Time, in other words, is the difference between contradiction and difference. My claim that Bakhtinian otherness entails contradiction rather than mere difference is buttressed by the fact that temporality is itself fundamentally articulated as contradiction in the speculative tradition which Bakhtin seeks to continue. Contradictions are after all the propulsive moments of Hegelian dialectic. Bakhtin seems to aspire to a Hegelian order of historical determinations in his much touted pledge to restore the time of social reality to artistic language. But Bakhtin is plausibly even more radical than Hegel and therefore even more congenial to recent materialist thinkers because his dialogue does not ultimately render the threshold of contradiction timeless through *geist*, but effectively proliferates historically determinate moments by insisting upon the obstinate irreducibility of their contradictions. Or at least Bakhtin points this epistemological path by foregrounding the intrinsic recursiveness of the social exchange upon which dialogue is premised. If the dialogic voice can only be intelligible in terms of the response it elicits, we might justifiably surmise that the meaning of the whole "utterance" can only be elucidated as a deliberate proliferation of contextual contingencies upon which interpretation will thereafter subsist.

The importance of this point is best observed when we recall that the most popular strawman of Bakhtinian argument is Saussure, who privileged the systematic (synchronic) and thus timeless aspect of language over the temporally bounded performance (diachrony) of individual speakers. Saussure's aim was precisely to escape the "unscientific" contingencies of *parole*. Bakhtin evokes a striking contrast with the Saussurean stance in *Marxism and the Philosophy of Language*, where he observes that dialogic utterance is fundamentally a "value judgment" generated out of the contradiction between two aspects of the word: theme, which designates the historical instant of utterance, and meaning, which designates the parts of utterance which are repeatable, the self-identical components of systematic language. The relationship between theme and meaning is necessarily expressed as contradiction, but it becomes quite clear that contradiction here may be construed as constitutive of utterance precisely insofar as utterance (meaning) is recursive for theme. Bakhtin specifically elaborates this point:

> ... *there is nothing in the structure of signification that could be said to transcend the generative process, to be independent of the dialectical expansion of social purview. Society in process of generation expands its perception of the generative process of existence. There is nothing in this that could be said to be*

*absolutely fixed. And this is how it happens that meaning–an abstract self-identi-
cal element–is subsumed under theme and torn apart by theme's living contradictions so as to return in the shape of a new meaning with a fixity and self-
identity only for the while, just as it had before.*[3]

Because theme is articulated in the instant of speech and is thus, by definition, unreproducible, the contradictions it engenders are not expressible except as theme is differentially related to the contingencies of its expression. In
other words, theme may only be said to be "torn apart by living contradictions," as Bakhtin claims, if we acknowledge that such contradictions constitute a figural "return" of meaning–that is, the transformation of the relations between theme and meaning, self and other. Bakhtin generalizes that
value, issuing from this threshold of contradiction, always depends on an
"evaluative orientation" with the proviso that "a change in meaning is essentially always a re-evaluation: the transposition of some particular word from
one evaluative context to another." We must appreciate how Bakhtin's notion
of "evaluative orientation" here explicitly recalls and re-emphasizes the transitional moment of ritual crowning and de-crowning in carnival. We will note
that for Bakhtin such a moment always redounds to a transformation of the
terms which articulate it. Its intelligibility, then, is intrinsic to its
recursiveness and its recursiveness is a proliferation of its contingencies.

We might now conclude that it is precisely the contingencies of expression
which dialogue preeminently expresses, rather than the mere fact of its own
intrinsic otherness. Thus dialogism no longer floats free as a term designating
the radical otherness of "joyful relativity." It is more meaningfully anchored
in the determinations that change it; transition is assimilable to formal/social
totality. If, in dialogue, contingencies are proliferated through contradiction,
we could say that in the dialogic novel contradiction is revealed rather than
resolved through a mode of representation that, as a result, entails the temporality of reflection. This mode of representation, after all, follows the original epistemological path of dialogue, which was intended to move language
toward the status of act. Following this deduction, I believe we can more con-
fidently conceptualize novelistic dialogue (in accord with Bakhtinian intentions) as a mediation which preserves the subject's own historical particularity
but nonetheless transcends the idealism of intentional consciousness through
which we first objectified it.

---

[3] V. N. Volosinov, *Marxism and the Philosophy of Language,* Ladislav Matejka and I. R. Titunik, trans. (New York: Seminar
Press, 1973), p. 106.

The Novel as Ethical Paradigm

The second panel, on "The Novel as Ethical Paradigm (guiding readers to values, enlarging sympathies, teaching us 'how to live')," was introduced by NOVEL's Book Review Editor Richard Pearce, a teacher at Wheaton College in nearby Norton, Mass., himself an author of several studies on contemporary fiction. Professor Pearce began by citing Thomas **Kuhn** to the effect that "paradigm embodies a set of shared methods, shared standards, knowledge, modes of explanation, and theories." He then illustrated the point with an anecdote about discovering his first literary paradigm in his student days from an admired teacher (female) who told him he should not read novels for suspense, but should "read the end first, and then you can see how everything relates." This introduction to the novel "as a lyric or ... a well-wrought urn," rather than an ethical paradigm, seemed in retrospect an example of how "ethical questions were moving [even then] from the center to the margins," and made him ponder the consequences of "today's topic," which "brings the question of ethics back from the margins into the center." That prospect might well please Secretary of Education William Bennett, and/or the National Endowment for the Humanities, but for Pearce it had raised a number of troubling questions:*

> Are we bringing back some of [Bennett's] notions of shared assumptions which have been attacked and discredited, argued against so eloquently by so many critics in such different kinds of paradigms recently? Are we bringing back a paradigm, for instance, that doesn't question its own assumptions about the nature of language, about unified character and unified texts, about the production and distribution of novels, about the canon? In fact, what are the implications of talking about ethics now in a period when maybe we should be talking about politics? Or is the focus on ethics or on individual action as opposed to public action and politics a positive thing? These are some of the questions that occurred to me and there are lots of others. And into this sea of contradictions, I hope, will step our three panelists.

In effect, he had already introduced the first speaker, Patricia Spacks, by remarking earlier how J. Hillis Miller, in his new book on the ethics of reading, had said "that ethical theory depends on story," that you can't have ethics without narration. Patricia Spacks was now going to turn that premise around and ask "can you have narration without ethics?"

The Novel as Ethical Paradigm*

PATRICIA SPACKS

I keep thinking about the postmodern answering machine messages that, I am told, now abound in New York City. "You know what to do," the machines say. "You know when to do it."

One feels tempted to interpret. Refusing imperatives of action, the message responds to a cultural situation in which machines have usurped human functions. It rejects fictions of courtesy or amiability or exchange in favor of ironic economy. It declares a minimalist aesthetic.

Or does it? I shall return to this problem after investigating communications of relationship in rather different terms.

The operative words in the rubric under which I write, *ethical* and *paradigm*, suggest a currently implausible cultural coherence. *Ethical*, from Greek *ethos*, "character, custom, man's normal state"; *paradigm*, "a pattern, example, or model." Such words imply normative values and moral hierarchy. Joined, they convey the possibility of moral comprehension and hint prescriptive rigor. Although *paradigm*, since Thomas Kuhn, possesses up-to-date overtones, *ethical* sounds old-fashioned. The very word may evoke Richardson's conclusion to *Pamela*: "the Editor of these sheets will have his end, if it inspires a laudable emulation in the minds of any worthy persons, who may thereby entitle themselves to the rewards, the praises, and the blessings, by which PAMELA was so deservedly distinguished" (533). Or Dr. Johnson in *Rambler* 4, insisting that the purpose of fiction is "to increase prudence without impairing virtue" (23). Statements like this condense obvious meanings of "the novel as ethical paradigm." And whether we envy the moral security or condescend to the apparent critical naïveté of our forebears, we rarely posit the kind of unified moral universe that they apparently believed themselves to inhabit. What have ethical paradigms to do with us, in our postmodern skepticism about textual as well as universal orderings?

But I want to sketch some possibilities for late twentieth-century reading that might incorporate a notion of the ethical, even of the ethical paradigm, in ways facilitating engagement with the text. Let me, by way of introduction, quote more recent critics than Dr. Johnson: Michael Holquist and Walter Reed, writing in 1980 about the nature of the novel. Toward the beginning of their essay, they define what they call the "novelistic" level of the novel–by which, I take it, they mean the level at which it distinctively constitutes itself a novel–as "a diacritical space where other cultural codes, including the literary, intersect and interfere with one another" (415). A careful antihumanistic definition, I'd say. Later, though, Holquist and Reed make a rather different point: "It is the elusive space of the boundaries between individual and group that the novel has taken as its own, the interface between the potentially

---

* I am greatly indebted to Myra Jehlen and Aubrey Williams for their contributions to the final form of this essay.

utter uniqueness of the myriad contingencies in any single life on the one hand, and on the other, the patterns particular cultures provide for giving cohesion, shape, and meaning to those contingencies–without which they would not even be comprehensible *as* contingencies" (422).

The notion that novels occur at the intersection of the individual with the social is hardly startling. In this particular instance, though, the idea evolves from the definition of the novel as "diacritical space": a fact suggesting that no matter how one abstracts the concept of *novel*–as discourse, space, cultural artifact, whatever–finally we understand novels as having reference to people. The interference of cultural codes means something human. We may articulate in various ways the shape of novelistic structures, but their substance remains human relationships; that's what "the boundaries between individual and group" means. An ethical dimension inheres in the nature of narrative.

But we need to consider *how* the ethical resides in literature and what it might mean to speak of the paradigmatic in this connection. An ethical paradigm comprises an image of social behavior. Although the word *paradigm* suggests a pattern for imitation, the idea of ethical paradigms need not imply a view of fiction as rule book. On the contrary, the paradigmatic force of narrative derives from its orderings of action, those fundamental dramatic structures that underlie plot. Novels more lucidly than life investigate available sequences of cause and consequence: that is, we discover or generate such sequences by reading (as well as by writing) fiction. They help us inhabit our "as if" universe. To try to suggest how, I shall reflect briefly on the first paragraph of *Clarissa*. Precisely because we can no longer accept its heroine as a simple model of conduct (she provides a *theater* of conduct rather than a model), we may use the novel to investigate more subtle creation and examination of ethical possibilities in fiction.

The book opens with a letter from Anna Howe to Clarissa asking for information about recent events in the Harlowe family. Let me quote its first paragraph:

> I am extremely concerned, my dearest friend, for the disturbances that have happened in your family. I know how it must hurt you to become the subject of the public talk; and yet upon an occasion so generally known, it is impossible but that whatever relates to a young lady, whose distinguished merits have made her the public care, should engage everybody's attention. I long to have the particulars from yourself; and of the usage I am told you receive upon an accident you could not help; and in which, as far as I can learn, the sufferer was the aggressor. (1)

The "accident," we will soon learn, is the duel between Lovelace and Clarissa's brother James, in which the aggressor, James, suffered an injury to his arm.

On the basis of scanty information, Anna Howe here tries to construe Clarissa's emotional situation and to elicit more information. She considers her friend a model woman, Clarissa's virtue attested by the attention everyone pays her and underlined by her putative reluctance to attract such attention. Allegedly made an object of obsessive public speculation ("whatever relates to" her, Anna claims, provides subject for talk) despite her preference and despite the sensitivity Anna assumes in her, Clarissa presents for her friend a shadowy ethical dilemma as well as a pretext for fascinated imaginings. Within the few sentences I have quoted, Anna constructs two mini-narratives. Knowing how the situation *must* hurt Clarissa–a tiny imagined drama right there–she fancies also that "everybody" is talking, that it is "impossible" for the world *not* to attend to this young lady of "distinguished merits." The tension between "public" observation and "private" virtue exists not as observed fact but as imagined inevitability. It exemplifies that intersection of public and private integral to the novel as genre. Only slightly less apparent is the analogous tension between the desire to be noticed and the desire to remain obscure, dramatized in Anna's prose.

Although at the moment engaged in writing, Anna figures also the situation of the reader in her frustrations of passivity and temptations of mental action. One notes immediately the urgency with which she "longs" for information. The intensity of her longing measures the need for facts as the ground for judgment. Only by *knowing* can Anna lead her life, become an ethical agent. Despite her intimate acquaintaince with the woman about whom everyone speaks, she finds herself in an epistemological quandary which also constitutes a moral dilemma.

Anna has various sources of information ("Mr. Diggs the surgeon," Mr. Symmes, Mr. Wyerley, and unspecified others); the reader, only one. Frustrated, like Anna, by inadequate knowledge, readers may be tempted into usurping the role of author, the presence who articulates the immediate moral situation. Like Anna, readers must generate their own coherence by organizing facts and surmises into stories. The less we know, the more we invent. We may tell ourselves stories, for instance, about Anna's desire. Perhaps we believe that the young woman's avidity for authentic detail betrays not only hunger for knowledge but a shadow of gloating: something in the misfortune of her dearest friend possibly does not displease her. Anna appears to reproach as well as praise Clarissa. We may imagine a narrative of female competition in the background. If so, we are inventing a bit of moral knowledge: making an ethical judgment.

These and the other possible stories constructable on the basis of an opening paragraph constitute only hypotheses, later to be substantiated or repudiated; so do Anna's stories of Clarissa's suffering from being talked about and of the universal preoccupation with what has happened in the Harlowe household. One can have little stake in them as yet; later, each reader's narrative hypotheses may be passionately held, as Anna's view of what has happened between Lovelace and Clarissa will be passionately defended.

The reader's first participation in the plot involves him or her in efforts of discovery comparable to Anna's; like Anna, we find ourselves involved in

anxieties of uncertainty as we struggle for moral understanding. Anna, paradigmatically ignorant, paradigmatically eager for knowledge, exemplifies in
simple form the dilemma of autonomy that will focus so much attention in
Richardson's novel. Powerless to gain firsthand information, she duplicates in
epistemological terms Clarissa's powerless situation. If Clarissa finds herself
victim of "an accident [she] could not help," Anna is weakened by her social
situation, by difficulties of communication, by problematic possibilities of interpretation. The reader, already assessing Anna as a character even through
Anna's insistence that only Clarissa matters, faces comparable problems:
every novel makes vivid the question of readerly autonomy, conceived, like
Anna's situation, as a problem of social relations. To what extent, in what
ways, can one, should one, resist the pressure of other consciousnesses? If
we construct and perceive stories around characters, we also inevitably construct judgments. If we function as ethical agents in the world, we bring ethical categories to bear on the imagined actions of imagined people as they do
on human facts they encounter.

But Richardson is easy. Even if one reads him against the author's manifest
intention, one is reading a fiction that insists on the pressure of ethical meanings. What about more recalcitrant texts? What about, for instance, that answering machine message: "You know what to do. You know when to do it"?
These words send the caller back to herself, denying the conventions of relationship; they suggest a society from which ordinary forms of politeness have
vanished. Yet they also assume a powerful bond between the mind controlling the machine and that of the caller. Indeed, they define an entire relational mode. No need for imperatives, this utterance says, given our shared
awareness. We all know what it's proper to do. The message, then, rejects
one form of ethical protocol only to establish another.

My second reading of the eleven-word message exemplifies the ambiguity
of ethical meanings as well as their inevitability: my first reading, after all,
was also ethical. I wish to claim that novels, in their typical concentration on
depictions of human speech, thought, and action, like machine messages
about knowing and doing, necessarily allude to the ethical, however they
avoid the schematic. We focus on the erotics, the politics, the semiotics of
texts, all themselves ethical matters; we need to be reminded about textual
ethics.

Hillis Miller argues that ethical theory depends on story. "Without storytelling there is no theory of ethics," he writes. "Narratives, examples, stories
. . . are indispensable to thinking about ethics" (3). You can't have ethics
without narrative, in other words. But what about the converse: can you have
narrative without ethics? Part of the fundamental pleasure of reading novels
depends on the opportunity to try out attitudes, venture moral danger, interrogate sequences of cause and effect. The traditional realistic novel depicts a
world full of agents; it delights readers partly by the fantasies of agency it
corroborates, the space of freedom for fantasy it provides. Although novels
may not supply direct models of behavior, they evoke patterns of action by

which to test our own. Even that first paragraph of *Clarissa* supplies an ethical paradigm in this meaning of the term: the miniaturized drama of relationship Anna Howe sketches heightens ethical self-consciousness.

To repress our ethical responses to the reading of fiction denies the fundamental nature of generic power and leaves fiction incomplete, possibly incoherent, incapable of its own meanings. The process of reading allows us to construct and deconstruct a shifting series of ethical paradigms. Clarissa's complex and ethically problematic action of self-presentation succeeds Anna's attempt at interpretation; Lovelace in action will follow James Harlowe in action; each character is represented as constantly engaged in processes of willing, self-justified in relation to divergent ethical schemes. If we can no longer accept fictional figures–or, probably, any figures–as adequate models for our own conduct, we can yet interrogate in an ethical mode such representations of human behavior.

Alertness to ethical possibility in textual representations also involves acts of resistance. Because novels have the power to engage us morally, they give us choices–not merely acceptance versus non-acceptance, but acceptance versus refusal. The kind of reading I have suggested is essentially ahistorical, based on the assumption that fiction's performative power makes something happen in readers' minds and feelings in a continuing, ever-changing present. But more encompassing versions of reading begin in historical recognitions that originate processes of resistance as well as of acceptance. Richardson imbued his text with assumptions about class and gender, about family, about virtue and villainy, about social stability–assumptions no longer automatically acceptable. One must read attentively enough, *historically* enough, to notice such assumptions. They carry ethical as well as political imperatives, these notions about class and gender and family, and we can only disobey their implicit coerciveness by elucidating them. Which returns us to moral epistemology: to judge appropriately, to make choices, it is necessary to *know*.

Paradigms are not imperatives but possibilities. The paradigms of fiction provide an opportunity for moral playfulness: cost-free experimentation. The play and the work of reading, its freedom and its urgency, oddly duplicate one another. That fact suggests another view of the novel as ethical paradigm, one already hinted at in my discussion of Anna Howe. What I have said so far implies a mimetic notion of fiction, but the novel's paradigmatic possibilities do not depend on its mimetic fidelity. Although not every novel creates, like *Clarissa*, unmistakable figures for the reader in the text, every novel generates unique interactions with its readers; these interactions too create paradigmatic possibilities.

In our current obsession with reading as interpretation, we risk forgetting that reading, first of all, constitutes, as play and as work, experience: specifically experience of agency or its illusion. At the simplest–but absolutely necessary–level, we feel our power over the book as physical object; we peek at the end, reread, close the book. More importantly, we choose to attend

closely or casually and choose what to attend to; we must choose to discrimi-
nate, or choose not to; we permit ourselves to make or reject connections between the text and the world outside it. As that great discriminator Henry
James pointed out, even minimal acts of distinction-making have moral
weight. Here is a sentence from the first page of *The Wings of the Dove*: "To
feel the street, to feel the room, to feel the table-cloth and the centre-piece
and the lamp, gave her a small, salutary sense, at least, of neither shirking
nor lying" (5). Minute aesthetic discriminations, registered on the pulses,
possess moral weight–or so this tiny paradigmatic representation of Kate Croy
suggests. Really to see the world, fully to realize words on a page–thus we
create our moral dignity. Ultimate clarity of perception, like fullness of realization, remains an unattainable ideal. The sentence about Kate inaugurates a
novel in which strenuous effort at discrimination will not forestall self-delu-
sion. Yet the effort itself remains valuable.

To be sure, we need not acknowledge the moral force of the sentence or of
the novel. As we help to generate the novels others have written, we can refuse to grant that what we are willing to notice matters in moral terms. But if
we refuse to accept, we resist; we continue to exist in relation to the problem,
functioning still in the ethical realm.

The hypothesis that novels provide us with ethical paradigms helps de-
emphasize verisimilitude. Paul Ricoeur, discussing the history of the novel,
writes, "It was this concern for being true–in the sense of being faithful–to reality, or for equating art and life, that most contributed to covering over the
problems of narrative composition" (11). At the heart of these problems,
Ricoeur believes, is the matter of literary convention, long occluded for both
critics and novelistic practitioners by the novel's claim to transcribe reality.
Realism itself, as Ricoeur reminds us, constitutes only a convention.

We no longer talk about "truth" in the sense to which Ricoeur alludes. To
claim the paradigmatic possibilities of texts and of the act of reading them
shifts critical focus from mimesis to another relation between text and world,
directing our attention toward the texture of ethical life. Instead of inquiring
what a literary action imitates, we may once more wonder–anticipating rather
different answers from those our forebears found for similar questions–what
moral utility it asserts. Jane Austen, in *Northanger Abbey*, reflects about this
matter in ways that summarize better than I can the richness and the unex-
pectedness available through ethical investigation of fiction.

The novel concludes, you may remember, by offering its readers
alternative ethical interpretations: "I leave it to be settled by whomsoever it
may concern, whether the tendency of this work be altogether to recommend
parental tyranny, or reward filial disobedience" (252). The joke at the expense
of conventional moralizing echoes earlier comments on literary and social convention: the ostentatious compliance with "the rules of composition" (251) involved in making Eleanor Tilney's lover the gentleman who left behind his
laundry list; the allusion to the reader's expectation about the relation
between the remaining number of pages and probabilities for the ending;
Henry Tilney's badinage about women's journals and letters and about Bath

conversation; and so on. Although *Northanger Abbey* is usually read as mockery of Gothic romance, these jokes do not direct themselves specifically at such romance. They concern conventional expectations for fictional narrative and for social behavior–the latter as arbitrary, often as ridiculous, but as necessary as the corresponding expectations about fiction, and not unrelated to them.

The ethical alternatives of Austen's final sentence derive from romance convention. If the narrator ridicules the two morals she suggests, she implicitly challenges the reader–as Mark Twain does in denying the existence of a moral in *Huckleberry Finn*–to generate more satisfying, less simplistic, interpretations. One might venture, for instance, that the novel's most provocative ethical paradigm explores the question of convention itself. Catherine Morland learns to use social and literary convention fruitfully: her predilection for Gothic helps her articulate General Tilney's tyranny; her concern for social mores helps free her from John Thorpe by teaching her that she need not go off with him in his carriage; her eagerness to be taught rules for everything engages Henry's ridicule but also his attention. On the other hand, Catherine's innocence and directness enable her to evade conventional restrictions. In contrast, Isabella Thorpe remains trapped by her reliance on empty conventions. Even Henry Tilney, who wittily demonstrates how society's rules deconstruct themselves, succumbs to convention. He sees in Catherine the feminine foolishness his culture has trained him to perceive and loves her for the flattery of her female admiration. Morality operates both through and despite convention.

One can debate about the nature of morality, itself a convention, but the fact that we operate necessarily within the ethical sphere seems to me undebatable. The question is only whether we choose to deny this fact in our critical procedures. Accepting it, I'm arguing, proves more fruitful. Even the most ungiving text, like my telephone message, lends itself to ethical analysis. Inquiries about the principles of conduct stated and modeled in a text help us construct "thick" interpretations. Political and social questions inform ethical ones: new feminist awarenesses, for instance, shape formulations and investigations of ethical possibility. Ethical interpretations prove no more univocal than any other variety, but interpreters' voices, for all their multiplicity, remain inevitably and invariably ethical.

Works Cited

Austen, Jane. *Northanger Abbey*. 1818. Vol. 5 of *The Novels of Jane Austen*. Ed. R. W. Chapman. 3rd ed. Oxford: Oxford University Press, 1969.

Holquist, Michael and Walter Reed. "Six Theses on the Novel–and Some Metaphors." *New Literary History* 11 (1980): 413–423.

James, Henry. *The Wings of the Dove*. 1902. New York: Penguin Books, 1982.

Johnson, Samuel. *The Rambler*. Ed. W. J. Bate and Albrecht B. Strauss. Vol. 3 of the Yale Edition of *The Works of Samuel Johnson*. New Haven: Yale University Press, 1969.

Miller, J. Hillis. *The Ethics of Reading: Kant, de Man, Eliot, Trollope, James, and Benjamin*. New York: Columbia University Press, 1987.

Richardson, Samuel. *Clarissa, or The History of a Young Lady*. 1747–48. 4 vols. London: Dent, 1932.

———. *Pamela, or Virtue Rewarded*. 1740. New York: Norton, 1958.

Ricoeur, Paul. *Time and Narrative*. Vol. 2. Tr. Kathleen McLaughlin and David Pellauer. Chicago: University of Chicago Press, 1984.

The Novel as Ethical Paradigm?

ROBERT SCHOLES

> ... *a conference featuring panels designed to explore and bridge differences between old humanistic and new "posthumanistic" approaches to traditional aspects of fiction.*
>
> (from the flyer for this conference)

> *Prudence suggests that I stop here.*
>   (Ortega y Gasset)

Having elected, imprudently, to extend this text beyond its epigraphs, I wish to offer some general observations on the modern novel. Just as every animal belongs to a species, every literary work belongs to a genre. A literary genre, the same as a zoological species, means a certain stock of possibilities. It is erroneous to think of the novel–and I refer to the modern novel in particular–as of an endless field capable of rendering ever new forms. Rather it may be compared to a vast but finite quarry. There exist a definite number of possible themes for the novel. The workman of the primal hour had no trouble finding new blocks–new characters, new themes. But present-day writers face the fact that only narrow and concealed veins are left them. Not only is the difficulty of finding new subjects steadily growing, but ever "newer" and more extraordinary ones are needed to impress the reader. This is the second cause of the difficulty with which the genre as such is faced in our time.

Proof that the present decline is due to more fundamental causes than a possibly inferior quality of contemporary novels is given by the fact that, as it becomes more difficult to write novels, the famous old or classical ones appear less good. Only a few have escaped drowning in the reader's boredom.

At this point I must stop and confess to an unethical act. Every word I have written since the opening sentence of this paper has been plagiarized from an essay written sixty years ago by José Ortega y Gasset, called "Notes on the Novel."[1] I have done this both in order to raise certain questions about the novel as a literary form and as a way of making concrete the question of what an ethical paradigm might be. To begin with the latter of these two questions, we should note the way in which, by acknowledging my plagiarism and naming the source of the formerly plagiarized words, I have transformed an unethical act into an ethical one. What began as theft has ended as the quotation and citation of authority. The unethical has become the ethical by the uttering of a few additional words which have served to invoke what we might properly call an "ethical paradigm"–a paradigm, you will notice, that is not located in my text itself, but in a code situated outside my utterance, in a cultural space, in this case that of a certain academic or professional discourse that supports and enables my particular practice. If we are to consider the relationship between any specific textual practice and some behavioral paradigm that we can call "ethical," a major question will have to be how a particular text, for example this or that fictional narrative, can be connected to a general code of behavior. This question–of the relationship between a narrative text and some ethical paradigm or code–will preside over my inquiry on this occasion, but before posing it more concretely I should like to return to those provocative statements about the decline of the novel that I stitched together from a few pages of Ortega y Gasset.

It would be absurd to subscribe to what Ortega says in the passage I have quoted from, because he is simply wrong about nearly everything he mentions in it; moreover, his metaphors are careless and inept as well–but I did not quote him to aggrandize myself or contemporary criticism at his expense. I think he is very much alive as a writer, and I believe that in those "Notes on the Novel" from which I quoted he says some things that are both eloquent and important. Consider this, for instance: "The titles of certain books are like the names of cities in which we used to live for a time. They at once bring back a climate, a peculiar smell of streets, a general type of people and a specific rhythm of life" (87). Now that is not only well said; it is also true. And there–even in the passage I plagiarized earlier, and then cited as an authority, and then rejected–even there, in those admittedly inadequate sentences–a perspective on the novel is introduced that we cannot afford to ignore.

---

[1] José Ortega y Gasset, "Notes on the Novel," *The Dehumanization of Art and Other Essays on Art, Culture and Literature*, Helen Weyl, trans. (Princeton, N.J.: Princeton University Press, 1968), pp. 58, 59–60. Page references in the text are to this edition.

Ortega reminds us that literary genres exist in time, that they rise, flourish, and decline, and that the talent of individuals is enhanced or diminished by the possibilities for artistic production that a particular genre makes available at a particular time. He also reminds us that history brings with it a changed perspective on the novels of the past. In 1925 it seemed to him that most of the famous or classical texts in the genre were, in his pungent phrase, "drowning in the reader's boredom." Sixty years or so later, Ortega's sentiments themselves have a "period" flavor, a modernist intolerance that is quite different from our present view, for it is now the case that many people–including academic and professional critics and reviewers–are actually indifferent to the serious art and literature of our own time but take delight in the painting, music, and fiction of the nineteenth century. Ortega, though he might not have anticipated this, can help us understand it:

> Let us observe ourselves the moment we have finished reading a great novel. Is it not as though we were emerging from another world where we were held in-communicado? That there can have been no communication is clear; for we were aware of no transition. A second ago we were in Parma with Count Mosca and La Sanseverina, with Clélia and Fabrice: we lived their lives with them, im-mersed in their atmosphere, their time and place. Now, abruptly we find our-selves in our room, our city, our time; and already our accustomed preoccupa-tions begin to stir. There is an interval of indecision and suspense. Perchance a sudden wave of recollection washes us back into the universe of the novel, and with a certain effort, as though struggling through a liquid element, we must re-gain the shores of our existence proper. Were someone to find us in just that mo-ment, our dilated pupils would betray our shipwrecked condition. (91)

To read a novel is indeed to dwell in another place, to exchange one's own horizon for the horizon of the narrative, so that the transition from the fic-tional world to actuality may easily leave us momentarily disoriented. This situation becomes even more complicated and consequential when the "actual" world to which we return causes us to feel "shipwrecked" or cast away. This metaphor–of "the shores of our existence proper" to which we must struggle through a "liquid element" of imagination–becomes even more powerful if we find our "proper" existence itself an alienating experience.

In his discussion of the exhaustion of the novel as a genre Ortega allowed himself, at least momentarily, to consider the problem in terms too exclusively formal. A literary genre is *not* like a quarry with only so much rock in it, but is a variable structure that waxes and wanes through its rela-tionship to other cultural variables. The novel as a genre has in fact always been linked with certain other cultural phenomena. Like democratic or repub-lican forms of government and the capitalistic economic system, it has been preeminently the creature of that form of decadent Christianity known as Protestantism.

I do not mean the word *decadent* as an insult here–anything but. I think of Protestantism as the fairest flower of Christian thought, with Deism and Unitarianism as the loveliest petals on that flower, of which social democracy is the finest fruit. Capitalism, as an economic system, and the novel, as a literary form or genre, have grown from the same branch of the same tree. If the novel is in trouble as a form–and I think it is–this is because the culture of enlightened Protestantism is itself in trouble, because capitalism is in trouble, and because social democracy is in trouble, for the ethical paradigm of which the novel has been an expression is precisely that of Protestant, capitalist, democracy. Thus, if the plight of the novel is a concern, it is not for any purely formal reason. It is because the plight of an entire cultural heritage and a whole way of life is a concern.

I am not saying that fiction can no longer be written. It will never stop. Narration is as elemental a feature of human existence as language itself. I am saying only that a particular narrative form–the novel–is so tied to a certain ideology and a certain cultural practice that its life span is indissolubly linked to that ideology and that cultural practice. Nor am I saying that a writer's individual faith will prevent him or her from writing novels within a culture dominated by the Protestant/capitalist/democratic paradigm. One may profess any religion or none at all and still write novels. What counts is the strength of what I am calling the Protestant paradigm within a given cultural situation. At the present moment, this strength varies from place to place in this world and even within different segments of the population in a single country.

This linkage between a literary form and a cultural or ideological structure is in no way describable in terms of causes in one sphere leading directly to effects in the other. No ideology can generate a perfect transmission of its values–even with a ministry of propaganda established to accomplish that very feat. Nor can any artifact single-handedly bring about a massive cultural change. *Uncle Tom's Cabin*, for instance, had its enormous effect on a certain audience only because that audience had already been constituted by the very Protestant ethical tradition that I have been alluding to as the cultural matrix of the novel. Dante's *Commedia* (to name another powerfully ethical narrative) was not aimed at changing minds but at giving concrete embodiment to what its readers already knew. The novel, on the other hand (as opposed to the epic, romance, and allegory), assumes that consciousness is *defined* by its changeability, and that a narrative text should aim at that very dimension of consciousness, which is called conscience. Harriet Beecher Stowe did not have to deploy a new ethical paradigm. She had only to make concrete the tension between the practice of slavery and a paradigm already in place for many of her readers.

To make this discussion itself more concrete, I should like to turn now, however briefly, to a novel which is not only paradigmatically ethical but is the very model and type of everything I have been saying about the relationship between this narrative form and a particular ethical paradigm: George Eliot's *Middlemarch*. I want to discuss *Middlemarch* not only for its many virtues, which led Virginia Woolf to call it "one of the few English novels written for grown-up people;"[2] nor simply because Eliot has been regularly charged–as F. R. Leavis ruefully acknowledged–with being "peculiarly addicted to moral preoccupations",[3] I have selected *Middlemarch* as a paradigmatic ethical novel because I can remember vividly my own first reading of it forty years ago–and the ethical shock of finding myself far too closely mirrored in the character of Fred Vincy, who is nicely summed up by the narrator as one of those "young gentlemen whose consciousness is chiefly made up of their own wishes" (Riverside Edition, 89).[4] That, as a dear friend of mine observed upon hearing this confession, "was before you grew up and turned into Casaubon"–an observation that, despite its wickedness and gross inaccurary of reference, suggests that the book can still function in a normative fashion, as a table of behavioral exemplars that can be matched with the names of actual people, who may then be judged according to the ethical values assigned the characters in the novel, who have themselves already been judged and assigned positive or negative ethical weight by the author and narrator of the novel, in terms of that larger pattern of Protestant values to which everything in the book has been referred.

This power of normative ethical discourse is characteristic of the great nineteenth-century novels. In recent years, it has often been discussed in terms of some art of characterization that has been unaccountably rejected or just plain lost by what must clearly be an inferior breed of contemporary writers. Or, in terms such as those suggested by Ortega y Gasset in his "Notes on the Novel," this "decline" in characterization has been attributed to the exhaustion of a vein, all the types of character having already been quarried by previous generations of laborers. I am suggesting, on the contrary, that what is lacking–in both life and art–is not at all a matter of skill or talent or disposition but precisely that sense of consciousness as conscience that is so central to George Eliot's work but so difficult to recapture at our present moment in our astonishingly commodified entrepreneurial culture. To be more precise about this it will be necessary to look more closely to the way George Eliot's narrative voice describes the consciousness of characters in the novel. Here are some samples (with emphasis added):

> (p. 149–of Dorothea) *It was not indeed entirely an improvisation, but had taken shape in* inward colloquy, *and rushed out like the round grains from a fruit when sudden heat cracks it.*
>
> (p. 209–of Dorothea) *In her indignation there was a sense of superiority, but it went out for the present in firmness of stroke, and did not compress itself into an* inward articulate voice. . . .
>
> (p. 255) *Any* inward debate *Lydgate had as to the consequences* . . . .

---

[2] Virginia Woolf, *The Common Reader*, First Series (New York: Harvest Books, 1964), p. 172.

[3] F.R. Leavis, *The Great Tradition* (New York: Doubleday, 1954), p. 42.

[4] George Eliot, *Middlemarch*, G. S. Haight, ed. (Boston: Houghton Mifflin, 1986). Page references in the text are to this edition.

(p. 264) *Will Ladislaw on his side felt that his dislike was flourishing at the expense of his gratitude, and spent much* inward discourse *in justifying the dislike.*

(p. 299) *The Vicar was holding an* inward dialogue. . . .

(p. 322–of Casaubon) *"She knows that I know," said* the ever restless voice within. . . .

(p. 439) *"There really is nothing to care for much," said* poor Rosamond inwardly. . . .

(p. 483–of Lydgate) *. . . he took no notice of it, and went on with an* inward drama and argument. . . .

(p. 516–of Bulstrode) *He* inwardly declared *that he intended to obey orders.*

Dorothea, Lydgate, Ladislaw, Farebrother, Casaubon, Rosamond–even Bulstrode–all hear that "ever restless voice within," which is not simply a novelistic device but a conception of character as defined by conscience, in terms of what George Eliot calls inward colloquy, inward articulate voice, inward debate, inward discourse, inward dialogue, and inward drama and argument. Now the notion of inward debate is as old as Homer, but the coupling of it with the Protestant notion of individual conscience is the special domain of the novel, a matter that George Eliot's powerful text clearly illustrates.

This ethical Protestantism is visible everywhere in *Middlemarch*. It is in the dozens–perhaps hundreds–of moments when the narrative voice turns away from a particular occasion or event to make a moral generalization–often by shifting into the first person plural in midsentence, as the following two examples, which are entirely typical, will illustrate:

Will was not without his intentions to be always generous, but our *tongues are like little triggers which have usually been pulled before general intentions can be brought to bear.* (267, emphasis added)

He [Mr. Brooke] had never been insulted on his own land before, and had been inclined to regard himself as a general favorite (we *are all apt to do so, when* we *think of* our own *amiability more than of what other people are likely to want of us).* (291, emphasis added)

These invocations of general principles are indispensable to George Eliot as a means–as *the* means–of connecting singular characters and events to the larger ethical field that justifies the writing and reading of novels as a serious matter. The justification for novels, in George Eliot's view, is tied to her suspicion of ethical paradigms or, as she puts it, "general doctrine," and nowhere is she more the voice of Protestant consciousness than when she criticizes such doctrines: "There is no general doctrine which is not capable of eating out our morality if unchecked by the deep-seated habit of direct fellow-feeling with individual fellow-men" (453). By opposing "morality" to "general doctrine," Eliot takes her stand on quintessentially Protestant ground, and by making "fellow-feeling" for individuals the center of that morality she makes a case for the novel as a major locus in the development of such fellow-feeling. But this passage is not presented directly as a justification for fiction in a serious world, but in another connection entirely, which we should now examine. The narrator is talking about that excellent capitalist, Mr. Bulstrode:

> The service he could do to the cause of religion had been through life the ground he alleged to himself for his choice of action: it had been the motive which he had poured out in his prayers. Who would use money and position better than he meant to use them? Who could surpass him in self-abhorrence and exaltation of God's cause? And to Mr. Bulstrode God's cause was something distinct from his own rectitude of conduct: it enforced a discrimination of God's enemies, who were to be used merely as instruments, and whom it would be as well if possible to keep out of money and consequent influence. Also, profitable investments in trades where the power of the prince of this world showed its most active devices, became sanctified by a right application of the profits in the hands of God's servant.
>
> This implicit reasoning is essentially no more peculiar to evangelical belief than the use of wide phrases for narrow motives is peculiar to Englishmen. There is no general doctrine which is not capable of eating out our morality if unchecked by the deep-seated habit of direct fellow-feeling with individual fellow-men.
>
> But a man who believes in something else than his own greed, has necessarily a conscience or standard to which he more or less adapts himself. (453)

Max Weber's *Protestant Ethic and the Spirit of Capitalism* can be seen as a somewhat belated gloss upon passages like this in *Middlemarch*. Eliot was aware of the close connection between Protestantism and capitalism—and of the complex web of support and contradiction in which they were bound. Her awareness—and its limits—are perhaps most accessible to us in the ethical center of the book: her portrait of Caleb Garth. Garth is presented to us as a man of the highest ethical probity and—what is more important than mere righteousness—of genuine and effective good will. The evolution of the concept of benevolence in the English novel, from Fielding to George Eliot, is a fascinating theme, and far too vast for the present occasion, but we should notice that Caleb Garth's benevolence takes the form of what he himself calls "business," in which the Protestant ethic and the spirit of capitalism are indeed hand in glove. Listen to Garth holding forth on this theme:

> "No, no; but it's a fine thing to come to a man when he's seen into the nature of business: to have a chance of getting a bit of the country into good fettle, as they say, and putting men into the right way with their farming, and getting a bit of good contriving and solid building done—that those who are living and those who come after will be the better for. I'd sooner have it than a

fortune. I hold it the most honourable work there is . . . . It's a great gift of God, Susan." (295)

"Business" in Caleb Garth's view is doing good, making the world a better place to live, "a great gift of God." Within Garth's speech business is specifically set against the acquisition of a "fortune," though it is clearly seen as creating prosperity for both present and future inhabitants of the country where such good business is done. It is, I should say, capitalism without capital, and once we think of it that way we can see how the entire character of Caleb Garth has been constructed in such a way as to avoid or hide the contradiction between Protestantism and capitalism that lies at the heart of their union. We can observe this best in the extended passage devoted to Caleb's vocation and his character in Book 3:

> *Caleb Garth often shook his head in meditation on the value, the indispensable might of that myriad-headed, myriad-handed labour by which the social body is fed, clothed, and housed. It laid hold of his imagination in boyhood. The echoes of the great hammer where roof or keel were a-making, the signal-shouts of the workmen, the roar of the furnace, the thunder and plash of the engine, were a sublime music to him; the felling and lading of timber, and the huge trunk vibrating star-like in the distance along the highway, the crane at work on the wharf, the piled-up produce in warehouses, the precision and variety of muscular effort wherever exact work had to be turned out,—all these sights of his youth had acted on him as poetry without the aid of the poets, had made a philosophy for him without the aid of philosophers, a religion without the aid of theology. . . .*
>
> *Though he had never regarded himself as other than an orthodox Christian, and would argue on pervenient grace if the subject were proposed to him, I think his virtual divinities were good practical schemes, accurate work, and the faithful completion of undertakings: his prince of darkness was a slack workman. But there was no spirit of denial in Caleb, and the world seemed so wondrous to him that he was ready to accept any number of systems, like any number of firmaments, if they did not obviously interfere with the best land-drainage, solid building, correct measuring, and judicious boring (for coal). In fact, he had a reverential soul with a strong practical intelligence. But he could not manage finance: he knew values well, but he had no keenness of imagination for monetary results in the shape of profit and loss: and having ascertained this to his cost, he determined to give up all forms of his beloved "business" which required that talent.* (185)

The passage is far too long to be quoted fully here, and I have had to omit much that is of interest, but I think we can see even in this brief excerpt how George Eliot has tried to insulate Caleb Garth from the capitalist side of capitalism by giving him a marvelous talent for what she and he call "business," and no ability at all in the area of finance—which leads to a picture of a man with a keen sense of "values" but no imagination of "profit and loss." As a result, she is able to conclude this portrait by saying that he devoted himself to those kinds of "work which he could do without handling capital."

Contemplating the character of Caleb Garth, one cannot help but feel that the loveability of the character has been purchased not simply at the expense of his believability but at the cost of the conflict between Christianity and capitalism being put into brackets and disposed of–or, in a word, repressed. This particular repression, I should say, constitutes the essence of late Protestantism. In the case of Caleb Garth, it is interestingly correlated with another repression–that of the division of labor, and, in particular, that crucial separation between labor and management, for Caleb Garth's attitude toward rank in the world of business is described as follows: "he thought very well of all ranks but he would not himself have liked to be of any rank in which he had not such close contact with 'business' as to get often honourably decorated with marks of dust and mortar, the damp of the engine, or the sweet soil of the woods and fields" (185). The rhetoric of this passage is fascinating, designed as it is to allow the marks of toil to appear only as badges of honor or decorations–and in that phrase, "honourably decorated," we have both valor and frivolity, nicely balanced.

Surely the portrait of Caleb Garth is a miracle of balance–or of the repression of conflicts that threaten the Protestant paradigm itself. Garth is a hero of business but uncontaminated by capital and only decorated with the badges of labor. He exists in a pastoral world, forty years before the time of the novel's composition, which suggests that already, in George Eliot's time, the contradictions between the Protestant ethic and its economic concomitant, capitalism, were making themselves felt. *Middlemarch*, unquestionably the greatest work of English realism, was already marked by a nostalgia, a repression of its own world's actualities, a repression without which the Protestant paradigm essential to its realization might not have remained viable. Now, a century later, that paradigm lies broken beyond all reconstitution, and both our world and the art that inevitably reflects that world suffer from our inability to find a viable replacement for it.

The Ethics of Reading:
The Case for Pluralistic and Transactional Reading

DANIEL R. SCHWARZ

My project is to define humanistic formalism as an ideological and theoretical alternative to deconstruction even while calling into question the hierarchical role that ideology and theory have been playing in literary discussion. This project began with my book *The Humanistic Heritage: Critical Theories of the English Novel from James to Hillis Miller* (1986), in which I sought to define the theoretical underpinnings of Anglo-American criticism, and continues in my *Reading Joyce's "Ulysses"* (1987) and my forthcoming *The Transformation of the English Novel, 1890–1930*. Within my larger project of defining a theoretical base for humanistic formalism, I shall in this essay focus on the reader.

Here and elsewhere I call for a revised humanistic criticism that insists on the inseparability of such formal matters as rhetoric and narrative codes from the content, meaning, and significance of imaginative literature. While continuing to emphasize interpretation of literary texts, my revised humanistic criticism–what I call humanistic formalism–would require of literary theory that it develop concepts about how texts behave and how readers respond. Humanistic formalism seeks to understand how texts function within their own ontology and how the rhetorical effects–usually, but by no means always, consciously built into the text by the author–affect the reader in her or his world. It regards reading as an active quest to discover what words mean and signify within the imagined world. Humanistic formalism unembarrassedly asks, "What happens to characters within an imagined world?"; "Who is speaking to whom and for what reason?"; "What is the nature of the voice that speaks to us? Specifically, what are her or his attitudes, values, and feelings, and how does the artist convey them?"; "What do we learn from the representation of human behavior within that world?"; "What is the relation of form–including structure, mode of narrative, patterns of language (syntax, diction, rhythm, metaphors and metonymies)–to meaning?"; "What does the imagined world reveal about the author and the actual, historical world in which she or he lived?" Since humanistic criticism assumes that texts are by human authors for human readers about human subjects, a humanistic criticism is interested in how and why people think, write, act, and ultimately live.

I. Introduction

For many of us, educated in English departments between 1950 and 1970, it seems as if we are, in Arnold's words, "Wandering between two worlds, one dead / The other powerless to be born." We are caught between two worlds; one is interpretive humanistic criticism, not dead, but called into question by the challenge of recent theory. The other is deconstruction, fully born but un-satisfactory to many of us for three reasons: its failure to understand or ac-count for the entirety of a text; its tendency to read reductively so that all texts seem much the same; and its polemical tone and at times arrogant stance which looks down on other approaches from a steep and icy peak.

Perhaps we can distinguish between deconstruction and humanistic formal-ism by using the metaphors of a mirage and Zeno's paradox. For deconstruc-tion, it is a mirage to believe that an author can approach anterior reality or reveal his own psyche; for no sooner do we approach reality than it is de-ferred and thus recedes; what we have is traces of meaning, not the presence of meaning. By contrast, an apt metaphor for humanistic formalism is Zeno's paradox, for humanistic formalism believes that an author's efforts to present his view of the world or of himself can be seen as akin to bisecting one's way across a room without ever quite reaching the other side. Moreover, the im-ages of mirage and Zeno's paradox are appropriate to contrast deconstruc-tion's view that it is hopeless–a mirage–to believe that we can recuperate the intended text, with the humanistic view–again figured by Zeno's para-dox–that the critic can discover the conscious and unconscious meaning that the author built into a text. The process of bisection becomes more difficult as we move towards the unapproachable point–the infinity–of complete recuper-ation. With each succeeding bisection, the process of reaching a meaning in-tended by the author and one on which diverse readers might agree becomes more difficult; it is as if the process were on an incline or were meeting physi-cal resistance.

I would like to suggest that as readers we can and should belong to multi-ple interpretive communities; rather than propose unitary stories of reading and choose between the either-or of possible readings, we can and should en-joy multiplicity and diversity in our readings. The kind of pluralistic criticism I imagine sees criticism as a series of hypotheses rather than as a final prod-uct. In its healthy and open pluralism, it is inclusive rather than exclusive. Even as we answer each question and pursue each line of inquiry, we become aware that each explanation is partial. It may be time to back off from the no-tion that the critic is *vates* and return to the more modest Socratic question and answer structure in order that we leave rhetorical space for other expla-nations.

Recently, Don Bialostosky has argued in his splendid *PMLA* article that we need a dialogic criticism which "will not try to decide among [the] competing claims or synthesize their opposing beliefs but will try to imagine and enter their unrealized conversation" (Bialostosky, 792). To an extent, my book, *The Humanistic Heritage*, is an effort to do this by imagining what the voices of di-verse critics would be saying to one another if they were discussing the tradi-tional English novel from Defoe through Joyce. As Bialostosky puts it, "Those who take turns speaking and listening, representing others and being repre-sented by them, learn not just who these others are but who they themselves may be, not just what others may mean but what they themselves may mean among others" (Bialostosky, 792). We need to acknowledge the impossibility of reaching one determinate meaning, while creating a flexible dialogic field in which plausible meanings may contend and from which we may propose theoretical hypotheses derived from close reading. The more we can maintain a dialogue between contending interpretive communities, the more the theoretical explosion will produce powerful readings rather than parochial and remote debates; by powerful readings, I mean not merely unitary narratives produced by self-assessed wizards or super-readers on whom the text's sense depends, but the more humble figure of an exegetical reader whose compelling interrogatives take account of diverse approaches. As T.S. Eliot reminds us in *Little Gidding*, "We shall not cease from exploration / and the end of all our exploring / will be to arrive where we started / and to know the place for the first time."

If we can be aware of why we disagree and of what assumptions or predilections take us in diverse paths, we will be in a position to have a dialogue about the problems of reading each text. Thus, in my recent *Reading Joyce's "Ulysses,"* I have tried to establish how, within a contemporary reader, a dialogue takes place between, on the one hand, reading *Ulysses* as a polysemous text that disseminates its linguistic phenomena but fails to achieve coherence and order, and, on the other, reading *Ulysses* as a traditional novel that has the kind of organic unity that we find in elaborate literary texts, the genetic code, and complex mathematical functions.[1] To an extent, I have become what Bialostosky calls a dialogic critic, that is, a critic who "not only ... respond(s) to ... diverse voices ... but [invents] the responses they have not made to one another" (Bialostosky, 792).

II. The Use and Abuse of Literary Theory

In this age of literary criticism and literary theory, the ethics of reading require us to be honest about what criticism and theory do. For many of us the problem in English studies today is how to apply the work of the theoretical explosion to close reading of texts. Put another way, we want to maintain a balance between the interpretation of texts–studies that seek to recreate or represent a text–and speculation about how language behaves. How can we describe the dialogue between reader and text without acknowledging that each reader brings diverse experiences–notably, but not exclusively, the other texts he has read–to the text? Do we not need interpretive criticism that maintains the uniqueness of each text and indeed values the interpretive process more than the teleological goal? Critical explanations should be perceived as an ongoing dialogue; talk of "cracking a poem," of arriving at a final interpretive destination, deprives us of the very spirit of reading as intimate sharing of consciousness. We should eschew criticism that fulfills the teleology of one dominant concept–whether it be irony, tension, ambiguity, or more recently, "aporia," "absence," and "phallo-centricism." We should be wary of valuing

---

[1] To be sure, in my book, *Reading Joyce's "Ulysses,"* I see the dialectic as finally being resolved in favor of mimesis, plot, and theme.

the challenges to unity and meaning in the form of gaps, fissures, and enigmas–as if *not to mean* and *not to signify* were better than *to mean* and *to signify*.

When we enter into an imagined world, we become involved with what
Nadine Gordimer calls "the substance of living from which the artist draws
his vision," and our criticism must speak to that "substance of living" (Gordimer). In Third World and postcolonial literature this involvement is much
more intense. Thus the recent interest in postcolonial and Third World literature–accelerated by Soyinka's Nobel prize–challenges the tenets of deconstruction. Literature written at the political edge reminds us what literature has always been about: urgency, commitment, tension, and feeling. Indeed, at
times have we not transferred those emotions to parochial critical debate
rather than to our response to literature? While it may not be completely irrelevant to talk about gaps, fissures, and enigmas and about the free play of signifiers in the poetry of Wally Serote ("Death Survey") and Don Mattera
("Singing Fools"), we must focus, too, on their status as persecuted blacks in
South Africa and the pain and alienation that they feel in the face of persecution. Nadine Gordimer has written–and Joyce might have said the same thing
about Ireland: "It is from the daily life of South Africa that there have come
the conditions of profound alienation which prevail among South African artists" (Gordimer). When discussing politically engaged literature, we need to
recuperate historical circumstances and understand the writer's ordering of
that history in his imagined world. We need to know not merely what patterns of provisional representation are created by language but the historical,
political, and social ground of that representation. We need to be open to
hearing the often unsophisticated and unironical voice of pain, *angst,* and
fear.

When we read literature we journey into an imaginary land, while at the
same time remaining home. Reading is a kind of imaginative travelling;
unlike real travelling, it allows us to transport ourselves immediately back
"home." Travel is immersion; home is reflective. How we take our imaginative journeys depends on how we are trained to read: what we as readers do
with the available data–how we sort it out and make sense of it. Although the
text has a kind of stability because it cannot *change,* our ways of speaking
about texts are always somewhat metaphoric. In our interpretive criticism we
cannot fully represent a text. When we describe or interpret a text we inevitably order and distort it. Our language is metaphorical–or as de Man would
have it, allegorical. But the metaphoricity of our efforts to represent a text in
part mirrors the metaphoricity of the author's efforts to mirror the world.
Since interpretive criticism does not–cannot–provide transparent or literal language for understanding texts, interpretive criticism creates in part its own
text.

Theoretical discourse is far more metaphoric than interpretive exegesis–or
at least what exegesis wished to be when it was a nominalistic report of the
imagined world evoked by a text. We should understand that theories are
metaphors, and like all metaphors they need to show the relationship

between the "image" (in this case, the conceptual framework proposed for a group of texts) and the "thing imaged" (here, the individual texts). We should remember that when theoretical discourse tries to represent the texts about which it is generalizing, it becomes more metaphorical–and hence more rhetorical and disfiguring–than interpretations. In other words, each stage of telling is inevitably a disfiguration, not an imitation. Or as Stevens puts it in "The Man With the Blue Guitar," "[T]hings as they are / are changed upon the blue guitar." For is not the Blue Guitar the basic impulse of the imagination–and of its surrogate in literature, namely language–to be metaphorical, disfiguring, and performative?

Literary theory seeks to offer hypotheses about how literary texts behave, what they do to readers, what readers do to them, and how language means; it seeks to find rigorous principles akin to those of science to explain what happens in literature. To the degree that literary theory is as rhetorical as it is descriptive, it cannot claim to have the status–as it often implies–of a scientific hypothesis explaining how texts behave. Yet to the degree that it is descriptive and pragmatic, it may help us understand individual texts. Theories, like genres, propose models; they become useful, I believe, when we examine the models in detail and find the ways that the models both adhere to and do not quite fit the theory, causing us to rethink the theory to accommodate new data. Theory always imposes its own ordering text. Because language distorts and disfigures even as it generalizes, theory is to interpretations as interpretations are to literary texts and as literary texts are to the anterior world. Yet all too often theory depends on our need and desire to have a unitary narrative in the form of a pattern or hypothesis to explain our diverse reading experiences of actual texts. Because we read in multiple ways, even contradictory ways, we need many tentative and often contradictory hypotheses–or theories–to accommodate one specific reading experience. If theoretical formulations do not seem to represent actual relationships to texts, if they do not seek a dialogue between specific and abstract, then their language becomes truly signifiers without signifieds; or in other terms, they become dead metaphors because they are detached and separate from what they are imaging.

III. Reading Pluralistically

It is unfortunately true that we are in a period where, for many, commitment to a dominant interpretive strategy shapes stories of reading every text–that is, the critic brings the same strategy to each text and finds the same things. Paradoxically, the very deconstructive criticism that objects to critical telos in unitary narratives of a text's meaning finds its own *telos* in both its readings and its theory. But need that be so? Should we not have an array of strategies which we use depending on the text and, to a lesser extent, on our interests? Should we not allow the text to shape our readings? Put another way, as readers we are members of diverse interpretive communities which should be in a unique dialogic relationship with each text. I am much more interested in the socio-economic implications of *Nostromo* than I am, say, of *The Secret Sharer*, where my concerns are more weighted to the psychology of the young captain as revealed by his first-person narration.

Should interpretive strategies create texts, or can we imagine a process by which a critic is sufficiently eclectic that he draws upon his familiarity with a range of interpretive strategies, choosing those that are most appropriate for each text and author? We need to learn how to enter into a dialogue with diverse approaches, to see their point of view, to understand that interpretive communities become narrow enclaves unless they conceive themselves as part of larger intellectual communities. What is appealing to me about Bakhtin is the implicit acknowledgment of pluralism within a novel's style and imagined world:

> The novel as a whole is a phenomenon multiform in style and uniform in speech and voice.... The novel can be defined as a diversity of speech types (sometimes even diversity of language) and diversity of individual voices, artistically organized.... Authorial speech, the speeches of narrators, inserted genres, the speech of characters are merely those fundamental compositional unities with whose help heteroglossia [raznorecie] can enter the novel; each of them permits a multiplicity of social voices and a wide variety of their links and interrelationships (always more or less dialogized). These distinctive links and interrelationships between utterances and languages, this movement of the theme through different languages and speech types, its dispersion into the rivulets and droplets of social heteroglossia, its dialogization—this is the basic distinguishing feature of the stylistics of the novel.[2]

The same multiplicity of contending voices is inherent not only in critical dialogue about a text, but is and *should* be present in the criticism of any one critic.

Just as an author "rents" multiple linguistic systems to create what Bakhtin calls heteroglossia, the reader "rents" diverse interpretive strategies—or perspectives—depending upon his prior experience. But we each belong to multiple interpretive communities; and as we read, we draw upon our participation and experience in several interpretive communities. Not only do those interpretive communities change as well as modify and subvert one another, but our relationship to them varies from text to text. How we read the texts—and the world—depends on an ever changing hierarchy of interpretive strategies. These hierarchies constitute our reading of texts—and the world—even as they are constituted by it. That is, as we read, our interpretive

---

[2] According to Bakhtin, "the internal stratification of any single national language into social dialects, characteristic group behavior, professional jargons, generic languages, languages of generations and age groups, tendentious languages, languages of the authorities, of various circles and of passing fashions, languages that serve the specific sociopolitical purposes of the day, even of the hour (each day has its own slogan, its own vocabulary, its own emphases)–this internal stratification present in every language at any given moment of its historical existence is the indispensable prerequisite for the novel as a genre. The novel orchestrates all its themes, the totality of the world of objects and ideas depicted and expressed in it, by means of the social diversity of speech types [*raznorecie*] and by the differing individual voices that flourish under such conditions" (M.M. Bakhtin, *The Dialogic Imagination*, ed. Michael Holquist [Austin: University of Texas Press, 1981], pp. 261–63).

strategies are challenged and modified even as they modify what we read. When reading criticism we need to be aware of the theoretical and methodological assumptions that produce a reading and examine whether we belong to the community of readers who share those assumptions.

Our ethics of reading needs to account for the subjectivity inherent in our reading. For may not subjectivity idiosyncratically deflect us from the decision about which interpretive communities we shall use? Need we be self-conscious about the distinctiveness of our position as to the text that we are describing or responding to? If someone were to read my interpretive criticism or come to my classes, he would be aware of my propensity for seeing texts in historical, mimetic, and formal terms—especially my propensity as a pragmatic Aristotelian to hear the voice of narrators and to stress the relationship between *doesness* and *isness*. And what about my personal background and experience? My biases and shortcomings? Do I not have a greater professional and personal stake in some texts than in others?

What I am suggesting is that the reader as *übermensch* or as super-reader is a disguise for the human reader with all his tics and quirks as the recent de Man revelations remind us. Thus if we wish to enter into a dialogue with other approaches, we need to understand the deflection caused by our subjectivity and that of the interpretive critics we read. It may be worth the effort to induce from each interpretive text a persona of the critic to see if we can explain his subjectivity and thus understand his underlying perspective, approach, values, methods, and theory. That is, we must read critical texts as if they too were spoken by a human voice to a human audience, and—as if we were hearing a first-person narration—we must attend to what is missing or distorted.

Since my ethics of reading depends upon the litmus test of "for example," I want to propose the kinds of inquiry that would constitute a dialogic or pluralistic reading of Joyce's "Araby," a work chosen because it is short, well-known, frequently taught, and understood in many different ways. If we see "Araby" as belonging to a sequence of stories that thematizes the moral paralysis of Dublin; as a product of the socio-economic reasons for that paralysis; as the third story of the sexual initiation of a young boy in a series beginning with "The Sisters" and "An Encounter"; as an earlier version of Joyce's *A Portrait of the Artist as a Young Man;* as a confession that carries heavy autobiographical freight; as a polemic urging us to see what happens when we are limited and defined by systems of perceptions not our own; as an elegy for boyhood; as a satire on the inhibiting and debilitating effects of a Catholic education; as an artistically organized structure of linguistic effects; as a dramatic monologue; and as an instance of early modernism in several ways (including its turn-of-the-century fascination with masks, its biographical relationship to the author, and its demands upon the reader to weave the meaning of the text)– if we see "Araby" in all these ways, then we *begin* to define what kind of story we are dealing with.

When reading "Araby," each of us becomes a member of a number of different audiences:

1. The 1895 audience to whom Joyce imagines that the adolescent speaker is narrating his story—a story based on the young Joyce's visit to an actual bazaar in 1894. This narrative audience, whom the speaker addresses, is an implied audience within an imagined world who knows the customs, politics, routines of Dublin, and even the popular culture of Dublin, including its songs and folk legends.

2. The 1904 historical audience that the author had in mind as he wrote the story.

3. The 1988 contemporary audience. Those of us who teach Joyce are conditioned by the interpretive history of "Araby" and our varying knowledge of Joyce's life and text. Does the reality of a text include not only its interpretive history, but our memory of our last rereading—*i.e., our* interpretive history? When we discuss books or poems, do we not present the shape we put upon it? When we "speak" of our reading to a class or colleagues or friends, do we not "write" our text of that reading experience? Because we draw upon our own anterior experience, as we *reread* we modify our understanding because our intertextual and real experience have changed. But, in a process akin to pentimento, past readings peek through; what we did to the text and it did to us in our prior readings shape each new reading, just as we live in the texture of past association when we meet an old friend. The students coming to a text for the first time will respond differently, moreover, depending on age group, social-economic group, nationality, education level; their response can be further broken into fragments depending on interest and learning—including knowledge of Catholicism and Ireland. In fact, each of us has her own particular response—subjective, disfigured, a function of who we are when we read and how that uniquely shapes our response to each word. Finally, the largest interpretive community—the largest interpretive entity or unit—is each reader—you or me.

As readers, we create a version of events other than the one the author wrote; in varying degrees, we weave the texture of an open text—open in the sense that it requires our sense-making to complete it—especially with modern texts such as Joyce's which are more open to varying interpretation. But an open text need not be indeterminate merely because a reader needs to *interpret it*. Acts of interpretation depend on answering a series of hypothetical questions that determine the ground of the inquiry and become the cause of interpretive effects. One might conceive the reader at the center of a series of concentric circles—each representing an interpretive strategy. Depending on the literary text and what interests that reader, the ordering of the circles from closest to most distant varies. My ideal reader is a pluralist who centers herself at a radial center of concentric circles of diverse interpretive communities and draws upon the appropriate circles for each text and each reading, even while understanding that what is appropriate for her reading would not necessarily be appropriate for another reading or her next reading. With each rereading the circles of interpretive strategies that the reader brings closest to her radial centerpoint will change.

A pluralistic interpretation of Joyce's "Araby" might address the following interrelated questions, and as it found answers, would then–depending on the reader's interests–establish a hierarchy of issues:

1. What is the *point of view*? Who is speaking to whom and for what purpose? Who is telling the story, and on what occasion? What is the speaker's relation to Joyce? What does Joyce expect of the reader? My own reading of "Araby" argues for a triple perspective. An indeterminate time has passed between the boy's original experience and his retrospective first-person telling of that experience. Joyce expects us to share his ironic perspective towards a retrospective teller who is myopic and limited in his understanding, embedded in the ecclesiastical language he would disavow, and, as a very young artist, infatuated with what he believes is poetic and literary language. The young speaker's interior verbal world–excessive, colorful, elegant–contrasts poignantly with his inability to *speak* to Mangan's sister. Indeed, does not the *lack* of dialogue between the speaker and Mangan's sister poignantly comment on the rest of his world which seems full of talk–the talk of the priests, his uncle and aunt, his friends–that does not speak to his soul? For the boy, as for Stevens in "An Ordinary Evening in New Haven," "the words of the world are the life of the world."

2. What is the genre? What kind of text are we reading? As discourse, "Araby" needs to be generically defined in terms both of the dramatic monologue and what Adena Rosmarin has recently called, in her magnificent study *The Power of Genre*, the mask lyric. As a story, it needs to be seen as having aspects in miniature of confession, *künstlerroman*, and *bildungsroman*. It also may be seen in terms of Joyce's generic distinction between lyrical, dramatic, and epical as presented in *A Portrait of the Artist*.

3. What does "Araby" reveal as an *expression* of Joyce's life? In what way does Ellmann's monumental biography become part of our intertextual response to the story?

4. How is "Araby" a socio-economic text produced by Ireland's historical circumstances–in Joyce's view, by Ireland's twin servitude to the Catholic church and England? How is "Araby" a satire of Catholicism which–along with England–is the social and political antagonist of the story? Isn't Joyce using the boy to demonstrate the values of a representative preadolescent in Dublin and showing what forces–notably Catholicism and British domination of Ireland–shape the boy's epistemology and language, even as the speaker performs for us the consequences of that upbringing?

5. How is "Araby" a study of sexual repression? Can it be discussed in psychoanalytic terms?

6. How is "Araby" a chapter in the evolving collection called *Dubliners*? How do we link the speaker to the younger first-person narrators of the two prior stories, "The Sisters" and "An Encounter"? Because of the continuity among the three stories, does he not become a shadowy version of a portrait of the artist as a *very* young man? In that vein, how are these three stories part of a fictional sequence, including *A Portrait of the Artist,*

and *Ulysses*, about a young man's growing up in Dublin? How do we link his sexual repression with the frustrated and guilty sexuality of the title character of the subsequent story, "Eveline"?

7. How is "Araby" part of Joyce's cityscape–his representation of Dublin–and how does that look forward to, and become part of, his later depictions of Dublin's characters in *Ulysses* and *Finnegans Wake*?

8. How is "Araby" a 1904 text that depends on historical and literary allusions which have to be recuperated by historical scholarship? (Harry Stone's excellent essay in the Viking Critical Edition of *Dubliners* does this as do the footnotes in that edition.) As a 1904 text, "Araby" is an historically determined production written by a specific author at a particular time. One critical task is to reconstruct the expectations that existed when the story originally appeared and to understand the distinction between that response and a contemporary response. Of course, Joyce had no one "horizon of expectation," but rather had several in mind at the same time: Dublin's drowsing citizens whose consciences and consciousness needed arousing; the Catholic hierarchy; the Irish artistic and intellectual elite, including Yeats; the British public; and perhaps a prospective publisher for his story.

9. How does "Araby" enact a dialectical linguistic drama in which realistic, descriptive language describing the pedestrian world of Dublin struggles with the language of the romance world? Within the boy's mind the language of sexual desire, religious education (especially the ritual of confession), Irish songs, and literary naturalism not only struggle with one another, but also with his own desire and efforts as a putative artist to invent stylized and mannered forms to render his past experience. The boy's romance language–the language borrowed from his reading rather than his experience–is transformed and undermined by the pedestrian world of Dublin and the obsessive hold of the church.[3]

10. How does "Araby" fulfill the conventions of the modern short story–including endings that are the fulfillment of prior hints; dense verbal textures in which the linguistic subject reinforces the theme and action, as well as the compression of storytime (several weeks) into a few pages to be read within a twenty-minute reading? How does "Araby" look back to the naturalism and realism of nineteenth-century fiction?

---

[3] Bakhtin's concept of heteroglossia is particularly useful to discuss the dialogues among styles in "Araby." As Bakhtin notes:

> *Languages do not exclude each other but rather intersect with each other.... All languages of heteroglossia, whatever the principles underlying them and making each unique, are specific points of view on the world, forms for conceptualizing the world in words, specific world-views, each characterized by its own objects, meanings, and values. As such they all may be juxtaposed to one another, mutually supplement one another, contradict one another and be interrelated dialogically. As such they encounter one another and co-exist in the consciousness of real people–first and foremost, in the creative consciousness of people who write novels. As such, these languages live a real life, they struggle and evolve in an environment of social heteroglossia. Therefore they are all able to enter into the unitary plane of the novel, which can unite in itself parodic stylizations of generic languages, various forms of stylizations and illustrations of professional and period-bound languages, the languages of particular generations, of social dialects and others (as occurs, for example, in the English comic novel). They may all be drawn in by the novelist for the orchestration of his themes and for the refracted (indirect) expression of his intentions and values* (291–92).

11. How is "Araby" a story of what happens to the ideal reader–although we realize an ideal reader is a fiction–as he or she moves from the beginning to the end, making sense of the story as he or she responds to the structure of effects that results from the voice, organization, conventions, and linguistic patterns?

12. In what way is the text an experience, like other experiences, which resists full understanding, but iterates the boy's quest for understanding–a quest which is the subject of the boy's adventure and of his retelling? As readers, we find what we look for: our readings may be creative, open, and part of our realization of the world; or they may be narrow, stilted, unimaginative, and controlled *completely* by the text. The adolescent speaker's reductive reading of his experience teaches us what happens when we read in either extreme way.

13. Finally, my pluralistic reading would include a story of *my* personal experience of reading "Araby": my identification as an adolescent with the boy's love of language and prepubescent sexual anxiety, my visit to Dublin a few years ago, and my twenty-four years of pleasure in teaching and speaking about the story. As teacher and critic should I not try to explain how and why I am touched at every stage of my life by the story of a young boy whose quest for love and language mirrors, parodies, and tropes aspects of my own quest?

IV. A Transactional Theory of Reading

I would like to propose the concept of transactional reading to stress how reader and text meet in the seam of the reading experience. In my view, text and reader are engaged in a transaction where each does something to the other.[4] Peter Ruppert has put it nicely in his *Reader in a Strange Land*: "In a dialectical model of the reader/text relationship, neither reader nor text is a stable entity or a finished product; each constitutes, rather, an active component in a mutual transaction that produces discord, disagreement, and transformation" (Ruppert, 27).

The equivalent to squaring the hermeneutical circle is to bisect the distance between, on the one hand, reader-response criticism which argues that the reader creates the text and which is epitomized by Stanley Fish, and, on the other, Aristotelian principles which assume that texts shape readers and are epitomized by Wayne Booth and his followers. What Fish and Booth both do is focus on the structure of affects generated by the text and the process of the sense-making that continually goes on in the reader's mind. Both are interested in *doesness*, in reading as action, but whereas for Booth it is the text that transforms, modifies, qualifies, and reformulates the reader's emotions

---

[4] As Iser in his essay "Interaction Between Text and Reader" has written: "Communication in literature, then, is a process set in motion and regulated not by a given code, but by a mutually restrictive and magnifying interaction between the explicit and implicit, between revelation and concealment. What is concealed spurs the reader into action, but this action is also controlled by what is revealed; the explicit in its turn is transformed when the implicit has been brought to light. Whenever the reader bridges the gaps, communication begins" (*The Reader in the Text*, Susan Suleiman and Inge Crosman, eds. [Princeton: Princeton University Press, 1980], p. 111).

and values, for Fish it is the reader who does these things to the text. For Booth, language represents non-linguistic aspects such as theme, plot, character, and structure. While Fish claims that the language is itself the focus, in practice he too is reading through language to what it represents.

Traditional Aristotelian criticism argues that the author–or the implied author–speaking to an implied reader, *produces* the effects based on prior causes built into the text by the author in his *making* of the fiction. Such criticism moves from author as maker to the made object–the text–to what the text or made object does. The traditional paradigm is:

(from the) anterior world ⟶ the author (makes) the text

(or imaginary universe) (which produces effects on) the reader.[5]

Reader-response criticism argues that ultimately readers produce the text and infer a hypothesis of the author: it moves backward from reader to text to author. When Fish reads seventeenth-century poetry, he is something of a closet Aristotelian in his concern with the structure of effects and its relationship to the enactment of a plot and the genre of the text. Fish reverses the method of inducing *doesness* from the text and ultimately the author; he induces the text from what it does to the reader and then induces the author from the text he creates. So we can graph Fish:

the reader (unmakes/creates) the text (or imaginary universe)

(from which he induces) the author as well as the anterior world that the author attempts to describe.

Since in practice both include a dialogue between reader and text, Aristotelian criticism and most reader-response criticism are transactional.

Let me distinguish what I am calling transactional reading from the theoretical underpinnings if not the practice of reader-response criticism. For Fish, "[I]nterpretation is the source of texts, facts, authors, intentions" (Fish, 16). But I would argue that interpretation is the way we organize and give shape both to the experience of reading texts and what they do as a class of objective phenomena. As a reader, Fish believes that he does not recuperate texts, but rather *makes* texts. Fish wants to focus on the temporal flow of the developing responses of the reader to the words as they succeed each other on the page; the critic describes his experience of that process. As Fish puts it, "[T]he meaning of an utterance . . . is its experience–all of it–and that experi-

[5] 1. The author's account   4. The reader's account

2. The imaginary universe evoked by the author ⟶ 3. The imaginary universe constructed by the reader

ence is immediately compromised the moment you say something about it" (Fish, 65). For Fish, "[I]nterpretive strategies are not put into execution after reading; ... they are the shape of reading, and because they are the shape of reading, they give texts their shape, making them rather than ... arising from them" (Fish, 13). But while interpretation, cognition, and perception are inseparable from reading, are they not also part of the reflective process that succeeds reading? Even if we accept Fish's view that "the formal features ... are the *product* of the interpretive principles for which they are supposedly evidence...." and that "formal units are always a function of the interpretive model one brings to bear," does that mean they–the units–are not "in the text"? (Fish, 12–13). What we see in the experiential world depends on our perspectives, but what we do not see is still there and perhaps the very things that others will see. For Fish, criticism cannot be demonstrative, but only persuasive.[6] Yet, I would argue, stories of reading–like all telling and writing–are partly demonstrative and partly persuasive or performative. Cannot a discussion of the *isness* and *doesness* of the text, its original author, and its historical context be *demonstrative* rather than merely rhetorical?[7]

Transactional reading is, for me, a crucial component of the informed pluralism essential to humanistic formalism. In my transactional model the reader is a savvy figure–part picaro, part hero–who lives by his wits, intuition, and humor as he moves through time engaged in the process of sense-making. But he is also a reflective figure who lives at the center of concentric circles of epistemologies–interpretive communities, if you will–and moves outward from a passage to read synchronically. For the odyssey of reading requires both a wily, shrewd, canny, linear reader as well as a reader who resists temporal narratives of reading, and who sees the multiplicity of meanings generated by literary texts and the primitive mystery of combinations of words. The transactional reader does not take signs for wonders; she establishes in the adventure of reading a hierarchy of meanings, even while understanding that such a hierarchy varies depending upon her interests and values at the time of reading. Such a reader has the openness, flexibility, and humility to allow the text its occasion, and gives it space to perform its meaning. Open to new experience, she is not intimidated by the possibility that texts will not fit preexistent patterns. She is willing to use diverse interpretive strategies for different texts, and she has no preexisting formula for reading.

While a transactional approach does not arrive at one valid meaning, it permits a dialogue between phenomena discovered in the text and the reader's sense-making; it also seeks to demonstrate how that sense-making derives from a dialogue of interpretive strategies within the reader's mind. It is in those passages where determinacy comes into question and ambiguity exists

[6] Fish writes, "That is why, as I said, the stakes in a persuasion model are so high. In a demonstration model our task is to be adequate to the description of objects that exist independently of our activities; we may fail or we may succeed, but whatever we do the objects of our attention will retain their ontological separateness and still be what they were before we approached them. In a model of persuasion, however, our activities are directly constitutive of those objects, and of the terms in which they can be described, and of the standards by which they can be evaluated. The responsibilities of the critic under this model are very great indeed, for rather than being merely a player in the game, he is a maker and unmaker of its rules" (Fish, *Is There a Text in This Class?* p. 367).

[7] We should note that Fish shares the binary fallacy with deconstruction–that is, he assumes that if something is not absolutely irrevocably true, it must be false.

when the most interpretive cognition and analysis are required of our transactional reader. The reader weaves patterns of meaning from implication, imagines unseen motives not articulated in dialogue, interprets more knowingly
than characters or narrator, and supplies unwritten threads of plot to tie
discrete episodes together. Do we not make our world from our responses to
experience and do not authors write because they assume that we do so?

My transactional model stresses both the private nature of our story of
reading and the public nature of our sharing knowledge generated by the
text. It seeks to give account of the multiple and contradictory kinds of reading that are part of the critical process of reading, a process that has disruptions and short circuits. Fish argues that stability exists not in texts, but in interpretive communities defined by literary, political, and cultural
determinants. But I believe that it is just as correct to say that communities of
words–i.e., literary texts–make readers. All Fish is really saying is that a
text–or a tree–depends on human cognition; the text or tree cannot look at
me. This is, of course, Stevens' point in "The Idea of Order in Key West"–our
imagination responds to experience and makes ghostlier demarcations and
keener sounds–and a major point of the entire Romantic movement of which
reader-response criticism is so much a part.

If texts are the products of interpretive acts, interpretive acts are the products of texts. Doesn't an author encode a response? Doesn't she use her
words to structure her effects? Do not texts produce effects in readers? The
problem with speaking exclusively of what the reader does to the text is that
it deflects attention from the way readers respond to an imagined world created by the words and the anterior world which gives it shape. It tends to
stress moments of disunity rather than seeing patterns of unity. Do we not
read to *know*, to learn about behavior? Do we not need to account for why
one kind of imitation interests more readers than others; what attracts us to
some imagined ontologies more than others; of what are pleasing fictions constituted; why we need organization and unity; why necessity and probability
are aesthetically pleasing; and why we wish to allegorize universals from details?

Let us for a moment consider codes. Just as we respond to baseball games,
social behavior, and academic conferences by reference to codes based on
prior knowledge of the purposes, goals, and practices of those activities, our
responses to texts depend on the conventions and customs of the prior texts
that we have read. What is important to stress is that texts contain the potential for provoking our knowledge developed from prior reading. Authors
build a narrative code into their texts, a code that instructs the reader how to
respond to each text; when the reader adds a supplement of his reading experience, the decoding becomes a transaction. Yet the perception of the author's code varies with readers and changes with time. When Eliot defined
"objective correlative," was he not talking about narrative coding? "The only
way of expressing emotion in the form of art is by finding an 'objective correlative'; in other words, a set of objects, a situation, a chain of events which
shall be the formula of that *particular* emotion; such that when the external

facts, which must terminate in sensory experience, are given the emotion is immediately evoked" (Eliot, 124–5). Wasn't Eliot speaking of the inadvertent *effects* of polysemous signifiers when he complained that "Hamlet (the man) is dominated by an emotion which is inexpressible, because it is in *excess* of the facts as they appear" (Eliot, 125)?

Let me tentatively propose five stages of the hermeneutical activities involved in reading and interpretation. Even while acknowledging that my model is suggestive rather than rigorous, I believe that we do perceive in stages that move from a naive response or surface interpretation to critical or in-depth interpretation and, finally, to understanding our readings conceptually in terms of other knowledge. My stages are:

1. *Immersion in the process of reading and the discovery of imagined worlds.* Reading is a place where text and reader meet in a transaction. As we open a text, we and the author meet as if together we were going to draw a map on an uncharted space. We partially suspend our sense of our world as we enter into the imagined world; we respond in experiential terms to the episodes, the story, the physical setting, the individualized characters as humans, the telling voice. In "Araby" we live in the world of 1895 Dublin, see it from an adolescent's point of view, and experience his quest for meaning and understanding. While it has become fashionable to speak dismissively of such reading as "naive," or the result of the "mimetic illusion," in fact how many of us do not read in that way with pleasure and delight? Who of us would be teaching and studying literature had he not learned to read mimetically?

2. *Quest for understanding.* Our quest is closely related to the diachronic, linear, temporal activity of reading. The quest speaks to the gap between "what did you say?" and "what did you mean?" In writing, as opposed to speech, the speaker cannot correct, intrude, or qualify; she cannot use gestures or adjust the delivery of her discourse. Because in writing we lack the speaker's help, we must make our own adjustments in our reading. As Paul Ricoeur notes, "What the text says now matters more than what the author meant to say, and every exegesis unfolds its procedures within the circumference of a meaning that has broken its moorings to the psychology of its author" (Ricoeur, 191). We complete the sign of the imagined world by providing the signified, but no sooner do we complete a sign than it becomes a signifier in search of a new signified. In modern and postmodern texts, our search for necessary information may parallel that of many major characters. Where we cannot rely upon the teller or have sufficient information, the quest for necessary information will be much more of a factor than in traditional texts. In this stage we are actively unravelling the complexities of plot; we also seek to discover the principles or world view by which the author expects us to understand characters' behavior in terms of motives and values.

The text of "Araby" invites–indeed, demands–an ironic reader who shares with Joyce an objective view of the adolescent teller; because of his cynicism, hyperbole, verbal extravagance and syntactical disruptions, we understand that this is not the normative style of *Dubliners*. Until recently, I would have claimed that "Araby" is a prose version of a dramatic monologue, but Adena

Rosmarin has taught us that such a first-person confessional work might bet-ter be called a "mask lyric." For Joyce does not expect us to judge the speaker by a set of values he lacks and of which he is unaware, but expects us rather to share empathetically the speaker's vision. By thinking of unreliable speak-ers in modern fiction as having much in common with dramatic monologues, we explain the story in terms of a recognized genre. Yet isn't Joyce's speaker–the younger, retrospective, imperceptive, sensitive poet who is in love with language–also a version of the author? Indeed, as I have argued elsewhere, collectively Joyce's works are striking examples of how the author enters into the text of modern British literature (Schwarz, 1982, 279–92).

3. *Self-conscious reflection.* Reflection speaks to the gap between "what did *you* mean?" and "what does *that* mean?" Upon reflection, we may adjust our per-spective or see new ones. What the interpretive reader does–particularly with spare, implicatory modern literature–is fill the gaps left by the text to create an explanatory text or *midrash* on the text itself. As Iser puts it, "What is said only appears to take on a significance as a reference to what is not said; it is the implications and not the statements that give shape and weight to the meaning" (Suleiman and Crosman, 111). While the reader half-perceives, half-creates his original "immersed" reading of the text, he retrospectively–from the vantage point of knowing the whole–imposes shape and form on his story of reading. He discovers its significance in relation to his other experi-ences, including other reading experiences, and in terms of the interpretive communities to which he belongs. He reasons posteriorly from effects to causes. He is aware of referentiality to the anterior world–how that world in-forms the author's mimesis–and to the world in which he lives. He be-gins–more in modern texts, but even in traditional texts–to separate his own version of what is really meant from what is said.

Here Todorov's distinction between signification and symbolization is use-ful. "Signified facts are *understood*: all we need is knowledge of the language in which the text is written. Symbolized facts are *interpreted*: and interpreta-tions vary from one subject to another" (Suleiman and Crosman, 73). A prob-lem is that, in practice, what is understood by one reader may require inter-pretation by another. What is a pre-interpretative fact within a first-person discourse like "Araby"?[8] The more interpretive work she finds to do, the more the reader *acts.* Even as we discover the meaning of implication, we are aware of challenges to unitary reading.

4. *Critical analysis.* The principle metonymic reading of "Araby" depends on placing it in the context of a sequential reading of *Dubliners,* but as we read each of the stories, does not each become the centerpoint of a concentric circle of episodes, including our memories of other stories in *Dubliners*? And it also becomes a centerpoint in the consciousness of our memory of other Joyce texts; other texts of the period; intellectual and cultural history of Ireland; and the modernist movement in England and its counterparts in Europe, including developments in painting and sculpture.

---

[8] As I have argued elsewhere, indeed, even pre-critical facts provided by an omniscient narrator involve selection and ar-rangement; we must interpret his psyche and character from what he includes, emphasizes, evades, and omits. See my "The Narrator as Character in Hardy's Major Fiction," *Modern Fiction Studies* 18 (Summer 1972), 155–72; and my "'I Was The World in Which I Walked': The Transformation of the British Novel," *The University of Toronto Quarterly* 51:3 (Spring 1982), 279–97.

For example, in "The Sisters" the boy "felt that I had been far away in some land where the customs were strange–in Persia." To the reader of "Araby," the dream of escape inevitably ties him to the younger boy of the prior story. What these recurring references do is modify our reading to understand the boy in "Araby" as an evolving figure who *continually* meets paralysis and disappointment. "Araby" becomes the third unit in a narrative code and "Eveline" is the fourth. We begin then to think of "Araby" in terms of its place in *Dubliners*. We place the text into an historical, authorial, generic, or theoretical context. As Paul Ricoeur writes, "To understand a text is to follow its movement from sense to reference, from what it says to what it talks about" (Ricoeur, 214). In the process, we always move from signifier to signified; for no sooner do we understand what the original signifiers signify within the imagined world than these signifieds in turn become signifiers for larger issues and symbolic constructions in the world beyond the text.

While the reader responds to texts in such multiple ways and for such diverse reasons that we cannot speak of a correct reading, we can speak of a dialogue among plausible readings. Drawing upon our interpretive strategies, we reflect on generic, intertextual, linguistic, biographical relationships that disrupt linear reading; we move back and forth from the whole to the part. My responses to my reading are a function of what I know, what I have recently been reading, my last experience of reading a particular author, my knowledge of the period in which he wrote as well as the influences upon him and his influence on others. My reponses also depend on how willing I am to suspend my irony and detachment and enter into the imagined world of the text as well as on how much of a text my memory retains.

Isn't the self-dramatizing speaker, with his highly charged metaphorical imagination and his love of language–its sounds, sights, textures–a portrait of a very young artist? If one reads "Araby" aloud, one can hear how the speaker savors the sensuality of language and realizes that he has transferred his sublimated sexuality to his telling. Indeed, his image of the physical intimidating crowd contrasts with his own abstract, solitary, idealized and platonic need for love. How oddly he describes his view of Dublin life in terms of his clerical education–"the shrill litanies of shop-boys," the "nasal chanting of street singers." "Araby"–the name of the bazaar–is the soul, the chant, of Desire: "The syllables of the word *Araby* were called to me through the silence in which my sort luxuriated and cast an Eastern enchantment over me." And the narrator recaptures the excitement of this magic even as he retells it. The telling, like the bazaar, is the antidote to the pedestrian world that imprisons him and Mangan's sister. It is his response to sights, sounds, and texture of words which may save him, despite his veering round to darkness at the end–the reference is to Sue's renunciation of freedom in *Jude the Obscure*. For doesn't the speaker's plight remind us of how, in late nineteenth- and early twentieth-century British literature, inhibiting social conventions stifle the soul's urge to be free? Isn't that the subject not only of *Jude* but of *A Room with a View*, *Heart of Darkness*, *Mrs. Dalloway* and *To the Lighthouse* as well as so much of Eliot's and Yeats's poetry?

5. *Cognition in terms of what we know.* Drawing upon our interpretive strategies, we reflect on generic, intertextual, linguistic, and biographical relationships that disrupt linear reading; we move back and forth from the whole to the part. As Ricoeur writes: "The reconstruction of the text as a whole necessarily has a circular character, in the sense that the presupposition of a certain kind of whole is implied in the recognition of the parts. And reciprocally, it is in constructing the details that we construe the whole" (Ricoeur, 204). We return to the original reading experience and text and subsequently modify our conceptual hypotheses about genre, period, author, canon, and themes. We integrate what we have read into our reading of other texts and into our way of looking at ourselves and the world. Here we consciously use our categorizing sensibility–our rage for order–to make sense of our reading experience and its way of being in our world. In the final stage, the interpretive reader may become a critic who writes his own text about the "transaction" between himself and the text.

That "Araby" reflects Joyce's boyhood in Dublin in 1894 is part of "cognition in terms of what we know." Indeed, isn't our understanding of what Rosmarin calls a mask lyric increased by knowing about Joyce and the world in which he lived? Expressive issues include the relationship between "Araby" and the first two stories in *Dubliners*, between the boy and Stephen Dedalus in *Portrait* and *Ulysses*–including the way that "Araby" can be understood in terms of Joyce's aesthetic theories in both works–and between Joyce and the evolving persona of the volume *Dubliners*.

Let us pursue the relationship between the boy and Joyce, and see briefly how the boy is a surrogate for Joyce. Were it not for Ellmann's biography–and, of course, the letters–"Araby" would read differently; but if we know that it is biographically and historically grounded in anterior reality, that knowledge becomes part of our pluralistic response from the first reading. Joyce tells us that these first three stories are of "my childhood" (he is much more ambiguous about the biographical origins of the subsequent stories in *Dubliners*). His narrator's self-indictment, his escapism, his fascination with the sounds of words–"Her name was like a summons to all my foolish blood"–reflect Joyce's own history. Harry Stone has written of the importance of the literary allusions; and while we might differ on how he makes sense of these sources, he has shown that they are essential to biographical and historical contexts (Stone, 344–68). And if we know the bazaar took place in Dublin in May 14–19, 1894, when Joyce was thirteen, we can hypothesize that the story may have taken place in springtime of the boy's thirteenth year. If we know also that in late 1894 Joyce lived at North Richard Street, a dead end near the Christian Brothers' School, we have a specific locale for the story.

The boy's hyperbolic language is meanwhile at odds with a stifling respectability which has ground his life to dust ("decent lives," "safely housed"), in part because respectability itself had been revealed as a sham to young Joyce as his father's fortunes declined and as alcoholic scenes became embedded in his memory. Can the reader who does not know Joyce's vision of Dublin here and elsewhere–the pervasive idleness and sloth of adults–quite understand the resonance of the word "work" in the cliché: "All work and no play makes Jack a dull boy"? So, yes, eroticism and sublimated sexuality are part of the texture, but so is the cityscape of Joyce's imagined Dublin, a cityscape that reflects a Dublin in which Joyce lived and walked.

Paradoxically, when we speak of a work as an expressive tale, we talk about it as an historically determined product. Didn't Joyce write from self-imposed exile about the political and social realities of Dublin? Isn't "Araby" a story that comes from the depth of conscience and commitment? Just as I believe referents in art are necessary, so are referents in criticism. Criticism must take account of how literature is an historically determined product, how both the author and the reader are products of the worlds in which they live. To quote Mary Louise Pratt, "[J]ust as textual reception can be shown not to be the private personal exercise in semantic promiscuity that it was feared to be, so it can be shown that textual production is not simply a matter of individual authors acting out inscrutable intentions, personal prejudices, and private anxieties. Just as the subject who reads a text must be seen not as an autonomous, self-consistent essential self but as constituted by its social reality, so must the same be said for the subject who produces a literary text" (Pratt, 30). In treating literary interpretations as historical human productions, both the new historicism and Marxism have more in common with what I call humanistic formalism than with criticism that ignores representation. Indeed, I would agree with Pratt that "what the theory of socially constituted reality says is that what people actually do and the interpretations they produce are attached to *everything* outside themselves, to the whole of their social and material life"–although I might not agree with her about the definition of "socially constituted reality" (Pratt, 46).

While within my paradigm the above stages of reading occur in order, in fact we continually move back and forth through the stages. Cognition in terms of what we know is less a part of actual reading than immersion in the text, but most reading experience includes all five levels interacting simultaneously. In other words, my paradigm has both a synchronic and diachronic dimension. Different texts not only elicit different components of each phase, but each reader will respond differently depending on her interests. Within our own minds, *each* reading of a text is different because *we* are different; indeed, one difference when we reread is that we have more experience of the text than when we originally or last read it. Our first reading cannot be said to precede our critical activity any more than we can say that the events in our lives are separable from our first efforts at understanding. Even in our first reading we move from immersion in a text to interpretive reflection, particularly for complex texts and/or for those texts in which we have a personal or professional investment. Not only when we teach and write about texts, but when we reread them, we should be self-consciously aware of the stages and evolution in our responses to texts.

V. Theoretical Implications:
Towards a Pluralistic Theory of Interpretation

I have been arguing that "Araby" is about the problem of a way of telling and reading–about the continuity between perceiving experience and reading texts, between reading and writing. In "Araby," while the church's monologic perspective, and its imposition of that perspective on its acolytes, excludes, narrows and limits the young speaker, he resists that perspective enough to give the reader a sense of what is missing, even though he finally submits to that perspective in the story's closing lines. Like his contemporaries Conrad, James, and the Cubists, Joyce favored multiple perspectives–witness *Dubliners* and *Ulysses*. Finally, "Araby" shows language, perspective, sexuality to be problematic; it asks rather than answers questions and by asking questions invites a critical methodology that would do the same.

To think of fictions only as textual events rather than representations diminishes them. I am doubtful that we ever suspend our representational sense of reading and forget that we are listening to a human voice. Test "Araby" on a class of educated readers and they respond in terms of a young boy's psychological and sexual maturation in an inhibiting culture. For does not the boy align the work of his life–his classroom world–with life itself? Does not the alternative play world of his adolescent desire become inevitably synonymous with his hopeless romantic quest? My undergraduates see "Araby" in terms of what we might call a thematic genre or an experiential archetype. Can we sensibly discuss fiction without reference to character and plot? As I have shown, Hillis Miller, in his deservedly praised *Fiction and Repetition*, reveals the difficulty in doing so as he enacts his own private *aporia* between deconstructive and humanistic criticism in his discussion of major English novels (Schwarz, 1986).

My own approach depends on self-consciousness about theory and method, with the understanding that interpretations–powerful, sensitive readings–are still a primary business of literary criticism. By powerful reading, I mean readings that take account of a text's unity and the factors that challenge it; readings that have an awareness of how texts are metaphorical in relation to anterior worlds and authors; readings that show a sense of which audience the writer had in mind; readings that realize how each of us reads uniquely and self-consciously; readings that have knowledge of relations to other texts by the same author as well as to authors in the same culture; readings that convey generic decisions made by the author and an awareness that what makes genre interesting is both similarity to and difference from models; readings that are attentive to patterns of syntax, diction, and tropes; readings that understand the characters' and speaker's grammar of personal motives and how historical cause and effect shapes characters, implied author, and implied reader; readings that have a complex understanding of how political, social, and economic reality produces effects that not only shape the author's creative process but also the response of his original and all subsequent readers.

What are the ethics of reading? Should we not teach our students how the pleasure and purpose of reading complements experience? Can we not show our students how reading teaches us how to *see*–how to read human situations, including how to respond to various uses of language? Because of their ontological status as fictions, novels can be used as reference points to learn about ourselves. By reading we extend our knowledge of ourselves and of the real world; novels enable us to see ourselves by showing us versions of not-ourselves and versions of ourselves. Because novels are representative of recognizable experience, they explore, test, question, and, at times, confirm ourselves. "Araby" of course is about interpretation–that is why, as you have surely realized, it has been my example; because the speaker is locked into a monologic way of seeing, he has to "read" his disappointment as a way of resolving his complex prepubescent emotions into an acceptable *telos*. That is Joyce's point. We learn from "Araby," among other things, the danger of seeing our experience as a replica of prior experience. The boy has been taught to believe sexuality is sinful and sees himself as a kind of St. Augustine figure who must turn his back on sexuality and turn to spirituality if he is to avoid damnation.

Humanistic formalism seeks to practice a criticism that is honest about its theoretical and methodological assumptions and dialogic in tone. An ethical reader speaks as if there were a response, another way of looking at things, and implies that when he stops his own demonstrative and rhetorical performance, he will listen and give space to a different view. The ethical reader seeks to understand the perspective of other readers. He is tactful, judicious, modest, wide-ranging, open, and pluralistic in his response to texts and to other critical views. Yet he is aware of the mysteries of language, the possibility of indeterminacy, disorder, and misunderstanding. He is wary of proposing flamboyant and hyperbolic readings in the name of being interesting. Regarding self-knowledge as a value, an ethical humanistic reader seeks to discover how and why authors create imagined worlds that mime real ones. An ethical teacher acknowledges his responsibility in teaching students what literature is *about* without sacrificing a focus on formal issues. Ethical teaching recalls why each of us began to be interested in literature in the first place, and insists on maintaining the excitement of responding to content. Finally, the ethical reader imagines himself in the role of an odyssean figure seeking meaning rather than in the position of *vates* or super-reader. He feels a responsibility to try to recreate both the text *and* the anterior world on which the text is based. Indeed, does not an ethical reader understand a moral responsibility to try to recreate the text as it was written for its original audience, as well as to define what that text means to us now?

Works Cited

Bakhtin, M.M. *The Dialogic Imagination*. Ed. Michael Holquist. Austin: University of Texas Press, 1981.

Bialostosky, Don. "Dialogics as an Art of Discourse in Literary Criticism," *PMLA* 105:5 (October 1986), 788–97.

Eliot, T.S. "*Hamlet* and His Problems." *Selected Essays, 1917–1932*. New York: Harcourt Brace and Company, 1960. Pp. 121–26.

Fish, Stanley. *Is There a Text in This Class?* Cambridge Ma.: Harvard University Press, 1980.

Gordimer, Nadine. "The Arts in Adversity: Apprentices of Freedom," *New Society* (December 24, 31, 1981).

Pratt, Mary Louise. "Interpretive Strategies/Strategic Interpretations: On Anglo-American Reader Response Criticism." In *Postmodernism and Politics*, ed. Jonathan Arac. Minneapolis: University of Minnesota Press, 1986. Pp. 26–54.

Ricoeur, Paul. "The Model of the Text," *Social Research* 51:1 (Spring 1984), 185–218.

Rosmarin, Adena. *The Power of Genre*. Minneapolis: University of Minnesota Press, 1986.

Ruppert, Peter. *Reader in a Strange Land: The Activity of Reading Literary Utopias*. Athens: University of Georgia Press, 1986.

Schwarz, Daniel R. *Reading Joyce's "Ulysses."* London: Macmillan; New York: St. Martin's Press, 1987.

——. *The Humanistic Heritage: Critical Theories of the English Novel from James to Hillis Miller*. London: Macmillan: Philadelphia: University of Pennsylvania Press, 1986.

——. "'I Was the World in Which I Walked': The Transformation of the British Novel." *The University of Toronto Quarterly* 51:3 (Spring 1982), 279–97.

——. "The Narrator as Character in Hardy's Major Fiction." *Modern Fiction Studies* 18 (Summer 1972), 155–72.

Stone, Harry. "'Araby' and the Writings of James Joyce." In *Dubliners*, ed. Robert Scholes and A. Walton Litz. New York: Viking Press, 1969. Pp. 344–368.

Suleiman, Susan, and Inge Crosman, eds. *The Reader in the Text: Essays on Audience and Interpretation*. Princeton: Princeton University Press, 1980.

The Novel as Cultural Discourse

The last panel on the first day, "The Novel as Cultural Discourse (its relation to other kinds of discourse—e.g., legal, medical, political—in establishing its own expressional context)," was in some ways the most satisfying session of all. Conceived and moderated by NOVEL's *managing editor Roger Henkle, author of* Comedy and Culture *and for many years a shaper of Brown's literature and society programs, the panel most clearly approximated the conference ideal of addressing a function of the novel through new and old approaches. Thus, in his paper on the novel's mediation of the contradictions inherent in Darwin's theory of evolution, George Levine gave a model demonstration of bridging possibilities; Khachig Tölölyan's political refinements of those possibilities, as applied to war-and-peace novels by Pynchon and Tolstoy, were equally solid; and Charles Altieri's more abstruse engagement with Joyce's attempt to resolve the problematics of history in* Finnegans Wake, *and to go beyond the egoism of "mememormee," was at all times closely, candidly, and vigorously pursued. In such ways these panelists furthered Professor Henkle's opening observation that the study of discourse was itself a new way to approach old problems, and that "Michel Foucault's work, particularly* The Archaeology of Knowledge, *had brought [it] into our own discourse about the novel":*

Although Foucault, both in the *Archaeology* and in works such as "What is an Author?" had problematized the role of individual novelistic expression, and had given the creative work a less privileged position in cultural expression, he had nonetheless sensitized us to the discursive qualities of the novel working with other social texts. Thus the papers presented here deal with the novel as an element of broader discourse, and perhaps even of its formation; as an expression in itself of a set of discourses; and, less hesitantly, as the *dynamic* element in the interaction with broader cultural discourse.

The Novel as Scientific Discourse:
The Example of Conrad

GEORGE LEVINE

The word "discourse" in its traditional meaning implies rationality, thematic coherence, and sustained argument; it also obviously carries the suggestion of non-fiction. Discourses are about something (presumably). In modern theory, "discourse" implies something else again. With Foucault it implies a cultural and political context so that when, in a characteristic contemporary move of intellectual imperialism, we want to argue that science is only another form of discourse, we mean to be diminishing, or challenging its truth claims, and implicating it in the ideologies it has, by defining itself, excluded. Like other kinds of discourse, the argument implies, science is not exempt from epistemological limitations; it has no more claim on the real than biography, or history, or perhaps even fiction. As discourse, science is subject to the kinds of criticism to which we have been trained to subject any text. And as text, it ceases to be a transparent description of nature; it is rather a marker of difference, of absence rather than presence. It becomes a set of linguistic conventions, or of ideological predispositions. So non-fictional, even scientific discourse very rapidly becomes indistinguishable from fiction.

Important as recent concentration on "discourse" has been, differences remain after the assimilation of science to other discourses of power has been completed. There is, after all, more than a little fluttering after power, as well as much silliness, in the move to blur entirely the distinction between fiction and non-fiction. Certainly, science does need to be considered in contexts other than those professionally affirmed by scientists; and certainly, science from many perspectives can be seen as participating in the myths of power that dominate within the culture and as developing within the contexts of social and political and economic pressures (and theories). Recent studies by Adrian Desmond, Martin Rudwick, and Simon Schaffer and Steven Shapin provide superb case studies of the way this happened in different phases of English science.[1] Moreover, Malthus did, after all, provide the "Eureka" for Darwin's theory of natural selection; and Adam Smith had laid out in the world of Economics the kinds of mechanisms that Darwin was to find propelling evolution, so that Marx could argue that Darwinism simply extended laissez-faire economics into nature. Yet Darwinian theory requires different kinds of argument and different kinds of authorization than do political arguments or literature. The equation between a work of fiction and of what we might still call non-fiction must become trivial since the equation would be appropri-

---

[1] See Adrian Desmond, *Archetypes and Ancestors: Palaeontology in Victorian London* (London: Blond and Briggs, 1982); Steven Shapin and Simon Schaffer, *Leviathan and the Air Pump* (Princeton: Princeton University Press, 1985); and Martin Rudwick, *The Great Devonian Controversy: The Shaping of Scientific Knowledge Among Gentlemanly Specialists* (Chicago: University of Chicago Press, 1987). Rudwick, however, is concerned to demonstrate that the process of scientific thinking and argument, deeply rooted in social and biographical causes, is nevertheless epistemologically sound. In a fascinating final chapter, he considers the question of whether "consensual victory of one particular interpretation was due to its objective superiority in explanatory terms or to the superior rhetorical skill and firepower of those who advocated it" (p. 438).

ate for *any* works. Short of universal homogenization, there are differences that remain to be accounted for and assimilations that need to be queried.

I don't, however, want to ask for an exemption for science, or to privilege it; I am only suggesting that science is obviously not simply a "fiction," whatever we might mean by that. Moreover, it needs special attention because it carries with it an authority within the culture that other forms of discourse have often attempted to imitate but have not achieved. Scientific discourse offers itself as non-fiction, as a transparent description, however tentative, of the real. It proposes to be a means to understand the workings of the world, or to the manipulation of that world beyond words. Moreover, it makes an argument, asks to be falsified, and provides quite elaborate procedures for testing; it insists on replication. Now while every aspect of this self-presentation has been importantly challenged by philosophers of science, it would be absurd not to recognize that scientific discourse is another kind of thing from the discourse of the novel. At the very least, we might allow Bas van Frassen's almost minimalist point that science asks acceptance of its propositions even if, as he says, "acceptance is not belief."[2]

The discourse of Newton's *Principia* obviously offers itself on terms very different, say, than *Tom Jones*. One gains nothing from treating them as equivalent, although something might well be gained by thinking of them as related, as expressing in alternative ways certain shared assumptions. Consider, first, how one might think about the relation between two less obviously disparate texts ostensibly from different worlds of discourse, say, Arnold's *Culture and Anarchy*–very much a cultural discourse in the most obvious senses–and *Jude the Obscure*, which found itself, willy-nilly, in the middle of social battles that Arnold would have recognized if not approved. The two books might be seen as alternative discourses, Arnold's constructing an argument by using materials drawn from social and historical worlds accepted as real by its readers, and Hardy's implying an argument by using fictional materials that are understood to "represent" a real world overlapping and contiguous with the "real" world of *Culture and Anarchy*.

But my interest in the question hasn't so much to do with the truth claims a novel might seem to be making. In the case of *Jude,* for example, what is interesting is not its obvious place in cultural battles–the marriage question, the woman question–that its first readers, like Mrs. Oliphant, recognized immediately. Hardy's novel evoked such antipathy and passion because it *felt* authentic, and it felt so because of its use of familiar terms of cultural discourse, many of which were borrowed from Arnold's analysis. The fiction oddly confirms Arnold's outrageous division of culture into the Hebraic and Hellenic, while wildly complicating it. In any case, *Jude* participates in a discourse already established as descriptive of the culture; and that we might, from another perspective, want to talk of that discourse itself as fictional in no way

2 Bas C. van Frassen, "Empiricism in the Philosophy of Science," in *Images of Science,* ed. Paul M. Churchland and Clifford A. Hooker (Chicago: University of Chicago Press, 1985), p. 247. Van Frassen's theory of "Constructive Empiricism" is anti-realist, but attempts to account for the success of science by, among other things, demonstrating the irrelevance of truth claims to scientific argument, whose acceptance does not require belief.

diminishes the point that the novel uses, participates in, even reshapes cultural discourse.

The case might be more difficult with Newton and Fielding, a connection which, as far as I know, hasn't been made; perhaps it shouldn't be made. And certainly, I don't know enough to make it. But I want to suggest the possibility that the formal structure of *Tom Jones* owes something to the way Newton's imagination of the world as a mathematically organized phenomenon reflecting intelligence, and accessible to the abstract intelligence of humanity had permeated the culture. The more obvious model is the Christian/providential one; but Fielding's book might be seen as bringing together various Christian and narrative traditions within the assumptions about order and the constitution of nature itself that Newton's work had fairly recently authorized.

Here as elsewhere, the assumptions and fundamental values of a culture, as they are formulated in the discourse taken generally to be its most authoritative, will almost certainly inform its art. In a way, that is a truism. But the play of assumptions within fiction is often no mere replication of ideas and attitudes already available elsewhere. While the novel will inevitably work with unarticulated cultural assumptions, its form can entail a rich exploration of their implications, sometimes a raising of them to consciousness and a demystifying of them, sometimes direct subversion. The symmetries and the polarities of *Tom Jones*, the solidity of characterization, the sharpness of definition and the precision of elaboration, the confidence in sequence of cause and effect in unrolling the narrative–all participate in an imagination of experience at least consonant with the Newtonian world, which was, after all, the eighteenth-century world, as well. Traditional narrative, in which cause and effect determine sequence, and in which intrusions implying design are conventional, is largely homologous with the scientific world view of early modern Western history.

However wildly unrealistic it often is, the novel as a genre speaks into (or defines itself against) a recognizable world, made recognizable because it works with the unself-conscious discourse of its own culture. The peculiar interest of science is that against the threats of various kinds of relativism and, indeed, the modern dominance of anti-foundationalist theory, it has seemed to provide one ultimate foundation. Since Newton, at least, it has become the most authoritative discourse, the one by which most people are likely to be intimidated, the one whose assertions are most likely to be accepted. Science clearly did replace religion as the definer of our faith in what the world is really like; and even the most fanatic of believers in the West are likely to seek the sanction of science for much of what they argue and believe. Creationist, anti-evolutionary arguments, note, are themselves full of scientism, insisting that Creationism is a science, and that it is more scientific than evolutionary theory, which is after all, they complain, only a "theory."

But to see it as having achieved the kind of authority hitherto belonging to religion is not to mistake its particular base in power. The very epistemological (and therefore, implicitly, social and even "spiritual") authority it has achieved makes it extremely valuable in social discourse. That is, ideology puts scientific discourse to use precisely because science, at least, seems disinterested, objective, concerned to tell the truth as in itself it really is; science is the most important discourse by which ideology is naturalized. It is the discourse that power needs to use, and the discourse that most needs to be demystified. Its pervasiveness in literature testifies to this double use.

Using scientific metaphor is as commonplace now as using Biblical metaphors would have been two hundred years ago. Most obviously, in contemporary writing, there is Pynchon's use of thermodynamics and entropy and his transformation of scientific ideas into something very like fantasy. It's worth recalling, as well, how Lawrence drops into scientific metaphor in his well-known argument against the traditional stable ego of character in *The Rainbow*: denying the individual, he talks of the ego passing through "allotropic states," of his interest being not in diamond, nor in coal, nor in soot, but in the underlying single element, "carbon." This is old stuff by now, of course, but Lawrence was importantly right in finding the conception of character linked to ostensibly unrelated aspects of science. Equally famous, if perhaps more discredited, is Zola's project described in "The Experimental Novel"–based on Claude Bernard's *Introduction to the Study of Experimental Medicine*, and realized in The Rougon-Marquart series. And although the differences are obvious, George Eliot in *Middlemarch* also self-consciously reflects on narrative as a scientific activity.

But the novelists who really know a lot about science and who self-consciously use it make a small minority. The power of science within our culture is reflected in the way it infiltrates consciousness that knows very little about it. Perhaps to put it more carefully, it shares, as Michel Serres has shown, in the dominant concerns of the culture, is in fact a powerful myth whose shape can be discerned well outside the realms of specifically scientific discourse.[3] Scientific ideas are absorbed, used, and created by a culture that is only partially aware of science as a professional practice.

While there has been much debate about how legitimate it is to transfer scientific ideas to other forms of discourse, literature makes the move frequently and easily through metaphor, sometimes to deny or satirize the transference, sometimes to accomplish it. "Social Darwinism" has often been attacked as an illegitimate metaphorizing of Darwin's biological theory; sociobiology insists that the move is not metaphorical. The constraints of biology determine the constraints of culture. In any case, literature is the place where, in the absorption, use, or rejection of science–consciously or not–the transference most frequently takes place. Criticism requires an alertness to the presence of scientific discourse, or its metaphors, not only because it helps clarify what the texts are doing, but because the texts themselves often constitute a fictional test of the science and of the transference. Participating equally but differently in the culture's myths and ideologies, science and literature support, reveal, and test each other.

---

[3] See *Hermes: Literature, Science, Philosophy*, ed. Yosué V. Harari and David F. Bell (Baltimore: Johns Hopkins University Press, 1982).

To make my point, I will concentrate for the rest of this paper on a particular scientific idea, evolutionary gradualism, to suggest how it becomes a part of narrative discourse, is reflected in, reenforced, and ultimately subverted by English nineteenth-century realism and the developing modernism of Joseph Conrad.

The English nineteenth-century novel, reflecting and inspiring dominant assumptions about what reality and nature are really and naturally like, seemed to entail a gradualist reading of change. At the same time, those guiding assumptions about what is real, usually also implying an ethical imperative to behave "naturally," concealed their own incoherence. Darwin's argument stands behind both the gradualism and the incoherence. Geological and biological gradualism was so fundamental an aspect of the way reality was understood that it helped determine the way novels were written and was almost automatically transferred from the realms of science to the realms of society and politics.[4]

Certainly, within Victorian realism, which in narrative method stresses continuity and connection, attempt at radical change is perceived as violent, a disruption of normal human and social relations: the disruption of the idea of the organic community or the natural human bond, as in Hetty Sorrel's murder of her illegitimate infant, or Sikes's murder of Nancy.

Victorian realism and Darwinian evolution tend to be mutually supporting imaginations of the real, whose structures are most obviously threatened by the possibility of catastrophic change. Darwin staked everything on the view that Nature does not take leaps. So did Victorian novelists. When Razumov, in *Under Western Eyes*, scrawls "evolution not revolution," he says no more–though more desperately–than George Eliot did: "what grows up historically can only die out historically."[5]

The language of *The Origin of Species* is the nineteenth century's most imaginative and powerful denial of catastrophic change, and became its most powerful text for the denial of revolutionary change as well. Here is some rather neutrally formulated language, but one can see how easily it could be adapted to political argument:

> *Why should all the parts and organs of independent beings, each supposed to have been separately created for its proper place in nature, be so invariably linked together by graduated steps? Why should not Nature have taken a leap from structure to structure? On the theory of natural selection, we can clearly understand why she should not; for natural selection can act only by taking ad-*

---

[4] Since this paper was completed, Stephen Jay Gould's impressive study of uniformitarian ideas in geology has appeared. Gould brilliantly demonstrates how the idea of deep time in geology and the idea of gradual, directional change were implicated in major ideological and religious attitudes. Neither Hutton nor Lyell, the two great British propagandists for gradualism, produced their theories out of empirical evidence, though both writers were persuasively "scientific." The crossing between "scientific" and cultural discourses was constant and powerful. See Stephen Jay Gould, *Time's Arrow, Time's Cycle* (Cambridge, Mass: Harvard University Press, 1987).

[5] Joseph Conrad, *Under Western Eyes* (Garden City, N.Y.: Anchor Books, 1963), p. 54. *Essays of George Eliot*, ed. Thomas Pinney (New York: Columbia University Press, 1963), p. 287.

*vantage of slight successive variations; she can never take a leap, but must ad-
vance by the shortest and slowest steps.*[6]

For Darwin, this is not merely a description of Nature, but a defense of science; for science itself was at stake in this argument. Uniformitarianism, allowing no causes but such as are now in operation, was what Darwin learned
from his mentor in geology, Charles Lyell. Once the possibility were allowed
of intrusion beyond the explanatory power of natural law, natural law could
not be relied upon either for inference or prediction. George Eliot, we remember, similarly depended heavily for her moral teaching on laws of necessary
sequence, and the deterministic implications of her narratives issue from the
same extension of scientific law to human activity.

But there is a gap in the Darwinian argument–as in realist narratives–through which chance and potential disruption emerge. We may understand why natural selection allows some variations to survive and others not,
but the variation is a sudden and unexplained intrusion on the lawful processes of nature. The variation appears as "chance" (although Darwin wished
to avoid the implication) and as sudden and unexplained as the intrusion of
Haldin into Razumov's rooms at the beginning of *Under Western Eyes*. Into the
law-bound system that Darwin was attempting to create, lawlessness immediately thrusts itself.

While the uniformitarian basis of Darwin's arguments, which parallel
closely the methods and themes of realistic fiction, implicitly denies the possibility of successful revolution, the true generating power of Darwin's theory
was what he could not reduce to law, nor account for by gradualism.[7] The
great spokesman for gradualism, Darwin needed to disguise or downplay
those aspects of his theory and argument that would not fit uniformitarian
theory. And in its duality, Darwin's theory exposes by analogy fundamental
contradictions in the Victorian realist project, which also entails an implicit
commitment to gradualism but invariably must include in its resolution elements that resist gradualist interpretation. The determination to view all experience from the perspective of the ordinary closes out the possibility of real
change and locks all characters into an organic-determinist system. But the
conventions of coincidence by which even a novel like *Middlemarch* releases its
protagonists from social or psychological imprisonment do not so much represent a retreat from the ideals of realism as a necessary element in any imagination of the possibility of real change and growth in the realist's world.

[6] Charles Darwin, *The Origin of Species by Means of Natural Selection, or The Preservation of Favoured Races in the Struggle for Life*,
first edition, ed. J.W. Burrow (Harmondsworth, Middlesex: Penguin Books, 1959), pp. 223–224.

[7] Although it was possible to derive from Darwin's arguments, stripped of their creative multivalence, a strictly determinist
and rather bleak view of the workings of nature, his language and the structure of his argument left a wide space for creativity. Gillian Beer has analyzed his language in several works to show how important to Darwin's science was the unresolved excess of meaning in his language. "He gives room," she says, "for mystery, for exploration, and insists upon the
dark space behind the summary formulation of 'the struggle for life.'" See "Darwin's Reading and the Fictions of Development," in David Kohn, ed., *The Darwinian Heritage* (Princeton: Princeton University Press, 1985), p. 572. Beer also argues
that "it was the element of obscurity, of metaphor whose peripheries remain undescribed, that made the *Origin* so incendi-
ary–and that allowed it to be appropriated by thinkers of so many diverse political persuasions" (p. 574). This is certainly
partly the case; but I would want to argue that *any* scientific argument might be put to almost any political use because scientific argument allows metaphorical extension.

Conrad's fiction is at least as ideologically conservative as that of the real-ists who preceded him and whose techniques he was coming to reject. The use of science for such ideologically conservative purposes suggests again how the authoritative discourse of science is implicated in a broader cultural discourse. Science can be used spuriously to authorize political positions. What is interesting about Conrad in this respect is that while his narratives reflect the breakdown of belief in Darwinian gradualism, that very breakdown is taken for authority for an even more intense and irrational conservatism. That is, as he rejects the conventions of narrative that have traditionally been allied with anti-revolutionary political attitudes, he explicitly commits himself even more ferociously to such attitudes while–as, say, with the famous figure of the sailor in *Heart of Darkness*–he invokes arbitrarily the discredited tradi-tional realist and gradualist positions to reaffirm the necessity of political sta-bility.

Most narratives turn on the convergence of at least two narrative lines, as when Haldin and Razumov meet. But such convergence almost always has the effect of surprise or even shock. We can even detect this in the way Dar-win uses it, for in order to bring home to us the interdependence of all organ-isms he seeks for examples that emphasize the unlikeliness of convergences. There is a quality of wonder as Darwin explains how the enclosure acts helped "determine the existence of Scotch fir": careful study had shown him that where cattle graze the fir gets no chance to grow. Then he goes on to show that "in several parts of the world insects determine the existence of cattle."[8] Clearly, the enclosure acts were not designed to affect the growth of Scotch fir, nor do the flies of Paraguay act in order to affect the life of cattle. Any "design" to be inferred from the intersection must be the consequence of omniscience. In fiction, novelists must devise plausible ways to bring narra-tive lines not ostensibly related to each other by design or intention into con-tact. Seen from this perspective, the device of omniscient narrator is not an accident of nineteenth-century realism, but a condition of it. Once allow not only that limitation of perspective is a condition of all actors, but that omnis-cience is impossible, and the realist project of discovering the paths of neces-sary sequence breaks down. It becomes conceivable not only that none has the power to discover the paths, but that the paths are not there in the first place.

The conservative Professor of *Under Western Eyes* radically subverts the gradualism of Darwinian evolution in the very way he tells his story. He be-comes spokesman for other aspects of the Darwinian program–the element of chance, and the fundamentally irrational and inhuman energies of nature. The Professor's story implies–with the authority of Darwinian science behind it–the arbitrariness of the very civilization that Darwinian science had been used to authorize in the earlier tradition. "Words, as is well known," the Pro-fessor notoriously says, "are the great foes of reality."[9] Ironically, science lies

[8] *The Origin of Species*, p. 124.

[9] *Under Western Eyes*, p.1.

behind this, the science that posits an irrational source and material explanation for life. In *Under Western Eyes*, narrative is a series of disruptions, and explanations are delayed as long as possible, in some cases never clearly made. The realist preoccupation with ordinary details becomes, in Conrad, phantasmagoric. Ironically, in every respect Conrad's world and Conrad's fiction announce the separation of language from its material base, the unnaturalness, then, of language, and of fiction itself.

The scientific discourse of Conrad's fiction leads to the positing of a reality beyond language, but a reality from which fictions protect him. That reality is, indeed, revolutionary, in the sense that it is governed not by regularities, but by irrationalities, by forces incomprehensible to human consciousness, and violently threatening. Aware of the artificality of human constructs, Conrad does not move to a revolutionary displacement: instead he is committed to supporting them in their artificiality against the deep irrationality of phenomena.

Absorbing scientific ideas, Conrad writes narratives filled with the pain of living in a world governed by the assumptions of the scientific enterprise and the traditions by which science had come to assert its Huxleyan imperialism in relation to all knowledge. Conrad explores the difficulties of seeing the human within the context of the nature science was describing. Conrad's modernism is not an escape for scientific discourse but another selective use of it; and its profound authority shapes his world. It informs his critique of a realism which was itself based in a "scientific" discourse. His techniques of disruption, discontinuity, of elaborating a radical distrust of language, lead to a vision of the world that totally undercuts the gradualism in which Darwin and Victorian realism had invested so much. As he describes a revolutionary, chance-ridden, disruptive nature, he sees the anti-revolutionary stance of realism itself as a conventional and arbitrary construction of nineteenth-century bourgeois imagination, like the domestic dullness of Geneva presided over by a statue of Rousseau. He exposes the contradictions latent in that construction in the image of the revolutionary cabal developing in the heart of Geneva. Razumov, ironically, is saved by being thrust into the irrational truth of nature; he becomes a scientist in that by losing his capacity to hear words, he stops being a foe of reality.

Conrad finds sanction for his chancy world in the very Darwin whose gradualism was a scientific manifestation of realist ideology. He finds in Darwin's revelation of the irrational sources of human rationality evidence for the arbitrariness of civilization. He finds in the mechanical and mindless and anti-teleological structure of Darwin's world clues for the writing of a new kind of disruptive and fragmented narrative. And ironically, he seeks in the gradualist conventions of Darwin's narrative, his overt refusal of mystery and irrational disruption of law, the moral sanction for an anti-revolutionary position which he did *not* find endorsed in nature.

The relation between science and narrative here is characteristically complex. The two discourses provide a running commentary and critique of each other. And the critic gains immensely from learning how to hear the dialogue.

Discoursing with Culture:
The Novel as Interlocutor*

KHACHIG TÖLÖLYAN

The composition of a paper usually takes its cue, either obediently or in rebellious departure, from the title provided by the organizers of the conference where it is presented. Now, when I was first asked to participate, I was told that the topic of the panel would be "The Novel and Discourse." Even as I accepted the invitation, I wondered what verbs I would choose to take the place of that "and," to specify the mediations that connect Novel to Discourse. I also wondered which of the technical and ever-divergent meanings of discourse I would privilege.

These meanings are legion, but seem to me to cluster along three main lines of development worth enumerating at the outset. One notion of discourse probably makes its first appearance in Benveniste's opposition of *histoire* and *discours* and culminates in Gérard Genette's analysis of the relations between story and narrative discourse.[1] While the pair history/discourse enables an admirable precision in formal analysis, its structuralist and binary logic has hampered inquiry into certain aspects of the complex intercourse between the two terms. I shall be suggesting that both this intercourse and other relations between elements of narrative often serve as figures of–even isomorphs of–the dialogue between the novel and culture, a dialogue which inevitably has a political character.

A second, even more familiar notion of discourse appears in the work of Foucault, who distinguished "initiators of discursive practices" like Marx and Freud from novelists by saying that no novelist is "more than the author of his own text."[2] If taken as definitive, this suggests that novels may exist at the margins of one discourse or at the intersections of several, but that they will never be able to participate in culture as initiators of new discursive practices. In *The Discourse of Modernism*, which is perhaps the most satisfactory extended application of Foucauldian theory we have, Timothy Reiss implies that the novel's rise need not be viewed as always initiated by the intersection of pre-existing discourses.[3]

It can also be seen as part and parcel of European culture's larger, evolving response, in the period 1590 to 1650, to the imperatives which simultaneously resulted in the development of science, (utopian) narrative and other instanti-

---

* This essay retains the structure of the talk I gave at the NovEL-sponsored conference commemorated by this issue. I am grateful to Professors Mark Spilka and Roger Henkle of Brown University for providing me with the occasion, and to Professor Ellen Rooney, also of Brown, for her detailed critique of an early draft.

[1] Emile Benveniste, *Problèmes de linguistique générale* (Paris: Gallimard, 1966), esp. Ch. V, "L'Homme dans la Langue," pp. 238–39; Gérard Genette, *Narrative Discourse: An Essay in Method*, tr. Jane E. Lewin (Ithaca: Cornell University Press, 1979), esp. pp. 25–112.

[2] "What Is an Author?" *Language, Counter-memory, Practice*, ed. and tr. Donald F. Bouchard and Sherry Simon (Ithaca: Cornell University Press, 1977), p. 131.

[3] Timothy Reis, *The Discourse of Modernism* (Ithaca: Cornell University Press, 1982).

ations of an "analytico-referential" master-discourse. In Reiss's account, the dialogue between prose fictions (not yet quite the novel) and culture is enacted within each text by the simultaneous representation and critique of this discourse, which promises power, knowledge and progress.

Finally, Bakhtin's notion of discourse, which he elaborates out of his description of society as an arena and theater of linguistic competition, posits powerful institutions, like the Church, as laying claim to the possession of "a single language of truth." Against the ideological desire of such institutions to shape and master a monoglot society, Bakhtin juxtaposes the possibility of heteroglossia in certain historical moments and genres. He celebrates what his biographers describe as the proclivity of language for "breaking down into separate discourses."[4] He privileges the *oeuvre* of Rabelais as an ancestor of the novel, an ancestor which works not just by foregrounding the undecidability of competing meanings and interpretations, but rather by dramatizing the struggle between discourses. By implication, Bakhtin saw the competition between dominant, emergent and residual literary discourses of the 1530s as significantly related to a contemporaneous struggle in French society, which was torn by religious dissent, challenged by new geographical discoveries, and strained by the attempt to curb a peasantry that had grown self-confident after the Black Death and the Hundred Years' War, both of which had made their labor, and therefore them, more important.[5]

Such a historical criticism of the novel, like the novel itself, functions as an interlocutor in cultural discourse. In the late 1920s and in the 1930s, when Bakhtin began to think about heteroglossia, he had more in mind than just Dostoevsky or Rabelais; he was also addressing obliquely the problems of a Soviet society which was then strained by Stalin's effort to impose a vulgarized dialectical materialist discourse of "scientific" truth as the master discourse of all intellectual endeavor, ranging from biology to literary history. It is under these conditions that he began to elaborate the theory of discourse which retains the most direct relevance to our present consideration of the relation between the novel and discourse. That relevance is due both to Bakhtin's account of what happens in the novel, and to the politics of his intervention in cultural criticism, through his deployment of literary history. Surprisingly, such a cultural politics is more ambivalently present in Foucault, who has been plausibly read both as an advocate of active political intervention and as a quietist. In contrast to the tendencies initiated by both of these men, the Benveniste-Genette tradition retains a formalism that resists implication in cultural criticism, except of course when further empowered by feminist, Lacanian or Althusserian approaches.

As I was pondering how best to say something about, or in, the interstices of such a mass of material, a written description of this conference arrived, informing me that I had been misinformed: the full topic title was "The Novel as *Cultural* Discourse." I confess that the addition of the word "cultural" did not immediately clarify my task. After all, most familiar uses of "discourse"

---

[4] Katerina Clark and Michael Holquist, *Mikhail Bakhtin* (Cambridge: Harvard University Press, 1984), p. 265.

[5] An interesting, if unusual, presentation and critique of Bakhtin's views on Rabelais can be found in Richard Berrong's *Rabelais and Bakhtin* (Lincoln: University of Nebraska Press, 1986), esp. pp. 52–79.

have presupposed its inevitable implication in culture, while studies of culture always break down (in our part of the human sciences) into a discussion of specific discursive and institutional practices. It seemed to me that the now redundant title could be parsed in several ways. For example, it might be appropriate to write on the novel's role as a constitutive discourse in culture between the years 1720 and 1885, say, and as–at the very least–a contributing discourse since then. In the long early phase, the Western European novel intervened directly in the construction of the order of Reality; it engaged–as my discussion of Tolstoy, below, will substantiate–other narrative and non-narrative discourses which aspired to a similar major role. Eventually, as Modernism was born in the acknowledgment of the exhaustion of realism, novelistic discourse resorted to miming conceptual formulations and narrative practices increasingly shaped by the dynamics of other artistic and social-scientistic discourses; along with them, sometimes as a camp-follower, it continues to infiltrate the workings of the quotidian.[6]

Contemplating this development, I began to consider writing on the ways in which one or more of the discourses dominant in contemporary culture shape the novel even as the latter engages, selectively reflects, foregrounds, underplays and subverts such discourses. Since I have written on Thomas Pynchon's work, I was considering his *oeuvre* as a possible text when a draft of Professor George Levine's paper on "The Novel as Scientific Discourse" arrived.[7] I was enlightened by its account of the influence of science on Victorian Realism, and by its analysis of Conrad's position *vis a vis* both science and realism. At the same time, I found myself disagreeing with the hypothesis that science has probably been the most authoritative discourse of Britain since Newton and down through the nineteenth century. This is a hypothesis which has many supporters, of course, and a variant of this assumption about the primacy of scientific discourse is prevalent among many critics of Pynchon's work: not just of *Gravity's Rainbow* but also of stories like "Entropy" and the short novel *The Crying of Lot 49*. In both instances, the view is plausible, but not altogether true. My reading of Bakhtin suggests that if discourses are neither always autonomous nor merely interpenetrating, but rather exist at certain historical conjunctures in a loose hierarchy in which some are more determining than determined, then it may be argued that scientific discourse has often functioned as an instrument and convenient legitimator of more powerful discourses and institutions of domination, in particular those of Capitalism. Both in the nineteenth century and today, it is not "I think, therefore I am," but rather "I own, therefore I am" that is synecdochic of the discursive practices of domination.

In Pynchon's work, this is fully acknowledged by the attention paid not just to science, but to technology as owned, developed, appropriated and put into practice by corporations and cartels, by Shell and General Electric and IG Farben, and by their parodic twins, like Yoyodyne.[8] Furthermore, Pynchon's

---

[6] Alexander Gelley, *Narrative Crossings* (Baltimore: Johns Hopkins University Press, 1987), p. ix, echoing de Certeau.

[7] Ms., April 1987. For a final version, see elsewhere in this panel's pages.

[8] For a detailed substantiation of this claim, see my study of Pynchon's uses of the history of technology in "War as Background in *Gravity's Rainbow*," *Approaches to Gravity's Rainbow*, ed. Charles Clerc (Columbus: Ohio State University Press,

texts elaborate a master-discourse of Control, of the cybernetics of society, which occupies a central, if much criticized and undercut position in them. However important and richly narrativized, the discourses of Capitalism, Technocracy, Behaviorist Psychology and Film are viewed as agents of this discourse. It is intriguing evidence of the *zeitgeist* at work that Pynchon fashioned his narratives of the master-discourse of Control between the years 1961 and 1973, perhaps just slightly anticipating Foucault's analytics of control. Of course, both were readers of Weber, Freud and the Frankfurt School.[9] More recently, a handful of writers of fiction have acknowledged the centrality of the discourse of control in Pynchon's work; especially since the appearance of William Gibson's odd postmodern version of science fiction, *Neuromancer*, what is now being called cyberpunk has become a fad, while Pynchon and one of his mentors, William Burroughs, have been recognized as the progenitors of this narrativized cybernetic discourse of control. Of course, Burroughs mastered early the strain of paranoid narrative which shapes not just *Gravity's Rainbow* but also Norman Mailer's *An American Dream*. He was also the bitter bard of addiction; his narratives of chemical control and therapeutic imprisonment anticipated work as primitive as Ken Kesey's *One Flew Over the Cuckoo's Nest* and as complex as Pynchon's. The point requiring reiteration is that the full-fledged cybernetic discourse of control engendered within the realm of novelistic narrative by Pynchon's fusion of Burroughs and Norbert Wiener *uses* science and technology as its handmaidens. They figure and are metaphors for a genuinely authoritative discourse of control.

From the perspective of this conference, novels in which a socially powerful discourse appears unmodified and untransformed are the least interesting; that very lack of fertile transformation is what makes–for example–so much of American science fiction of the interwar period uninteresting. There and elsewhere, the lack of intercourse between discourses in the novel too often restages a similar poverty of contact between the text's and the culture's discourses. Bakhtin believed that the best novels always staged a struggle between discourses. I would like to extend his insight by suggesting that the most compelling texts are those which represent the relationship between the novel and its cultural context *as* a conflict between two competing discourses, embedded within the novel itself. For me, this formulation is central to a discussion of "The Novel as Cultural Discourse."

Two difficulties haunt the critical effort to unpack such representations of the relation between the novel and culture. On the one hand, one can err by a sort of literalism that misconstrues a familiar discourse privileged by the cultural context–Science in the case of Pynchon, History in the case of Tolstoy–as ruling the text itself; one can fail to see that when a culturally important discourse is imported into the novel it becomes a novelistic strategy. It no longer retains the authority it has in the world, precisely because it has entered into

1983), pp. 31–68.

9 For further details concerning these claims, see: Vincent Balitas, "Charismatic Figures in *Gravity's Rainbow*," *Pynchon Notes* 7 (June, 1982), 38–53; Lawrence Wolfley, "Repression's Rainbow: The Presence of Norman O. Brown in Pynchon's Big Novel," *PMLA* 92:5 (Oct. 1977), 873–89.

new relations with other discourses of the heteroglot text in which textuality and fictionality take precedence. At the other extreme, the complement to such misreading is the consequence of a particular reader's lack of familiarity with cultural codes. If the reader is innocent of relevant knowledge of the cultural situation, then the novel's attempt to figure its relationship to that situation by representing a clash of discourses will obviously be overlooked. To elucidate these difficulties of discussing discourse in the novel, and the novel as cultural discourse, I want to draw on two large and great novels of war and peace: Tolstoy's *War and Peace* and *Gravity's Rainbow*. They portray threatened and straining societies on a continental and global scale, respectively. In each, War intensifies and concentrates the effort to control and direct all social resources, including humans regarded as resources; such concentration lays bare certain discursive practices of control, stripping them of euphemism and occultation. On the one hand, then, such novels–which, for reasons elaborated elsewhere, I call cosmographies–are catalogues and cornucopias of discourses active in the culture. On the other hand, even here, much specialized discourse is permitted to enter the novel only as story-telling, in the guise of traditional elements of the plot.

The mapping of discourses in *War and Peace* may seem a simple task at first glance. The text is shot through with historiographic discourse. A strain of such discourse, that of military history *per se*, is used to comment on the strategic councils of Prince Bagration, General Kutuzov and Napoleon, and to represent and chart the course of both minor skirmishes and major battles like Borodino. Finally, Tolstoy presents his readers with the lengthy Epilogue in two parts, whose primary purpose seems to be to denounce the great man theory of History. It is this Epilogue that has attracted the lion's share of attention from critics, since in it the concentration of a different and almost alien kind of prose and of Tolstoy's own historiographic intention are both unmistakable, as well as embarrassing to purist-practitioners like Henry James. The latter's friend, Turgenev, dismissed the lump of historiographic discourse in the Epilogue as Tolstoy's hobby-horse. Other Russian contemporaries, many of whom had praised Tolstoy for the realism of his depictions of the Crimean War in the *Sebastopol Sketches* (1855), gleefully focused on the details of the specialized discourse of military history deployed in *War and Peace* (1869), questioned the accuracy of his accounts and interpretations of strategic decisions, and chastised him, after all a novelist, for the degree of his dependence on non-imaginative sources, on what they saw as a historical and historiographic discourse threatening to the novel. Novel-readers, it seems, knew what was fitting novelistic discourse; they had chosen to forget the genre's origins in *Tristram Shandy* and *Don Quixote*, of which the Russian Formalists would remind a later generation, and whose mixture of discourses Bakhtin was to celebrate. At any rate, Russian critics–let alone Western readers–misread the role of military history and historiographic discourse in *War and Peace*. Guided by the nineteenth century's exaltation of History and by simultaneous timorousness about its ability to engulf the novel, they invested the historical discourse in Tolstoy's novel with the authority it had acquired in their lives. They reacted accordingly, with ambivalence, both because the history was not always faithful to the prevailing version, and because when it was accurate, it seemed to threaten the novel's own claims. The situation began to change decades later, when Eikhenbaum's *Tolstoy in the Sixties* appeared (1930) and hinted at Tolstoy's more complex use of History.

Eikhenbaum chronicles the intellectual currents and cultural discourses which influenced Tolstoy in the decade of the 1860s, during which *War and Peace* was written, serialized and finally published as a book. He shows how the work changed from its original conception as a novel of domestic life to an "epic," a work which contained both military history and historiographic discourse that dealt with national and pan-European problems. Departing from the critical tradition preceding him, Eikhenbaum implies that both the specialized discourse of historiography and the familiar language of realistic depiction make full sense only when viewed as part of a larger cultural conversation, indeed an angry debate, in which Tolstoy was engaged.[10] Tolstoy obliquely intervened in the argument between Tsarist authoritarianism and the "nihilist" opposition who, differing in all else, shared a belief that Society was held together by a heroic figure or could be transformed by a small group of heroic figures, the young and the dedicated. This debate runs through Turgenev's *Fathers and Sons* and, I would add, a generation later it still provides material for Georgii Plekhanov's *The Role of the Individual in History* (1898).[11] To Tolstoy, both imperial authoritarians and nihilists seemed to subscribe to some version of the great man theory of history and of social change. Eikhenbaum's point is that in *War and Peace* Tolstoy argued against this view even when he did not mention it and only seemed engaged in a debate about generalship and the historiography of war.

Consider, for example, the episode depicting the battle of Schöngraben. Prince Bagration is in command. Prince Andrei, who conveys his orders to scattered units, also acts as Tolstoy's observer of the swirl of battle. Phases of the prolonged battle are described over some forty pages. One point emerges immediately: incompetent and sometimes cowardly officers of aristocratic lineage bungle, yet at the end of battle are found lounging in Prince Bagration's tent, giving accounts of the events and of their behavior which, Tolstoy intimates, will eventually be transformed by and coalesced into historiographic discourse and the "truth" of the battle of Schöngraben. It is clear from his ironic tone that he disapproves and solicits his readers' disapproval: the great men are bumblers who have the advantage of belonging to the Tsar's and Tolstoy's own aristocratic class, which controls the discourse pertaining to battles and history. But if the debate with the rulers of Russia and with official discourse is out in the open, the cultural conversation with Russian nihilism emerges in full only with the assistance of Eikhenbaum's work. As an example of the effect his work can have on our reading, I want to attend to Tolstoy's depiction of Captain Tushin.

---

[10] Boris Eikhenbaum, *Tolstoy in the Sixties* (Ann Arbor: Ardis, 1982; or. 1930). See especially pp. 195–244. I am deeply indebted to my colleague, the translator of this book, Professor Duffield White, to whose interpretation of Eikhenbaum's work I owe as much as to the text.

[11] Professor Noël Carroll of Wesleyan first pointed out this connection to me.

One can't miss him in the section devoted to Schöngraben. Transparently not an aristocrat, a stumpy officer of low rank who is literally not of heroic stature and is depicted as an extension of the pipe he puffs on, he is first a comic character uttering the wisdom of the folk. Yet his actions as the commander of a small artillery battery save the day, even after his unit is carelessly positioned and then abandoned by panicked superior officers. These same superiors try to blame failure on Tushin, and only Andrei's intervention as a witness rescues Tushin from possible disgrace. It is easy enough to read this scene, too, as polemic against the military aristocracy. But with Eikhenbaum's help, its function as anti-nihilist discourse can be discerned beneath the ordinary novelistic language which describes Tushin's actions and motives. Tushin directs the world for which he is responsible, four cannon and attendant artillerymen and horses, with alternating fussiness and glee. In battle, he becomes increasingly peculiar but retains his technical competence: "Although he remembered everything, considered everything, did everything the very best of officers could have done in his position, he was in a state resembling a feverish delirium or intoxication."[12] In the heat of battle, talking to himself, the guns, the horses, the soldiers and the enemy, Tushin hardly considers "everything": not Tsar nor Mother Russia nor Heroism, nor even his unit's desperate situation after the infantry on his flanks retreats. Literal and symbolic smoke obscures his vision of the whole, while "a fantastic world of his own had taken form in his mind, which afforded him pleasure at that moment. The enemy's guns, in his fancy, were not cannons but pipes from which an occasional puff of smoke was blown by an unseen smoker" (242). This is the state of mind and level of military analysis which saves the day at Schöngraben. Neither Tsar nor nihilist can theorize or anticipate it; nor, by implication, can they control the events that will shape history, as Tolstoy understands history. Furthermore, neither the discourse of military history nor that of radical theory can accommodate the truth of Tushin's essentially petty mind. But Tolstoy thought his own unadorned prose could and did. Whatever we think of such claims, it must be admitted that Tolstoy, perhaps more than any other Russian author and in contravention of Foucault's claims about novelists as initiators of discourse, succeeded in putting his version of narrative discourse into play as a force in Russian political culture. All the way down to Solzhenitsyn, and perhaps also in the work of Hemingway, Tolstoy's discourse operates not merely as a stylistic example but as a peculiar regime of truth, whose categories are the untrustworthiness of official discourse, version and vocabulary, the predictable unpredictability of modest muzhiks and Spanish guerrillas, their potential for unpredictability and unsung greatness. It is easy enough to dismiss all this as the illegitimate progeny of official humanist discourse, fashioned outside the novelistic realm. But ever since the French Revolution and the reactions to it, figures as diverse as Carlyle and Michelet had been involved in a discursive struggle whose oppositional elements included individual great men and the masses. This discourse is not only clarified and given potent narrative form in *War and Peace*,

---

[12] *War and Peace*, tr. Ann Dunnigan (New York: Signet, 1968), p. 241. Further references to this work will be given in parentheses in the text.

but also enlarged by the addition of the figure of the unsung, unpredictable men whose behavior can alter the course of great events. Given the situation of Tsarist Russia, where institutionalized, professional thinkers (philosophers, for example) had a relatively smaller and more officially circumscribed existence than novelists, critics, journalists, all functioning within the broad definition of the intelligentsia, it seems tenable to argue that Tolstoy's synthetic version of previously existing discourses became definitive and initiatory for Russian culture, and indeed for the Marxist culture that inherited its terms and criticized it.[13] Both the recuperation and the critique of Tolstoy's version underscore the participation of his work in the struggle to shape a broader cultural discourse.

Pynchon's lush prose is a far cry from Tolstoy's or Hemingway's. War is a matter of V-2 rockets rather than artillery batteries in *Gravity's Rainbow*, and it comes as no surprise that for this as well as other reasons, his work is a catalogue of the various strains of technological, scientific and pseudoscientific discourse. These are displayed as prominently as historiographic discourse in *War and Peace*. Less transparently and with less open moralism than Tolstoy, Pynchon too is present in his fiction, stacking the deck against certain characters, institutions, discourses and practices, inviting us to align our moral and ideological indignation with his. And as in *War and Peace*, the discourses present in his work appear in guises which only become transparent when the reader is assisted by knowledge of cultural issues and debates, sometimes conducted in the language of science and at others in colloquial versions of that language. Let me address two small and manageable examples.

For many scientists, and for readers otherwise informed about the discourses of science, Pynchon's work is a constant source of small pleasures. The chemist Larry Rosenhein points to the possessive delight with which he encountered a very minor and seemingly pointless passage in *The Crying of Lot 49*, where he discerned traces of a scientific discourse and was sure most non-scientists would not.[14] In the passage in question, the heroine, Oedipa Maas, meets a poker player who complains that in every game he almost but never quite wins back his stake, and certainly never wins. "To lose" is rarely just another verb in Pynchon's novels. It alerts us to the loss of energy, of communicable content, or of collective memory stored in real or metaphoric circuits. Armed with this knowledge, someone already versed in physics will hear in these lines a rephrasing of the colloquial gloss of the Second Law of Thermodynamics, which states that, first, you can't win and second, that you can't even break even.

From a formal perspective, there is nothing "necessary" about this passage. It does not forward the plot, shed light on the development of character, or comment in any but the most general way on the social world represented in the fiction. It is a piece of camouflaged discourse seeking fit audience, though few. Above all, it is in the text because Pynchon is committed to bringing scientific formulations to bear on every conceivable aspect and fictional repre-

---

[13] Note, for example, Sidney Hook, *The Hero in History* (Boston: Beacon Press, 1955), for its critique of the Tolstoy-Plekhanov line of argument.

[14] "Letter to Richard Pearce," *Pynchon Notes* 17 (Fall, 1985), 45.

sentation of the human condition. He does not claim that the discourse of science provides a more adequate representation of human reality; neither science nor technology have real advice or comfort, let alone solutions to offer. But they do provide his narrative with a discourse that operates at a high level of abstraction and generalization, inscribing human experience as a special case of the impersonal and constraining laws that control our material lives. Like Joseph Conrad, who, in Professor Levine's formulation, "explores the difficulties of seeing the human within the context of the nature [that] science was describing," Pynchon locates the human within the scientific and natural, though he does seem occasionally perplexed by the results of the instantiation of the human as yet one more facet of the material universe. His inscription of the human in these terms enables him to intervene in our ongoing cultural debate concerning the possible foundation of any but the most nihilistic action. In Pynchon's novels, science and technology, two discourses of knowledge and mastery, are used to show the extent to which, when they seem to work best, they lead only to our being mastered by the illusion of mastery, by our misconception of ourselves as masters of nature's creatures and of our own creations.

Gravity's Rainbow explores the omnipresence of control coupled with the illusion and failure of mastery. Perhaps the most important element of its plot is the search for a missing V-2 rocket. Historically, the V-2 was to be the ancestor of all our guided missiles. Given that errors in its trajectory could be corrected in flight, it can be thought of and represented as being under the control of those who construct and launch it, a mastered weapon whose phallic shape, often and at times tiresomely invoked by Pynchon, is an obscene icon of presence. Yet a crucial rocket in the V-2 series is missing in the story. Its absence and the quest for it provide the narrative impetus of the novel. This absence structures the text and is inscribed in and by all its discourses, including the mathematical. Mathematical absence–which I shall discuss in a moment–in turn comes to stand for the absence of, indeed the impossibility of attaining certainty in literal or interpretative realms. In one singularly condensed passage, Pynchon uses statistics to drive home the inescapable paradox of power and mastery, simultaneously illustrating the way in which detailed knowledge of an important cultural discourse (in this case statistics), is essential to proper interpretation of his work and of its relation to the world. Roger Mexico, a fictional statistician, charting the distribution of V-2 rocket hits on Greater London in 1944, hears an intellectual "music, not without its majesty, in this power series

$$\mathrm{Ne^{-m}}\left(1 + m + \frac{m^2}{2!} + \frac{m^3}{3!} + \dots \frac{m^{(n-1)}}{(n-1)!}\right),$$

terms numbered according to rocketfalls per square, the Poisson dispensation ruling not only these annihilations no man can run from, but also cavalry accidents, blood counts, radioactive decay. . . ."[15]

---

[15] *Gravity's Rainbow* (New York: Viking, 1973), p. 140. Further references to this work will be given in parentheses in the text. For a longer discussion of this statistical formulation, see my "The Fishy Poisson," *NMAL* 4:1 (Winter, 1979), n.p., note 5.

The name of "Poisson" is our clue. He was the first statistician to show that this now eponymous formula could be used to calculate the probability of the occurrence of random events. Subsequent work demonstrated that the formula did have applications quite as broad as Poisson had envisioned. In 1898, Von Bortkiewicz showed that it could predict a random and whimsically selected event, such as the number of men who would be kicked to death by horses in a Prussian cavalry regiment in any given year; hence the otherwise puzzling reference to cavalry accidents in the passage cited. In 1946, R. D. Clarke showed that the Poisson could have predicted the distribution of V-1 "flying bomb" hits over South London; hence Mexico's fictional calculation, which actually repeats the historically real, as is so often the case with Pynchon. Having introduced it, Pynchon uses scientific discourse to expose its status as knowledge without mastery, as knowledge which controls yet radically lacks the certainty its possessors yearn for. Roger can tell the people of London that a certain number of rockets will strike in a certain area over a certain period of time, and will kill an uncertain number of people. Neither the killers nor the killed will know just who will die, or where, or when. The absent rocket (n *minus* one) embodies this absence of certainty. When it returns as a prediction of the nuclear future in the last pages of the book, it fictionally enacts the return of the repressed. As far as Pynchon is concerned, in a technocratic and information-oriented society, the repressed is the anxiety over the lack of certainty, an anxiety engendered in part by the explosion of information and of claims about the control and certainty that is allegedly made possible by such an explosion. But the only certainty the text ultimately offers is that this absence of certainty will continue unabated, Strategic Defense Initiative or no. In predicting what can be predicted, Pynchon suggests, statistics–like his own apocalyptic pages–simultaneously affirm that which will remain irreducibly unpredictable.

What I am claiming is that the reader has to know something about scientific discourse and its mathematical dialect in order to have a full grasp of the meditation on control, certainty and the absence thereof in Pynchon's fiction. Yet that very familiarity with the scientific discourse makes it possible to mistake it for a privileged discourse of certainty and control. After Chernobyl and the Challenger, it may be that our cultural tendency to attribute privilege to the technological byproducts of science is diminishing; we may thus be less likely to mistake the scientific and technological discourses as the locus of authority in Pynchon's texts. Pynchon urges us along this path by dramatizing the persistence of claims in behalf of these discourses, and their promise of control and certainty; he does so not just explicitly, but also by re-enacting these claims and their deconstruction in scenes not explicitly concerned with technology. To offer but one example, he introduces a wild and dangerous horse into his narrative, an appaloosa called Snake, which functions at what seems to be a decidedly unscientific level of discourse. Traded from Texas to Saudi Arabia to Kirghizistan, it is said to be "homicidal ... unpredictable.... with no warning ... he could manage to kill ... simply [with a] gesture of a hoof" (342). Even a reader who knows nothing about the Poisson distribution and Von Bortkiewicz's demonstration of its applicability to deaths in the cavalry due to kicking horses can read Snake as a figure of predictable unpredictability set loose in the garden of certainties. But when this reading is mediated by a knowledge of the statistical discourse, it becomes linked to the rocket and far more ambitious thematics of control that speak to the real world that the V-2 made, in which we dwell, where the only certainty is that there will always be an absent rocket, as much beyond our control as death is beyond mastery.

Finnegans Wake *as Modernist Historiography*

CHARLES ALTIERI

Rather than concentrate on how the novel might be positioned within a set of competing discourses, I want to try the opposite tack. Here I shall try to flesh out one Modernist example of deliberately setting the novel against the historical models that had been its allies in the nineteenth century. A moment of real history sets the stage. Having been invited to present a paper on Vico and Joyce, I assumed that most of the participants would praise the mythographic typology of imaginative universals central to both figures. Therefore I decided to argue that that faith in pattern and recurrence was in fact an abuse of history. Such emphases make it easy to evade the agent's own place within historical flux, and they provide a contemplative, often determinist sense of that place which tempts us to avoid taking responsibility for what we make of our history. As Joyce himself realized when *Finnegans Wake*'s Four Elders carry out their endlessly learned trial of Pegger Festy, such ideals of comprehension must result in a "standing verdict of Nolans Brumans whereoneafter King, having murdered all the English he knew, picked out his pockets and left the tribunal scotfree."[1] To understand all the determinants of his action is necessarily to forgive all, or at the least to acknowledge an insuperable gap between the order of reflection and the domain of power to which the king is permitted to return, free of all categories which such judges can bring to bear.

My righteous indignation was to receive a considerable shock from the actual history that was the conference. Virtually everyone at the conference took exactly the same critical attitude towards Joycean versions of history, most going so far as to argue that Joyce was a "failure" compared to the more socially responsible work of novelists like Mann. Therefore I was confronted with two features of my own historicity not so easy to bask in: 1) that my own newfound faith in the moral importance of history seemed itself historically determined, so that the responsibility I sought might just be an evasion of responsibility aligning me with the comforting pieties of academic fashion[2]

[1] James Joyce, *Finnegans Wake* (New York: Penguin Books, 1976), pp. 92–93. All subsequent references will be to this edition.

and raising the difficult issue of whether conforming with one's times can provide an adequate imaginative stance for understanding the past; and 2) that my own shame at this discovery was historically problematic–does the shame offer a glimpse of individualist needs and values that can sustain a theoretical and readerly alternative to the dominant historicist reliance on de-mystified third person stances or engaged political ones, or is it "merely" a residue of an individualist ideology that must be expunged if one is to be consistent with something that might be called either historical necessity or integrity to the logic of analysis? The more suspicious alternative has all the authority of contemporaneity behind it, but that does not quite suffice to en-compass the shame, provide sufficient alternative investments to the imagina-tive states that individualism fostered, or align those investments with a posi-tive program that would justify subordinating individual values to the constraints required by real political action.

I do not have a theoretical alternative capable of dialectically incorporating what had been alienated by my efforts to find identity within the new histori-cism. I do, though, have a substantially modified capacity for sympathizing with the efforts of Joyce and other Modernists to set an insistently historical imagination against the historicist models for understanding those materials which prevailed then and prevail now. While that sympathy cannot in itself produce sufficient alternatives to the prevailing views, it can at least try to distribute embarrassment by pointing to authorial attitudes much more capa-cious and complex than the critical models that would judge them. What bet-ter beginning for such a project than to have experienced on one's own some of the ways that history can be a nightmare from which one wishes one could awaken? And ultimately what better text to search for alternative histories than *Finnegans Wake*, in which Viconian themes are crossed with the adven-tures of a hero whose own effort to read his first person concerns within a culture irreducibly other traps him into elaborate anxieties and rhetorical de-fenses about a letter purportedly either revealing his unsavory actions or exonerating him by making clear what actually happened? While everyone has heard of this letter, no one actually possesses it. So since we encounter not historical reality but hopes and fears which the idea of an explanation of it produces, we find history irreducibly a matter of how we read the inten-tional lives of the characters and how that reading forces us to reflect on who we become by our participation in their quest. In the place of third person analytic explanations and critiques we find ourselves forced to explore ways of treating history in first person terms as a locus of forces within which iden-tifications are possible and a version of identity necessary.

Joyce's fullest statement engaging Vico's historiography takes place as a mysterious questioning of Shem, the ephebe sufficiently alienated from his-tory to need a reflexive means of realigning himself with its products. Its terms dramatize the plight of all Enlightenment ideals of explanation and cul-tural progress:

---

[2] For a good recent description of the orthodoxy governing the New History in Modernist studies see Robert von Hallberg, "Editor's Introduction," *Critical Inquiry*, 13 (1987), 415–20.

*Now, to be on anew and basking again in the panaroma of all flores of speech, if
a human being duly fatigued by his dayety in the sooty, having plenxty off time
on his gouty hands and vacants of space at his sleepish feet and as hapless
behind the dreams of accuracy as an camelot prince of dinmurk, were at this auc-
tual futule preteriting unstant, in the states of suspensive exanimation, ac-
corded, throughout the eye of a noodle, with an ear-sighted view of old hopeinha-
ven with all the ingredient and egregiunt whights and ways to which in the
curse of his persistence the course of his tory will had been having recourses, the
reverberration of knotcracking awes, the reconjungation of nodebinding ayes, the
redissolusingness of mindmouldered ease and the thereby hang of the Hoel of it,
could such a none ... byhold at ones what is main and why tis twain, how one
once meet melts in tother wants poignings ... then what would that fargazer
seem to seemself to seem seeming of, dimm it all?
Answer: a collideorscape.* (143)

Obviously this collideorscape has its contemporary counterpart in deconstructive treatments of history, especially as represented in Linda Orr's
superb essay, "The Revenge of Literature."[3] But rather than remain "as hapless behind the dreams of accuracy as any camelot prince of dinmurk," Joycean history also sets itself the task of exploring the values made possible by
the play of the main and the twain as one tries nonetheless to capture the
"hang of the Hoel of it." Vico's role for Joyce consisted largely in showing
that such values were possible for an art devoted to a philological intricacy;
then Joyce's task would be to free the values from the Enlightenment rationality that still pervaded Viconian thought. First Vico showed that secular
history had to be materialist, at least to the degree that it concentrated on the
concrete ways that language shaped institutional life. Such knowledge promised both to elicit a profound humility before the inventive beneficence of
Providence, and, more important, to establish a *sensus communis* on terms
very different from those proposed by Cartesian rationalism. Where Descartes
hoped to deduce what was essential to humanity by elaborating clear and distinct first principles, Vico thought one might define the human by
interpreting the forces it produced within the history that records them. Like
God, man is revealed in the forms its makings disclose. Then Vico proposed a
reading of that history that relied to a large degree on the capacity of poetic
language to render the energies of those makings and to cast the universals
which then define social values.

---

[3] "The Revenge of Literature: A History of History," *New Literary History* 18 (1986), 1–22. For Derrida's comments on *Finnegans Wake*, which I think are not fully responsive to the complexity of investments that Joyce performs, see his "Two words
for Joyce," in Derek Attridge and Daniel Ferrer, eds. *Post-structuralist Joyce* (Cambridge: Cambridge University Press, 1984),
145–59. Jean-Michel Rabaté's "Lapsus ex machina" in that volume strikes me as a richer response to the deconstructive,
anti-narrative features of Joycean writing (79–101). I should add that I have taken my sense of the play of the main and the
twain, as well as much of what I know about *Finnegans Wake*, from Hazard Adams' class on that text. In his writings Adams first fully worked out the levels of authority involved in narrative in his *Joyce Cary's Trilogies: Pursuit of the Particular
Real* (Tallahassee: University Presses of Florida, 1983), pp. 246–64. Then he turned to Joyce and recognized the need to
adapt what I am calling the anti-story into his theoretical model. The results are most impressively set out in his "Critical
Constitution of the Literary Text: The Example of *Ulysses*," *New Literary History* 17 (1986), 595–616.

Both Viconian discoveries, however, seemed severely undermined by Vico's general Enlightenment stance. The claims about poetic language, for example, could not themselves be cast in poetic language. For in Vico's eyes the presence of those imaginative, fabricating energies muddles any possible analytic clarity: a language that can give life to the gods cannot clearly analyze the institutions of men. On the more general level of materialist analysis, Vico once again based his Enlightenment versions of freedom on an impersonal lucidity that hoped to purchase progress at the cost of analyzing its own versions of making: the historian who analyzes the makings of others is not significantly a historical maker in his or her own right because that stance tries to escape the collideorscape.

We smile knowingly, all too aware of the historian as maker. But from a Joycean perspective it is possible to say that contemporary writing does very little with that awareness except try to expose the blindnesses it entails. That is no way to encounter the dualities fundamental to the "hang of the Hoel of it." Rather we must begin by confronting the basic contradiction which Enlightenment historiography continues to foster, and then we might engage the full collideoscape that focuses our investments in history and histories. That contradiction is as simple as it is inescapable: as Foucault saw, the very ideals of lucidity and individual freedoms projected by Enlightenment rationality have fostered their own undoing. Those ideals had generated models of expressive individuality and myths of the endless proliferation of differences (ultimately taking form as dreams of infinite irony) which made rationality itself suspect and, more important, made it extremely difficult to trust in the political balances of individualism and collective interest sustaining the political orders engendered by that rationality. As we generalize about history we must put ourselves in categorical terms; but as we try to understand the import of those generalizations we inevitably unmake their generalizing force by betraying the particular structure of interests and selections which reveals both the power and the pathos of our local situation. Yet if we respond to such conditions simply by telling stories of interests pursued or blindnesses revealed which stem from that pathos, we merely confirm our historicity without either gaining fresh insight into the general condition or projecting alternative modes of engaging it.

Finnegans Wake posits a Modernist historiography capable of treating these contradictions as the basis for recasting the principles of making that Vico at once developed and suppressed.[4] This history would have to discover a

[4] Beckett's "Dante ... Bruno. Vico ... Joyce," reprinted in Richard W. Seaver, ed., *Samuel Beckett: I can't go on, I'll go on* (New York: Grove Press, 1976), 105–26, provides what is still the best analysis of why and how Joyce takes up the Enlightenment stance that Vico posits. In order to show how keen that analysis is I first quote from Vico:

> *Our Science therefore comes to describe at the same time an ideal eternal history traversed in time by the history of every nation in its rise, development, maturity, decline, and fall. Indeed, we make bold to affirm that he who meditates this Science narrates to himself this ideal eternal history so far as he himself makes it for himself by that proof "it had, has, and will have to be." For the first indubitable principle posited above is that this world of nations has certainly been made by men, and its guise must therefore be found within the modifications of our own human mind. And history cannot be more certain than when he who creates the things also narrates them.... these proofs are of a kind divine and should give thee a divine pleasure, since in God knowledge and creation are one and the same thing.* (Giambattista Vico, *The New Science,* trans. Thomas Goddard Bergin and Max Harold Fisch [Ithaca: Cornell University Press, 1968], 104–5, paragraph 349.)

mode of poetic language that would allow the author to play Enlightenment insight against Enlightenment myths of progress by showing how such a dense language might be precisely the vehicle necessary for disclosing the modes of making that go into the pursuit of the ideal, yet undiscoverable letter posited as the goal of historical knowledge. As Beckett realized, the Viconian ideal of poetic language promises to capture the intricate relationship between maker and made which is basic to human truth and then to communicate that knowledge with an immediacy that literally testifies to its relevance as well as demonstrating the powers of agency necessary to reflect on what one encounters. The novelist, like the modern painter, need not confine himself to writing about something. He can make that writing the thing itself, the force that demonstrates the reality of what it discusses. Then one can render quite literally a historicity in which we come to know ourselves both in what we have made and in what we make as we engage those phenomena. Joyce's text becomes a model for the consciousness capable of containing the diversity, complexity, contrariety and duplicity of our historical being within the confines of a single book, which in turn reflects the potential power of a single imaginative commitment.[5] And on that basis it can explore two basic features of that poetic language which make its playful deconstruction the basis for new possibilities of historical understanding—not because one is thereby free to contemplate history but because thereby one realizes certain expressivist first person ways of participating fully in its complex demands which cannot be incorporated within explanatory models for that history.

This new language must begin with a strong deconstructive component. If history is made by beings as divided as ourselves, we need a kaleidoscope adapted to a strange Providence sustained by a constant interaction of collision and escape—from the level of the pun where collision implicates us in dualities which it becomes increasingly difficult to imagine escaping, to the most abstract shape of the narrative action where the main and the twain remain in constant conflict as we simultaneously posit underlying principles of fatality or Providence and exercise a sceptical intelligence attentive to the anti-story produced by the workings of desire and difference. Hoels breed Iseults whom they cannot control. But suppose that the proliferation of Iseults also gives us

---

Beckett then insists that Joyce adapts this Vico to "the problem of style," where it becomes necessary to render the "cyclic dynamism" of history by reducing "various expressive media to their primitive economic directness, and the fusion of these primal essences into an assimilated medium for the exteriorisation of thought" (120). And, Beckett adds, adapting Viconian poetics to Viconian historical principles offers the opportunity of projecting a possible *ricorso* which need not be a repetition, and a possible historicity which "is not the result of Fate or Chance–in both cases the individual would be separated from his product–but the result of a Necessity that is not Fate, of a Liberty that is not Chance." If the result is a vision of Providence, it is of a "providence" one names only with one's tongue "very much in his cheek" (110–11).

[5] Here and in remarks I make later about the reading process I rely on other essays where I have tried to work out from Modernist painting the idea of art as testimony, that is as work less concerned to base its authority on what it asserts about the world than on what it creates as indubitable conditions of experience for the spectator. However one might interpret a Mondrian or even a Picasso collage, one simply has not looked carefully at the work if one has not felt certain balancing forces possess one as one looks, or, in the case of Picasso, if one has not undergone complex processes of unmaking and reconstructing what counts as a material object. Modernism we might say takes very literally the iconic dimensions of Vico's imaginative universals. I make my clearest case for this in "Picasso's Collages and the Force of Cubism," *Kenyon Review* 6 (Spring 1984), 8–33, "Modernist Abstraction and Pound's First Cantos: The Ethos for a New Renaissance," *Kenyon Review* 7 (Fall 1985), 79–105, and "Why Stevens Must be Abstract, or What a Poet Can Learn From Painting," in Albert Gelpi, ed. *Wallace Stevens: The Poetics of Modernism* (New York: Cambridge University Press, 1985), pp. 86–118.

new perspectives on what it meant to dream of, or even to be part of, a Hoel. That was Vico's ambition, and therefore it would play an important role in Joyce's recasting. For our recasting of that we must concentrate on two fundamental features of that Viconian heritage–the way it enables us to characterize the overall action of the text and the model of individuality that derives from Joycean anti-Enlightenment.

The traditional view of the overall action of *Finnegans Wake* posits the imaginative site of the story as a single dream within which HCE takes on different identities and states of being as he enters different levels of sleep. This hypothesis does establish a rationale for the multiple levels generated by Joyce's language. But it also pays the enormous price of having to rely on Enlightenment models for dispelling embarrassment about the confusions that comprise "his tory." So long as we view the work as fundamentally a dream we remain subordinated to the quest for an explanatory typology; we keep the authorial subject in the text distinct from any object which the text can be said to engage; and we leave the writing subordinate in principle to the authority of a Freud or Jung. All of those moves minimize the power of the letter to compose its own imaginative reality, and more important, greatly simplify our relation to the history that humans make.

Joyce tries to correct the picture by giving a new twist to Vico's ideal of humanity coming to know itself in the history it has made. For him the knowing is indistinguishable from our actual participation in the making and the demands which they produce for what Joyce called "an ideal reader suffering from an ideal insomnia." Where traditional history tries to describe events and structures, Joyce extends Modernist presentational principles to project something like a holographic human mind trying to encompass in a single structure the main and the twain informing the history it has made and is still making. The maker of history, or the synthetic language whose competent speaker could be the maker, is always present in our expressions, but in such a twain form that we must project a virtual source of the complex utterances which is beyond the control of any speaking character (including the author). To know ourselves in history and history in ourselves we must simultaneously occupy a point of view within history–in one's "preteriting unstant," and at its margin where "all the stranger things that ever not even in the hundrund and badst pageans of unthowsent and wonst nice ... [depend upon] the untireties of livesliving being the one substrance of a streamsbecoming. Totalled in toldteld and teldtold in tittle-tell tattle" (*FW* 597). Historical evidence becomes the degree of cultural information the text can project as continuous with the virtual "I" who must as its writer and its reader encompass this archetypal set of processes. And then Irish Wakes over historical loss call up states of being in which "gramma" can speak "on the impetus of her imperative" (*FW* 268).

Beckett brings Dante to bear in order to show how poetic language can try to embody that collective imperative. For Dante faced his own version of Post-Enlightenment fragmentation in a political climate where no actual dialect could be seen as either mirroring the world or bearing the epic weight once sustained by Latin. Every choice of a language also established particular allegiances and oppositions by tying the utterance to specific social conflicts with all the attendant suspicions and fears. Thus Dante (like Joyce six hundred years later) had to construct his own "synthetic language" that might get beyond specific historical investments to project an overall account of who we are as beings who must work out identities within those historical conditions. By writing "a vulgar that *could* have been spoken by an ideal Italian who had assimilated what was best in all the dialects of his country, but which in fact was certainly not spoken nor ever had been" (Beckett, 122), Dante found the necessary level of ideality required to replace the world Latin had composed. Poetic language could no longer be content to capture the imaginative life of particular social groups but must make possible new realities and generate models of agency capable of inhabiting the domains thereby created. Joyce then relocates the ground of Dante's ideal language so that it comes to constitute the secular realm of historical self-awareness which all subjects can use to define their own historicity.

But stressing such potential universals brings Joyce dangerously close to Idealism, however intricately ironized. The second feature of his poetic language provides the necessary counterbalance by projecting a radical interpretation of what it means to be bound to the specificities of one's historical being. Amidst the quintessential Bakhtinian carnival where all fixed identities collapse into a fluid sense of sharing the multiple roles that history imposes upon us, reading remains an irreducibly individual "cyclological" (220) process. Clearly no one mind can encompass all that this writing has made. In fact the density of signs forces the reader into the position of hopeful "fargazer seem[ing] to seemself to seem seeming of." Yet in this fall there emerges a considerable consolation–the realization that the embarrassment of being an individual brings with it certain visions of lack and of limit which cannot be incorporated within any historical schema. We know our individuality less from any positive content than from the properties of lack and limit that we gradually see developing in our readings of the world. It is only as we project inadequate meanings for Joyce's text that we become something like characters within it. We do not fill out the author's intentions, as is the case in traditional readings of traditional fictions. Instead we become aware ourselves as both creators and occluders of imaginative paths made available by the text, as if this reading activity typified our state as simultaneous narrators and makers of histories that in turn allow individual expression in a world written through by typologies. While basking in the "panaroma of all flores of speech," and while constantly wondering at the "differances" between the written and the sounded word, one finds "his tory" taking shape only through the "knotcracking awes" and "nodebinding ayes" that at once negate and form various holes and wholes preventing us from a full reading of the letters.

These activities seem to me not only the fundamental semantic focus of the book but also its ethical core. What happens as we read provides actual testimony for relations to the world and to other imagined readers and actors which the text then leads us to reflect upon–not by some illusionary picture of events and structures in the world but through the dispositions that the reading shows us are fundamental to our own "cyclological" processes. It is as if Joyce creates a set of fictive exemplars that we come to see dramatizing the determined individualism that we observe in ourselves as we read. And then these exemplars focus the dispositional responses that we can turn to as possible ways of valuing what we now see are necessary features of our being as readers of and in history. Therefore I shall conclude by briefly spelling out what is dramatized in two of these exemplars so that I can draw my anti-historicist morals.

With such attention given to the act of writing, the first exemplar is the au-thorial presence as it vacillates between the extreme arrogance of the synthetic maker and a rediscovered modesty that stems from recognizing how one's individuality calls up a profound humility before something like Provi-dence. The Promethean author clearly offers his linguistic ambitions as ana-logues to the synthetic dreams. All language in effect becomes a dialect of some grander synthesis that must be called Joycean. Yet the very grandeur of the synthesis assures its constant undoing. At one pole the scope of significa-tion makes it impossible to be impersonal, impossible not to continually over-determine what arises with the most personal of memories of his own family romance and fantasies of escape. At the other pole the personal becomes a mark of a more encompassing fall, where Viconian humility reenters the epic dream. For there is also no more humbling experience–for the writer as well as the readers (themselves divided between the pride of making sense of this book and the pain of sensing how much they miss)–than the process of seeing one's distortions of the language continuously yielding a range and depth of possible meanings that surpass what one intended to produce. Willed distortion becomes the vehicle by which one comes to appreciate just how complex and capacious must be the mind or site that holds what lan-guage makes possible. Thus our greatest moments of self-gathering are also moments where we recognize a strange dialectic between what blind individ-uality reveals and the transpersonal field of play it opens. The textually pro-duced and sanctioned heroic agency makes a self in puns that also unmake the desired identity in the service of some larger anti-historical principle "celebridging over the guilt of the gap in your hiscitendency" (305). In that gap, where the main becomes irreducibly twain, we begin to recognize the strange harmony between our lacks and the immarginable nature of the grounds we reveal in our composings and decomposings. The epic and the joke become necessarily fused elements in a process of losing and finding the letters which can return "his tory" to the state of the anagogic book, which must therefore also be an anti-book.

While Joyce could insist on the perverse transcendental qualities of his inescapable personal investments in his tellings, he could not allow himself to give the writing any more overt ethical role. For that he needed his charac-ters, in part because ethical projections are necessarily theatrical and must be rendered in that quasi-distanced register. Let us then glance briefly at what the two main characters HCE and ALP project as possible ways of organizing the range of emotional investments that this history elicits and frustrates.

For the male principle, history is that resistance which calls up dreams of a phallic "unstant" where for the moment the self escapes all external authority. Because the sexual cry of such triumph allows an "earsightedness" that is no longer bound to the differential structure of language, HCE's fullest expression of this desire occurs as he dreams he can play Wagner's Tristan dallying with an Iseult "deaf with love" (and free of the genealogical chain defining her as his daughter):

> No, No, the dear heaven knows, and the farther the from it, if the whole stole stale mis betold, whoever the gulpable, and whatever the pulpous was, the twooned togethered, and giving the mhost phassionable wheathers, they were doing a lally a lolly a dither a duther one lelly two dather three lilly four dother. And it was a fiveful moment for the poor old timetetters, ticktacking, in tenk the count. Till the spark that plugged spared the chokee he gripped and (volatile volupty, how brieved are they lunguings!) they could and they could hear like of a lisp lapsing, that was her knight of the truths thong plipping out of her chapellledeosy, after where he had gone and polped the questioned (396).

The imaginary dimension of male sexuality projects a phallic energy capable of inhabiting dualities as if they could all be unified in a fiveful moment where questions are polped and lisps heard lapsing into the pure state–physical and psychological–of being "her knight of the truths thong." As Lacan would eventually elaborate, the male ego is inseparable from this imposition of the mythic upon the material because its very gendering depends on the ideal of a phallic potency with the power to adapt the world to the demands of the ego. Joyce, though, is not content to trace those projections. He insists on the eternal return of historical necessity–here in the fact that HCE's fantasies entail his also having to play the role of victim required by the identification with King Mark, everywhere in the awareness that sexual ecstasy is essentially the realization in time of desires that make it impossible for the male ego to reconcile itself to time. Because the dream of sexual potency is continually forced to confront the mocking pressures of temporality, the aging lover is condemned to play simultaneously the masterful Tristram and the miserable King Mark.

The opposite irony ties ALP to history. Rather than worry about the inevitable loss of ecstasy that undoes imaginary kingships and inaugurates a course of resentments, she must come to terms with the horror of having to realize the truth about the ones she loves. ALP's resistance to history takes the form of a constant temptation to despair over its truths about others rather than about the self. Yet that danger also provides the psychic resources for facing the fact that there is no way to reconcile opposites in order to transcend the constant undoing of selves and objects of desire. Instead the best one can do is to try out modes of identification that can align the full psychic energies of subjectivity with the fated divisions permeating all the fundamental constituents of history–narrative, narratee, and narrator. By taking this path ALP can fully participate in the erotic opera without assuming herself to be its hero or heroine and without having to resort to the asceticism that is Lacan's only alternative to the male imaginary. Because she does not need to justify herself, ALP can turn the clarity of seeing into a profound acceptance which allows her to identify with the endless contrariety that is life itself. Book and anti-book, narrative time and the resistance to it, then become correlatives that take us far beyond the textual play which gives us access to them.

When ALP begins speaking, she seems a more perceptive version of HCE's desperate quest to transform his own banality into imaginatively satisfying states. But she also has two abilities he lacks. She can turn on her fantasies in bitter understanding, and she can see herself in typological terms which provide partial relief from time while also establishing terms for a more insistent individualism responsible to the differences which her own caring has produced. Both abilities are most pronounced, and most significant, in perhaps the most remarkable passage of this remarkable book, where ALP sees, as her husband never could, that despite one's desires for grandeur the fall is a pervasive and inescapable reality:

> *I could have stayed up there for always only. It's something fails us. First we feel. Then we fall.... Let her rain for my time is come. I done me best when I was let. Thinking always if I go all goes. A hundred cares, a tithe of troubles and is there one who understands me? ... How small it's all! And me letting on to meself always.... I thought you were all glittering with the noblest of carriage. You're only a bumpkin.... But I'm loothing them that's here and all I lothe. Loonely in me loneness.... My leaves have drifted from me. All. But one clings still. I'll bear it on me. To remind me of. Lff! So soft this morning, ours. Yes.... End here. Us then. Finn, again! Take. Bussoftlhee, mememormee! Till thousendsthee. Lps. The keys to. Given! A way a lone a last a loved a long the* (627–28).

Even in this concluding moment, Joyce will not allow a simple, emotionally satisfying imaginary relation to the problem of the imaginary. ALP seems capable of accepting the fact that everyone falls. But reconciliation to a common fate still elicits judgment–of the whole, of herself, and most of all of the one to whom she had been devoted. Yet as she turns critically on her life, one principle seems able to resist these dark truths. That principle takes figurative form as the leaf that continues to cling even as all her other individuating traits surrender to time's laws. But how comprehensive is this figure? How can Joyce hope to have it suggest a general reflexive attitude earned by this entire text's obsession with the letter that cannot be found? The answer lies in the opera available for ALP after she confronts a poverty more excruciatingly simple and concrete than that facing any other modern hero. What remains is memory–not the memory of specific scenes or exalted moments but memory in something close to a pure form that can survive the linguistic deformation of the past which is basic to the work as a whole.

Joyce's pun on memory defines the enabling difference, and establishes an expressivist version of history that one can only win by resisting its historicist formulations. Her state is of a memory inseparable from something like a pure condition of identity, a "me, me, me" that becomes at once a purely private mode of assertion and an abstract principle aligning her with the intimate source of all care about history's collideorscape. Her desolation is so intense that it purifies memory of all contents and leaves only its pure form, the form that makes history matter as the precondition of individuality. Thus her dominant memory is of making love that morning to HCE, but the focus is not on him nor on the pleasure of polping questions. All she remembers is the way that their action possessed the morning so that the event attached to them in the same way that the leaf does. So purified, however, this memory becomes an emblem of an intensity of care and of identification that provides the novel's Nietzschean answer to Viconian *ricorso*. Facing the despair of lucidity about what one loves casts the loving itself as a principle that can meet the stringent criteria for happiness posed in Nietzsche's doctrine of the eternal return of the same. "Mememormee" projects a mode of intensity that as a force establishes the Hoel by which an individual can embrace what is irreducibly twain and thereby spur the novel to turn back once more on its commodious recirculation.

Memory, then, need not tie one to the specular mirror of specific scenes. The discipline of searching for the letter establishes another level of the life of the mind where its action has a kind of force only marginally (or immarginably) attached to particular passing phenomena. ALP can affirm her desolation because she has come to be able to see incompleteness as a profound form of fulfillment allowing even these banal, "loothesome" characters a typological immortality–less for what they are in themselves than for eliciting the condition of desire that is inseparable from the investments allowing us to make history. "Mememormee" is the pure cry of selfhood that will only be distorted by more factual and explanatory encounters with history because those efforts only add features that have very little to do with the underlying dynamics of psychic life. ALP's sense of individuation, like her sense of time, can be complete because it is so simple. She asks only that she remain open to the thousand thees that are still to make their appearances in the collideorscape. Then she can hope to find in the activity of caring the principle of individuation that survives all the imaginary distortions which it creates. Those moments too will fail, but in the fall fragments shored from the experience of historicity provide the will to pass on to others the desire to live and to love. Viconian *ricorso* has a totally human providential core.

The Joyce we have been reconstructing remains devoted to ideas of type and recurrence that are not compatible with contemporary historicism. But under the pressure created by that criticism, we come to see that rather than being escapes from history these Joycean values may define crucial principles for appreciating who we are because of our investments in history and because of the imaginative work we do within or upon that historicity. In *Finnegans Wake* we encounter a version of historical determinism so total that it can reject all foundational tales which purport to explain the mechanism imposing causal shape upon events (tales that are themselves necessarily determined by their historical situation). For Joyce, we are determined to a density of differences that no generalization can capture or theory erase, so the dream of science ironically fosters a radical individualism. It is precisely those overdetermined features generating and generated by individual cares that make one embarrassed to find oneself merely repeating social nostrums and that therefore elicit the "mememormee" at once dependent on a social order and mobilizing constant resistance to it. As in Spinoza, the determined nature of a person's differences creates the possibility of fleshing out an individual *conatus*.

This model is not compatible with the work of the historian, who must try to provide explanations within whatever cognitive limitations the culture can teach her to acknowledge. But it should prove extremely useful for the humanities because it provides a sense of history capable of explaining why the arts tend to resist those historical explanations. Ironically that case has its clearest claims upon us when its opponents turn to the anti-foundational attitudes towards history that now govern academic literary historicism. Those attitudes have generated two basic contemporary strategies for doing history without relying on the myths of progress that undermined Enlightenment and whig historiography. At one pole we find the suspicious, morally judgmental history which I tried to practice. Convinced that historical agents spend most of their psychic energies creating false foundations to fool themselves or fool others by naturalizing what is in fact in their interest, this stance is committed to debunking those self-flattering constructions and putting in their place a more accurate (or more politically useful) version of how those interests are actually constituted and deployed. But how then can this model construct a society for such interests that is not as appalling in its selfish blindness, with its attendant manipulations and suspicions, as the bourgeois order that it proposes to resist? The only answer I find plausible is to shift to a second anti-foundational strategy emphasizing the capacity of some kind of dialogical model to negotiate exchanges both with the past and with other ways of interpreting its discourses. These models too, however, have a great deal of trouble with irreducible differences and the very particular passions that elicit and reinforce "mememormee." Usually they fudge the difference between hearing a play of voices and somehow adapting to those differences without relying on that now villainous concept of dialectic.

Those difficulties can be negotiated by the tact and rhetorical skill of a Stephen Greenblatt. But if we simply negotiate them we avoid the lesson implicit in the pains and embarrassments which we encounter when the models are more adamantly faithful to their theoretical underpinnings. Joyce directs us in just the opposite direction, forcing us to see that the strange blend of determinist thinking and anti-foundational attitudes towards the grounds on which we posit those determinations must lead away from suspicious attitudes towards more speculative and engaged blends of psychology and ontology. If anti-foundational theory is correct in its claims that there are no givens or universals, and if all phenomena are culturally constituted, then we are back in some version of Vico's faith that the way to understand what is human is to see how that humanity comes to express itself within history. This need not lead to an eager debunking of those constructions or even to the kinds of dialogue which allow Gadamerian "application" by subsuming the past under the needs of the present. A world free of foundations is a world that is constantly being created anew *as* it comes under the provenance of different desires and cares. Before we debunk we need to understand just what occupies the operatic stages in which individuals form attachments, react to embarrassments, and base the self on a way of holding both in memory. Attending carefully to that variety comprises what I call an expressivist view of history, a view whose terms were first elaborated by Vico and by Hegel but which required Joyce before it could be fully separated from Enlightenment desires for a structure to explain the nature and sequence of those expressions. Joyce then shows that while recognizing the intensity and variety of those expressivist commitments may take a background of recurrent forms, the forms themselves must function very much along the lines of the abstract yet intensely personal "me" that clings to ALP. Expressivist history is the tracing of the "mememormees" created by those falls from common sense that eventually forge a *"sensus communis"* about what we have made of and as our history. That history takes form in a collideorscape continually adjusted to the means by which resources elaborated in a culture's past become available for distinctive recombinations in some present.

Without an intense ironic and critical spirit we are likely to miss the intricacy of those elements and their combinations: "You wish to ave some homelette. . . . your hegg he must break himself" (59). But once those elements actually enter the making of histories, we may lose more than we gain by imposing explanatory categories on at least the more engaging "mememormee"'s that emerge. That way the best we can hope to foster is a society of Shaun the Postmans. Joyce's way, on the other hand, is to imagine a social order based on the pursuit of collective identifications that are knowable only in and as our differences as we make and unmake particular histories. There both academic conformity and the impositional expressivist individualisms of Pound, Yeats and Lawrence give way to a plausible homology between a workable aesthetics and a workable politics.

The Novel as Therapeutic Discourse

The first panel on the second morning of the conference was "The Novel as Therapeutic Discourse (its readerly or emotional satisfactions and functions)." Whether it was the topic itself that generated the lively discussion that followed, or the provocative speakers, or the fact that the four panels of the previous day had made for a crowded schedule with little or no time for discussion, or some combination thereof, is hard to say. The result in any case was therapeutic, in terms of conference spirit, which rose prodigiously, for all of which panel moderator Carol Singley, then NOVEL's assistant editor, now teaching at Swarthmore, then and now an Edith Wharton scholar, deserves much credit. Moderator Singley began at any rate with a modification of the panel's descriptive subtitle:

> In retrospect, perhaps we should have also included [the novel's] "readerly" frustrations and perplexities. Certainly the topic evokes a number of questions about reader involvement with and response to texts, and it invites our investigation from several directions and angles. How ... does the novel affect our emotional, intellectual, and psychological well-being? Can novels make us better, and if so, what is the process by which relationships between text and reader are affected? And what are the notions of this self that engages in the meaning-making activity with the text? These are some of the issues that our speakers, coming from a wide variety of perspectives and experiences, are going to address.

There followed the "little drama," as New Critics might have it, of Canadian bibliotherapist Joseph Gold's confrontational pitch for the utility of "systems theory," psychologist Murray Schwartz's more personal account of his own early addiction to novel-reading, and comparatist Susan Suleiman's playful feminist scenario on the relations between modernity and play.

The Function of Fiction: A Biological Model[1]

JOSEPH GOLD

Not all the king's horses, nor all the king's men
Could put Humpty Dumpty together again.

The novel is the latest and most highly evolved form of story-making. Its development is an extremely complex communication system that can now be seen to characterize human species development. I am only beginning to formulate, after ten years of work, some description of just how complex this system of information storage the novel is. That extended prose narrative should be therapeutic ought not to be surprising. Had we not been so distracted by the religious origin and the economic and political goals of our own profession, we might have seen long ago that the novel is a language model of human behavior, the function of which is to increase human self-awareness, and consequently social awareness, with a view to improving the chances of community survival.

To talk about the novel as therapeutic is to turn our attention to its uses. We are now in the realm of applied literature. In looking at the novel's function, we are shifting our attention away from the trends of recent criticism, whether "new," formalist, structuralist, poststructuralist, or postmodernist as these attitudes have come to be called. What I want to do in this paper is look first at some problems that have arisen in consequence of certain lines of thought in contemporary criticism; then to discuss the nature of narrative phylogenetically, as a biologically evolved human activity; and finally to offer some theoretical framework and some illustrative applications for the novel as a medium of helping, of therapy. Before we can see the therapeutic value of fiction, we need to glimpse the theoretical ground that is the foundation for potential value.

Academics love to argue and the attractions of this entertainment can easily divert us from our larger and more important responsibilities. We are almost ready, I hope, to move beyond the fear and insecurity which keeps us behind our earlier battle lines. The dust is settling. We can now appreciate the importance of the work done by those scholars, whose names are familiar to us all, exemplified for instance in Jane Tompkins' valuable anthology, *Reader Response Criticism.*[2] They have led us to some key questions. What we need now is a methodology that will enable us to answer them. For instance, we are pretty well now all agreed that the text (by this I mean the novel as experienced, not the book of paper on which it is written), is not an object, it

---

[1] I am extending a line of thought developed by Eric Lenneberg's wonderful book, *Biological Foundations of Language* (New York: Wiley & Sons, 1967), and the essay by William Orr Dingwall, "Human Communicative Behavior: A Biological Model," in *The Signifying Animal: The Grammar of Language and Experience,* ed. Irmengard Rauch and Gerald F. Carr (Bloomington: Indiana University Press, 1980), pp. 51–86.

[2] *Reader Response Criticism: From Formalism to Post-structuralism,* hereafter, *Reader Response Criticism,* ed. Jane Tompkins (Baltimore: Johns Hopkins University Press, 1980).

is not a thing. Poulet, Iser, Fish, Bleich, and many others are all agreed on this. At the same time it is not a no-thing, since readers do have neural experience of it. Then what is it? This is by no means our most difficult question, though I can find no modern writing that gives a clear answer to it. It is a question Louise Rosenblatt, to her credit, has been trying to answer for decades. Her discussions of transaction and afference have perhaps come closer than most.[3] A much more difficult question is this: where does personal response begin and end and communal/social response take over? Or to put it another way, *can* we sort out the personal from the communal, or should we put our energy into trying? Does a community of readers replace individuals? Professors Holland and Bleich seem to be approaching this question. I am left by their answers with the somewhat uncomfortable feeling that their paths lead to seeing the literary work of art as almost purely diagnostic. For them, the novel's value seems to lie in uncovering the reader's personal neuroses or idiosyncracies, more than in its value as an instrument of healing and comfort. The more traditional view of the novel, as a diagnosis of the culture's dysfunction, is described in Walker Percy's elegant essay in the June 1986 *Harper's* magazine, where the writer argues that the value of the novel consists in its ability to make the reader aware of society's ills. The novel in this view becomes a corrective of social and political disease. Neither of these positions addresses the relationship between novel, reader, and culture, because neither position emanates from a systemic view of human perception and behavior, though all these views, doubtless, tell a part of the story.

How did we literary critics get bogged down in a discussion that leads us without a thread into a maze? In the middle of this maze is a mirror that derides us with the reflection of our own bewilderment. We got here, I suspect, through our disposition to philosophize. A survey of any typical list of postmodernist critical writings reveals to us that we are in the realm of modern philosophy, as practiced by, dare I say it, amateur philosophers. I mean by this, those whose training was not in philosophy. Professional philosophers do not discuss the nature of the novel. I gather that they like to reason about the nature of the reasoning process. Since philosophy seems to be a discipline devoted to thinking about the nature of knowledge, it is obviously possible to philosophize about anything. New Critics like Tate, Ransom, Warren and Empson and mythologists/taxonomists like Frye and Campbell tried to practice criticism modeled on their view of science, albeit a nineteenth-century view of science. They tried to analyze or organize the constructs of literature as though these were material art objects. Contemporary criticism is modelling itself on a philosophic logic whose goal was not the formulation of a theory, but the perfecting of a practice of controllable discourse. By examining variables, postmodernist criticism arrives at the absence of all constants. Modern philosophy *per se* or in its lit-crit costume will not help us to formulate a theory of the novel. Literary criticism requires a new direction.

[3] See, for instance, Louise M. Rosenblatt, "The Transactional Theory of the Literary Work: Implications for Research," in *Researching Response to Literature and the Teaching of Literature: Points of Departure*, ed. Charles R. Cooper (Norwood, N.J.: Ablex, 1985), pp. 33–53.

As we know literary criticism, its family of origin was father theology fertiliz-
ing the history of ideas, parents from a leisured class, largely isolated from
applications, experiment, and utility, certainly not used to manual labor and
making ends meet, and preoccupied with pure, or impure, speculation. Because professional literary criticism had its origins in this kind of philosophy,
it read literature as thought rather than art, or versions of experience. The
shift from moral discourse and the history of religion to the history of literature as moral discourse was almost imperceptible and literature was divine. Is
deconstruction a belated secular backlash? Courses in the history of ideas
were until recently commonplace in departments of English. Here again English critics lacked no temerity. They would do the work of three, four, or five
disciplines exclusively from the information in literature, or in John Stuart
Mill. We have been not only philosophers, but historians, priests, political scientists and psychologists, though our only credentials may have been a Ph.D.
in ambiguous sentences in Henry James. It is little wonder then that we
follow our latest critical forays into some dead ends from which we will have
to backtrack.

Literature is not experienced by readers as philosophy but as experience. It
appears to be rooted in observed, concrete, sensory data and in human behavior. It presents a verbal model of these observations. Those who eschew
affect and detail will turn away from literature and towards philosophy. I
have recently observed two students who did just that. When literature
proved resistant to postmodernist abstract discourse, they became philosophy
majors. Those who love abstraction will not love literature or will convert literature into something that fits their tastes. But observation of discrete matter
and behavior is one distinguishing characteristic of literature. It is time for literary criticism to grow up and leave home. It has clung to its neo-classical
parents long enough. It must now create a home of its own, one made of
new combinations of old and new materials.

It is instructive to examine Stanley Fish's confession, the cry of the
magician who has surprised himself, "I have made the text disappear,"[4] in
the face of our daily experience of the pleasures of novel reading, our recall of
these experiences in astonishing detail, and our pleasure in sharing reading
as mutual experience and as confirmation of that experience. As readers who
know that we love particular books or poems, what are we to make of this or
of David Bleich's assertion that response is a "symbolic object,"[5] or of Jonathan Culler's tentative agreement with what he believes he finds in Empson:
"the poem offers a structure which must be filled up."[6] All this suggests that
notwithstanding the agreement that the text is not an object, or that some of
us have shifted our attention to the subject, i.e. the reader, abstract philosophic musings by critics have yet to find an epistemology, and therefore a
theory, that can move or help to move them out of subject-object or cause-

[4] Stanley E. Fish, "Interpreting the *Variorum*," in *Reader Response Criticism*, p. 183.

[5] David Bleich, "Epistemological Assumptions in the Study of Response," in *Reader Response Criticism*, p. 152.

[6] Jonathan Culler, "Literary Competence," in *Reader Response Criticism*, p. 113.

and-effect thinking to something that speaks to the reality of our encounter with imaginative language. Contemporary criticism evidently wants to leave its old dualism but it cannot find the way, or cannot find a way that does not lose faith in literature itself. When criticism abandoned its old humanistic territory it set out in search of a new absolutist refuge. It will never find this place, for it does not exist. Not only is the map not the territory, as Korzybsky pointed out long ago, but we don't have the right map because we don't know what we are looking for.

I want to suggest here that to get to new ground we will have to retrace our steps and then return with a new language, new to our discourse that is, one not based on the old Cartesian dualism and one not imprisoned in the metaphors of architecture–the structures, layers, containers, foundations, steps, doors and windows, edifices with which the discussion has so far been cluttered. This structural language, which persists even in poststructural discourse, inevitably reifies our percepts. We are *en route* to the novel as therapeutic experience, but to get there we must begin where the novel begins, in the fundamentals of language. The novel is simply one organization of language with certain properties. How it works rests on how language functions. Curiously, contemporary criticism seems disarmingly innocent of a knowledge of the recent thinking about language and brain function, of work in the fields of psychology, biology, physiology, neuroanatomy, and psycholinguistics. In literary criticism we may look in vain for Eric Lenneberg, Jerrie Levy, Karl Pribram, David Premack, Albert Bandura, Fernando Nottebohm, Robert Tees, Alexander Luria, Thomas A. Sebeok, Michael S. Gazzaniga, for example, all of whom have something to say to English scholars. In the realm of communication theory we do not teach Gregory Bateson, Paul Watzlawick and others; we do not teach systems theory as it applies to literature. What seems to have happened is that critics trained in an English/Philosophy/Religion matrix have recreated literature in their own image and thus the text is the center of ontological speculation. Even the Freudian psychoanalytic root, instead of following its pragmatic and experimental path as it did in psychology, branched off and was re-directed back into the stream of a philosophic mode, via Lacan and the swirling eddies of what I venture to call literary theology. "I have made the text disappear" is like a belated cry of "God is dead."

Let us look at a passage of remarkable confusion in which Stanley Fish, whom we know as a disciplined and persuasive critic, gives us a seminal insight into the kind of problem we have. Arguing that "the objectivity of the text is an illusion, Fish tells us that "kinetic art," being not static, escapes this illusion, "it makes inescapable the actualizing role of the observer." Since Fish does not illustrate this I do not know what he has in mind by kinetic art–ballet, movies, gymnastics? This is a telling omission; we will have to become less fuzzy if we are to get anywhere. Similar obscurity and imprecision persist when Fish continues, "Literature is a kinetic art but the physical form it assumes prevents us from seeing its essential nature...." He explains that "we" think of a book "as a stationary object" but we forget it was moving–"pages turning, lines receding into the past. . . ."[7] What was moving? How tangled even Fish's thought can become when his concepts about perception are not grounded in an appropriate paradigm! Fish has asserted the illusoriness of the text's objectness (rather than its objectivity, as he calls it) and then proceeds to lose himself in the very illusion he has described. This confusion of language with the sensory sources that lead to language is compounded even further by Fish's assertion that "literature is a kinetic art," because "pages turn" and "lines recede"–to use his astonishing phrases. Literature is not defined by pages, and it is eyes that move, not lines. A novel can be written on a wall, as Timothy Findley's *Famous Last Words* suggests.

What we need to learn from this is that we must acquire a more disciplined understanding and discourse for describing the characteristics of literature, its variant forms, and the human response to them. We will not further our discipline or our profession by chatting off the tops of our heads or avoiding hard questions. We have to begin, not end with, a theory. I don't want to argue with Professor Fish. I single out his remarks only by way of illustrating a professional problem. Literature has its origins in a phonetic code. Verbal language is primarily acoustic. Whether or how or if narrative "moves" seems less important to me than what neural processes we use in creating and apprehending it and to what purpose. What are the cognitive strategies that translate language into meaning? What is meaning in the language/information transaction? These are the sorts of questions we must address, along with our associates in other disciplines.

If we can hold onto narrative as sound we can perhaps escape this subject-object dualism, because we are not likely to think of sound as material. We need to think of the reading or story *process*. Thinking about sensory deception will inevitably confuse us as to the nature of literature; the neural activity that creates story is so complex and so little understood that our concepts and language will simplify and distort if we reify literature *even to deconstruct it*. This is what happened to Professor Fish. We do not think of story as object when someone tells one, or when we hear a radio play. In speaking of literature we must change from thinking of *works of art*, like sculptures, to thinking about information exchange. Language is not dependent on a material form, unlike the plastic arts where the matter and the information are inseparable. Language is a code, a sound notation system for recording responses to environmental and somatic experience. The neural modalities function differently in decoding verbal language and in assessing objects. The fact that we use hands in both reading by braille and exploring a statue does not mean the processes are the same. The novel is a concept or behavioral model somehow left in the mind through the agency of language. Language stays in short term memory only long enough to convey meaning which is remembered long after the language is forgotten.[8] A good question for us might be, what is left after the language vehicle is forgotten? I mention this to point to the ur-

---

[7] Stanley E. Fish, "Literature in the Reader: Affective Stylistics," in *Reader Response Criticism*, pp. 82 and 83.

[8] J. Sachs, "Recognition memory for syntactic and semantic aspects of connected discourse," *Perception and Psychophysics* 2 (1967): 437–41.

gency of shifting our thinking away from dualism and into process, system, and above all function. The novel is coded *experience*. As literary critics we will be obliged to enter fully the realm of theory and research as to those cognitive processes peculiar to the transmission and reception of language forms, if we are to survive as a credible discipline. We might as well get on with it.

The old humanistic criticism attributed absoluteness to literary information which it called "the text" or "work of art" as though the reader were not a function of the information. Rebellion against this has led to a great deal of nonsense. The value of literature is not diminished by understanding the reader's role in the feedback loop that is communication. Let us think of narrative as a form of language sound transmission constituting a coded experience of the total environment and capable of being integrated into an information store. Then let us acknowledge that human beings are primarily engaged in the business of survival: eating, begetting, staying warm, etc. In support of the survival process, language evolved, I believe, in the service of organizing, storing and using a sound code, as the most efficient system for the mapping of sensory data. Story is in turn the most efficient arrangement of that sound code. Robert J. Baron, describing a neural network model for natural language processing, proposes that "storage is the conversion of information from the temporal to the spatial domain, and recall is the conversion of information from the spatial back to the temporal."[9] I suggest that prior to storage encoding is the translation into temporal order (language) of spatial data. So we have the sequence: Sensory Experience (spatial ["S"]) › Language (temporal ["T"]) › Storage (spatial ["S"]) › Recalled (temporal ["T"])–S›T›S›T . . . in a series of embedded loops.

Language seems to be genetically authorized to code and store sensory data for communication in an extra-genetic information bank–a library. The more information the organism can store from experience, the better the chance of managing new information, both secondary and primary, on the principle of once bitten, twice shy. Ernst Von Glaserfeld asks us to see language as "purposive behavior."[10] This concept is important in getting critics back on track, in redirecting our attention to the value of our profession, *the study and use of literature being nothing less than the discipline attached to the most complex set of message formations created by our species*. Von Glaserfeld takes his model of language from cybernetics. Sensory data he calls a cluster of sensory signals in response to objects in the environment. To internalize this world, in my view to control it, we need a code, for instance naming. This code becomes equivalent to a representation, though it is not an isomorph in the brain. The concept of representation is metaphoric. Rather, the code is a secondary feedback loop, a series of activated pathways, to be used as a means of managing new first-hand experiences, percepts, so as to reduce their level

9 Robert J. Baron, "Brain Architecture and Mechanisms that Underlie Language: An Information-Processing Analysis," in *Origins and Evolution of Language and Speech*, ed. Stevan R. Harnad, Horst D. Steklis, and Jane Lancaster (New York: New York Academy of Sciences, 1976), p. 245.

10 Ernst Von Glaserfeld, "The Development of Language as Purposive Behavior," in *Origins and Evolution of Language and Speech*, pp. 212–26.

of disturbance to the experiencing, sensory organisms.[11] Story is to human beings what the pearl is to the oyster. It is active adaptation, fitting the environment to our processes–humanizing it. The "momentous step" as Von Glaserfeld calls it, is the human ability to create a mental model, a cluster of recorded signals no longer dependent "on signals in the channels of sensory perceptions." Von Glaserfeld points us to thinking of language as a tool for managing the environment, by analogue to the termite-fishing chimpanzees as filmed by Jane Goodall. The primate chooses a twig, not for its own sake, to chew on for instance, but for its virtues as a tool in a second, environment-controlling situation.

As Eric Lenneberg pointed out in 1967, naming or language response is not a signification of the data in the external environment, *but a coding of the mental registration of that data.* The word "tree" does not refer to an object, but to the conceptual categorization of tree-like objects in the mind of the tree-perceiver. This model applied to narrative means that story is always saying: "This is not how the world is, of course, but how I see the world." The reader then, in turn, does not describe what she/he reads "out there," but describes in "translation" his/her reading of the text or his/her own view of the world in relation to the world of the storyteller which has now modified the reader's version. The value of this process is precisely in its amplification of versions of shared experience of environmental data.

If critics have not sufficiently called upon the discipline and languages of neuropsychology, biology, systems theory, cybernetics and psychotherapy to help them, these disciplines have similarly so far failed for the most part to understand the power and significance of story in shaping human cognition. For if naming, and simple sentence structure, is a quantum leap in the evolution of human information processing, a natural outcome of such a process in the phylogeny of human beings is the power of narrative. Story is the primary postlinguistic device for organizing and storing important information. We story everything. Here we find the most sophisticated temporal sequencing, the primary characteristic of story and memory retrieval, of event, experience and sensory response. It is through story that we accomplish identity-formation, a never-ending process of writing and rewriting the story of our lives. As Sir Oliver Sacks so elegantly attests in his recent book on neural dysfunction:

> We have, each of us, a life-story, an inner narrative–whose continuity, whose sense, is our lives. It might be said that each of us constructs and lives, a 'narrative', and that this narrative is us, our identities.
>
> If we wish to know about a man, we ask 'what is his story–his real, inmost story?'–for each of us is a biography, a story. Each of us is a singular narrative, which is constructed, continually, unconsciously, by, through, and in us–through our perceptions, our feelings, our thoughts, our actions; and, not least, our discourse, our spoken narrations. Biologically, physiologically, we are

[11] For further discussion of the brain as a holistic, energy-exchanging process, see Karl H. Pribram, *Languages of the Brain: Experimental Paradoxes and Principles in Neuropsychology,* (Englewood Cliffs, N.J.: Prentice-Hall, 1971).

not so different from each other; historically, as narratives–we are each of us unique.

   To be ourselves we must have ourselves–possess, if need be re-possess, our life-stories.[12]

This story-identity of ourselves is the record of our relationship to the data of sensory experience. The most elaborate story of all, in our culture, takes the form of what we call the novel, a story that characteristically takes many hours to read. The novel tries to engage the reader affectively and invites imaginative role-play participation by presenting a fairly elaborate sequence of simulated life-experiences. The novel's code is available for decoding to those who have knowledge of the language being used, enough proximate memory of the sensory experience being described, and enough freedom from pathology to permit experience of the emotions that are targeted for arousal, for instance sadness, disappointment, joy, shame, nostalgia, lust, and so on. The novel is not available to someone blocked off from these and I would not prescribe it for such a person. A novel is a story, the reading of which creates for the reader the illusion of having lived through a period many times greater than the actual reading time and of having experienced a range of affect that would normally be experienced only over months or years of developmental time. Moreover, the novel elicits response by showing human feeling, thought, and behavior in relational contexts.

   The novel-reading experience can mediate between the reader's actual life experience, in relationships, career, physical environment, somatic reality, etc., and a simulated life that can be placed on a scale of very similar to utterly unlike. In the process of decoding the novel's representational code, the reader must necessarily undertake some form of life review, often unconsciously. Since most memory has some affective hook that keyed it into place, there is some necessary degree of evoked feeling in responding to the discoveries that the decoding entails. So we now have a model in which the novel's decoded life is reviewed and lived on one plane, as an acknowledged fiction, while the reader's own life record is reactivated for comparative or differentiated experience in the present. As a consequence of this, the linguistic experience of the novel is integrated into the story that is the reader's identity, which the novel modifies by forcing the existing system to accommodate it.

   There are many benefits potentially accruing from this re-cognition process, too many to describe in detail here, but some of them, stated briefly are: normalization, the power of fiction to overcome the isolation of traumatic life events and so produce a sense of not being alone in suffering; access to painful or uncomfortable experience, originating in the distant or recent past, a benefit particularly useful to someone who is blocking recall or examination of memory and is afraid of confrontation; new ways of looking at familiar

[12] Oliver Sacks, *The Man Who Mistook His Wife for a Hat and Other Clinical Tales* (New York: Summit, 1985), p. 105. For another version of story as identity formation, see the work of George A. Kelly, *The Psychology of Personal Constructs* (New York: W.W. Norton, 1955), and the more recent commentary on Kelly in James C. Mancuso and Jack R. Adams-Webber, eds., *The Construing Person* (New York: Praeger, 1982).

material, of reframing cognitive structures that seem fixed or hopeless; re-lief–sometimes called escape–from temporal and/or spatial entrapment, mak-ing possible the encounter with alternatives. Other therapeutic outcomes from reading fiction include the acquisition of information in greater volume and in more accessible and memorable storage form (by means of affective associa-tion) than from any other source, and the learning of new language to aug-ment the decoding system that is used in reading, so making possible more and more complex reading. Since it appears that the novel experience can be detached from and independent of the percept cluster that lies in its origin in the mind of the novelist, in other words we do not have to have had the same identical set of experiences to decode the record, the novel can be pro-cessed as a new experience for ourselves. All these benefits are greatly en-hanced if readers are encouraged to think of reading fiction as potentially use-ful, rather than as trivial diversion or cultural duty. This question of attitude is profoundly important and usually ignored.[13] I do not have space here to describe the concept of immunization by reading, based on Seligman's classic experiments that led to his concept of learned helplessness and the antidotes; nor to explain the relevance to literature of the cybernetic concept of feedfor-ward. I have no doubt, however, that literature can take its place in the fore-front of mental health treatment and preventive mental health care.

My own research strongly suggests that our educational, or critical teaching posture, has been to invite our population not to take reading seri-ously, to treat their reading as frivolous distraction rather than as life-giving experience or survival training. Bruno Bettelheim points out in his *Uses of En-chantment* the invaluable role of fairy tales in the cognitive lives of children. He maintains, and I agree with him, that simplifying and laundering chil-dren's literature will render it useless to them, worse than useless since its ir-relevance to them will breed a distrust of all reading and thus condition them aversively to the very resource that might assist their survival and enhance their lives. Much of what Bettelheim says of the fairy tale is equally valid for adolescent and adult literature and for what happens to students in our schools. Students and clients frequently tell me that they liked reading until they experienced the teaching of literature in high school. How much has English contributed to, or failed to prevent, the alarming dropout rate we are now witnessing?

We English professors are, I believe, in some obscure way, afraid of the power and relevance of literature. We are all a bit like the Lady of Shalott, unable or unwilling to see the continuity between art and life and afraid of participating in the continuum. Certainly it is true that shifting our focus to the life-experience of reading, to personalize and share literature in the class-room, will entail an encounter with feeling, with individuals. It will be harder to be remote and intellectual. It will be harder to hide. The teacher of litera-ture must become, not a professor of information, not a priestly custodian of one truth, not a resource–we have libraries for that–but a mediator, a live

---

[13] Cf. Joseph Gold and Fred Gloade, "Affective Reading and its Life Applications." Forthcoming in *The Arts in Psychotherapy*.

reading demonstrator, a facilitator of literary experience. Such facilitating skills as are necessary can be learned, and since most of us were taught nothing about method or process in teaching, we may have to overcome the erroneous conviction that we have nothing to learn. The Ph.D. program would have a very different look in a short time if we were to take these new directions seriously.

In short, our discourse about language, what we have called criticism, must continually remind itself that its goal is a return to the experience, in response to which the language, the signals comprising the poem or story, originated. The purpose of this return is to re-experience the map of the world that the novel provides in the service of our survival. The old humanism at least knew that the territory was the world in which we must find a way to be. This humanism operated in a Cartesian mindset which saw literature as the word of God, of truth, which the writer had somehow found in the world "out there." Posthumanist contemporary criticism has turned away from the world. The question is, are we going to continue bickering about how many novels can be written on the head of a pin, or are we going to address the reality of the novel as cognitive experience for readers? Our credibility, our very professional existence, rests on the answer to this question.

It is time to think of literature as our special human way of describing and organizing our relation to the world, the system of which we are part. The function of literature is to help us live safely, creatively, and communally. It is time for us to practice functional criticism, a criticism that explores the role of individual novels in individual and communal living, a criticism that will ask not what is it, but what does it do? Critics of the functional school will, as teachers, help to make novels available to all, enjoyable to all, and useful to all. They will teach the theory of the novel as therapeutic discourse and their research will explore the ways in which literature functions to help people. I like to think that day is coming when not only will critics encourage their students to write in the first person, but they themselves will acknowledge the truth that their truths are strategies of response arising from the stories of their own lives.

Beyond Fantasy: The Novel as Play

MURRAY SCHWARTZ

Let me begin by thanking Carol Singley for giving me an opportunity, a respite from administrative work–this is the first time I've thought in about three years. This has also been an opportunity to hear some of the thinking of Joseph Gold, with whom I find myself in a great deal of agreement, and whose talk is in many ways a kind of introduction, or in any case, overlaps with things I would like to say.

The first thing I thought when I saw the title of this panel, "The Novel as Therapeutic Discourse," was therapy for whom? The writing of a novel can, I believe, be a therapeutic process for a writer. I think of Sylvia Plath's writing of *The Bell Jar*, to take a relatively recent example, as at least temporarily a kind of therapeutic process which later on in her life became increasingly difficult and finally impossible because of her own complex relation to language. But what I'd like to talk about is the way in which there are therapeutic uses of novels for readers that may or may not be a parallel to the uses of writing novels for writers.

I want to start with a confession. I was trying to think of an example of how this process might have worked for me in my own history, and most of the examples I thought of came from my own adolescence, where I think novel reading begins for most people. I myself went from comic books to serious literature without any transition. I went from "Superman" to *Crime and Punishment*, as I think of it. When I was fourteen years old I confess I skipped a day of high school in order to read *Crime and Punishment*. In the last week I've been thinking about that. Why did I read *Crime and Punishment*? I do believe that was a therapeutic day, and I'm trying to understand why. Well, I read *Crime and Punishment*, now as I look back on it, for many reasons. It was probably quite an overdetermined day. There was some crime and punishment involved in the act itself. There was also a considerable amount of fantasizing going on. There was a lot of pleasure in the fantasy content of that book. There were a lot of powerful feelings, some of them murderous, and there were a lot of complex processes going on in me that had to do with being a fourteen-year-old. But now that I look back on it and try to understand a kind of abrupt transition from something much more directly the material of fantasy to a novel like *Crime and Punishment*–I think there was something else going on. There was a search of a kind going on that I found a field for and a response to in *Crime and Punishment*. That is to say I came away from reading that book and other big novels in those years with the sense that I had experienced not just an alternate world but one that was more vivid, more coherent, more real, than much of the actuality around me.

Now, one can get stuck in such a process. D.W. Winnicott, whom I'll talk about a little more in a few minutes, actually describes a young boy who could not stop reading–that is to say, this did literally become a substitute reality for him.[1] But as I remember this experience, it actually vivified my perception of family relations, relations with peers, the actuality that was there when I emerged from the reading experience. In other words, the novel became a very complex object–I use the word in the psychoanalytic sense–not simply a book, not simply a text, not simply language, but a much richer object in which I mixed a great deal of my own fantasy life and in which I found a kind of narrative holding environment which I could make use of. It was actually the total style of the book which created that sense of a vivid reality, something very hard to pin down by talking about particulars, a kind of coenesthetic experience that I'll refer to a little later on also.

The point I want to make is that the novel was a much more complex object than I had ever used in fantasy, in comic books, in other kinds of texts, and I think we use novels this more complex way. Observe people sometime in a bookstore. They're not relating to things. They're relating to complex interactions of their own inner life with the objects. You flip through it, you open it a little, you peek in it, you contemplate devouring it, you browse in it–the novel is a highly charged set of expectations before we even open it, before we read its title, before we decide whether or not certain fantasies will or will not be permitted, before we become voyeurs or secret sharers in its content. In other words, books are in many ways richly and sometimes very privately parts of our own object world, whether or not we immerse ourselves in the reading of them.

But when we do immerse ourselves in the reading of them, the more complex, potentially therapeutic process can occur. This comes from what I will call a deep rapport with the transformative potential of the narrative structure. Here I am borrowing language from a psychoanalyst, Christopher Bollas.[2] The experience, I think, is one of becoming the narrative structure itself. That is to say, self-consciousness is lost, we become merged with, absorbed in, a process in which we are in a sense distributed, in which our energies and perceptions and memories can be distributed. This is not a process Freud understood in his model of literary creation and response. The classic essay in 1908, "The Poet and Daydreaming," lays down its arms before the secret of the writer's *ars poetica*. Freud couldn't understand precisely this dimension, how the writer overcomes what he called a resistance to this merger, this distribution. And I think that's because Freud, despite his own discoveries, clung to a model of reality which placed play and daydreaming in opposition to some set of external definitions of the real, so that he could imagine the writer and the daydreamer and the playing child retrieving aspects of their own childhood, of their own prior experience, and synthesizing them in some way in the fantasy or the game or the text, but he could not imagine how this moved from one person to another, because for him the whole process was in opposition to what is real.

---

[1] D.W. Winnicott, *Playing and Reality* (London: Tavistock Publications, 1971).

[2] Christopher Bollas, *The Shadow of the Object: Psychoanalysis of the Unthought Known* (London: Free Association Books, 1987).

But consider daydreaming from a kind of phenomenological perspective as Roy Schafer has. The best discussion in all the psychoanalytic literature of daydreaming, I think, is in Schafer's *Aspects of Internalization.*[3] He says the common feature of all daydreams is not their content or the particular modes of fantasy that we make use of within them, but what he calls the suspension of reflexive self-representations. That is to say, as in a dream, we're not there when we daydream. We become the daydream. We do this every day. I sometimes think it's a main function of driving in America—so that people can daydream. But the function of the daydream is not merely to suspend reality-testing, to escape, although it does that among other things. It can also be to return to an external world, that is to say, a kind of inner reality testing goes on which enables a fresh perception of the world. I watch people do this in meetings all the time. It's one of the ways we survive meetings, at least in the administrative world. To put it dramatically, I think, in a sense we murder reality to recreate it by a process of daydreaming—that the daydream is a mode of interaction and not simply a mode of suspended participation in reality. This is something that Freud did not understand, though in a kind of paradoxical way, his own discoveries prepared the way for it.

A much richer idea has some of its classical statements in Winnicott's notion of playing, which is resolutely paradoxical. Winnicott clung throughout his writing to a paradoxical notion of playing, in which a choice between inner and outer reality was not to be made, was not being asked to be made. So that when we play we are not simply fantasizing. He reserved the term "fantasy" for a kind of reworking of already structured material. When we're playing, we're using fantasy, using memory, using every form of internal representation at our disposal, in order to reimagine or reshape or reengage the world. So that there is something beyond the suspension of normal reality testing involved here. There is a kind of in-mixing of self and other.

Let me come back to my experience of *Crime and Punishment.* I believe that in my discovery of the novel, what I had discovered was the aesthetic dimension of reading, the very suspension of boundaries which allows a return to the world in a vivified way. This is not only a function of the creation of characters, of plot, of narrative coherence—like the content of a waking dream—but has something to do with the ways in which these elements become a field of play, and evoke states of being that may be beyond particular memories, or may have something to do with the way memory works in the first place.

I think finally that that evocation of states of being, of affective states, is something that has its roots in preverbal realities to which we somehow find ways of attaching language or encoding narratives. There is not only an internalized anthology of possibilities here. I think one of the things that happens when we read or we learn to use literature, is that we do get this internal anthology, we get possibilities for character, for relations, and so on. But there's something beyond that content, a kind of shaping of states of being that al-

[3] Roy Schafer, *Aspects of Internalization* (New York: International Universities Press, 1968).

lows us not only to use style as a whole, but to evoke and remember very basic kinds of experience.

Recent research by baby-watchers, who are trying to use empirical means and the apparatus of experimental psychology to formulate the notions of emergent self in very early experience, prior to the acquisition of language, discover more and more how we seem to be innately amodal. That is to say, we can use one mode of experience, and the brain seems capable of translating it into another. To take a simple example, if an infant just a few weeks old tastes something without seeing it, the infant can identify it visually later on. That is to say, the taste, the shape in the mouth can be seen, can move from one mode of perception to another, and later on when these amodal, preverbal experiences become attached to language, they seem to become generalized in ways that a word or a phrase or a metaphor might encode, so that the acquisition of even a simple word carries with it a generalization of affective states that were experienced first in nonverbal or in other modes of perception.

Now when I'm talking about the evocation of states of being, that's what I'm referring to, something very fundamental, very basic, very absorbing, very important to remember or retrieve in the experience of reading narrative. This is a coenesthetic and not a diacritic process. It can give reading novels an important cultural and therapeutic dimension beyond their particular narrative uses. So when I read *Crime and Punishment* I felt understood in a way that went beyond the vicarious participation in the novel's fantasy life. This is something, I think, that continues throughout life, and is a way of becoming, by becoming distributed in the field of literary play.

Playing and Modernity

SUSAN RUBIN SULEIMAN

I. Prologue

You might be wondering why, in a session on "The Novel as Therapeutic Discourse," I am presenting a paper titled "Playing and Modernity." Could it be that I had just finished this paper when Mark Spilka called to ask me to participate in this session, and knowing that I wouldn't have time to write another, I proposed this one? While having the advantage of no-nonsense empirical fact, this explanation tells only part of the story. After all, I have other papers in my drawer that I did not propose. If this paper is in some immediate sense beside the point, it is so in a way that I would like to think of–nevertheless–as suggestive.

You notice that I have not invoked the idea of "play therapy," although it would be an obvious reference–an easy way out. But as an easy way out, it does not get us very far. For if reading (and writing) novels can be thought of as a form of play, and if playing is a form of therapy, the question still remains what the function and aim of such a play therapy might be. Do we read, and play, in order to "understand ourselves better," to find ourselves, to integrate the fragments of our lives into a harmonious whole? Or is the pleasure of the text, as Roland Barthes would have it, necessarily perverse, seeking not the integration and consistency of the self but its dissemination, its loss? And which self are we talking about–the writer's or the reader's? Is the writer's play the reader's play? Does it make any difference if one is a man, the other a woman? And if we want to write or speak about these questions, especially where modern texts are concerned–those which approximate that impossible ideal Barthes posited as *"le scriptible,"* the texts of *jouissance*–can we do so from a position safely outside, the position (let us say) of the adult, nonperverse therapist or analyst?

II. Theory

There is nothing quite like the idea of play to get us into a muddle.

Consider: Does all playing involve a game? Are all games playful? What's the difference between playing with and playing against? Playing at and playing on? Playing up and playing down, playing to and playing around? And what about "just playing?" Do all games have players? Does all play have players? Does the game stop if there is no one around to see it–or to play it?

Little wonder that, when trying to explain what he meant by a "concept with blurred edges," Wittgenstein chose the example of "game."[1] And that Gregory Bateson, a playful man, when faced with such questions, invented

---

[1] Ludwig Wittgenstein, *Philosophical Investigations*, trans. G. E. M. Anscombe, 3rd edition (Oxford: Blackwell, 1972), paragraphs 66–70.

the metalogue. "A *metalogue* is conversation about some problematic subject. This conversation should be such that not only do the participants discuss the problem but the structure of the conversation as a whole is also relevant to the same subject. Only some of the conversations here presented achieve this double format."[2] In Bateson's metalogues, the speakers are himself, the Father, and his daughter Catherine, the Daughter. The Daughter asks: "Daddy, why do things get in a muddle?" "Why do Frenchmen?" "Why a Swan?" "Daddy, are these conversations serious?" The Father answers, mostly, in one form or other. "What do you mean?" And then the conversation starts. How it ends, varies–never with an answer, though. And the metalogue on games and being serious ends with the Father replying, to the Daughter's question, "Why do kittens and puppies play?" "I don't know–I don't know."

Why is playing modern? Why is the modern playful? I don't know, I don't know. But the rules of the game we are playing now require that I speak for about twenty minutes, coherently if at all possible, and not waste time playing games. Therefore, with a lingering *au revoir* to the Father and his daughter (for I shall come back to them, you may be sure–and to the mother too, if she is somewhere to be found), I turn my discourse down a more disciplined and clearly laid out path.

That modern art and literature, and modern writing about art and literature, are centrally preoccupied with the question of play is a truism–which according to my dictionary is a statement so self-evident as scarcely to need to be stated. From Mallarmé's dice-throw in *Un Coup de dés* (which appears to be an obligatory reference point, if not necessarily a point of origin, for any discourse about the modern) through Surrealist parlor games, Oulipian exercises, Joycean punnings, Steinian button games, Beckettian endgames, Cooverian baseball games, Robbe-Grilletian mirror games, Borgesian labyrinths, Bataillean rituals, Barthian funhouses, *etcetera, etcetera*–modern writing is rife with play. Any thematics of modern writing must therefore be, at the same time, a thematics of play. So we may conclude. In its tidiest form, such a thematics is descriptive and classificatory. Bracketing the philosophical questions which might get it into a muddle, this tidy thematics (and by calling it tidy I am in no way suggesting that it is valueless–merely that it has the values proper to it, no loose ends) starts with questions it can answer by working at them. For example: How are games and playing thematized in literary texts? What are some specifically modern modes of such thematization? By looking at a great many different texts, or choosing a single writer whose work offers a particularly rich field for investigation, one can arrive at extremely interesting and potentially generalizable results. Thus, in a short essay on "Games and game-structures in Robbe-Grillet," published already some years ago, Bruce Morrissette suggested three different, mutually non-exclusive ways in which games are inscribed in Robbe-Grillet's fiction and films: the game as internal reduplication or *mise en abyme*, as for example the various games played

---

[2] Gregory Bateson, *Steps to an Ecology of Mind* (San Francisco: Chandler Publishing Company, 1972), p. 1. Bateson's metalogues are on pp. 3–58.

by the characters in *L'Année Dernière à Marienbad;* the game as "inner principles of organization left unrevealed to the reader," like the Tarot game which
(together with the Oedipus myth) structures but is never explicitly mentioned
in *Les Gommes (The Erasers)*; and the game as a metaphor or allegory for the
activity of writing, like the labyrinth pattern in *Dans le labyrinthe.*[3]

Although Morrissette did not attempt to generalize his observations or pursue them beyond the descriptive level (other than to say, in conclusion: "It
would be possible to argue that since Raymond Roussel the creation of novels
on game premises has given rise to certain tendencies in fiction leading away
from the 'serious' thematics ... associated with the novel in the mind of the
public"), I find his essay, even today, full of interesting implications. His
three categories, for example, can obviously be extended to works other than
Robbe-Grillet's. Georges Perec's extraordinary novel, *La Vie mode d'emploi*
(translated into English by David Bellos as *Life: A User's Manual*) uses the jigsaw puzzle as both a *mise en abyme* (the main character, one Percival Bartlebooth, literarily spends his life creating and unmaking puzzles) and as a metaphor for the kind of writing that Perec is practicing, as well as for one kind
of reading that his novel solicits. In addition to the jigsaw puzzle, which is
explicitly thematized and is accompanied by other explicitly thematized games
such as riddles, crossword puzzles, mathematical games, and so on, *La Vie
mode d'emploi* uses at least two systems of implicit formal constraints, modeled
on an expanded chessboard and on a complicated mathematical figure, the *bi-
carré latin orthogonal d'ordre 10*. For details on all this, I refer you to Warren
Motte's delightfully informative book on Perec, *The Poetics of Experiment.*[4] My
point here is simply that Morrissette's categories are applicable, and serve interestingly to order, many other texts besides Robbe-Grillet's.

Furthermore, these categories allow one to raise other theoretical
questions. For example, what is the role of the unstated "inner principles of
organization" in a reading of the text? Its role in the *writing* of the text is clear
enough, for it functions like any other formal constraint: it sets a "task" for
the writer's ingenuity to solve. Perec was notoriously fond of this kind of
game, and was diabolically clever at it; witness his "hypogrammatic" novel,
La Disparition, which in over two hundred pages of intelligible narrative never
once uses the most frequent vowel in the French language, the letter e. What
is almost unbelievable is that some of *La Disparition*'s first readers didn't
notice the disappearance in *The Disappearance*. Much more likely, however, is
that most readers of *La Vie mode d'emploi* would never notice, without being
told, the expanded chessboard structure and the "bi-carré latin orthogonal d'-
ordre 10." In *La Disparition*, I believe, a great deal of the reader's pleasure
consists in following–and admiring–*as one reads* the author's verbal resource-
fulness, his veritable *tour de force*. Therefore, not to notice the absence of the
E is to be deprived of an essential pleasure, and in fact no one nowadays
reads that book who doesn't already know, and enjoy, the game. In *La Vie
mode d'emploi*, however, I wonder whether a knowledge of the organizing

[3] Bruce Morrissette, "Games and Game Structures in Robbe-Grillet," *Yale French Studies* 41 (1968), 159–67.

[4] Warren F. Motte, Jr., *The Poetics of Experiment: A Study of the Work of Georges Perec* (Lexington, Ky: French Forum Publishers, 1984).

principles adds much to the actual pleasure of reading? I tend to think not, although I may be wrong.

That is the kind of question that we tidy thematicians savor. Here are a few more to sink our teeth into: Is the game of pebbles in Beckett's *Molloy* a *mise en abyme* or a metaphor for writing, or both? Ditto for the bullfight and the obscene games with eggs and bull testicles that the narrator plays with his friend Simone in Bataille's *Story of the Eye*. Should we distinguish between "primary" games and "secondary" games (like the puzzle versus other represented games in *La Vie mode d'emploi*) in our thematic readings? Are there comic versus tragic thematizations of play? For example, when Malone says, "Now it is a game, I am going to play," and soon after says "Now I have to play," and not long after that says "What tedium. And I call that play,"[5] is that progression comic or tragic–or is the question itself badly put? Besides being a metaphor for writing, can play also be a metaphor for living? Perec's Bartlebooth (whose name is itself a game, calling other texts into play: Parsifal, Bartleby, Barnabooth) dies while working on his 439th puzzle; Malone dies while spinning out his most ambitious piece of narrative invention–which is what he calls play–and so on. Finally, can we define criteria for distinguishing the *modern* "playful" text and modern thematizations of play from earlier ones (for obviously, thematization of play in literature is not a new phenomenon: cf. Rabelais, the *Grands Rhétoriqueurs*, as well as nineteenth-century realist fiction: *The Gambler*, etc.)? Might we say that it is the overdetermined *coexistence* of play as *mise en abyme*, as implicit organizing principle, *and* as metaphor for writing and/or living that is specific to modern texts? Or should we, in addition (or instead?) try to categorize and distinguish specifically modern kinds or clusters of kinds of games and playing: sado-erotic play (in which case our starting reference point would have to be not Mallarmé but the Marquis) and more generally playing as fantasy, or playing as free invention, as mastery, as mockery, as parody (which is a form of what Roger Caillois calls *mimicry*), as self-mutilation (which Bataille would call *"le jeu majeur"*), as transgression, as perversion, as *jouissance*, as "an absolutely de-centered game," as . . .

Hello, Mr. Bateson. I didn't expect to see you again so soon.

In other words, there is no such thing as an absolutely tidy thematics of play–or of anything else, probably. The very search for tidiness and no loose ends, if carried far enough, leads to the recognition of blurred edges.

But if that's the case, then we might as well have fun. Or as Barthes would say, we might as well take our pleasure wherever–and however–we can. I therefore offer a bit of conversation, in the spirit of Gregory Bateson doubled by that of (perhaps) Julia Kristeva.

---

[5] Samuel Beckett, *Malone meurt* (Paris: Editions de Minuit, 1951), pp. 9, 13, 25. Unless otherwise indicated, all translations from the French are my own.

III. Metapolylogue: On Playing and Modernity

FATHER, *reading aloud from a book*: "As has rightly been noted, girls' fantasy toys are meant to imitate local, domestic, realistic behavior, whereas those for boys evoke activities that are faraway, fantastical, inaccessible or even downright unreal."[6]

Enter DAUGHTER.

DAUGHTER: Daddy, when I play at being Mommy, am I serious?
FATHER: I don't know, dear. Are you?
DAUGHTER: It depends. If I'm telling my doll to do her homework or to wash her hands before dinner, then yes, I'm very serious. But if I'm tickling her to make her laugh, then I'm joking.
FATHER: I see. And what happens when I tell you to stop playing and come help me take the garbage out?
DAUGHTER: Daddy, don't be dumb. Then we're working.
FATHER: But don't we sometimes have fun–like when I bang the lids together and you go Oompa–Ooompa–Oompapa?
DAUGHTER: Yes, but then we're playing.
FATHER: Oh, I thought we were taking the garbage out.

Enter the Mother, disguised as GEORGES BATAILLE, bearing a plate of bull testicles.

"BATAILLE": "Reason . . . is the opposite of play. It is the principle of a world which is the exact opposite of play: that of work."
DAUGHTER: Who is that?
FATHER: Why, I think it's your . . . It's a famous author, who is dead. You'll read him when you get older.
"BATAILLE": "An authentic game demands such an unleashing of violence that the aspect of play, which seduces, is not immediately visible in it: on the contrary, it is terrifying, and ravishes only in horror."

Exit "BATAILLE."

DAUGHTER: Daddy, I don't think I like that man. What was he carrying?
FATHER: Eggs. But where were we?
DAUGHTER: I forget. Daddy, what did he mean, that a real game is terrifying? Is it sort of like a roller coaster, when you're scared to death but still want to do it?
FATHER: Yes, sort of like that. Except he meant *real* death, I think, not just fooling.
VOICE OF "BATAILLE," *offstage*: "Frazer tells the story of a king of the province of Quilacare, in Southern India: '. . . This province is governed by a king, who, from one jubilee to the other, has only 12 years to live. . . . At the end

---

[6] Roger Caillois, *Les Jeux et les hommes* (Paris: Gallimard, 1967), p. 62n.

of the 12 years, an immense crowd assembles.... The king has a platform built, covered with silken coverings.... He mounts the platform; and before the assembled crowd takes sharp knives and starts to cut his nose, his ears, his lips, his members and as much flesh as he can ... until finally he loses so much blood that he begins to faint. At that point, he cuts his throat.' I doubt that I can cite an example of a game played more sovereignly and more extremely...."[7]

DAUGHTER: Daddy, I'm scared.

FATHER: Don't worry, dear. He was only talking. He died in his bed, like a good bourgeois.

DAUGHTER: What's a good bourgeois?

FATHER: Hm ... let's see. It's somebody who takes himself very seriously.

DAUGHTER: You mean, he doesn't play?

FATHER: Well, he does–but only at certain times and in certain places. He wants to draw the lines very clearly, you see–everything in its place.

DAUGHTER: Oh, then he's tidy. Like me. I like things in their place.

FATHER: Yes, I guess you do. In a way, we all do. Why do you think that is?

DAUGHTER: I dunno. It's kind of ... safe, you know? I feel ... all mixed up inside when I'm in a messy place, almost as if I didn't know who I was.

Enter JACQUES DERRIDA and the Mother disguised as D. W. WINNICOTT, riding bicycles.

"WINNICOTT": "The searching for the self can come only from desultory formless functioning, or perhaps from rudimentary playing, as if in a neutral zone. It is only here, in this unintegrated state of the personality, that that which we describe as creative can appear."[8]

DERRIDA: "There are thus two interpretations of interpretation, of structure, of sign, of freeplay. The one seeks to decipher, dreams of deciphering, a truth or an origin which is free from freeplay and from the order of the sign.... The other, which is no longer turned toward the origin, affirms freeplay and tries to pass beyond man and humanism, the name man being the name of that being who, throughout the history of metaphysics ... in other words, through the history of all of his history–has dreamed of full presence, the reassuring foundation, the origin and the end of the game."[9]

DAUGHTER: What were they saying? They went by so fast I couldn't hear.

FATHER: Me neither. Something about a reassuring foundation and the end of the game.

DAUGHTER: Well *I* never like to stop playing, even if it's my bedtime.

FATHER: Which it soon will be, I'd like to remind you.

---

[7] Georges Bataille, "Sommes-nous là pour jouer ou pour être sérieux?," *Critique* no. 51–52 (1951), 736, 740, 742–43.

[8] D. W. Winnicott, *Playing and Reality* (New York: Basic Books, 1971), p. 64.

[9] Jacques Derrida, "Structure, Sign, and Play in the Discourse of the Human Sciences," in *The Structuralist Controversy*, ed. Richard Macksey and Eugenio Donato (Baltimore: Johns Hopkins University Press, 1972), pp. 264–65. (Name of translator not given).

DAUGHTER: I know I know, but this is fun. Daddy, do you believe in God?

FATHER: Hm ... sometimes. Sometimes when something terrible happens, I say "Dear God, please help me."

DAUGHTER: Yes, but that doesn't count. I mean, every day all day long. Did God create the world? Does he know what we're doing? Is he behind it all?

FATHER: You are asking very difficult questions today. To tell you the truth, I don't know. I rather doubt it, though.

DAUGHTER: If you believed in God, would you be more sure about things? I wish you wouldn't say "I don't know" so often!

FATHER: Aha, you want me to be strict and stern and lay down the law? Up to bed you go, then!

DAUGHTER: No. I like you just the way you are, Daddy. But sometimes I feel it would be nice to be certain of things–what's good and what's bad, what everything *means* when you really get down to it.

Enter ALAIN ROBBE-GRILLET, carrying a pack of what appear to be oversized playing cards.

ROBBE-GRILLET: "What is called serious, what is upheld by values (work, honor, discipline, *etc.*) belongs ... to a vast code, situated and dated, outside of which the idea of depth loses all of its meaning; the serious supposes that there is something behind our gestures: a soul, a god, values, the bourgeois order ... whereas behind the game, there is nothing. Playing affirms itself as pure gratuitousness."[10]

DAUGHTER: Could you say that again, sir? It sounds interesting.

ROBBE-GRILLET: Yes, my charming girl–I'll be happy to explain. You see, each one of us plays a game with the cards they've got–like these in my hand. "In themselves they have no meaning or value, but each player will give them meaning, his own, by arranging them in his hand and then throwing them on the table according to his own ordering, his own invention of the game that's being played."[11] That's what I call freedom.

He throws a card on the table: it is a still photograph from Robbe-Grillet's film, Glissements progressifs du plaisir, *showing a beautiful young girl tied eaglespread to a bed, naked, with blood running down her legs. The DAUGHTER looks at the picture, then jumps back in surprise and fright.*

ROBBE-GRILLET: Don't be frightened, my dear. It's only make-believe–see, that's red paint we smeared on the legs of the actress. Remember, there's nothing behind this, it's only me playing.

[10] Alain Robbe-Grillet, in discussion recorded in *Nouveau Roman: hier, aujourd'hui*, Direction: Jean Ricardou, Françoise Van Rossum-Guyon, vol. 1 (Paris: Union Générale D'Editions, 1972), p. 127.

[11] Unnumbered text inserted as a separate *"prière d'insérer"* in Robbe-Grillet, *Projet pour une révolution à New York* (Paris: Editions de Minuit, 1970). The passage quoted is on the last page.

FATHER, *steering him toward the door*: Monsieur, I admire your work. Someday I'll explain it to my daughter. For now, *au revoir*.

Exit ROBBE-GRILLET

DAUGHTER: Daddy, you didn't have to make him go. I was scared at first, but then I saw it was just pretending. He was kind of nice, Monsieur Robbe-Grillet.
FATHER: Yes, he's charming.
DAUGHTER: Daddy, do you ever dream of tying girls to a bed?
FATHER: ——
DAUGHTER: You can tell me, I know you'd never do it for real.
FATHER: There are some things we'll talk about when you get older. Now it's time for you to go to bed, young lady. Off with you!
DAUGHTER: Goodnight, Daddy.

She kisses him and starts to leave the room. Just then, a soft knocking is heard at the door. The FATHER goes to open, and the DAUGHTER stops to see who is there. In the doorway stands the Mother, disguised as ROLAND BARTHES.

"BARTHES": Good evening. May I come in?
FATHER: Monsieur! Why, of course. I am delighted to see you again. (*To DAUGHTER*): Come here, dear. I want you to meet an old teacher of mine, who was very important in my life. (*To BARTHES*): Monsieur, this is my daughter.
"BARTHES": I am pleased to meet you, my dear. (*To FATHER*): Forgive me for coming unannounced. I could not help overhearing your conversation with Robbe-Grillet. He and I were good friends, you know. I wrote about his very first books, back in the structuralist days. A very writerly writer.
FATHER: Yes, I remember.
"BARTHES": We did not see eye to eye on everything, of course. Especially about the body of the mother. I never understood why he was so intent on attacking it–for you agree, do you not, that playing with the female body is always, in the end, playing with the body of the mother?
FATHER: Yes. But Monsieur, do you remember the famous sentence you wrote, which has so often been quoted: "The writer is someone who plays with the body of his mother"?
"BARTHES": Ah, yes. "No object is in a constant relationship with pleasure. For the writer, however, this object exists: it is the *mother tongue*."
FATHER: "The writer is someone who plays with the body of his mother: . . . in order to glorify it, to embellish it, or to dismember it, to take it to the limit of what can be known about the body. I would go so far as to take *jouissance* in a *disfiguration* of the . . . "[12]

___

[12] Roland Barthes, *Le Plaisir du texte* (Paris: Editions du Seuil, 1973), pp. 60–61.

"BARTHES": Hm ... Yes, I did write that. But it was not my last word. As you know, I was very attached to my mother. Do you remember what I said in my inaugural lecture at the Collège de France? "I would therefore like the speaking and listening that will be woven here to resemble the comings and goings of a child who plays around his mother, leaving her and then returning to her to bring her a pebble, a piece of yarn, thus drawing around a peaceful center a whole area of play ... "[13]

FATHER: Yes, that was very beautiful. I was very touched by that image–the mother as peaceful center, a necessary still point around which the child weaves his play. But tell me, did you ever imagine the mother moving, joining in the play?

"BARTHES": Hm ... to tell you the truth, that thought never occurred to me.

FATHER: As I recall, you said in that same lecture: "Only the son has fantasies. Only the son is alive." Of course you meant in opposition to the Father, who is always dead. . . .

"BARTHES": Yes–the symbolic Father. The Father who stands for the Law.

FATHER: Yes, I know. I suppose you also meant that the daughter is alive, the daughter also plays.

"BARTHES": Yes–yes, of course. Now I really must be going.

Exit "BARTHES"

DAUGHTER: He didn't say goodbye to me. Daddy, is fantasy play? I have lots of fantasies!

FATHER: Yes, dear, I know you do. Monsieur Barthes didn't mean to exclude you–he just didn't think of it.

In the meantime, the Mother has come in, still carrying her Roland Barthes mask.

MOTHER: That's why we have to think of it for ourselves!

The daughter sees her, understands the game, and starts to laugh. They are all laughing now; hugging each other, they start to dance around the room to the strains of the Blue Danube Waltz. Offstage, a chorus of women's voices, including those of Luce Irigaray, Hélène Cixous and Julia Kristeva, is heard chanting.

CHORUS:
    Revise, re-view
    To see things anew
    Teach the daughter to play
    Imagine the mother playing.

---

[13] Roland Barthes, *Leçon* (Paris: Editions du Seuil, 1978), pp. 42–43.

Discussion

SINGLEY: Well, we made good on our promise, we have time to play with some of the insights our speakers have given us, and they're now willing to answer questions. Yes?

ALTIERI: That's an impossible act to follow so I have a rather hostile question as the only way to reenter the discourse. I'm struck by how much philosophy occurs in Professor Gold's talk, and I want to raise some questions in relation to that. I'd cite, for example, three statements: "Critic's truths are opinions arising from stories of personal history"; ... second, "Critics are afraid of continuity between art and life"; and third, "Literature is not experienced as philosophy but appears to be rooted in observation of discreet matters of behavior." I want to ask one question about each of those statements. They're fairly brief. First of all, is it conceivable that the philosophical notion of truth could be a way to negotiate between stories of our lives, or at least that might be its presumed social role? Second, if one takes the nature of "appear" seriously in the quotation about "literature not experienced as philosophy but appears to be ..." *etc.*, then doesn't there have to be some framework of discourse about what drives those appearances? That is, on the one hand, some kind of sociological discourse which might, for example, notice the history of the ideological use of experience as you used it and as British criticism has used it all through the twentieth century. Or on the other hand something that worries about warrants and ways of engaging and judging experience, that is, thoughts about the reflective processes that it seems to me have to be a part of that reading activity. And finally, the notion of critics being "afraid of life" seems to me to reintroduce a kind of hierarchy of attitudes based on a model that denies that hierarchy. I would like you to respond to that and ask what kind of discourse within *your* discourse allows the correction of that kind of really arrogant and pompous usurping of a moral standard in terms of critical work. If you could make it playful I would love it!

GOLD: Could I make it brief, too? I don't know how to engage so much material as you raised there, but I suppose if one presses far enough then philosophy covers all our discourse and ... if pushed to some wall that I dislike, yes, I suppose all of our dialogue is in a sense philosophic and all disciplines stem from that kind of discourse about the significance of what we're doing. But I dislike what I am calling "philosophy" in the sense of that kind of discipline which discusses ideas removed from the reality of individual life-responses that are not always filtered through a thoughtful process. And I don't think it's arrogant to say this. I mean, I've paid my dues, I've done all the criticism that was required, and I published the things that were *au fait* at the time that they were *au fait*. But it seems to me that now we have to hear what people say about their actual experiences directly; and that the way in which ... a story in process works *does* engage some understanding of a kind of system, using systems theory, of very complex interactions with each other and the environment. We are not fixed entities and we are continuously in the process of exchanging moments and developments from the encounter with time and space. So, to put it very simply, my butcher reads novels–he told me when I was buying meat. He took me to one side and he said–after he read something in the local paper about something I said about literary theory–he said "I read novels, you know." And I said, "Great. What are you reading?" And we had a little chat at the side of the shop while people were buying coldcuts and I would never have heard that had I not started to engage in some sort of public dialogue about the validity of the reading process without a hierarchy of museum pieces and university approved material. There are millions of closet readers and they are not from my point of view philosophers and they are not engaging in philosophy.

SCHWARTZ: I must say I feel my own position comes close enough to that of Joseph Gold that I am very anxious to dissociate myself from him. What worries me in what you've said–though it was very eloquent–was essentially that your making the novel into therapeutic discourse makes the criterion for the novel "what is good for us." I think first of all that represses a long tradition of dissent, of literature which is black in its statement. Does *Crime and Punishment* really act as therapeutic discourse if one takes the issue it raises seriously? The distinction between the position you're taking and the one Dr. Altieri was just suggesting is that in order to move from therapeutic discourse to something usable one has to pass through a cognitive stage. One has to turn therapeutic discourse into cognitive discourse so that it is sharable and so that one can analyze it other than in terms of feeling good. It seems to me this is where what you propose is in fact dangerous, because it sets up cognitive discourse and reasoned discrimination.

GOLD: Well, I'd like to respond to that. There is a discipline, a very demanding discipline of personal response. Perhaps more demanding than the particular game of learned strategies that we are used to in some of our critical discourses. Of course, there is a cognitive process that has all kinds of levels of development depending on the nature of the reader's learning, and whether we talk about discriminating readers or informed readers. There's reading in all kinds of ways and of all kinds of materials, and obviously people will try to make sense of what they read, and they do that, they do not merely feel–I'm not suggesting in the brief time that I took that merely granting approval is sufficient in response to understanding how a piece of reading illuminates one's own experience or integrates with it as a language code....
Of course people have to make sense of what they read. My students say that to write coherently about their real personal understanding of experience of the material that we deal with is the hardest thing they have ever had to do, and they would in some cases rather revert to the playing of a game that was familiar to find out what would please the particular professor. It is very difficult if you say what pleases me is to hear what you have to say about your own response. They find they're not trained to do that in our school system in Canada. They're trained by people who were trained in New Criticism. So

I'm not clear, really, where the danger is because this does not lead to anarchy or to casualness. It leads to the most serious kind of engagement with material that is useful. I confess I do not really understand what is tainted about the notion, what is disfunctional about the idea, that fiction is useful. It seems to me *that* really is the ultimate criterion for the validity of the art that we take seriously. Our credibility, may I add, depends precisely upon our willingness to say that what we do is useful, and that the literature we read is useful. Until we say that, I think we're going to have a real problem communicating with the rest of our culture. We can easily dispense with ourselves, we can wash ourselves right off the educational map, if we don't engage with the issue of the utility of what we do.

SCHWARTZ: I also want to comment about a possible misunderstanding that can come from the title of this panel, the therapeutic uses of the novel. It's easy to think of the kind of broad, adaptive function of reading as a form of social adjustment: that is to say, people learn how to cope better, they learn how to identify themselves better, they get in touch with themselves, and so on. I'm not too interested in that. That does go on, and it's one of the uses one can make of stories or narratives of all kinds. What I was trying to get at when I talked about evoking states of being is something that may not be very socially acceptable at all. It may be at times very profoundly subversive of social arrangements. It's not a question of feeling good, it's a question of feeling real. It's a question of engaging in certain experiences of self-transformation that may be profoundly antagonistic to social arrangements.

SULEIMAN: That is what I wanted to say, too. It's one thing to say that literature is useful, that reading novels is useful, but as I tried to suggest in the very brief opening section of my paper, that still leaves open every important question. Useful for what? What does it mean to be useful? What kind of use? What is the aim of this kind of system? If you just wanted to derive some sort of self-help thing, you don't really need to read novels. You could pick up a million books that are all best sellers on all the shelves–*How to Save Your Own Life*–well, that's a novel. But anyway, the point is that all of the really significant questions are begged by suggesting–I'm not saying that what you said was not useful, all I'm saying is after what you said one still has to ask a whole lot of other questions which I think are extremely important.

QUESTIONER: Dr. Suleiman in her prologue explicated Bateson's notion of discourse in a certain way. I'm intimidated by the cluster of primary activities, namely ridicule, hostility, aggression, denunciation, she finds in highly structured play forms, especially as applied to Bataille and Barthes.

SULEIMAN: Did you feel that it was aggressive and hostile? Oh, no. Barthes is one of my all-time intellectual heroes, and I thought that what in fact I was doing–it's called a metapolylogue–is something that Barthes was trying to do all his life, which was in a sense to write a novel. He didn't think he was doing it, and then Robbe-Grillet said, "But you have written a novel, it's all your work." So it seems to me if you interpreted it in a very aggressive and hostile way, that would be interesting to discuss.

DANIEL SCHWARZ: I'd like to thank Susan Suleiman a lot [and address another question to Joseph Gold]. Could you give us an example of exactly how you would proceed with therapeutic reading? Specifically, as something of an Aristotelian, I wonder how you are able to describe what happens to the reader without rhetorical and linguistic terminology that describes the structure of effects. It seemed at least in your abbreviated version you were moving directly to cosmic theory and behavioral descriptions but without the transactional language.

GOLD: That gives me an opportunity to say something in response to Susan. . . . How did I get to this point in my life through the whole system of education and not really come to grips, or be invited to come to grips, with this issue of the validity of fiction and reading and literature in my and others' and my peers' and fellow students' personal lives? I agree with you there are a lot of important questions still to be answered. But we are going across a bridge here to the notion that literature is somehow intimately to be applied to people's experiences outside of the reading. In the study of literature that is part of my educational understanding—and I teach in the same places as the rest of you, I teach in universities and English departments—there has not been the pattern of dialogue or the interest of discourse between professors and students or professors and each other. That may have been the private agenda for reading that they kept by the bedside table. But it's not what they brought to the classroom. That distance between those two kinds of experiences is what I'm trying to address now. So yes, useful for what; useful in ways of seeing. In therapy, the goal is change. Literature as reframing experience is an absolutely crucial tool. I must say that I do not agree that other kinds of writing will serve the purpose that literature serves. When you say pick up thousands of self-help books—they do not aim to be affective, they aim to use a language that is deliberately designed to be nonaffective. They want to be as much like scientific discourse, as mathematical, if you like, as possible. They want to shed affect and the evocation of feeling very often. The peculiar attributes of literature are that it is memorable as experience because it has its own special techniques for hooking into shared affective history, and certainly these are the questions we should be researching: what the difference is between visual media and reading media, and how we store one set of information as opposed to another set of information, in intermodal structures. So your question about how we do it in dialogue is, in a practical case, you mean, how would I work with an individual? By asking someone to read something that somehow had been suggested to me in an explicitly therapeutic situation, suggesting a reading that occurred to me when doing an assessment, or in the course of treatment or making a profile of a situation as experienced in his life or her life by the client, and I say, "You know, that reminds me of a story," and I suggest it. Then we talk about the reader's experience of the story in whatever terms the reader chooses. It's not a teaching situation; it's a sharing situation.

SCHWARZ: Well, is it applicable though . . . ?

GOLD: I think it is applicable to a teaching situation because we are asking students to consult an affective response as part of the information they have for understanding. It is we who have taught about the separation of an intellectual kind of process from a feeling response. But, I mean, my dog has no problem with this. The feeling response is a source of information. When it hears footsteps on the path, it gets agitated and barks. That's telling it something very important. We all knew that it was somehow important when we cried or laughed at reading, but did we use it as information? No, we never talked about that in the classroom. I never heard one professor while I was doing my doctorate talk about his own feelings about the literature. Never. And I did a Ph.D. . . .

SULEIMAN: I've been thinking of the reading of the gentleman who asked the question about interpreting this as very, very hostile. If you take Bateson's notion of the metalogue seriously, in other words a conversation whose very structure has something to do with the problem at hand, and what a muddle it is, I cannot say that I'm ridiculing or opposing any single one thing. I'm merely trying to problematize a certain number of notions. For example, I would not even be against the idea of suggesting that one of the ways in which you can teach the daughter to play is not to play with dolls and just normalize and integrate herself into the everyday world. . . . You know, girls play safe, good little homey games and boys play far-away fantastical games, Cowboys and Indians or whatever. I would say that one of the ways I would want to put things into movement would be to allow girls to play–even in violent ways–ways that we don't think of as "feminine" at all. But at the same time, it's not that I want the daughter to totally play out the Robbe-Grillet fantasies either. I appreciate the way you put it. All I would have right now would be suggestions for what one might do to dislodge certain notions that have not been helpful, such as the idea of the daughter playing with dolls, and only that way to become normalized in a very narrow way to become a mother, and the idea of the mother as the center around which–and I was really astonished that that passage is so poetic and beautiful, that text of Barthes, because it obviously is only when you look at it in a certain way that it suddenly reveals the problem. On the one hand it's a very beautiful text, envisaging the child playing while the mother is the peaceful center. But then what happens? In a way I want to be able to move that mother and one of the ways she can move is by first of all endorsing all kinds of mimicry or trying on [of] different roles. It doesn't mean that's her last vision, but at least let her get out of that sort of madonna position of sitting there while all the world goes by her and pays homage to her. So I certainly do appreciate the question. I wish I had a positive answer.

QUESTIONER: I had this feeling as you talked, it's very difficult, I don't mean just for women writers but for all of us, to do what you are striving to do. That is to say, to actually reach that next stage in which one can engage the mother as an actor in the playful scene; it's in some ways very threatening to us. We should ask why that is.

SINGLEY: We know there's a difference in gender in reading, but we're only exploring the beginning levels of those differences. In the same way I would suggest with class and different types of orientation.

SCHOLES: Weren't you playing?

SULEIMAN: Yes, and I've been mother, too.

DIANE ELAM (Brown graduate student, to Gold): You accuse the New Critics of being amateur scientists, and then you accuse many literary critics today of being amateur philosophers. I think you yourself could be accused of being an amateur systems theorist. I wonder if you would comment briefly on what you think is the status of these categories of professional and amateur, and if there is a therapeutic discourse involved here.

GOLD: It's a very difficult question. It's a dangerous game. I'm grateful to New Criticism. It trained me to take texts seriously. But I guess I've become really frustrated and see great danger in some of the dialogue, some of the writing that's taking place in what's been called modernist criticism. I think it's hard to follow; I think it's obscure; I find it unrelated to the discourse of ordinary daily life and I guess it's that people trained in a whole variety of fields—most of these people work with literature mostly, and they drop into a kind of discourse. People are doing it now at younger and younger ages. It seems to be something people with graduate degrees in English have learned to be able to do very quickly. That's what you were saying this morning, Murray. I just find it a very dangerous trend and I want to talk [instead] about ways to read that you can identify with in experience. It seems to me to learn it off the top is not authentic somehow. I guess I'm just trying to express that, and I would defend myself on the grounds that the discipline of family therapy as practiced now in North America, the American Association of Family Therapists of which I'm a member, is a systemic based on Gregory Bateson's work with communication theory. It really is a discipline of systems theory. I think I've read just about everything I can find in systems theory.

LANGBAUM: I'm addressing Joseph Gold here. I actually approve of what both you and Murray Schwartz are saying. I think it's time that literature be brought back into real life. I think you're both talking about why we all began reading novels in adolescence. I think of course that explains particularly the adolescent influence. Not only is the adolescent interested in working on his own fantasy but also in finding out about things. He's exploring novels to find out about sex, or to find out how the other half lives. But it's just because I do approve—and also I like the fact you've delivered us from the claustrophobic cloud of language—it's just because I'm so interested that I'd still like to bring up some questions that require the spirit to be corrective in practice. I think of two things. One, it seems to me [that] you have ignored the question of genre, as a part of decoding in literature. I have a perfect example. I was on an M.A. oral just before I left. We were talking about E.M. Forster's *Where Angels Fear to Tread* and the candidate was carrying on about the psychology and the sexual problems and so on, and I said, "I would never know from what you were saying this is a howlingly funny novel." Now once you talk about that, then you realize that ... you don't want a way to heaven. You realize that the psychology is deliberately thin. You realize that in a comic novel too much projection is not wanted. That strikes me as one kind of question you have to take into account. Another question would be, how do you raise the level of discourse? It's easy enough to say ... it gives a picture of the way, it shows just the way you feel. Somehow you have to get your students to talk a little more interestingly than that. I had a perfect example of this situation when I had a paper in an undergraduate course and the boy very, very frankly said, I have just learned that I have diabetes. I am making an adjustment to this, and therefore I'm finding in this novel ... an amazing message to me about my problem. Well, the boy, of course, was misreading the novel entirely. There was no message at all. Those are the dangers. I think you have to try to work if you're going to use your method, you have to try to modify to work out those questions.

SINGLEY: I'd like to ask a question that may not be able to be answered quickly, but are we working with the notion of discovery of the self, that is, the assumption of the whole self, which it seems to me that Murray Schwartz and Joseph Gold help us toward, or are we working with the notion of the creation of the self by different means which strikes me as what Susan Suleiman's work about gender and representations leads us toward? Does it make any difference for our use of fiction in therapeutic discourse?

SCHWARTZ: When I pointed to the paradoxical dimension of playing I was trying to briefly indicate that under certain reading conditions when we're absorbed in a novel, that's not a real question, that is to say, if we need to differentiate between the discovery and the creation themselves we are already in a different state of being. In the play state, that question is suspended; that's a paradoxical state of being. I think a part of the answer to the question has to do with teaching. I was describing reading experience; that's not the same as teaching literature, and I think that in teaching literature we do something beyond that that can, but doesn't necessarily, connect with it. We can make connections between the actual states of being experienced in the reading of a novel of one kind or another, or the reading of one genre or another, and its actual structure, content, and language can become very intellectual, abstract in ways that are good and bad, well done or poorly done. I wouldn't want to rule out any of that. I think the important thing in the teaching of literature is to make the connection and say "what does this state of being have to do with what we identify and talk about and learn the history of when we teach literature?" So there is an added dimension which is potentially continuous with that experience, but they are not automatically the same thing.

GOLD: Well I would just endorse that response and say that it is not my concept nor my intention to suggest that a shift to an additional dimension or activity will lead to a displacement of all interest in the history of literature or in the influences of literature, the development of language in all kinds of forms and genres and so on. What interests me very much is the kind of question that Susan suggested when she said there is the question of books that are helpful but are not literature. It's those kinds of distinctions, not just a matter of impressions. It's something we can find out about the very structure of the language chosen in such texts, in the use of language for those texts, the differences between poetry and prose and the amount of lexical reference there is. Is there a code difference there that needs to be explored–some sort of investigation as to how people respond to these different things? I think our discipline needs to get into those sorts of questions. Music is a code without a lexicon, therefore is it in fact referential to anything? If so, to what? I'm interested in those questions. I think we are going to have to address questions about the difference between reading and watching television and images of various kinds. I think the situation–I don't know–we're very calm here. Have you noticed how we can hold conferences about these issues and be very calm? It seems to me that this is a critical issue for our time. We are an endangered species. I'm really concerned about this question whether people can continue reading. I take [Ray Bradbury's] *Farenheit 451* seriously. I'm not crazy to think there is a danger to our cultured civilization in this matter. I think it's a matter of great import, and therefore I say we need to address all those questions that will help us say to the rest of the world we are specialists in something, we care about reading, and really believe it's seminally important and central to a developing and free democratic culture. That's where I'm trying to move somewhat.

SULEIMAN: If you're going to talk about reading as therapy then I think you must be misreading, that is to say, in a therapeutic contact, or a personal contact, I don't see how one can speak about misreading. Everybody gets what they can, or what will be "useful" to them and how you move from that to a classroom exam situation is another problem.

GOLD: Except that what I would think if the reading moves so far away from a common area of language understanding of the text, it doesn't appear to have the same reference at all to what I've read, then I think I'm getting near the pathology, and I say this is psychopathic.

SULEIMAN: Is it sort of like when Proust says in the beginning of *A la recherche du temps perdu* that sometimes he would wake up in the middle of the night and think that he was a string quartet or an article that he was reading?

SCHWARTZ: I just wanted to say that I'm worried about books disintegrating because of acid, but I'm not worried about reading. I think there's more reading going on, that visual media do not necessarily contradict reading. If you look at the history of new technology–even over the last 150 years, to say nothing of the last two thousand years–there isn't much evidence that new technology has obliterated reading.

LANGBAUM: I'd like to add that there's nothing better for a book than to have a movie made of it, then they put out a neat paperback with pictures of the stars on the cover and more people are reading it than ever before.

SINGLEY: We have time for one last question.

GAYLE GREENE (visitor from California, to Gold): You really clarify for me a lot of what I've been doing in the past two years without exactly knowing it. I teach women's literature at a women's college. I always wondered why I had more fun than my male colleagues. When I teach freshman writing, and I teach it as female writing in a women's college, there is absolutely no problem in that connection. The students immediately understand why it's important. Now we don't stay on that level. Once you've got their attention, you do more interesting things. You can do what we've even done here. Of course, you don't call it that.

GOLD: I appreciate that, and I agree with you. What I said was that the attitude towards reading does have an effect on reading. I would suggest to you that we can unabashedly add usefulness to it as well as pleasure because I think that people always, in my experience, apologize in our culture for reading. I think it's important to say, this is a very valuable activity–and this is what I mean by giving permission. I would not say this is going to be good for you, or you might not like it, but you are doing a useful thing and not just filling the time.

SINGLEY: Thank you.

The Novel as Psychosocial Design

The second panel of the second day, "The Novel as Psychosocial Design (its ordering characteristics as plot or action, à la Freud and/or Marx," proved to be the most elusive topic of the conference. Peter Brooks would take it down the byroads of surviving oral traditions within that industrialized and commodified urban form, the printed novel; Robert Caserio would follow the low roads of total ambiguity in postmodern fictions with sadomasochistic propensities; and Nancy Miller would remap the lost trails of eighteenth-century French fictions by women writers excluded from male canons. No wonder that moderator Karen Newman, a Shakespeare scholar and teacher of Comparative and English literatures at Brown, would retitle the occasion as "The Plot Panel" and dwell on its darker implications:

> I think words like design and plot would seem innocent in the context of a conference on the novel–[a context] that is compromising only because plot and its partner character get rather bad press these days from a still dominant formalism, or alternatively, from newly constituted ideologies. The work of our panelists today should, I think, belie such prejudices. But I would suggest briefly that a word like plot or a word like design has other [and more sinister] meanings. Plot means not only the design of the story, but as you know, a secret and usually evil scheme.... And despite my general resistance to theories of conspiracy, stories about canon formation, about inclusion and exclusion, often read more like plots in the second sense than in the first.

Nancy Miller, she went on to say, would tell one such story in her turn, and, she might well have added, the other panelists would pursue that sinister turn in their comments on sadomasochistic tales and the lost innocence involved in the lost art of storytelling.

The Tale vs. The Novel

PETER BROOKS

To be asked to consider the novel "as psychosocial design" leads me, some-what perversely no doubt, to think about a certain tradition of dissent from the overwhelming importance the modern era, from Romanticism onwards, has assigned to the novel as the vehicle of our collective anxieties and their workings-through. The tradition of dissent I have in mind is suggested by a kind of oral residue in a literature—that of the dominant modern novelistic tra-dition—that by its modes of production and consumption is absolutely allied with writing and printing.[1] Next to the "great tradition" of the novel, which appears to be wholly aware that it is a purely bookish phenomenon, depen-dent on the new industrial processes of printing and distribution, there is also the tale, short story and novella, that appears to insist, somewhat perversely, on its authentic relation with a tradition and a communicative situation that are clearly obsolete. If the familial and communitarian circles which fostered the telling of the Tales of Mother Goose and the *Kinder- und Hausmärchen* col-lected by the Grimm Brothers—the evening watches around the hearth which the French called "veillées"—may survive in peasant culture in the nineteenth century, they clearly have little to do with literature, which is in the process of becoming commercial, even industrial, and, certainly in France, urban.

One can, for example, find in the work of Maupassant a notable instance of such an urban literature, self-consciously a commodity in a marketplace, which nonetheless returns again and again to fictive situations of oral com-munication. Maupassant's *contes* and *nouvelles* abound in examples of "framed tales," where one tale is embedded within another, where the storyteller speaks to someone who listens, where every narrator has one or more explicit narratees. What is at stake in these tales is perhaps less the "message" of the story than its reception. To use the terms of Roman Jakobson, at issue is per-haps less the "poetic" function of language than its "phatic" and "conative" functions: how, and by what means, the message is received, and with what results.[2] The tale told may present an attempt at seduction, or even some-thing close to rape, as in the rather sordid little tale called "Une ruse," where the ruse is not simply the theme of the story told by the doctor who has just been examining a newly-wed woman, but also the ruse of narrating itself. When the young woman has listened to this fierce story of marital infidelity and dissimulation, she asks, now "tense" ("crispée"), "Why did you tell me this dreadful story?" To which the doctor, smiling, replies, "In order to offer you my services, should the occasion arise."[3] The services are of course

[1] A more extended version of this essay, which includes not only my discussion of Walter Benjamin but also the study of Jules Barbey d'Aurevilly's "Le Dessous de cartes d'une partie de whist," from *Les Diaboliques*, can be found in the *Yale Jour-nal of Criticism* 1, No. 1 (Fall, 1987).

[2] See Roman Jakobson, "Closing Statement: Linguistics and Poetics," in *Style in Language*, ed. Thomas A. Sebeok (Cam-bridge, Mass.: MIT Press, 1960), pp. 350–77.

[3] See Guy de Maupassant, "Une ruse," in *Mademoiselle Fifi*, from *Oeuvres complètes* (Paris: Conard, 1908), Vol. 4, p. 149. Eng-

rather shady ones, and their very offer constitutes a kind of violation of the newlywed, a forced loss of innocence. In other cases, the force of a narrative is such that it can provoke an interpretative discussion among its listeners, or the radical conversion of a whole life. Narrating is never innocent, and the narrative that frames another allows the writer to dramatize the results of the telling. And this no doubt gives a signal to the reader that the tale told can and should react on his own life: that literature is not inconsequential.

One could at this point return to the *Decameron* and the whole literary tradition that insists that narrative implies narrating, which dramatizes a situation where a group of people is, for one reason or another, called upon to exchange stories; and to the picaresque tradition, where the chances of the highway ever lead to meeting new characters, who become characters precisely because of the stories they have to tell; and finally to *The Thousand and One Nights*, where one loses one's way in the attempt to follow the levels of embedding–tales within tales within tales within ... –which give the impression of a possible infinite regress, were it not that finally telling cures: cures the murderous neurosis of the Sultan, provoked by his wife's infidelity, brings about the happy marriage of the Sultan with Scheherazade, and thus saves the state threatened by a parlous disequilibrium. Scheherazade knows perfectly well that narrating is never innocent, that telling a story can change a life. But what needs explanation, or at least exploration, is the survival of this oral tradition in the literary culture of the nineteenth century, and in texts that have nothing to do with the fantastic or the infantile, with the "veillée" or the circle of storytellers. Are we faced with a vestigial infancy of storytelling? Do we rather find the confirmation of the Bakhtinian conception of narrative discourse as the meeting place of diverse voices? Or should we speak of a kind of nostalgia for a communicative situation that the modern writer will never experience?

I find it significant that the work of Balzac, the first novelist to be fully aware of the new conditions of an industrializing and commodified literature, very often stages situations of oral communication where the exchange and transmission of narrative is at issue. The most striking example might be *Autre étude de femme*, which presents a group of initiates gathered late at night in a noble hôtel of the Faubourg Saint-Germain for an exchange of stories that constitutes "a happy protest by the ancient spirit of our joyous country."[4] It is thus under the sign of a preservation of the customs of the *ancien régime* in a new world where everything tends to "mechanize itself"–"*se mécanifier*"–that several narratives are going to be offered by the members of this elite society. We detect in *Autre étude de femme*, as in so many other tales of Balzac, the desire of a novelist who has fully assumed the conditions of the modern professional writer–who indeed founded his own print shop in an effort to control

---

lish translations my own. This tale was first brought to my attention by Angela S. Moger: see her "That Obscure Object of Narrative," *Yale French Studies* 63 (1982), pp. 129–38. My use of the terms "narrative," "story" and "narrating" generally corresponds to Gérard Genette's "*récit*," "*histoire*" and "*narration*," in "Discours du récit," *Figures III* (Paris: Editions du Seuil, 1972); English translation Jane E. Lewin, *Narrative Discourse* (Ithaca, N.Y.: Cornell University Press, 1980).

[4] Honoré de Balzac, *Autre étude de femme*, in *La Comédie humaine* (Paris: Bibliothèque de la Pléiade, 1976), Vol. 3, p. 674. Further references to this tale will be given in parentheses in my text. English translations my own.

the means of production of the written–to recover the oral context of narrative, to be in touch again with a lived situation of exchange between narrator and narratee, creator and public. At the same time he assigns this oral context to a past which just barely survives in the modern world: it is seen as an anachronism, an object of nostalgia. One comes upon this nostalgia once again–now in a highly nuanced and "modernist" form–in Walter Benjamin's remarkable essay, "The Storyteller" [Der Erzähler].

According to Benjamin, "the art of storytelling is coming to an end," which means that we are losing "the ability to exchange experiences": the very communicability of experience is threatened with loss.[5] From which it follows that "the art of storytelling is reaching its end because the epic side of truth, wisdom [die Weisheit], is dying out" (413; 87). Benjamin identifies traditional storytelling with the traveller, who returns from his wanderings with something to tell, but also with the preserver of local traditions, rooted in his native place. In the Middle Ages, these two types of storytelling interpenetrated because of the craft structure, whereby the resident master craftsman and the traveling journeyman came together in the workplace. Benjamin writes: "If peasants and seamen were the old masters of storytelling, the artisan class was its university" (411; 85). But through the workings of "the secular productive forces of history" (413; 87), narrative has been taken from the realm of living speech, which now permits us to discover a new beauty in what is vanishing.

What stands in opposition to storytelling, what is in the process of replacing it entirely, is of course the novel, inseparably linked to the invention of printing and the notion of the book. For Benjamin–who is here closely following the Lukács of The Theory of the Novel–"The birthplace of the novel is the solitary individual, who ... is himself uncounseled, and cannot give counsel to others" (413–14; 87). For the novelist is necessarily isolated, invisible, a hidden god who does not have the capacity to enter into colloquy with his fellow man, and thus cannot communicate that wisdom that is good counsel. The novel is complicit with "information," the typical modern form of communication, the domain of the newspaper which, in providing explanations for everything, impoverishes our experience of narrative. Storytelling does without explanation and without psychological analysis, giving narrative a "chaste compactness" that commends it to memory and integrates it into the experience of the listener. It is in a state of relaxation, even a state of boredom [Langeweile] that the listener best assimilates the story told, makes it his own, in order to repeat it. As Benjamin writes in a quasi-Surrealist sentence, "Boredom is the dream bird that hatches the egg of experience" (417; 91). And this kind of boredom, already extinct in the cities, is dying out in the country as well. With it the "gift of listening" is disappearing, and the community of those who know how to listen. For, says Benjamin, "storytelling is

5 Walter Benjamin, "Der Erzähler: Betrachtungen zum Werk Nikolai Lesskows," in Illuminationen (Frankfurt: Suhrkamp Verlag, 1955), pp. 409–36, English translation Harry Zohn, "The Storyteller: Reflections on the Works of Nikolai Leskov," in Illuminations (New York: Harcourt, Brace and World, 1968), pp. 83–109. I shall generally follow the translation by Harry Zohn, introducing a few modifications to emphasize the literal sense of the German text. I shall give in parentheses in my text first the page number of the German original, then the page number of the English translation.

always the art of repeating stories, and this art is lost when the stories are no longer retained. It is lost because there is no more weaving and spinning going on while they are being listened to. The more self-forgetful the listener is, the more deeply is what he listens to impressed upon his memory. When the rhythm of work has seized him, he listens to the tales in such a way that the gift of retelling them comes to him all by itself" (417–18; 91).

For Benjamin, then, storytelling belongs to the world of the living word, the world of a communication that is authentic because it concerns the transmission and the sharing of experience, and that can thus become wisdom, the counsel of man to his fellow men. Once again, such storytelling is for Benjamin closely tied to artisanal work:

> Storytelling as it long prospers in the realm of artisanry–the rural, the maritime, then the urban–is itself so to speak an artisanal form of communication. It does not aim to convey the pure essence [an sich] of the matter, like information or a report. It sinks the matter into the life of the storyteller, in order to bring it out of him again. Thus traces of the storyteller cling to the story the way the handprints of the potter cling to the clay vessel. (418;91–92)

Benjamin's interest in Nikolai Leskov–the ostensible subject of his essay–may be explained most of all by Leskov's view that writing "'is for me no liberal art, but a craft [ein Handwerk]'" (418; 92). Benjamin also cites a similar comment from Paul Valéry, praising the traditional artisan and asserting: "'the time is past in which time did not matter. Modern man no longer works at that which can't be abbreviated'" (419;93).

It would appear thus far that we are faced with a fully nostalgic and romantic view of storytelling, one we may even judge to be utopian and mystified, especially when one considers that Benjamin is discussing a nineteenth-century writer who can at best give us a *simulacrum* of the "hand-made" story that would seem to be the only authentic illustration of his argument. One of the many difficulties presented by Benjamin's essay arises from his choice of an example which strikes us as an inauthentic instance of the matter under discussion. But this may be a signal that Benjamin is on the track of something that goes well beyond nostalgia, at least in any simplistic form. We need to pursue for another moment the meanders of his argument. He ends his quotations from Valéry with a sentence in which Valéry asks himself if the "'increasing aversion to patient tasks'" might not coincide with "'a weakening in men's minds of the idea of eternity'" (420;93). And the idea of eternity, Benjamin adds, has its source in death. From which he will draw the conclusion that one might establish an equivalence in the changes–changes that are all losses–in the idea of eternity, in the figure of death, in the communicability of experience, and in the art of storytelling. The idea of death itself is dying, according to Benjamin, in that it has lost its public presence. "There used to be no house, hardly a room, in which someone had not once died," whereas modern man dies in the hospital. Yet it is true that "not only a man's knowledge or wisdom, but above all his real life–and this is the stuff that stories are made of–first assumes transmissible form at the moment of his death" (420; 94). Thus Benjamin can say, in a striking epigram, "Death is the sanction of everything that the storyteller has to tell."

I don't intend to pursue in detail all that derives, in Benjamin's argument, from this primordial role assigned to death as the authority of narrative. It is sufficient perhaps to note that with the decline of the epic, memory–"the epic faculty *par excellence*" (424; 97)–loses its original unity, to become on the one hand "remembrance" [*Eingedenken*], characteristic of the novel, and on the other "reminiscence" [*Gedächtnis*], characteristic of the story. For in the novel, where according to Lukács the writer and the reader are both solitary individuals, and where the essential and the temporal are radically separated, it is the creative work of "active memory" that transforms everything, that confers on the struggle against time a certain meaning. It is the "meaning of life" that is at the center of any true novel. And since the meaning of a life is only revealed at the moment of death, one reads a novel in order to know death, that death that we will never know in our own life, that which, through the figuration of a fictive life, gives us an image of what might constitute meaning. The novel is significant, says Benjamin, "because this stranger's fate by virtue of the flame which consumes it yields us the warmth which we never gain from our own fate. What draws the reader to the novel is the hope of warming his shivering life at a death he reads about" (428; 101).

If it is thus the "meaning of life" which is at issue in the novel, we must on the other hand talk of the "moral of the story," that is of a participation and a sharing in wisdom between the storyteller and his listener. At the very end of his essay, Benjamin returns to the image of the flame: "The storyteller–he is the man who could let the wick of his life be consumed completely by the gentle flame of his story. This is the basis of the incomparable aura about the storyteller, in Leskov as in Hauff, in Poe as in Stevenson. The storyteller is the figure in which the righteous man encounters himself" (436; 108–109). The mention of Poe and Stevenson may well surprise us here, and leave us in some confusion concerning the historical coördinates of Benjamin's argument. But once again, we should understand that the apparent nostalgia of his evocation of the oral tale and its teller is in essence strategic: that he is not urging a return, even fictively, to a situation of storytelling which is gone for good (and which was perhaps always a myth), but rather waging a combat–whether in the advance guard or the rear guard it is hard to say–against the situation of any text in the modern world.

Anthropologists and linguists have taught us that, in oral cultures, meaning depends in large measure on the context of any speech act. Writing, on the other hand, by its very nature abolishes context to create an "autonomous discourse," a discourse that one cannot directly question or respond to because it is detached from its author and belongs, strictly speaking, to no one.[6] I detect in Benjamin's essay a protest against the

---

[6] On these questions, see the excellent exposition by Walter J. Ong, in *Orality and Literacy: The Technologizing of the Word* (London and New York: Methuen, 1982), especially chapter 4, "Writing restructures consciousness."

decontextualization of discourse, an effort to rediscover certain contextual co-ördinates of narrative in narrative voice, in the transmission of a certain "wisdom" from narrator to narratee, in the transaction or transference that takes place every time that one recounts something to someone. Paradoxi-cally, where it is a question of modern narrative, Benjamin's argument points the way less to an impossible return to the past than to a new attention di-rected toward the most subtle signs of context in the most highly elaborated texts, those that are the most self-conscious about their communicative situ-ation and status. Our reading of Benjamin suggests that what needs to be scrutinized in narrative is less its "message," less its ostensible affirmations, and much more its interstices, its gaps, its moments of passage, the moments where something falls silent to indicate a transference, the moment where one begins to be able to hear other possible voices in response.

To pursue this line of thinking, I need one more quotation from Benjamin:

> A man listening to a story is in the company of the storyteller; even a man reading one shares this companionship. The reader of a novel, however, is iso-lated, more so than any other reader. (For even the reader of a poem is ready to utter the words, for the benefit of the listener.) In this solitude of his, the reader of a novel seizes upon his material more jealously than anyone else. He is ready to make it completely his own, to devour it, as it were. Indeed, he destroys, he swallows up the material as the fire devours logs in the fireplace. The suspense which permeates the novel is very much like the draft which stimulates the flame in the fireplace and enlivens its play. (427; 100)

We begin to understand that Benjamin's evocation of the sociable situation of storytelling, of the lived exchange that it fictively implies–as simulated in and through the written–should be set in opposition to a situation of consumption of narrative in what he also calls "the age of mechanical reproduction." Benja-min is reacting against the aesthetics and the ethics of reading implied by the solitary consumption of the printed novel: against a reading that interiorizes and devours, which races like a flame through discourse the better to reach the signifying end. Lost in this kind of reading is the experience, or the illu-sion of the experience, of an exchange between living creatures, that human transaction which leads to reflection–and to reflexivity–and in its wake to wis-dom, in the form of counsel given and received. What Benjamin would wish to restore, or to create, is perhaps most of all a certain attitude of reading that would more closely resemble listening, which would elicit the suspension of meditation rather than the suspense of consumption, and which would fore-ground the exchange, the transaction, even the transference–in a fully psy-choanalytic sense–that can take place in the offer and the reception of a narra-tive. If Roland Barthes defined accurately the nature of modern narrative as contract, Benjamin proposes rather the notion of narrative as *gift*: an act of generosity to which the receiver should respond by an equal generosity, ei-ther in telling another story (as in the model of the *Decameron* and its tradition), or in commenting on the story told, but in any event by the proof that the gift has been received, that the narrative has made a difference.[7]

If we return to our preliminary examples of the nineteenth-century oral in the written–Balzac's *Autre étude de femme*, Maupassant's "Une ruse"–we note that in fact the whole structure of embedding, the play of narrators and narratees, exists above all to verify and validate the reception of the narrative, to mark the difference that narrative makes. "Why have you told me this dreadful story?" asks the newlywed in "Une ruse" (p. 149). By indicating in this manner that she would have preferred not to hear the doctor's story, the young woman signals the modification that has been produced by the story. She will never again be as she was. Her listening to the story has produced a loss of innocence. Even if she will never need the doctor's "services"–even if she will remain faithful to her husband–the coördinates of her moral universe have been altered. In the knowledge of good and evil that she has acquired, however trivial it may be, there has been something of a fall. The transmission of narrative has cognitive value.

The attraction of nineteenth-century writers to situations of oral communication may be explained above all by their deep wish to believe in the cognitive value of narrative, its capacity to make a difference through the transmission of experience. This wish to believe might be the best starting point for a study of all that is deployed by modern narrative to signal, to underline, to dramatize the reception and the transmission of the narrated, and of narrative itself. This would be the moment, had we the time, to discuss the pertinence of theoretical models suggested by Jakobson, Benveniste, Bakhtin–and by the Freudian concept of "transference."

But what of Benjamin's bipolar opposition of the oral, or the "orally-simulating," tale to the novel? The opposition itself may by this point appear largely strategic, a commentary on and a critique of the typical modern novel as the realm of the lonely individual and the solitary reader. By its example, the tale that recreates the oral situation of storytelling challenges the novel to reclaim something that it has largely lost from its heritage: the situation of live communication, the presence of voice. These can now only be simulated, fictive, the object of conscious artistic creation, but even as such they may represent an essential aspect of narrative, which is always also narrating, the transmission from one person (if merely grammatical) to another. Those writers whose works are strongly marked by nostalgia for storytelling may appear to look to the past, toward a lost *ancien régime* of narrative, yet at the same time they may be opening the way toward a more "writeable" literature (to use the term which Barthes sets in opposition to "readable"), one where the reader must engage the very medium and communicative situation of narrative. And this, I would argue, has been a prime concern of many of

7 See Roland Barthes, *S/Z* (Paris: Editions du Seuil, 1970), pp. 95–96; English translation by Richard Miller, *S/Z* (New York: Hill and Wang, 1974). On narrative as contract and as gift, see also the fine article by Léo Mazet, "Récit(s) dans le récit: l'échange du récit chez Balzac," *L'Année balzacienne*, 1976 (Paris: Garnier, 1976), pp. 129–61. On the pertinence of the psychoanalytic notion of transference in the exchange of narrative, see Peter Brooks, *Reading for the Plot* (New York: Alfred A. Knopf, 1984; rpt. Vintage Books, 1985), pp. 216–37; "Constructions psychanalytiques et narratives," *Poétique* 61 (1985); and "Psychoanalytic Constructions and Narrative Meanings," *Paragraph* 7 (1986).

the narratives we loosely categorize as "postmodern": narratives by such as John Barth, Donald Barthelme, Carlos Fuentes, Julio Cortazar, Milan Kundera. In the place of authoritative narrative voices, they propose stammering and self-cancelling ones; in the place of the Flaubertian ideal of impersonality and impassibility, they present idiosyncratic and engaged narratives. Above all, they appear–often in a mood bordering on desperation–to propose a dialogue with the reader, to ask for the reader's response in exchange for counsel given. What is difficult to judge is whether this attempt to engage a dialogue marks a renewal of the oral communicative situation in the novel, or rather a last, desperate, and doomed action to react against decontextualization and consumerist reading. The narratives we most often take as avant-garde may in fact represent a rear-guard maneuver attempting, in vain, to counteract the fate of the sign in the era of textuality.

Mobility and Masochism:
Christine Brooke-Rose and J.G. Ballard

ROBERT L. CASERIO

1. On the road with *hypercrite lecteur*

From *Xorandor*, the name of Christine Brooke-Rose's latest (1986) novel, we can derive *xorandoric*, an adjective describing postmodern fiction. For in *A Rhetoric of the Unreal*, Brooke-Rose says that postmodern fiction–surfiction, metafiction, the novel novel novel–is a wholly ambiguous or wholly indeterminate text, which is what xorandoric denotes. In such a text we find information gaps in both the story and the plot, gaps "prevented from being filled in by two mutually exclusive systems of gap-filling clues" (228). The structural rule for such mutually exclusive systems would combine the co-presence or coherence of items of information in a narrative with the same items' simultaneous disjunction or incoherence. Brooke-Rose finds instances of the rule in James's proto-postmodern *The Turn of the Screw*, in narratology, and in computer science. Shlomith Rimmon's narratological work, *The Concept of Ambiguity–the Example of James*, explores (in Brooke-Rose's summary)

> disjunction as the source of ambiguity. But disjunction itself is of two
> types: inclusive (a $\vee$ b) and exclusive (a $\wedge$ b), often confused.... Rimmon adds a sign of her own to denote ambiguity: $\wedge$. That is, ambiguity combines co-presence (•) with exclusive disjunction ($\wedge$), it is: a *and* b
> (•) + a *or* b ($\wedge$). This in order to distinguish the absolute ambiguity she is dealing with from looser uses of the term. (226–27)

For her latest novel Brooke-Rose enlists computer science to reformulate $\wedge$ as the adding of the computer operand ANDOR, which means non-exclusive *or*, to the operand XOR, which means exclusive *or*; hence *Xorandor*.

Now, because the logic of events and meanings in the absolutely ambiguous or indeterminate text can be both rigorous and self-contradictory at crucial points, the xorandoric text needs a reader who is critically hyperactive. He who runs may not read any longer, unless he runs and reads with an unparalleled quickness to catch up with and catch hold of meanings that are rigorous and self-contradictory, determinate and indeterminate, at crucial points. The ambiguous, indeterminate character of postmodern fiction demands the reader's hyperactivity because the reader will never be reading only where events and meanings conjoin or only where they literally *take place*. Disjunctive and indeterminate meanings instance a displacement of meaning. The hyperactive reader must be restlessly on the move to keep up with meanings whose displacement, no less than whose disjunction and indeterminacy, will be a sure thing in the totally ambiguous text.

Brooke-Rose calls this mobile reader *hypercrite lecteur*. Herself a great *hypercrite lecteur*, in *A Rhetoric of the Unreal* she illuminates similarities and contrasts between xorandoric and nonxorandoric forms. Because xorandoric fiction confuses the real and the unreal, and makes all reality ambiguous, what is most at stake in this illumination is the relation of structures of modernist and postmodern fiction to structures of traditional novelistic realism. According to Brooke-Rose's strongly argued theory, most twentieth-century SF (science fiction) is not xorandoric because it shares structural procedures with the rhetoric of RF (realistic fiction). RF and most SF both depend on exhaustiveness of description, on neutral "transparent" style and on "defocalisation"–*i.e.*, de-emphasis–of the hero. Above all, both RF and SF reduce to certainty any ambiguity that arises in narrative. Yet while RF and SF procedures tend to merge, RF has a disambiguating procedure that SF does not share. This procedure is the realist's appeal to our agreed-upon and unambiguously recognizable history. The realist makes this appeal by relying on a kind of narrative supplement, a parallel-story structure he identifies with history as the reader knows history from outside of fiction. By being tied to a shared understanding of the past and the present, ambiguity or indeterminacy in the meanings or events–even in the ontological status–of a realistic narrative becomes resolved. Here history is the story that fills in the gaps in the fictional plot. This history is understood to be external to the fiction, and not made up. In contrast, when SF uses history to fill in information gaps it invents unreal chronicles to do so. The disambiguating parallel-story structure in SF is thereby a virtual (albeit mostly unconscious) parody of RF procedure.

In spite of the strength of Brooke-Rose's theoretical treatment of these disambiguating procedures, I shall point out later two exemplary postmodern fictions–one by J.G. Ballard and one by Brooke-Rose herself–which suggest that the treatment has its vulnerable side. But the intellectual and emotional flexibility which is part of Brooke-Rose's strength of argument is the more valuable for the vulnerability it risks. Preferring xorandoric texts, Brooke-Rose does not like RF's disambiguating, determining procedures. When those procedures bulk too large in SF–as they do in Tolkien–she turns away from their product, reserving her enthusiastic interest for non-normative xorandoric SF, like Vonnegut's *The Sirens of Titan* and Joseph McElroy's *Plus*. But Brooke-Rose persists in linking formalist likes and dislikes with meditations on reality and on the very historical dimension whose exploitation in RF she finds uncongenial. As a result a moving conflict of interests pervades *A Rhetoric of the Unreal*. The critic-novelist is drawn away from and towards reality, away from and towards thinking of the real and the unreal in oppositional *and ontological* terms. What if the real and the unreal continue to have an ontological importance for us? What if the real and unreal not only *are,* and are different, but–as a result of a twist in the history of Being–have come to intertwine their differences? Because Brooke-Rose begins and ends her book with thoughts about how for even *hypercrite lecteur* the real and the unreal now might merge ontologically and historically she is led to make her book vulnerable to a worry that punctuates her last page. She says there that, since we have not shown "the slightest capacity for solving the world's real problems, only a brilliant capacity for displacing them, ... more and more words and formulas and forms, continuous or discontinuous, theoretical or intuitive, not only [seem] to me yet another displacement, but also [have] me dead scared, even if like everyone else ... I am contributing to it." This worry was predicted in 1975 by a curious aspect of her novel *Thru,* where stylized and parodied discourses of disjunction, displacement, and indeterminacy, from linguistics to Lacan, are turned into a sublime poetry. The curious aspect of *Thru* is the way it makes one feel that the free-for-all thruway of the text can become a roadblock, and that what the road blocks is more important than the formulas and forms of mobility.

In a recent essay, "The Dissolution of Character in the Novel," Brooke-Rose hints that what the road blocks is a regenerative feminine something, which she denominates (*another* word-formula) *lalangue*. But insofar as *lalangue* is also a term for an indeterminate displacement, what *is* there to be "dead scared" about? To judge from a recent joining of forces between narrative theory and Freudian metapsychology, the solution to anxiety on the critical thruways is not less disjunction and displacement but more. We are now influenced by two opposed yet complementary schools of Freudian narratology, both of them derived from *Beyond the Pleasure Principle*. Both of them see a vital conjunction in bringing together displacement and restlessly mobile xorandoric indeterminacy with Freudian Eros. One school–Peter Brooks's *Reading for the Plot* is an example–presents narrative as the vehicle of erotic desire, binding the death-instinct libidinally by displacing or mastering life's tendency towards closure. The other school presents narrative as the vehicle of the death-instinct, binding Eros destructively by inhibiting or fixing life's tendency towards ever-restless openness. Obviously both schools agree that the all-important thing is mobility of meaning, *hypercrite lecteur*'s specialty, not narrative itself or anti-narrative itself. The agreement oddly revises the dualism Freud wanted to maintain when thinking about Eros and death. As if uneasy about being recruited for a dualism, the narratologists transform the indeterminacy and displacement of fused antithetical instincts feared by Freud into an indeterminacy and displacement of meanings, now asserted to be the ally of Eros and of *hypercrite lecteur* against death.

An anti-narrative argument in this vein is Leo Bersani and Ulysse Dutoit's *The Forms of Violence: Narrative in Assyrian Art and Modern Culture*. The book is a polemic against the forms of art least suitable to "the desiring imagination" (71). The least suitable forms are narrative ones, because "traditional" narrative does not represent a psychic or cultural investment in displacement and indeterminacy. The latter are Bersani and Dutoit's sources of what authentic human desire takes most pleasure in, so here we again find *hypercrite lecteur*'s mobility and the totally ambiguous aesthetic objects that correspond to his mobility. "The desiring imagination," one reads, is inseparable from

> *a pleasurable movement toward an absent (and . . . unlocatable) source of satisfaction. The pleasure of desire is inseparable from the tension created by the lack in desire. Desire constitutes a mobile and indeterminate sensuality.* (105)

The Assyrian palace reliefs, eliciting this sensuality, present art and art's pleasure as "the very tension of the displacing movement itself" (105). Now it is this tension which "the dominant esthetic *and* ethic of mimesis in our culture" (37) denies. And it uses narrative–pre-xorandoric narrative, at least–as a prime instrument of the denial. The writers argue that pre-xorandoric narrative reifies and fixes its characters and scenes, and that such narrative thereby inspires a nefarious mimetic fixation, which ties down the reader's restless desires, and produces a life-denying arrest. The type of this fixation is sadomasochism.

How does our culture involve sadomasochism, narrative, and the "dominant" form of mimesis? Bersani and Dutoit portray sadomasochism as a psychosexual dependency on a rigid determination of experiences and persons. Both are transformed by sadomasochism into objects that are cut away from an inherent infinity of indeterminate meanings and relations. Once they are thus cut away and dismembered, the reified phenomena are then fixed into immobilized forms. Bersani and Dutoit see Sadian narrative as archetypal narrative because they see pre-xorandoric storytelling as the product of a cutting and fixing, dismembering and immobilizing of experience, of desire, and of what desire pursues. Narrative of this type gives us not displacement and indeterminacy, but rigid assignment of our experiences and wants to fixed places or to fixed images or to fixed satisfactions. This dismembering, immobilizing process or determination makes sadomasochism and narrative be types of each other. Both stimulate in their proponents, according to Bersani and Dutoit, a mimetic fascination with dismemberments and fixations, and hence with violence and immobilization:

A coherent narrative depends on stabilized images; stabilized images stimulate the mimetic impulse. Centrality, the privileged foreground, and the suspenseful expectation of climaxes all contribute, in historical and artistic narratives, to an immobilizing self-displacement. (52)

The immobilization is itself an aggression (in the name of a fixed "self") against desire; only a *mobilizing* self-displacement would not be aggressive. For such self-displacements there would be no narrative, and no violence. "Desiring fantasy is displaced fantasy," the writers say; "and displacement is nonnarrative representation" (116). Liberated from narrational cuttings and fixings, the restlessness of desire is thereby presented as averse to sadomasochism; indeed, "the very restlessness of desire," the writers conclude, "is a guarantee of its curiously mild and pacific nature" (125).

Bersani and Dutoit say that the argument of *The Forms of Violence* is for the sake of "rightly ... humane or morally liberal responses" (38), that the curiously mild and pacific restlessness of desire is "an ontological safeguard against a fanatically organized interest in any part of the world" (125). Nevertheless, like Brooke-Rose I think that something is wrong with this insistence on an aesthetic and ethic of displacement and indeterminacy. When *The Forms of Violence* speaks about sensual "mobilization," about the way looking at Assyrian sculpture "trains us to formalize psychic mobility" (39), or about "fantasies always on the move" (105), it sounds like the argument is marching in the boots of the enemy. *The Forms of Violence* points out an example of the enemy, "the dominant esthetic *and* ethic of mimesis in our culture," in the narrative movie images of Leni Riefenstahl. This example shows by contrast how the Assyrians were *not* Nazis. But within a few pages Jane Austen, James, and Proust turn out, by virtue of the fixating procedures of their RF narratives, to be Riefenstahl's allies, and sadomasochistic as well. The suggested images that arise here of Austen in stormtrooper's leather or James in a spiked dog collar may verge on insight, and certainly Proust is bound to Charlus; but the aesthetic and ethic of mobility loses insight by being quickly on the defense against what is not mild and pacific. The pacific defensiveness exerts its own coercive violence. Throughout the discussion of narrative's dismembering procedures and incitements, Bersani and Dutoit use a vocabulary of figurative violence which, in spite of its figurative nature, they require their readers to take as literal. The narrative dismemberments the writers speak of are scarcely matters of the real bloodshed that appears to be under discussion in their book. And the mimesis the authors speak of is, in any actual practice, scarcely a matter of the literal copying—on the part of both authors and readers—that seems to be what Bersani and Dutoit mean by the term. The writers exploit metaphorical latitude of meaning in the terms *violence* and *mimesis* in order to fix rigidly in their readers' minds highly determinate denotations of those words. Given the writers' aesthetic and ethic of indeterminacy, this is an indeed *curiously* mild and pacific expository strategy.

To be sure, one is always too quickly on the defense. But are determinations and arrests of thought and perception as destructive as Bersani and Dutoit make them out? I cannot avoid the idea that in one's reading of fiction, of RF especially, there is an experience of violent arrest, of a suffering of a text's revelatory determinations or disambiguations of meaning, which our critical theory has not yet appreciated for its *vital* importance. The value of *The Forms of Violence*—the value justifying attention and challenge—results from a form of masochism that is, I submit, indeed operative in the nature, and in the necessary response to, some of our culture's honored works. Bersani and Dutoit are not mobilizing against a chimera. Like them I hypothesize the relevance to art of masochistic suffering and arrest. Unlike them, I hypothesize a different value for that relevance. In what follows I speak of masochism—*apart* from sadism—to focus on a psychic or intellectual pleasure or benefit in psychic or intellectual (rather than bodily) injury or puncture; and I lean towards a figurative meaning—albeit a determinate one—of the term. It will be seen that the benefit of pain I hypothesize is connected with being determined in some way, as by some binding power of experience or thought; and that this determination is rooted in phenomena that precede adult sexual development. My inspiration for this way of speaking is Freud, in "The Economic Problem of Masochism" (1924), and Jean Laplanche's development of Freud's essay. I shall follow Laplanche in suggesting, most unlike Bersani and Dutoit, that Freud adumbrates a conjunction of masochism and vital function, in fact of masochism and creativity. This possible conjunction is glanced at yet skipped over by *The Forms of Violence*, with the result that the writers deny any final link between vitality and masochism. And because they see an inevitable coupling of masochism and death, they speak throughout of sadomasochism as an indissoluble entity. Of course, for me to speak of vitality in conjunction with masochism will be not to speak of anything cozily vital. What there is in postmodernism to be dead scared of might find its alternative in only another fright. But to be open to fright and pain is not to be closed to life.

What evidence, then, in Freud's thoughts about masochism might give pause to *hypercrite lecteur*, and might help to hypothesize the vitality of a demobilizing or binding text and an arrested or bound reader? A moment in *The Forms of Violence* debates the book's own assumptions and provides a starting-point. The writers say,

> If we understand fantasy here as the imaginary expression and fulfillment of a desire, then the psychic disturbance produced by fantasy is . . . experience of pleasure as pain; . . . it is a masochistic . . . excitement. . . .
> . . . In one sense, [then,] masochism serves life. The threat to psychic wholeness in each destabilizing fantasy is an enrichment of being. (34)

The writers have consulted *Life and Death in Psychoanalysis*, Laplanche's great commentary, and are following out Freud's idea that masochism in the child produces—as a marginal derivative, to begin with—the adult form of sexuality.

Yet the masochism at issue, as Freud pointed out in "The Economic Problem of Masochism," has three forms: primary or erotogenic masochism, female masochism and moral masochism. Interrelated as these masochisms are, they are misleadingly treated if lumped together, as they are in *The Forms of Violence*.

Female masochism (which Freud says we are especially familiar with in men!) and moral masochism are expressions of desire for punishment. They are derivative forms of sadism, itself a derivative of primary erotogenic masochism. The latter as I understand it is not a desire for punishment. Perhaps because *The Forms of Violence* equates erotogenic masochism with female and moral masochism, and perhaps too because it treats sadomasochism as an unbreakable monad, the book's appreciative address to the phenomenon stops abruptly: "The logical 'end' of [masochistic] excitement . . . is the destruction of life itself" (34).

But the 'end' of erotogenic masochism, in Freud and in Laplanche, does not follow the logic just claimed for it. To be sure, any logic in Freud's idea of erotogenic masochism is difficult to make out, since what Freud says about it is confined to over-condensed remarks in his 1924 essay. And, as if the condensation were not enough to insure an absence of helpful commentary, exegesis of erotogenic masochism has been overshadowed by *Beyond the Pleasure Principle* and *The Ego and the Id*–or rather by our attachment to the pages in Freud that undermine any difference between death-instincts and life-instincts. But by assigning a collaboration with death to female and moral masochism rather than to erotogenic masochism, in the 1924 essay Freud's differentiation of the masochistic economy might be taken as another attempt to hold on to the logic of instinctual dualism he wants to maintain. Laplanche's commentary, I think, follows out Freud's possible intention; even though erotogenic masochism is only a fine thread in Laplanche's densely-woven book, Laplanche does not assign the phenomenon to Freud's periodic compulsion–as Laplanche puts it–"to carry death back . . . to the very level of biology, as an *instinct*. . . . to demolish life" (123). But this thread in Laplanche's book has been ignored, partly because of the thread's fineness, and partly because of the postmodern stress on indeterminacy in Freud's thought. And, in a sense, in Freud's thought the arbitrary displacement of life into death, of death into life, has the attraction of logic; that is, his thought ends *logically* in the idea of such indeterminacy. But what if this logic is not at one with the "logic" of biological life as it might exist despite the pessimistic side of Freud's thought? Probing Freud's lead and Laplanche's follow-up, then, I will set out the way whereby erotogenic masochism might be said to enrich biological and intellectual life–keeping an eye as I do so on the bearing on literature of this curt exposition.

On the basis of "The Economic Problem of Masochism" one might say that erotogenic masochism is the effect of a libidinal reserve which, on the one hand, represents the coalescence or fusion of the death instinct and Eros and, on the other hand, represents a defusion of them. A masochistic pleasure in tension due to pain and unpleasure would originate the defusion. Such pleasure would unbalance the static equilibrium of the fused antithetical instincts, and so it would effect an advance–the excitation of sexual instinct, for example–in the liberation and consolidation of a purely libidinal Eros. Thus this vitally unbalancing excitation would be the source of the enrichment of life that masochism might be said to instigate. But Freud's few pages on the subject need supplementation by Laplanche's idea of erotogenic masochism as an anaclitic crossroads.

Laplanche suggests that, in terms of psychic development, primary, erotogenic masochism is situated between an organism's primary, nonambiguous and nonarbitrary coordination of instinct, aim and object, and a later ambiguous and arbitrary coordination. For example, instinctive hunger, the aim to preserve bodily functions essential to life, and food, represent the nonambiguous coordination. Biological function essential to life is what Laplanche calls the vital order. In what might be a deliberate challenge to Freud's idea of a primary fusion of the death instinct and Eros, Laplanche hypothesizes a primary, direct functioning of the vital order in nonambiguous coordinations of instinct, aim, and object. But in human growth, as of course Laplanche points out, this direct functioning is not present for long. Here we find the beginning of psychic mobilization or displacement–although the displacement, it will be seen, is not unchecked. Intellectual and cultural development requires the substitution of ambiguous or arbitrary secondary aims and objects for what in early development are the undisplaced matchings of instinct with its complements. In this process the development of life is excited by a painfully pleasurable unbalancing of a present match of instinct, aim, and object for the sake of a new and potentially more arbitrary match. When and where these masochistically pleasurable and hence stimulating unbalancings occur there is an anaclitic crossroads.

At this psychic site, the vital order is called upon by the libido to act as a model, as a prop or stay, to support the functioning of arbitrary substitutes for prior, more determinately vital coordinations of instinct. Freud says "erotogenic masochism accompanies the libido through all its developmental phases" (164). If so, then the libido is bound to return to the masochistic site of the anaclitic crossroads, perhaps because the libido is originally closest there to the vital order. It appears, at least, that in a masochistic posture the libido comprehends simultaneously the pleasurable stimulation of the vital order and the unpleasurable stimulation of the vital order's substitutes. But, excited though it is by both the vital order and the vital order's displacement, erotogenic masochism functions as a brake on displacement. It seeks to form any arbitrary, ambiguous, or indeterminate displacement of vitality on the pattern of the vital order–on a pattern, that is, of the nonarbitrary, nonambiguous coordination of instinct, aim, and object. Now in language and literature the cratylistic fantasy of a nonarbitrary match between the components of a sign might be an ideational recollection or projection of the vital order's unambiguous matching of instinctual components. Likewise, realistic fiction's claims to be truly side-by-side with life, unambiguously matching descriptive language with described things, might be also a projected recollection of the vital order's integrated components. Put this way, of course, linguistic craty-lism and literary realism can be seen as erotogenic, insofar as they seek to bind different elements into a fixedly integrated unity; but what would be the masochistic component here? The latter might show itself in the prestige given by cratylism and realism to the passive, nonarbitrary motivation of signs or of discourse by painfully coercive external things or by an all-determining life-force.

In speaking of erotogenic masochism in a way that emphasizes its agency–as a *seeker* of coordinating bonds, or as an *active* brake on mobility and displacement–one must not lose sight of the passivity of the phenomenon. Arguably, libido starting out on the road of life's displacements would not re-gain access to the vital order were it not stimulated to do so by the pleasure of a painfully passive determination or arrest by the vital order's substitutes, which first appear to be alien and invasive. Now the veritable highway of dis-placements is in the intellect, in the realm of ideas. At the anaclitic crossroads the organism's vital functioning is invasively determined by *ideas* of life, of life in its present (and past) mode and of life as it might be extended in future by novel and ambiguous substitutes. Indeed, ideation and intellectual devel-opment as Laplanche describes them involve the libido in erotogenic maso-chism. Laplanche describes this involvement, to which *he* adds literary allu-sions, by speaking of how *"the very movement of fantasmatization"* emphasizes "the privileged character of [erotogenic] masochism in human sexuality. The analysis ... of an essential fantasy–the 'primal scene'–would illustrate it as well ...: the child, impotent in his crib, is Ulysses tied to the mast or Tanta-lus, on whom [the spectacle] is imposed" (102). Laplanche emphasizes the child's bound passivity not just in relation to activity but in relation to fantasy and thought. The bound nature of the Ulyssean child is what makes possible his fixation on all ideational representatives from ego to ideal, and La-planche–in what seems, very significantly, a dissent from Lacan–assigns this binding not to sadistic aggression or to the desire for punishment, but to the love of life. "A human being can supplement a love of life that is occasionally deficient only by a love of the ego or of the ideal agencies which are, in turn, derived from it" (125). Both ego and ideal are the products of an arrest of mo-bility. Laplanche goes on: "Even an unconscious fantasy ... could not come into existence without ... the minimum of imaginary inertia allowing ... the precipitation of those concretions that are 'object-like' in that ... they can be surrounded and cathected" (126). So to be tied to the mast of ideation is cre-ative, and abets life. This binding is figured last by Laplanche as punctua-tion–a figure that suggests fixation and also, in the light of the intrusive or in-vasive character of ideation, suggests puncturing. "It is the ego, derived from the vital energy form, that introduces the punctuation of recognizable and *re-producible* perceptual elements. It is a punctuation that is perhaps necessary for the fixation of every discursive sequence" (126).

Invasion or intrusion, punctuation, stopping: in the medium of these excitational hurts the libido meets the death-instinct and binds it erotically, or uses the meeting to defuse Eros and death under the influence of excitement by pain. In Laplanche's light I suggest that the reader who suffers punctuation by an intrusive, determining text is not bound to death, and that his experience of arrest is not logically or necessarily a move into sadism or moral masochism. *Hypercrite lecteur* is not the only hero of reading; the bound and determined figures of Ulysses and Tantalus–I might add, of Shelley's supine visionary Prometheus–have a role to play even in responses to xorandoric fiction. Yet before I move on to bound figures in Brooke-Rose's and J.G. Ballard's postmodernism, there is one more theorist I want to enlist in the attempt to gain attention for Freud's primary masochism. In Fredric Jameson's great book on Wyndham Lewis, *Fables of Aggression* (with *The Forms of Violence* in mind, should it be called *Fables Are Aggression*?), another extraordinary last page reveals a desire to end displacement, and–unintentionally–forges a link between erotogenic masochism and the disambiguating procedures of RF. Up until his last page Jameson has been arguing that a mimesis which seeks a fixing or binding of the forms of real life in a representational "beyond" reproduces the reifying procedures of Lacan's Imaginary, of capitalism, and of proto-fascism. Because Lewis is a satirist his representational aim is particularly urgent. Lewis sees the human objects of his satire as unreal and unalive. He wants to use representation to give them a determinate life so that his aggressive attack can give them a determinate death. Yet how can art be a life-and-death matter if the difference between Eros and death is ambiguous? Lewis' work asks this question all the more urgently because Lewis sees all art as a bottomless abyss of displacements and indeterminacies. Lewis is a proto-postmodernist. *The Revenge for Love* (1937), the novel about the Spanish Civil War, presents its characters and its parallel story, history, as factitious structures of mutually exclusive systems, ambiguously combining co-presence and disjunction. At the end of the novel, however, the nasty character Percy (named after Lewis) weeps. He weeps because the xorandoric rhetoric of the unreal in life itself has produced two deaths which he finds perplexingly determinate and real. How can the unreal–and the dead–have real life-and-death effects?

Jameson's comment on the ending is astonishing. He asserts: "On the closing page of *The Revenge for Love*, ... there hangs and gleams forever the realest tear in all literature" (177). This is astonishing because in these words Jameson implicitly turns his back on his Lacan-derived idea that the binding aims of determinate representations are death-inspired. That the realest tear, inspired by an idea of life, is seen to hang forever on the page argues in the critic's mind a commitment to a binding nonarbitrary and unambiguous representation. Suddenly, not the Lacanian symbolic, but the imaginary and the real conjoined, are given pride of place. Jameson's penetration by this ideational reversal is preceded by a political commentary–by Jameson's expression of fright at the way mere words, in their slippery mobility, are used by those in power to produce and evade politically-caused real deaths. A sadistic polit-ical and historical determination causes the critic to regress to the posture characteristic of the anaclitic crossroads. And this regress, in which Jameson is invaded by a critical position not his own, is for the sake of the vital order. "There hangs and gleams forever the realest tear in all literature." Could one mobilize the words to fix them anew in the spirit they are penetrated by? The realest tear also means the realist tear. By tearing or puncturing the reader with a finally unambiguous, determinate representation of life, by binding the reader to a fixed understanding of the parallel-story structure called history, the rhetoric of the real produces erotogenic effects. In this bound state, my speculation means to suggest, more can be seen about the nature of the sub-stitute forms of life that lean upon and are stayed by vital function and vital order, than could be the case otherwise.

2. Crash

Vaughan, Ballard's hero in the novel *Crash* (1973), spends his life cruising the thruways and hoping to be in auto-accidents. Already a multiple-accident vic-tim, he has collected a fellowship of perpetrators or victims of collisions, among whom is the novel's narrator, one Ballard. To these friends, no matter what their sex, Vaughan makes love, focussing his sexual acts on their scars and mutilations. But this love-making pursues not sex but an idea: to wit, that aggression on the road only *appears* to be the triumph of accident or of a desire for punishment or of a death-drive. Vaughan has made himself the delegate of Eros to convince highway victims that the roadside slaughter really represents death's binding and defeat by love. And in plotting his own death in a crash with the limousine of movie-star Elizabeth Taylor, he plans an apocalyptic demonstration of the way Eros inspires even suicide and mur-der.

Which school of narratology would find an exponent in Vaughan? Would he be a hero for Peter Brooks, a villain for Bersani and Dutoit? Certainly for the latter Vaughan's idea-driven monomania would seem a throwback to–Riefenstahl. In *The Mythopoeic Reality* Mas'ud Zavarzadeh says that post-modernism undermines the possibility of totalizing the present human situ-ation. Vaughan is no postmodernist, then, because his idea about the acci-dents that accompany our restless mobility seeks to totalize the meaning of vehicular casualty. Accordingly, Peter Brooks would not like him any more than Bersani and Dutoit, for Vaughan wants to limit the meaning of what he plots, and to see desire stilled by consummation. What then of Ballard the au-thor–is he drawn into Vaughan's project in a way that makes him a literary and ethical reactionary? To say so would ignore how Vaughan's idea and its totalizing impulse seems to be offered us, as much as not, as a parody of *Be-yond the Pleasure Principle*. Ballard has said that he devoured Freud in his ado-lescent years, and that consequently he set out on a medical career to become a psychoanalyst. But, after giving up medicine and psychiatry for science fiction, Ballard seems to have turned against his inspiration. At least, in *Crash*–which is thoroughly typical of Ballard's work before *Empire of the Sun* (1984)–we find a totally ambiguous text, because the novel projects mutually exclusive clues to its author's attitude about his subject and his Freudian sources. The novel about Vaughan hovers among three stances toward the story and its presentation: earnest application of Freud to plausibly concrete experiences; parody of Freud; and "pop" stylization of Freud (something between endorsement and subversion). The deadpan earnestness with which Ballard and "Ballard" present *Crash* makes it impossible for the reader to determine if the novel is, after all, a joke. But as we watch Vaughan enact Freud's hope to see Eros free itself from fusion with death, the hope looks like the symptom of an absurd speculation. And, at the same time, *Crash*'s literalization of the idea that Eros and death are fused makes the idea of fusion look no less preposterous than the enactment of defusion. Freud's presence in the novel is displaced by parody, which is displaced in turn by earnest Freudianism, which is displaced once more by parody. The wavering between seriousness and play cannot be resolved, and so the case for the total ambiguity–and for the postmodernism–of Ballard's text is a strong one.

This total ambiguity makes the generic identity of Ballard's text no less indeterminate. *Crash* shows signs of being SF or RF; but what in fact is it? The novel uses recognizable sociological codes to situate its story in contemporary London, but the contemporaneousness remains uncertain because Ballard does not use the RF parallel-story structure to attach the novel to a recognizable *historical* code. The name of the film-star is the only link between the novel and a determinate historical period. Moreover, when Ballard–before *Empire of the Sun*–does provide his reader with more contemporary sociological and historical matter than he does in *Crash*, the reader is made to feel that the realistic matter is stereotyped, the product of clichéd and factitious interpretative codes. As a result, the sociohistorical analysis that plays teasingly through *High-Rise* (1975) looks again like parody, especially where the analysis is offered as a disambiguation of the mysterious events that take place in the titular building. The tale is about a condo full of well-off upwardly mobile professionals who are all alike, but who take to internecine warfare. It's suggested that this is because of a natural tendency towards class-division: the turmoil begins with the *ressentiment* felt by the lower floors against the upper. But since this analysis explains everything and nothing, its suggestion is made to look like claptrap, an architectural convenience on which to build a tale about a building. And as a working-class hero named Wilder emerges from the fighting and makes his way to the building's top, slaying (Oedipus-like) the structure's patriarchal architect, the Marxist and Freudian machinery of ascent is interwoven with modernist heart-of-darkness absurdity in an apparent abetment of analytic claptrap. The effective causes of what happens in the novel and of the novel's structures are the by-now sclerotic codes of psychosocial and literary analysis. The RF reader would expect to use these codes to disambiguate the mystery of the novel's warfare, but

High-Rise only frustrates the expectation. At best the codes are deployed here xorandorically; they are both helpful and useless in determining the story's events and meanings. The hyperactive reader's pursuit of meanings is left on the run–or, appropriately to this novel, on an upward climb to nowhere.

Yet as Ballard's career has unfolded, a stubborn figuration has come to take a place within it, in a way restless ambiguity does not dislodge. Ballard's work starts up where mobility breaks down, because the breakdown, it seems, stimulates interest; the arrest of life, reception of life. Immobilization and its pleasurable pain, informing all Ballard's work, are Ballard's unambiguous building blocks. And so it is, I think, that in even Vaughan and Wilder the tied Ulysses of erotogenic masochism reappears. In spite of the active restlessness of Vaughan's experimentation with sex and collisions, throughout the novel Vaughan is pinned down by ideational obsession. So is "Ballard," from the moment the latter's car fatally pins to its hood the first driver with whom the narrator collides. This means that the vital interest of *Crash*'s story inheres in the wonder of what is produced by passivity, by mobility under arrest. And mobility under arrest is figured as ecstasy at the climax of Wilder's climb to the top in *High-Rise*. The warfare in the building has sealed it off–with the consent of the combatants–from the rest of the city. Because the building thereby loses its food supply, the eating of family pets by the combatants comes to be supplemented by cannibalism. At the top of his ascent Wilder is to be killed by a band of mothers that includes his own wife–and is to be fed to his children. This denouement could suggest a misogynistic fantasy of women's role in any new social order–but like all the other sociohistorical considerations in the novel, this one is ambiguously endorsed and ridiculed. Yet the last view of Wilder in the novel focusses on his feeling like a happy child as he goes blithely towards death. With this focus, the ambiguity of meaning in the women's ascendancy is pushed aside. The reader is directed instead to the bliss of Wilder's halted mobility, to his regression to what is in effect the bound state of the infant in his crib, contemplating a psychic invasion as pleasure. The presentation suggests that this state is beyond–or prior to–ambiguity, even though ambiguities environ Wilder's condition. In his halted state, Wilder is possessed and determined by a receptivity to pain that is vital.

As if to disambiguate fully the meaning of the figure of arrested Ulysses, Ballard has made this figure the focal point of *Empire of the Sun*, his first historical novel in an RF mode and, according to the book's prefatory note, an autobiographical work. The novel's tied Ulysses is Jim, a boy imprisoned in Shanghai from 1942 to 1945 by the Japanese invaders of China. Jim is the bound recipient of an extraordinary historical vision, and it is his bound state that enables the vision's reception. The vision is coordinated by the novel with what the reader already knows, more or less, about World War II. The effect of the coordination is to pass on to the reader Jim's state of being bound by a life-determining historical revelation. And this transfer of state effects an unmasking of *hypercrite lecteur*. He is shown to have invested himself in mobility and displacement in order to refuse and to hide from an historical conditioning that incites his proud restlessness, and punctures it. In attempting to uncover and to reverse this refusal *Empire of the Sun* gives a privileged place to erotogenic masochism.

As Ballard presents it, the Second World War's global conflict disjoins and displaces things and relations, and produces the world as a totally ambiguous postmodern text. One of the first of the novel's surprises is that, instead of being destroyed by the displacement, Jim immediately likes the strange dislocations of the war. The boy gathers from the immediacy of history the pleasure of experiencing life as an *hypercrite lecteur*. Yet the novel shows that the pleasure can be experienced only from a point of arrest. In the novel this point is the fixed and fixing site of the prison camp. Having been separated from his parents, Jim lives an insecure Crusoe-like existence in the deserted houses of the Shanghai British Concession. His ambition is to surrender to the Japanese, to trade his isolated drifting for security. So he actively seeks entry into a detention camp's order of restraint. Awful as it is to think of, his detention once secured turns out–as he expects–to foster enrichments. For one thing, living on the edge of starvation in the camp keeps him so close to the vital order that he clings to life without aggression, as if aggression were a waste of life. The boy feels he has no enemies: he identifies with his Japanese jailers, with the occupied Chinese, with the American liberators. They provide him with what he needs, which is not just food, but an array of idealized agencies, supplements of a love of life that is frequently deficient; object-like identifications whose painful imposition on his psyche stills and stays him with the promised pleasure of *future* mobility.

Outside the bound campsite, mobility is a deadly wandering from the capacity to be imposed on. Outside, being imposed on has been transformed into universal imposing, due to a restlessness of desire which is not mild and pacific. And the impositional agent is not just the war, but the ambiguity and arbitrary displacements of linguistic agency. Jim's imprisonment returns him to his crib as a child acquiring language. He is hungry for names. But Ballard assigns supervision of his language-acquisition to Basie, whose function in the novel is to equate treachery with language as a form of restless displacement, which the coming of the Americans intensifies. In *Empire of the Sun*, the restlessness of desire and the totally ambiguous text are consummately American products. The liberating American airlifts drop Spam, *Reader's Digest* and *Life*. The magazines to Jim "were filled with headlines and catch phrases from a world he had never known, and a host of unimaginable names. . . . they described an heroic adventure on another planet . . . a universe away." But entranced as he is by this acquisition of arbitrary displacements of his own wordless experience, Jim wonders if "despite all the new names that it had spawned, was the war recharging itself here [in eastern Asia], to be fought forever in that far more ambiguous language that Jim had begun to learn?" (228).

The far more ambiguous language is the rhetoric of the unreal. In this rhetoric, what goes on displaces the truth of what is going on historically and politically, *moving* the determinate reality of history and politics into the indeterminate, totally ambiguous text. Because of the link between Jim and James G. Ballard, *Empire of the Sun* throws a retrospective light on Ballard's SF and fantasy, revealing his past work as the formally organized displacement of a response to World War II. And just as the novel disambiguates the author's past work, it disambiguates our knowledge of World War II. But in saying that our historical knowledge is disambiguated by an RF novel, I must take the occasion, as earlier I promised, to address the vulnerable side of Brooke-Rose's comparison of RF with both SF and xorandoric fiction. Brooke-Rose believes that RF uses history as we know it to disambiguate indeterminate aspects of an RF narrative. But history as we know it has little certainty. The bedrock of historical events is ambiguously suspended in change, is waiting for some future all-determining transformation. According to *Empire of the Sun*, the history of World War II is highly ambiguous. We only more or less know that that war ended, because the nuclear arms generated by the conflict terminated the war's hostilities, and yet also continued them by displacing them. We can be certain of the end of the last global conflict only insofar as we more or less know that the nuclear arms emerging from the war can be disarmed, depending on whether or not we more or less use the free will we more or less have. Which is to say we have no certainty about the war's end and effect. Picturing our history in this way, *Empire of the Sun* does its structural duty to use history for its parallel-story; but it thereby also upsets Brooke-Rose's argument. In Ballard's book history does not disambiguate RF; instead, RF disambiguates history.

Empire of the Sun disambiguates the aftermath of World War II by imaging it as a universal death already effectively accomplished, because to remain within the uncertainty of freedom of choice not to disarm is to have already lost the last war—and life itself. Ballard's novel suggests that we have not survived the war, but have survived our collective death. Individual life appears to go on, in all its immediate vitality; but the collective commitment to nuclear war nullifies this life. The living have become restless ghosts playing dangerous games with their posthumous condition. This assertive determination of our history is climactically dramatized in the novel's next-to-last chapter. On the verge of liberation Jim comes upon the bayonetted body of a Japanese airman, one of his ego-ideals. He sees the flyer as "this imaginary twin he had invented, a replica of himself whom he watched through the barbed wire. If the Japanese was dead, part of himself had died" (269–70). Although the airman's signs of life are ambiguous, the boy decides to feed him. But the feeding turns into a nightmare in which the boy and his double attack each other. It is clear to the reader that the flyer's aggressive movements in the struggle are only galvanic spasms derived from the bayonetting. But Jim decides to see the ambiguous movements as, after all, signs of resurrection. He leaves the airman, thinking that the attempt at feeding has "made a small space in [the flyer's] death" and that he is called to resurrect all his other friends, most of them lost, whom he refers to as "the impatient dead" (271–72).

What the reader is made to see is clearly different from what the child decides to see. Ambiguity mobilizes the boy so that he can walk forward into life out of the camp. But as his illusion saves him, it also displaces the truth: the dead airman *is* the child's double, because now the child is showing ambiguous signs of life. In earlier Western history such ambiguity might have been closer to the vital order. But this child's saving illusion is determined by the epoch in which the sons of the earth have empire over the sun by dominating its nuclear energy. This empire's primal scene is the maintenance of vital function illustrated by the sadistically feeding child and the devouring dead flyer. Dominated by such a scene, in which this displacement of vital function has gone so far, can the anaclitic crossroads do its reparational work? In defense against the recognition of displacement's extremity, postmodern life recommends further displacement. The recommendation might be a way for the dead to pretend to life, as Jim pretends that his life and the life of his time have not been in essence extinguished. *Empire of the Sun* exhibits what Jim really knows, in spite of pretending: his experience coordinated with the phenomena of his world-historical time and place determines living as a living death.

The narrator of Ballard's *The Unlimited Dream Company* (1979) begins his story with the crash of an airplane and is never sure thereafter if the crash has left him alive or dead. In *Empire of the Sun* this uncertainty in a postmodern fantasy about whether life is death is resolved into certainty. Postnuclear history, the productive agent of postmodern fantasy, is pre-deceased. Ballard's disambiguation of his fantasy via his grim determination of the historical present reveals postmodernism to be postmortemism. No wonder Ballard's characteristically deadpan style, with its ambiguous effects, seems numb: flatness is appropriately postmortem, and also might express the shame of a ghostly survival. This is not a congenial style for *hypercrite lecteur*, who wants to feel life in the lively ambiguity of language and the restless mobility of desire. But *hypercrite lecteur*, according to *Empire of the Sun*, has one genuine hope of vitality. It is in being bound, no matter how painfully, by the novel's historical vision and by an arrest of restlessness. When in the novel Jim leaves the camp, the novel leaves the reader there, suffering the novel's disambiguating determination of history. If this determination is plausible, what hope of escape from global death would there be in alternative, arbitrary or ambiguous versions of the present? *Hypercrite lecteur* will respond impatiently to the question, scarcely stopping to point out that fictions, like facts, are arbitrary constructions, having no binding or all-determining effect or value. But such response, emphasizing the fictiveness of all things, shirks the possibility that Brooke-Rose, for all her advocacy of the rhetoric of the unreal, does not evade. We might live in a state whose intertwining of real and unreal, no less than whose intertwining of life and death, cannot be disjoined or displaced by those on the run from it.

The postnuclear primal scene Ballard describes in his novel's scene between Jim and the dead airman might well be a secondary derivative, via sadism, of masochism; or an Oedipal tangle expressing a derivative collective desire for punishment. But the origin is not the disease, which is the long distance between the mobilized derivative and the origin. The reader who submits to Ballard's version of RF's painful binding of his and his world's restlessness might recover the long distance by returning to the libidinal passivity of the anaclitic crossroads. This submission would be therapeutic, I think, since it gives the reader a state of detached fixity in which to feel the pressure of the vital order and to contemplate ideas of life in the painfully exciting way that keeps Jim alive in the camp. Even if in this state one envisions the historical present as moribund, the energizing pain of the vision can incite one to act in future against the present determination of history. It has always surprised me that readers of SF should devote themselves to the passive contemplation of the developments and disasters of a future in which they could play no part. By provoking this attitude to spectacle, I have thought SF could only flatter the worst form of supine passivity to the world. But in Ballard's light I now see this as the use of a literary form to recover a psychic state which is, after all, a restorative primary masochism. To be fixed by an intrusive spectacle even of global horror and death is to be shocked back to where one began, at the verge of the vital order, remembering unambiguous vital function. And no matter what one sees there, whether ambiguities or determinations, perhaps this memory is in itself the best fight for life. Interestingly, in experiencing a form of regression to the crossroads of the vital order and its substitutes, SF readers and RF readers find themselves on the same ground.

3. ENDXORANDOR

Ordinarily Christine Brooke-Rose's novels depend upon underdeterminations of the action-code and of the symbolic-code. In plain words, ordinarily we cannot *know* what happens in her texts or just what she *means* by them: they are totally ambiguous. But at the end of *Xorandor* there is a reversal. Until just before the novel's finale we find–not surprisingly, given Brooke-Rose's usual practice–increasing information gaps in both the story and the plot. These gaps cannot be filled in because of the symbolic underdetermination of the text; and we expect the text to "end" by maintaining the underdetermination. But the unexpected occurs: an overdetermination of the action-code–that is, a disambiguating event–halts, and lays waste or consumes, the text's accumulated symbolic underdeterminations, its ambiguities and displacements. This is what happens: Xorandor, a self-originating computer who feeds on radioactive materials, faces a dilemma. His computer offspring have begun to feed on the fissile material of nuclear warheads, thereby defusing the bombs. To protect their arsenals the world governments decide to deport the computer race to where they come from, Mars. But they do not come from Mars. The computer has told a totally ambiguous story about his origins, and he has been misinterpreted in the light of an SF cliché. Yet rather than once more ambiguate what has become disambiguated, Xorandor decides to be bound by the disambiguation of his story, and to swallow his postmodern printout. His deportation means his extinction. But– with the help of twin *human* computer whiz-kids–unknown to the great powers, Xorandor will secretly leave behind two of his own missile-eating offspring to carry on disarmament–and save children. Now this is Ballard's latest story over again. Like Ballard's Jim, in the era of empire over the sun when nuclear arsenals make the living into the living dead, Xorandor suffers immobilization, and he thereby understands the necessity of being punctuated by an idea of real life yet to come. Determined by comparison of the vital order with its current substitutes, the computer's alliance with life puts an end to restless ambiguity's displacement of vital function. In effecting the alliance through the disambiguating event of his self-sacrifice, Xorandor acts in a painfully masochistic way. On the showing of Brooke-Rose's story, the pain is psychosocially erotogenic.

Works Cited

Ballard, J.G. *Crash*. New York: Farrar, Strauss, & Giroux, 1973.

——. *Empire of the Sun*. New York: Simon and Schuster, 1984.

——. *High-Rise*. New York: Holt, Rinehart and Winston, 1975.

——. *The Unlimited Dream Company*. New York: Holt, Rinehart and Winston, 1979.

Bersani, Leo, and Ulysse Dutoit. *The Forms of Violence: Narrative in Assyrian Art and Modern Culture*. New York: Schocken Books, 1985.

Brooke-Rose, Christine. *The Christine Brooke-Rose Omnibus: Four Novels*. Manchester and New York: Carcanet, 1986.

——. "The Dissolution of Character in the Novel." In *Reconstructing Individualism*. Ed. Thomas C. Heller *et al*. Stanford: Stanford University Press, 1986. Pp. 184–96.

——. *A Rhetoric of the Unreal: Studies in Narrative and Structure, Especially of the Fantastic*. Cambridge: Cambridge University Press, 1981.

——. *Xorandor*. Manchester: Carcanet, 1986.

Freud, Sigmund. "The Economic Problem of Masochism." *The Standard Edition of the Complete Psychological Works of Sigmund Freud*. Ed., trans. James Strachey. London: The Hogarth Press and the Institute of Psycho-Analysis, 1940–68. Vol. 19. Pp. 157–70.

Jameson, Fredric. *Fables of Aggression: Wyndham Lewis, The Modernist as Fascist.* Berkeley, Los Angeles, London: University of California Press, 1979.

Laplanche, Jean. *Life and Death in Psychoanalysis.* Trans. Jeffrey Mehlman. Baltimore and London: Johns Hopkins University Press, 1976.

Rimmon, Shlomith. *The Concept of Ambiguity–the Example of James.* Chicago: University of Chicago Press, 1977.

Zavarzadeh, Mas'ud. *The Mythopoeic Reality: The Postwar American Nonfiction Novel.* Urbana: University of Illinois Press, 1976.

Feminist Writing and the History of the Novel*

NANCY K. MILLER

I. Prelude

I have been asked to speak *as a feminist* about why the novel matters. I am happy to do so. I would like to begin with some remarks by the ultimate feminist critic of the novel, Virginia Woolf, in her 1929 essay, "Women and Fiction." I will then turn to Colette's 1910 fiction of a woman novelist's return to writing, *The Vagabond*, and Christiane Rochefort's reflection on women and writing. These short takes are the prelude to my paper.

> For a novel, after all, is a statement about a thousand different objects–human, natural, divine; it is an attempt to relate them to each other. In every novel of merit these different elements are held in place by the force of the writer's vision. But they have another order also, which is the order imposed upon them by convention. And as men are the arbiters of that convention, as they have established an order of values in life, so too, since fiction is largely based on life, these values prevail there also to a very great extent.
>
> It is probable, however, that both in life and in art the values of a woman are not the values of a man. Thus, when a woman comes to write a novel, she will find that she is perpetually wishing to alter the established values–to make serious what appears insignificant to a man, and trivial what is to him important. And for that, of course, she will be criticized; for the critic of the opposite sex will be genuinely puzzled and surprised by an attempt to alter the current scale of values, and will see in it not merely a difference of view, but a view that is weak, or trivial, or sentimental, because it differs from his own. (48–49)

* This essay, for which I hold the copyright, appears in a somewhat different form under the title "Authorized Versions" in *French Review* (February 1988), an issue which focuses on the canon in French.

* * *

At the beginning of Colette's novel, the heroine, author of three novels (including, in her own words, one "unrecognised masterpiece," *mon 'chef-d'oeuvre inconnu' à moi*), reflects upon the economics of a writing life. Now working as a music-hall performer, who describes herself as "a woman of letters who has turned out badly" (13), she wonders about a woman's letters:

> To write, to be able to write, what does it mean? It means spending long hours dreaming before a white page, scribbling unconsciously, letting your pen play round a blot of ink and nibble at a half-formed word, scratching it, making it bristle with darts and adorning it with antennae and paws until it loses all resemblance to a legible word and turns into a fantastic insect or a fluttering creature half butterfly, half fairy. (14)

This celebration of writing, the pleasures and passions of the hand, the pen and the page, the negotiations between an unconscious graffitti and the conscious need to "note and describe" (14), continues for three more paragraphs, in a kind of ironized poetics oddly evocative of Hélène Cixous's call for a writing of the body in "The Laugh of the Medusa." It then moves to register another note, to evoke another regime of materiality:

> It takes up too much time to write. And the trouble is, I am no Balzac! [Et puis, je ne suis pas Balzac, moi.] *The fragile story I am constructing crumbles away when the tradesman rings, or the shoemaker sends in his bill, when the solicitor, or one's counsel, telephones, or when the theatrical agent summons me to his office for "a social engagement at the house of some people of very good position but not in the habit of paying large fees."*
>
> The problem is, since I have been living alone, that I have had first to live, then to divorce, and then to go on living. To do all that demands incredible activity and persistence. And to get where? (15)

Colette's novel asks the question: what does it mean to be a novelist who is not Balzac, who is no Balzac? What does it mean for a French woman writer to take Balzac as the measure of the genre? "No body of novel writing can be compared to Balzac's," Colette writes in 1944, looking back on a career (*Oeuvres*, 1297).

* * *

This is Rochefort in 1983, telling her story (written directly into English):

> When I finished my first book—it was a novel of course, it is easier for women to begin with a novel, for this is what they are supposed to do more or less and this

is another story, the influence of discrimination on choices–when I finished my novel, my first movement was to show it to the man I lived with at the moment. He said: "My poor girl, you better darn stockings." I stopped writing on the spot for three years–till I parted from my husband, swearing that never again in my life was I going to show anything to a man who loves *me. Recently, I found this forgotten manuscript, which in my memory was the pretty bad work of a beginner; not only did it have some qualities–but it was feminist: I had even forgotten this remarkable point, congratulations. I had a good moment laughing at me, at us, at History. . . . I gave the book a title: "You better darn stockings." And I put it back in its tomb. . . .*

Well. So, here you are now, sitting at your writing table, alone, not allowing anybody anymore to interfere. Are you free?
. . . .

Has literature a sex? With dignity, I, and most of my sisters, we would answer: No.

But. But. But, do we have the same experience? Do we have the same mental structures? The same obsessions? . . .

After all, we don't belong to the same civilization. (In *New French Feminisms*, 185–86).

***

As I imagined myself delivering this paper, knowing I would have missed the entire first day of a conference devoted to The Novel, one question kept nagging away at me: whose novel? Whose–or which–subjective mode, ethical paradigm, prophetic mode and cultural discourse would have been dissected and debated, deconstructed and reconstructed, by a group of critics and writers chosen to speak, if I have understood the mandate of the event, *because* they would not agree upon an answer to that question; they would, at the very least, agree to disagree.

I more specifically wondered about The Novel of the panel to which I had been assigned: whose psyche, whose social, whose design was to be at stake in a discussion of what Mark Spilka in his letter to our group also named by its alias: the plot?

The question–whose novel, whose plot–is for me bound up with a range of critical issues that have everything to do with the novel in its relation to the psychosocial, even though they are not uniquely generated by the novel as a *form*: canon-formation, readership, and what Barthes famously called the pleasure of the text. In the argument I will be making today, whose examples are drawn from the eighteenth-century novel, the French and occasionally the English novel, since the two track each other in this period, my concern will be to frame the problem of that literature within the context of a more general feminist reflection on the designs of inclusion and exclusion that have resulted in the history of the novel as we know it.

I have chosen to focus on the eighteenth-century novel for a variety of reasons: in part because after a series of major infidelities, I am working again
on the novel of this period as part of a larger project on the French canon, a
special issue of *Yale French Studies* I am co-editing with Joan DeJean called *The
Politics of Tradition*. And less fortuitously, because I think that the novel of the
eighteenth century in this formative moment of its history delineates with
great clarity the cultural arrangements and social dilemmas of the human subject we have come to identify with the project of the Novel itself. Peter
Brooks has offered a reading of these issues in his first book, *The Novel of
Worldliness*, to which my own early work on the novel is much indebted. My
particular territory now is those novels that articulate and explore with particular emphasis what I will call, following the famous phrase of feminist historian, Joan Kelly-Gadol, "the social relations of the sexes" (822–23), the differentially gendered experience of a socially constructed sexuality. More
specifically, though I will only touch upon it here, I am interested in the particular, memorialized figure of the human subject who emerges from this literature and the ways in which this subject is kept alive at the expense of others by a type of reading and a specific repertory of values.[1]

Let me frame this discussion with yet another narrative epigraph. This is
the story of a footnote, a real one and a metaphorical one that I place here
now as a *mise en abyme* of the fable of this presentation. I am indebted to my
friend Rachel Brownstein for the reference, which I might otherwise have
missed.

About six hundred pages into Frances Burney's nine-hundred page novel,
Camilla, the heroine receives the visit of the ebullient Mrs. Mittin. Mrs. Mittin
eagerly tells Camilla the story of her getting to know Mrs. Berlinton, a story
about novels and their readers:

> *I happened to be in the book shop[1] when she came in, and asked for a book; the
> Peruvan Letters[2] she called it; and it was not at home, and she looked quite
> vexed, for she said she had looked the catalogue up and down, and saw nothing
> she'd a mind to; so I thought it would be a good opportunity to oblige her, and
> be a way to make a prodigious genteel acquaintance besides; so I took down the
> name, and I found out the lady that had got the book, and I made her a visit,
> and I told her it was particular wanted by a lady that had a reason; so she let me
> have it, and I took it to my pretty lady, who was so pleased, she did not know
> how to thank me. (606)*

Burney's 1796 novel was republished by Oxford University Press in 1983. The
editors' footnotes are abundant, informative and useful, authoritative in tone,
and, on the face of it, carefully documented. Thus on this passage, for "book
shop" they offer: "obviously a circulating library. In *The Southampton Guide*
(6th edition., c.1801, pp. 74–75) [the story takes place in Southampton] there

---

[1] A longer version of this discussion will be part of a special issue of *Yale French Studies*, *The Politics of Tradition* (editors, Joan
DeJean and Nancy K. Miller). The issue, scheduled to appear in the fall of 1988, will be devoted to the place of women
writers and questions of canon-formation in French literature and literary history from the Middle Ages to the present.

is a description of such a library: 'T. Baker's Library, in the High Street, contains a well chosen selection of nearly seven thousand volumes, forming a
more general collection of useful and polite literature than is usually found in
circulating libraries. The books are lent to read, at 15s. the year, 4s.6d. the
quarter, and 5s. for the season.'" As someone who rarely does this kind of research herself, I love having access to information provided with such detail.
The precision of it–"5s. for the season"–feeds the fantasy (which I
occasionally entertain) that one might be able to reconstruct the true past of
reading; the material history of letters; the grass roots of novel readership;
what is called by some the "sociology of the book" (Pomeau, 29).

Despite the seductions of its information, however, this is not the footnote
I just referred to; merely its context. The note in question comes (next in sequence) to explain the title of the volume requested, the "Peruvan Letters."
The editors write: "Mrs. Mittin meant either Charles de Secondat Montesquieu's *Persian Letters* (tr., 1722) or George Lyttleton's *Letters from a Persian in
England to his Friend in Ispahan* (1735). In her ignorance she failed to
distinguish between Persia and Peru" (949–950). The failure to distinguish between Persia and Peru, however, is neither securely nor uniquely a matter of
Mrs. Mittin's ignorance. The editors themselves, I think, fail to distinguish
between Persia and Peru, between Montesquieu and Graffigny. Françoise d'-
Issembourg d'Happoncourt Graffigny's *Lettres d'une Péruvienne*–one of the
most widely read novels of the eighteenth century–were translated as the
Peruvian Letters in England in 1771, 1774 and 1782. (At least English Showalter, who knows about these things, tells me that *my* source of
information–the Italian editor of a critical edition of the novel, Gianni Nicoletti–missed a few himself.)

What follows here are notes occasioned by this omission of a woman
writer from the record of cultural production. Gestures like these, born less of
prejudice than oversight and happenstance–after all, why Burney and not
Graffigny?–have come nevertheless *collectively* to constitute the set of references that through its exclusions (either/or) make up the standard history of
the novel.

II. "Least Forgotten" Writers

In his still timely study on the eighteenth-century novel, Georges May makes
the observation that the history of the French novel remains to be written.
"The volume devoted to the 18th-century novel," he goes on to argue, "is especially lacking" and he wonders about this missing piece of literary history.
(All the more, since, to quote Lanson, which he does, "the novel is the only
genre that can be said to be evolving in the 18th century" [1]). Twenty-five
years later, as a feminist critic concerned with imagining a history of the
French novel still to be written, I find in his introduction and in the long
chapter, "Feminism and the Novel," many of the elements we need in order
to begin. By this I mean that May supplies a gendered–though this is of

course neither his category nor his discourse–account of authorship: male *and* female. Thus, in a rollcall of novelists publishing between 1715 and 1761, he names (in this order): Prévost, Marivaux, Crébillon, Duclos, Mme de Tencin, Mme de Graffigny, and Mme Riccoboni and characterizes them as the "least forgotten" writers of this period (*"les moins oubliés"* [3]). The inclusion of women's names–as a matter of course, among the least forgotten, may not be taken for granted–twenty-five years ago, or today.

Let me review a few symptomatic (if randomly chosen) cases. My first example is Etiemble's collection in the two-volume Pléiade, 1966, *Novelists of the 18th Century* [*Romanciers du XVIIIe siècle.*][2] Of May's list Etiemble includes only the men to which he adds others. Now, Etiemble has read Georges May, and concurs with his sense that one needs a history of the eighteenth-century novel; that it is wrong to justify the ignorance of the general reading public who see in the French novel only Balzac and Stendhal instead of Rétif, or Duclos, or Crébillon and miss the eighteenth century completely. But nowhere, in a preface and introduction both of which demonstrate a high degree of self-consciousness about the grounds for inclusion and exclusion at work in the anthology, and a sympathy for what he calls the "human reference" (*"référence à l'humain,"* II, xx), does it seem to cross the critic's mind that women writers were central to the production and formation of the very fictional forms he is so eager to present to a sophisticated reading public (*"aux gens cultivés,"* [I,8]).

Etiemble explains that a reader who wants a more complete picture of the evolution of the genre ought to "*reread*" *other* works not included in his volumes. (Not included because unlike his selection these have received their own individual Pléiade "consecration"–which is one way of going about things I suppose.) Readers, he specifies, are to *return* to the novels of Montesquieu, Marivaux, Diderot, and Rousseau interweaving them in chronological order along with his authors if they are to have a complete picture, more than "a glance of what the French novel becomes in the 18th century" (I, 7). Thus, despite Etiemble's awareness of the importance of women novelists of this deconsidered form in the seventeenth century–he names Scudéry and Lafayette (I, 7)–and his admiration for Georges May's mapping of the terrain, neither Graffigny, Tencin, nor Riccoboni, for example, figures in this "tableau" of the French novel. Why does Etiemble, who is not beyond a major saving operation in this anthology, not moved to make a case for women writers? (Why Sénac de Meilhan, or Cazotte, and not Riccoboni or Tencin?)[3]

One could argue that the category of the "woman writer" was not a vivid one in 1966. One could also argue that what attracts Etiemble to his corpus is the lure of identification, a form of "reading as male bonding" that Susan Winnett, in a shrewdly argued paper on "narrative and the principle(s) of pleasure" at a recent MLA convention, identifies as a "homoaesthetic sub-

[2] I chose this volume precisely because, as Etiemble himself argues, the Pléiade edition constitutes a form of recognition that assures a posterity of reading, confers legitimacy and provides authorizing versions.

[3] In his defense of Sénac de Meilhan, Etiemble even manages to work in a swipe at Germaine de Staël (the only woman mentioned in this volume). He uses the literary historian Albert Thibaudet to set her up.

text," a set of assumptions that follow from a "legalized, entirely male circuit of desire."[4]

Etiemble is drawn in particular to the form of male memoir, the novel as list of serial pleasures, epitomized in Louvet's *The Loves of the Chevalier de Faublas* (*Les Amours du Chevalier de Faublas*). In the list of "if I like *Faublas* it's because" ["*si j'aime le* Faublas *c'est* . . ."] let us retain this formulation: "It's in particular because of the slightly disreputable women who work at satisfying Faublas for the amusement of the well-endowed reader" (II, xxv). Although to be fair, this figuration of the well-endowed reader ("*du lecteur bien consti-tué*"–red-blooded might be a better translation) is not Etiemble's *only* explanation for textual preference, it is difficult to resist the impression that his evaluation of Crébillon, Duclos, Denon and company is profoundly involved with a highly masculinist mode of critical pleasure (very specifically, reading as a French, relentlessly heterosexual, terminally misogynistic though always elegant and gallant male [II, xxvi]): reading *like* a man.

I want to suggest further that if Graffigny, Tencin and Riccoboni do not appear on Etiemble's screen it may also be because in addition to being women writers, hence generally invisible, they specifically produce what I will call *feminist writing* on the same subjects. The novels of women writers in eighteenth-century France and England may be characterized by what Rachel DuPlessis has called a "poetics of . . . critique" (32). These fictions of dissent call into question the fulfillment of virile subjectivities that typically structures libertine texts (by which I mean here the recollections of a man's life as organized by and narrated through his sexual experience–whether a list of encounters or the obsession of a single passion, like *Manon Lescaut*). I am willing to argue that this plot of heterosexual engagement is in fact the basic "psychosocial design" of the memoir novel, one of the two dominant novelistic forms in the eighteenth century. Feminist fiction takes another, harsher and less jubilant view of the social relations of the sexes; in these novels female subjectivity is the figure and not merely the figure of representation against which these tropes of masculine performance display themselves.[5]

Perhaps things have changed in France since 1966. Let us turn now to a more recent example, then, this time not an anthology, but another legitimating instance of eighteenth-century letters, a mainstream exercise in literary history; the volumes published in 1984 by Arthaud (specifically the volumes

---

[4] "Coming Unstrung: Women, Men, Narrative and Principle(s) of Pleasure." At this same MLA convention, Jane Tompkins offered a paper entitled "Reading Like a Man." I find the macho resonance of the phrase apt. See also Robert Scholes's contribution to the debate, "Reading Like a Man," in *Men in Feminism*, ed. Alice Jardine and Paul Smith (New York: Methuen, 1987).

[5] I've of course no idea whether Etiemble ever read any of the women's novels I'm thinking of; what interests me here is the effect of his selection, the authorization of a form of ignorance. Two types of examples come to mind. In the first, Riccoboni's *Lettres de Mistress Fanni Butlerd* and *Histoire du Marquis de Cressy* offer clear instances of feminist critiques of male advantage in the social relations between the sexes and are obvious candidates for a more balanced account of eighteenth-century fiction. In the second, if within the genre of the male memoir as psychosexual recollection we shift the emphasis away from novels that feature the list of conquests to the obsession of a single passion, one might interestingly contrast *Manon Lescaut* with Tencin's almost contemporaneous *Mémoires du Comte de Comminge* for another view of masculine subjectivity.

of *Littérature Française, 5, De Fénelon à Voltaire* and *6, De L'Encyclopédie aux Méditations;* the former edited by René Pomeau and Jean Ehrard, the latter by Michel Delon, Robert Mauzi and Sylvain Menant).

The difference in treatment of men's and women's novels is related to a question of category and definition: the men appear in the table of contents with their names under the large headings: "Great Works, Great Authors" (*"Grandes Oeuvres, Grands Auteurs"*). Except for Staël (and she is part of an ensemble along with *"Benjamin Constant et le groupe de Coppet"*) no women's names appear in the table of contents, or in the bibliographical sketches at the back of the book. But the exquisite cadavers are there, of course, slotted into the subset of a literary historical category: the sentimental novel, under "Forms and Genres." Under the promising heading, "toward a new novel" (Vol. 5), Tencin and Graffigny are located within the subheading, "the novel of/for sensitive hearts" (*"le roman des coeurs sensibles"*). (They cannot have read Tencin.) We also find: Riccoboni–less talented than Richardson and Diderot in her ability to create the illusion of reality (Riccoboni *"ignore le pittoresque,"* Delon 6: 216). And at the end of the century, we find in a short list, as servile imitators of Rousseau, the women novelists Krudener, Charrière, Cottin, Staël (*"Staël elle-même"*[!]), "who borrow from Rousseau their characters, situations, settings and the means of moving their female readers, for these women are primarily addressing a female audience" (Delon, 221).

Although in their analyses of the production, distribution and consumption of books, the authors of these manuals rarely distinguish by gender, they do pay attention to the role of education in the formation of a reading public (Pomeau, 45) and note the situation of women excluded from the scenes of knowledge; with a few exceptions women are seen as not fit for studying serious subjects: "women are granted the novel, the frivolous genre, without anyone suspecting that it is to them that the novel will owe its surprising development" (Pomeau, 45). The problem is that this acknowledgment of women's crucial role in the production of the novel and its paradoxical relation to women's social inferiority stops there and congeals into commonplace. It does not take the next step to reflect upon its own categories of analysis, categories that by their language–Great Works, Great Authors–return women to invisibility, to the clichés of a female novel-reading public on the one hand, the *lectrice,* and of women writers as inferior imitators of a perfected male model and novel of the feminine to boot!–Richardson and Rousseau. In their blind admiration for the masterpieces of the dominant tradition, they fail to see women novelists in the eighteenth century, on the one hand, as the continuers of a powerful tradition of seventeenth-century women writers, and on the other as the producers of new forms. I cannot stress too emphatically the degree of canon-*de*formation this failure of vision represents. By this I mean the process of selection by which the authorial and reading practices as well as the "preferences" of a given cultural moment are erased, forgotten and rewritten as a transcendent literary history; or worse still, a matter of taste.

What we need to write a history of the eighteenth-century novel are some new ways of thinking about what goes on in a republic of letters (Pomeau,

43–57), restoring its heterogeneity, looking at the social values that subtend its literature. By looking at the feminist novels of critique and dissent, it becomes possible to understand better what Jane Tompkins in her provocative study of American fiction calls "cultural 'work'" (xv) within a national tradition: to understand the ways "that literature has power in the world, to see how it connects with the beliefs and attitudes of large masses of readers so as to impress or move them deeply" (xiv).

Let me return now to the case of Mrs. Mittin's mistake. Graffigny's *Peruvian Letters* is a novel that like most women's novels in France enjoyed tremendous popularity when it was published, and in this case even a certain posterity: thirty editions, including ten in English and Italian, until 1777, and then continuous publication until 1835. Despite its contemporary critical recognition, the novel rarely figures in the standard accounts of eighteenth-century fiction, nor until recently has it been collected in standard editions. Unlike many female-authored novels, however, the *Peruvian Letters* has had a reprieve of sorts. In 1967 an Italian scholar, Gianni Nicoletti, brought out a critical edition of the novel, the first republication since the early nineteenth century. And in 1983, perhaps more important, a paperback edition based on Nicoletti's work was published by Garnier Flammarion in a collection of epistolary, love-letter novels. This volume has made it possible for the first time to teach the novel as a matter of course. Will this be the case?

Despite the work's material availability, without a rethinking of the criteria that consigned the novel to oblivion in the first part of the nineteenth century, without a critical reflection about the act of women's writing as a type of cultural intervention, it is not at all clear that the Peruvian letters will emerge from the margins to be read alongside, for example, the Persian ones. The very fact of classifying the novel as a "love-letter novel" maintains the hierarchy of classifications that, as I suggested, in the standard manuals, trivializes female authorship.

The reconstructive project of reading women's writing necessarily involves textual strategies that acknowledge the peculiar status of this literature in the library: there, but as I have argued, in opposition to the *déjà lu*, the "already read" of the canon–"underread"–"*sous lu*," cut off from the kind of historical and metacritical life that characterizes the works of the dominant tradition (Miller, "Arachnologies," 7). Learning to read women's writing entails not only a particular attentiveness to the marks of signature, it also involves "reading in pairs," in Naomi Schor's coinage, "*intersextually*" (84). By this I mean looking bi-focally, bi-nocularly at the literature of men's and women's writing side by side to perceive at their points of intersection the lines of another history of the novel, a history more like the one that actually took place: Persian *and* Peruvian.

It does not require major archaeological skills to begin this task. It is a question, rather, of looking again. In closing, I will offer an example of this re-vision that will ultimately bring us full circle. At the end of his long essay on Fanny Burney's *Cecilia* in which he makes the claim that women are particularly well suited to novel writing because it requires the skills of observing, feeling and depicting (*"observer, sentir et peindre,"* 501), Laclos concludes: "Finally, we think that this novel must be counted among the best works in this genre, with nevertheless the exception of *Clarissa*, the novel in which one finds the most genius, *Tom Jones*, the best constructed novel, and *la Nouvelle Héloïse*, the most beautiful work ever produced under the title of the novel" (521). Although we find here of course the now classic move of putting the woman in her place, what interests me in Laclos's poetics of the novel is its explicitly gendered approach to comparative literature. But there is yet another comparison to be made.

In the original preface to *Evelina,* Burney begins with a paragraph almost identical in its language to the beginning of Laclos's review article: "In the republic of letters, there is no member of such inferior rank, or who is so much disdained by his brethren of the quill, as the humble Novelist," but in her conclusion she places herself differently in this fraternity. Despite the various powers of Johnson, Rousseau, Richardson, Fielding and Smollett, Burney will not pursue, she explains, "the same ground": "In books," she argues, "imitation cannot be shunned too seduously; for the very perfection of a model which is frequently seen, serves but more forcibly to mark the inferiority of a copy" (n.p.).

In the preface to *her* "letters," Graffigny, in the familiar ironic style of eighteenth-century philosophical discourse, also raises the problem of imitation in what I see as a similar defense of new ground, and that I read as a claim for the originality of a woman writer. She regrets the power of prejudice that leads "us" (the French) to scorn other nations, notably the Indians, "except to the extent that their customs imitate ours, that their language resembles our idiom" (Flammarion, 249). "We" might today as feminist critics interpret this as a gloss on the status of women's writing in the dominant culture: the canon retains what it knows how to read, when it recognizes its own idiom.

By way of a conclusion, I now want simply to summarize the two local points I hope to have made here: the first is that in the range of works that are retained in the standard account of "the eighteenth-century novel," one might want to see the ways in which the very categories that define this corpus effectively serve to suppress a wide range of women's writing which I will call feminist texts. When women's novels are placed in the category of the sentimental (for *"coeurs sensibles"*) and not read as fictions of social life, what results is a distortion of the fabric of literary exchanges–not to mention, a distorted account of a highly dialogic sociality. My second point is that the exclusion of these voices of critique is supported and naturalized by a critical discourse of male bonding that gets caught up in the mirrors of representation (Etiemble, the masculinist critic, sees himself in *Faublas, etc.* This identification, which is bound up with another kind of mirroring, bears upon the general ignorance of a female and feminist tradition of writing and rewriting that did not in the history of the novel wait for Rousseau or Richardson to take shape.

Works Cited

Burney, Fanny. *Camilla*, 1796; rpt. Ed. Edward A. Bloom and Lillian D. Bloom. Oxford and New York: Oxford University Press, 1983.

——. *Evelina*, 1778; rpt. New York: Norton, 1967.

Colette, Sidonie Gabrielle. *The Vagabond*. Trans. Enid McLeod. New York: Farrar, Straus and Giroux, 1955; repr. 1980.

——. *Oeuvres*. Ed. Claude Pichois. Paris: Gallimard, 1984.

Delon, Michel, Robert Mauzi, Sylvain Menant, eds. *Littérature Française 6. De L'Encyclopédie aux Méditations*. Paris: Arthaud, 1984.

DuPlessis, Rachel. *Writing Beyond the Ending: Narrative Strategies of Twentieth-Century Women Writers*. Bloomington: Indiana University Press, 1985.

Etiemble, ed. *Romanciers du XVIIIe Siècle*. 2 Vols. Paris: Gallimard, 1966.

Graffigny, Françoise de. *Lettres d'une Péruvienne*, 1747, rpt. in *Lettres Portugaises, Lettres d'une Péruvienne et autres romans d'amour par lettres*. Ed. Bernard Bray and Isabelle Landy-Houillon. Paris: Flammarion, 1983.

——. *Lettres d'une Péruvienne*. Ed. Gianni Nicoletti. Bari: Adriatica Editrice, 1967.

Kelly-Gadol, Joan. "The Social Relations of the Sexes: Methodological Implications of Women's History." *Signs: Journal of Women in Culture and Society* 1, 4 (Summer 1976): 809–824.

Laclos, Choderlos de. *Oeuvres Complètes*. Paris: Gallimard, 1959.

May, Georges. *Le Dilemme du Roman au XVIIIe siècle: Etude sur les rapports du roman et de la critique (1715–1761)*. New Haven and Paris: Presses Universitaires de France, 1963.

Miller, Nancy K. "Arachnologies." In *The Poetics of Gender*. Ed. Nancy K. Miller. New York: Columbia University Press, 1986.

Pomeau, René and Jean Ehrard, eds. *Littérature Française 5. De Fénelon a Voltaire: 1680–1750*. Paris: Arthaud, 1984.

Rochefort, Christiane. "Are Women Writers Still Monsters?" In *New French Feminisms*. Ed. Elaine Marks and Isabelle de Courtivron. Amherst: University of Massachusetts Press, 1980.

Schor, Naomi. "La Pérodie: Superposition dans *Lorenzaccio*." *Michigan Romance Studies* (1982) 1: 73–86.

Tompkins, Jane. *Sensational Designs: The Cultural Work of American Fiction, 1790–1860.* New York: Oxford, 1985.

Winnett, Susan. "Coming Unstrung: Women, Men, Narrative and Principle(s) of Pleasure." Unpublished ms.

Woolf, Virginia. "Women and Fiction." In *Women and Writing,* Ed. Michèle Barrett. New York and London: Harcourt Brace Jovanovich, 1980.

The Novel as Narrative Process

The last panel of the conference, "The Novel as Narrative Process (its mimetic and self-reflexive characteristics)," was chaired by Naomi Schor, Nancy Duke Lewis Professor of French Studies at Brown, herself adept in narrative and feminist studies. Like other enlisted moderators, Professor Schor found the title of her panel and the "helpful parenthesis" that went with it in the NEH conference proposal "somewhat enigmatic":

Confronted with *this* postmodern perplex–what is the narrative process, and how does it relate to the familiar questions of mimesis and self-reflexivity–I decided to look the words up in the dictionary.... Among the several meanings of the word "process" I discovered two whose antithetical meanings seemed to me to be at work in different ways in our panelists' papers. For process means both continuous forward movement, procedure, progress ... and a series of actions, motions, or operations definitely conducing to an end. In other words, process signifies both open-endedness–process as opposed to the finished product–and closure, the inexorable movement toward a *telos*. Whether placed in the service of a feminist or a formalist critique of the mimetic claims of classical realism, the recent emphasis on narrative process subverts traditional notions of causality, identity, and univocal meaning. At the same time, however, because process itself is by definition end-oriented, process in narration is not finally incompatible with closure representation and interpretation. Our panelists are uniquely qualified to both valorize process and to mediate between its opposing meanings and claims.

Schor's introduction proved apt. In the two papers that followed, Rachel Blau Duplessis pursued a feminist critique, Elizabeth Ermarth a formalist critique, of the claims of classical realism; and Ermarth especially tried "to mediate between ... opposing meanings and claims."

Feminist Narrative in Virginia Woolf

RACHEL BLAU DUPLESSIS

In homage to one of the great modes of the novel in our time, I am basing this paper on some of the narrative possibilities offered by Reader's Digest Condensed Books. The book I am condensing is *Writing Beyond the Ending,** offering some of the background arguments and summarizing how the cultural work of Virginia Woolf exemplifies certain feminist strategies of narrative. By feminist I mean the explicit critique of existing gender arrangements and the sex-gender system as part of the necessary and enabling cultural work of a writer.

In nineteenth-century fiction dealing with women, authors went to a good deal of trouble and even some awkwardness to see to it that *Bildung* and romance could not co-exist and be integrated for the heroine at the resolution, although works combining these two discourses in their main part (the narrative middle) are among the most important fictions of our tradition. This contradiction between love and quest in plots dealing with women as a narrated group, acutely visible in nineteenth-century fiction, has one main mode of resolution: an ending in which one part of that contradiction, usually quest or *Bildung*, is set aside or repressed, whether by marriage or by death.[1] It is one of the projects of twentieth-century women writers to solve the contradiction between love and quest and the alternate endings in marriage and death that are the writers' cultural legacy by a different set of choices. They invent a complex of narrative acts, which themselves draw on two contradictory oscillations in the psychological and the social spheres, narrative acts which are my general subject, and which I have termed writing beyond the ending.[2]

Significant twentieth-century female authors have taken the romance plot as summarizing some intransigent set of relations which they will not accept in the broadly cultural and specifically narrative forms in which it had appeared at the resolution of nineteenth-century texts (and in which it still appears in both modern and contemporary works). Hence the romance plot is a major focus of their intrepid scrutiny which constitutes one aspect of their poetics of critique and their transformation of narrative.

---

* *Writing Beyond the Ending: Narrative Strategies of Twentieth-Century Women Writers,* Indiana University Press, 1985, © Rachel Blau DuPlessis, 1985. Material drawn from this book is reprinted with the permission of the publisher and the author.

[1] This either/or choice was the subject of considerable comment; for example, Mona Caird, *The Morality of Marriage* (London: Redway, 1897): In the future "women will no longer have to choose between freedom and the affections of the home–now the stern alternatives," p. 145. Nancy K. Miller's study of this contradiction for the eighteenth-century novel is exemplary: *The Heroine's Text: Readings in the French and English Novel, 1722–1782* (New York: Columbia University Press, 1980).

[2] My use of narrative convention as a site of struggle, involving "the embodiment and performance of known but excluded and subordinated experiences and relationships; the articulation and formation of latent, momentary, and newly possible consciousness," is deeply indebted to Raymond Williams, for whom "The reality of conventions as the mode of junction of social position and literary practice remains central," *Marxism and Literature* (Oxford: Oxford University Press, 1977), pp. 212 and 179.

This concern to examine romance enters their artworks, not only in overt content and critical remarks but more drastically in the place where ideology is coiled: in narrative structure. As a narrative pattern, the romance plot muffles the main female character, represses quest, valorizes heterosexual ties as opposed to homosexual, incorporates individuals within couples as a sign of their personal and narrative success. The romance plot separates love and quest, values sexual asymmetry including the division of labor by gender; it can be based on extremes of sexual difference, and it evokes an aura around the couple. In short, the romance plot, broadly speaking, is a trope for the sex-gender system as a whole. Writing beyond the ending means the transgressive invention of narrative strategies, strategies which express critical dissent from dominant narrative as a branch of dominant values.

Virginia Woolf conducted a serious and continual scrutiny of these issues throughout her career. Woolf's discussion of *"Life's Adventure,"* an imaginary book by an imagined contemporary novelist named "Mary Carmichael," proposes two critical acts for modern women writers: breaking the sentence and breaking the sequence.[3] Both are ruptures with conventional literary practice. Breaking the sentence severs dominant authority and ideology. Breaking the sequence is a critique of narrative, restructuring its orders and priorities precisely by attention to specific issues of female identity.

The formal questions about fiction which Woolf raised in "Modern Fiction" are elaborated and socially grounded a decade later in "Women and Fiction" (1929), a work related to *A Room of One's Own.* Here the sentence, the plot, narrative convention and subject matter will alike be subjected to revisionary scrutiny by the female novelist because these narrative forms and modes carry an ideological and interpretive freight about gender. Woolf argued repeatedly that the prevalent values of fiction are androcentric, devaluing or rendering minor and suspect female experiences.

> . . . *as men are the arbiters of that* [social] *convention, as they have established an order of values in life, so to, since fiction is largely based on life, these values prevail there also to a very great extent.*
>
> *It is probable, however, that both in life and in art, the values of a woman are not the values of a man. Thus, when a woman comes to write a novel, she will find that she is perpetually wishing to alter the established values—to make serious what appears insignificant to a man, and trivial what is to him important.*[4]

---

[3] Virginia Woolf, *A Room of One's Own* [1929] (New York: Harcourt, Brace and World, Inc., 1957), abbreviated in the text as *AROO:* "I am almost sure, I said to myself, that Mary Carmichael is playing a trick on us. For I feel as one feels on a switchback railway when the car, instead of sinking, as one has been led to expect, swerves up again. Mary is tampering with the expected sequence. First she broke the sentence; now she has broken the sequence. . . . Perhaps she had done this unconsciously, merely giving things their natural order, as a woman would, if she wrote like a woman. But the effect was somehow baffling; one could not see a wave heaping itself, a crisis coming round the next corner. . . . For whenever I was about to feel the usual things in the usual places, about love, about death, the annoying creature twitched me away, as if the important point were just a little further on," pp. 85 and 95.

[4] "Women and Fiction," *Granite and Rainbow* (New York: Harcourt, Brace and Company, 1958), p. 81.

Trying to make fiction talk about women and their concerns, especially when a woman is the speaking subject, may necessarily lead to a critical transformation of narrative structures, to reversals, reassessments, reweightings of all sorts. Woolf's argument here strongly proposes female difference. The question therefore follows: what is different about women, or at least sufficiently different to make these claims plausible.

The psycho-sexual and socio-cultural structures of female identity are elucidated in two oscillations repeatedly visible in the texts and careers of women writers. The process of oedipalization traced by Freud contains the crucial "admission" (in the Freudian context) that this crisis of gendering ineluctably contains a massive oscillation between oedipal and pre-oedipal situations and resolutions, so the goal of heterosexual object choice is repeatedly colored by, and in some tension with, female bonding, mothering, and the mother-daughter dyad.[5]

The narrative and cultural implications of this neo-Freudian picture of gendering are staggering. With no easy or one-directional passage to "normal femininity," women as social products are characterized by unresolved and continuous alternations between allegiance to males and to females, between heterosexuality and female-identified, lesbian, or bisexual ties. The "original bisexuality" of the individual female is not easily put to rest or resolved by one early tactical episode. Further, the emotional rhythms of female identity involve repeated (and possibly even simultaneous) articulations of these two principles or states, which are taken (ideologically) as opposing poles.[6]

Many twentieth-century women writers undertake a reassessment of the processes of gendering by inventing narrative strategies, especially involving sequence, character, and relationship, that neutralize, minimize, or transcend any oversimplified oedipal drama. Effort is devoted to depicting masculine and feminine "sides" of a single character who contains her/his own "plot" involving semi-conjugal relations–in Woolf's androgyny and in similar procedures in Dorothy Richardson. Original bisexuality is extended the length of a character's narrated life in Woolf and in H.D. Women writers readjust the maternal and paternal in ways that unbalance the univocal sequence of object choice. Such narratives, notably female *Künstlerromane*, may invent an interplay between mother, father and female hero in a relational triangle. These changes are often accompanied by pointed remarks about the plots, characters, and situations once expected in narrative: gender polarization, patrisexual romantic love, the arrest of female quest, the "happy ending"–remarks that underline the self-consciousness of this critique of narrative scripts.

---

[5] The relevant texts are Sigmund Freud, "The Psychology of Women" (1933), in *New Introductory Lectures on Psycho-Analysis*, trans. W.J.H. Sprott (New York: W.W. Norton and Company, 1933); the same essay is called "Femininity" in *The Standard Edition of the Complete Psychological Works of Sigmund Freud*, Vol. 22, trans. James Strachey (London: The Hogarth Press and the Institute of Psychoanalysis, 1964); Nancy Chodorow, *The Reproduction of Mothering: Psychoanalysis and the Sociology of Gender* (Berkeley: University of California Press, 1978).

[6] Chodorow summarizes the female's "emotional, if not erotic bisexual oscillation between mother and father–between preoccupation with 'mother-child' issues and 'male-female' issues," p. 168. I am indebted to Chodorow for the concept of oscillation which I have extended in certain ways.

The new, contradictory paths back and forth through oedipal materials, the psycho-sexual oscillation of the gendering process, so distinctly theorized, interact with another systemic aspect of female identity, which shows the same wavering, dialogic structure: a socio-cultural oscillation of hegemonic processes.

In the social and cultural arenas, there is a constant repositioning between dominant and muted, hegemonic and oppositional, central and colonial, so that a woman may be described as (ambiguously) nonhegemonic, or, with equal justice but less drama, as (ambiguously) hegemonic if her race, class and sexuality exist within dominant paradigms.[7] Virginia Woolf envisions this oscillating consciousness in *A Room of One's Own*:

> *It* [the mind] *can think back through its fathers or through its mothers, as I have said that a woman writing thinks back through her mothers. Again if one is a woman one is often surprised by a sudden splitting off of consciousness, say in walking down Whitehall, when from being the natural inheritor of that civilization, she becomes, on the contrary, outside of it, alien and critical.* (*AROO* 101)

Note how, interestingly for this argument, Woolf passes from the oedipal-preoedipal division in object relations to the social oscillation, suggesting the deep but unarticulated connection between both processes in the creation of female identity. The debate between inheritor and critic is a movement between strong identification with dominant values and alienation from them. The way the passage proposes an opposition between "natural" and "critical" focuses its intent. "Natural" is what every ideology happily claims it is; the beliefs, social practices, senses of the self are second nature, assumed. The word "critical," however, has the force of a severe and transgressive dissent from cherished mental structures and social practices. In relation to this oscillation of hegemonic process, writers like Woolf undertake a reassessment of the mechanisms of social insertion for women through the family house, the private sphere and patriarchal hierarchies, inventing narratives that offer, in the multiple individual and the collective protagonist, alternatives to individual quests and couple formation.

Virginia Woolf's career as a novelist makes two great lines crossing on one major problem–the formation of narrative strategies that make a critique of both gendering and hegemonic processes by rupturing the sentences and sequences of romance and related materials in quest plots. Both of her very first novels draw on the traditional concerns of love plots–the production of newly joined heterosexual couples, and of quest plots–the *Bildung* of the protagonist. That is, in *The Voyage Out* (1915) and *Night and Day* (1919) Woolf considers the endings in engagement to marry and death.[8] After these novels, heterosexual

---

[7] "(Ambiguously) nonhegemonic" from my essay "For the Etruscans," in Elaine Showalter, ed., *The New Feminist Criticism: Women, Literature and Theory* (New York: Pantheon Books, 1985), pp. 271–91.

[8] *Jacob's Room*, which I do not discuss in my book, could be seen as the symbolic displacement and death of the male hero, which clears the way for the female hero and her plots. Obvious abbreviations will be used for the works cited in the text:

romance is displaced from a controlling and privileged position in her work.[9] It will never again appear as the unique center of narrative concern; it will never again appear assumed or unquestioned. *Mrs. Dalloway* (1925) offers thematic and structural debates about romantic love, the structural debate centering on the cunning device of a nonsexual yet secretly bonded couple–Mrs. Dalloway herself and Septimus Smith–as the bifocal center of the work. *To the Lighthouse* (1927) has a critical relation to the marriage plot and proposes a special passage through "reparenting" for Lily. *Orlando* (1928) and *Flush* (1933) close the issue of heterosexual love by drastic changes in its definition–the latter by describing the burning and yearning passions of a jealous pooch.

To the Lighthouse is able in a different way to express the desire for a female bond which also emerges in *Mrs. Dalloway*'s Clarissa-Sally materials, by fashioning a story which displaces the heterosexual love plot in favor of the parent-child tie, a bisexual oscillation between mother and father. The love of Lily for Mrs. Ramsay, which creates vision, and the moment of empathy for the widowed Mr. Ramsay, which creates sociability, are both formative events of far greater importance than the traces of heterosexual courtship plots in the novel. In the first section of *To the Lighthouse*, community (the dinner party) had depended extensively on couples and the bait of romance; Minta's golden haze of love helps the emotional entanglements of family life; Lily reluctantly attends to the young man to whom she has been assigned, after rich meditations on refusal and rebellion. But Woolf supplants the formation of a new couple as plot center. Lily is fabricated deliberately to avoid the romantic involvements that are proposed, and Mrs. Ramsay is explicitly criticized for proposing them. The detailed consideration of an old couple always in the process of reformation and affirmation is put in the context of many other networks, communities and ties: "geniality, sisterhood, motherhood, brotherhood" as another novel says (*MD* 209). And by the death of Mrs. Ramsay at midbook, the affirmation of the romantic, polarized couple is put definitively in the past. In the third section, community and selfhood must be negotiated in the absence of the promise of couple love that once mediated them. This occurs through a concerted use of the pre-oedipal materials of female identity, to dissolve the purely romantic telos of the oedipal drama. In *Mrs. Dalloway* and then in *To the Lighthouse*, Woolf has redefined the story of romance by posing the pre-oedipal alternatives, lesbian bonding and the mother-child dyad, to rupture the cultural hegemony of the love plot.

The novels along the second major line of Woolf's career–*The Years* (1937) and *Between the Acts* (1941) as well as *The Waves* (1931)–ask a fundamental ideological and structural question: what "social" desires will empower stories and characters if a writer does not depend on the emphases and motivations of romance? Here Woolf displaces the emotional aura and structural weight of

---

MD is *Mrs. Dalloway* (New York: Harcourt, Brace and World, 1925); Y is *The Years* (New York: Harcourt, Brace and World, 1937); TG is *Three Guineas* (New York: Harcourt, Brace and World, 1938).

[9] Woolf investigates where to put romance even at the absolute beginning of her writing career, in "The Journal of Mistress Joan Martyn" (1906); although unfinished, the work asks questions that Woolf's whole *oeuvre* answers. The work appears in *Twentieth Century Literature* 25, 3/4 (Fall/Winter 1979), ed. Susan M. Squier and Louise A. DeSalvo.

individual quest and of hero and heroine onto a communal protagonist. This protagonist–a large family, a group of friends, an audience, containing many close bonds and, importantly, including equalized members of all ages and sexual persuasions–creates a structure in which couples, individuals, walls between public and private, polarized sexes, and closures in (and of) family houses are subject to strong oppositional formations. In general, Woolf separates *eros* from any forced or conventional bonds, especially such institutions as heterosexuality and marriage.

In 1927 Woolf foresaw intergeneric works which were to reject the realistic sociological novel of facts, incomes and environment; the psychological novel with "the incessant, the remorseless analysis of falling into love and falling out of love . . . ," plots, in short, of quests ending in success or failure and of romance.[10] Her later novels substitute for these discredited narratives the invention of a communal protagonist and a collective language.

The communal protagonist is a way of organizing the work so that neither the development of an individual against a backdrop of supporting characters nor the formation of a heterosexual couple is central to the novel. The collective protagonist makes the group, not the individual, the central character.[11] Not based on individual *Bildung* or romance, but rather on a collective *Bildung* and communal affect, the novel can suggest (a plausible utopia of) social change in the structures of narrative. The promotion of any given character to a position of greatest importance in a narrative indicates values and marks social hierarchies.[12] To discredit this social practice of narrative, in *The Years* and *Between the Acts*, Woolf has equalized the characters. No one stands higher in the plot than any other: the final conveyor of value is plural. Several of Woolf's discarded titles for *The Years* show her thinking: *The Caravan* is a collective ramshackle journeying, *Ordinary People* evokes the multiple and humdrum at once.[13] Altogether, the books express "'I' rejected; 'we' substituted."[14]

Woolf makes community plausible by rhetorical and stylistic tactics. She interpenetrates choral remarks so that each character is continuing, adding, intuiting, and humorously modifying the other's longing. She makes a concerted use of the ellipses of conversational outreach, of space for desire and possibility. She uses a question mark as a political statement about dialogue, openness.

---

[10] Woolf, "The Narrow Bridge of Art," *Granite and Rainbow*, p. 19.

[11] Indeed, in an essay on Turgenev written in 1933, after the completion of *The Waves* and during the inception of *The Years*, Woolf reflects that for the novel combining fact and vision, the poetic and the commonplace, poetry and realism–that is, the work she excitedly contemplated as *The Years*–character as it is known in English novels must be sacrificed. Characters "dominate" and "destroy" the balance she sought. See "The Novels of Turgenev," in *The Captain's Death Bed and Other Essays* (New York: Harcourt Brace Jovanovich, 1950), p. 57.

[12] Raymond Williams makes this point in *Marxism and Literature*, p. 175.

[13] Evidence for the rejected working titles is found in *A Writer's Diary*, ed. Leonard Woolf (New York: Harcourt Brace and Company, 1954), pp. 228, 229.

[14] *A Writer's Diary*, p. 279, planning for *Between the Acts*.

> "But how ..." she began, "... how can we improve ourselves ... live more
> ..." she dropped her voice as if she were afraid of waking sleepers, "... live
> more naturally ... better ... How can we?"
> "It is only a question," he said–he stopped. He drew himself close to her–"of
> learning. The soul ..." Again he stopped.
> "Yes–the soul?" she prompted him.
> "The soul–the whole being," he explained. He hollowed his hands as if to en-
> close a circle. "It wishes to expand; to adventure; to form–new combinations?"
>
> (Y 296)

And what prevents this expansive, interrogative possibility? "Each is his own
little cubicle; each with his fire, his wife ..." (Y 296). Allegiances to particular
romance, private property, and defensively maintained values are the barriers
to "new combinations"; it is the business of The Years not to attack but rather
to dissolve these barriers, whose knotlike bastion is the private sphere. Hence
a narrative dissolution of the institution that produces a private/public dichotomy, related to and upheld by conventions of gender, becomes central to the
novel. I mean the family.

By transforming the family into a group protagonist, Woolf goes to the
heart of the Victorian ideology of the dichotomous division of the world into
separate and opposing spheres: public/social and private/domestic, which are,
in apparently natural fashion, allocated to the sexes in a division of labor and
activities. The family, Woolf shows oppositionally, is the institution that reveals the interpenetration of public and private, "the tyrannies and servilities
of the one are the tyrannies and servilities of the other" (TG 142). She dedi-
cates the texture and structure of her later novels to elaborating that inseparable connection and to contesting the ideology of separate spheres.

So out of her critique of romance, with its icon of couple formation, its
idealization of the family house, the private sphere for women, and the often
hierarchical division of labor by gender, Woolf has formulated an oppositional
narrative strategy expressing a set of critical values: the collective protagonist.
This protagonist functions, to allude back to the citation from A Room of One's
Own, to allow inheritor and critic to coexist in one narrative space. For while
Woolf wanted strongly to propose changed values and ideas, she resisted, for
political reasons of great power, coercion and promulgation; she resisted the
authoritarian both in idea and in narrative practice.[15] Hence the new center
of vision represented by North, Eleanor, Nicholas, Peggy and Sara remains in
a willing dialogue with hegemonic values and characters, desiring not to
coerce but to welcome them. This is why, during the resolution, Nicholas
never makes a public celebratory speech (coded by Woolf as a ridiculous

[15] During the long and painful process of composition of The Years, Woolf engaged in an intense debate about its narrative
politics, asking how to bring the dominant order into question without being tainted by dominant values. One solution
was her wrenching rejection of a brilliant mixed-genre design for the novel–The Pargiters design–which alternated didactic
essay with narrative. The values she wanted the work to express were being undermined by the preachy patriarchal tone
of the essays. Woolf feared that The Pargiters had been Creonesque: commanding assent, making it possible to interpret
certain incidents only one way, brooking no argument. In contrast, Woolf projected an Antigonesque narrative: tolerant,
humane, forgiving.

presumption of authority), but responds to Kitty's individual need for a toast by a personal gesture. This is why the novel ends as emergent Eleanor extends welcoming hands to her retrograde brother Morris and inquires, "And now?" having seen from the window yet another bourgeois house close with a thud on yet another young couple. Woolf constructs the work so that the whole collective protagonist includes both vanguard outsiders and the "old brothers and sisters," and all may step into the postbourgeois world together.

Conspicuous Construction; or, Kristeva, Nabokov, and The Anti-Realist Critique

ELIZABETH DEEDS ERMARTH

The conflict between realists and anti-realists re-enacts a powerful cultural habit of dualistic formulation. No sooner do we stop assuming representational values, a state aggravated, no doubt, by reading realistic novels, than we proceed to find reflexiveness everywhere; and, whether the shocking impulse is James Joyce or French philosophy, we proceed to apply that new norm with the same zeal once reserved for the old one. For those who thrive on the agony of combat my presentation will perhaps sound a dull note because I find no abyss between representation and reflexion, or between their counterparts, the symbolic and semiotic; no abyss even between realist and anti-realist conceived as two halves of a similar dualism. The differences look to me more like matters of position on the same playing field and the distinction more like a net across which a certain game is played. By emphasizing one or the other half of a dualism we reinforce a deeply rooted mental habit that not only easily contains shifts of 180 degrees–for example, the shift from mimesis to reflexion–but that also survives such shifts and actually thrives on them. How to move away from this time-honored playing field to something really new is not only a problem for critical discourse but also a much broader cultural issue.

I will concentrate on the work of two writers, one a French theorist, one a Russian-American novelist. Both participate in the current critique of Western discourse in ways that not only are mutually informative but that also suggest new directions for the energies of interpreters like ourselves. By inviting Julia Kristeva and Vladimir Nabokov into the same paragraph I suggest that they act as accomplices–perhaps unwitting ones–in that redefinition of fundamental premises which I take to be central to postmodernism. Both begin with language and its processes and for both a key step, perhaps *the* key step, is the reinstatement of semiosis into the symbolic order. Privately I think that the novelists were telling us earlier and better some things that have since emerged into theoretical debate; but this putative priority means only that we might look for critical tools in fiction as well as in more theoretical writing, now that theory has contributed so much to our general understanding of interpretive and cultural discourse. Nabokov's work shares with Kristeva's an emphasis on semiotic powers in language.

When Kristeva identifies the two dispositions in language as the symbolic and the semiotic she insists that neither alone exhausts linguistic function and that both are necessary. The symbolic function is the one that "communicates meaning," the one that constitutes itself by predication, the one that is thetic and syntactical. The semiotic disposition, by contrast, remains "heterogeneous" to meaning; to it belongs the musical, rhythmic, non-sense effects of language, the ones evident in poetry or in the echolalias of children (Kristeva also cites "carnivalesque discourse, Artaud, a number of texts by Mallarmé, certain Dadaist and Surrealist experiments"). These dispositions of language, Kristeva argues, cannot be severed and the practice of emphasizing one at the expense of the other leads to disorder. Language depends on the joint function of symbolic and semiotic disposition, the joint operation of syntax and parataxis, the combined effect of rhythmic and thetic utterance.

Achieving such balance in language is not a simple matter, to put it mildly, and in part the complexity proceeds from the fact that the achievement depends upon renouncing familiar mental habits. What linguists and, presumably, the rest of us need is a theory that, in Kristeva's words, "would search within the signifying phenomenon for the *crisis* or the *unsettling process* of meaning and subject rather than for the coherence or identity of either *one* or a *multiplicity* of structures." In other words, what we need is a theory of process rather than of product, but process forever separated from the product which formerly subverted it: process conceived as an unsettling maneuver whereby meaning and subject cease to be structures of static forms and become permanently questionable, always unfolding activities.[1]

Such linguistic matters belong for Kristeva at the heart of philosophical, aesthetic, and theological matters, or rather, those matters are at heart linguistic ones. It is crucial for understanding so many of the best contemporary writers that their work addresses such problems of meaning at the level of language and with the assumption that language in its full power is poetic as well as symbolic. Poetic language, we note, is not equated *with* but is opposed *to* symbolic language. In other words, language exercised in its full power as both semiotic and symbolic and understood as a process of construction fundamental to all other conscious construction, such language does not merely point to philosophical, aesthetic, or theological discourse, it *is* philosophical, aesthetic, and theological discourse. This point seems worth emphasizing because many who are alarmed by semiotics (and hence by the anti-realists and their French theoretical cronies) suppose that its linguistic emphasis signals the end of clarity and morality.

[1] Julia Kristeva, "From One Identity to An Other," *Desire in Language: A Semiotic Approach to Literature and Art*, trans. Thomas Gora, Alice Jardine, and Leon S. Roudiez (New York: Columbia University Press, 1980), pp. 132, 133–35, 125.

It is true that Kristeva, Nabokov, and their accomplices do reemphasize what is heterogeneous to meaning, and this is tantamount to qualifying an entire cultural and conceptual disposition. The symbolic disposition of language confers identity on the speaking subject by positioning it as the transcendent motivating and originating agent of meaning, the provider of thesis and conclusion. Thus the symbolic disposition insures that the signifying economy creates and supports the speaking subject. This creation is perhaps its most important function, far more profound a function than the meanings and significations to be found in philosophical or other thematic terms. This symbolic disposition, with its subject and structure, and with its thetic impulse for results, provides a sort of linguistic Beyond, or, in Kristeva's terms, a guarantee of "a transcendence, if not a theology." It is this speaking subject that the semiotic disposition of language unsettles (along with meaning and signification) and replaces with a "questionable *subject-in-process.*"[2]

If Kristeva is correct that there is more to language than meaning and signification (*i.e.*, more than the symbolic disposition), then this unsettling process is not an arbitrary production of an idle French intelligentsia or of novelists who just like to show off; instead this unsettling process is normative for, fundamental to, definitive of the proper functioning of language and its constructions. "It is poetic language [the semiotic disposition] that awakens our attention to th[e] undecidable character of any so-called natural language, a feature that univocal, rational, scientific discourse tends to hide."[3] Rational discourse has become arrogant towards its semiotic sibling during several centuries of positive science. By reinstating semiosis Kristeva implicitly displaces the view of language that takes it to be primarily symbolic, that is to say, referential, and with that view are displaced other cultural shibboleths, especially a thetic view of temporal process: the view that is usually invoked by the word "time" and that implies the kinds of history, causality, and moral possibility that presuppose natural law. It is this symbolic view of language, then, that *seems* to be implied by the great realistic novels of the nineteenth century, "a narrative form which," as Robbe-Grillet says, "understandably remains a kind of paradise lost of the novel."[4] It is a view of language that certainly has been implied by much interpretation of fiction.

As I read the bottom line of Kristeva's project, it suggests we exorcize the scientism that has crept into our methodologies and into our transactions with the word, a scientism that has paralyzed language's potent energies and constrained it to a narrowly conceived representational function: one in which a sign simply refers, without any unsettling influence, to a world where language functions chiefly as an instrument of information. With its semiotic disposition restored language always also refers to itself as an entire formulating system wherein the sign has its place and its function as an instrument of human agency and as an entirely human invention. I should not have thought

[2] Kristeva, *Ibid.*, pp. 124, 135.

[3] Kristeva, *Ibid.*, p. 135.

[4] Alain Robbe-Grillet, *For a New Novel: Essays on Fiction*, trans. Richard Howard (New York: Grove Press, 1965), p. 32. Published between 1953 and 1963, the essays were first collected as *Pour un Nouveau Roman* by Les Editions Minuit in 1963.

that professors of literature and language would have objected to this, although certainly they have. The disrupted representational view of language naturalizes it–takes it out of human hands–by the implication that things preceded their names. It is a view represented by Milton in *Paradise Lost* where Adam wakes to find a cosmos, the ultimate *objet trouvé*, and exercises his power over it by assigning names to things. This is also the view parodied by García Marquez in *One Hundred Years of Solitude* where the village falls victim to memory loss and everyone goes around putting little signs on things in order not to forget their names.

As far as I know it is nobody's ambition to establish an exclusively semiotic linguistic practice; but to emphasize the semiotic helps to demonstrate how far gone we are on the road to the other extreme. An exclusively symbolic literary theory masks the semiotic function in order to encode a supposed transcendence which is really a function of linguistic habits. What Kristeva's theory rejects is not at all the symbolic disposition of language but only such disrupted representational or symbolic practices and the theories they imply. This extends by implication to narrative and, perhaps most importantly, to the interpretation *of* narrative that has emphasized meaning and signification at the expense of semiotic and reflexive value. Such disrupted practices do not merely obscure the full range of value in literature, they disturb the renewal of social codes; in other words they block a moral process and often in the name of morality. Kristeva comments explicitly on this important synapse between social order and interpretive practice: "While poetic language can indeed be studied through its meaning, such study reduces it and obscures the very thing that in the poetic function ... makes of what is known as 'literature' something other than knowledge: the very place where the social code is destroyed and renewed."[5]

What Kristeva describes, Nabokov does. His word play is familiar enough. One well-known example is the sentence in *Lolita* where Humbert Humbert reflects, apropos of Lolita's sexual excursions at camp Climax, on the difference between "the rapist" and "therapist": "The rapist was Charlie Holmes; I am the therapist–a matter of nice spacing in the way of distinction" (II:ii). The pun is auditory, it is visual, *and* it is saturated with meaning. A more extended instance of Nabokov's conspicuous construction is this passage from *Ada*, a novel which is one long sustained example of the restoration of semiosis into the symbolic project. Here Van Veen is being interrupted (during an assignation with amorous Lucette) by a telephone call from his secretary, Polly, who is typing his treatise on time. [The confusion between the French for "adored" and the French for "duration" is not entirely a fault of my reading]:

> At this point, as in a well-constructed play larded with comic relief, the brass campophone buzzed and not only did the radiators start to cluck but the uncapped soda water fizzed in sympathy.

---

[5] Kristeva, "One Identity to An Other," *Desire in Language*, p. 132.

*Van (crossly): "I don't understand the first word ... What's that?
L'adorée? Wait a second" (to Lucette). "Please, stay where you are." (Lucette
whispers a French child-word with two "p"s.). "Okay" (pointing toward the cor-
ridor). "Sorry, Polly. Well, is it l'adorée? No? Give me the context. Ah–la durée. La durée is not ... sin on what? Synonymous with duration. Aha sorry
again, I must stopper that orgiastic soda. Hold the line." (Yells down the 'cory
door,' as they called the long second-floor passage at Ardis.) "Lucette, let it run
over who cares!"*

*He poured himself another glass of brandy and for a ridiculous moment could
not remember what the hell he had been—yes, the polliphone.*

*It had died, but buzzed as soon as he recradled the receiver, and Lucette
knocked discreetly at the same time.*

*"La durée ... For goodness sake, come in without knocking ... No, Polly,
knocking does not concern you—it's my little cousin. All right. La durée is not
synonymous with duration, being saturated—yes, as in Saturday—with that particular philosopher's thought. What's wrong now? You don't know if its dorée
or durée? D. U. R. I thought you knew French. Oh, I see. So long.*

*"My typist, a trivial but always available blonde, could not make out durée
in my quite legible hand because, she says, she knows French, but not scientific
French." (II:v)*[6]

A whole lot of construction is going on here. With the simultaneous com-
mencement of phone buzz, radiator cluck, soda fizz, and door knock, we
have the emphasis on coincidence, parodying well-constructed plots: a sort of
temporal collage. The soda is "orgiastic" but alas, and despite long anticipa-
tion, Van and Lucette are not. The rhymes between "cory door" and "second
floor" link this occasion to an amorous moment with Ada in Ardis. Another
conjunction with sense as well as play is the one between "synonymous" and
"sin on" which, though Polly doesn't know it, may be a good comment on
the whole notion of synonymous meaning. "Saturation" and "Saturday" mu-
sically join a condition and a moment. The variations on English and French
words for temporal persistence (*la durée*, "duration," the "long" of "so long")
make a regular little rondo in themselves and allude to the variations on the
theme of time both in Van's treatise and also in Nabokov's *Ada*. The echo between *la durée* and *l'adorée* is a typist's mistake in the symbolic order but is a
luminous conjunction in the Nabokovian play on the theme of time where
time and love are the same. Thematically speaking, of course, I am grateful
for Polly's closing distinction between French and "scientific" French. The
whole situation here is not so much a domestic comedy as it is a linguistic
commentary. There could scarcely be a more literal competition between the
symbolic and semiotic impulses than the interruption of Lucette's whimper of
bliss by the secretary typing a treatise. Of course Lucette's problem always
has been that, unlike her sister Ada, she makes eros "mean" something and
so always fails with Van because she turns sex into a symbolic project. In this

---

[6] Vladimir Nabokov *Lolita*, annotated edition by Alfred Appel, Jr. (New York: McGraw Hill, 1955), pp. 152; and *Ada or Ardor:
A Family Chronicle* (New York: McGraw Hill, 1969), pp. 286–87.

passage we have an instance of rampant reflexiveness, if not severe semiosis, which nevertheless carries meaning; the vigorous restoration of the semiotic apparently does not destroy the symbolic project but, on the contrary, colludes with it.

The emphasis on reflexive play in Nabokov and others seems to me historically intelligible as a response to the almost insane lengths to which we have transformed language into a symbolic instrument. The emphasis on artificiality in language, far from being mere dandyism or anti-bourgeois assault, is an act of restoration of full power to a language that has been bound by a thousand threads in Lilliput. Nabokov's conspicuous construction has little to do with mere self-indulgence, as is sometimes charged, and much to do with the creation of reader-accomplices who will metamorphose through such exercise from being novices to being experts at the art of walking on water, that is, at the art of performing the miracle of language without sinking into this or that message. The alliteration of *Ada*, its time warps, and echoes, and constantly crossing digressions, its always surprising English, mortifies the mind in flight from pleasure. Its digressiveness and its exquisiteness unsettle the reading subject, clearing it off the map for a few hours; its openness is erotic, opposed to closure and to the meanings that belong to systems more or less coherent and ruined. This novel differs from *Middlemarch*, certainly, but how much is a question; the answer partly depends on how much our interpretive habits favor the symbolic view of language.

Our interpretive habits notwithstanding, the novel in differing degrees seems always to have relied on both symbolic and semiotic functions. The nineteenth-century novel was no stranger to semiosis or to "the unsettling process of meaning and subject," nor is the most unsettling contemporary novel estranged from symbolic function. The time has come for me to confess my inability to separate reflexiveness from representation on any grand scale. For example, highly reflexive paintings or novels contain all kinds of representational elements. Escher's prints, cubist collages, and Magritte's bourgeois gentlemen depend for their effect on representational values; so do reflexive fictions by Kafka, Robbe-Grillet, and Nabokov, including the exactitudes of *The Metamorphosis*, the parquet floor in *The Voyeur*, and the motels in *Lolita*. Even where the governing convention is reflexive, not representational, the whole could not function without both dispositions. On the other hand, the most representational painting or novel contains all kinds of reflexive elements and in fact depends on them for the creation of symbolic value. Whatever calls attention to the organizing motives of art is a reflexive device. Tintoretto's "Finding of the Body of St. Mark" (Brera, Milan), a picture organized by the most rigorous representational conventions, vigorously calls attention to its own organizing principles by making the plunging diagonal of the barrel vault converge to the vanishing point just at the upflung hand of the saint. The mirrors in *Vanity Fair*, the multiplied acts of waiting in *Middlemarch*, or of baptism in *Our Mutual Friend*, are reflexive functions, as are the prisons of *Charterhouse of Parma* and *Little Dorrit* and the walls, windows, and ladders of *The Red and the Black*. Pure abstract reflexiveness would be positively pata-physical: pure representation, too, perhaps. There is plot in *Ada* and *Travesty*, there is parataxis in Jane Austen and Stendhal. The shift to semiosis restores a balance, it does not cancel the symbolic disposition of language.

This restoration of semiosis, however, does undermine the privilege of certain ideas based on the disrupted representational view of language, especially the conventional idea of historical time as it has been reflected in fiction for more than two centuries. This linear, causal, teleological time–what Kristeva calls "the time of project and history"[7]–is closely identified by Kristeva with the symbolic function of language and by Robbe-Grillet with the nineteenth-century novel. In *Ada* the time of Balzac or Trollope scarcely exists at all or it exists as something constantly destabilized along with other systems of meaning and value.

To those for whom history means the relativization of every system except history, the anti-historical effort in fiction may seem urgent, violent, perhaps overstated. But the modern idea of history is not the only one and, even to the Renaissance humanists who inspired it, it might seem a bit odd to suppose that *history* could have the power to stabilize meaning.[8] Current efforts at linguistic restoration can appear as one further step in a methodological revolution that began five hundred years ago, that corresponds to the rise of print culture, and that has often been betrayed by a thetic impulse for resolution which has been aimed primarily at saving essences. The continuity of that tradition, its central dispute between dogma on the one hand and, on the other, history broadly conceived as open-ended process, accommodates Kristeva and Nabokov, although they are sometimes carelessly excised from it. Primary conventions, for better or worse, have massive staying power and the news of their demise is usually premature.

Once reflexiveness and semiotic function have regained their rightful place in theory and usage, we may seem to have replaced an Either/Or with a Both/And. The illusory appearance of renovation, however, should not mask the fact that Both/And merely reencodes the same dualisms with their same mental and linguistic baggage rather than gesturing toward a new modality. Such subversion is familiar to feminists, who have always faced a major problem in trying to avoid the trap of simply inverting privilege within the same old dualistic constructions. (The importance of this problem makes most unfortunate Kristeva's eventual move to gender the two dispositions of language, so that the semiotic becomes maternal and the symbolic paternal. Although she disclaims any biological basis for this gendering, holding instead for cultural function, still the gendering invokes biology as destiny and seems an unnecessary subversion of her linguistic argument.) The problem with dualism is its capacity to achieve the appearance of change by merely inverting an already established power structure. The previously depreciated Other, whether it is called semiotic or maternal, now assumes priority and privilege over its for-

---

[7] Julia Kristeva, "Women's Time," trans. Alice Jardine and Harry Blake, *Signs*, Vol. 7, no. 1 (Autumn, 1981), 18.

[8] Their recognition that the past was past–one of the truly original moments in the history of consciousness–included a far different understanding than that of positivist historians backed by two centuries of science.

merly depreciated opposite, changing the terms but retaining the system. In terms of expediency as well as in terms of ethics such reincarnation is undesireable; it subverts the impetus for change. Sooner or later the designated Other—whether it is the symbolic or the semiotic disposition of language, the maternal or paternal function, the reflexive or representational convention—becomes depreciated as the dualism asserts its apparently inevitable tendency to resolve into hierarchy. Women have been perpetual carriers of the depreciated half of binarisms, whatever the changing content of those binarisms may be. Even when that content changes radically over time, women's position in the (rarely explicit) hierarchy remains the same. In short, the trouble with dualisms is their well-known repressions; unsexing dualisms, if that were possible, would still leave them to function as disguised hierarchies.[9] No sooner does imbalance appear, for example, in the reflexion-representation duo, than combat ensues and victory is claimed. The disguised hierarchy generates teleology which in turn generates transcendence.

Anti-realists and theoretical feminists both attack the abuses of a deeply entrenched but manifestly eroded system of assumption and privilege. Together they affirm and extend the massive reexamination of Western discourse itself: its obsession with power and knowledge, its constraint of language to primarily symbolic function, its ethic of winning, its categorical and exclusive modes of definition, its belief in the quantitative and objective; its linear time and individual subject, and above all its common media of exchange (time, space, money) which guarantee certain political and social systems. While the emphasis in such critiques sometimes seems to elide any of the demonstrable virtues of this metaphysic, still it seems important to look beyond its dualisms. Kristeva, despite her unfortunate gendering of linguistic dispositions, looks beyond them to something more dynamic, something with more play: in short, to the unsettling process that qualifies but does not unseat meaning and subject. The semiotic, she says, is "a disposition that is definitely heterogeneous to meaning but always in sight of it": a statement that also might serve as a definition of parody, that favorite Nabokovian and anti-realist device.[10]

This process, this play in language that makes way for imagination, is constitutive in *Ada*. This novel confirms Nabokov's claims: first, that the plot of great literature lies in the style and, second, that readers should be construction workers not consumers. The style of *Ada* is a tissue of little moments that act more like intersections than like stages along the way of plot. The language moves from one exquisite detail to the next leaving none of the mnemonic residues of realism. In the polliphone passage the stock plot is no more than a vaudevillian echo; meanwhile an activity of alliteration radiates from one center after another. Adoration invokes duration, saturation calls up Saturday, absent Ada is more present than visible Lucette; the clatter of

---

[9] For discussion of the hierarchy lurking in dualistic formulation see Margaret Homans, "The Masculine Tradition," in her *Women Writers and Poetic Identity* (Princeton: Princeton University Press, 1980), pp. 12–40.

[10] Kristeva, "One Identity to An Other," *Desire in Language*, p. 133.

coincidence mimics the amorous conjunction sought so desperately by poor Lucette and makes more poignant still the exquisiteness of the truly erotic as we experience it everywhere in Nabokov's style. The rhythm of language and love overriding time and death in *Ada* could not be more demonstratively remote from the "action" of the sober novel of meaning and signification produced by our critics if not our writers. In *Ada* the detail is not a base for transcendental excursion but rather a moment among paratactic moments; it belongs not to the development-and-climax plot that Nabokov parodies but to the imaginative activity involved in riding through one anticlimactic departure after another. Surprising, digressing, recurring: Nabokov's details support a thematic anthemion, a floral pattern where words do not point to a Beyond of structure and meaning but *are*, in the essential participation of readers, all there is of structure and meaning.

This unsettling process, moreover, is not entirely new; the explicit effort to dispose of the teleological tic is at least a century old. What semiosis implies for humanism is an open and important question; we have nothing like adequate preparation for answering it. If humanism is synonymous with causality, Judaeo-Christian morality, and historical time as it was conceived between (roughly) 1500 and 1900, then perhaps humanism is in deep trouble, but I am not persuaded that the problem or so-called crisis has yet even been fully conceived. Humanism preceded and provided the basis for much of the cultural metaphysic currently challenged by anti-realist writers; certainly it preceded the modern idea of historical time, an idea that it generated; but if humanism has been incorrectly identified with the time of history and project then humanism needs redefinition before it can be understood to be in crisis or not. If humanism can be defined in philological terms (there is, shall we say, a certain precedent for this), if it involves care for textuality and language, attention to difference between textual moments, an expanded sense of language as a model not just for well-made urns but for each human system in all its complex multivalence, then perhaps humanism is only just finding its own demystified way. In any case, the current emphasis on semiosis does move us well beyond some complacencies and does dispute the privilege of representational language; however this does not seem tantamount to a cultural bonfire. Those who identify themselves by means of privileged positions based on hidden hierarchies and teleologies may be irritated, but their irritation is not about the end of morality or humanism; it is about the end of hegemony.

As for Kristeva and Nabokov, the unsettling of meaning and subject seems consistent with social and moral function. The crises where Kristeva wants us to locate are "inherent in the signifying function and, consequently, in sociality."[11] That is scarcely a world-denying remark. The author of *Lolita* has demonstrated that crime is not a legal matter; that what has been denied a certain girl-child is the right to her own imagination, something that Humbert Humbert buys for himself at her eternal expense. The restoration of semiosis

---

[11] Kristeva, *Ibid.*, pp. 124–25.

makes possible the renewal of social codes that would otherwise fall victim to disrupted linguistic habits. Reflexion and representation, rather than being disarticulated halves of a disarticulating dualism, simply may be two among a variety of motives. The construction of conventions where various motives can coexist without finality and defeat: this enormous literary and linguistic effort has begun. Its fortunate rhythms are most evident in the work of contemporary novelists.

The Windup Session

The windup session was held on the third morning of the conference, April 25, 1987. Along with remaining panelists, editors of NOVEL *and other moderators from Brown, interested staff and students, and visitors to the conference like Gayle Greene from Scripps College in Claremont, California, the session was also attended by most of the twelve guest respondents to the conference. It was their last chance to speak up as they had been doing after conference panels. In the discussion that follows the moderator's opening remarks, their names are listed in full to distinguish them from panelists and moderators already identified, and here listed only by their last names. Meanwhile the moderator of the final session, Marianna Torgovnick, was introduced by Professor Emeritus Edward Bloom,* NOVEL's *former Editor-in-Chief, also currently from California, who began by reminding everyone that* NOVEL's *twentieth birthday party was nearing its end, and that the time had come for the conference's summation:*

> I think it's not going to be terribly formal. It will give us all a chance to review the thoughts which have come to mind over the last few days.... Maybe this is the time [also] when we discover that a perplex is no longer a perplex. Maybe some things have been resolved. And perhaps also [as with our tenth anniversary conference] we may conclude that nothing really has been concluded and that nothing is conclusive....

He then introduced moderator Torgovnick, who had been chosen for this task because of her initial work in organizing the MLA conference called "Still Towards a Poetics of Fiction?" which had appeared in NOVEL's *pages as the first in a series of items on "Why the Novel Matters," the series from which the present conference drew its theme. Before presenting her prepared remarks, Professor Torgovnick set the ground rules for the discussion which followed. She said that her own responses would be governed by what she might be telling her colleagues about the conference back at Duke University, how she had felt about it, how she had drawn on "little comments" made by moderators and speakers that helped to reveal the implicit values behind the conference and its overall shaping, how she hoped discussion would be directed at such ends. As indeed it was.*

Did We Meet Your
Expectations?

MARIANNA TORGOVNICK

One of the hotels housing the Conference solicited evaluations with cards that asked, "Did We Meet Your Expectations?" The cards gave me the title for this response, which asks two questions: first, did the Conference meet the expectations it set for itself? second, did it meet my expectations?

The Conference brochure clearly stated its goal–to "explore and bridge differences between old humanistic and new 'posthumanistic' approaches to traditional aspects of fiction." The Conference's title reproduced the doubleness of humanistic and "posthumanistic": the first half of the title, "Why the Novel Matters," encapsulated the humanistic approach to fiction; the second half, "A Postmodern Perplex," conveyed a puzzled, almost bemused, reaction to "posthumanism." As Robert Scholes pointed out in remarks prefacing his talk, *humanistic* did not go into quotation marks, and hence seemed knowable, definable, real. *Posthumanistic* went into quotation marks and hence seemed questionable, nebulous, tenuous. Perhaps as penalty and compensation, *humanistic* was preceded by the adjective "old," but *posthumanistic* was preceded by the adjective "new"–an adjective that is usually a winner in literary studies. I couldn't help wondering, perhaps a little wickedly, whether all the participants knew whether we had been invited as humanists or posthumanists–and whether we would have been pleased by the designation.

Lodge: Somebody said people might have been invited as bridges.

Scholes: Some of us are old posthumanists.

Torgovnick: Yes, *bridge* is another key word for conference expectations. So is *traditional*, to which I'll return in a moment. But consider [first] what it means "to bridge" the gap between humanistic and posthumanistic approaches. This sounds like a neutral architectural metaphor–but was the act it urged really neutral? It seemed clear that getting people together to talk about the novel was a good idea; but didn't the formulation of two approaches that leave a gap needing to be bridged (approaches that did not, presumably, ever overlap or exist in any sort of continuum) invite polarization, with its accompanying aggressivity and defensiveness? Intellectual "bridging" is a form of synthesis, and syntheses can be powerful or weak, a bringing together of the best in two things or a dilution of the best into a swamp of compromises. When the gap between two opposing approaches is "bridged," we avoid the military metaphors that often prevail (confrontation, battle, war)–but do we still have a winner and a loser–or just two-way traffic?

Based upon the advance materials, my own expectation was that the conference, held under the auspices of the National Endowment of the Humanities, favored the humanistic side, though perhaps unconsciously. I had the uneasy sense that the questions which most interested me differed substantially from those implied by the Conference's organization. And I feared that the Conference might miss an important chance to examine the institutional structures within which we study novels–NOVEL itself being one such institution. My uneasiness grew as expectations passed into response.

At the Conference, the sessions united humanistic and posthumanistic critics on panels devoted to "traditional" aspects of fiction. Mixing traditional and non-traditional critics on panels had the strategic value of avoiding the kind of explicit isolation of critical tendencies on separate panels I sense happened at NOVEL's tenth anniversary conference. But it also had the uncomfortable effect of grouping critics who would (as Nancy Miller put it) "necessarily have to agree to disagree," because some of the panelists, presumably the posthumanists, would not be interested in "traditional" topics or not interested in "traditional" ways. Our organization around "traditional" aspects of fiction made some participants uncomfortable; many speakers made comments about not knowing whether or how their paper "fit" their session's title. The "traditional" topics of the sessions may also have caused certain omissions in the kinds of approaches represented at the Conference. Certainly, one of the ways that the Conference did not meet my expectations (and may or may not have met its own) was in its omission or blunting of some anticipated angles on the novel.

Before I list the omissions, let me say, as clearly as possible, that I know that some of them may have been caused by declined invitations and other factors beyond the control of the Conference's organizers. Missing nonetheless were: Marxist approaches and more generally political approaches, despite their prominence in criticism today; New Historicist approaches (perhaps absent because stronger in period fields like the Renaissance than in novel studies); and Deconstructionist approaches (the humanists' opponents at the 1977 NOVEL Conference). Feminist approaches were pretty much missing until the second day, when they made themselves felt in the "Psychosocial Design" and "Narrative Process" sessions. When feminism surfaced, some male members of the conference seemed to feel anxious and uneasy–even threatened; I thought that was a very interesting phenomenon, but I don't want to accuse everyone of having felt they were . . .

Suleiman: Why do you use the word "accuse"?

Torgovnick: Because I can't help but give away my own point of view. Perhaps I should add that later in the Conference some feminist critics seemed to feel hostile and separate, despite widespread interest in their work.

As I anticipated the Conference and now, as I look back on it, our division into "humanistic" and "posthumanistic" camps seemed most consequential. The division encouraged (and I think produced) a sense that the Conference's guiding question–Why the Novel Matters–could best be answered by reasserting the novel's connection to experience, something most of the participants had no problem accepting. But it also suggested that the "old humanistic" positions provided the clearest ways, perhaps the only ways, of making such a reassertion and of answering the question of why the novel matters. Most of all it suggested that those nasty posthumanists were a threat to the novel's mattering. The danger here was that humanistic approaches would be (as in the English tradition) fearful and suspicious of developments in the last decade, and therefore *regressive* even while aggressively trying to reclaim the center. This seems to me a danger which many of the most explicitly "humanistic" papers did not avoid.

What bothered me most about the guiding dichotomy of "humanistic" and "posthumanistic" is that it led to a falsification of issues and therefore of arguments. Our ostensible question at the Conference was "Why the Novel Matters: A Postmodern Perplex." A more pertinent question for the wrap-up session seemed to me, "Does NOVEL matter as much as it could and how could it matter more?" As a representative body of the journal's readers and contributors, *that* was a question we could usefully address. A second pertinent question might be, "For whom does the question 'does the novel matter' not arise? For whom is it clear that the novel *does* matter?" If humanistic academics find this a troubling question posed by posthumanism, some members of the Conference did not and identifying them will, I think, be helpful.

First, the novelists invited to the Conference seemed to feel that the novel mattered a great deal. For novelists in countries like South Africa (Gordimer), for black women (Marshall), for Latin Americans (Puig, who unfortunately missed the Conference, but was scheduled to come), the novel *does* clearly matter. For David Lodge, who illustrated his opening remarks with approving references to a number of contemporary novelists, the novel also clearly matters. For the Russian-American Nabokov (discussed in Elizabeth Ermarth's paper) the novel clearly matters. For the feminist critics at the Conference (and for the women students in the audience) the novel also, clearly, matters. It may be that the question of why the novel matters only arises in economically and socially privileged cultures or in segments of such cultures free to bask in what Robert Newman calls "the post-modern aura," which depends upon an inflated rhetoric of cultural crisis. In this sense, it will not do to see the novel (as some speakers saw it) as a Protestant or capitalist genre, threatened by the weakening of those traditions. In traditions neither Protestant nor capitalist (the Russian, the Latin American, for example) the novel has flourished and does flourish. We can articulate a sense of crisis in our discipline in order to make ourselves feel embattled, and therefore important. Or we can recognize and extend the ways we already are important. As critics of the novel, an authentically popular form of literature in this as in earlier centuries, we should, I think, do the latter.

What I would urge for NOVEL's third decade are some of the following paths. First, I would urge NOVEL to return to an interest in the fortunes of theory and in recent critical trends both here and abroad. Its involvement with the current state of the profession was something I valued in NOVEL when I first knew it as a graduate student in the mid-seventies, and something I have missed in it lately. Second, I would urge a heightening of the comparative, cross-national focus NOVEL has always maintained. By heightening, I mean more frequent inclusion of articles on the kind of fiction represented at the Conference (contemporary, women's, and third world). Third, I would like NOVEL to broaden its sense of comparative studies to include more cross-disciplinary work, especially work on literature (narrative) and the other arts, the social sciences, and the sciences. Very exciting work is being done by scholars of narrative with anthropology and psychology, for example, disciplines in a greater state of crisis than our own. This kind of interdisciplinary work extends, not threatens, how the novel matters; it is a large part of the current power and prestige of literary studies. Fourth, recognizing the novel's status as a popular genre, I would urge some inclusion of what are often called "cultural studies," especially as popular phenomena interact with the novel as a written and read genre.

Fifth, I would urge that we turn from the articulation of "old" and "new" positions towards an openness towards those positions which seem most compelling now. That turn would involve not just a rhetorical substitution, but would encourage work that is intellectually and culturally consequential. It might, for example, encourage more work written for the educated public rather than for a small group of specialists. In our receptiveness to approaches which seem compelling now, our model should not be "eclectic humanism," but something closer to "dialectical pluralism." If our work, if our ideas matter to us, they should be worth others' attention, others' responses, others' agreement or disagreement. Professors of literature may no longer have a shared sense of the best that has been known and thought. But we can do our best to know and think and to share the products of our thought with the general culture.

Discussion

HENKLE: Before we begin, Marianna, can you articulate what you mean by the different kinds of fiction that you think came up at this conference that have not currently been presented in NOVEL and also what you mean about the more compelling issues now, that are being evaded or avoided through the posturing of all the new humanism?

TORGOVNICK: Well, the second question is maybe too big for me to do right now, because I think other people should jump in as well. But the kinds of people that were properly, I think, invited, were: a South African novelist who is actively engaged in political struggle–who is still writing; a British novelist who is still writing; a black woman novelist; and (if he had come) a Latin American novelist in exile. (But again, all very contemporary). Now I haven't done a statistical study, but my sense is that NOVEL, by and large, tends to feature articles about novels in the English or French tradition; that tends to be pretty much the scope of the comparision. Occasionally, something Spanish or German or further afield will come out–but it tends to be pretty much English and French. There aren't that many things on contemporary fiction. While there's probably been at least one article on Alice Walker, there isn't that much on black women writers. So, it just seemed to me interesting that there was this disparity or gap between the kinds of novels–I mean, obviously, you can't invite Charles Dickens, he won't come–between the kinds of articles that are published and the kinds of people that we've seen here.

BERNARD DUYFHUIZEN: I want to point out that as far as the conference was concerned, one category that was conspicuously missing in defining the panels was the political one–although you had an extraordinary political novelist say in Nadine Gordimer– but there was no address to the political novel as a genre in the forum.

SPILKA: Her panel, the fifth one, the Prophetic Mode, was supposed to include the political.

ALTIERI: Calling politics "prophecy" seems to me to be very old humanism indeed!

SPILKA: Well, the "prophetic" means being critical of one's conscience, which I think is what politics is certainly about, as well as being predictive. And we had two novelists who were in that sense politically critical and predictive.

ROBERT LANGBAUM: I'm particularly sorry that we didn't have a session on the Latin American novel, since there's been so much talk that the novel has declined–what can you do with the novel? I just finished teaching *One Hundred Years of Solitude*; García Marquez has imagined something completely fresh. On the other hand, one might consider it a kind of revival of the novel by doing things that are not novelistic–bringing back epic, tragedy, all of those old forms–and by trying also to understand what there is in the political, social, and historical milieu that makes the novel so fresh and vital. I do have a sense that the novel is freshest and most vital when people are reading a political code in it; when it's really important; when messages come through; when we have a society in transition. I would think of Russia, for example, as analogous to Latin America now. They too are modernizing, coming out of a backwards state into the ferment of modern ideas–and that was the great moment of the Russian novel.

TORGOVNICK: People like Paz and Fuentes make very interesting comments about the precarious status of the middle-class in these countries. I don't know enough about the tradition to do very much work with it, but it seems to me that someone who does can do [helpful] work, ... partly because in this country so few of us know Spanish as a foreign language. I know when I tried to work with Latin-American fiction a year ago, I found that the only books on Latin-American fiction had, by and large, been published by the University of Texas Press, which is a curious kind of assumption of responsibility by a university press closest to Latin America, geographically. There was only one book published by a major university press–Chicago–by a critic named McAdam; and the introductory chapter set forth the problem of the Latin-American novel, as placing it within the Western tradition, as a way of avoiding the view that it was a *lusus naturae*. Either the Latin-American novel had to be part of the Western tradition or it was going to be a freak of nature. That's an interesting move, because it ignores all the things Paz and Fuentes, for instance, say about the highly ambivalent relationship of Latin-American fiction to the Western tradition, because of its colonial status, because of its lateness, because of all of these things.

LANGBAUM: We had a chairman of Latin-American studies in our Spanish Department–he's an Englishman, came to us from Edinburgh–and he was complaining: "You have no idea what goes on in that world with Latin-American novelists. The Latin Americans insist that this is stuff only they can understand; we've no way of talking about international terms," and so on. That doesn't apply to ... Englishmen–who say no, now we really must be able to apply international categories.

SPILKA: May I remind you that we had a category called "The Novel as Cosmic Mode," in the original state of ten panel discussions, in which we hoped to get Latin-American novelists to talk to the different sense of the world they're functioning in, from the "Western" novelists. Coover was going to do one part of it, but he's off on leave, and Puig couldn't come.

ELIZABETH WEED: I liked your list of what was excluded, although one thing I would have added, and I think this is not entirely contained within the category of political, and that is staying even within the Western novel, critiques of the novel from the postcolonialist view. And I say this particularly because there are a number of black and other people who are doing such critiques, and I felt that this conference was so painfully within the family–it's almost entirely white and Eurocentric. And I particularly felt that being on stage with Paule Marshall, and realizing that this is a black woman novelist performing before a largely white audience. And I think that this is something that I would have preferred to have avoided. And I think not only because it's awkward, but also because there is a great deal we can learn from the black and other postcolonialist critics, who could have participated nicely in the critical discourse .

ERMARTH: Well, I've been looking for a place to drop a remark. Nancy Miller said something yesterday about the material availability of texts, and I just wanted to bring that phrase back and say that it is crucially important. In talking about contemporary fiction for example, I couldn't teach *Ada* this semester because it's not available. I couldn't teach *Ada* last year because it's not available; I can't teach the foreign novel because it's not available. And this seems to me, in effect, a form of censorship. What's happened is that for some reason or other, pressure has not come to bear in the proper places to suggest that maybe this is as important as putting *Anna Karenina* out of print. *Anna Karenina* probably isn't as available as it should be any more either, but it doesn't have that same sort of strange status. And I think something that NOVEL might do ... is to help keep us aware of the fact that a lot of books are not available or are in print for just six months.

DUYFHUIZEN: I think that raises a crucial point, because the whole book production industry is very much tied to what we try to do, and as you move away from, say, the Ivy colleges, where the money is there for the students to buy a lot of books, and move into the state universities and even further afield down to the community colleges, where students are really struggling with their dollars, they won't take a course that asks them to buy too many books sometimes simply because they can't afford it. And we run into this problem of always having to find the least expensive paperback, and those are going to be the ones that are in the public domain, where the publisher doesn't have to pay out royalties, whereas some of the contemporary fiction, because it's tied to the royalty system and so forth, is going to be more expensive, and therefore harder to produce in more than just one edition, and then even more easily taken out of print for a while. So there's a real problem in terms of availability that I think needs to be addressed if we're going to be able to look at the novel from its present, on back, instead of saying there are these cut-off points for periodicity which say: these books are available now because they're in the public domain and published by a number of presses, whereas these other books only exist in one edition. Khachig Tölölyan was mentioning that he can't get *Gravity's Rainbow* right now in paperback, that for some reason Bantam and Viking have pulled it.

TORGOVNICK: I couldn't get *Lost in the Fun House*.

HENKLE: Maybe this is following along the lines of what wasn't covered, but the novel, of course, is the great bourgeois form; it rose essentially with the rise of the middle class and served the middle class beautifully.... You know, as rich as I thought these panels were, I was struck by the fact that this was a very comfortable bourgeois positioning with respect to all of us about the novel. There are indications, here and there, in people's talks, about the novel forming resistance, or allowing for dialogue, a dialogue that constitutes contradiction. There are issues raised, quite obviously, about the way in which the novel has gender-coded itself or the tradition has. But essentially, for this group, as far as I could see, nobody was really raising any kinds of crucial doubts about the novel and certainly not interrogating the way in which the novel has been so centrally a conservative, recuperative operation. We're trying to expand it so that it has a little edge to it, in its resistances, and maybe so that it recuperates marginal parts of the culture that it hasn't. But ... I didn't get much of a sense that anybody's unhappy with the novel's continuing nicely positioned role ... as a genre.

ALTIERI: I would like to complicate that by saying what I was most struck by, in Gordimer and Marshall, was how much in the service of resistance to that bourgeois tradition they relied on radically bourgeois means–I mean completely conventional models, to my eyes, of what their actual fictional work involves. There's this strange situation where those of us who are–I'll use myself as an example–comfortable with the discomforts of being bourgeois, and therefore like experimental fiction which these novelists–who have actually engaged [in the] political operation–don't ... enjoy, [though] at least in the evidence of this panel, they have enormous stakes in precisely those means [of resistance] which you're attributing to the bourgeois order. I don't have an explanation for this, I just think that the two sides make for an interesting dilemma.

MILLER: It seems to me that's placing the problem of canon formation, placing an impossible burden on creative writers. Elizabeth Weed's comment about Paule Marshall said "Here, do the polite part, do the third world, do the political, be the only minority member of the conference and do what we ourselves won't and here I think in fact it's probably our charge, not theirs–that that should be in our panel, not something we expected them to show better.

SCHWARZ: I would ask rhetorically, because I want to ask both Charles Altieri and Roger Henkle, I would ask, for example, what is the subject left out? But to Charles' comment I would say this, Gordimer is using very traditional means of communication because she's very interested in–she wants–a large audience. She cannot write experimental fiction. She speaks in her essays about her public in South Africa, about how fiction must be about what's derived from the substance of living from which the artist draws his vision. And she thinks that not only the fiction that she writes should speak to that, but the criticism of the fiction that she writes should speak to that. In fact, it's very interesting to me how the recent interest in postcolonial and third-world literature often challenges the tenets of deconstruction, textuality. These people are very concerned with representative and mimetic problems. I think what Gordimer has written–and Joyce might have said the very same thing about Ireland, if I may insert something about my own approach–it's from the daily life of South Africa that the conditions of profound alienation come which prevail among South African artists. But she's also stressed that the way to recuperate historical circumstances, and to introduce history into the imagined world, is to use very traditional means of communication. And in a sense, one can't be experimental, one can't also talk about the free-play of signifiers, and gaps and fissures; one has to talk about substance and representation.

LODGE: I'd like to comment on this question of the relationship between creative writing and criticism because I spoke about it in my lecture and I drew attention to what I saw as a radical discontinuity in the way the novel is talked about in academic contexts and the way it's actually written and received and circulated. And I can't help feeling that this conference confirmed that judgment and it confirmed it in curious social ways, as well as in discursive ways. I mean there was almost an apartheid between the creative writers and the critics. I mean I'm here as a bridge, so I think I've been pressed on all these occasions. I don't know if I'm suggesting anything designed about all this, but ... I don't remember Nadine Gordimer or Paule Marshall ever being involved in a discussion in one of the panel sessions, and I think that when I accepted the invitation to come I got the impression it was going to be a more evenly balanced conference in terms of writers and critics. So I'm slightly disappointed that the presence of writers was so small, and that while they were here they were not present at most of our critical discussions. So that, to me, was a bit disappointing. It bears on the question of: is the sense of crisis that is implied in the title of the conference supposed to be in the practice of the novel, or in the practice of criticism and teaching in the academic industry of the novel. And it seems to me that it's in the second, though occasionally the conversation swerves over into supposing that there's some crisis in the novel. I think the novel is alive and well–immensely pluralistic and international. But I think there were signs which erupted rather vividly in Joseph Gold's talk and the response to that, a talk which was both rather annoying and yet provocative, and touched certain nerves while offending at the same time. And the nerve it touched was a sense that academic discourse about the novel, and particularly as a result of the theorization of the subject, has alienated a large number of people who write and read novels from that discussion. Gore Vidal in the *New York Review of Books* talked about the academic theorists who have presided over an eighty percent drop in English studies. Even if that is only half true, it's rather alarming. I don't think that the conference addressed itself to that question. Maybe there is a way of justifying and defending the type of theorization of the subject that has taken place, all the jargonizing that's been a consequence of that. But a lot of the papers that were given employed that elaborate meta-language which is actually an excuse; it asserts a mastery over the subject that authenticates the professional mastery of the critic. It doesn't actually communicate any sense of the value of the meaning of the text to the ordinary educated reader. I would have wished for more debate about that, for it seems to me the most constructive thing that's happened here.

SPILKA: A propos of that, I'd like to add or recall that Marshall was in the back clapping when Joseph Gold said fiction should be useful. She was cheering. But that's the only participation. I don't think Nadine Gordimer came to any sessions except her own panel.

SCHOLES: I want to comment on part of what David said. Though I agree that there was a certain amount of meta-language flowing about, there was a lot less of it than I expected. I suspect that one of the things going on here was the enactment of, in fact, the entry into the post-theory phase–that theory was all very well and doubtless good for us all, but that we were in fact coming through it and about to ask, "Well, now what should we do with it?"

LODGE: The only paper which actually made a positive proposal was Joseph Gold's, and I rather recoiled against that.

SCHOLES: That's not the answer.

ALTIERI: Caserio had five-hundred proposals on every possible level.

TORGOVNICK: All of the anti-theory talks strike me as remarkably theory talk.

SCHOLES: Let me clarify. I'm not suggesting that this is either a return to something that existed before theory, or that it's a judgment on theory. What I'm suggesting is that perhaps there's a working through theory going on which will enable us to get a little beyond the meta-language and talking only to one another and to begin to speak in language that will reach other people but will be informed by having been through theory.

SINGLEY: Speaking from my conversation with Paule Marshall, I can tell you that she was very pleased to be part of a conference where she was involved with critics talking about novels instead of coming in and just giving a reading and leaving. So one of the things that the conference did that does not normally happen was to put the novelist and the critic in closer proximity, even though I agree with you that it was not done to the extent that we all might wish. But that raises the question which we feel ourselves compelled to be involved with–that of the novelist, or the writer, and our critical pursuits. My impression of the discipline is that our function is to work with the product that the artists produce and that we're not very involved with literary production. Our interests are often quite divergent. [Paule Marshall] was extremely confused, perplexed, and a little bit bothered by the first day's events as she heard them and told Mary Helen Washington: "They treat the novel as if it's a construct." And clearly for her, what the term meant was some sort of an object not representing life. Later she told me that someone she had known did a study of her fiction in terms of its structures, the rooms in houses, and she felt that extremely interesting, because, in fact, rooms had been important to her as she grew up, and this person had seen an inherent structure. In that way criticism was interesting to her, and informative, perhaps even inspiring for the rest of her work. But my impression was that until the last day–Mary Helen Washington's response to the feminist session I take as another barometer of this–until the last day there was very little sense of how what we were doing was tied directly to what novelists intend to do when they write. I think it's a very interesting question for us, and again Joseph Gold comes back as a fulcrum to discuss it. Is there another bridge that we want to make, and in what way do we want to make it? Nadine Gordimer's part, as far as I can see, was to remain rather distant from the conference events by choice, and put her energy into her reading schedule and so forth, although she was invited to be a part of it. But I don't think by and large [the novelists] think about our concerns a great deal.

CHRISTINA CROSBY: I think one of the interesting things here is that the novel remains as a sort of uninterrogated category. Nobody ever said what we meant by the novel; we all assumed we knew what it was. There was no real discussion of the kinds of issues Henkle and Scholes were raising, about whether it's a genre tied to a particular moment that is bound to do particular things, or whether there are other possibilities, other ways of thinking about it. It seems to me that we just took it as a given, and it doesn't seem to me at this point, at least, that there's any sense of it being a given; there are so many different kinds of novels being written, there are so many different readerships, and different ways of reading, that I was in a sense perplexed that we never got around to thinking about that topic explicitly in our conversations. And that means we never thought enough, I think, about the problem of readership. I don't think we can rely on the kind of notion that you were referring to, David Lodge, about the ordinary, educated reader. That seems to me to be a throw-back to the phrase, the "common reader," that you used early in your keynote address. I don't think that those are useful categories anymore. Again because there are so many different kinds of readers, so many different sorts of readerships—we just can't do that usefully, it seems to me, without dropping out a whole lot of really determining differences.

BLOOM: As a sometime humanist I'm concerned, also, by what seems to be a lack here. We're talking about criticism, we're talking about the novel *qua* novel—and this picks up what Christina [Crosby] has been saying—we seem to be paying very little attention to the kinds of audiences who are going to be reading novels. How much attention are we to pay to the audience? There really seems to be a dichotomy within this group between the fiction and the criticism, and the bridge there does not seem to be a very conclusive or cohesive one. And it seemed to me ... as we address ourselves to the question "Why the Novel Matters," perhaps we should really reverse that a little bit to "Does the Novel Matter?" and try to come to terms with that particular question. I don't think you can ignore, or at least set the reader to one side, in this kind of discussion because it is, in effect, I would say, the reader who is the bridge in all of this.

CASERIO: The reader is always a political person, and I think the novel matters most to the female students that Gayle [Greene] was talking about, to the blacks that read Paule Marshall, to white middle-class South Africans who are criticized by Gordimer. And I agree with Marianna [Torgovnick] that politics was absent in so many of our discussions. But I think the discussion of the readership is always a political one.

BLOOM: But not every novel is going to address itself to every reader. And there is such great diversity. This is one of the frustrating things about the novel itself: it's almost amorphous.

HENKLE: It's a real question whether it matters to those people you're talking about, simply because we are using it as an incorporative device. People who are excluded from power in society like the novel's form because it is the great accepted form; it centralizes the subject, it creates the illusions of the constructs of individuality; it presumes some kind of integration of a variety of discourses, and so forth; in a sense, it serves to move them back into the main stream, which the novel seems to be serving very well. And maybe that's who the readers are, but . . . what is it doing to those readers to use a form that is such a privileged form?

AVROM FLEISHMAN: I think that for a young black woman to have read *The Color Purple* and found a powerful feeling of identification reading it, does not necessarily move her into the main stream of white, middle-class culture. But it uses the white, middle-class form for something else. There are a lot of main streams.

EUGENE GOODHEART: And a lot of thoroughfares.

MILLER: I want to add on to that comment. Barbara Smith has made some very strong statements about what she wants the novel to be and what she calls for–and there are other black women critics who have taken similar positions. She wants the novel that will give an account of her reality and she will not be able to sleep until that happens . . .

GOODHEART: Yes, there is this constant desire to find something recognizable in the novel which can't be found and recognized in other discourses. And that hasn't materialized enough. And yet in a way, it's one of the most traditional aspects of the novel. But then you run into the idea that the novel is a construct. It's a construct in which you displace the search for yourself and never find yourself by virtue of your putting it into a construct. So how to talk about that construct which is an obstacle to representation and a means of representation at the same time makes one talk in a difficult way . . . When I asked Nadine Gordimer and Paule Marshall why they wrote fiction, why they didn't write journalism, I couldn't get an answer from them that was helpful. Except that Paule Marshall said, "I think of my characters as being in the world." Well, where are we? I think she meant that . . . there's a difference between a world understood as a context and a world understood as an imminent totality, so I thought she was saying, "I had to write fiction because it is only in fiction that what is either hidden or implicit in the world comes to some kind of totalized realization." Since David Lodge is here, and since I also feel very much disappointed about how the novelists and we didn't talk together–I want to ask you a big question. Just why do you write novels? If it matters, it must matter most in terms of what makes you write them, or any writer write them? But why do you feel this to be? Couldn't you say what it is about novels that makes you want to write them more than you would want to write criticism or autobiography or some kind of journalism?

LODGE: I think in my own case I would say that the wish to write novels grows out of the experience of reading them. In other words, I felt powerfully moved and excited and stirred by literary fiction as an adolescent. And I wanted to perform that feat for other people. It seemed to me a way of, I guess, coping with the inevitable imperfections of life–I mean you turn a negative positive by writing about it. I think a number of other novelists have said similar things–I won't say this is a universal explanation, but I suspect Nadine Gordimer would have been a novelist wherever she happened to grow up and I suspect she would have been the same way wherever she was. The fact that she happens to be a South African in that political situation means she was saturated with that political consciousness. I don't think that the singular form of her fiction is dictated by a specific experience that she has. That is my guess.

GOODHEART: So partly you're doing a constructive performance, and an imitative performance–a fooling around with what has excited you in terms of somebody else's construction. Again at the same time you're negotiating some life difficulty, so it is not just a fooling around.

LODGE: No. Let's take a classic example. One of the great books of my adolescence was *A Portrait of the Artist as a Young Man*, about that Catholic subculture, and I guess I then would brood on my own experience in a way that Joyce did on his and try and see what kind of public significance it had for me. He developed it out of that by means of narrative structure. I think that that was missing a bit from the conference, except for the panel on the narrative process, as a kind of system of seeing nature, as a way of organizing the world. But you ask the question, "Why write fiction, why not just write confession or history or journalism?" It's because of the freedom of the narrative convention that the novel allows you to incorporate bits of real experience and put them in a more dramatic focus–you can change things, reverse them, turn them inside out, and it's that freedom to invent the narrative level of the text, I think, that is the reason why one writes novels rather than non-fiction.

STEVEN COHAN: The discussion so far is that the crisis, the problem, is not with the novel or the novelist, but with people who professionally talk about novels, either in criticism or in theory–I think mostly in theory. Ask novelists why they are doing what they are doing. You can ask them in such a way that it becomes very difficult for them to answer in a way that will be fruitful for theorists' work. But they generally answer it very spontaneously and naturally–they write novels because they're compelled to write novels. It's not really problematic; it's a way of expressing yourself. I think the real problem comes–as David Lodge says–there is a chasm between the activity of writing novels, writing novels for a readership, and finding ways of talking about those novels in the academy, which illuminates the novel, illuminates the relationship between the novels and readers. And we haven't yet addressed it so far in the conference. Maybe we should address it in this discussion. We have lost the vernacular, we have lost the ways of talking about novels. And it hasn't always been the case. There's been a body of criticism, historically, very bright and brilliant, concise and illuminating about novels in an available connection.

LODGE: Let me say I don't think we want to go back to the early days . . .

COHAN: There doesn't necessarily have to be a relationship . . . between why people write novels and why people write about novels, and why people read novels and teach novels; that is, one assumption has always been that the process of reading and the process of writing and teaching about novels is a recovery of that original imperative that motivates the writer, but I'm not sure that they're not necessarily very different projects that give the novel its currency but can be confused.

GAYLE GREENE: I too wanted to speak about that difference David Lodge has articulated between the novelists' assumption that the novel is alive and well and matters–and I would extend that to many readers, critics, and teachers of the novel–and the crisis one feels among critics in the profession, as to ways of talking about the novel that Joseph Gold articulated yesterday. And I wonder if that difference isn't related to the absence of the political–something else that came up–because I see that as a bridge–the political. And what I wish that Paule Marshall had answered to your question, "Why does she write novels if she thinks so politically?" What I really wanted her to say was because some of us think that the personal is political, which, as you will recognize, is something that is a basic tenet of feminism, and I think it's a very important one. I think the absence of the political from this conference is striking in all sorts of ways–and I don't mean the political as another metalanguage that Jameson would have come and given us the word on. I don't think that's terribly helpful in many ways. I mean, the political is some kind of informing dimension of our lives, and I think that it's lacking in American fiction–as a matter of fact, in contemporary American fiction. I think talking about the political would have been a very useful way into the different types of contemporary fictions: why does South American fiction feel able to deal with it, why do many Canadian writers feel able to deal with it, and still some British writers feel able to deal with political awareness? In America it seems to be a very difficult and often absent subject from our best contemporary writers, and absent in a really striking way from this conference, not only in the session on the political, but in a sense of the political as some kind of informing dimension of our lives. And I suspect that's why we're in crisis right now; I think that's where we sort of drifted away from "real life"–a very loaded and suspect term right now. But, I think the problem that someone [Joseph Gold] was pointing to yesterday is a real problem: we are an endangered species, however you want to account for it, and however you want to deal with it in the future. And I would just say that is definitely related to the absence of political and of the Marxist approach, but not solely Marxist, a deeper sense of the political, from this conference. . . .

SULEIMAN: I don't have anything terribly well organized, but I guess there are three different things that I find myself wanting to respond to. One is Charlie [Altieri's] remark, "Isn't it interesting how some of the more obviously political novelists are using traditional modes of language and ways of speaking?" I think it's a very old problem–you know, the old thing in the thirties–what one writes when one dreams about revolution: should one write traditional novels or should one be a surrealist? It is also a question that haunts all the debates in the late sixties and seventies. Again it's this whole question of do you change the world by changing the form? I think my sense is that there is a general way in which what we are struggling with here is in fact a question of language. How should we talk about the novel in a way that matters to us as critics–which raises the question that Barthes raised, why does one need criticism? Also because it gives you a kind of pleasure seeing how someone else reacts to the text. So that the question of language is just as important, I think, for the critic, for the person who is trying to say something about fiction, as it is to the writer of fiction. Incidentally, I don't react, necessarily, to Paule Marshall and Nadine Gordimer as absolutely traditional novelists, and certainly not Alice Walker. I think that the way they use language–Paule Marshall's comments yesterday–the narrative voice as very classical and traditional–is almost off-putting to me, because she's not doing anything, it seemed, with what were ultimately repetitions that she didn't need that I found jarring in the work of a black woman writer. But then when the characters speak there's all kinds of very interesting stuff that is going on in the language which has to do with what she was talking about yesterday–the mother, the poet, what they did with language–that there's a real disjunction in her work between that narrative voice which is so, in fact, closed, traditional, and in a way not opening anything up. The same with Gordimer. I don't think Gordimer is that traditional. I think if you read her work–often I'm asking myself, who's speaking here? Suddenly, I've lost track; it's not your ordinary repetitive thing. So that raises the next thing I'm responding to in Nancy [Miller's] statement: people want more positive representation. But then again, do we want positive representations of the kind that you find in Harlequin romances, where the language itself is so dead and so repetitive that all you get is the psychological projection and kind of identification it allows? Or are we looking for some ways in which one can do things with the language that imply a genuine engagement with the language? That's the ultimate criterion whereby I decide whether I want to keep on reading a novel. Then I think that could also be the ultimate criterion that I struggle with in writing, which is why I also respond to Bob [Scholes'] notion about working your way through theory. Somehow, for me the biggest question is how can one still say anything vital or interesting to one's peers in an academic conference or to whomever one is writing to about criticism, and it seems to me the only way is to somehow engage oneself in a way that puts yourself on the line, the way I think the best novelists also put themselves on the line. In David [Lodge's] novels there's also a fantastic lot of play with language; all this stuff in the whole world taking place–it's the kind of fooling around which is not merely just telling a story but really worrying through or being concerned with where one is in relation to the language.

SCHOLES: David is a post-novelist.

ALTIERI: I didn't say there were traditional depictions, I said I was struck by the traditional understanding. I just want to make three points, I think in the same spirit. The first one I think is Nancy [Miller's] and that is whether it is an important role for the critic to point out, let's say, the risks of identifying with the main values in *The Color Purple*, and for whom would that job be important, because I think that particular question may put bite to what Gold seems to have missed–the range of uses of fiction and the range of audience perception. Now the second problem, it seems to me, is that a lot of this discussion has to do with things that are splits inside the history of the novel itself, between high art and popular art, and inside the history of the academy where it seems to me the whole notion of the English Department is increasingly absurd, partially because it has a commitment somehow to art, partially because it doesn't want to be teaching composition, and some enormous sense of its crossing to the world gets lost because of those dichotomies. Now, the third point is that there are two ways in which English department crossings to the world are lost by the structuring of the English department. One is towards the social import of the various kinds of figures that it discusses. The other, for me, is towards the philosophical. What does that mean? This is where I want to come back to David and to get at something that happens in American criticism that may not be right, but ought to be defended. I think we've been saying the same thing. For some of us at least, the notion of instructing an audience–that is, a general literate audience, but not quite as attuned to some things that we possess–is not part of the way American academia works. American academia exists in a large country, and–this may be our limitation–tends to ask us to talk to one another, to represent ourselves to one another. That has its limitations. But, it also has a crucial kind of alchemy which gets us back to the Alice Walker question. And that is my version of academic discourse, not to appropriate writers to the discourse that I possess, but to try to honor those writers by showing how much they can elicit, flesh out, elaborate, fill out all those discourses that I possess. And I think that the dream of academic discourse is a kind of bringing to bear all the kinds of education we've had on what the writers produce, and trying to show how much then can be carried off. That produces an enormous class difference in many ways with other kinds of uses of fiction. And it produces what I think ought to be an uneasiness about how we relate to Alice Walker and to reading about an Alice Walker who has social needs and to readers who have other kinds of needs in relation to that kind of text. There are enormous risks and trade-offs in these various kinds of options, and I don't think it's ever easy. I don't think there's going to be a dialectical pluralism; you can't do the range of things that have to be done together. You have to be sort of wary about what these primary notions are. Torgovnick put it beautifully, I think: there may not be, any longer, a best that has been done and thought, but there are ways of trying to represent ourselves as doing the best we can about thinking and saying. It seems to me that's the only value. Then we can hate each other, but we can at least honor that.

FLEISHMAN: Torgovnick's introduction was set up to and kind of invites the responses that have been given to disclose all sorts of gaps in what we did do. I think people have expressed all the things that they wanted to have happen and found didn't happen. I don't want to sound like Pollyanna–that's not my usual stance–but I found that according to some standards of what makes a good conference this was a good conference. One of the standards is that there are some good papers presented. There were some good papers presented. But I do find myself in the position of speaking up for a neglected minority in that the papers that stand out in my mind were not the ones that people are discussing. For example, Charles Altieri's paper, and George Levine's paper. But those really good analyses of individual discourse that function in the world of art and the depiction of life did not seem to me the kinds of things that we were getting involved in and getting excited about. I'm curious to know whether I'm speaking for a neglected minority of another sort in suggesting that those papers were very well done. . . .

LANGBAUM: I would like to be a devil's advocate for a moment and suggest that maybe there's no crisis at all. But if there is a crisis, the crisis is not in the language of fiction. It is a crisis in the language of criticism. It seems to me that I see a parallel to this. The critic must inevitably be coming from another place than the novel's history. Novelists are always amazed by what a critic makes of his or her work. I experienced this first when I was working on my book on Isak Dinesen. I didn't deal with interpretation–I just stayed away from it. Every now and then I would suggest something and she would say, "I never thought of it that way, but, you know, you're right." I think that would be a kind of relation that a critic and a novelist might have. In other words, the novelist might never have thought of it that way, but may see that is an authentic insight. So we have to come from different angles inevitably. On the other hand, I think within the language that accounts for what the novelist is doing and intending and what we're doing–I think we had a language that had nothing to do with either the actions used in reading or the actions used in writing. People are living in a dream. There's a lot of people maybe being pushed aside. I think maybe that's the price of finding another language. I'd like to say one other thing. I think in talking about what the novel is–I'm going to repeat what I said earlier: we do have to take into account the different kinds of novels and different ages at which we read them. So that to say that the novel is a construct which we then try to write again is simply over-simplifying. I think at a stage of adolescence we're probably trying to find our identity in life. I doubt by the time anyone reaches my old age he's trying to find his identity. Some novels will help you find your identity. Others won't do anything about that. So I think you have to consider the different kinds of things that novels can do. The thing that amazes me is when I look at the *New York Times* best seller list, I'm horrified to realize I don't know any of them. I've never heard of those people. And yet these are the best sellers. So we academics really are living in a completely different universe.

SCHOLES: I want to say that I think there is a crisis, but it's not an academic crisis or a literary crisis–it's a cultural, social, political, economic crisis. And the absence of the political in this conversation–or this conference–is a sign of our desire not to attend to this larger crisis. I think for myself–and I was partly trying to get at this in the piece I delivered–that one of the things that has happened culturally is that we now have a necessity for a fictional discourse that speaks to more collective entities than the individual conscience and consciousness, which I called "Protestantism." I think that the new kinds of characterization, new kinds of emplotment, that might represent our world adequately are not so easy to come by right now. It's only certain cultural situations where it's possible to write novels of worldwide influence and impact. South Africa may well be one of those situations. The South African novel is important because South Africa is on everybody's mind. Every college campus has a South African drama being enacted in terms of divestiture or some other representation of this issue. I mean, South Africa is a novel, really, a fiction which is being created and participated in and enacted by students on many, many campuses. It's not a real cause and effect relationship to South Africa, I think, but a need for moral engagement with South Africa that drives people to demonstrate. What I mean to say is that we might well have engaged the political more properly here, but we would have had to pose it *against* the ethical–that is, acknowledge the claims of a collective consciousness against the individual consciousness. And to stage that particular opposition would be to see it as another version of the opposition between the aesthetic and the political which has come out in a number of papers. To be radical aesthetically and to be radical politically are, I think, not harmonious. My position on that would be that aesthetic radicalism is a displacement of political radicalism or a sublimation of it. What you need to be effective with discourse is to reach audiences, and anti-novels or aesthetic experiments simply displace themselves from the large audience and reach a small audience of one sort or another. . . .

BLOOM: Along those lines, though, I wonder why we can't consider the aesthetics of the novel–to use the simpler term, the pleasure principle in the novel within the political framework or whatever else is involved. We seem to be–we are indeed intellectualizing the novel as though the pleasure that is involved, its aesthetic qualities, either don't exist or we simply take them for granted. I wonder why we aren't speaking more about the pleasurable qualities, about what is a matter of style, a matter of metaphor, whatever else happens in terms of the aesthetic sense. And that I suspect is the last of this session.

CLAYTON KOELB: I thought that was what Elizabeth Ermarth's talk was all about–in the sense it was the pleasure of the novel. I understood the great agreement there seems to be that there is a crisis–the rhetoric of crisis does seem to have become as [Lodge] suggested a permanent part of our discourse–and though I don't necessarily share that view that we are in crisis, I think that the rather consistent rhetoric of crisis in this particular discussion says something important. And I think it's quite in keeping with the topic of the conference which seems to me to reflect in the very question the kind of anxiety that novels–or at least those who read novels or teach novels–have been displaced to the margin, perhaps. And it is certainly an anxiety in the profession that all of us literary critics have been pushed to the margin. I think that one of the things that seem to me to be consistent in the presentation ... was an interest in the problematics of marginality. One of the things that seems to matter to us most about the novel is the way in which it challenges precisely that question–is our own discourse marginal? To what extent does the way in which we have been talking about the novel put certain groups on the margin, and to what extent is the novel a cure potentially, politically, for the marginality of people who have been subject to colonialism or sexism, or whatever. These are important questions. I do sense very much a kind of unity in that concern, that desire to overcome that marginality best expressed, perhaps, in the sentence in Professor DuPlessis's presentation which I realize was not perhaps meant to be central, but I thought so, which was "Don't throw the baby out." I think that was very important and right on many levels and expressed what we want to express in this conference.

QUESTIONER: I think in some ways we're saying does the right kind of novel matter to the right kind of people. Do we and what we say about it matter? We're not really talking about does it matter but ... whether it's modernism or very high culture. We again reject the marginal. I'm intrigued by our returning to a kind of comfortable sameness or homogeneity as critics and the ways in which we are adept in enacting the refusal of the marginalization. I'm caught up this morning simply by seeing [the separation of men and women] in this room.

ALTIERI: Do I matter? It seems to me that's the subtext. That's the academic concern.

SCHOR: Right. But who is "us?" who is "them?" who is speaking for whom? I come back to what you were saying about a crisis. To paraphrase Nancy's comment yesterday about "whose novel is this," I would ask: whose crisis is this? For feminist critics this is not a moment of crisis. This is a moment of extraordinary fulfillment, creativity, a sense of effectiveness for the academician. We like being marginal. We are slowly being pushed, propelled in some bizarre setting which is not really the center, but somewhere around there.... [On that marginal note, HERE ENDS OUR TAPE].

LIST OF CONTRIBUTORS

MARK SPILKA has been teaching English at Brown University since 1963 and has held teaching or visiting posts at the University of Michigan, Indiana University, Tulsa University, and Hebrew University. He is the editor of *Novel: A Forum on Fiction* and of an earlier anthology drawn from its pages, *Towards a Poetics of Fiction* (1977), also for Indiana University Press. His books include *The Love Ethic of D. H. Lawrence* (1955), *Dickens and Kafka: A Mutual Interpretation* (1963), *Virginia Woolf's Quarrel with Grieving* (1980), and *Hemingway's Quarrel with Androgyny* (1990).

CAROLINE MCCRACKEN-FLESHER teaches English at the University of Wyoming. She has recently published in the Soviet Union on the state of novel studies. Her current writing focuses on narrative formulations of cultural marginalization in nineteenth-century Scottish novels.

CHARLES ALTIERI teaches modern literature and literary theory at the University of Washington. His latest book is *Infinite Incarnations of Ourselves: Abstraction in Modernist American Poetry* (1989).

NANCY ARMSTRONG writes on literary theory and the novel and is now working on a book about domestic fiction from *Clarissa* to *Mrs. Dalloway*. She teaches English and comparative literature at the University of Minnesota.

LEO BERSANI is Professor of French at the University of California, Berkeley. His most recent books are *The Freudian Body* (1986) and, with Ulysse Dutoit, *The Forms of Violence* (1985).

DON H. BIALOSTOSKY teaches romantic literature and literary theory at SUNY, Stony Brook. His work on narrative theory includes recent articles on Chatman and Bakhtin, Wordsworth and Plato, and a book called *Making Tales* (1984), on Wordsworth's narrative poetics.

PETER BROOKS is Tripp Professor of Humanities at Yale University and Director of the Whitney Humanities Center. His most recent book is *Reading for the Plot: Design and Intention in Narrative* (1984).

ROBERT L. CASERIO is Associate Professor of English at the University of Utah and co-director of the University's Humanities Center. He is the author of *Plot, Story, and the Novel* (1979). His recent essays have appeared in *Antaeus, Grand Street, Novel, SAQ,* and *Contemporary Literature;* and he is at work on *The British Novel since Conrad: Theory and History.*

STEVEN COHAN, Associate Professor of English at Syracuse University, is the author of *Violation and Repair: The Paradigm of Experience in the English Novel* (1986) and co-author of *Telling Stories: A Theoretical Analysis of Narrative Fiction* (1988).

TERRENCE DOODY is Professor of English at Rice University and the author of *Confession and Community in the Novel* (1980). He has just completed a study entitled *Among Other Things: Recent Theory and the Structures of the Novel*. The essay on realism included here will be part of that book.

RACHEL BLAU DUPLESSIS has written two scholarly studies, *Writing Beyond the Ending* (1985) and *H. D.: The Career of That Struggle* (1986), and a book of poetry, *Tabula Rosa* (1987). She teaches at Temple University.

BERNARD DUYFHUIZEN is Associate Professor and Director of English Graduate Studies at the University of Wisconsin—Eau Claire. His work on narrative and critical theory has appeared in such journals as *Novel, Comparative Literature, College English, Modern Fiction Studies,* and *Pynchon Notes.* He has completed a book-length manuscript on narrative transmission theory and is currently working on a study of the reader in Thomas Pynchon.

ELIZABETH DEEDS ERMARTH teaches narrative and theory at the University of Maryland, Baltimore County. Her publications include *Realism and Consensus in the English Novel* (1983) and *George Eliot* (1985). She is now writing a book on contemporary fiction and a volume of Routledge's five-volume *Novel in History.*

JOSEPH GOLD teaches English at the University of Waterloo, Canada, co-directs the Southern Ontario Counselling Center, and belongs to the American Association for Marriage and Family Therapy. He is currently completing a book on reading fiction as a life source. His earlier work includes books on Faulkner and Dickens.

GEORGE LEVINE has evolved from Chairman of English at Rutgers to Director of The Center for the Critical Analysis of Contemporary Culture. His most recent work includes *Darwin and the Novelists* (1988) and an anthology called *One Culture: Essays in Science* (1987).

DAVID LODGE is Honorary Professor of Modern English Literature at Birmingham University in England, from which he retired in September 1987 to become a full-time writer. His new novel is *Nice Work* (1989), and his new anthology is *Modern Criticism and Theory* (1988).

NANCY K. MILLER is Distinguished Professor of English at Lehman College and the Graduate Center, CUNY. She is author of *The Heroine's Text: Readings in the French and English Novel, 1722–1782* (1980) and *Subject to Change: Reading Feminist*

Writing (1988). She has also edited *The Poetics of Gender* (1986) and, with Joan DeJean, *The Politics of Tradition: Placing Women in French Literature* (Yale French Studies 75).

The late ROY PASCAL taught at the University of Birmingham, England, where he wrote and edited several books on Kafka and on a variety of issues in foreign literature and criticism.

RICHARD PEARCE has worked as an NEH Fellow on problems of discontinuity, absence, and wholeness in modern literature. A teacher at Wheaton College, he has edited the book review section of *Novel* for several years.

ROBERT SCHOLES, a Joyce scholar in his youth, has since written and edited a great many books on narrative theory, fabulation, structuralism, and semiotics. He is the Andrew W. Mellon Professor of Humanities at Brown University.

MURRAY M. SCHWARTZ is Dean of Humanities and Fine Arts at the University of Massachusetts at Amherst. He teaches literature and psychoanalytic theory there, and has written many essays in both fields. Most recently he co-edited with Kathleen Woodward *Memory and Desire: Literature, Psychoanalysis, Aging* (1986).

DANIEL R. SCHWARZ teaches English at Cornell University. His most recent books are *The Humanistic Heritage: Critical Theories on the English Novel from James to Hillis Miller* (1986), *Reading Joyce's* Ulysses (1987), and *The Transformation of the English Novel: 1890–1930* (1989). He is also the author of books on Conrad and Disraeli.

KAJA SILVERMAN took her degree at Brown and now teaches at the University of Rochester. She is the author of *The Acoustic Mirror: The Female Voice in Psychoanalysis and Cinema* (1988), *The Subject of Semiotics* (1983), and numerous articles on feminist theory, psychoanalysis, film, and literature.

ALAN SINGER teaches literary theory at Temple University. He is the author of *A Metaphorics of Fiction: Discontinuity and Discourse in the Modern Novel* (1984) and of a novel called *The Charnel Imp* (1988). His essay is part of a work entitled *Narrative Knowing: The Subject of Action in Ideology and the Novel*.

PATRICIA MEYER SPACKS is now Professor of English at the University of Virginia. Best known for *The Female Imagination* (1976) and for her work in eighteenth-century studies, she is currently writing a book on boredom.

SUSAN RUBIN SULEIMAN teaches Romance literatures and comparative literature at Harvard University. Her books include *Authoritarian Fictions: The Ideological Novel as a Literary Genre* (1983) and a volume she edited, *The Female Body in West-*

ern Culture: Contemporary Perspectives (1986). Her latest book is *Women and the Avant-Garde: From Surrealism to Postmodernism*.

KHACHIG TÖLÖLYAN teaches fiction and critical theory at Wesleyan. He is the editor of *Pynchon Notes* and has published widely on Pynchon, Barth, and Borges.

MARIANNA TORGOVNICK teaches English at Duke University and is the author of *Closure in the Novel* (1981) and *The Visual Arts, Pictorialism, and the Novel* (1985). She is writing a book on modern primitivism in art, literature, and popular culture.

Guest respondents to the *Novel* conference, some of whom spoke in the recorded discussions, were STEVEN COHAN (Syracuse), CHRISTINA CROSBY (Wesleyan), TERRENCE DOODY (Rice), BERNARD DUYFHUIZEN (Wisconsin–Eau Claire), AVROM FLEISHMAN (Johns Hopkins), EUGENE GOODHEART (Brandeis), JANICE HARRIS (Wyoming), CLAYTON KOELB (Chicago), ROBERT LANGBAUM (Virginia), MICHELLE MASSE (Louisiana State–Baton Rouge), and MARY-HELEN WASHINGTON (Massachusetts–Boston).

INDEX